A Guide Book of
LIBERTY SEATED SILVER COINS

SECOND EDITION

A Complete History and Price Guide

Q. David Bowers

Foreword by
Kenneth Bressett

Whitman
Publishing, LLC
PUBLISHING SINCE 1934
Whitman.com

A Guide Book of
LIBERTY SEATED
SILVER COINS
SECOND EDITION

© 2023 Whitman Publishing, LLC
1974 Chandalar Drive, Suite D, Pelham, AL 35124

THE OFFICIAL RED BOOK is a trademark of Whitman Publishing, LLC.

Correspondence concerning this book may be directed to
Whitman Publishing, Attn: Liberty Seated, at the address above.

ISBN: 0794850510

Printed in China

Disclaimer: Expert opinion should be sought in any significant numismatic purchase. This book is presented as a guide only. No warranty or representation of any kind is made concerning the completeness of the information presented. The author, a professional numismatist, regularly buys, sells, and holds certain of the items discussed in this book.

Caveat: The value estimates given are subject to variation and differences of opinion. Before making decisions to buy or sell, consult the latest information. Past performance of the rare-coin market or any coin or series within that market is not necessarily an indication of future performance, as the future is unknown. Such factors as changing demand, popularity, grading interpretations, strength of the overall coin market, and economic conditions will continue to be influences.

Other books in the Bowers Series include: *A Guide Book of Morgan Silver Dollars; A Guide Book of Double Eagle Gold Coins; A Guide Book of United States Type Coins; A Guide Book of Modern United States Proof Coin Sets; A Guide Book of Shield and Liberty Head Nickels; A Guide Book of Flying Eagle and Indian Head Cents; A Guide Book of Washington Quarters; A Guide Book of Buffalo and Jefferson Nickels; A Guide Book of Lincoln Cents; A Guide Book of United States Commemorative Coins; A Guide Book of United States Tokens and Medals; A Guide Book of Gold Dollars; A Guide Book of Peace Dollars; A Guide Book of the Official Red Book of United States Coins; A Guide Book of Franklin and Kennedy Half Dollars; A Guide Book of Civil War Tokens; A Guide Book of Hard Times Tokens; A Guide Book of Mercury Dimes, Standing Liberty Quarters, and Liberty Walking Half Dollars; A Guide Book of Half Cents and Large Cents;* and *A Guide Book of Barber Silver Coins, A Guide Book of Modern United States Dollar Coins; A Guide Book of the United States Mint; A Guide Book of Gold Eagle Coins; A Guide Book of Continental Currency and Coins; A Guide Book of Quarter Eagle Gold Coins;* and *A Guide Book of American Silver Eagles.*

Whitman Publishing is a leader in the antiques and collectibles field.
For a complete catalog of numismatic reference books, supplies, and
storage products, visit Whitman Publishing online at www.Whitman.com.

Whitman®

CONTENTS

FOREWORD

It is easy to become a fan of Whitman Publishing's Bowers Series of books about United States coinage. They cover a broad range of subjects from the beginning of U.S. coins to the present, and each book is chock full of valuable information and colorful background stories to both educate and entertain readers. Most of the more than two dozen volumes in this corpus are now in their second or third editions, with the most popular, *A Guide Book of Morgan Silver Dollars*, recently celebrating its seventh.

A Guide Book of Liberty Seated Silver Coins by Q. David Bowers is very much like Dave's many other works in its scope and thoroughness. It embraces virtually everything one could ever need to know about this highly specialized subject. The book appeals to its targeted audience of active collectors, as a hands-on guide to building a valuable collection. It also serves as a classic reference for these coins, with benchmark information to assist future researchers. In its second edition numerous comments, new discoveries, and other helpful information have been added to keep the book up to date. This newest edition is also an updated revision in terms of coin valuations, and other edits gleaned from recent research since the first edition was published in 2016.

Many of the new additions have been contributed by members of the Liberty Seated Collectors Club, and other users of the first edition, who have generously provided their insights, research, and knowledge of the subject to benefit others and to enliven and even broaden interest in these silver coins.

There are some coin collectors who are not particularly fond of Christian Gobrecht's controversial Liberty Seated design. They will find enough background information in Dave Bowers's analysis to either change their attitude, or to confirm their belief that it should never have been used as a national emblem of Liberty, much less continued in use for more than 55 years. Whatever your feelings, you will find this account like the proverbial box of assorted chocolates, with something exciting and unexpected in every bite.

Taking readers beyond the usual boundaries of numismatic research is a hallmark of Bowers's writing. By adding colorful anecdotes and other related material to his factual narrative he holds the reader's attention and interest, sharing an encyclopedic knowledge of every aspect. This is a trait attributed to the past century, where numismatic scholars were expected to be fully acquainted with a broad range of knowledge about all kinds of coins, medals, paper money, and tokens. Sadly, far too many of today's researchers limit their expertise to a single area of personal interest, and could not distinguish a Roman *sestertius* from an Armenian *half-double tram*. Reading a Q. David Bowers book will expand your knowledge and inspire you to broaden and deepen your own studies.

Among the plethora of useful information presented here in each year's detailed account of Liberty Seated coinage are stunningly detailed pictures of each coin that show all of the features clearly with their distinguishing designs and points of interest. References like this are invaluable to both collectors and researchers. Collectors will find them particularly important when attributing their coins, and especially so when attempting to distinguish genuine pieces from the many counterfeit issues that were as prevalent in the 1850s to 1880s as they are today with the new crop of fakes that are currently being imported from overseas.

The contemporary fakes (forged to circulate alongside the real coins then found in commerce) were most often cast copies made from crude molds, or less often struck from hand-cut dies. Occasionally the die-struck pieces were very well made; in fact, one example, an 1861 dime, was mistakenly thought to be a pattern coin struck in copper.

Among counterfeit Liberty Seated coins, dimes were the most plentiful, likely because they were easiest to make and less likely to be suspected. Ten cents was a substantial amount of money in the 1800s, making the dime profitable to counterfeit.

You never know where Dave Bowers's trails may lead when exploring the history, background, related myths, and stories surrounding his subjects. Every coin has tales to tell. Some will inspire you to learn even more about the topics that appeal most to you. In this account he provides a solid basis for collectors who specialize in the fascinating coins featuring the familiar figure of Lady Liberty. Was she really the woman who was described in 1876, by a writer in *Galaxy* magazine, as "That young woman sitting on nothing in particular, wearing nothing to speak of, looking over her shoulder at nothing imaginable, and bearing in her left hand something that looks like a broomstick with a woolen nightcap on it"?

I'll leave it up to you to decide.

Kenneth Bressett
Colorado Springs, Colorado

Kenneth Bressett is Editor Emeritus of *A Guide Book of United States Coins* (the hobby's best-selling *Red Book*); a past governor and president of the American Numismatic Association; and a well-known teacher, researcher, and writer. Among his recent books are *Bible Lore and the Eternal Flame: A Numismatic, Historical, and Archaeological Trip Through Biblical Times*, and *A Penny Saved: R.S. Yeoman and His Remarkable Red Book*.

INTRODUCTION

Welcome to my study of Liberty Seated silver coins. These pieces from the half dime to the silver dollar and trade dollar have been numismatic favorites for a long time, and each year draws new enthusiasts. The Liberty Seated Collectors Club (www.lsccweb.org), with the *Gobrecht Journal* and the online *E-Gobrecht*, serves as a meeting place for specialists. In a wider frame, thousands of other enthusiasts form sets of certain denominations and, most often, seek one of each major design change to include in a type set of U.S. coins.

I began serious work and compilation of this book in 2014. By that time, I had files dating back to the 1950s when I began taking careful notes on coins, collectors, market conditions, and other aspects of numismatics that interested me. Research has always been high on my list of enjoyable activities. At the time the *Red Book*, as the annually issued *A Guide Book of United States Coins* was nicknamed, was the be-all and end-all as a source for market information. As a young dealer (I started part-time in 1953 after having discovered numismatics in 1952), I priced my coins per that reference, which was timely for most but not all series. Each July when a new edition came out I went through my inventory and marked up each coin. Prices *always* went up, it seemed! At the same time there were little booms now and then in certain series such as Uncirculated and Proof coins and commemoratives. At one time I offered to "pay over *Guide Book*" for Liberty Seated Proof coins. For the latest information on these I would consult advertisements in the *Numismatic Scrapbook Magazine* and the prices realized in auctions. To this I would factor in what other dealers were asking.

In late 1953, with my business not even a year old, veteran dealer Abe Kosoff (he started in 1929) contacted me to say he was going to Cairo to attend the Sotheby's auction of the Palace Collections (King Farouk's holdings), and to ask if he could represent me. My two specialties at the time were colonial and pattern coins. I asked him to contact me when he returned. He did, and I bought hundreds of pattern coins from him and from his business associate, Sol Kaplan.

I spent a lot of time while in Forty Fort High School and Pennsylvania State University attending coin conventions on weekends and setting up exhibit spaces. At Penn State many classes met Mondays, Wednesdays, and Fridays. By getting permission to skip Fridays, I could drive to New York City to visit New Netherlands Coin Company, Stack's, and others (it took two full days to "do" the many dealers—this in an era before certified grading, when nearly all coins were in 2x2–inch paper envelopes), or to go elsewhere to attend coin shows.

I also started doing many interviews with old-timers ranging from Stephen K. Nagy to B. Max Mehl and more. At the time there were not many people interested in numismatic research. I talked with and corresponded with perhaps a dozen who were, including Kenneth Bressett, Walter Breen, and Eric P. Newman, to mention just three. Today there are dozens of highly qualified researchers and writers. Along the way I became interested in American history and finance (later my university degree) and their relationship to numismatics. I read through each and every issue of *Niles' Weekly Register*, published in Baltimore beginning in 1811. (In the late summer of 1814 editor Hezekiah Niles gave a first-hand account of the British approaching the city, but the "Star-Spangled Banner" prevailed, as we all know.) I read Mint reports, other histories, and newspapers, filled out call slips at the Library of Congress, interfaced with the National Archives, and more. Chapter 3 of this book touches lightly on many relationships between the economy, the prices of gold and silver, and other aspects which were directly responsible for fluctuations, often wide, in mintage figures from year to year. To me such information is an integral part of understanding Liberty Seated coins.

The business was very *personal* when I started back in the 1950s. On my Royal typewriter I wrote hundreds of letters to customers each year. Probably for every one coin I advertised I sold ten privately. Today, for some people a check of auction catalogs determines rarity. In fact, only a tiny percentage of rare coins then or now cross the auction block. *Coin World* (1960), the Teletype system (early 1960s), *the Coin Dealer Newsletter* (1963), and other sources of weekly or even daily information were not dreamed of. No one could imagine an era in which the Internet would instantly, at the touch of a pad or key, reveal millions of coins for sale worldwide. When I graduated from Penn State with a degree in finance in 1960, there were no courses on computers, although to turn out IBM punch cards for its own use the university had installed a huge computer in the Boucke Building that required a special air-conditioning system to cool. Today an inexpensive notebook computer is probably more powerful!

I was a very "fussy" buyer in an era in which hardly anyone else was. I sought what today would be called "choice" and "gem" quality coins, to the extent that such were available. If you read some old auction catalogs, *A Guide Book of United States Coins*, or magazines from the mid-1950s you will see that Uncirculated and Proof coins were nearly always listed without any numbers or agreed-upon adjectives accompanying them. Probably 90 percent or more of buyers would accept *any* Uncirculated or Proof coin unless it had obvious defects or had been polished or harshly cleaned. Today, in a way, this is still true—nearly everyone buys based on the grading number seen on a third-party grading slab. Sharpness of strike and quality of eye appeal don't count for very much—an observation I repeat in this book under the "Being a Smart Buyer" heading for each denomination and also in the next section, "How to Use This Book."

For some of my specialties, such as colonial coinage, a high-quality coin might be Very Good or Fine. For patterns, for which I was probably the most active retailer in the 1950s and 1960s, high quality was the standard as they did not move around from collection to collection as much as regular nineteenth century Proof coins did and were not dipped or cleaned as often. This attention to selecting coins with good eye appeal had its pluses and minuses. On the plus side, I developed hundreds of customers who bought everything I sent them. For more than just a few I was their exclusive source. On the negative side, my prices were often undercut by other dealers who advertised as I did, but delivered coins that I considered to be lower-level in quality. This prompts me to repeat that a huge amount of information already in print about Liberty Seated coins is based on the pieces offered at auction over the years. In reality, the vast majority of such coins are bought and sold privately without any public record. In my own career in the 1950s probably nine out of ten coins I sold never appeared in print. A few years ago in the space of one hour I sold two MCMVII (1907) Ultra High-Relief double eagles for more than a million dollars each, and neither transaction ever reached print.

About 1954 I decided to form a collection of Proof Liberty Seated and Barber half dollars starting with 1858, the earliest date for which Proofs were listed in *A Guide Book of United States Coins*. My Proof Barber halves of 1892 to 1915 were completed within a few months, with most costing $8 to $10 each, except for a gem 1913 I bought from Harvey Stack for $25. The 1914 and 1915 were the last to be acquired, for two reasons: Most I saw were extensively hairlined, and these two cost more than $200 each as a Virginia collector, R.L. Miles Jr., was hoarding them. Liberty Seated half dollars were a different challenge entirely. The dates from 1879 to 1891 were acquired in gem quality rather quickly. Most in the 1870s were hairlined, and those from 1858 through the 1860s were extensively so. Not one in ten early Proofs met my criteria.

As a dealer I "trained" other dealers to offer only high-quality coins to me. Otherwise, I would send them back—a wasteful exercise for both parties. Art and Paul Kagin operated the Hollinbeck Coin Company in Des Moines, Iowa, and produced a string of mail-bid sales that included many half dollars simply described as "Proof," as was standard. I would call Art on the sale date and ask about the coins I needed. "This one is not for you," he would say for one coin; "You'll like this," for another. It took a very long time to fill out the early years in my set. There was a situation that seems curious today: the *Guide Book* did not list or price Proofs dated prior to 1858. I was offered these and in time bought perhaps half of the dates from 1839 through 1857 by paying only slightly more than the Uncirculated values for them! Today there is a truism: If a coin is listed in *A Guide Book of United States Coins*, the demand for it is much, much higher than if it is not listed. Such pattern coins as the 1856 Flying Eagle cent, 1838 Gobrecht dollar, and 1879 and 1880 $4 gold Stellas are examples. If they could be found only in the *United States Pattern Coins* book by J. Hewitt Judd, not many people would know about or desire them.

As the years went on, I handled many Liberty Seated coins of all denominations, in all grades and covering, eventually, all known varieties (including the unique 1870-S half dime and 1873-CC, No Arrows dime). Along the way I have been honored and privileged to offer at auction some of the finest collections ever formed.

The Garrett Collection, consigned by Johns Hopkins University and sold in a series of four auctions from 1979 to 1981, had countless gem Liberty Seated coins that had been acquired by T. Harrison Garrett in the 1870s until his passing in a boating accident on Chesapeake Bay in 1888. In 1979 I wrote a book, *The History of United States Coinage as Illustrated by the Garrett Collection*, that quickly sold out its first printing of 4,000 copies and went on to be issued to the extent of about 15,000 copies, if I remember correctly. A pleasant aspect of my involvement was spending time at the Evergreen House, the Garrett mansion on North Charles Avenue in Baltimore, and on the university campus at the library, copying more than 4,000 pieces of early correspondence regarding the collection. Up until this time the "brilliant is best" guideline was nearly universally in place. As a result, cleaning and dipping coins was the rule, not the exception (otherwise *all* Proof Liberty Seated coins would have remained perfect or nearly so from the time of issue to today). The Garrett sales changed that when beautifully toned coins brought record prices. Since then, toned coins have been in favor, and dipping and cleaning has decreased. Johns Hopkins University had an outside appraisal of nearly $9 million for the Garrett Collection. When the last coin was sold, the realization was $25 million—and this partly in a weak market (caused by the end of wild speculation in silver and gold in the late 1970s).

Emery May Holden Norweb was one of my favorite clients. She took a liking to me when I was a teenager as did her husband, Ambassador R. Henry Norweb. I visited them at their summer seaside home in Boothbay Harbor, Maine, in their home base in Bratenahl near Cleveland, and in their New York City top floor of the River House. (*Time* magazine founder Henry Luce had a lower floor.) Mrs. Norweb, as I called her, was very particular about quality and wanted the best. As a result she built her collection very slowly over a long period of years. When she bought coins from me, including Liberty Seated issues, price was not important (I always tried to be fair), but quality was. I knew that and would only offer her the best. In the same era, John J. Pittman of Rochester, New York, had a penchant for high quality, and always examined his coins through a thick brass-rimmed magnifier that looked like it was taken from some piece of laboratory equipment.

The Liberty Seated silver coins that were part of the Louis E. Eliasberg Collection were consigned to my company by his son Richard and were auctioned in New York City in 1996 and 1997, again memorable occasions. Most of these were of very high quality and came from the collection of Pennsylvania oilman John M. Clapp, who also had a very discerning eye.

Given the time and space, I could tell much more about my involvement with Liberty Seated coins, the collectors who sought them, and the dealers who handled them—including several who have specialized in the series past and present.

While the coins themselves have always been fascinating, equally so has been their history. Liberty Seated silver dollars and trade dollars form an important part of my two-volume series, *Silver Dollars and Trade Dollars of the United States: A Complete Encyclopedia*, published in 1993, still a standard reference. Up to that time trade dollars in particular were widely ignored. Today they are collected with enthusiasm. I like to think that my book was the catalyst.

In the pages to follow I share a lot of my knowledge and research, with some information concerning the distribution of coins (such as the exporting of Liberty Seated dollars) never before available in any single volume. This study would not have been possible—not even close—without the help of the many people I credit in the acknowledgements section. Without exception, everyone I contacted for information was willing to share it. I wonder if any other historic or research pursuit in science or art would have as many people of such a generous nature. If someone wants to write a book, *Who's Who in Numismatic Research and Scholarship*, the acknowledgements listing is a good place to start.

With the above said, enjoy!

Q. David Bowers
Wolfeboro, New Hampshire

HOW TO USE THIS BOOK

The typical entry for a coin by date and, in many instances, mintmark contains the following information:

Circulation strike mintage: Nearly all figures are from official records, including from *The Annual Report of the Director of the Mint*. In relatively few instances, the mintages are estimated and noted accordingly. The mintage figure is often unrelated to the numismatic rarity of coins today due to exportation, melting, and unusual distribution. Many such circumstances are explained in the text.

Proof mintage: Treasury Department records are the source for most Proof mintage figures from 1859 to 1891. Earlier mintages are estimated.

A beautiful Proof twenty-cent piece of 1875, the first year of issue of the short-lived denomination.

Availability in Mint State: Estimates are given by the author based on long-time personal experience plus other sources including specialists, specialized texts, and information published in the *Gobrecht Journal* and elsewhere. Population reports issued by Professional Coin Grading Service (PCGS) and Numismatic Guaranty Company of America (NGC) have been reviewed, but are used with a grain of salt. Countless coins graded, for example, MS-63 in the 1990s have "graduated" to be MS-65 today, the result of "gradeflation." A glance at population reports from the early 1990s shows very few MS-66 coins in proportion to MS-64 and 65. Today MS-66 coins abound.

The 1884 dime is an example of a Liberty Seated coin that is very common in Mint State. (shown at 150%)

Some numbers in population reports represent just a single coin submitted for grading multiple times. Adding to this is the popular practice of submitting a coin to both leading grading services to see which gives a higher grade. This is an important caution for sophisticated readers, as many offerings of coins quote such reports as the ultimate definition of rarity. Moreover, many collectors seek just one example of each date and mint. Accordingly, in surveys of collectors, such as in the holdings of members of the Liberty Seated Collectors Club, a collector might have one quarter of 1858-S, a rare issue, and one of 1876, which is very common; in a survey both would seem to be equally available.

Furthermore, as explained in the "Being a Smart Buyer" comments under the introduction to each denomination, the certified grade of a coin sometimes has little to do with its overall numismatic desirability. Most connoisseurs would prefer a sharply struck MS-63 coin with beautiful eye appeal to a much more expensive MS-65 that is dark and unattractive. Perhaps unique in the overall field of collectibles and antiques, most non-connoisseur coin buyers would rather have an ugly coin that a third-party grading service says has a high numerical grade than a beautiful and much less expensive coin in a slightly lower grade. This defies logic. The explanation is simple, however: By simply looking at a number, a buyer who wants to take the quick path and not learn much about coins can have instant gratification. In another complication, Registry Sets, which are venues for the popular pursuit of trying to have a collection with the highest total of grading numbers, do not consider sharpness of strike or eye appeal. A very expensive Ugly Duckling 66 trumps a moderately priced beautiful White Swan 64.

Many high-end coins are footnoted with "Population reports may exaggerate the number known." Many coins that were earlier certified at one level of Mint State have in later years graduated to one or two steps higher. Accordingly, for some issues coins for which few MS-64 and 65 coins were known in the late twentieth century now have populations significantly higher. This poses the question: Is a coin that used to be MS-63 now an MS-65 if it is certified as such?

Availability in circulated grades: These figures are educated guesses based on the relative quantities and grade levels seen by the author and many consultants and noted in sources including often extensive information in the *Gobrecht Journal.* Surveys in the journal need to be taken with a grain of salt regarding populations in certain grades. Many of the much rarer higher-grade EF and AU coins have been purchased by Liberty Seated Coin Club members, thus skewing survey data.

The 1871-CC Liberty Seated half dollar is scarce in any grade. Nearly all show evidence of circulation, often extensive. This VF-30 coin would be a nice addition to any advanced collection. (shown at 125%)

Characteristics of striking: Often within a given date and mintmark many different die pairs were used. One rule does not fit all. There are, however, some general observations for many varieties, and these are given. New Orleans coins of the 1840s are often weakly struck in areas. In contrast, Philadelphia coins of the same era are usually sharp. For many coins, cherrypicking will result in buying sharp coins at no extra cost, for the certification services do not mention this aspect.

Detail of a weakly struck 1838 quarter with weak striking and planchet lines certified as MS-67 by a leading service. Sharpness is important, but most buyers do not know this.

Proofs: Comments are given concerning the dies or other characteristics of certain Proofs together with approximated numbers of certified coins.

Notes: Under this heading are unusual varieties, comments on distribution, historical notes, and other information that may be interesting or relevant.

Market values: These values represent estimated market averages for typical coins in given grade categories. Especially attractive examples of rarities may sell for more at auction. In all instances these are given as a general market guide. As this book is expected to be in print for a number of years, consult current sources before buying or selling for current prices, as well as for certified populations.

Liberty Seated Collectors Club
Founded 1973

Founded in 1973, the Liberty Seated Collectors Club (LSCC) is an organization of over 600 enthusiasts dedicated to the study and collecting of Liberty Seated coinage.

Our membership is diverse and includes variety experts, those pursuing date and mintmark sets, and type collectors.

Our print publication, The Gobrecht Journal is issued three times per year, while the electronic E-Gobrecht is distributed monthly.

The LSCC maintains an active presence at the largest conventions and also conducts events at regional shows throughout the year. Club meetings and educational sessions are open to all.

For more information or to join the LSCC, visit our website at *www.lsccweb.org.*

THE LIBERTY SEATED SERIES

Christian Gobrecht, Engraver

It was a time of transition in 1835. By this time U.S. Mint engraver William Kneass, in office since January 28, 1824, was recognized as a good technician and fine craftsman for reproducing and multiplying images from models, but not as a creative artist.[1] In contrast, Philadelphia engraver Christian Gobrecht, who had worked for a decade or more on selected contracts with the Mint for medals (and possibly other things), and who was also an engraver of bank notes and designs on calico-printing rolls, was recognized as an artist of high caliber. He was also an inventor and mechanic par excellence—in 1817 he had invented the first medal-ruling machine. This made Gobrecht a candidate for an engraving position at the Mint, not for the first time.

Years earlier, on December 1, 1823, Gobrecht had written this letter to the president:

Christian Gobrecht.

> To His Excellency, James Monroe
>
> Sir:
>
>   The situation of engraver to the Mint of the United States having become vacant by the death of Mr. Robert Scot, I beg leave most respectfully to present myself to your consideration, as an applicant for the appointment that is in consequence to be made. My pretentions as an artist, as a member of the community, and as the head of a family, I cheerfully submit to the scrutiny which you will without doubt cause to be made and indeed it is upon the result of such an inquiry rather than upon any [petition] on my own part, that I risk my hopes of receiving your confidence.

The gentlemen under whose fidelity and skill the institution of the Mint has been so long successfully and usefully conducted have the means as well as the inclination to ascertain the nature of my pretentions, and therefore I venture to make an appeal to them especially. Should this application be successful to the motives already existing for serving my native country and my family, will be added the ardent desire that I shall feel to testify my gratefulness to you, for the honor and benefit conferred upon.

Your most Obt St.
Christian Gobrecht.
Philadelphia
1 Dec. 1823.[2]

The appeal was unavailing, and the nod went to William Kneass, another bank-note engraver in Philadelphia. This was a political appointment. The Mint director probably would have chosen Gobrecht.

Gobrecht was likely disappointed. Years later, a letter from G.M. Eichelberger to Gobrecht, dated March 5, 1838, told much: "I was much gratified to hear that at last you were drawn forth from your retirement and employed by the government, which ought to have been done 20 years earlier if justice had been done to all concerned."[3]

An entry in Mint records paying $25 to "Chas. Gobrecht" on January 27, 1825, surely referred to Christian Gobrecht.[4]

On February 14, 1825, Mint Director Samuel Moore wrote to President John Quincy Adams and solicited his permission to introduce, "in the character of assistant engraver, Christian Gobrecht of this city, an artist of great merit." Moore related:

His taste with regard to it [die engraving] has been well proved by some medallions, executed at my request, during the period of my early conversation with him respecting the Mint's models for a new head of Liberty. They were much admired by our best judges and among others by Dr. R.M. Patterson, whose opinion the Department will duly appreciate.

From the commencement of my charge at the Mint in 1824, when my knowledge of this very ingenious artist began, I have much wished to obtain for the public, his services as die sinker. I know that this was the earnest desire of my excellent predecessor, and I entertain the hope that such a preliminary arrangement may be

A bank-note engraving-plate Proof by Christian Gobrecht for the Bank of Orleans in New Orleans, Louisiana. Depicted is the seated figure of Liberty with a pole and cap.

made on the present occasion as will secure this result. It appears to me a most auspicious measure toward beautifying our coins.[5]

Through the years Gobrecht kept in touch with the Mint. On December 30, 1826, he was paid $100 for "executing designs and models of dies for the mint which were not adopted."

During the 1820s and 1830s, Gobrecht engraved the dies for a number of medals. The best known are the Franklin Institute medal made in 1825 but dated 1824, after a design by Thomas Sully; an admission pass for Philadelphia museum owner Charles Willson Peale; a portrait medal of Charles Carroll of Carrollton; a medal for the Massachusetts Charitable Mechanic Association; and an 1826 medal with a portrait of Archimedes for the New England Society for Promotion of Manufactures and Mechanical Arts.[6]

The New England Society was so impressed with Gobrecht's dies that their first medal was presented to Gobrecht himself. The Society wrote to Gobrecht on February 19, 1828, "You have done yourself and your country honor, in the beautiful sample of your talents and proficiency furnished to our Society."[7]

Gobrecht was active in the Franklin Institute as one of its earliest members and served on the board of managers from 1828 to 1830. He also served on the Committee on Inventions, an unsurprising role given his mechanical inclinations.[8]

Gobrecht's admission pass to Peale's Philadelphia Museum in Philadelphia. 32 mm. (Julian UN-23.)

Gobrecht's medal depicting Archimedes for the New England Society for Promotion of Manufactures and Mechanical Arts, 1826. 64 mm. (Julian AM-55.) (shown reduced)

Gobrecht's medal of Charles Carroll of Carrolton, the oldest living (at the time) signer of the Declaration of Independence, and detail of the engraver's signature, 1826. 52 mm. (Julian PE-06.) (shown reduced)

Robert M. Patterson

Returning to 1835, Mint Director Samuel Moore resigned his position in May, and on May 26 his brother-in-law, Dr. Robert Maskell Patterson, was appointed to the post. For the next month or so an easy transition was made. On June 16, Moore, still concerned with Mint matters, wrote to Secretary of the Treasury Levi Woodbury seeking permission to hire Christian Gobrecht as a member of the Mint staff.

Robert Maskell Patterson.

There was a lot of work to do; Kneass was strained to the limit, and the preparation of dies for the branch mints authorized for Charlotte, Dahlonega, and New Orleans would, in time, require a lot of additional work. Clearly, help was needed. Traditionally, the Mint had a chief or main engraver, not necessarily formally titled as such at this early time. Any other engraver on the staff was designated as an assistant.

Levi Woodbury. (Engraving by James B. Longacre, *National Portrait Gallery of Distinguished Americans*, 1835)

The Liberty Seated Design

After the production of silver dollars in 1804, coinage of this denomination was suspended. Nearly all had been exported, and the Treasury Department felt that their usefulness for domestic commerce was lost. After the dollar was discontinued, the half dollar became the largest silver coin of the realm. They became a familiar sight in commerce and in bank reserves.

In 1835, as Patterson settled into his office, he advanced the idea of having a new silver dollar made. On August 1 he wrote to Thomas Sully, one of the most highly regarded artists in Philadelphia:

> In entering upon the execution of my office here I have felt it to be one of the first objects requiring my attention, to endeavor to introduce a change in our coin that may make it a more creditable specimen of taste and art. To accomplish this purpose, I look naturally to your valuable aid and accordingly beg that you will execute for the Mint a drawing of what you shall judge a suitable design for the face of the coin.
>
> The only law which governs us in this matter is the following: "Upon the said coins there shall be the following devices and legends, namely: upon one side of said coins there shall be an impression emblematic of liberty, with an inscription of the word Liberty, and the year of the coinage; and upon the reverse of each of the gold and silver coins there shall be the figure or representation of an eagle with this inscription, United States of America, and upon the reverse of each of the copper coins there shall be an inscription which shall impress the denomination of the piece, namely cent or half cent, as the case may require."
>
> For the impression emblematic of liberty you know that our coins have heretofore used a bust. It appears to me that it would be better to introduce an entire figure. When a likeness is to be given as on the European coins the head alone is very properly used in order that the features may be distinctly represented. But, when

an emblem only is called for it would seem rather desirable to avoid this individuality in the features. Besides, there is certainly more room for a display of taste and beauty of form when a full figure is used.

The round form of the coin, its small size, and the practical necessity of covering as much of the face as possible seem to require that the figure be in a sitting posture, sitting for example on a rock.

To be distinctly emblematic of liberty, I would propose that the figure hold in her right hand the liberty pole surmounted by the pileus, an emblem which is universally understood. I would also suggest that the left hand be made to rest upon the United States shield on which the word Liberty required by law may be inscribed.

For the reverse of the coin I propose an eagle, flying, and rising in its flight amidst a constellation, irregularly disposed, of 24 stars and carrying in its claws a scroll with the words E Pluribus Unum, of many stars our constellation, of many states one union.

As I am desirous that the real American bald eagle should be represented and not, like the heraldic eagle, a mere creature of imagination I have requested Mr. Titian R. Peale to make a design in conformity with the above suggestions and therefore will not trouble you with the reverse of the coin, at least not for the moment.

The Liberty Cap and Pole

By 1835 the liberty cap, or *pileus*, was a very familiar motif, indeed "universally understood," dating back to at least the era of ancient coinage when it was featured on many coins. Such a cap was presented to slaves when they were given their freedom.

In colonial America the liberty cap was widely used to represent freedom from the shackles of British rule. Many towns and cities had liberty poles set up in prominent places—tall and with a cap at the top. Such were common sights into the early 1800s.

On coins, the liberty cap with pole was a popular motif. It was used on certain American coppers of the 1780s (with the seated figure of Liberty being the motif of Connecticut coins from 1785 to 1788), on various Britannia counterfeits (made at Machin's Mills in Newburgh, New York), and on various other issues.

Somewhat related to the preceding, but without a liberty cap, are many motifs of seated female figures such as Britannia on ancient coins and later renditions of her holding spears and tridents.[9]

Connecticut copper coin with Liberty seated with pole and cap on the reverse. The inscriptions refer to AUTHORITY OF CONNECTICUT and LIBERTY AND INDEPENDENCE, 1785. 27 mm. (Die variety is known as 1785 Miller 3-1A.)

IMMUNE COLUMBIA obverse combined with NOVA CONSTELLATIO reverse, illustration of a copper coin. 27 mm. (S.S. Crosby, *Early Coins of America*, 1875)

The Kneass Sketch

It is seen that Patterson originated the conception of the design later carried out for coinage, except in its final form the eagle held nothing in its claws. On August 1 engraver Kneass made a rough sketch of a seated figure with a pole and cap, based on his conversation with Patterson.

Concerning this, Elvira Eliza Clain-Stefanelli, director of the National Numismatic Collection at the Smithsonian, wrote:

The earliest rendition of Britannia as a seated woman appeared on an ancient Roman sestertius of Antoninus Pius, circa AD 140. 32 mm.

Seated Britannia holding a spear, as seen on a King Charles II medal dedicated to the signing in July 1667 of the Treaty of Breda between the British and the Dutch, who had been at war for more than ten years. John Roettier was the engraver. If not seated on rocks, Britannia was close to them on this die. 56 mm.

Seated Britannia holding a trident, as seen on a 1797 Soho Mint farthing of King George III. 35.8 mm.

I am very grateful to Mr. Robert W. Julian, who pointed out to me that Patterson spent several years in France during the Napoleonic and post-Napoleonic periods, which explains his preference for the "French cap of Liberty," in place of Britannia's trident, symbol for England's maritime power. This "French connection" of Patterson might also explain the very unusual appearance of the first drawing of the American Liberty. She is the only Liberty who does not wear a "classical" garment; she wears instead a dress of the period reminiscent of the empire-style dresses worn, for example, by Josephine Beauharnais, Napoleon's wife.

Sketch of Liberty seated made on August 1, 1835, by engraver William Kneass.

The high bodice, the short sleeves, and the faint lines in the back of the head (possibly indicating a standing lace collar, not a falling hair lock), in addition to the coronet or high diadem over tightly gathered hair with a bun in the back, could testify in favor of Patterson's strong inclinations toward France and his vision for a new American Liberty. A few additional awkward design elements of the "Kneass Liberty" point again toward some remarks made by Patterson, namely the very shape of the rock, more like a pillow, on which Liberty is seated, as well as the poorly drawn right hand of Liberty holding the pole with the liberty cap. Also awkward is the distance at which she holds the pole as if she was about to hand it to somebody—but Kneass was not famous for his artistic skills.[10]

Gobrecht at the Mint

Recently retired Mint Director Samuel Moore wrote to his successor, R.M. Patterson, on June 16, 1835:

> The necessity of having an additional engraver in the Mint, which has for many years been sufficiently manifest, may be considered as imperative now in order to supply the branch mints with the requisite dies . . . No provision was made in the acts of last session [of Congress] for a second engraver here but all the branches are left dependent on this source for dies.

Moore wrote back to Patterson on June 26, 1835:

> The term "assistant engraver" as employed by Mr. Woodbury without however appearing to lay any stress on them, as indicating a distinctive station. Certainly the conception of any inferiority of rank would be very unsupportable [?] to Mr. G[obrecht] and this it will be proper to exclude which can easily be done. No inferiority in this respect was within my contemplation in the arrangement proposed.

There was no "chief engraver" office title at this time, only "engraver" and "assistant engraver."

While full-time employment of Gobrecht was being considered, Kneass suffered a debilitating stroke on August 27, which in effect made it impossible for him to perform the full work of engraver. Director Patterson reiterated his predecessor's request for help in the engraving department, and Christian Gobrecht began work at the Mint in September. As noted previously, to call Gobrecht an assistant, when he was more talented artistically and had a larger repertoire of medallic products than did Kneass, would have been an insult, and it was thus suggested that he be called the "second" engraver. His salary was $1,500 per year.

Regarding the design for the reverse, Titian Peale responded to Patterson on September 14 suggesting that Mr. Persico (E. Luigi Persico, a sculptor who had created medal dies for the Mint in August 1824) be hired to make bas-relief models from the sketches, as these would be more suitable for the die engraver to study. Peale subsequently sent three renderings to Patterson. On October 5 Patterson wrote to Treasury Secretary Woodbury seeking his and presidential approval for creating coins from the designs. Once this was received, information relating to the new design was made available to the press.

In November the *Philadelphia Gazette* told of work in progress:

> We learn that a new die for the coins of the United States, is now in a state of preparation, and will be ready for use in the ensuing year. The design was prepared by Sully, and is said to be exceedingly beautiful. It is a full length image of the Goddess of liberty, in a sitting posture, with one hand resting on a shield containing the coat of arms of the United States. On the reverse, will be the American eagle, as at present, without however the shield and coat of arms with which his breast is disfigured, and which somewhat resembles a gridiron, exhibiting the bad taste of broiling a bird with his feathers on. The first coin struck with the new device, will be the dollar, of which there have none been coined for thirty years.[11]

On January 8, 1836, impressions of the obverse design in fusible metal were sent to Secretary Woodbury in Washington, D.C., for him to show to President Andrew Jackson. On January 12 Woodbury advised Patterson that the president had approved of the design but suggested some modifications. In the same month Gobrecht started work on the reverse.

Drawing of Liberty by Thomas Sully.

A rendering of Liberty, oil on cardboard.

Coinage by Steam Power

A steam-powered toggle press of the Uhlhorn type, designed by Franklin Peale and made in a local machine shop, the first such device at the Mint, was inaugurated in a special ceremony on March 23, 1836. This was a postponement of an event that was intended to take place on George Washington's birthday, February 22, but the press was not ready.[12] Christian Gobrecht prepared dies for medals commemorating the new machine, depicting on the obverse a liberty cap with rays (similar to that used on Mexican coins since 1824), and on the reverse an inscription. Quantity production of copper cents on the press began on March 23, the day of the ceremony.

It was envisioned that the new Liberty Seated coinage, as it became known, would be struck on the new press. The liberty cap was used by Gobrecht on a pattern gold dollar that year, as there had been some discussion of initiating this new denomination.

One of the new
steam presses of 1836.

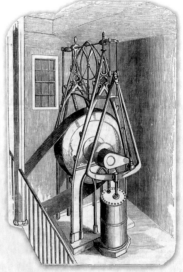

The main steam engine at the
Mint (boiler not shown).

Christian Gobrecht's medalet for the
planned ceremony launching steam coinage
on February 22, 1836. The press was not
ready, and the event was postponed. 28 mm.

The date on the reverse die was
altered for the ceremony that took
place on March 23, 1836. 28 mm.

Gobrecht's pattern
gold dollar of 1836,
Judd-67, with liberty
cap and rays. (actual
size: 15.5 mm)

The New Dollar Becomes a Reality

Sketches were prepared for a new reverse of the silver dollar featuring an eagle. Director Patterson wrote to Secretary Woodbury on April 9, 1836:

> The die for the reverse is not commenced, but I send you the drawings which we propose to follow—the pen sketch being that which we prefer. The drawing is true to nature, for it is taken from the eagle itself—a bird, recently killed, having been prepared, and placed in the attitude which we have selected . . . The absurdity of the shield sticking to the breast of the bird is avoided, the shield with its 13 stripes being placed with the figure of Liberty on the face of the coin. The arrows and branches are also removed from the eagle's claws, as contrary to nature and good taste. A constellation of stars equal to the number of states is distributed irregularly over the sky supposed to be seen beyond the eagle, instead of having 13 equal stars simply arranged around the margin.

Woodbury responded on April 11, noted that the suggestions were satisfactory with the pen-and-ink sketch being best, and recommended the mouth of the eagle be closed. Patterson wrote back to Woodbury on April 14:

> I am glad to find that our dies and designs for the new coinage met your approbation. Your suggestion that the mouth of the Flying Eagle should be closed had also been made by me to the artist, and a change was tried; but the effect was thereby injured on two accounts—first by taking away the spirited appearance of the bird, and secondly by smoothing down the feathers on the neck that are never ruffled except when the mouth is open.[13]

> There has been great difficulty in getting a good design for the eagle. I am confident that not less than 30 sketches had been rejected; indeed we feared, that at one time, that the flying eagle would have to be abandoned entirely.

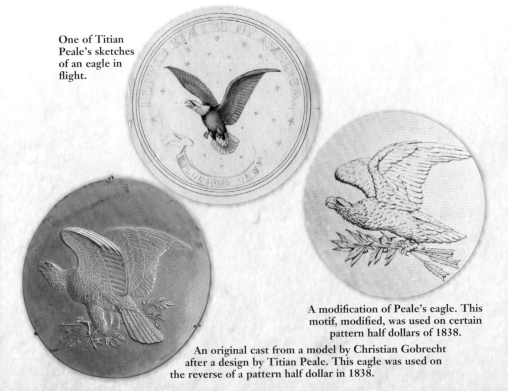

One of Titian Peale's sketches of an eagle in flight.

A modification of Peale's eagle. This motif, modified, was used on certain pattern half dollars of 1838.

An original cast from a model by Christian Gobrecht after a design by Titian Peale. This eagle was used on the reverse of a pattern half dollar in 1838.

No account of the reverse of the Gobrecht dollar would be complete without adding a Mint tradition, the twice-told folkloric tale of Peter, the Mint eagle, this version from Harper's *Young People*, March 21, 1893:

Peter, the Mint Eagle

If you have a silver dollar of 1836, 1838, or 1839, or one of the first nickel cents coined in 1856, you will find upon it the true portrait of an American eagle that was for many years a familiar sight in the streets of Philadelphia.

"Peter," one of the finest eagles ever captured alive, was the pet of the Philadelphia Mint and was generally known as the "Mint Bird." Not only did he have free access to every part of the Mint, going without hindrance into the Treasury vaults where even the treasurer of the United States would not go alone, but he used his own pleasure in going about the city, flying over the houses, sometimes perching upon the lamp-posts in the streets.

Everybody knew him and admired him, and even the street boys treated him with respect. The government provided his daily fare, and he was as much a part of the Mint establishment as the superintendent or the chief coiner.

He was so kindly treated that he had no fear of anybody or anything, and he might be in the Mint yet if he had not sat down to rest on one of the great flywheels. The wheel was started without warning, and Peter was caught in the machinery. One of his wings was broken, and he died a few days later. The superintendent had his body beautifully mounted, with the wings spread to their fullest extent, and to this day Peter stands in a glass case in the Mint Cabinet, where you may see him whenever you go there. An exact portrait of him as it stands in the case was put on the coins named.[14]

Director Patterson concluded to Secretary Woodbury on April 9, 1836, this being slightly more than two weeks after the first steam press was put into use (during which

Peter as photographed in the Visitors' Center at the Philadelphia Mint, May 25, 2015.

Peter, the Mint eagle, watched over the U.S. Mint display at the World's Columbian Exposition in Chicago in 1893.

time Peter's demise may have occurred): "The eagle is flying, and like the country of which it is an emblem, its course is outward and upward. . . ."

Production coinage of large copper cents soon commenced on the steam press. Hundreds of thousands had been struck by early November when the first half dollars were made. Some quarter dollars were made as well in late 1836 or early 1837.

Continuing Developments

By April impressions of the dollar reverse were ready, with the eagle in flight and nothing in its claws—the branches and arrows omitted as a matter of "good taste." On June 18, 1836, Director Patterson wrote to Secretary of the Treasury Levi Woodbury, noting in part: "Mr. Gobrecht will commence the die for the reverse immediately." This silver dollar reverse die was completed by the last week in August. After other correspondence, Secretary Woodbury approved the final reverse design on August 27. Some type of reducing lathe, details of which are not known today, was employed in the process, perhaps even a derivation of the improved engraving machine that Gobrecht had invented in 1817. Later, in December 1836, such a lathe was received from Victor Contamin, an inventor and expert on steel in France.[15]

On September 22 Director Patterson instructed chief coiner Adam Eckfeldt, who had been at the Mint since the 1790s, to have hubs and working dies prepared and to strike dollars on a screw press using a "reeded or ground" collar. Accordingly, the coins were made with a plain edge. It was anticipated that a large-capacity, steam-powered press would be used for the regular-production coinage, but the press was not ready. On September 22, 1836, Patterson wrote to Eckfeldt:

> The dies for the new dollar having been sunk by Mr. Gobrecht and the impressions approved by the Treasury Department, I am exceedingly desirous that you shall take without delay the necessary measures for an early issue of dollar coins.
>
> For this object I pray you to have the hubs and working dies prepared and the proper arrangements adopted for the cutting and milling of the planchets, and coining them in the larger screw press, the pieces being struck in close reeded or ground [plain] collar.
>
> The employment of the screw press is only to be temporary, and you are aware it is of great importance that the lever-press for dollars should be completed in as early a day as possible.

On November 8 the first coinage production of Capped Bust half dollars with reeded edges took place on the steam press. It was not until after March 1837 that a steam press capable of striking large-diameter silver dollars was completed by Franklin Peale and installed. Accordingly, the 1836-dated Gobrecht dollars were struck on a traditional screw press operated by three or four men, a fact not widely known today. On December 31, 1836, 1,000 silver dollars were delivered. (Further details are in chapter 9.)

Thus began the Liberty Seated coinage.

Other Denominations
and the Adding of Stars

The Liberty Seated design was widely admired. In 1837 it was extended to the half dime and dime denominations using the same style as on the obverse of the 1836 dollars—Liberty in a plain field. The reverses of the half dime and dime featured an open wreath enclosing the denomination.

In 1838 the director of the Mint and engraver Gobrecht decided to make additional silver dollars. The design of 1836 had been reviewed by Franklin Peale in January 1837 and was considered by him to be too "medallic."[16] The 1838 patterns were made with stars on the obverse (rather than a starless obverse field as in 1836), the proper place for stars perhaps (considering their placement on other silver and gold coins dating back to the 18th century), and the edge was made reeded rather than plain. The tiny C. GOBRECHT F. letters on the base of Liberty were effaced from the hub before the 1838 (and later 1839) master dies were sunk, and more neck feathers were added to the working die.[17]

In the meantime, in early 1838 the half dimes and dimes struck at the New Orleans Mint were without stars—the type of 1837. On May 12, 1838, Superintendent David Bradford of the New Orleans Mint sent "a specimen of our coinage, a dime," to Mint Director Patterson.

Following the style of the 1838 pattern dollars, stars were added to the obverse of the half dime and dime, creating a second type for the year.[18] On September 14, 1838, Patterson sent $5 face value of quarter dollars of the new design to Secretary of the Treasury Levi Woodbury in Washington, D.C. Liberty Seated half dollars made their debut in 1839 and had stars on the obverse.

The first Liberty Seated coins had no drapery at Liberty's elbow. In 1839 drapery was added to her elbow in the half dollar series. The half dime, dime, and quarter dies all featured the drapery the following year. In 1840 the shield was slightly modified, and other subtle changes were made for the half dimes, dimes, and quarters. The drapery was made considerably larger and was continued until the end of the series.[19] Liberty Seated dollars with a perched eagle on the reverse made their debut in 1840. This denomination circulated only sporadically, and in the 1840s they often traded at a premium, due to demand from exporters who bought them for use as coins valued for their bullion content at their destinations.

Two other Liberty Seated denominations were made. The twenty-cent pieces with the standard obverse combined with an eagle reverse designed by engraver William Barber (in office from 1869 to 1879) was made from 1875 to 1878. The trade dollar was introduced as a new denomination in 1873 and was coined through 1885, with issues after 1878 limited to Proofs for collectors. The obverse featured Liberty seated on bales and the reverse an eagle similar to the design later (1875) used on the twenty-cent piece. The designer was Barber.

A Gobrecht sketch of Liberty seated on a smaller rock than that finally used on coinage and with drapery at her elbow, date of rendering unknown.

A Gobrecht sketch of a perched eagle.

Another of many of Gobrecht's sketches for a perched eagle, this closely resembling the style first used on the quarter dollars of 1838.

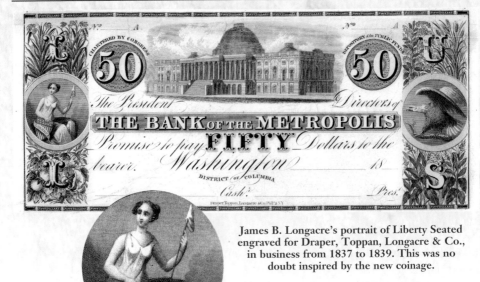

James B. Longacre's portrait of Liberty Seated engraved for Draper, Toppan, Longacre & Co., in business from 1837 to 1839. This was no doubt inspired by the new coinage.

Coinage at Several Mints

From 1838 onward, production took place at the Philadelphia and New Orleans mints. The New Orleans facility struck half dimes, dimes, quarters, half dollars, and dollars intermittently until it closed early in 1861 at the advent of the Civil War. It reopened in 1879 to coin Morgan-design silver dollars. Liberty Seated dimes and quarters were struck there in 1891.

In 1854 the San Francisco Mint began business. Its first silver coinage consisted of quarters and half dollars in 1855 followed by dimes in 1856, silver dollars in 1859, half dimes in 1863, trade dollars in 1873, and twenty-cent pieces in 1875. Many, if not most, San Francisco coins of the early years were shipped to China, where silver was appreciated and was a base of the economy, but gold coins were not wanted. Many Chinese-Americans in California sent coins to their relatives back home, and many of the half dollars were shipped there by merchants desiring to buy goods.

Beginning with the official acceptance of American silver dollars in China in 1842, large quantities of Liberty Seated dollars were shipped to the port of Canton. At the destination, various countries had trade buildings and facilities, called *hongs*, to receive coins

Trade buildings on the waterfront of the port of Canton, China.

The new cent design
with shield reverse as
approved in December 1859.

The cereal wreath
on the 1860 half dime.

The cereal wreath
on the 1860 dime.

In 1860 the new wreath was adopted on the half dime and dime. The French Liberty Head was never used on any circulating coins. Snowden's *A Description of Ancient and Modern Coins, in the Cabinet Collection at the Mint of the United States* was published. In December 1860 Secretary Cobb resigned his position and went to the South to become a leader in the secessionist movement and the establishment of the Confederate States of America.

In 1861, shortly after Snowden left his position at the Mint, *A Description of the Medals of Washington* was published under his name. This 412-page volume was and still is highly regarded. Both books were primarily researched and written by William Ewing Dubois and George Bull (co-curator of the Mint Cabinet at the time).

The Civil War and Later

When the Civil War began on April 15, 1861, Northerners envisioned an easy win. The North was the home of industry while the South was mainly agricultural. President Abraham Lincoln called for 90-day enlistments, after which time the war would surely be over. Reality proved otherwise. The first major battle did not take place until late July when Confederate and Union forces clashed at Bull Run in Manassas, Virginia, not far from Washington, D.C. Crowds of curiosity seekers went to watch the Yankees thrash the Rebels. The Rebels won, and the Union troops scattered in disarray. By late December of 1861, the outcome of the war was still uncertain, and gold coins began to be hoarded. By January 1862, they were available only at a premium from banks and exchange brokers.

In March of that year Legal Tender Notes were authorized by the government. As the federal Treasury had very little money, such notes were exchangeable only in other notes, not in gold or silver coins. This catalyzed a rush to hoard silver coins, and by early summer all were gone from the channels of commerce. Peace was declared in April 1865, after which it was thought that silver coins would soon return to circulation. This did not happen, as citizens were uncertain about the strength of the Treasury and the monetary system and still disliked Legal Tender Notes. It was not until

A $1 Legal Tender Note. These could not be redeemed at par in
silver or gold coins. Citizens were concerned about the stability of
the Union, and silver and gold coins disappeared from circulation.

years later—after April 20, 1876—that silver coins were on par with paper bills, and such coins were again plentiful in commerce. The Treasury geared up for a new demand for silver and made large quantities. This proved unnecessary when the public released long-hoarded older coins, creating a glut. As a result the mintages of new dimes, quarters, and half dollars were very low beginning in 1879.

Silver three-cent pieces and half dimes were a separate case, the production of these denominations having been ended under the provisions of the Coinage Act of February 12, 1873. When large quantities of these came out of hiding later in the decade, they were pulled out of circulation through banks and were sent to the mints to be melted.

Meanwhile in California

A curious situation developed on the West Coast after silver coins began to be hoarded in early summer 1862. The Constitution of the State of California, adopted in 1850, prohibited the use of paper money in circulation. Many of the gold-seekers had unfortunate memories of certain bills becoming worthless during the Panic of 1837 and its aftermath. When Legal Tender Notes were introduced in the East and Midwest, they had no place on the West Coast. Silver coins remained in circulation for face value. If anyone brought a Legal Tender Note it was accepted only at a deep discount. From 1861 until 1876, silver coins aplenty were in circulation there. Issues of the San Francisco Mint went into circulation. Many were exported, including to western Canada, where they were legal tender, but those that remained stateside were well used and became worn.[22] Today, Liberty Seated coins of the Philadelphia Mint from that era are seen with much-higher average grades than are those of San Francisco.

Coins Go to Canada

Historian Neil Carothers wrote:

> From 1858 to 1862 a steady stream of subsidiary silver [coins of less than the $1 denomination] went across the border. After the greenbacks fell to a discount in 1862, the profit on export to Canada became large, and in a short while Canada was over-run with United States silver. When the saturation point was reached in the fall of 1862, the Canadian market was wiped out. . . .
>
> Before the end of 1862, United States silver was at a discount of 3% in Canadian gold. The *Detroit Advertiser* said that the city treasurer of Toronto had half a ton of U.S. silver coins that he could not dispose of. In this country [the United States] a greenback dollar would buy about 80 cents in subsidiary coin. Across the line a Canadian paper dollar would buy $1.03 in the same coin.[23]

Some Canadian merchants would receive U.S. silver coins only at a discount. No one wanted to ship them back to their country of origin and exchange them for paper notes of uncertain value. For a period of years during the 1860s, it was estimated that in the city of Montreal alone there were 30 or more brokers and exchange offices that derived most of their income from trading in U.S. coins in bulk, often at the rate of more than $80,000 per day.[24]

As U.S. silver coins had no fixed values in Canadian commerce and traded at varying discounts, they were complained about by the public, as those holding such coins were always fearful of sustaining losses. In 1869 William Weir, an agent of the Canadian government, made arrangements with merchants to export $2 million worth of American silver coins to New York City to be sold to brokers there. A January 27,

1870, proposal by Sir Francis Hincks, government finance minister, to fix the rates of U.S. coins at a 20-percent discount was circulated to various merchants and bankers.[25]

> [This resulted in an] official proclamation, February 12, which fixed April 15, 1870, as the last day of grace for 'the old lady with the broomstick' and other barbarisms of the United States Mint. After that date our half dollars must take forty cents for themselves or give up passports, and all the other coins, even to five cent pieces, in the same ratio.[26]

In 1870 more than $3.5 million in U.S. silver coins went from Canada to brokers in New York City, causing a glut there, after which additional pieces were said to have been shipped to England as bullion.[27]

The Mint Act of 1873

In the meantime, the Mint Act of February 12, 1873, was authored for the Treasury Department by John Jay Knox, comptroller of the Treasury, whose interests included numismatics. This legislation ended the silver three-cent coin and half dime and discontinued the Liberty Seated dollar. It also altered the weight of subsidiary silver coins so that two half dollars equaled the French five-franc coin. This brought the U.S. silver coins (except the dollar) in line with the Latin Monetary Union.[28]

In a draft, Knox considered dropping the weight of the silver dollar from 412.5 grains to 384 grains, but then decided against it, saying that silver dollars had not been seen in general commerce since 1806, and there was no domestic demand for them.[29] In actuality, silver dollars circulated in the far West, these including the issues of Carson City and San Francisco.

John Jay Knox, author of the Coinage Act of February 12, 1873.

A new denomination, the trade dollar, was created. Weighing 420 grains as opposed to 412.5 grains for the silver dollar, the heavier trade dollar was made expressly for the export trade with China. These were very successful, and millions were struck from 1873 to 1878.

In 1875 the twenty-cent piece was launched as a convenience for making change in the West (as silver coins did not circulate in the East). These were confused with quarters and were discontinued after 1876, except for Proofs made for collectors in 1877 and 1878.

Beginning in the mid-1870s, the price of silver bullion fell sharply. Several European nations discontinued making full-value silver coins, while at the same time many new mines opened in America. What to do? Western interests persuaded Congress to pass the Bland-Allison Act on February 28, 1878. This mandated that the Treasury buy two to four million ounces of silver each month and coin it into dollars. The trade dollar was discontinued.

After circulation strikes of the trade dollar were discontinued in 1878, the remaining denominations—the dime, quarter, and half dollar—were minted until 1891. Production quantities fell sharply in 1879 due to the overabundance of silver coins on hand.

In the 1890s continuing into the early 1900s, the Treasury Department made a heroic effort to redeem noncurrent silver coins, from silver three-cent pieces to half dollars, then in circulation. From fiscal year 1891 to 1905 inclusive, $69,940,694 in face value was redeemed, melted, and recoined into Barber dimes, quarters, and half dollars.[30] By the second decade of the twentieth century, nearly all were gone.

Old Silver Coins Reappear

In addition to the silver coins melted and recoined by the U.S. Mint, quantities remained in Canada and a few Latin American countries to which coins had "fled" in the 1850s and early 1860s. Finally, in the spring of 1876, the premium on silver coins in relation to Legal Tender Notes disappeared. Anticipating a tremendous demand for new silver coins, the Treasury Department minted large quantities of dimes, quarters, and half dollars, a production that continued into 1878.

Neil Carothers takes up the story in 1877, by which time the U.S. government had been minting record quantities of silver coins and had recently exchanged about $36 million face-value worth of them for paper money:

> Further exchanges of newly-minted silver coins for paper notes were brought to a complete stop by an unexpected and dramatic development. In the winter of 1877 there suddenly reappeared in circulation literally hundreds of millions of the silver three-cent pieces, half dimes, dimes, quarters, and half dollars that had as suddenly departed in 1862. They streamed in from Canada, from Central America, from South America, and from the West Indies. A small quantity, probably, was brought out from domestic hoards. With the value of silver going down and the value of greenbacks rising toward parity with gold a point had been reached where these long absent coins were worth more at home than they were in foreign countries.
>
> The most interesting feature of this unexpected homecoming was the information it afforded as to the fate of the coins in 1862. It showed that they had not been melted or exported to Europe as bullion, although there was a definite profit in melting the coins at that time. They had gone to Latin America, served as local currency for 15 years, and then returned. Senator John Sherman in 1880 estimated the value of the coins returned in the preceding two years at $22,000,000, and a large amount came back after that time.[31]

New Designs Wanted

Familiarity breeds contempt, it has been said, and that was true of the Liberty Seated design. Starting in a large way in the 1870s there were proposals that new motifs be adopted.

The Galaxy, June 1876, published a lengthy commentary on the design of American coins, inspired by the recent re-emergence of silver coins in circulation that had not been seen since hoarding began in 1862:

> Now that we see real money again our attention is naturally attracted by its appearance, the look of it. That is pleasant enough in one respect. A bright silver piece, no matter what design is stamped upon it, is a much more attractive thing than a little scrap of paper, generally crumpled and greasy. But now that we see our national money again, notwithstanding all our reasons for welcoming it, we must confess that it is not as handsome as it ought to be, as it might be, or even as it once was. It does us no credit as an exhibition of our skill in designing, in die sinking, or coining. Why is it that we have the ugliest money of all civilized nations? For such undoubtedly our silver coinage is. The design is poor, commonplace, tasteless, characterless, and

the execution is like thereunto. Our silver coins do not even look like money. They have rather the appearance of tokens or mean medals.

One reason of this is that the design is so inartistic and so insignificant. That young woman sitting on nothing in particular, wearing nothing to speak of, looking over her shoulder at nothing imaginable, and bearing in her left hand something that looks like a broomstick with a woolen night-cap on it—what is she doing there? What is the meaning of her? She is Liberty, we are told, and there is a label to that effect across a shield at her right, her need of which is not in any way manifest. But she might as well be anything else as Liberty; and at the first glance she looks much more like a spinster in her smock, with a distaff in her hand. Such a figure has no proper place upon a coin.

On the reverse the eagle has the contrary fault of being too natural, too much like a real eagle. In numismatic art animals have conventional forms which are far more pleasing and effective than the most careful and exact imitation of nature can be. Compare one of our silver coins with those of Great Britain, France, or Germany, and see how mean, slight, flimsy, inartistic, and unmoneylike it looks. Our coins of forty or fifty years ago were much better in every respect, and looked much more like money, the reason being that they bore a head of Liberty which was bold, clear, and well defined in comparison with the weak thing that the mint has given us for the last thirty years or so. The eagle too, although erring on the side of naturalness, was more suited in design to coinage. But still better were the coins struck at the end of the last century and the beginning of this one. The eagle was a real heraldic eagle, the head of Liberty had more character, and the whole work was bolder and better in every way. . . .

In this hundredth year of our national independence we could not do a better thing to mark the time than to give real character and significance and beauty to our coinage, particularly as we distinguish the year by a return to the use of a real money currency. This could be done only by a change in the design and in the workmanship. The latter needs no advocacy; but the former of course requires the most careful consideration. In looking at our coinage we find that the greatly superior appearance of the old silver—that is, of the pieces up to about 1835—is owing to their breadth and to their having on the obverse a large boldly designed head. It was the reduction of the width, the substitution of the weak meaningless sitting figure in place of the head, and the low relief and feeble execution of that figure, that gave our silver currency the mean and insignificant look that it now has and has had for forty years. But even this head, although so much better than the sitting figure, is quite insignificant. It really means nothing, and might as well be called anything else as Liberty. It has, of course, no historical association whatever, nor is there about it any particular pertinence to our nationality. It might just as well be on the coins of any other republic in the world as upon ours. . . .

The narrative in *The Galaxy* continued at length and suggested that the portraits of George Washington and Benjamin Franklin, if placed on coinage, would have true American meaning.

Gaston L. Feuardent, born in Cherbourg, France, in 1843, and the son of art dealer and consultant for the Louvre Felix Feuardent, came to America in 1876. On January 16, 1877, he was elected a resident member of the American Numismatic and Archaeological Society. To the *American Journal of Numismatics*, October 1881, he contributed a scathing article which included these comments:

Government as an Art Educator

Permit me to say a few words in reference to the evident want of that artistic and aesthetic taste, which should preside over the engraving of the dies from which the coins of the United States are struck. A comparison of American coins, as to their artistic value, if made with those of other modern nations, would be by no means to the advantage of the former, although we all know how poor is the work displayed on the coins of other countries, excepting France, who has retained in her coinage the artistic culture shown in the works of the close of the Renaissance period, and whose coins excel in art all other modern nations. The reason of this excellence is not to be found in the fact that French die-sinkers of to-day are greater in their art than those of other nationalities, but that the ancient dies engraved by Dupré for the Republic of 1793 are still used for striking the coins of the Republic of 1880.

The importance of having designs of real and artistic merit impressed on all objects intended for a large circulation cannot be overrated, and by thus forcing every inhabitant of a country to be constantly in contact with results of a taste guided and inspired by a true art, any Government would be a great benefactor to its country, and the greatest art educator of its people. Museums and schools of art are being established all over the land, and are doing commendable work, but while comparatively few persons have the means or the leisure to profit by these institutions, we may estimate at once the benefit which could be derived from them, if such things as coins, bank notes and stamps were in themselves models of artistic beauty.

Now let us examine some of the issues of our own government. We have the new silver dollar [by Morgan], a very minute and clever piece of handiwork, but showing more plainly, by the very excellence of the mechanical execution, the complete absence of mental labor in the composition of the subject; it is only the work of an artisan, and of an artisan without taste.

As to the half dollar and the smaller pieces, the figure represented on them is simply horrible; and in circulating such an object, the government is doing nothing less than propagating and encouraging the taste for what is ugly and repulsive. The aesthetic worthlessness of the goddess of Liberty on these coins is evident; as to her artistic value, it may be called still less, for there is no life in the figure, and a study of its anatomy will demonstrate that no life is possible in a being of such construction. The idea of Liberty, so dear to us, is here represented by a figure, seated; her head turned towards her right shoulder, a movement which naturally ought to bring her chin nearly over that shoulder; but, on the contrary, by an inexplicable fancy of the artist (?) her head remains entirely over her left shoulder. As to her limbs, they are if possible, still more extraordinary; they are without any kind of modeling, and the left arm, curiously bent, is hanging to the "wand" that the Latins called the Rudis or Vindicta, and a little object which must be intended for the cap of Liberty. But the most astonishing part of the anatomy of the goddess is certainly her right leg, which, instead of being attached to the hip of the imaginary being, is simply fixed to her dress; so that, when our goddess will take off her dress, supposing that goddesses do so, she is sure to take off her leg at the same time. . . .

After considering what is done in the way of official issues, and having pointed out what good may be derived from an artistic currency, we must try to find the remedy and ascertain the means to attain it. It must be remarked, however, that since the mediaeval period, numismatic art has never retaken the place it occupied in antiquity. In the middle of the period of the Renaissance—when the monuments and most of the objects made seem to have been "kneaded" with art; and, when medals were so beautiful, the work on coins was relatively poor; this singular fact may be explained by considering that, at that time, there was no idea of educating the masses; the art objects were made for a few rich persons who had ordered them; now, wealth is so much greater, and consequently more generally diffused, nearly everyone is seeking for art to adorn the household; and from this comes the great demand for industrial objects inspired with art, and the desire to educate the artisan and refine his taste, so that he can model pleasing objects. . . .

I believe that the American Numismatic and Archaeological Society would deserve the gratitude of all Americans, if, by starting a movement in that direction, it would succeed in showing the Government how much good might be effected in presenting to the nation coins, stamps, and bank notes, which would be so many models of art to be followed by all.

In 1890 and 1891 the Treasury Department called for new designs for the dime, quarter, and half dollar. (The Morgan silver dollar, being of more recent adoption, would not be changed.) A competition among invited artists was held, but none of the submissions were found to be satisfactory. By default, Charles E. Barber, who had been the main engraver since 1880, was given the task but was told by the director of the Mint to use a head seen on coins of France (again, France to the fore!) as a model. The result was the Liberty Head or Barber design that was used from 1892 to 1916.

Scattered Liberty Seated coins remained in circulation for many years until the 1930s, when they finally disappeared.

2

COLLECTING LIBERTY SEATED COINS

Today Liberty Seated silver coins are among the most dynamic specialties in numismatics. Thousands of collectors enjoy them, and those with an advanced interest usually join the Liberty Seated Collectors Club (online at www.lsccweb.org). Founded in 1974, it issues the *Gobrecht Journal*. Dr. John McCloskey was editor from near the beginning until 2014. *E-Gobrecht*, published monthly on the Internet and archived at the LSCC website, includes news and information.

While many newcomers to numismatics come to believe that Mint State and Proof coins are the way to go—the higher the grade, the better—those in the hobby, the old guard so to speak, usually concentrate on older issues, most of which have seen extensive circulation. Members of the Colonial Coin Collectors Club (www.colonialcoins.org) specialize in issues that are mostly in grades from Good to Very Fine. The same goes for collectors of early copper half cents and cents. Similarly, Liberty Seated enthusiasts typically seek nice coins in various circulated grades. The vast majority of articles, surveys, and other information in the *Gobrecht Journal* deal with pieces that have seen circulation, often extensive, with not much said about the latest ultra-graded coin. Of course, Mint State and Proof Liberty Seated coins are the *crème de la crème*, but for many issues these either do not exist at all or are extremely expensive. No one

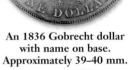

**An 1836 Gobrecht dollar
with name on base.
Approximately 39–40 mm.**

**A very sharply struck 1844-O half dollar
with nice eye appeal. This was graded
MS-63 when offered at auction. 30.6 mm.**

has ever assembled a complete collection of Liberty Seated coins in Mint State, but Eugene H. Gardner, a dedicated collector in Lancaster, Pennsylvania, came close.[1] The National Numismatic Collection at the Smithsonian Institution has many Proofs, but hardly any Mint State Liberty Seated coins of any denomination.

To study Liberty Seated coins is to fall in love with them, many collectors have found. Most if not all varieties are surrounded by a generous measure of historical information. Tapping into this will enhance anyone's enjoyment. In this book I endeavor to include notes that add to the appeal of the various issues.

Early Collecting Interest

From their inception with the Gobrecht dollar of 1836, Liberty Seated coins attracted the attention of at least a few collectors. The numismatic community was very small at the time. Although specific information is elusive, probably at least 100 people were interested. Colonial American coins, coins of ancient Greece and Rome, and medals were focal points. There was relatively little attention paid to current coins made at the Philadelphia Mint. Proof coins were supplied to collectors who requested them. The new Gobrecht dollar was an exception, and beyond numismatics, specimens were desired by congressmen and others. President Andrew Jackson had at least a passing interest in numismatics. His display of coins, tokens, and medals included two Proof 1836 Gobrecht silver dollars—one being from among the first pieces struck and the other given to a Jackson family member by Martin Van Buren.[2] On January 27, 1837, John Guest presented President Jackson with a small group of coins as a gift. Included were a 1792 silver Washington half dollar and a 1662 Oak Tree silver twopence.[3]

As the years went on, Proof sets were made in small quantities, probably not exceeding more than 10 or 15 sets of most silver coins in the 1840s. The first Liberty Seated mintmarked coins, the 1838-O half dime and dime, attracted no numismatic attention at all at the time they were issued. William E. Dubois and Jacob R. Eckfeldt, curators of the Mint Cabinet formed that year, did not add these or later mintmarked coins to the display. Continuing for decades afterward, collector interest was for *dates*, and whether a coin had a mintmark on the reverse was not important. There were no checklists of branch-mint coins and production quantities.

Mintmarks

A pioneering article about mintmarks was published in the *American Journal of Numismatics* in July 1876:

Issues of the U.S. Mint at New Orleans

This list of issues of the branch Mint at New Orleans was prepared with great care and trouble by Mr. Wm. E. DuBois of the Mint at Philadelphia, and has been revised by him and by myself. It may not be absolutely perfect, but is thought to be very nearly so. If omissions are found, I hope to be informed of them. I believe the same facts cannot be read elsewhere. —W.S. Appleton.[4]

Dollars were coined in 1846, 50, 59, 60, 61.[5]

Half-dollars were coined in every year 1839-61.

Quarters were coined in 1840, 41, 42, 43, 44, 50, 51, 52, 53, 54, 55, 56, 57, 58, 59, 60.

Dimes were coined in 1838, 39, 40, 41, 42, 43, 45, 49, 50, 51, 52, 53, 54, 56, 57, 58, 59, 60.

Half-dimes were coined in 1838, 39, 40, 41, 42, 44, 48, 49, 50, 51, 52, 53, 54, 55, 56, 57, 58, 59, 60.

Interest in branch-mint coins remained minimal. This changed after May 1893 when Augustus G. Heaton advertised his monograph, *Mint Marks, A Treatise on the Coinage of United States Branch Mints*, in *The Numismatist*. Heaton, a writer of great facility and soon to be elected president of the American Numismatic Association, listed 17 "causes of attractiveness" for collecting mintmarks, as delineated below:

Causes of Attractiveness

1st. Mint Marks in their progressive issue at New Orleans, Dahlonega, Charlotte, San Francisco, and Carson City show the direction of our country's growth and its development of mineral wealth.

2nd. Mint Marks in their amount of issue in varied years at different points offer the monetary pulse of our country to the student of finance.

3rd. The denominations of any one Branch Mint, in their irregular coinage and their relation to each other at certain periods, indicate curiously the particular needs of the given section of the land.

4th. A knowledge of the Branch Mint coinage is indispensable to an understanding of the greater or less coinage of the Philadelphia Mint and its consequent numismatic value.

5th. A knowledge of the coinage of the different Branch Mints gives to many usually considered common dates great rarity if certain Mint Marks are upon them.

6th. Mint-Mark study gives nicety of taste and makes a mixed set of pieces unendurable.

7th. Several dies were used at Branch Mints which never served in the Philadelphia coinage, and their impressions should no longer be collected as mere varieties.

8th. The very irregularity of dates in some denominations of Branch Mint issues is a pleasant exercise of memory and numismatic knowledge.

9th. This irregularity in date, and in the distribution of coinage, gives a collection in most cases but two or three, and rarely three or more contemporaneous pieces, and thus occasions no great expense.

10th. As the Branch Mints are so far apart their issues have the character of those of different nations, and tend to promote correspondence and exchange, both to secure common dates in fine condition and the rarities of each.

11th. The United States coinage has a unique interest in this production at places far apart of pieces of the same value and design with distinguishing letters upon them.

12th. As Mint Marks only occur in silver and gold coins they can be found oftener than coins of the baser metals in fine condition, and neither augment or involve a collection of the minor pieces.

13th. As Mint Marks have not heretofore been sought, or studied as they deserve, many varieties yet await in circulation the good fortune of collectors who cannot buy freely of coins more in demand, and who, in having access to large sums of money, may draw there from prizes impossible to seekers after older dates.

14th. The various sizes of the mint marks O, S, D, C, and CC, ranging from the capital letters of average book type to infinitesimal spots on the coin, as well as the varied location of these letters, defy any accusation of monotony, and are far more distinguishable than the characteristics of many classified varieties of old cents and 'colonials.'

15th. Mint Marks include noble enough game for the most advanced coin hunter, as their rarities are among the highest in value of United States coinage, and their varieties permit the gathering in some issues of as many as six different modern pieces of the same date.

Augustus Goodyear Heaton.

16th. The face value of all the silver Mint Marks to 1893, being less than one hundred and fifty dollars, they are within the means of any collector, as aside from the economy of those found in circulation, the premiums for rarities are yet below those on may coins of far inferior intrinsic worth.

17th. As the new Mint at Philadelphia will have a capacity equal to all existing United States Mints, it is probable that others will be greatly restricted or even abolished in no long time, and that Mint Marks will not only cease as an annual expense, but be a treasure in time to those who have the foresight to collect them now.

The *Treatise* sold well. Within a year at least several dozen numismatists were in the pursuit of mintmarked silver coins, and some of these wrote to the various mints to seek current issues. It was not until well into the twentieth century, however, that such interest became widespread. As a result, relatively few Mint State Liberty Seated coins still available were saved, and mintmarks in the current Barber or Liberty Head series attracted little attention. Generations later, many issues with originally large mintages were found to be rare in high grades.

The Friesner Sale

In *The Numismatist* in January 1894, William M. Friesner advertised his collection for sale:

> The collection is complete except for the dollar of 1803, quarter of 1827, and half cents of 1836 and 1846. There are complete brilliant Proof sets of 1850 and 1855 to 1893, both inclusive. Nearly everything else is Uncirculated. There are many varieties but no duplicates.
>
> My collection of Postal Currency is complete with a number of essays, all Uncirculated. Fine collection of Jackson cents almost complete. My collections of the New Orleans, San Francisco, and Carson City mints almost complete with many of the rare varieties Uncirculated.
>
> Prefer to sell the collection as a whole, which I will do at a discount.

No buyers stepped up to buy the collection, and after advertising it again in February he consigned it to New York dealer Édouard Frossard to be auctioned. The sale took place on June 8. A complete listing of the branch-mint Liberty Seated coins, descriptions, and prices follows, lightly edited for clarity, but in no instances have the meanings been changed:[6]

Carson City Mint

Dimes:
1872-CC: Very Good; rare; $0.60.[7]
1875-CC, CC Above Bow: Very
Fine; $0.10.
1875-CC, CC Below Bow: Very
Good; $0.10.
1876-CC: Uncirculated; $0.10.
1877-CC: Uncirculated; $0.10.
1878-CC: Very Fine; $0.80.

Twenty-cent piece:
1875-CC: Uncirculated; rare; $2.75.

Quarters:
1870-CC: Very Fair; scarce; $4.00.
1872-CC: Poor; very scarce; $0.75.
1873-CC, With Arrows: Good; scarce;
$0.55.
1875-CC: Fine; $0.25.
1876-CC: Uncirculated; $0.35.
1877-CC: Extremely Fine; $0.45.
1878-CC: Uncirculated; $0.30.

Half dollars:
1870-CC: Very Good; scarce; $1.00.
1871-CC: Good; scarce; $0.60.
1872-CC: Fine; scarce; $0.95.
1873-CC, With Arrows: Large CC;
Good; $0.60.
1873-CC, With Arrows: Small CC;
Very Good; scarce; $0.60.
1874-CC: Fine; $1.05.
1875-CC: Fine; scarce; $0.60.
1876-CC: Brilliant; Sharp Uncirculated;
rare; $1.00.
1877-CC: Extremely Fine; $0.60.
1878-CC: Brilliant; Sharp Uncirculated;
rare; $2.90.[8]

Silver dollars:
1870-CC: Fine; rare; $4.40.
1872-CC: Uncirculated; very rare;
$35.00.
1873-CC: Pin scratches; Very Good;
rare; $9.25.

Trade dollars:
1873-CC: Fine; scarce; $4.60.[9]
1874-CC: Fine; scarce; $4.60.
1875-CC: Fine; scarce; $3.00.

New Orleans Mint

Half dimes:
1838-O, No Stars: Fine; $2.50.
1839-O: Extremely Fine; $0.55.
1840-O, No Drapery: Very Fine; rare;
$2.00.
1840-O, No Drapery: Fine; rare; $0.50.
1841-O: Very Fine; $0.55.
1842-O: Circulated; Good; $0.30.
1844-O: Fine; $0.60.
1848-O: Very Fine; $0.55.
1849-O: Nick on edge; Very Fair; rare;
$0.20.[10]
1850-O: Very Fine; $0.40.
1851-O: Sharp Uncirculated; $0.60.
1852-O: Fine; rare; $1.00.
1852-O: Good; rare; $0.10.
1853-O: Uncirculated; $0.15.
1854-O: Uncirculated; $0.80.
1855-O: Very Good; scarce; $0.40.
1856-O: Uncirculated; $0.35.
1857-O: Extremely Fine; $0.40.
1858-O: Uncirculated; $0.20.
1859-O: Uncirculated; $0.20.
1860-O, O Below Bow: Fine; $0.20.

Dimes:
1838-O, No Stars: Very Fine; scarce;
$2.10.
1839-O, Small O: Good; $1.00.
1840-O: Very Good; $0.75.
1841-O: Fine; $0.45.
1842-O: Very Good; $0.20.
1845-O: Very Good; $0.20.
1849-O, Large O: Very Fine; $1.55.
1849-O, Small O: Fine; $1.50.
1851-O: Fine; $0.40.
1852-O: Very Fine; $0.55.
1853-O: Very Fine; $0.25.
1854-O: Uncirculated; $0.45.
1856-O: Very Fine; $0.20.
1857-O: Uncirculated; $0.20.
1858-O: Very Fine; $0.40.
1859-O: Extremely Fine; $0.80.
1860-O, O Below Bow: Small nick;
Fine; rare; $4.00.
1891-O: Uncirculated; $0.25.

Quarters:
1840-O, No Drapery: Reverse O Over A; From circulation; $0.25.
1840-O, No Drapery: Reverse O to Right of R; Uncirculated; rare; $2.70.
1840-O, Drapery: Reverse O Over R; Uncirculated; $0.95.
1841-O: Very Fine; $2.20.
1842-O, Large Date: O High to Right of R; Very Fine; $0.80.
1842-O, Large Date: O Lower to Right of R; Circulated; $0.50.
1842-O, Small Date: Very Good, $2.00.
1843-O: Fine; rare; $1.30.
1844-O: Extremely fine; rare; $1.50.
1847-O: Very Good; $0.45.
1850-O: Fine; $0.50.
1851-O: Circulated; $1.15.
1852-O: Pin puncture; Extremely Fine; $2.10.
1853-O: Very Fine; $0.60.
1856-O: Very Good; $0.50.
1857-O: Extremely Fine; $0.50.
1858-O: Very Fine; $0.50.
1859-O: Extremely Fine; $0.50.
1860-O: Uncirculated; $0.70.
1891-O: Sharp Uncirculated; $1.45.

Half dollars:
1840-O: Uncirculated; rare; $2.70.
1841-O: Uncirculated; scarce; $2.80.
1842-O: Fine; $2.00.
1843-O: Extremely Fine; $1.00.
1844-O: Extremely Fine; $1.15.
1845-O: Brilliant; Uncirculated; $2.00.
1846-O: Tarnished; Very Fine; $1.00.
1847-O: Extremely Fine; $1.00.
1848-O: Uncirculated; rare; $1.50.[11]
1849-O: Uncirculated; rare; $1.00.
1850-O: Uncirculated; $1.10.
1851-O: O in angle formed by stem of twig and feather of arrow; Sharp Uncirculated; rare; $2.00.
1851-O: O farther to right, close to stem of twig; Fine; $1.75.
1852-O: Bold impression; Extremely Fine; rare; $3.00.
1853-O: Very Fine; $0.55.

1853-O: Duplicates; Very Good; 2 pieces; $0.50 each.
1854-O: Extremely Fine; $0.50.
1855-O: Pin scratch in field, following arm; Sharp Uncirculated; $0.80.
1856-O: Sharp Uncirculated; $0.80.
1857-O: Very Fine; $0.85.
1858-O: Sharp Uncirculated; $0.65.
1859-O: Extremely Fine; $0.55.
1860-O: Uncirculated; $0.60.
1861-O: Sharp Uncirculated; $0.95.

Silver dollars:
1846-O: Very Fine; rare; $4.10.
1850-O: Extremely Fine; $3.40.
1859-O: Extremely Fine; $1.20.
1860-O: A few pin dots; Uncirculated; rare; $2.10.

San Francisco Mint
Half dimes:
1863-S: Very Fine; scarce; $2.10.
1864-S: Fine; scarce; $1.00.
1865-S: 5 Over 3; Fine; Scarce; $2.00. [This variety is unknown today.]
1866-S: Very Fine; scarce; $2.10.
1867-S: Very Fine; scarce; $2.30.
1868-S: Very Fine; scarce; $1.25.
1869-S: Fine; scarce; $1.25.
1872-S, S Above Bow: Uncirculated; scarce; $2.30.
1872-S, S Below Bow: Uncirculated; scarce; $2.00.
1873-S: Very Fine; scarce; $1.25.

Dimes:
1859-S: Good; $0.70.
1860-S: 13 Stars; Uncirculated; rare; $5.00.
1863-S: Circulated; Good; scarce; $0.35.
1864-S: Uncirculated; $0.65.
1865-S: Good; scarce; $0.45.
1867-S: Uncirculated; $0.45.
1868-S: Good; scarce $0.35.
1868-S, Duplicate: Very Fair; $0.15.
1869-S: Uncirculated; scarce; $0.55.
1870-S: Good; scarce; $0.55.
1872-S: Uncirculated; scarce; $0.55.
1873-S: Uncirculated; very scarce; $0.55.

1874-S: Fine; $2.00.

1875-S, S Above Bow: Uncirculated; $0.20.

1875-S, S Below Bow: Uncirculated; $0.20.

1876-S: Very Fine; $0.10.

1877-S: Uncirculated; $0.15.

1884-S: Fine; $1.35.

1885-S: Very Good; rare; $0.60.

1886-S: Uncirculated; $0.10.

1887-S: Uncirculated; $0.35.

1888-S: Uncirculated; $0.25.[12]

1889-S: Uncirculated; $0.35.

1890-S: Uncirculated; $0.15.[13]

1891-S, Large S: Very Fine; $0.10.

1891-S, Small S: Uncirculated; $0.30.

Twenty-cent pieces:

1875-S: Sharp; Uncirculated; $0.25.

1875-S, Duplicate: Uncirculated; $0.25.

Quarters:

1855-S: Very Good; $0.90.

1858-S: Fair; $0.30.

1860-S: Fine; scarce; $2.40.

1861-S: Fine; scarce; $3.00.

1862-S: Good; $0.40.

1864-S: Fine; scarce; $0.30.[14]

1865-S: Very Good; $0.30.

1866-S: Good; $1.00.

1867-S: Very Good; $3.00.

1868-S: Very Good; $0.35.

1869-S: Rather poor; scarce; $0.35.

1871-S: Very Fine; rare; $2.00.

1872-S: Very Good; $0.55.

1873-S: S in angle; Fine; scarce; $0.40.

1873-S: S to left; Very Good; $0.40.

1874-S: Uncirculated; scarce; $0.60.

1875-S: Uncirculated; $0.50.

1876-S: Uncirculated; $0.25.

1877-S: Uncirculated; $0.25.

1878-S: Uncirculated; $0.40. [Later this would be recognized as a rarity.]

Half dollars:

1856-S: Sharp; Uncirculated; $12.00.

1857-S, Large S: Very Good; scarce; $1.30.

1857-S, Small S: Fair; $0.55.

1858-S, Large S: Very Good; $0.80.

1858-S, Medium S: Very Good; $0.60.

1859-S: Fine; has been cleaned in acid; $0.65.

1860-S, Large S: Fine; scarce; $1.25.

1860-S, Medium S: Very Good; $0.60.

1861-S, Large S: Very Good; $0.55.

1861-S, Medium S: Good; $0.70.

1862-S, Medium S: Very Fine; $0.85.

1863-S: Fine; $0.75.

1864-S: Fine; $1.00.

1865-S: S over center of F; Fine; $0.70.

1865-S: S more to the left of F; Fine; $0.65.

1866-S, No Motto; A beautiful Uncirculated impression; rare; $31.00.

1866-S, With Motto: S under arrow's feathers; Very Good; $0.60.

SILVER COINS, CARSON CITY MINT.

CARSON CITY MINT.

803	**Dollars.** 1870.	Fine. Rare.
804	— 1872.	Uncirculated. Very rare.
805	— 1873.	Pin scratches. Very good; rare.
806	— 1873.	Trade Dollar. Fine; scarce.
807	— 1874.	Trade. Fine.
808	— 1875.	Trade. Fine.
809	— 1878.	Standard. Sharp, uncirculated.
810	— 1881.	Sharp, uncirculated; scarce.
811	— 1883.	Sharp, uncirculated; scarce.
812	— 1885.	Brilliant, sharp, uncirculated; very scarce.
813	— 1890.	Sharp, extremely rare.
814	— 1891.	Brilliant, sharp, uncirculated.
815	— 1892.	Uncirculated.
816	— 1893.	Brilliant, sharp, uncirculated.
817	— 1893.	Uncirculated.
818	**Half Dollars.** 1870.	Very good; scarce.
819	— 1871.	Good.
820	— 1872.	Fine; scarce.
821	— 1873.	Without arrows. Fine; scarce.
822	— 1873.	Arrows. Large cc; good.
823	— 1873.	Arrows. Small cc; very good, scarce.
824	— 1874.	Fine.
825	— 1875.	Fine; scarce.
826	— 1876.	Brilliant, sharp, uncirculated. Rare.
827	— 1877.	Extremely fine.
828	— 1878.	Brilliant, sharp, uncirculated. Scarce.
829	**Quarter Dollars.** 1870.	Very fair; scarce.
830	— 1872.	Poor; very scarce.
831	— 1873.	Arrows; good, scarce.
832	— 1875.	Fine.
833	— 1876.	Uncirculated.
834	— 1877.	Extremely fine.
835	— 1878.	Uncirculated.
836	**Twenty Cents.** 1875.	Uncirculated; rare.
837	**Dimes.** 1872.	Very good; rare.
838	— 1875.	c.c. within wreath. Very fine.
839	— 1875.	c.c. beneath wreath. Very good.

A page from the Friesner catalog with annotations showing the prices realized.

1866-S, With Motto: S in angle formed by stem of twig and feather; Very Good; $0.70.

1867-S: Very Fine; $0.65.

1868-S: Fine; $0.60.

1869-S: Very Fine; $0.75.

1870-S: Fine; $0.55.

1871-S, Medium S: Very Fine; $0.70.

1871-S: Small S in angle; Very Fine; $0.60.

1871-S: Small S to left of angle; Very Fine; $0.70.[15]

1872-S: S high; Very Fine; scarce; $0.70.

1872-S: S low; Very Fine; scarce; $0.75.

1873-S: Fine; scarce; $0.65.

1874-S: Fine; scarce; $0.80.

1875-S, Large S: Uncirculated; $0.90.

1875-S, Small S: Uncirculated; $0.85.

1876-S: Sharp; Uncirculated; $0.60.

1877-S: Sharp; Brilliant Uncirculated; $0.60.

1878-S: Proof surface; Sharp; Uncirculated; very rare; $7.70.

Silver dollars:

1859-S: Sharp; Extremely Fine; rare; $5.30.

1872-S: Good; rare; $3.00.

Trade dollars:

1875-S: Fine; $1.75.

1875-S: Very Good; $1.00.

1876-S: Extremely Fine; $1.80.

1877-S: Uncirculated; $1.10.

Although the Friesner Collection had many gaps, it was the most-extensive auction offering of branch-mint coins up to this time. In ill health for a long time, William M. Friesner passed away on August 1, 1894. At the ANA convention later that month, a "Resolution of Respect" was passed.

A second important branch-mint collection (including die varieties) was sold by Frossard in its auction held on March 8 and 9, 1898.

Decades slipped by. Finally, in the 1930s, interest in mintmarks became widespread. This was due to several factors. In 1930 Wayte Raymond, manager of the coin division of the Scott Stamp & Coin Co. and owner of Wayte Raymond, Inc., acquired from Martin L. Beistle the right to market coin pages and albums under a patent issued to Beistle in 1927. The National line of albums eventually included Liberty Seated issues by date (not by mintmark).[16] For the first time, such coins could be mounted in convenient pages, safely stored, and under clear cellulose acetate slides could be viewed from both sides. Now a collection could be watched as it grew, and an unfilled hole represented a coin to be obtained. Silver coins placed in these albums acquire a halo of iridescent toning over a period of time from sulfur in the cardboard. In modern times such holders have been used often to impart rainbow toning to brilliant coins by heating the holders slightly to accelerate the process.

A few years later, Raymond issued the *Standard Catalogue of United States Coins*, the first reference book to list prices as well as mintage quantities. This was published in succeeding editions until 1957. These two Raymond products revolutionized coin collecting. Whitman Publishing, then based in Racine, Wisconsin, was part of the boom. Whitman issued "penny boards" and other sheets, albums, and folders, but did not become involved in Liberty Seated coinage.

In November 1946 Whitman launched *A Guide Book of United States Coins* with a cover date of 1947. Based on research and information gathered by Stuart Mosher and edited by Richard S. Yeo (*nom de plume* R.S. Yeoman), the cumulative later editions have placed the book among the best-selling non-fiction titles of all time (with more than 23 million copies in print). In later decades, numismatic magazines added to the interest with news of the latest discoveries, auction offerings, and market guides.

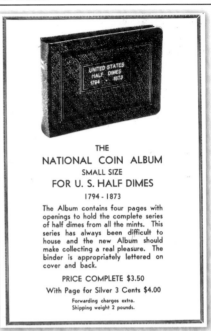

July 9, 1929.   M. L. BEISTLE   1,719,962
DISPLAY HOLDER
Filed Oct. 26, 1927   2 Sheets–Sheet 2

U.S. Patent No. 1,719,962 filed on
October 26, 1927, granted on July 9,
1929, for Beistle's "Display Holder."

THE
NATIONAL COIN ALBUM
SMALL SIZE
FOR U. S. HALF DIMES
1794 - 1873

The Album contains four pages with
openings to hold the complete series
of half dimes from all the mints. This
series has always been difficult to
house and the new Album should
make collecting a real pleasure. The
binder is appropriately lettered on
cover and back.

PRICE COMPLETE $3.50
With Page for Silver 3 Cents $4.00

Forwarding charges extra.
Shipping weight 2 pounds.

The National Album for Liberty Seated
half dollars by date. A hole could
be filled by a coin from any mint.

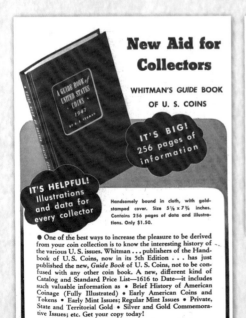

New Aid for
Collectors

WHITMAN'S GUIDE BOOK
OF U. S. COINS

IT'S BIG!
256 pages of
information

IT'S HELPFUL!
Illustrations
and data for
every collector

Handsomely bound in cloth, with gold-
stamped cover. Size 5½ x 7¾ inches.
Contains 256 pages of data and illustrations. Only $1.50.

● One of the best ways to increase the pleasure to be derived
from your coin collection is to know the interesting history of
the various U. S. issues. Whitman . . . publishers of the Hand-
book of U. S. Coins, now in its 5th Edition . . . has just
published the new, Guide Book of U. S. Coins, not to be confused with any other coin book. A new, different kind of
Catalog and Standard Price List—1616 to Date—it includes
such valuable information as ● Brief History of American
Coinage (Fully Illustrated) ● Early American Coins and
Tokens ● Early Mint Issues; Regular Mint Issues ● Private,
State and Territorial Gold ● Silver and Gold Commemorative Issues; etc. Get your copy today!

See Your Coin Dealer or Write to the

WHITMAN PUBLISHING COMPANY
DEPT. HV ● RACINE, WISCONSIN

THE NATIONAL COIN ALBUM
Designed and Published by Wayte Raymond, Inc.

A smaller-format National Album
for half dimes 1794 to 1873.

An announcement for the first edition
of A Guide Book of United States Coins,
popularly known as the "Red Book."

Proof Coins for Collectors

By the time the Liberty Seated design was inaugurated in 1836, there were several-dozen numismatists who collected American coins along with medals, ancient coins, and foreign issues. Proof coins with mirror-like finishes, called Master Coins or Specimens in early Mint correspondence, were often supplied for face value on request as an accommodation. After the Mint Cabinet was formed in June 1838, collectors had a meeting place in Philadelphia to trade coins and discuss the hobby. Records concerning the making and distribution of Proof coins are virtually non-existent prior to 1858. Some were produced as parts of sets containing all copper, silver, and gold denominations. The earliest known is dated 1821 and is in the National Numismatic Collection in the Smithsonian Institution. The full sets of 1834 Proof coins made for diplomatic presentation to the sultan of Muscat and the king of Siam are the most famous of such early issues.

The number of Proof coins known today for each issue prior to the late 1850s varies widely. It is certain that most were struck singly and not in sets. Remarkably, Proof Capped Bust quarters of 1827, one of America's most famous rarities, appear at auction more often than Proof Liberty Seated quarters of any given date from 1838 into the early 1840s.

Proof coins were issued yearly by the Philadelphia Mint for the Liberty Seated series except for 1851 and 1853. Restrikes of the 1851 silver dollar from a die with the date centered were made beginning in spring 1859 or later.[17] Sometime during the 1860s, George F. Jones noticed that no numismatists owned a Proof 1853 silver dollar and none had been reported. Obligingly, the Mint restruck 12 coins for collecting purposes. A few scattered coins of other 1853 denominations attributed as Proofs have come on the market from time to time, but their circumstances of issuance are not known. Breen's 1989 revision of *Walter Breen's Encyclopedia of United States and Colonial Proof Coins, 1722–1989* assumes that various Proofs were struck (but provides no sources for mintage times or quantities) and cites certain auction appearances. David W. Akers suggested that the only true Proofs of this year are restrike silver dollars (see note under the 1853, With Arrows, quarter in chapter 7).

James Ross Snowden was appointed Mint director in June 1853. He became very interested in Washington tokens and medals and set about making restrikes and unusual die combinations for private sale to collectors, as previously noted (see chapter 1). Proofs of regular-issue coins were in strong demand.

A letter written in 1860 provides information concerning the number of Proof sets made in 1858, a year before the Mint began publicly releasing mintage figures for silver and gold Proof coins.[18] The writer was J. Ledyard Hodge, a Philadelphian who actively bought, sold, and traded coins. This letter was sent to Robert Alonzo Brock, a collector in Richmond, Virginia:

A half dollar of 1868 from a silver Proof set of the year; 600 sets were coined. 30.6 mm.

Phila-March 13th, 1860
R. Alonzo Brock, Esq.

Dear Sir,

I have delayed answering your last letters, hoping every day to pick up something that might increase your collection, but I find things remarkably dull in the coin line, and when any fine or rare pieces do make their appearance it is with such prices attached as to frighten any one. I however send you some pieces by Adams Express which please enquire for the cost of them being in annexed list.

The Mint has raised its price for Proof sets this year to $3; until now they charged merely their actual value of $2.02 but last year the demand was so great that it kept the time of one person occupied nearly the whole year, attending to getting up the pieces and delivering them., they being all struck on the hand press, with special care. So this year they justify the additional charge on the ground of the trouble and time used. These Proof sets of back years increase in value rapidly. Those of 1859 are already worth $4.50 to $5 and of previous years $8 to $10, and perhaps even more. Previous to 1859 there were very few struck in each year, not over 200 sets. The set of 1858 possesses a value on this account that there were no silver dollars at all struck of that year, except about 210 to go in the Proof sets, so that these dollars will soon be very rare indeed. In fact they are worth $5 already.[19]

I was offered a set of 1858 same pieces as in the one of 1860 I send you for $8, but declined having it myself, and not knowing whether you cared for it at that price, though if you wish it at all you will probably have to give that or more. If you wish these Proof sets of back years, let me know and also how much you are willing to give. I would advise you if you wish them at all to take them at once, especially the 1858 and 1859 at present prices. The previous ones I think have attained nearly their fixed price, and besides are not often to be met at any price. I have also declined buying any of the pattern pieces of the Mint cents or others, or any of the rare silver or copper coinage as half cents of the 1840s etc., not feeling authorized to invest $4 or $5 on a single piece without direction from you.[20] If you wish any of these pieces I think you had better make out a list of the pieces you wish and their value to you as a guide for me.

Have you come across any new store cards, etc. I find one or two almost every day, but must say I do not admire the prices. As the ones I want now are almost invariably rare ones. I am put in for at least $1 apiece for them, and it is awful to look over my list of pieces specially wanted and seen over 100 blanks, of ones I know of besides any quantity unknown.

In haste,
Yr's very truly,
J. Ledyard Hodge

On December 20, 1859, Mint Director Snowden issued a circular detailing the charges for Proof coins. The gold sets with the denominations of $1, $2.50, $3, $5, $10, and $20 had face value of $41.50 and sold for $43, reflecting the face value of each coin plus a 25¢ per coin proofing charge.

In 1859 each Proof set contained a one-cent piece, three-cent piece, half dime, dime, quarter dollar, half dollar, and silver dollar for a face value of $1.94 and were sold for $3. Snowden's circular stated:

> To carry with effect the direction as to the passing out of Master Coins, contained in the circular of the 20th of December, 1859, the following regulations are made:

1. The chief coiner will deliver them to the treasurer as other coins are delivered and shall, as in other cases, be checked as by the weight of the coins.

2. The Treasurer will be charged for the same as in similar cases.

3. The premium on the sets or single pieces delivered to applicants will be paid monthly with the ordinary funds of the Mint to meet the expenses which have been incurred in preparing and striking these master coins.

4. When single pieces are desired, their price is as follows:

Silver dollar $1.60   Half dime $0.08
Half dollar $0.75   Three-cent piece $0.05
Quarter dollar $0.35   Cent $0.02
Dime $0.15

This, of course, adds up to $3.00. On speculation and anticipating large sales, the Mint struck 800 Proof sets of silver coins in 1859 and 1,000 sets each in 1860 and 1861. In addition, extra cents were made. Sales fell below expectations, and most of the silver coins were placed into circulation to avoid wasting the work.[21] Beginning in 1862, the Mint was more cautious with the quantities produced.

In later years the prices of Proofs varied, new denominations were added, others were dropped, and so on. For example, the *American Journal of Numismatics* gave this information in April 1883:

At the opening of each year, demands are made at the Mint by coin collectors, numismatic societies, and others, for Proof coins, or sets representative of a year's coinage. To meet this demand, special coins are struck as is well known, and sold at rates proportional to the extra labor involved. These sets are in gold, silver, nickel, and copper. The regular Proof set of gold coins is sold for $43; the silver and minor $4.05; and exclusive of the trade dollar $3.05. The minor coins, embracing the old and new 5-cent coin, the 3-cent piece, and the bronze penny, are sold at 18 cents the set. The stamping of the new 5-cent coin has increased the interest among collectors, and many requests are made for the set containing the old and new half-dime piece.

From the late 1850s onward, yearly figures were given for gold coins individually and silver Proofs in sets, but additional silver coins of specific denominations were made upon request. Although it was thought that unsold supplies were melted, Mint correspondence reveals that quantities were kept on hand for years afterward, even though other Mint records say "melted."[22] The coins presumed to have been destroyed mainly went to numismatists. By June 15, 1875, the Mint had on hand, unsold, complete gold Proof sets dating back to 1862 that were offered for sale via letter.[23] In a phrase: information released from the Mint regarding the total production, distribution, and melting of Proofs of this era is unreliable in many instances.

Expansion of Interest and Information

There was a time when the majority of numismatists interested in Liberty Seated coins sought as many different basic dates and mintmarks as possible, as well as overdates and other varieties listed in the *Guide Book of United States Coins*. Many others limited their purchases to Proofs by date, usually commencing with 1858. There was a limited interest in varieties—such as minute variations in dies—beyond this point. Such pursuits were aided by Daniel W. Valentine's *The United States Half Dimes*, published by the American Numismatic Society in 1931, and M.L. Beistle's *A Register of Half Dollar Die Varieties and Sub-Varieties, Being a description of each die variety used in the coinage of United States Half Dollars*, published in 1929.

The hobby of coin collecting expanded dramatically beginning in 1960 with the launching of *Coin World*, the first weekly publication in the hobby, followed by nationwide publicity surrounding the "rare" 1960 Small Date Lincoln cent.[24] Prices rose across the board, especially for federal coins minted from 1792 onward. It became very expensive to collect multiple series. By that time there were only two American-specialized clubs or groups devoted to a specific discipline: the American Vecturist Society founded in 1948, devoted to transportation tokens, and the Rittenhouse Society established in 1957, a group of researchers and writers. The decades of the 1960s into the 1980s saw a dramatic expansion. New groups included the Token and Medal Society, the Society of Paper Money Collectors, Early American Coppers, the John Reich Collectors Society, the Numismatic Bibliomania Society, and more.[25] Each issued a newsletter or magazine, had meetings annually and sometimes on other occasions, and made it possible for collectors of like interest to share news and findings.

The Liberty Seated Collectors Club was formed in 1974 through the efforts of Kam Ahwash, a specialist in Liberty Seated dimes, who in 1977 published the *Encyclopedia of U.S. Liberty Seated Dimes, 1837–91*, the first modern study of die varieties among coins of this design. Today, the club and its *Gobrecht Journal* are the focal point for the series studied here. For most of the period up to 2014 John W. McCloskey was editor and a major contributor to the *Journal*.

Interest expanded, and more books were published to cover and assign numbers to die varieties, including: *The Comprehensive Encyclopedia of United States Liberty Seated Quarters*, by Larry Briggs (1991); *The Complete Guide to Liberty Seated Half Dimes*, by Al Blythe (1992); *The Complete Guide to Liberty Seated Dimes* by Brian Greer (1992); *The Complete Guide to Liberty Seated Half Dollars*, by Randy Wiley and Bill Bugert (1993); and *Double Dimes—The United States Twenty-Cent Piece*, by Lane J. Brunner and John M. Frost (2014). This was succeeded, in large part, by Gerry Fortin's "Liberty Seated Dimes—Die Varieties, 1837–1891" on the Internet.

Many other books have added to this knowledge, including *Walter Breen's Complete Encyclopedia of U.S. and Colonial Coins* (1988) which gave much information about die varieties, including the Liberty Seated series. Bill Fivaz and J.T. Stanton's *Cherrypickers' Guide to Rare Die Varieties* became immensely popular and describes interesting and often valuable varieties that in many instances can be purchased unattributed at no more than a common coin of the same date and mint would cost. Kevin Flynn has published the *Authoritative Reference* series giving enlarged illustrations and descriptions of many varieties.

The Study of Coins and Dies

Most of the specialized books on Liberty Seated coins, as well as many articles in the *Gobrecht Journal* and the *Cherrypickers' Guide*, give information on interesting coin features and die characteristics. These include:

Misplaced dates: Abbreviated as MPD, these include dozens of coins in which tiny elements of the four-digit date logotype punch can be seen hidden in denticles or in the lower part of the seated figure—such as the top of an eight barely visible between two denticles. Although there are a number of theories and some controversy as to why many dozens of such varieties were made, mine is this: A workman about to impress a date punch into a working die did not know if the die had been hardened. To test this he gently tapped the punch into an inconspicuous spot. If the die was too hard to receive a punch impression it was softened, the punch entered, then rehardened. If the die metal was unhardened to begin with he punched the logotype into its place below the base of Miss Liberty. In most instances MPDs are not identified when coins are offered for sale, giving the collector an opportunity to cherrypick them for no additional cost.

Repunched dates: Abbreviated RPD, hundreds of these have been described. They were caused by a worker punching a four-digit logotype into a working die, then tapping the punch again but off-register. The 1844-O half dollar with the first date punched high and into the base of Miss Liberty is the most outstanding example of this. Others range from double- and triple-punched dates to dates in which only a small part of one digit is doubled.

Repunched mintmarks: Abbreviated as RPM, these show one or two traces of an earlier mintmark punch below the final one. The most dramatic examples show a large mintmark over a smaller one or a regular mintmark punched over one erroneously set in a horizontal position.

Repunched stars: On certain early Liberty Seated dies with obverse stars, 1838 to 1840, the 13 stars were individually punched into the dies by hand. Many coins show one or more stars with repunching.

Date positions: Ideally, the four-digit date is centered approximately between the base of Miss Liberty and the denticles. There are many variations in which the date is obviously too high, sometimes with one or more digits touching the base, or too far left or right.

A misplaced date on an 1871 Liberty Seated dollar. The top of an eight digit can be seen in the denticles.

A repunched date on an 1844 half dime.

An 1875-S quarter with the S mintmark over a previous erroneous horizontal S.

Mintmark positions: Variations in which a mintmark is away from its normal position create interest. Certain half dimes and dimes of the 1870s exist with the mintmark on the reverse below the bow and also above the bow. These are major and are listed widely, including in *A Guide Book of United States Coins*.

Rotated dies: Normal alignment of Liberty Seated issues is coin-wise, with the obverse and reverse dies 180 degrees apart. A few were deliberately made medal-wise with the obverse and reverse dies aligned in the same direction; certain restrike Gobrecht dollars, for example. Many coins of all denominations had the anvil or lower die slightly loose in the coining press, allowing it to rotate. Rotated or misaligned dies of varying degrees have been featured extensively in specialized studies.

Die deterioration: As a die was used to strike coins, it became worn. Some developed cracks, after which a Mint worker would remove it from use. In some instances they were kept in the press with multiple cracks, almost to the point of shattering. Sometimes a small piece would fall from the die, usually at the edge, with the result that a coin struck from such a die would show a blob or *cud*. In some instances dies were ground down slightly or *relapped* to remove irregularities from the field or elsewhere.[26] This process caused certain features such as the drapery at Liberty's elbow, the stars, or the date to lighten or, in instances of drapery, to disappear. Many coins struck from relapped dies have mirror-like surfaces. Dies stored in damp surroundings rusted, with the result that coins struck from them show myriad tiny raised dots or lumps.

Extensive die cracks on the obverse of an 1838 Large Stars dime.

The obverse die of this 1855-S half dollar was relapped, removing the drapery from the elbow and giving it a mirror-like surface, in this instance enhancing its value.

Selected examples of the preceding varieties are treated in the present work, but the vast majority will be found in the published and Internet sources mentioned throughout and in the bibliography.

THE AMERICAN SCENE
1836–1891
A chronicle of selected national and numismatic events during the era of Liberty Seated coinage.

The Years 1836 to 1838

CURRENT EVENTS. The year 1836 saw a great interest in building railroads, a relatively new type of transportation which eventually supplanted canals, which were still prominent during this decade. The Erie Canal, built from 1817 to 1825, was the most famous.

The *American Almanac* for 1836 reported that as of January 1, 1835, there were 2,867 miles of completed canals and approximately 1,600 miles of completed railroad track. In 1835, 465 miles of new railroad track were laid, followed by 175 miles in 1836, 224 in 1837, 416 in 1838, and varying amounts from that point onward. The anticipation of land opening up due to the laying of track also furnished an incentive to buy real estate.

On March 6, 1836, after 188 men defended themselves against an 11-day siege, the Alamo in San Antonio fell to 4,000 troops under the command of General Antonio López de Santa Anna. Among the dead, the names of William B. Travis, James Bowie, and Davy Crockett would live on in history. A little over a month later, the Texan side would win the war, and the Republic of Texas was founded with Sam Houston serving as president.

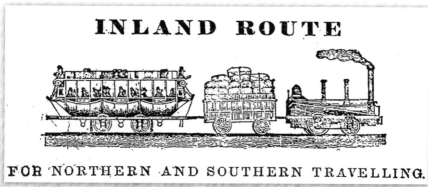

An engine and cars on the Richmond, Fredericksburg, and Potomac Rail Road Company. (From a broadside dated May 30, 1836)

Andrew Jackson had been in the White House since his inauguration on March 4, 1829. A controversial figure, his policies were widely criticized by many. Following the Tariff Act of 1828, which protected American industry, the economy had been very good. There were problems now and again, but overall the course was upward. The Treasury showed a favorable balance and, for the first and last time in history, the government refunded money to the various states.

By 1836 unbridled speculation in federal Western land had caused problems. Many buyers of tracts west of the Allegheny Mountains had paid for their purchases in bank notes, some of which had questionable value. To counter this, Jackson issued the Specie Circular which mandated that after August 15, 1836, only hard money—gold and silver coins—could be used in transactions. This and other factors had a chilling effect on the economy. Contemplating the presidential election of November 8, 1836, Andrew Jackson opted for retirement, and Vice President Martin Van Buren ran on the Democratic ticket against William Henry Harrison, Hugh Lawson White, and Daniel Webster. Van Buren won.

The second Bank of the United States, which had received a 20-year charter that was not renewed, wound down its business in early 1836, by which time the various branches had closed. Trouble began early in the year 1837 when the "Flour Riot" erupted in New York City's Chatham Square. A crowd had gathered to protest the high prices of bread, meat, and fuel. They drove off the mayor and the police, and stormed a warehouse holding flour. In March stock prices on Wall Street fell across a wide front of issues. Anxiety gripped the financial community. New Orleans, the trade center of the Mississippi Valley, was hit hard, and Herman Briggs & Company, a leading cotton-brokerage house, failed. In a domino effect, other brokers and factors went bankrupt, and banks experienced a cash shortage.

At the time, there were 788 banks in the United States (as of one reporting period in 1837; the number was constantly changing) with a combined capital of $291 million. These institutions had $149 million worth of paper money in circulation backed by $38 million worth of specie. Deposits totaled $127 million. Outstanding loans amounted to $525 million. The credit and cash crunch went from bad to worse, and on May 10, 1837, New York banks suspended specie payments under a state law which permitted them to do so for a one-year period. No longer was paper money exchangeable at par for gold and silver coins. Thus began the Panic of 1837, a period of hard times that lasted into the spring of 1843. Although hundreds of banks failed, most of those that remained in business resumed specie payments within a year or so. To fill the need for a circulating currency, change merchants and others issued millions of Hard Times tokens (as they are known today), most of which were the size of a copper cent.

Many varieties of copper and brass tokens were privately issued during the Hard Times era. This one (Whitman-11-520a, HT-32) satirized Martin Van Buren (who stated he would follow in the footsteps of Andrew Jackson) and also the slow movement of federal funds to banks. (shown at 150%)

The rules were that congressmen could receive their pay in specie—gold and silver coins. This became a great advantage in 1837 when banks were no long paying out such coins. An account of October 16, 1837, said that the Treasury had no gold coins (!), and that the Bank of the Metropolis, which had no gold coins either, was able to loan Congress some half dimes, dimes, and half dollars.[1]

THE NUMISMATIC SCENE. It was a time of innovation at the Mint, and steam was used for the first time to power coinage presses. A new denomination, the gold dollar, was proposed, and patterns were made, but no circulating coinage materialized. Second engraver Christian Gobrecht created the Liberty Seated design.

In June 1838 the Mint Cabinet was organized, and on March 31, 1839, Congress voted approval for a $1,000 appropriation to launch it as well as a $300 annual maintenance sum. The curators, William E. Dubois and Jacob R. Eckfeldt, assembled a collection of current and past coins as well as mineral samples. Adam Eckfeldt, who had been with the Mint since the 1790s, contributed many coins he had saved. In the same year branch mints were opened in New Orleans, Charlotte (North Carolina), and Dahlonega (Georgia). The last two minted only gold coins.

The Year 1839

CURRENT EVENTS. In the *United States Magazine and Democratic Review*, John L. O'Sullivan commented: "The far-reaching, the boundless future will be the era of American greatness. In its magnificent domain of space and time, the nation of many nations is destined to manifest to mankind the excellence of the divine principles to establish on earth the noblest temple ever dedicated. . . ." This statement was made in an era of slavery, the oppression of women, the abuse of children—all biblically rationalized—as well as the exploitation of Native Americans, massive fraud in banking and medicine, and widespread, grinding poverty.

Britain started the Opium War with China after Chinese officials destroyed $6 million worth of opium from India (mostly owned by Britons) stored in Canton warehouses. The East India Company promoted the use of opium to keep workers complacent and to provide profitable trade goods to a captive Chinese clientele. Elsewhere, especially in America and Europe, opium was a common ingredient of patent medicines, especially sleeping potions, painkillers, and tranquilizers for babies.

In 1839, 1,046 people were employed in gold mining, the capital invested in the industry totaled was $234,300, and the gold extracted amounted to $529,500, of which Virginia produced $52,000; North Carolina $256,000; South Carolina $37,000; Georgia $122,000; Alabama $61,000; and Tennessee $1,500. During the same year, the amount deposited for coinage came to $385,000, indicating that about seven-tenths of the annual production of gold from 1839 was converted into U.S. coins.

THE NUMISMATIC SCENE. Joseph Barlow Felt's *An Historical Account of Massachusetts Currency* was published, 248 pages in length (first edition). It was the first book with an American imprint to treat a numismatic subject in detail. The work was not intended for collectors, but, as the title indicates, it dealt with the history of money and media of exchange of the Massachusetts colony. Nevertheless, it was highly valuable and informative to numismatists.

Franklin Peale, in high regard at the Mint, was named to the post of chief coiner. By this time, new steam-powered presses had been in use at the Mint since 1836, and many improvements were in place. Almost immediately, Peale started to abuse his position and privileges, in effect stealing services from the government.

The Year 1840

CURRENT EVENTS. In 1840 the effects of the Panic of 1837 were still being felt, and although recovery was underway, many areas of business and finance were uncertain. The presidential election went to William Henry Harrison, the hero of the Battle of Tippecanoe, who captured 234 electoral votes to former president Martin Van Buren's 60. "Tippecanoe and Tyler, too" (John Tyler became vice president) had been a rallying campaign cry.

Temperance, abolition of slavery, and women's rights were three prime social causes, with abolition in the forefront. Canals formed the main focus for investment and development interest in the transportation sector, and about 3,300 miles of waterways were in service (as compared to an estimated 2,800 miles of railway operated by about 300 different companies, as most rail lines were quite short). During the next two decades, railroads would be in the ascendancy, and canals would gradually become obsolete. Track gauges varied widely because there were no standards in place, and it was not unusual for merchandise to be transferred several times to different cars during the course of a long trip.

THE NUMISMATIC SCENE. Beginning in 1838 and continuing into the early 1840s, there were many newspaper accounts (mostly published in the South) of counterfeit half dimes and dimes in circulation. These could be readily identified as they had no stars on the obverse. The *National Intelligencer* and other papers pointed out that these were actually not counterfeit but in fact genuine coins of 1837 that were made without stars. No matter, the warnings to the public continued.

A temperance medal of the 1840s. Such was put on a string and worn by advocates who had taken "the pledge." (shown at 150%)

There were no organized societies in numismatics, and in all of America there were probably no more than a few-dozen serious collectors. The center of activity was Philadelphia, where Mint officials were pleased to welcome numismatists who cared to come to visit the Mint Cabinet or acquire Proofs and other coins, which were obligingly furnished at face value. There were no coin dealers per se in the United States, but bankers and bullion dealers filled the gap. Indeed, these (and occasional numismatists who cared to trade) were nearly the exclusive source of rare specimens acquired by the Mint Cabinet during this period.

The Year 1841

CURRENT EVENTS. William Henry Harrison, elected president in 1840, caught cold on his inaugural day and a month later, on April 4, 1841, died. Taking his place in the White House was his vice president, John Tyler, age 51. On June 12 an act calling for a fiscal bank of the United States was introduced in the Senate and was passed by both houses, but it was vetoed by President Tyler. Tyler's entire cabinet, with the exception of Secretary of State Daniel Webster, resigned in protest over the president's action.

THE NUMISMATIC SCENE. For unknown reasons, the mintage of quarter eagles for the year was very limited, but these issues would not be generally recognized as rarities until 1909.

The Year 1842

CURRENT EVENTS. Abolition remained the most soul-searching and divisive issue on the American scene. In March the situation was greatly aggravated when the Supreme Court upheld the Fugitive Slave Act of 1793 but interpreted it by saying while slave owners could recover runaways, the states were under no legal obligation to render assistance to the slaveholder. In Massachusetts, children under the age of 12 were limited to working no more than 10 hours per day. This was an era of great expansion and prosperity for textile mills in New England towns, and young children were among those employed to tend the looms.

Child labor would be exploited for many decades, and it was not until the efforts of Jacob Riis and others after the turn of the twentieth century that there would be a widespread public outcry against it. However, in 1842 child labor was not at the forefront of social causes. After all, children were then legally property or chattels, like wives and slaves. Connecticut established the first system of public education in the United States. Elsewhere, few children, especially those in rural districts, had much in the way of formal education.

The Opium War that had begun in 1839 ended with the Treaty of Nanking on August 29, 1842. China ceded the city of Hong Kong to England. Amoy, Canton, Foochow, Ningpo, and Shanghai were designated as cities in which foreigners could conduct trade and have special privileges, including freedom from many legal restrictions.

A young girl tending a loom.

THE NUMISMATIC SCENE. The end of the Opium War would open up considerable opportunity for trade between China and other countries, particularly England, and would have great implications in years to come. The Chinese preference for silver would cause trading agents to pay in Mexican silver pesos (eight reales) and, later, after 1873, also in American trade dollars. Were it not for opium, far fewer trade dollars would have been coined.

The first significant book published in America with appeal to numismatists appeared. Titled *A Manual of Gold and Silver Coins of All Nations, Struck Within the Past Century*, it was written by Mint officials Jacob Reese Eckfeldt and William Ewing DuBois. Various coins, including the 1804 silver dollar (a coin whose existence was not known to numismatists earlier), were illustrated by means of plates made by the Saxton medal-ruling machine, a descendant of the original machine invented by Christian Gobrecht in 1817. Eckfeldt and DuBois were the numismatic experts at the Mint and managed the Mint Cabinet, which was growing each year as additions were retrieved from bullion deposits received at the Mint.

The Year 1843

CURRENT EVENTS. About 1,000 settlers followed the Oregon Trail with missionary Marcus Whitman to settle in the Columbia River Valley. Samuel Finley Breese

Morse, a man of many talents, including an expertise in oil painting, was the beneficiary of a $30,000 appropriation by Congress to facilitate the construction of an experimental telegraph line between Washington, D.C., and Baltimore. At the time, news could travel only as fast as the speediest train, with the average being about 35 to 40 miles per hour.

THE NUMISMATIC SCENE. On May 9, 1843, Matthew A. Stickney, a numismatist from Salem, Massachusetts, visited the Mint Cabinet and obtained an 1804 silver dollar by exchanging a 1785 Immune Columbia cent in gold for it.[2]

The Year 1844

CURRENT EVENTS. James Knox Polk, a relatively unknown figure, was nominated for the presidency by the Democrats who were deadlocked in convention. Polk became the first "dark horse" candidate to run in a national election, besting Henry Clay by 170 electoral votes to 105.

Samuel F.B. Morse harvested the fruits of his congressional backing and transmitted the first telegraph message ("What Hath God Wrought?") from the Capitol building to Baltimore.

THE NUMISMATIC SCENE. On July 23, 1844, engraver Christian Gobrecht, primary designer of the Liberty Seated coins, died. While in office, Gobrecht did his work quietly and competently. He was succeeded on September 6, 1844, by James Barton Longacre, an accomplished engraver of illustration plates, including 24 published in the highly successful 3-volume (or 4 in another edition) *The National Portrait Gallery of Distinguished Americans*. Longacre had not been employed at the Mint prior to his appointment to the main engravership.

The Year 1845

CURRENT EVENTS. Florida joined the Union on March 3 as the 27th state, and on December 29 the erstwhile Republic of Texas (established in 1836) became the 28th. Trade with China, opened to Western commerce in 1842, continued to expand. In New York City the "extreme" (a term for the new, high-speed design) clipper ship *Rainbow* was launched. Such vessels would proliferate during the next 20 years, despite

The National Hotel in Washington, D.C., as engraved by James B. Longacre (who in 1844 would succeed Christian Gobrecht as engraver at the Mint).

competition from an ever-growing worldwide fleet of steam-powered iron ships. In Annapolis, the U.S. Naval Academy was opened.

THE NUMISMATIC SCENE. *The Annual Report of the United States Treasury*, 1845, stated that in that year, coins of the United States amounting to $844,446 had been exported, as had foreign coins to the amount of $7,762,049. Imported coins amounted to $3,962,864. Further:

> Specie is, in a commercial sense, an article of merchandise, bought and sold at every commercial point, and entering largely into the channels of foreign trade. It is almost as much an article of trade as a barrel of port: with this difference, the former has a value approaching a fixed value while the latter has a variable value. Specie may be considered in Europe and America as an article of merchandise, forming one of the items of an ordinary price current: ever variable in value, commercially and legally, its value ascertained by the same standard as a barrel of flour, viz. its weight—worth more at one point than another, but finally, it is a basis of wealth, the measure of value of all property, its exportation lessening our real wealth; and its importation (and it can be imported only upon two grounds, 1st, as the adjusting weight in the balance of trade or idly, as capital, for investment), adding to our actual national wealth.

An accounting of the coins possessed by the Massachusetts Bank in Boston in 1845 showed "that there was very little silver in the hands of the cashier and teller and that the gold was largely English, with French and American trailing far behind."[3]

J.L. Riddell, melter and refiner at the New Orleans Mint, wrote an octavo book with 371 numbered pages, *Monograph of the Silver Dollar, Good and Bad, Illustrated with Facsimile Figures*. The main market intended for this book probably consisted of dealers in bullion, who might have found it useful to detect counterfeits.

The Year 1846

CURRENT EVENTS. The war with Mexico began on January 13, 1846, following President James Knox Polk's unsuccessful attempt to purchase the New Mexico Territory from Mexico. The conflict began when Polk ordered General Zachary Taylor to advance to the Rio Grande River, and on April 25 the first clash occurred when Mexican troops invaded U.S. territory and shed American blood upon American soil. On May 13 Congress declared war, appropriated $10 million to wage it, and provided for the enlistment of 50,000 troops. General Antonio López de Santa Anna, former dictator of Mexico, took command of the Mexican Army, and on September 24 in Monterrey his force of 10,000 succumbed to 6,600 under the command of General Taylor. On November 15 Tampico yielded to American naval forces, and on November 16 Saltillo fell to General Taylor's troops.

THE NUMISMATIC SCENE. In Washington, D.C., Congress utilized a bequest of £100,000 from James Smithson (an Englishman who never visited America) to found the Smithsonian Institution "for the diffusion of knowledge." Today, the Smithsonian Institution houses the National Numismatic Collection. The Smithson gift was in the form of a large deposit of British gold sovereigns made at the Philadelphia Mint.

In 1846 a 138-page catalog of the holdings of the Mint Cabinet was written by co-curator William E. Dubois and published as *Pledges of History: A Brief Account of the Collection of Coins Belonging to the Mint of the United States*.

The Year 1847

CURRENT EVENTS. Military engagements in the Mexican War moved towards conclusion with a string of American victories at Vera Cruz, Cerro Gordo, Contreras, Churubusco, and Molina del Rey, and were capped by General Winfield Scott's triumph at Chapultepec on September 13. The one-sided war was over.

About 15,000 Mormons who had fled persecution in a series of towns during their westward migration reached the shores of the Great Salt Lake. There they found their land of refuge, although at the outset the district was anything but promising. Salt Lake City was founded by Mormon leader Brigham Young, who, with more than 20 wives, was an ardent proponent of polygamy.

THE NUMISMATIC SCENE. Jacob Reese Eckfeldt and William E. Dubois, curators of the Mint Cabinet, welcomed collectors during this era. Proof coins were supplied on request for face value. Most coins were sold singly, not in sets.

The Year 1848

CURRENT EVENTS. The prohibition of slavery in new territories of the United States was the platform of the newly organized Free-Soil Party. Free-Soil presidential candidate Martin Van Buren snatched away enough votes from the Democrats that their candidate, Lewis Cass, lost to the carrier of the Whig banner, war hero General Zachary Taylor, who had won the nomination instead of those familiar Whig political war horses Daniel Webster and Henry Clay.

In 1848 Harvard University president Edward Everett made this statement concerning complaints over the admission of a black student to the venerable institution: "If this boy passes the examination he will be admitted; and if the white students choose to withdraw, all the income of the college will be devoted to his education." Elsewhere on the human rights front, the first convention of women's rights activists was held in Seneca Falls, New York, under the direction of Lucretia Coffin Mott and Elizabeth Cady Stanton with 260 women and 40 men in attendance.

THE NUMISMATIC SCENE. On January 24, James Marshall, an employee of John Sutter, discovered gold flakes in the tail race of a sawmill he and others were building on the American River. The course of history was changed forever.

Sutter's sawmill on the American River.

Philadelphia publishers Carey & Hart issued Thomas Wyatt's extensively illustrated book of 315 numbered pages, *Memoirs of the Generals, Commodores, and Other Commanders, Who Distinguished Themselves in the American Army and Navy During the War of the Revolution.* Bank-note engraver W.L. Ormsby prepared 14 plates using a medal-ruling machine.

The Year 1849

CURRENT EVENTS. Gold! Gold! Gold! Newspapers of 1849 carried little other national news. Fortune hunters flocked to California by sea and by land.

THE NUMISMATIC SCENE. In California several private minters issued coins. The first seems to have been Norris, Gregg & Norris, who had a mint in Benicia City and issued $5 coins marked San Francisco. Moffat & Co. was the most prominent of the coiners. Privately minted coins were highly prized locally in an era when federal coins were scarce. The Coinage Act of March 4, 1849, authorized two new federal gold denominations: the dollar and double eagle.

Forty-niners on their way to the Land of Gold. It was not an easy overland journey, particularly west of Salt Lake City. (*The Annals of San Francisco*, 1855)

$10 gold coin issued in 1849 by the Miners Bank in San Francisco. (shown at 150%)

$5 gold coins minted by Norris, Gregg & Norris were in circulation by June 1849. (shown at 150%)

$5 gold coin of Moffat & Co., the most prolific private coiner in San Francisco. (shown at 150%)

The Year 1850

CURRENT EVENTS. The Gold Rush to California continued apace. *The Bankers' Magazine and Statistical Register* commented on the rising price of silver on the London market, the center of silver trading at the time, noting that the metal was becoming scarce for three main reasons: (1) the influx of California gold; (2) the requirements for pay and maintenance of the German armies; and (3) the substitution of silver for gold in Holland. It was also noted that there was a demand for silver in California (a point that does not seem to have been raised by observers in America at the time).

Jenny Lind, the "Swedish Nightingale," was brought to Castle Garden, New York City, by P.T. Barnum. On opening night, September 11, 1850, the total receipts were $36,238. She quickly became the singing sensation of the age. Caterpillars were a nuisance in New York, and the Brooklyn Institute sought to eliminate them by importing eight pairs of sparrows from England. The American Express Company was formed by a merger of several different companies and would go on to achieve great success in transportation, security, and, years later, international exchange.

Jenny Lind at Castle Garden.

THE NUMISMATIC SCENE. The double eagle, authorized in 1849, appeared in circulation as America's largest denomination. Jacob R. Eckfeldt and William E. Dubois, curators of the Mint Cabinet, published a small book of 61 numbered pages, *New Varieties of Gold and Silver Coins, Counterfeit Coins, Bullion with Mint Values.* This was intended for use by bullion and exchange brokers and gave exchange rates for various silver and gold coins. It also furnished a useful supplement to the 1842 *Assay Manual* by the same authors. Included was information on gold coins privately minted in California. At the time, such coins were arriving at the Mint in large quantities.

The Year 1851

CURRENT EVENTS. The Gold Rush continued to dominate the popular news. The clipper ship with its sleek hull and billowing sails was becoming popular, and in the next few years many would be made.

The *New York Times* began publication on September 18, 1851, and would go on to become the most famous of all American newspapers. The London Great Exhibition opened on May 1, 1851, and was the first of many world's fairs the world would see during the next century.

THE NUMISMATIC SCENE. The first American rare-coin auction of importance was that of the collection of Lewis Roper, MD, sold in Philadelphia on February 20, 1851, by M. Thomas and Son. Among other things, it contained Proof Gobrecht dollars of 1836, 1838, and 1839. The buyer was Ammi Brown of Boston. Roper had become ill and died aboard a ship when sailing from San Francisco to Panama, returning from the California gold fields.

In July 1851 Director of the Mint Robert Maskell Patterson was replaced by George N. Eckert, who served until April 1853. In San Francisco Augustus Humbert, recently arrived from New York, began business as the official government assayer of gold, and on the premises of Moffat & Co., began making octagonal $50 gold coins.

The Year 1852

CURRENT EVENTS. In the November presidential election, Democrat Franklin Pierce of New Hampshire won over the Whig entry, Mexican War hero Winfield Scott. Harriet Beecher Stowe's narrative of "life among the lowly" (per the subtitle), *Uncle Tom's Cabin*, was published in book form in Boston in March. The first printing of 5,000 copies sold out in a week, and 7 weeks later 50,000 copies had reached buyers. Within a year the total climbed to 300,000.

THE NUMISMATIC SCENE. Bankers in the East were in receipt of $50 gold "slugs" issued in California starting in 1851. These were purchased by banks at a two-percent discount from face value.[4]

The Year 1853

CURRENT EVENTS. This was the peak year of gold production in California. The United States sought to intimidate Japan into opening up its ports for trade and commerce. At the time, U.S. trade was burgeoning in other areas of Eastern Asia, particularly China. Commodore Matthew Perry of the U.S. Navy, commanding two steam frigates and two sloops of war, arrived in Edo (later known as Tokyo) in July 1853 with a demand for trade relations: "a right, not a favor." He stated in no uncertain terms that he would return the following year to pick up a favorable reply. There was turmoil within Japan because of the situation, and opinions were divided as to which was the right course. The emperor died, and in 1854 his successor, his 29-year-old brother, told Perry he would open two ports to trade.

In New York City, the Crystal Palace opened on July 14, 1853. This privately funded enterprise operated under the management of none other than showman P.T. Barnum, who also published the *Illustrated News*, one of several newspapers to make extensive use of engravings for illustrations. Situated on the south side of 42nd Street between 5th and 6th avenues, the Exhibition of the Industry of All Nations took place in a glittering structure of steel and glass that measured about 365-feet square and 149-feet high

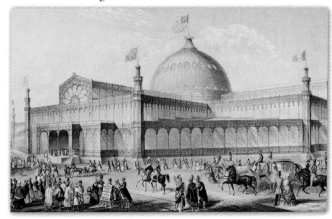

The Crystal Palace opened in New York City in 1853 under the aegis of P.T. Barnum and hosted many fairs and exhibits. A private enterprise, it never operated at a profit.

at the dome (which was 100 feet in diameter) and had about 173,000 square feet of exhibit space. Also in New York, Barnum's Museum—alternately called the American Museum—published a catalog of 153 numbered pages which included coins.

THE NUMISMATIC SCENE. In April 1853 Director of the Mint George N. Eckert was succeeded by Thomas M. Pettit, who served only a few weeks and was not confirmed—explaining why so little is heard of Pettit in numismatic chronicles. In June he was replaced by James Ross Snowden, who held the office until 1861. Snowden was quite interested in numismatics and wrote two books on the subject.

The Year 1854

CURRENT EVENTS. Due to political unrest in Germanic states during this era, many Germans immigrated to America, including 215,000 in 1854 alone. Many émigrés went to cities with already large German populations, such as Cincinnati and Milwaukee. Timothy Shay Arthur's novel, *Ten Nights in a Bar Room and What I Saw There*, was published. Sensational and full of lurid episodes with the backing of numerous members of the clergy, the tale was second in sales during the 1850s only to Harriet Beecher Stowe's *Uncle Tom's Cabin*.

Henry David Thoreau's *Walden* was published and included such aphorisms as "The mass of men lead lives of quiet desperation," and "If a man does not keep pace with his companions, perhaps it is because he hears a different drummer."

THE NUMISMATIC SCENE. Experiments to make cents thinner, narrower, and lighter (1854 and 1855) resulted in numerous patterns of designs similar to the Liberty Head motif on large cents (but without stars) or featuring a flying eagle copied from Gobrecht's dollar reverse. These were in copper, "French bronze" (95-percent copper, 5-percent tin and zinc, adopted in 1864), or other alloys. One especially curious coin (Judd-159) was made from an obverse die created by using a transfer lathe to reduce the obverse of an already-struck 1854 silver dollar. The San Francisco Mint was opened in March in remodeled facilities earlier used by Moffat & Co. and Curtis, Perry and Ward.

Chief coiner Franklin Peale's private minting operation within the Mint suffered a body blow after Colonel James Ross Snowden took office as Mint director in the early days of June 1853. Snowden justifiably viewed Peale's private business and other activities as illegal and of no benefit to the Mint. In 1854 Peale was fired. Many protests ensued, with Peale enlisting friends among Mint employees, scientists from around the city, and others to plead his case, stating that he was responsible for the modernization of the Mint facilities, the improvement of operations, and many other things. The Senate mounted an investigation, and Peale submitted testimony and a memorial on his own behalf.[5] However, Director Snowden examined the claims, and in a letter to Secretary of the Treasury James Guthrie, July 29, 1856, he demolished many of Peale's assertions by identifying other people who accomplished much of what Peale had claimed for himself.

Subsidiary silver coins from the three-cent piece to the half dollar were worth a 12.5-percent premium in the West Indies. Many were shipped there to buy goods.

The Year 1855

CURRENT EVENTS. In 1855 Congress voted to appropriate funds to construct a telegraph line from the Mississippi River to the West Coast. This would be completed in 1861. The Sault Ste. Marie (popularly called the "Soo") Canal opened and provided a water connection between lakes Huron and Superior. *Leslie's Illustrated Newspaper* began publication in New York City, to be followed the next year, 1856, by *Harper's Weekly*.

THE NUMISMATIC SCENE. Bullion dealers—these including speculators, banks, and exchange houses—were advised that Spanish-American dollars were generally received at $1.05 to $1.06-1/4, (proportionately for lesser denominations) at the Philadelphia Mint. The two-real or "two bits" quarter was received at $0.254, this contrary to speculation in countless newspaper articles of recent years that stated these were soon to become worth only 20¢ or even less. By this time most in circulation had seen extensive wear.

The auction of the Pierre Flandin Collection on June 5, 1855, was the most important rare-coin sale up to that point in time.

The Year 1856

CURRENT EVENTS. In the presidential election, James Buchanan, a Democrat from Pennsylvania, scored over his Republican opponent, the famous explorer John C. Frémont, and thus became America's only bachelor president. The Western Union Company, a consolidation of smaller telegraph firms, received its charter. In San Francisco a new vigilante group was formed, ostensibly to fight crime.

Cover of the "Valuable Collection," the cabinet formed by Pierre Flandin auctioned on June 6, 1855.

THE NUMISMATIC SCENE. At the Philadelphia Mint more than 800 small-diameter pattern cents with a flying eagle motif were made for distribution to Congressmen, newspaper editors, and others of influence. This set the stage to discontinue the large copper cent, minted since 1793, which had become expensive to manufacture and was widely viewed as being cumbersome to handle.

In 1856 Professor Daniel E. Groux, who had come to America from France in 1844, issued a 17 numbered-page *Prospectus of an Important Work in Three Volumes, to be called, Numismatical History of the United States, Comprising a Full Description of its Medals & Coins From the Earliest Period to Our Times.*[6]

The Year 1857

CURRENT EVENTS. The Supreme Court handed down the *Dred Scott* decision, which denied freedom to fugitive slave Dred Scott, who lived in the Minnesota Territory, a free area, and who brought suit to preserve his freedom. The Court decreed that black slaves could not bring suit in federal court, and that Congress lacked authority to ban slavery in the territories.

Financial markets suffered a chill in August when a leading New York City trading firm went bankrupt. This evolved into the Panic of 1857, which was mainly limited to banking and investment circles, not as much to the general public. The effects lasted well into 1858.

The Numismatic Scene. On September 12 the SS *Central America* foundered in a hurricane and sank, resulting in the loss of 425 lives and more than $1 million in gold coins and ingots.

The Act of February 21, 1857, had far-reaching numismatic implications. Among other provisions, the half cent, coined intermittently since 1793, was abolished, as was the large copper cent, which had been minted continuously since 1793 (with the solitary exception of 1815). The new cent, of the Flying Eagle design, copied Gobrecht's bird from the dollar reverse of 1836 to 1839, was of reduced diameter, and was made of a new alloy consisting of 88-percent copper and 12-percent nickel.[7]

Historical Magazine was launched, a monthly journal that contained many numismatic articles. For the *New York Dispatch* Augustus B. Sage initiated the first numismatic column to appear in a newspaper.

The Year 1858

Current Events. In Illinois, Abraham Lincoln accepted the nomination as Republican candidate for senator, stating that: "A house divided against itself cannot stand." Defeated by Stephen A. Douglas, Lincoln would go on to greater things. Slavery continued to be the main topic of discussion in Congress and in numerous state and local debates.

The American Bank Note Company was founded in New York City by a consolidation of seven engraving firms. The ABNCo. (as its credit line appeared on currency) would print federal bank notes until 1879 and postage stamps until 1894, after which it would continue to conduct a thriving business printing stock certificates, travelers' checks, currency for foreign countries (including Hawaii), and other security documents.

The Atlantic Cable, built by Cyrus Field and his associates, linked America and England by telegraph. Celebrations were held in New York City and elsewhere in August. Unfortunately, the signals soon failed, and an enduring connection was not made until after the Civil War. On October 27, 1858, the R.H. Macy Company opened its doors in New York City and eventually would become one of America's most famous retailers.

In the Kansas Territory the town of Denver was established, named after territorial governor James W. Denver. Placer gold was discovered at Cherry Creek, near Denver, setting off a gold rush. "Pikes Peak or Bust" was lettered on the sides of many wagons heading west.

Abraham Lincoln debating Stephen A. Douglas, 1858.

Celebrating the Atlantic Cable in New York City. (*Frank Leslie's Illustrated Newspaper*, September 11, 1858)

THE NUMISMATIC SCENE. In Albany, New York, J.H. Hickcox published *An Historical Account of American Coinage*, the first general-information guide of value to coin collectors. The American Numismatic Society was formed in March by teenaged Augustus B. Sage and friends and was active through this year and 1859. The fad of issuing historically themed medals began in the summer and became all the rage. In New York City, engraver George H. Lovett made many that were distributed by Sage, including the Odds & Ends, Numismatic Gallery, and Historical Series.

Mint Director James Ross Snowden began making restrikes and novodels openly to exchange for Washington tokens and medals needed for the Washington Cabinet being formed within the Mint Cabinet.

The Year 1859

CURRENT EVENTS. On October 16 John Brown led a party of more than a dozen white men and five black men to Harper's Ferry, Virginia, and took possession of the town and the federal arsenal there. It was the beginning of a hoped-for widespread insurrection by slaves. President Buchanan took action, and two days later Brown's remaining raiders were captured by federal troops under the command of Colonel Robert E. Lee. Brown was tried for treason, insurrection, and the murder of five men. He was found guilty and hanged.

The first medalet issued by Augustus B. Sage was Odds & Ends No. 1, from dies by George H. Lovett, observing the Crystal Palace disaster. 31 mm.

In the newly discovered vast ore deposit in Nevada that became known as the Comstock Lode, prospector George Hearst paid $450 for a half-interest in a mine that proved to be a bonanza. In Titusville, Pennsylvania, Edwin Laurentine Drake struck oil at a depth of 70 feet, and soon his well was yielding at the rate of 2,000 barrels per year. An "oil rush" ensued, and the district was soon teeming with drillers and prospectors.

THE NUMISMATIC SCENE. The Flying Eagle cent, in circulation only since 1857, was abandoned, and in 1859 the Indian Head cent made its appearance. Under Director James Ross Snowden, the Mint began the secret minting of restrikes of patterns and regular issues and the combining of illogical dies for private sale, mostly to William K. Idler, who then distributed them to the numismatic community. At the same time, he openly corresponded with some collectors who desired restrikes in exchange for Washington tokens and medals. (This activity was a very small part of such mintages; see chapter 9 for details.)

The *American Numismatical Manual* by Dr. Montroville W. Dickeson was published—large format, hardbound, and with embossed color illustrations. This was the first widely circulated volume issued on the coin hobby. Other editions were published in 1860 and 1865.

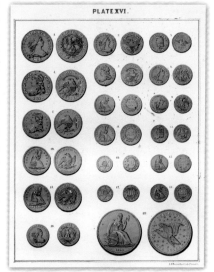

Plate XVI from the *American Numismatical Manual*, 1859.

The Year 1860

CURRENT EVENTS. In the presidential election, Abraham Lincoln garnered 40 percent of the popular vote and 180 electoral votes, while his main opponent, John C. Breckenridge, got 18 percent of the popular vote and 72 electoral votes. Stephen A. Douglas had 30 percent of the popular votes but just 12 electoral votes. John Bell gained 12 percent of the popular votes and 39 electoral votes. The election results were very distasteful to Southerners. On December 20, 1860, the South Carolina legislature voted 169–0 to secede from the Union.

The decennial census put the U.S. population at 31,443,321—twice that of 1820. New York City was the largest metropolis in the United States, with a population of 805,651, of whom 203,740 were Irish. The next-largest cities were Philadelphia with 562,529 inhabitants; Brooklyn 266,661; Baltimore 212,418; Boston 177,812; New Orleans 168,675; Cincinnati 161,044; St. Louis 160,773; Chicago 109,260; and San Francisco 56,802.

The Pikes Peak gold rush of 1858 had matured into several towns and a busy industry at the foot of the hills in and near Denver.

THE NUMISMATIC SCENE. The Washington Cabinet opened as part of the Mint Collection on Washington's birthday, February 22, with tokens and medals bearing his portrait being the center focus of the display. At the time, such pieces were the hottest items on the market. W. Elliot Woodward, who would become America's most honored rare-coin auctioneer in ensuing decades, conducted his first sale.

An ambassadorial delegation from Japan visited the Philadelphia Mint and was warmly welcomed. A full set of Proof coins was presented to them.

James Ross Snowden's *A Description of Ancient and Modern Coins in the Cabinet Collection at the Mint of the United States* was published. Today it is an important source for scholars. However, Snowden, who was heavily involved in the secret production of restrikes and rarities, did not see fit to disclose information on this activity.

The cased set of U.S. Proof coins from the cent to the double eagle presented to the Japanese delegation.

Reception of the Japanese delegation at the Philadelphia Mint on Thursday, June 13, 1860. (*Frank Leslie's Illustrated Weekly*, June 23, 1860)

The Year 1861

CURRENT EVENTS. The Civil War began on April 12, 1861, with the bombardment of federal Fort Sumter in the Charleston, South Carolina, harbor, and was officially declared on April 15. President Abraham Lincoln envisioned an easy win. He called for volunteers to enlist for 90 days, by which time the war would surely be over. In some of the larger Northern cities, parties and parades were held to send the soldiers off by train to the South.

Reality was different. The first major engagement was not fought until July 21, at Manassas, Virginia. In the Battle of Bull Run the Confederate troops vanquished the Yankees, who scattered to retreat to nearby Washington, D.C. and other safe places.

THE NUMISMATIC SCENE. The Dahlonega, Charlotte, and New Orleans mints fell into Confederate hands. At Charlotte, the Confederate States of America coined a few-hundred half eagles from worn Union dies. At Dahlonega, possibly as many as 1,000 1861-D gold dollars were made from unused Union dies. Following these ephemeral coinages, both mints closed, apparently from lack of a source of new dies, never again to reopen for coinage. The New Orleans Mint was operated for a brief time by the state of Louisiana and, later in 1861, the Confederacy. During this time, a pattern reverse die for a C.S.A. half dollar was made, and four coins were struck from it using a regular U.S. government Liberty Seated obverse die.

In late December concern for the outcome of the Civil War prompted the hoarding of gold coins, and banks stopped paying them out. James Ross Snowden's book, *The Medallic Memorials of Washington in the Mint of the United States*, was published this year.

The fall of Fort Sumter in April 1861.

The Battle of Bull Run in Manassas, Virginia, on July 21, 1861.

The Year 1862

CURRENT EVENTS. During the year, notable victories in the continuing Civil War were scored by both the Union and the Confederacy, with the Union's first significant success being the capture by General Ulysses S. Grant's forces of Fort Henry on the Tennessee River and Fort Donelson on the Cumberland River.

On March 8, the ironclad ships *Merrimac* and *Monitor* engaged each other off the coast of Virginia. Neither scored a victory, but the days of wooden ships were numbered. In November Lincoln relieved McClellan of his command and appointed General Ambrose Everett Burnside in charge of the Army of the Potomac. In January 1863 Burnside was given his walking papers following the general's defeat at the hands of Robert E. Lee at the Battle of Fredericksburg on December 13, 1862.

In its infinite wisdom, Congress offered 100 million acres of federal land to the Union Pacific, Central Pacific, and other railroads seeking to construct routes to the West Coast. The sale of land by the new owners would pay the large expenses involved. The railroads would repay the favor by forming trusts and charging the public erratic and often exorbitant rates.

THE NUMISMATIC SCENE. Fearful of the outcome of the Civil War, citizens began hoarding coins. Gold coins had been selling at a premium (in terms of paper money of sound state-chartered banks) since the final days of December 1861. On January 10, 1862, the *New York Herald* reported that brokers and exchange houses were paying a premium of one percent for subsidiary silver coins (denominations from three cents to a half dollar). Legal Tender Notes, not redeemable at par in gold or silver coins, were authorized in March. This increased the public's concern for the solidity of Union finances. By the second week of July hoarders had removed all coins from circulation, including copper-nickel cents. Brokers were paying an eight-percent premium for subsidiary silver coins. This spawned the issuance of tokens, encased postage stamps, postage currency, and scrip notes in large quantity.

A postage-currency
note of 1862.

The Year 1863

CURRENT EVENTS. President Lincoln's Emancipation Proclamation took effect on January 1, but it made little difference to the nearly 4 million slaves in the South who remained in bondage. The Civil War progressed on several bloody fronts. In the first week of July 1863, the Battle of Gettysburg marked the turning point of the war. Southern troops were routed in Pickett's Charge, although both sides sustained thousands of casualties. On November 19, 1863, vast tracts of land in the area were dedicated as the Gettysburg National Cemetery, and Edward Everett and President Lincoln were featured at the podium. Everett, erstwhile president of Harvard University, gave a well-prepared and quite lengthy speech describing in minute detail the battle that had taken place there. At the conclusion of Everett's oration, President Abraham Lincoln stepped forward to give brief remarks which he had composed by making notes on the backs of envelopes.

The draft of citizens for the Union Army began on July 11, under terms of the Conscription Act of March 3, but exempted anyone who paid $300. Draft riots broke out in several Northern cities. In New York City in July, a violent mob attacked the Colored Orphans Asylum on Fifth Avenue, but the more than 200 orphans had been evacuated earlier. An estimated 1,200 people were killed in the melee, and thousands were injured.

THE NUMISMATIC SCENE. By mid-1863 it took $140 to $150 in legal-tender "greenback" paper notes to buy $100 worth of gold coins. Later, that same $100 in gold cost $200 to $220 in paper, and paper was worth 45¢ to 50¢ on the dollar. During this time, the U.S. government would not accept its own paper money for the purchase of Proof coins and sets, and collectors were forced to pay in coin.

Copper (mostly) and brass Civil War tokens were issued by the millions to help fill the need for circulating small change. Numismatists took a fancy to them, and certain engravers produced rarities on order, such as the overstrike on an 1841-O Liberty Seated dime shown here.

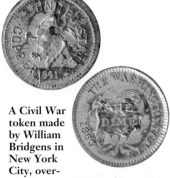

A Civil War token made by William Bridgens in New York City, over-struck on an 1841-O dime with the undertype showing clearly. Such tokens are great rarities today. (Shown at 150%, rotated to emphasize the dime.)

The Year 1864

CURRENT EVENTS. The Civil War continued to rage. On February 15 General William Tecumseh Sherman's troops occupied Meridian, Mississippi. On March 10 Ulysses S. Grant was placed in command of all Union armies. During the first week of June, Lee defeated Grant at the Battle of Cold Springs Harbor, after which General Sherman sustained extensive losses in Georgia in the Battle of Kennesaw Mountain. In July the Battle of Atlanta saw victory for Sherman. In November Sherman led his 60,000 troops on a 30- to 60-mile–wide swath of devastation through Georgia to the seacoast—an act remembered even today.

In the presidential election, Lincoln, with 55 percent of the popular votes, beat Democrat General George McClellan. Nevada became the 36th state in the Union.

THE NUMISMATIC SCENE. On July 11 a $10 paper note was worth just $3.90 in silver coins. In the Confederacy, a $10 note was worth just 46¢ in coin. The composition of federal cents was changed from copper-nickel to bronze.

In New York City the American Numismatic and Archaeological Society was formed, taking the place of the American Numismatic Society, which had expired in 1859. Later the new group changed its name to the American Numismatic Society, an organization that remains dynamic today (www.numismatics.org).

The Year 1865

CURRENT EVENTS. The Civil War ended with a string of Union victories. Northern troops occupied Columbia, South Carolina, on February 17; Charleston surrendered to the Union fleet on February 18; and Petersburg, Virginia, surrendered on April 3. General Ulysses S. Grant took the Confederate capital of Richmond on April 3. On April 9 General Robert E. Lee surrendered to Grant at Appomattox Court House, Virginia. More than one million men had been killed or injured in the conflict, making it America's bloodiest war.

President Abraham Lincoln was assassinated by actor John Wilkes Booth on April 14, 1865, while attending a performance of *Our American Cousin* at Ford's Theatre in Washington, D.C. Vice President Andrew Johnson succeeded to the presidency. The Reconstruction era began in the South, as so-called "carpetbaggers" arrived from the North to become involved in local and state governments and to help the former slaves. White Southerners who befriended their black neighbors and aided them in their newfound independence were called "scalawags."

THE NUMISMATIC SCENE. On the London market in January 1865, $100 in Confederate paper money was worth just $1.70 in gold, while $100 in Legal Tender Union bills was worth $46.

Silver coins remained absent from circulation in the East and Midwest, but banks often had large quantities. Sometime between Saturday night, February 11, 1865, and

John Wilkes Booth fleeing across the stage after shooting Lincoln
(in the draped box above). (*Harper's Weekly*, April 25, 1865)

the following Monday, burglars broke into the Traders Bank of Providence, Rhode Island, and absconded with one bag of silver three-cent pieces ($150 face value); one bag of half dimes ($214); one bag of dimes ($730); three bags of quarters ($144, $300, and $200); three bags of half dollars ($85, $300, and $342); one bag of mixed silver half dimes to half dollars ($550); one bag of mixed gold and silver ($193); one bag of $1 and $2.50 gold coins mixed ($280); and one bag of gold, "mostly in $20 pieces" ($1,353). Reflective of Liberty Seated dollars being out of circulation for many years, none were on hand. A $5,000 reward was offered for recovery.

The Year 1866

CURRENT EVENTS. On February 12, 1866, the United States demanded that French forces be removed from Mexico. Napoleon III had attempted to set up an empire in North America and had installed Emperor Maximilian as the ruler. In 1867 Mexican forces would depose and execute Maximilian. In the meantime, Mexican mints issued coins with his image. Chinese traders distrusted them, preferring the older pesos.

In New York City, Tammany Hall, the city's political ring, and William Marcy "Boss" Tweed were in full swing, with Tweed controlling the state legislature via illegal payments. Western Union acquired two telegraph companies and became the first significant industrial monopoly in the United States. The Washburn-Crosby Company was established in Wisconsin, and over a period of more than a century it would grow to enormous size and become known as General Mills. The Nestlé Company was founded by Henri Nestlé, who sold a formula for infants' liquid food.

In the West the Comstock Lode district at and near Virginia City continued to produce a record quantity of silver and gold. To make coins from the metal, Congress, under the Act of March 3, 1863, set forth the necessary details for a beginning, including salaries for those employed there. It was to be located at Carson, about 15 miles away. On July 18, 1866, construction began, but the mint did not produce coins until 1870.

THE NUMISMATIC SCENE. At the beginning of the year the director of the Mint was James Pollock, who took office in May 1861 and served until September 1866. He was succeeded in October 1866 by William Millward, who served until April 1867 (he was never confirmed by Congress).

IN GOD WE TRUST appeared on circulating coinage of the silver quarter, half dollar, and dollar, and on the gold $5, $10, and $20 for the first time.

The American Numismatic and Archaeological Society launched the *American Journal of Numismatics* in July, which became the publication of record for events in the hobby. Years later in the early twentieth century it was succeeded in fact by *The Numismatist* (which had been launched in 1888 and in time became the official magazine of the American Numismatic Association, a group formed in 1891).

The Year 1867

CURRENT EVENTS. Secretary of State William Henry Seward negotiated the purchase of Alaska from Russia for $7.2 million, which amounted to less than 2¢ per acre. The directors of the Union Pacific Railroad were making unconscionable personal profits on the construction of the rail link with the West. To avoid a government investigation they gave shares to congressmen and sold shares at low prices in the Crédit Mobilier Company, a newly formed enterprise intended to capture some of the profits from the construction.

THE NUMISMATIC SCENE. In April 1867 the Mint directorship of William Millward ended and that of Richard Henry Linderman began. Linderman used his office (his first term April 1867 to April 1869, and his second term April 1873 to December 1878) to feather his own numismatic nest and to create vast numbers of unauthorized (except by himself) pattern and fantasy coins.

The Year 1868

CURRENT EVENTS. In June Congress voted to readmit the seven states that formerly comprised the Confederate States of America, provided that black individuals were allowed to vote. In the presidential contest, Ulysses S. Grant, running on the Republican ticket, was elected by the support of bankers and creditors who held bonds and wanted them repaid in gold, as opposed to the Democratic platform which provided for payment in paper money (of lesser value).

THE NUMISMATIC SCENE. Specie payments remained in suspension, and paper fractional-currency notes took the place of dimes, quarters, and half dollars. Large quantities of silver began flowing into the Philadelphia Mint beginning in 1868 and swelling in the next two years, as bullion dealers became aware of a loophole in the Coinage Act of 1853 which permitted silver deposits to be converted into silver dollars. The dollars were then exported.

The Year 1869

CURRENT EVENTS. On May 10, 1869, at Promontory Point, Utah, railroad tracks from the East met those from the West, and the Union Pacific and Central Pacific railroads joined to complete the transcontinental rail link, thus rendering obsolete the passage from New York to California by way of Panama. The trip from New York City to San Francisco could thereafter be made in only eight days.

**Celebrating the completion of the transcontinental railroad
at Promontory Point, Utah Territory, in 1869.**

Susan B. Anthony started the Woman's Suffrage Association and campaigned for the right for women to vote. The year before, she had founded the *Revolution*, a newspaper with the motto "Men, their rights and nothing more; women, their rights and nothing less." The Wyoming Territory, newly formed, gave women the right to vote and hold public office.

The first of several notable "black days" in financial history occurred on Wall Street on "Black Friday," September 24, 1869, which saw many speculators ruined. Jay Gould, James Fisk, and others, one of whom was President Ulysses S. Grant's brother-in-law, attempted to corner the market on gold. They drove the price up to $162 per ounce, at which point Secretary of the Treasury George Boutwell began to sell government gold holdings to drive down the price.

THE NUMISMATIC SCENE. The director of the Mint was Henry Richard Linderman of Pennsylvania, who took office in April 1867 and continued through April 1869. From May 1869 through March 1873 James Pollock, who earlier served May 1861 through September 1866, was in office. James B. Longacre, chief engraver since 1844, died on New Year's Day and was succeeded in the post by William Barber, who would serve until 1879. At the Mint many sets of Standard Silver patterns were made in the dime, quarter, and half dollar denominations, each in silver, copper, and aluminum, with plain and reeded edges, either for Pollock or Linderman or both.

The Year 1870

CURRENT EVENTS. The federal decennial census reported the U.S. population as 38,558,371, including about three million immigrants who had arrived in the preceding decade. On July 24, 1870, the first through railway cars from California reached New York City. The 15th Amendment to the U.S. Constitution was ratified and forbade denial of the right to vote "on account of race, color, or previous condition of servitude." Women were not included, and black men still had a difficult time registering to vote in certain Southern areas.

The donkey symbol to denote the Democratic Party appeared for the first time in 1870 in the January 15 issue of *Harper's Weekly*. In 1874 Thomas Nast would create the elephant as a symbol for the Republicans.

THE NUMISMATIC SCENE. At the Mint the proliferation of unnecessary Standard Silver dime, quarter, and half dollar lightweight patterns continued, to which were added numerous varieties of Standard Silver dollars, although no one at the Mint seriously contemplated a new coinage of lightweight silver dollars. Proof coins of regular issues sold to collectors during this era were often struck from carelessly polished dies. (This did not apply to silver dollars, however.)

In Nevada the Mint at Carson (as the Carson City Mint was called at the time) began operations. It would continue coinage intermittently through 1893.[8] In San Francisco the cornerstone was laid for the new mint.

The Year 1871

CURRENT EVENTS. The Franco-Prussian War was fought in 1870 and 1871. Prussia and her allies triumphed, and her military prowess and munitions became world-famous. Germany obtained five billion francs as reparations from France, an amount equal to $965 million. The newly federated German Empire went on the gold standard, dumping several thousand tons of silver on the market. So much silver was on hand that France, Belgium, Switzerland, and Greece suspended silver coinage for a period. This signaled a decline in silver prices on the worldwide market, a fall that continued for the rest of the decade.

In its infinite wisdom, Congress declared under the Indian Appropriation Act (March 3, 1871) that Indians were now wards of the government—from then on, Indian tribes would not be recognized as separate nations or independent entities, and no further treaties would be made with them. (The Native Americans had honored every treaty, the white men none.)

The Chicago fire, said in legend to have been started when Mrs. O'Leary's cow kicked over a lantern, raged on October 8 and 9 and destroyed more than three-square miles of the city, causing an estimated $190 million worth of damage and killing about 250 people. Meanwhile, in Peshtigo, Wisconsin, from October 8 to 14, 1,182 people were killed in a devastating forest fire which wiped out the city.

THE NUMISMATIC SCENE. Silver and gold coins remained absent from commerce except on the West Coast. Active markets continued as usual in such coins as bankers and exchange houses bought and sold them at a premium. On one occasion a single steamship left New York City with 65 tons of silver coins aboard.[9]

The Year 1872

CURRENT EVENTS. The Great Epizoötic of 1872 saw an estimated four million horses killed by an equine virus suspected of having come from Canada. This wreaked havoc upon urban transportation. Commerce suffered, and the Epizoötic was given as one of the precipitating causes of the following year's Panic of 1873. In September in Philadelphia and New York, men were hitched to street cars to haul passengers and to carts to haul goods. In November a fire in Boston devastated 766 buildings and caused an estimated $75 million in damage, in part because the majority of horses to pull steam fire engines were incapacitated.

John D. Rockefeller's Standard Oil Trust refined 10,000 barrels of kerosene daily and received not only favorable transportation rates on railroads, but also "drawbacks," or rebates, from the railroads on rates they charged Standard's competitors (who in some instances had to pay five times more than Standard did). Cornelius "Commodore" Vanderbilt, who had his own monopolies, provided funds to establish Vanderbilt University in Nashville, Tennessee.

Susan B. Anthony and other advocates of women's rights dared to attempt to vote in the presidential election on November 5 and were arrested. The contest went to Ulysses S. Grant, who was re-elected on the Republican ticket even though his administration was poorly run and corrupt. His challenger was Horace Greeley, widely traveled editor of *the New York Tribune*.

THE NUMISMATIC SCENE. Specie payments continued in suspension and gold and silver coins still traded at a premium. Minor coins were in oversupply as they had been for some time. Two-cent pieces, minted since 1864, were unpopular with the public and were being called in, but despite this surplus the Mint inexplicably struck 65,000 for general circulation this year.

The Year 1873

CURRENT EVENTS. The so-called Panic of 1873 was centered in and about the stock market. Farmers reacted against the railroads' tariffs, and certain other railroad policies, not to overlook a generally poor reputation for integrity, caused many railroad stocks and bonds to drop. European investors withdrew much capital, causing prices to fall further.

On September 18, Jay Cooke & Company, agent for the Northern Pacific Railroad, failed. Black Friday, September 19, saw stocks fall precipitously. Numerous banks and brokerages houses failed, primarily in New York City. The stock exchange closed for 10 days, but the damage was done, and by the end of the year an estimated 5,100 businesses failed and millions were thrown out of work. The depression lasted through 1877. Wages dropped 20 to 25 percent and the prices of many goods and services fell as well. America went through a period of deflation.

Frightened investors in a "run" on the Union Trust Company. (*Harper's Weekly*, October 11, 1873)

THE NUMISMATIC SCENE. Engineered by Comptroller of the Treasury John Jay Knox, the Coinage Act of February 12, 1873, created a bureau within the Treasury Department in Washington, D.C., to supervise all of the assay offices and mints in America, headed by the director of the Mint. Previously, the director's office was within the Philadelphia Mint, and the other mints were considered to be branches subsidiary and reporting to Philadelphia. The weights of the silver dime, quarter, and half dollar were adjusted upward slightly, and arrowheads were placed alongside the date to signify the difference (which was minimal at best). The new weights were in the metric system and were consistent with Latin Monetary Union silver coins. The arrows were discontinued after 1874, although the new weight standard was continued.

The Year 1874

CURRENT EVENTS. In New York City the first electrically propelled streetcar went into service, but most transportation continued to be provided by horsepower in the literal sense. In Massachusetts a law was enacted which limited the daily working hours of women to ten. There were no effective child-labor laws in the United States, and it was not unusual to see six- to ten-year-old children working from dawn to dusk in textile mills, coal mines, and other hazardous occupations.

THE NUMISMATIC SCENE. In Philadelphia, patterns were made for Dana Bickford and James Dunning's international $10 piece (one of a string of ill-conceived proposals for a coin readily interchangeable across foreign borders; like the others, doomed to failure as it was created without any regard for constantly changing exchange rates).

The Year 1875

Current Events. Alexander Graham Bell conducted experiments which led to the creation of the telephone. The Kentucky Derby horse race was run for the first time.

The New York City Court House was finished for a total cost of $13 million, as compared to a pre-construction estimate of $250,000, thanks to the padding of bills by "Boss" Tweed of Tammany Hall.

Domestic production of gold and silver continued at a record pace with new mines in Colorado and elsewhere, adding to the supply from Nevada. On the international market the price of silver had been falling in the 1870s, causing problems with the Western economy.

Central City in the Rocky Mountains to the west of Denver was expanding its mining operations by leaps and bounds. There was a glut of silver in the marketplace, and the price was falling.

The Numismatic Scene. Congress passed an act on January 14, 1875, providing for the redemption of fractional currency (which had its beginning with postal currency in 1862) with silver coins of denominations from the dime to the half dollar. This was to take place "as rapidly as practicable." However, few new coins reached circulation. Immense quantities of newly minted silver pieces piled up in Treasury vaults as they were still worth a slight premium in terms of Legal Tender Notes. The Carson City Mint ramped up the production of silver coins and would maintain a strong output through 1877, less so in 1878. From 1879 onward the only silver coins made there were Morgan-design silver dollars.

The Year 1876

Current Events. The Centennial Exhibition opened in Philadelphia, the first world's fair to be held in America.

Agricultural Hall at the 1876 Centennial Exhibition held in Fairmount Park, Philadelphia. (*Centennial Portfolio*, Thomas Hunter, 1876)

The Battle of Little Big Horn on June 25, 1876, ended in an overwhelming victory for the Indians (one of only a few such instances in American history), led by Sioux Chief Sitting Bull. General George Armstrong Custer and his 264-man contingent were killed.

The presidential election of November 1876 ended in dispute in November when neither Democrat Samuel J. Tilden nor Republican Rutherford Birchard Hayes captured the needed 185 Electoral College votes to win, although Tilden had a plurality of popular votes. In early 1877 the mess was adjudicated by a commission of five senators, five representatives, and five Supreme Court justices, numbering eight Republicans and seven Democrats. Voting strictly along party lines (what else?), the committee declared the winner to be (who else?) Hayes. Former Confederate states were rewarded by having federal oversight removed, leading to segregation and rampant abuse of civil rights.

THE NUMISMATIC SCENE. Hundreds of different tokens and medals were issued in connection with the centennial observance. The Act of April 17, 1876, ordered the Treasury Department to pay out all of the silver coins from dimes to half dollars it had on hand, including substantial coinages of 1875. On April 20 this began, after which subsidiary silver coins and federal paper money traded at par for the first time since the spring of 1862. In anticipation of a great demand for new silver coins the mints increased production in 1876 and 1877. Then the unexpected happened: Immense quantities of long-hoarded coins were released by the public, and there were vastly more silver coins than were needed. The wheels of progress turned slowly, and in 1879 the production of new silver dimes, quarters, and half dollars was sharply restricted.

The Year 1877

CURRENT EVENTS. President Rutherford B. Hayes took office on March 4, in place of the popular-vote candidate Samuel Tilden. The editor of the *Washington Post*, founded later in the year (December 6, 1877), would call Hayes "His Fraudulency" and refer to "President Tilden" in discussions about "the crime of 1876." In the meantime, the United States continued in an economic slump that had commenced in 1873.

Augustus Pope opened the first bicycle factory in the United States in Hartford, Connecticut, and made the Columbia brand bicycle of the penny-farthing (large front wheel, tiny back wheel) style. Bicycling soon became a nationwide fad. The first bell telephone was sold in May 1877, and by August there were 778 instruments in use.

THE NUMISMATIC SCENE. There was a reduced call for minor coins this year. Indian Head cents were produced in what would be the lowest quantity in the nineteenth century, and nickel three-cent pieces and five-cent pieces were made only as Proofs for collectors.

The Year 1878

CURRENT EVENTS. Business remained in a slump, continuing the after-effects of the Panic of 1873. During 1878, more than 10,000 businesses failed. Thomas Edison developed methods for the cheap production and transmission of electricity, portending widespread use to light cities and homes. This had an adverse effect on gas company stock shares on Wall Street. Edison continued his experiments to develop a practical filament for an incandescent light bulb, but success would not come until the carbon filament of the following year. In the meantime, the inventor tried more than 500 different substances. White Soap, renamed Ivory Soap in 1882, was introduced by Procter & Gamble in Cincinnati.

THE NUMISMATIC SCENE. On December 17, 1878, greenback Legal Tender Notes achieved par with gold and silver (which would have happened soon thereafter anyway, as mandated by law to take place on January 1, 1879). For the first time in American history, paper dollars, gold dollars, and silver dollars all had the same value, at least in theory. At the time there was a limit of $5 to the amount of silver coins that could be exchanged for gold. As a result, citizens had to take a slight discount when trading for gold coins at the offices of money brokers and exchange houses (which were numerous in larger cities).

At the Philadelphia Mint, Goloid, a "dream metal" patented by Dr. William Wheeler Hubbell on May 22, 1877, was employed to strike numerous pattern dollars beginning in 1878 and continuing through 1880. This alloy contained silver and gold metal in the value ratio of 16 to 1, alloyed with 10-percent copper by weight (to add strength). Hubbell was only one of many who believed that a bimetallic standard could be maintained despite commercial pressure. The Bland-Allison Act of February 28, 1878, provided for what would, in time, be the mintage of hundreds of millions of dollars in unwanted Morgan-design silver dollars.

Coin dealers tired of excessive issues left over from the 1876 centennial. Ed Frossard complained:

> Mr. John W. Haseltine informs us that his next coin sale will contain many Centennial medals from a private collection, a number of which he had never seen or heard of. Mr. H. adds: 'There are now no new Centennial medals being made,' a welcome piece of information, for the interest in Centennial medals has of late decreased in a ratio proportionate to the increase of the posthumous article.[10]

The Year 1879

CURRENT EVENTS. On October 21, 1879, Edison claimed success in his search for a suitable material from which to make a filament for an incandescent lamp. This idea of lighting was not new, and others had demonstrated such lamps earlier, but none had lasted for an appreciable length of time. By this time, outdoor night illumination by arc lights had been in use for many years. William K. Vanderbilt acquired Gilmore's Garden and renamed it Madison Square Garden. It became a showcase for public events and in 1890 was replaced by a magnificent structure of the same name.

Frank Winfield Woolworth laid the foundation for his fortune made in five-and-dime stores when he set up a counter at which all merchandise cost five cents. "Twenty nickels make a dollar, you know." He then borrowed $400 to open a store in Utica, New York, which failed in three months. Undaunted, he opened a similar store in Lancaster, Pennsylvania. What happened changed the face of retailing in America.

THE NUMISMATIC SCENE. There had been a limit of $5 on the amount of silver coins that could be exchanged for gold at the Treasury, causing consternation in the early months of the year. The Act of June 9, 1879, removed the limit.

Horatio C. Burchard became director of the Mint in February 1879, replacing the infamous Dr. Henry Richard Linderman, and continued in office through June 1885. Shenanigans at the Mint continued under the Burchard administration (and the superintendency of the Philadelphia Mint by Colonel Archibald Loudon Snowden, the main culprit in all of this), and many fancy patterns were made for private profit to those connected with the institution. Included were metric issues, such as goloid $1, gold $4, and gold $20 patterns and trade dollars of 1884 and 1885. Although contemporary numismatists such as S.K. Harzfeld and W. Elliot Woodward protested Mint practices, it fell to scholars of the twentieth century to discover the vast extent of Mint improprieties and indiscretions of the period from the spring of 1859 to 1885. Years later in the early 1900s it was Snowden who sold two $50 gold patterns to William H. Woodin. An alarm was raised, the government wanted the coins back, and Snowden traded two large trunks filled with thousands of patterns to Woodin, who then used the opportunity to work with Edgar H. Adams to create *United States Pattern, Trial, and Experimental Pieces*, published by the American Numismatic Society in 1913.[11]

Dealers took notice of the reduced circulation-strike mintages of dimes, quarters, and half dollars, and investment interest increased. In late 1879 there was a speculation in Proof trade dollars that continued into early 1880, resulting in exceptionally high mintages.

RESUMPTION.
The Dance of the Dollars, January 1st, 1879.

Gold coins had been hoarded by the public since December 1861 when the outcome of the Civil War was uncertain. Finally, on January 1, 1879, gold coins were again on par with paper money, although this had been anticipated by the market on December 17, 1878. It was anticipated, as per this cartoon, that gold coins would become common in circulation. This did not happen. The public, now aware that paper bills could be exchanged for gold at any time, preferred to use bank notes. (*Frank Leslie's Illustrated Newspaper*, January 11, 1879)

The Year 1880

CURRENT EVENTS. In the presidential election contest of the year, traditional factions in the Republican party endeavored to have President Ulysses S. Grant run for a third term, but delegates to the nominating convention were deadlocked on the issue. Finally, on the 36th ballot James Abram Garfield was selected to carry the party banner, and in November he beat the Democratic challenger, Winfield Scott Hancock. The decennial federal census put the population of the United States at 50,155,783.

French actress Sarah Bernhardt ("Divine Sarah") came to the United States on the first of several tours and opened at Booth's Theatre in New York City on November 8, 1880. Alphonse Mucha would begin creating Art Nouveau posters featuring her 15 years later. Bernhardt is reported to have roused an audience to near hysteria by declaiming the *Marseillaise*, and is also reported to have brought another audience to tears by reciting the alphabet!

THE NUMISMATIC SCENE. At the Mint, numerous metric patterns continued to be produced, including Flowing Hair and Coiled Hair $4 Stellas. The existence of the Coiled Hair coins was kept secret, and the first photographs of them were not published until 1911.

The Year 1881

CURRENT EVENTS. President James Garfield said: "Whoever controls the volume of money in any country is master of all its legislation and commerce." On July 2, 1881, Garfield was mortally wounded by a gunshot from a rejected office seeker, Charles J. Guiteau, and on September 19 he died. Succeeding him in office was his vice president, Chester Alan Arthur. The Supreme Court ruled the Federal Income Tax Law of 1862 unconstitutional. The American National Red Cross was founded by Clara Barton in Washington, D.C.

THE NUMISMATIC SCENE. Earlier-minted silver coins were still abundant in circulation and in Treasury vaults. Thus, relatively few new dimes, quarters, and half dollars were struck. At the Philadelphia Mint, a new Liberty Head design was created in pattern form, which eventually was used on the 1883 Liberty Head nickel. The gold dollar was by now an anachronism and was rarely seen in commerce. However, a popular speculation in gold dollars had been going on since 1879, and quantities were hoarded by coin collectors and investors.[12]

The Year 1882

CURRENT EVENTS. The Chinese Exclusion Act, passed by Congress in 1880, took effect in 1882 and remained in force for ten years. Prejudice against the Chinese would continue for several decades, and immigrants from China would be referred to as "the yellow peril." A congressional committee reported that adulteration of food had caused many deaths and constituted as a fraud upon the people. Patent medicines were sold widely, were dominant advertisers in newspapers, and were further promoted by traveling shows, celebrity appearances, and far-fetched testimonials. William H. Vanderbilt's comment, "The public be damned," made to a reporter for the *Chicago Daily News* on October 2, added fuel to the fire of widespread antagonism against the "robber barons" of industry. The Standard Oil Trust was incorporated by John D. Rockefeller and his associates and brought 95 percent of the American petroleum industry under a single management.

On September 4, 1882, electricity was used for the first time to illuminate large sections of New York City. Power was generated by the Edison Illuminating Company, financed by J.P. Morgan. However, conditions would remain primitive for years to come. In 1882 just two percent of the homes in New York were connected to a water main, and nearly all private houses had privies in the backyard.

In Madison Square Garden, Jumbo, the elephant, appeared under the ownership of impresario P.T. Barnum, who had purchased the pachyderm, "the largest elephant in or out of captivity," from the Royal Zoological Gardens for $10,000, setting off a furor in England. The elephant was a star attraction in America until he met his untimely demise when hit by a freight train in Ontario in 1885. Jumbo's name entered the English language as an adjective for unusually large in size.

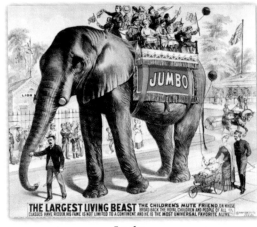

Jumbo.

THE NUMISMATIC SCENE. The country remained awash in silver coins, mainly dimes, quarters, and half dollars, while new Morgan silver dollars continued to be minted by the millions.

The Year 1883

CURRENT EVENTS. On March 3, 1883, Congress voted to build three new warships, the first constructed since the Civil War. America had fallen to 12th place among sea powers of the world. On May 24, 1883, the Brooklyn Bridge opened in a special ceremony (in which 12 people were trampled to death), and Brooklyn and Manhattan were linked by one of the engineering wonders of the world. The dormant volcano Krakatoa, located between Java and Sumatra in the Sunda Strait, exploded on August 27, 1883, in the greatest volcanic disaster since the demolition of most of the island of Santorini (Thera) in 1470 BC—an eruption that ended much of the Minoan civilization on nearby Crete. Krakatoa took an estimated 36,000 lives and spewed so much dust and smoke into the sky that sunsets around the world were bright red for a year thereafter.

THE NUMISMATIC SCENE. The Liberty Head nickel was minted and placed into circulation. With the denomination expressed only as V, these furnished the opportunity for sharpers to gold plate them to spend as $5 gold half eagles. The Mint added CENTS, after which word spread that the earlier coins would become very valuable. This even catalyzed numismatics to vastly increase in popularity and the prices of many coins to rise.

Dye's Coin Encyclopædia was published in Philadelphia. This immense volume comprised 1,152 pages and contained more than 1,500 illustrations. Distributed widely, the book did much to advance the cause of coin collecting in America in an era in which few textbooks or price guides were available.

The Year 1884

CURRENT EVENTS. In the 1884 presidential election, New York governor Grover Cleveland was swept to the first Democratic Party victory since Buchanan won in 1856. Leading contender James G. Blaine, long-term congressman from Maine, known as the "Plumed Knight," was defeated by the political slogan, "Rum, Romanism, and Rebellion."

In the field of entertainment, visitors to the New York seaside resort at Coney Island were enchanted by a new type of amusement device, the roller coaster, erected by L.A. Thompson, who would soon control much of Coney Island and would become famous as an amusement-park supplier. Mark Twain's *The Adventures of Huckleberry Finn* was published.

THE NUMISMATIC SCENE. The August 1884 issue of *Mason's Monthly Illustrated Coin Collector's Magazine* offered for sale a group of 200 Proof sets from 1860 to 1883, containing from one to 45 sets (the latter in the case of 1878) of each year, the lot for $800. The same issue offered an "1804" dollar for sale, "bearing a close resemblance . . . to the original dollar of 1804; but, as the piece is doubted by some experts, we will sell it for $50."

The Year 1885

CURRENT EVENTS. Chicago's first skyscraper, the Home Insurance Company building, opened to the public in the autumn and created a sensation. The National Audubon Society was formed.

Moxie Nerve Food was introduced as a cure-all by Augustin Thompson, MD. Moxie was said to have been compounded using a secret plant from the tropics found by the mysteriously elusive (to historians) Lieutenant Moxie. Advertising emphasis was soon changed to that of a healthful and refreshing beverage. By the 1920s, Moxie is said to have outsold Coca-Cola (first formulated in 1886) in its primary trading area, New England.

Mark Twain's *Huckleberry Finn* was the literary sensation of 1885.

THE NUMISMATIC SCENE. A change was made in the Mint directorship, and Horatio C. Burchard, who served from February 1879 through June 1885, was succeeded in July by James P. Kimball, who would hold the post through October 1889. The Treasury Department still had a large quantity of earlier-minted dimes, quarters, and half dollars on hand, so relatively few additional examples were minted, except of the dime denomination.

The Year 1886

CURRENT EVENTS. The labor movement in the United States, which had an uncertain status and future up until this point and had been largely at the mercy of industrialists, received worldwide attention and gained its first martyrs in Chicago's Haymarket Massacre. This disaster had its beginnings when police fired into a crowd of striking laborers on May 1, killing four and wounding others. Three days later, a peaceful mass meeting was held to protest police brutality when someone (never identified) threw a bomb, police fired into the crowd, and more casualties were added to the list.

On October 28, 1886, the Statue of Liberty, a gift of France, more formally known as *Liberty Enlightening the World*, was dedicated on Bedloe's Island in New York Harbor. Richard Warren Sears entered the merchandising business in Minnesota by buying a group of watches which had been refused by a local jeweler, thus sowing the seed for Sears, Roebuck & Co. On the soft-drink scene, Coca-Cola was sold for the first time in Atlanta, the Coca part of the name coming from the coca leaf.

THE NUMISMATIC SCENE. The Treasury-held supply of subsidiary silver coins was diminishing rapidly, and in 1886 the Mint began to receive calls for new coins.[13] Until recently, the government had a quantity of silver coins on hand, which had been minted in the 1860s and not distributed, and others which had been struck in the early 1870s (especially the 1873 arrows and later coinage) in anticipation of the resumption of specie payments. These stocks were augmented by the surprising return of about $30 million worth of silver coins that had been exported to Latin America circa 1862, coins that the Treasury and others had assumed had been melted.

The Year 1887

CURRENT EVENTS. The Interstate Commerce Act, approved by Congress, became effective on February 4, 1887, and regulated the rates of railroads. The Florida state legislature passed a law to segregate black individuals on railroad passenger cars. In Chatsworth, Illinois, about 100 people were killed when a burning bridge collapsed beneath a train.

Thomas Edison opened a new laboratory in West Orange, New Jersey. He produced an electrically driven phonograph—an improvement on his earlier models— intended for office dictation use. By the end of the year there were 200,000 telephone subscribers in America. The first social register published in the United States appeared and was the work of Lois Keller. Listed were about 3,600 names, primarily consisting of prominent New Yorkers who were white, not divorced, and not Jewish.

Nearly all inland travel between cities was done by train. Accommodations ranged from basic to elegant, as here in a drawing room car on the Boston & Maine Railroad in 1887.

THE NUMISMATIC SCENE. At the Philadelphia Mint the quantities produced of quarters and half dollars continued to be low, as they had been since 1879, due to a glut of coins in Treasury vaults. The coin hobby was entering a slump that would endure for more than a decade.

The Year 1888

CURRENT EVENTS. In November, Republican Benjamin Harrison (grandson of President William Henry Harrison) was elected president with 233 Electoral College votes, compared to 168 for his opponent, Democrat Grover Cleveland. However, Harrison received 100,000 fewer popular votes than Cleveland. Primaries held in Maine weeks prior to the national election gave Harrison the lead, giving rise to the popular phrase, "As Maine goes, so goes the nation."

The Washington Monument was completed in Washington, D.C., following four decades of intermittent construction. The first successful electric trolley cars (power taken from overhead wires) were introduced for public transportation in Richmond, Virginia, presaging the demise of the horse-drawn cars then in widespread service.

The year was best remembered for many years thereafter for the Blizzard of '88, which dumped many feet of snow on the Northeastern United States and which caused numerous homes and communities to be isolated for a week or more.

THE NUMISMATIC SCENE. Dr. George F. Heath of Monroe, Michigan, launched *The American Numismatist*. His aim was to produce an interesting, indeed chatty magazine that would appeal to coin collectors of all levels, including beginners. It seems that he did not realize that Charles E. Leal had published a magazine of similar title, so Heath dropped "American." Although this was unsaid, Heath's publication was in contrast to the *American Journal of Numismatics*, which appealed to advanced readers.

The Year 1889

CURRENT EVENTS. President Benjamin Harrison opened 1.9 million acres of former Indian lands to white homesteaders at noon on April 22. However, by morning many who had come earlier—"sooners," as they were called—had already staked their claims. By nightfall, communities were established at Guthrie, Oklahoma City, and elsewhere. In the same year, North Dakota, South Dakota, Montana, and Washington were admitted to the Union. On May 31 a dirt dam burst above the community of Johnstown, Pennsylvania, and in the ensuing flood more than 2,000 citizens were killed.

Nellie Bly (Elizabeth Cochrane Seaman), a reporter for Joseph Pulitzer's *New York World*, sought to better mythical figure Phineas Fogg's 80-day round-the-world trip and made the journey in 72 days, 6 hours, 10 minutes, and 58 seconds, finishing amidst much press-agentry. *The Wall Street Journal* began publication on July 8, an expansion of a daily financial newsletter issued by Dow Jones & Company, owned by Charles Henry Dow and Edward D. Jones.

THE NUMISMATIC SCENE. The director of the Mint was James P. Kimball, who served from July 1885 through October 1889. Serving from October 1889 through May 1893 was Edward O. Leech. At the Philadelphia Mint the superintendency changed from Daniel M. Fox (1885–1889) to Colonel Oliver C. Bosbyshell (1889–1894). Unlike Fox, who seems to have been indifferent on the subject, Bosbyshell had at least a passing interest in numismatics.

The Carson City Mint, which had last produced coins in 1885, reopened on July 1, 1889, and again struck gold and silver denominations.

The Year 1890

CURRENT EVENTS. The Sherman Anti-Trust Act was passed by Congress on July 2 and sought to curtail "restraint of trade or commerce" and limit the powers of monopolies, which at the time had a stranglehold on certain sectors of the American economy. However, "trust busting" with vigor would not take place until the administration of President Theodore Roosevelt in the first decade of the twentieth century. Interpretations varied, and it was not certain whether the provisions of the act applied to labor unions, which were engaged in their own monopolies.

The Chapman brothers, S. Hudson (left) and Henry, photographed in their library in 1890. Starting their partnership in 1878, the brothers were the leading American rare-coin dealers and auctioneers by 1890.

The McKinley Tariff Act, passed on October 1, increased certain tariffs to record-high levels but provided for reciprocal agreements with certain other countries. In November the failure of the Baring Brothers, London bankers, caused British investors to liquidate many American securities, thus precipitating a short-lived panic on Wall Street. At the time, the British were the main foreign investors in the American economy.

The 1890 federal census pegged the population at 62,947,714, two-thirds of whom lived in rural areas. Boom times were occurring in Los Angeles and its environs, and the population of the city, just 11,183 in 1880, soared to 50,000 by 1890. The richest 1 percent of the population earned more income than the poorest 50 percent combined. Of 12 million families in America, nearly half owned no tangible property, and 13 percent of citizens were illiterate.

THE NUMISMATIC SCENE. The coin market was in the doldrums. The collection of Lorin G. Parmelee was offered at auction, but prices were not up to expectations, and he did not allow many pieces to sell.

The Year 1891

CURRENT EVENTS. In Oklahoma, 900,000 acres of land formerly belonging to Native Americans was made available for white settlement. Thomas A. Edison filed for a patent on a motion-picture camera, not the first, but one of the more successful. Carnegie Hall was opened in New York City on May 5, the gift of steel baron Andrew Carnegie, who would give tens of millions of dollars to fund public libraries and other institutions. The initial program was of Tchaikovsky music conducted by the composer. In Springfield, Massachusetts, physical-education instructor James Naismith invented basketball as a sport for the season between the football and baseball seasons.

THE NUMISMATIC SCENE. In October the American Numismatic Association (www.money.org) was founded in Chicago when a small group of collectors met at the urging of Dr. George F. Heath, a Monroe, Michigan, physician (and town mayor), who published *The Numismatist*. The ANA would go on to become the world's largest non-profit coin-collecting group.

Operators at a multiple-telephone switchboard at the Cortlandt Street Exchange, New York City, 1891.

4

LIBERTY SEATED HALF DIMES (1837–1873)

Introduction

Half dimes were first minted in July 1792. The layout of the Philadelphia Mint, two old buildings and two to be constructed, was being planned, and certain equipment destined for the Mint was stored until autumn in the shop of mechanic John Harper, located not far from where the Mint would be ready. Silver for the striking of about 1,500 pieces worth 5¢ each was supplied either by the president, George Washington, or by the secretary of State, Thomas Jefferson, and the finished coins, called half "dismes," were delivered to Jefferson. The disme spelling was discontinued in time. It is thought that in October the new Mint struck 500 or so additional pieces struck, and by the end of that time the dies showed microscopic rust. Several "presentation" coins in existence today are from this later coinage.[1]

The first half dimes of the Flowing Hair design produced at the Mint were dated 1794 and 1795 and were of the Flowing Hair design by engraver Robert Scot. The Draped Bust, Small Eagle Reverse, design was produced in 1796 and 1797. The denomination was subsequently put on hiatus for the years 1798 and 1799. Coinage of the denomination resumed in 1800, now with the same obverse design but with the Heraldic Eagle reverse. These pieces were made through 1805, with the exception of 1804. Coinage then stopped.

Many years later, on the morning of July 4, 1829, half dimes were coined again, now for a ceremony for the laying of the cornerstone in the second Philadelphia Mint. The design was the Capped Bust style, with the obverse and reverse designed in 1807 by John Reich. It was first used on half dollars of that year, then later on dimes and quarters. Reich left the Mint in 1817. The engraver in 1829 was William Kneass, who had held that position since 1824. Kneass adopted the Reich design, made new hubs and master dies, and the denomination was reborn. These coins had raised rims and were struck in closed collars, unlike the half dimes of earlier designs. From 1829 onward Capped Bust half dimes were made continuously through part of 1837, after which the Liberty Seated design became standard.

Liberty Seated half dimes were made continuously through 1873, when the Coinage Act of that year discontinued this, two-cent, silver–three-cent, and silver-dollar denominations.

The *Annual Report of the Director of the Mint,* 1874, covering the fiscal year from July 1, 1874, to June 30, 1875, included this:

> Inquiry is occasionally made as to why the coinage of the silver five-cent piece was discontinued. The reason appears to have been that it would, on the resumption of specie payments, be likely to expel from circulation and drive into the Treasury for redemption the five-cent copper-nickel coins. At first glance this may appear improbable, but when it is considered that the original law authorizing the issue of the copper-nickel five-cent coin provided for its redemption in lawful money of the United States, it will be seen that there must come a time when it will be superior to the five-cent silver coin, and for the reason that it will be exchangeable for notes redeemable in gold coin. The silver coin, which would have a greater nominal than intrinsic value, and not redeemable in lawful money, or gold coin, would become the inferior currency. The five-cent copper-nickel coin having been issued to the extent of over $5,000,000 and the amount being sufficient for a token coin of that denomination, the provision of law discontinuing the issue of the five-cent silver coin appears to have been proper.

In the meantime, from 1837 coinage of half dimes was accomplished at the Philadelphia Mint each year, in New Orleans from 1839 intermittently until 1860, and in San Francisco continuously from 1863 to 1873.

The Design of the Liberty Seated Half Dime

Christian Gobrecht's Liberty Seated motif, used on half dimes from 1837 through the end of the series in 1873, was produced in 1837 at the Philadelphia Mint and 1838 at the New Orleans Mint, in the format without obverse stars, thus isolating these two issues as a separate type. The obverse depicts Liberty seated on a rock, her left hand holding a liberty cap on a pole and her right hand holding a shield inscribed LIBERTY. There is no drapery at her elbow, and there are no stars in the field. The result is a cameo-like appearance of rare beauty. The date is at the bottom border. The obverse design was inspired by the design of the Gobrecht silver dollars of 1836. The reverse consists of an open wreath tied with a ribbon, enclosing HALF DIME, with UNITED STATES OF AMERICA surrounding. Mintage figures reveal that 1,405,000 of the 1837 Philadelphia issue were produced while only 70,000 were made of the 1838-O.

In 1838 stars were added to the obverse of the Liberty Seated design. Otherwise, the motif is similar to the 1837 and 1838-O, Liberty Seated, pieces. In 1840 drapery was added to Liberty's elbow. From 1838 through 1859 many different varieties were produced. In 1853 the Liberty Seated design was modified by the addition of tiny arrowheads to the left and right of the date, to signify a decrease in the authorized weight from 20.625 grains to 19.2 grains. These arrows remained in place through 1855, after which they were discontinued, although the reduced weight remained in effect for later years as well.

There was a curious variation in the Liberty Seated figure in 1859. Anthony C. Paquet, an assistant engraver at the Mint, made some modifications, including giving Liberty slimmer arms, moving her left hand to be more separated from the liberty cap, and adding stars with hollow center points (*molets* or mullets). Such pieces were made only at the Philadelphia Mint. New Orleans half dimes continued with the standard figure.

In 1860 the obverse was modified by removing the stars and adding UNITED STATES OF AMERICA around the border. The reverse was changed as well, now with HALF DIME in two lines within a cereal wreath. This style was continued through 1873, at which time the half dime denomination was terminated.

Edge Reed Counts on Liberty Seated Half Dimes

The subject of counting the vertical ribs or reeds on the edges of Liberty Seated half dimes was detailed by John W. McCloskey, with findings as follows, lightly edited:[3]

Gauge 1: 86 reeds. This gauge reeding appears on later New Orleans pieces from 1852-O to 1860-O and is much wider than the corresponding reeding for Philadelphia pieces of this era.

Gauge 2: 90 reeds. This gauge reeding appears on most of the early New Orleans pieces from 1839-O to 1850-O. This reeding is closer to the Philadelphia reeding of the period, but can be distinguished with careful examination.

Gauge 3: 92 reeds. This gauge reeding appears only on 1838-O, 1842-O, and 1844-O pieces that I have examined. It is close to the other early New Orleans reeding but not identical.

Gauge 4: 98 reeds. This is the standard reeding of the Philadelphia Mint possessed by all Philadelphia pieces except for some in the 1850s.

Gauge 5: 106 reeds. This narrowest reeding for half dimes appears on Philadelphia pieces from 1854 to 1859 and on all San Francisco pieces from 1863-S to 1873-S. This gauge reeding distinguishes the San Francisco pieces from the rare Philadelphia pieces of the Civil War era.

Note: The three reeding gauges of the New Orleans Mint are very close but are certainly not identical. This information is not vital in authentication, however, since all three gauges are wider than the corresponding reeding at the Philadelphia Mint. The significance of these differences lies in the fact that one realizes not to expect a perfect match in the New Orleans reeding over the years. Furthermore, a San Francisco coin with a removed mintmark can be detected easily by counting the edge reeds.

Pattern Coins

There were no pattern half dimes made as steps to changing or modifying the designs, although in 1871 examples were struck using James Longacre's Indian Princess motif. In 1859 and 1860 transitional coins designated as patterns were made for the numismatic trade. They are listed in *A Guide Book of United States Coins* and are described individually in the following catalog.

There were many different Proof strikings in off metals such as copper and aluminum, dated 1863–1873 (1866 excepted). Popularly but incorrectly called trial pieces, they were made at the request of Mint officials for private use or for sale to collectors and are described in *United States Pattern Coins* by J. Hewitt Judd. All are rare.

1849 Half Dime Die Used for Patterns

In 1849 consideration was given to making a three-cent piece in silver, a new addition to the coinage lineup representing a value above the cent and below the half dime.[25]

On January 9, 1849, congressman and committee chairman Samuel F. Vinton wrote to Director of the Mint Robert M. Patterson: "Resolved, that the Committee of Ways and Means take into consideration the propriety of reporting a bill for reducing the size of the one-cent piece, and to authorize the coining of a three-cent piece—both to be composed of copper and some other precious metal." The coinage of pattern cents of a new format would wait until 1850, but pattern three-cent coins were made post-haste in 1849, with examples being ready by January 18.

For the rush to test the concept of a silver three-cent piece, a regular half dime obverse die used on regular issue Valentine-8 was combined with two hastily created reverses—one simply with the numeral 3 and other with the same value expressed as III.[26] A third issue, noted as "ugly duckling" in the Judd text, simply combined the number 3 numeral die with III die, creating a metallic disk with no other inscriptions! William E. Dubois, assistant assayer at the Mint, later wrote that certain patterns of this era were his idea and stated that "The 'artist of the Mint' [Longacre] did nothing but make III and the 3 as requested. It was at a juncture when a three-cent piece was talked of; two mixtures of base silver were made and these pieces were hastily struck, simply to show what the size would be."

Impressions of the three-cent piece were made in different alloys, one with 50 percent silver and 50 percent copper and another with 60 percent silver and 40 percent copper. Restrikes were produced at a later date, probably beginning in 1859, from normal silver planchet stock used for circulating coinage at that time (90 percent silver and 10 percent copper). Today, elemental analysis would be needed to differentiate the different coinage metals to assure proper attribution.

1849 Three cents (J–111 and 111a):

Obverse: A die of the regular Liberty Seated 1849 *half dime*. *Reverse:* The numeral three, with no further inscriptions. Originals struck in an alloy of 50 percent silver and 50 percent copper, average weight 22 grains. Restrikes may be in 90 percent silver. Elemental analy-

actual size: 15.5 mm

sis is required to tell the difference. J-111 is struck in an alloy of 50 percent silver and 50 percent copper and has a reeded edge. J-111a is struck in silver (regular alloy of 90 percent silver and 10 percent copper; restrike) and has a reeded edge.

1849 Three cents (J–112 and 112a):

Obverse: Another die of the regular Liberty Seated 1849 *half dime*, obverse same as preceding. *Reverse:* The Roman numeral III, with no further inscriptions. Original J-112 struck in an alloy of 60 percent silver and 40 percent copper, average weight 18.5 grains, per Judd,

actual size: 15.5 mm

although a text from a century earlier stated the composition of this and J-111 as "one half silver."[27] Restrikes may be in 90 percent silver. Elemental analysis is required to tell the difference. J-112 is struck in an alloy of 60 percent silver and 40 percent copper and has a reeded edge. J-112a is struck in silver (regular alloy of 90 percent silver and 10 percent copper; restrike) and has a reeded edge.

Aspects of Striking

Circulation strikes were produced for use in commerce, and little attention was given to the sharpness of details. As a general rule, most early issues including the 1837 and 1838-O, Without Stars, and the later 1838–1859, With Stars, varieties are fairly well struck. Weakness when it does occur is usually most noticeable on the head of Liberty and on the stars. Sometimes the higher-relief leaves in the laurel branches on the reverse show lightness.

Striking of the 1860 to 1873 coins with UNITED STATES OF AMERICA on the obverse is usually quite good, although the head of Liberty is weak on some.

Release and Distribution

Excepting Proofs made for presentation and for collectors, all Liberty Seated half dimes were intended for circulation. They served in commerce widely with the result that most became well-worn in time.

The Civil War was declared on April 15, 1861. In the North this was viewed as an easy win, and President Abraham Lincoln called for men to enlist for 90 days by which time it surely would be over. Reality was different. The first significant clash, the Battle of Bull Run in late July, resulted in a Confederate victory. Union troops scattered and fled. By late 1861 the outcome remained uncertain and gold coins were hoarded. In spring 1862 all silver coins disappeared from circulation. In the meantime on the West Coast, silver coins continued to be used at par in commerce, and any paper money brought into the area sold at a deep discount.

When the San Francisco Mint began producing half dimes in 1863, these went into circulation readily. It is said that these were especially popular with Chinese immigrants, many of whom had come to America during the Gold Rush and, later, to work in railroad construction. Many coins were sent back to relatives in China. After 1873 when the production of half dimes ended, many coins remained in circulation in the West for the next decade or so. Today the average grade of a surviving San Francisco Mint half dime of the 1860s is much lower than one made in Philadelphia. In addition, many San Francisco half dimes were made into buttons. Surviving examples have solder residue or tooling in the center of the obverse or reverse.

In the East, half dimes continued to be made after the spring of 1862, but they were not seen in commerce. The Mint sold them at par in exchange for gold coins, but only at a stiff premium if bought with Legal Tender Notes. Bullion brokers and banks maintained supplies for citizens who want to acquire them, again at a premium. It was anticipated that after the Civil War ended, in April 1865, that silver coins would reappear in circulation. The public remained wary of the solidity of the Treasury Department, and it was not until after April 20, 1876, that silver and paper were on a par, and silver coins, including long-hoarded half dimes, were again seen in circulation. Millions of half dimes reappeared and were deposited in banks, which sent them to the Treasury to be melted. In addition, large quantities held by brokers and others were melted. The result is that nearly all surviving Philadelphia Mint half dimes from the early 1860s onward are in relatively high grades. This situation has no counterpart with Liberty Seated dimes, quarters, or half dollars.

In November 1900 *The Numismatist* included this item reprinted from the *Havana Post:*

> Americans who visit the interior of Cuba are surprised beyond measure when they
> are given change for small purchases in cafes. The old American half dime, which

is no more in circulation in the United States, is used in the interior towns of Cuba, where it passes for two and a half cents. All of these coins are punched and were brought to Cuba many years ago. When the bangle craze had died away in America, and there were thousands of these half dimes which had been punched and were useless, some clever Yankee conceived the idea that they could be circulated in some way in Cuba and other West Indian islands. The plan worked well, and ever since that time they had been passing for two and one half cents.

Proof Liberty Seated Half Dimes

Proofs were struck at the Philadelphia Mint for all years from 1837 through 1873 with the possible exceptions of 1851 and 1853, although some of the With Arrows coins of 1853 are highly mirror-like. These have been called Proofs, but whether they were intended as such is a matter of debate.

From 1837 to 1858 Proof half dimes could be ordered at face value on request, sometimes single, other times as part of silver sets with all denominations. In 1858 about 210 silver Proof sets were made, per a letter from J. Ledyard Hodge.[4] The first official mintage figure for silver Proof sets is for 1859 when 800 were made. From that year forward figures were published regularly. In 1860 and 1861, when interest in numismatics was rising rapidly, production hit record levels of 1,000 sets per year. Curiously, Proofs of these two dates are far and away the rarest of the decade of the 1860s, for at the new price of $3 per set they were shunned by many collectors. It is likely that more than half of the coins were placed into circulation at face value.[5] Among later sets the figures reach lows of 460 and 470 in 1863 and 1864, respectively, although most survive today. Ordering Proofs from the Mint involved either paying in gold coins (only available at a premium in the marketplace) or by paying a strong premium in paper money. The Mint would not accept federal paper money at par.

Today, a complete run of Proof dates from 1858 to 1873 can be formed without difficulty. Typical grades are PF-63 and 64. Gems or PF-65 and finer coins are in the minority.

Grading Liberty Seated Half Dimes

1844-O, Small O; V-2. Graded MS-64.

MS-60 to 70 (Mint State). *Obverse:* At MS-60 some abrasion and contact marks are evident, most noticeably on the bosom, thighs, and knees. Luster is present, but may be dull or lifeless, and interrupted in patches in the large open field. At MS-63, contact marks are very few, and abrasion is hard to detect except under magnification. An

MS-65 coin has no abrasion, and contact marks are so minute as to require magnification. Luster should be full and rich, except for Philadelphia (but not San Francisco) half dimes of the early and mid-1860s. Most Mint State coins of 1861 to 1865, Philadelphia issues, will have extensive die striae (from the dies being incompletely finished). Some low-mintage Philadelphia issues may be prooflike (and some may even be mislabeled as Proofs). Clashmarks are common in this era. Half dimes of this type can be very beautiful at this level. *Reverse:* Comments apply as for the obverse except that in lower Mint State grades abrasion and contact marks are most noticeable on the highest parts of the leaves and the ribbon, less so on HALF DIME. The field is mainly protected by design elements and does not show abrasion as much as does the open-field obverse on a given coin.

Illustrated coin: This coin was struck in medallic alignment, as is seen with multiple examples of 1844-O, V-2.

1853, Arrows. Graded AU-50.

AU-50, 53, 55, 58 (About Uncirculated). *Obverse:* Light wear is seen on the thighs and knees, bosom, and head. At AU-58, the luster is extensive, but incomplete. Friction is seen in the large open field. At AU–50 and 53, luster is less. *Reverse:* Wear is noticeable on the leaves and ribbon. An AU-58 coin has nearly full luster—more so than on the obverse, as the design elements protect the small field areas. At AU–50 and 53, there still is significant luster, more than on the obverse.

1852-O. Graded EF-40.

EF-40, 45 (Extremely Fine). *Obverse:* Further wear is seen on all areas, especially the thighs and knees, bosom, and head. Little or no luster is seen. *Reverse:* Further wear is seen on all areas, most noticeably at the leaves to each side of the wreath apex, and on the ribbon bow knot. Leaves retain details except on the higher areas.

1846. Graded VF-35.

VF-20, 30 (Very Fine). *Obverse:* Further wear is seen. Most details of the gown are worn away, except in the lower-relief areas above and to the right of the shield. Hair detail is gone on the higher points. *Reverse:* Wear is more extensive. The highest leaves are flat, particularly the larger leaves at the top of the wreath.

1840-O. Graded F-15.

F-12, 15 (Fine). *Obverse:* The seated figure is well worn, but with some detail above and to the right of the shield. LIBERTY on the shield is fully readable, but weak in areas. *Reverse:* Most detail of the leaves is gone. The rim is worn but remains bold, and most if not all denticles are visible.

1846. Graded VG-10.

VG-8, 10 (Very Good). *Obverse:* The seated figure is more worn, but some detail can be seen above and to the right of the shield. The shield is discernible. In LIBERTY at least three letters are readable but very weak at VG-8; a few more appear at VG-10.

Reverse: Further wear has combined the details of most leaves. The rim is complete, but weak in areas. On most coins the reverse appears to be in a slightly higher grade than the obverse.

1837, Small Date. Graded G-4.

G-4, 6 (Good). *Obverse:* The seated figure is worn smooth. At G-4 there are no letters in LIBERTY remaining. At G-6, traces of one or two can be seen. *Reverse:* Wear is more extensive. The leaves are all combined and in outline form. The rim is clear but well worn and missing in some areas, causing the outer parts of the peripheral letters to be worn away in some instances. On most coins the reverse appears to be in a slightly higher grade than the obverse.

1837, Small Date. Graded AG-3.

AG-3 (About Good). *Obverse:* The seated figure is mostly visible in outline form, with no detail. The rim is worn away. The date remains clear. *Reverse:* Many if not most letters are worn away, as are parts of the wreath, though this and the interior letters are discernible. The rim can usually be seen, but is weak.

1873. Graded PF-66 Ultra Cameo.

PF-60 to 70 (Proof). *Obverse and Reverse:* Proofs that are extensively cleaned and have many hairlines, or that are dull and grainy, are lower level, such as PF-60 to 62. These are not widely desired, save for the rare (in any grade) date of 1846. Both the half dime and dime Proofs of 1837 were often cleaned, resulting in coins which have lost much of their mirror surface. With medium hairlines and good reflectivity, a grade of PF-64 is assigned, and with relatively few hairlines, Gem PF-65. In various grades hairlines are most easily seen in the obverse field. PF-66 should have hairlines so delicate that magnification is needed to see them. Above that, a Proof should be free of such lines.

Illustrated coin: Fully mirrored fields are seen when the coin is held at an angle to the light.

Collecting Liberty Seated Half Dimes

Although early half dimes, particularly those of the 1792 to 1805 years, and to a lesser extent the Capped Bust coins of 1829 to 1837, were eagerly sought after numismatics became a popular pursuit in America in the late 1850s, there was not much interest in Liberty Seated coins during the years they were issued. Proofs were an exception and were made every year from 1837 onward, with the possible exceptions of 1851 and 1853. Circulation strikes were ignored, including New Orleans and San Francisco branch-mint issues. The curators of the Mint Cabinet, which was organized in June 1838, had no interest in them. As a result, many half dimes made in large quantities range from scarce to very rare in Mint State today.

Liberty Seated half dimes were mentioned now and again in the two leading periodicals of the late 1800s and early 1900s—the *American Journal of Numismatics* and *The Numismatist*. A giant step forward was taken in 1893 with the publication of *Mint Marks, A Treatise on the Coinage of United States Branch Mints*. Interest in mintmarked coins increased, and in ensuing years the issues of New Orleans and San Francisco gained a following. By that time most coins in numismatic hands showed extensive wear. In August and December 1927 the first detailed study was published in *The Numismatist*. Will W. Neil's "The United States Half Dimes From 1829 Through 1873" described not only dates and mintmarks, but also die varieties within those categories.

The United States Half Dimes, by Daniel W. Valentine, was published by the American Numismatic Society in 1931. A supplement to this by Walter Breen was published in 1958. In 1992 the later entries in the Valentine book were succeeded by *The Complete Guide to Liberty Seated Half Dimes*, by Al Blythe, who continued using "V" or Valentine numbers. *The Authoritative Reference on Liberty Seated Half Dimes*, by Kevin Flynn, 2014, has much valuable information concerning legislation, minting, and interesting die varieties, most of which is not found in the books earlier mentioned. From the 1970s onward the *Gobrecht Journal* has published many items concerning Liberty Seated half dimes.

Liberty Seated half dimes are very collectible, and with the exception of the 1870-S, of which just one is known, all are readily available, although some are scarce. A dozen or more varieties are rarities in Mint State.

The *Gobrecht Journal* issued by the Liberty Seated Collectors Club furnishes a meeting place for the sharing of ideas, discoveries, and other information, as does the club's website.

A pleasant pursuit is the building of a half dime collection in circulated grades, such as Very Fine to About Uncirculated, with the addition of occasional Mint State and Proof pieces.

Being a Smart Buyer

First and foremost—and this is true of all Liberty Seated denominations—do not be a slave to grading numbers. There are *two more* factors that can be equally or even more important. Sharpness of strike is very important, and there are many half dimes that within a certain certified grade can have a needle-sharp strike or can be weak in areas. Eye appeal is equally important. Coins can be beautiful to view or they can be dark, stained, or otherwise ugly. I would rather have an MS-63 coin that is sharply struck and has good eye appeal than an MS-66 with lightly struck areas and that is not very attractive. Even better, the MS-63 is apt to cost but a fraction of the MS-66!

As is true of all Liberty Seated denominations, cherrypicking Liberty Seated half dimes for quality can pay dividends. The grading services pay little or no attention to strike or eye appeal. This provides the opportunity to acquire sharp coins, for varieties for which such exist, without paying any more for them. In addition there are many interesting varieties of which the public is not aware—such as repunched and misplaced dates—that often cost no more. The *Cherrypickers' Guide to Die Varieties of United States Coins* describes many such pieces. Kevin Flynn's *The Authoritative Reference on Liberty Seated Half Dimes* showcases even more.

For circulated coins, avoid those with nicks or scratches. Proofs are usually quite good, but some have light striking on Liberty's head and quite a few have scattered lint marks from residue on the dies. Eye appeal can vary.

1837 and 1838-O, No Stars on Obverse (Variety 1)

There are no stars on the obverse. A wreath is on reverse. This design is of the Small Letters variety. The mintmark is above the bow on the reverse for 1838-O.

Designer: Christian Gobrecht.

Specifications: *Composition:* 90 percent silver, 10 percent copper. *Diameter:* 15.5 mm. *Weight:* 20.625 grains (1.34 grams). *Edge:* Reeded.

1837, Small Date

Circulation-strike mintage: 1,405,000

actual size: 15.5 mm

Availability in Mint State: The Small Date variety is the less rare of the two styles. *MS-60 to 62:* 1,250 to 1,750. *MS-63:* 250 to 300. *MS-64:* 200 to 300. *MS-65 or better:* 125 to 175.

Availability in circulated grades: This issue is common in all grades.

Characteristics of striking: This issue is usually fairly well struck.

Detail of Small Date, showing Flat Top 1.

Notes: The Small Date numerals have a different style. The Flat Top 1 has a line, or *serif*, projecting to the left. The 8 is of a different style than the following. The knobs of the 3 are more open. While not arranged in a "straight line" as Valentine says, the arrangement of the digits is only slightly curved in a downward arc (the 83 numerals are lower than the 1 and 7).

G-4	VG-8	F-12	VF-20	EF-40	AU-50	MS-60	MS-63	MS-65
$50	$55	$100	$165	$265	$475	$700	$1,150	$2,650

1837, Large Date

Circulation-strike mintage: Portion of 1837, Small Date, mintage

Proof mintage: *15–20*

actual size: 15.5 mm

Availability in Mint State: As a class the two date styles of the 1837 half dime have had many auction appearances and are common in the context of the series. In 2014 the Eugene H. Gardner Sale featured three examples of this coin in MS-67. *MS-60 to 62:* 750 to 1,000. *MS-63:* 150 to 250. *MS-64:* 100 to 150. *MS-65 or better:* 75 to 100.

Availability in circulated grades: Thousands exist of this issue. This and the other date size are easy to buy in any desired grade.

Detail of Large Date, showing Pointed 1.

Characteristics of striking: This issue is usually well struck.

Proofs: Proofs of the Large Date variety have a triple-punched date. Some may have been struck on July 25, 1837, when the coinage of half dimes commenced. This die was also used to coin circulation strikes. This is the only Proof half dime prior to the 1850s that comes on the market with some frequency (in the context of early Proofs). Approximately ten examples have been certified.

Notes: The dates on 1837 half dimes are about the same size and differ mainly in the style of the numeral punches. The Large Date variety is slightly the rarer of the two. The 1 has a pointed top and the knobs on the 3 are closer than on the preceding. This die was made using the same date punches employed on 1837, Capped Bust, half dimes. The date numerals are arranged in a downward arc.

On July 25 Mint Director Robert M. Patterson sent 20 of the recently struck new half dimes to Secretary of the Treasury Levi Woodbury. These may have been Proofs.[6]

On September 18, 1837, E. Delafield of the Morris Bank of New York wrote to Mint Director R.M. Patterson: "I have forwarded to the Mint a box containing English silver of the British standard. Please receive the same for coinage into half dimes for the use of this bank."[7]

Unlike the related 1837, Liberty Seated, dime with Large and Small Date varieties, the half dimes of this year have digits about the same size, with the top of the 1 being the distinguishing characteristic. Thus, these might better be known as 1837, Pointed 1, and 1837, Flat Top 1.

G-4	VG-8	F-12	VF-20	EF-40	AU-50
$50	$55	$100	$165	$265	$475

MS-60	MS-63	MS-65	PF-60	PF-63	PF-65
$750	$1,150	$2,500	$7,000	$12,500	$32,500

1838-O

Circulation-strike mintage: 70,000

Availability in Mint State: In 2014 and 2015 the Eugene H. Gardner Sale featured examples of this coin in MS-66, MS-65, and MS-64. *MS-60 to 62:* 40 to 55. *MS-63:* 3 or 4. *MS-64:* 2 or 3. *MS-65 or better:* 2 or 3.

actual size: 15.5 mm

Availability in circulated grades: This issue is scarce in all circulated grades, but enough exist in proportion to the specialists desiring them that finding an example in a desired grade will be no problem.

Characteristics of striking: This issue is usually well struck.

G-4	VG-8	F-12	VF-20	EF-40	AU-50	MS-60	MS-63	MS-65
$165	$215	$500	$950	$2,500	$3,850	$5,750	$10,750	$27,500

1838–1840, Stars on Obverse
(Variety 2—No Drapery)

Stars on the obverse were punched individually into each working die. The reverse is the same as on the preceding variety. Mintmarks are above the bow on the reverse.

Designer: Christian Gobrecht.

Specifications: *Composition:* 90 percent silver, 10 percent copper. *Diameter:* 15.5 mm. *Weight:* 20.625 grains (1.34 grams). *Edge:* Reeded.

1838, Large Stars

Circulation-strike mintage: 2,225,000
Proof mintage: *4–5*

actual size: 15.5 mm

Availability in Mint State: This is one of the more readily available half dimes in various Mint State grades. In 2014 and 2015 the Eugene H. Gardner Sale featured examples of this coin in MS-68, MS-67, and MS-66. *MS-60 to 62:* 600 to 800. *MS-63:* 200 to 250. *MS-64:* 180 to 210. *MS-65 or better:* 100 to 125.

Availability in circulated grades: This issue is easy to find in circulated grades.

Detail of Large Stars.

Characteristics of striking: This issue is usually seen with sharp details.

Proofs: The coin from the 1996 Louis E. Eliasberg Sale is now PF-66. In 2014 the Eugene H. Gardner Sale featured an example of this coin in PF-67 (ex Pittman). Approximately two examples have been certified.

Notes: These have normal or medium-size obverse stars. Valentine lists more than a dozen varieties of this year. One with an extensively rusted reverse die is listed as FS-H10-1838-901. Dozens are known to exist.[8]

G-4	VG-8	F-12	VF-20	EF-40	AU-50
$30	$40	$50	$65	$125	$200
MS-60	MS-63	MS-65	PF-60	PF-63	PF-65
$300	$500	$1,350	$8,500	$10,500	$50,000

1838, Small Stars

Circulation-strike mintage: Portion of 1838, Large Stars, mintage

actual size: 15.5 mm

Notes: Valentine-1 to 3; Valentine mentions weak stars but not "small stars." These were struck from regular dies, but were relapped to remove some of the metal and to make the stars appear smaller. As such, it is not absolutely necessary for the completion of a collection. This style was not described by Valentine. These compose perhaps 15 percent or so of the population. In 2014 and 2015 the Eugene H. Gardner Sale featured three examples of this coin in MS-65.

Detail of Small Stars.

G-4	VG-8	F-12	VF-20	EF-40	AU-50	MS-60	MS-63	MS-65
$35	$55	$80	$175	$250	$375	$675	$1,000	$3,500

1839

Circulation-strike mintage: 1,069,150

Proof mintage: 5–10

actual size: 15.5 mm

Availability in Mint State: This is one of the more readily available half dimes in various Mint State grades, although it is not seen nearly as often as 1838. In 2015 the Eugene H. Gardner Sale featured examples of this coin in MS-68 and MS-66. *MS-60 to 62:* 300 to 400. *MS-63:* 100 to 125. *MS-64:* 75 to 90. *MS-65 or better:* 30 to 40.

Availability in circulated grades: This issue is plentiful in all grades.

Characteristics of striking: This issue is usually very sharp.

Proofs: Approximately three examples have been certified.

G-4	VG-8	F-12	VF-20	EF-40	AU-50
$35	$40	$45	$55	$105	$200

MS-60	MS-63	MS-65	PF-60	PF-63	PF-65
$300	$500	$1,600	$12,000	$15,000	$37,500

1839-O

Circulation-strike mintage: 1,291,600

Availability in Mint State: In 2015 the Eugene H. Gardner Sale featured examples of this coin in MS-67 and MS-65. *MS-60 to 62:* 75 to 100. *MS-63:* 15 to 20. *MS-64:* 7 to 9. *MS-65 or better:* 3 to 5.[9]

actual size: 15.5 mm

Availability in circulated grades: This issue is easy to find in any desired grade.

Characteristics of striking: This issue is usually well struck.

Notes: V-1 has a Large O mintmark, and is also the die used on 1838-O; these are rare but are not widely known outside of specialists. V-2, 3, and 6 have a small round O; V-4 and 5 have a medium-size elliptical O.[10] Only the most dedicated specialists collect by mintmark sizes, with the result being that scarcer varieties can be purchased at no extra cost by cherrypicking.

Reverses are seen in many degrees of misalignment from the normal 180 degrees.

G-4	VG-8	F-12	VF-20	EF-40	AU-50	MS-60	MS-63	MS-65
$35	$40	$45	$85	$200	$375	$950	$2,100	$8,500

1840, No Drapery

Circulation-strike mintage: 1,034,000

Proof mintage: 5–10

Availability in Mint State: In 2015 the Eugene H. Gardner Sale featured an example of this coin in MS-67. *MS-60 to 62:* 500 to 700. *MS-63:* 125 to 150. *MS-64:* 90 to 125. *MS-65 or better:* 30 to 40.

actual size: 15.5 mm

Availability in circulated grades: This issue is plentiful in all grades.

Characteristics of striking: These vary, but most coins of this issue are sharp.

Proofs: From the Louis E. Eliasberg Collection Sale, 1996, lot 950: "Stars 1, 8 and 10 doubled, the last sharply so. The 4 in the date has a flat top, with the apex of the interior triangular-space extending very close to the flat top; as time went on during the decade the third digit of the date was modified with a thicker top." Approximately five examples have been certified.

Notes: Per Walter H. Breen: "A tiny hoard of proof-like Uncs. turned up in Berkeley, CA, about 1961; these have weak details."

G-4	VG-8	F-12	VF-20	EF-40	AU-50
$35	$40	$45	$55	$105	$200

MS-60	MS-63	MS-65	PF-60	PF-63	PF-65
$300	$500	$1,500	$8,500	$10,500	$35,000

1840-O, No Drapery

Circulation-strike mintage: 695,000

Availability in Mint State: In 2014 and 2015 the Eugene H. Gardner Sale featured examples of this coin in MS-67, MS-66, MS-65, and MS-63. *MS-60 to 62:* 30 to 40. *MS-63:* 12 to 15. *MS-64:* 3 to 5. *MS-65 or better:* 3.

actual size: 15.5 mm

Availability in circulated grades: These are readily available in any desired grade.

Characteristics of striking: This issue is usually fairly well struck, but some are light at Liberty's foot.

Notes: V-1 has a large, round O. V-8 has the Large O reverse first used on 1838-O. Valentine lists four 1840-O, No Drapery, half dimes, V-1 to 4. Since then, several others have been identified, now numbered V-6 and V-8 to 10.

G-4	VG-8	F-12	VF-20	EF-40	AU-50	MS-60	MS-63	MS-65
$85	$100	$155	$250	$500	$650	$1,750	$5,500	$15,000

1840-O, No Drapery, Transitional Reverse

Circulation-strike mintage: 100

Availability in Mint State: *MS-60 to 62:* 4 to 6. *MS-63:* 1 or 2. *MS-64:* 1. *MS-65 or better:* 0. This issue is rare at any Mint State level.

actual size: 15.5 mm

Availability in circulated grades: *AG-3 to AU-58:* 100 to 200.

Characteristics of striking: This issue usually has some lightness on the head and star centers on the obverse, and on the highest parts of the leaves on the reverse.

Notes: V-6 is often called the "transitional" variety. This has the reverse type of 1841, with slightly larger letters, some "split" buds in the wreath, and the leaves in the cluster just to the left of the D in DIME reduced from four leaves to three. This issue has a small, round O mintmark. It is listed in *Cherrypickers' Guide to Rare Die Varieties* as FS-H10-1840o-901.[11]

1840-O, No Drapery, Normal Reverse, showing "whole" buds and four-leaf cluster.

1840-O, No Drapery, Transitional Reverse, showing "split" buds and three-leaf cluster.

G-4	VG-8	F-12	VF-20	EF-40	AU-50	MS-60	MS-63	MS-65
$300	$500	$675	$800	$1,200	$2,000	$3,500	$12,000	

1840–1853, Stars on Obverse (Variety 2—With Drapery)

The obverse has been redesigned slightly. Drapery has been added below the left elbow of Liberty, the most obvious change. The seated figure is slightly smaller, as is evidenced by the head being farther from the border than on the preceding variety, and there being larger spaces between the border and the lower–left and right of the figure. The liberty cap is smaller and more distant from the border, and Liberty's hand is closer to the cap. The shield has been rotated slightly to the right and is closer to being upright. The drapery to the right of the shield has been redesigned. The stars are now part of the hub, and henceforth there are no variations in their positions.

The reverse is of the same design, but the wreath is heavier and the letters are the larger, Large Letters, style. Some of the buds in the laurel wreath have split ends, widely called "split buds." See page 92 for illustrations. Mintmarks are above the bow through 1859.

Designer: Christian Gobrecht.

Specifications: *Composition:* 90 percent silver, 10 percent copper. *Diameter:* 15.5 mm. *Weight:* 20.625 grains (1.34 grams). *Edge:* Reeded.

1840, With Drapery

Circulation-strike mintage: 310,085

Proof mintage: Unknown

Availability in Mint State: In 2014 and 2015 the Eugene H. Gardner Sale featured examples of this coin in MS-67 and MS-65. *MS-60 to 62:* 80 to 100. *MS-63:* 20 to 25. *MS-64:* 18 to 22. *MS-65 or better:* 5 to 7.

actual size: 15.5 mm

Availability in circulated grades: This issue is readily available in relation to the demand.

Characteristics of striking: This issue is usually well struck.

Proofs: Proofs of this issue are very rare.

Notes: The reverse from this point on shows larger letters, with a few other differences occurring as well.[12]

G-4	VG-8	F-12	VF-20	EF-40	AU-50
$50	$60	$100	$150	$250	$360
MS-60	**MS-63**	**MS-65**	**PF-60**	**PF-63**	**PF-65**
$500	$900	$2,750			

1840-O, With Drapery

Circulation-strike mintage: 240,000

Availability in Mint State: In 2014 the Eugene H. Gardner Sale featured an example of this coin in MS-63. *MS-60 to 62:* 25 to 32. *MS-63:* 8 to 10. *MS-64:* 3 to 5. *MS-65 or better:* 0 or 1.

actual size: 15.5 mm

Availability in circulated grades: This issue is scarce in all grades.

Characteristics of striking: This issue usually has some weak areas, including the head.

Notes: Small, round O mintmark.

The 240,000 mintage was the New Orleans production in December 1840. It is assumed that these were With Drapery. The New Orleans Mint was very casual with some of its striking processes, and the present coin seems to reflect this. This variety was coined in December 1840 or early 1841 utilizing a pair of dies shipped from Philadelphia on December 2. As a general comment, it was the policy of the New Orleans Mint in the early days to keep using dies as long as they were serviceable. Accordingly, some dated obverses were used in the year following.

This is a cherrypicker's delight as nearly all certified 1840-O, With Drapery, half dimes make no note of the reverse style.

G-4	VG-8	F-12	VF-20	EF-40	AU-50	MS-60	MS-63	MS-65
$100	$115	$200	$350	$800	$1,550	$7,500	$22,000	

1841

Circulation-strike mintage: 1,150,000

Proof mintage: *10–20*

Availability in Mint State: In 2014 and 2015 the Eugene H. Gardner Sale featured examples of this coin in MS-67 and MS-65. *MS-60 to 62:* 500 to 700. *MS-63:* 90 to 110. *MS-64:* 60 to 80. *MS-65 or better:* 30 to 40.

actual size: 15.5 mm

Availability in circulated grades: This issue is common in all grades.

Characteristics of striking: This issue is usually sharp.

Proofs: All are of the V-1 variety and are very rare. Approximately six examples have been certified.

G-4	VG-8	F-12	VF-20	EF-40	AU-50
$30	$35	$40	$45	$75	$150
MS-60	**MS-63**	**MS-65**	**PF-60**	**PF-63**	**PF-65**
$190	$325	$1,000	$8,500	$12,500	$30,000

1841-O

Circulation-strike mintage: 815,000

Availability in Mint State: The 1841-O is unusual among New Orleans half dimes in that several dozen exist in Mint State, and examples in MS-64 and high grades are collectible within a relatively short time. In 2014 and 2015 the Eugene

actual size: 15.5 mm

H. Gardner Sale featured examples of this coin in MS-67, MS-66, and MS-64. *MS-60 to 62:* 20 to 25. *MS-63:* 7 to 11. *MS-64:* 5 to 9. *MS-65 or better:* 3 or 4.[13]

Availability in circulated grades: This issue is common, however New Orleans half dimes had a higher attrition rate proportionately than did Philadelphia coins.

Characteristics of striking: Varies within the issue.

Notes: V-1 and 2 have a Small O mintmark. V-3 and 4 have a Medium O. The V-5 has a Small O (0.8 mm). The last was listed later and was not known to Valentine. Al Blythe reported an unverified large wide O, originally listed by Neil (N-4) in his 1927 monograph.

G-4	VG-8	F-12	VF-20	EF-40	AU-50	MS-60	MS-63	MS-65
$80	$90	$155	$225	$325	$500	$1,100	$3,250	$8,000

1842

Circulation-strike mintage: 815,000
Proof mintage: *10–20*

Availability in Mint State: In 2015 the Eugene H. Gardner Sale featured two examples of this coin in MS-66. *MS-60 to 62:* 275 to 325. *MS-63:* 65 to 90. *MS-64:* 50 to 70. *MS-65 or better:* 15 to 20.

actual size: 15.5 mm

Availability in circulated grades: This issue is readily available in any desired grade.

Characteristics of striking: Striking of this issue varies but is usually quite good. Some show lightness on the denticles.

Proofs: Approximately six examples have been certified.

Notes: Relief and boldness can vary depending on how deep the master die was impressed into the working die (some deep impressions are called "Heavy Date" by Valentine) and whether the die was relapped (causing lightness).

G-4	VG-8	F-12	VF-20	EF-40	AU-50
$30	$35	$40	$45	$75	$165

MS-60	MS-63	MS-65	PF-60	PF-63	PF-65
$250	$400	$1,250	$8,000	$10,000	$20,000

1842-O

Circulation-strike mintage: 350,000

Availability in Mint State: In 2015 the Eugene H. Gardner Sale featured examples of this coin in MS-66 (2), MS-65, and MS-63 (2). *MS-60 to 62:* 75 to 100. *MS-63:* 25 to 30. *MS-64:* 12 to 16. *MS-65 or better:* 6 to 9.

actual size: 15.5 mm

Availability in circulated grades: This issue is scarce in all grades.

Characteristics of striking: This issue is often lightly struck in some areas.

Notes: The 1842-O has a Small O mintmark. All 1842-O half dimes were struck from the same die pair. Stephen A. Crain states: "I have never seen *any* variation in date or mintmark placement on any example I have studied, including the nine examples in my reference collection."[14]

G-4	VG-8	F-12	VF-20	EF-40	AU-50	MS-60	MS-63	MS-65
$75	$100	$125	$215	$600	$1,000	$1,275	$2,250	$13,000

1843

Circulation-strike mintage: 815,000
Proof mintage: *10–20*

Availability in Mint State: In 2014 and 2015 the Eugene H. Gardner Sale featured examples of this coin in MS-67, MS-65, and MS-63. *MS-60 to 62:* 350 to 450. *MS-63:* 110 to 140. *MS-64:* 90 to 120. *MS-65 or better:* 20 to 25.

actual size: 15.5 mm

Availability in circulated grades: This issue is easy to find.

Characteristics of striking: This issue is usually well struck.

Proofs: All are from an obverse die with the date triple punched.[15] Approximately eight examples have been certified.

Notes: Certain reverse dies were kept in service long after they developed cracks, some extensive.[16] V-6 has a double-punched date.

G-4	VG-8	F-12	VF-20	EF-40	AU-50
$30	$35	$40	$45	$75	$160
MS-60	**MS-63**	**MS-65**	**PF-60**	**PF-63**	**PF-65**
$225	$400	$1,350	$8,000	$10,000	$20,000

1844

Circulation-strike mintage: 430,000
Proof mintage: *15–25*

Availability in Mint State: In 2014 and 2015 the Eugene H. Gardner Sale featured examples of this coin in MS-67, MS-66, MS-65, and MS-64. *MS-60 to 62:* 200 to 250. *MS-63:* 70 to 90. *MS-64:* 50 to 70. *MS-65 or better:* 35 to 45.

actual size: 15.5 mm

Availability in circulated grades: Many of this issue exist. Finding one in any desired circulated grade will be easy to do.

Characteristics of striking: This issue is usually sharp.

Notes: V-1 and 2 are normal dates; V-3 is the significantly more common Repunched Date.

Proofs: The first three date digits are repunched, the first two both above and below. Approximately 12 examples have been certified.

G-4	VG-8	F-12	VF-20	EF-40	AU-50
$30	$35	$40	$55	$115	$200
MS-60	**MS-63**	**MS-65**	**PF-60**	**PF-63**	**PF-65**
$300	$500	$1,300	$8,000	$10,000	$22,500

1844-O

Circulation-strike mintage: 220,000

Availability in Mint State: From the
Louis E. Eliasberg Collection Sale,
1996, lot 962: "1844-O V-1. MS-65.
Finest known. Deeply frosty and
lustrous surfaces of virtual perfection.
Original brilliance delicately toned with

actual size: 15.5 mm

light blue and gold. Lightly struck at the centers as always. When 1844-O is seen it is
nearly always in very low grades. Even an MS-60 would create a major stir among afi-
cionados of the Liberty Seated series. This gem is believed to be the finest known. A
treasure for the specialist and one of the great highlights of the present offering. Most
of its high grade competitors are clustered far below at the AU or very low Mint State
level." In 2014 and 2015 the Eugene H. Gardner Sale featured examples of this coin
in MS-65 (ex Eliasberg) and MS-64. *MS-60 to 62:* 5 to 7. *MS-63:* 3 or 4. *MS-64:* 2
or 3. *MS-65 or better:* 2 or 3.

Availability in circulated grades: Both varieties are very scarce and are usually found
well worn.

Characteristics of striking: This issue varies, but usually has some lightness.

Notes: V-1 with Medium O is scarcer than V-2 with Small O. About 90 percent of
the 1844-O, V-2, half dimes have the reverse-aligned medal turn, and very few are
aligned coin turn.[17]

G-4	VG-8	F-12	VF-20	EF-40	AU-50	MS-60	MS-63	MS-65
$125	$200	$325	$750	$1,300	$2,750	$6,000	$10,000	$25,000

1845

Circulation-strike mintage: 1,564,000
Proof mintage: *10–15*

Availability in Mint State: *MS-60
to 62:* 350 to 450. *MS-63:* 120 to 140.
MS-64: 90 to 120. *MS-65 or better:*
50 to 65.

actual size: 15.5 mm

Availability in circulated grades: This is one of the most plentiful early dates.

Characteristics of striking: This issue is usually well struck.

Proofs: There are die artifacts just past stars nine and ten. In the date, the 5 is slightly
higher than the first three digits. Approximately 10 examples have been certified.

Notes: Valentine lists six varieties, and Blythe brings the total up to "at least 11." V-5
per Valentine: "All numerals show they have been twice punched, and the 5 looks as
if it had been made over from a 3." Al Blythe gives this a separate page listing. These
are relatively common. Repunched date FS-H10-1845-301, with the 8 and 4 protruding from the rock above the date, is an extremely rare variety (see next page).

Five pairs of dies were sent to New Orleans for an 1845-O coinage that never
materialized.

Misplaced Date: Bill Fivaz introduced a spectacular mis-placed date (MPD) variety for the 1845 half dime in Issue 70 of the *Gobrecht Journal* in 1997, with the date numerals first punched high into the base. Only a very few examples have surfaced of this rare early die state, including a Mint State coin in the Stephen A. Crain Col-

lection. *The Cherrypickers' Guide to Rare Die Varieties* lists this as FS-50-1845-301.

G-4	VG-8	F-12	VF-20	EF-40	AU-50
$30	$35	$40	$45	$60	$145
MS-60	MS-63	MS-65	PF-60	PF-63	PF-65
$225	$375	$1,150	$10,000	$15,000	$30,000

1846

Circulation-strike mintage: 27,000

Proof mintage: *10–20*

Availability in Mint State: This issue is very rare in any level of Mint State; a key to the series. The 1846 is far and away the rarest Philadelphia Mint half dime in high grades. In 2014 the

actual size: 15.5 mm

Eugene H. Gardner Sale featured examples of this coin in MS-63 and MS-64. *MS-60 to 62:* 3 or 4. *MS-63:* 2 or 3. *MS-64:* 1. *MS-65 or better:* 1.

Availability in circulated grades: This issue is scarce in all grades, but is particularly rare in EF and AU. The key to the Philadelphia Mint series.

Characteristics of striking: This issue usually has some slight lightness on the head.

Proofs: Proofs are from a different die not listed by Valentine. The point of the shield is directly over the 1. The most often (but not that often!) seen Proof of the era. Approximately 11 examples have been certified.

Notes: V-1 has the point of the shield over the serif on the right side of the 1 and the date slants slightly down to the right. The low-mintage 1846 half dime is one of the most famous coins in the series.[18] In terms of rarity, not including the 1870-S, it and the somewhat more available 1853-O, No Arrows, are the keys to the series.

G-4	VG-8	F-12	VF-20	EF-40	AU-50
$850	$1,300	$1,700	$2,400	$4,250	$7,500
MS-60	MS-63	MS-65	PF-60	PF-63	PF-65
$15,000	$35,000		$8,000	$12,500	$22,000

1847

Circulation-strike mintage: 1,274,000

Proof mintage: *8–12*

Availability in Mint State: *MS-60 to 62:* 500 to 700. *MS-63:* 90 to 110. *MS-64:* 60 to 80. *MS-65 or better:* 30 to 40.

actual size: 15.5 mm

Availability in circulated grades: This issue is common.

Characteristics of striking: This issue is usually fairly well struck.

Proofs: V-2 has numerals high and each touch the base. In 2014 the Eugene H. Gardner Sale featured examples of this coin in PF-67 and PF-65 (ex Eliasberg). Approximately eight examples have been certified.

Notes: V-1 to 5.

G-4	VG-8	F-12	VF-20	EF-40	AU-50
$30	$35	$40	$70	$95	$150
MS-60	MS-63	MS-65	PF-60	PF-63	PF-65
$225	$400	$1,100	$8,000	$10,000	$22,000

1848, Medium Date

Circulation-strike mintage: 668,000
Proof mintage: 6–8

Availability in Mint State: In 2015 the Eugene H. Gardner Sale featured an example of this coin in MS-65. *MS-60 to 62:* 200 to 250. *MS-63:* 40 to 50. *MS-64:* 25 to 30. *MS-65 or better:* 15 to 20.

actual size: 15.5 mm

Detail of Medium Date.

Availability in circulated grades: These are readily available in any desired grade.

Characteristics of striking: This issue is usually well struck.

Proofs: Date is touching the base of Liberty, although there is enough space below the date that this would not have been necessary. There is an artifact past star ten. This date is particularly rare. The Louis E. Eliasberg Collection Sale in 1996 had two gem Proofs![22] In 2015 the Eugene H. Gardner Sale featured an example of this coin in PF-64 (ex Pittman). Approximately two examples have been certified.

Notes: V-2 to 8, with the last a later discovery (Breen-3046). The Medium Date is actually fairly large in relation to the space on the coin provided for it. This is the date size usually seen. There is also a spectacular "Far Right Date" variety (V-9), with the date punched far to the right in the exergue. Only a few examples are known, including a Mint State coin in the Crain Collection.[23]

G-4	VG-8	F-12	VF-20	EF-40	AU-50
$30	$35	$40	$60	$95	$180
MS-60	MS-63	MS-65	PF-60	PF-63	PF-65
$300	$600	$3,000	$9,000	$12,000	$22,500

1848, 8 Over 6

Circulation-strike mintage: Portion of 1848, Medium Date, mintage

actual size: 15.5 mm

Availability in Mint State: A small fraction of the 1848 Medium Date. Data incomplete.

Availability in circulated grades: A small fraction of the 1848 Medium Date. Data incomplete.

Detail of 8 Over 6 Overdate.

Characteristics of striking: This issue varies, but is usually good.

Notes: Medium date 1848, 8 Over 6, overdate. Al Blythe designates as 1848, 8 Over 7 Over 6, discovered by Jack Collins. Kevin Flynn considers this to be the only true overdate of the year, 1848, 8 Over 6 (his OVD-001). Tom DeLorey says, "Not everybody agrees this is an overdate and not just a repunched date."[19]

Late die-state examples of V-7a exhibit die cracks at N through H of the denomination, and up through the E of STATES, as do late die states of the so-called 1848, 8 Over 7 Over 6. This appeared incorrectly as a new "V-10" in the 1994 LSCC half dime census survey (published in the *Gobrecht Journal*, March 1995), instead of correctly identifying it as V-7.[20] Bill Fivaz and J.T. Stanton assign FS-H10-1848-302. Overlays by Kevin Flynn show the outline of a 6 underneath the 8 with the left side extending through the serif of the 4. The repunching on the serif of the center horizontal bar is much wider than the serif on the 4 of the 1848 date punch and matches the width of the serif of the 4 on an 1846 date punch.

At the upper left of the 8 is what some say may be the upper-left tip of an earlier 7, except that it does not match the style of the upper left of the 7 on regular 1847 half dimes and is therefore discredited. Kevin Flynn lists this variety as refuted stating that the small vertical dash seen to the left of the upper 8 is simply part of the repunched 8 that is also seen to the left of the upper part of the lower loop.[21] Whatever it is, it is a rare variety.

Another variety, now thought to be a repunching, not an overdate, is called 1848, 8 Over 7, by Al Blythe, the discovery of Jack Beymer. Similar to the foregoing there is an earlier figure under the final 8.

G-4	VG-8	F-12	VF-20	EF-40	AU-50	MS-60	MS-63	MS-65
	$35	$50	$75	$125	$225	$375	$500	

1848, Large Date

Circulation-strike mintage: Portion of 1848, Medium Date, mintage

actual size: 15.5 mm

Availability in Mint State: In 2015 the Eugene H. Gardner Sale featured an example of this coin in MS-66. *MS-60 to 62:* 50 to 70. *MS-63:* 15 to 20. *MS-64:* 10 to 13. *MS-65 or better:* 5 to 8.

Detail of Large Date.

Availability in circulated grades: These are readily available in all grades.

Characteristics of striking: This issue is usually sharp.

Notes: V-1 is very scarce. This issue is made from the logotype used on dimes. The date extends into the base of Liberty and nearly touches the point of the shield. This is often misattributed. If the date does not overlap the base of Liberty it is *not* a Large Date.

Among half dimes of the 1840s there are numerous differences in letter spacing. For example, on the Eliasberg coin of this variety the letters in HAL join and the F barely touches; on others all letters are distinctly separated, and on still others HAL may be joined and F is entirely separate, etc. This is probably at least partially a function of how deeply the hub was impressed into the die or from relapping as there was no change in the hub.

G-4	VG-8	F-12	VF-20	EF-40	AU-50	MS-60	MS-63	MS-65
$35	$50	$80	$150	$190	$365	$750	$2,000	$4,000

1848-O

Circulation-strike mintage: 600,000

actual size: 15.5 mm

Availability in Mint State: This is the only New Orleans half dime of the decade that is readily available in upper ranges of Mint State. *MS-60 to 62:* 200 to 250. *MS-63:* 65 to 80. *MS-64:* 50 to 70. *MS-65 or better:* 30 to 40.

Availability in circulated grades: This issue is easy to find due to it being one of the more plentiful early New Orleans half dimes.

Characteristics of striking: The striking varies for this issue.

Notes: V-4 and 5 have the Small O; rare. V-2 and 8 have the Medium O. V-1, 3, 6, and 7 have the Large O. The Small O can be cherrypicked. When attributed it can sell for multiples of the price of the other two sizes.[24]

G-4	VG-8	F-12	VF-20	EF-40	AU-50	MS-60	MS-63	MS-65
$30	$35	$45	$85	$210	$365	$650	$1,400	$2,750

1849, 9 Over 6

**Circulation-strike mintage:
Portion of 1849 mintage**

actual size: 15.5 mm

Availability in Mint State: In 2014 and 2015 the Eugene H. Gardner Sale featured examples of this coin in MS-66, MS-65, and MS-64. *MS-60 to 62:* 50 to 65. *MS-63:* 15 to 20. *MS-64:* 12 to 15. *MS-65 or better:* 8 to 12.

Availability in circulated grades: This issue is a small fraction of the 1849 perfect date; slightly scarce.

Characteristics of striking: This issue varies, but is usually well struck.

Detail of 9 Over 6 Overdate.

Notes: The three obverse dies used on V-1, 2, 4, and 5 show traces of an earlier date. Over a period of time there has been much discussion and even controversy concerning these varieties. The earliest states of V-2 show an indisputable 6 or inverted 9 under the 9. Designations such as 1849, 9 Over 8 Over 6, and 1849, 9 Over 8, have not been confirmed by Stephen A. Crain (pre-eminent modern scholar of the half dime series). The illustrated detail is the most obvious of the overdates.

G-4	VG-8	F-12	VF-20	EF-40	AU-50	MS-60	MS-63	MS-65
$45	$50	$85	$120	$200	$350	$700	$1,200	$2,100

1849

**Circulation-strike mintage:
1,309,000**

Proof mintage: *8–12*

actual size: 15.5 mm

Availability in Mint State: In 2014 and 2015 the Eugene H. Gardner Sale featured two examples of this coin in MS-67. *MS-60 to 62:* 100 to 150. *MS-63:* 20 to 25. *MS-64:* 15 to 18. *MS-65 or better:* 12 to 16.

Availability in circulated grades: This issue is common in circulated grades.

Characteristics of striking: This issue varies, but often has some lightness on the head.

Proofs: V-8. This obverse die was also used for circulation strikes. In the date, the 1 and 4 are repunched, but not dramatically, while the 9 is more significantly repunched at the bottom. There is an artifact just past star ten. Approximately five examples have been certified.

Notes: Valentine lists eight varieties.

G-4	VG-8	F-12	VF-20	EF-40	AU-50
$30	$35	$40	$58	$100	$175
MS-60	**MS-63**	**MS-65**	**PF-60**	**PF-63**	**PF-65**
$265	$750	$1,650	$8,000	$10,000	$22,500

1849-O

Circulation-strike mintage: 140,000

Availability in Mint State: In 2014 and 2015 the Eugene H. Gardner Sale featured examples of this coin in MS-65 and MS-64. *MS-60 to 62:* 20 to 25. *MS-63:* 7 to 10. *MS-64:* 4 to 6. *MS-65 or better:* 2 or 3.[28]

actual size: 15.5 mm

Availability in circulated grades: This issue is scarce in all grades. While not a notable rarity, the 1849-O is a well-known key variety.

Characteristics of striking: These are usually lightly struck in areas on both obverse and reverse.

Notes: V-1 has the date logotype "heavy," or deep into the die, and V-2 is lighter; the latter seems to be a later state of the same obverse die.[29] All 1849-O half dimes have a Large O mintmark.

This is a well-known key issue and is nearly always seen well worn.

G-4	VG-8	F-12	VF-20	EF-40	AU-50	MS-60	MS-63	MS-65
$65	$95	$145	$300	$625	$1,200	$2,300	$4,000	$8,500

1850

Circulation-strike mintage: 955,000

Proof mintage: *8–12*

Availability in Mint State: *MS-60 to 62:* 1,000 to 1,500. *MS-63:* 130 to 160. *MS-64:* 100 to 125. *MS-65 or better:* 80 to 100.

actual size: 15.5 mm

Availability in circulated grades: This issue is common in all grades.

Characteristics of striking: This issue is usually sharp.

Proofs: V-2 is used for Proofs and circulation strikes. Approximately four examples have been certified.

Notes: V-1 to 5. Al Blythe notes that V-1 and 4 are slightly scarce.

G-4	VG-8	F-12	VF-20	EF-40	AU-50
$30	$35	$40	$60	$90	$180

MS-60	MS-63	MS-65	PF-60	PF-63	PF-65
$220	$375	$925	$12,000	$20,000	$40,000

1850-O

Circulation-strike mintage: 690,000

Availability in Mint State: In 2014 and 2015 the Eugene H. Gardner Sale featured two examples of this coin in MS-66. *MS-60 to 62:* 25 to 30. *MS-63:* 7 to 10. *MS-64:* 6 to 9. *MS-65 or better:* 4 to 6.[30]

actual size: 15.5 mm

Availability in circulated grades: This issue is easier to find, although many fewer exist than its Philadelphia Mint counterpart.

Characteristics of striking: This issue usually has areas of weak striking.

Notes: V-1, Large O; V-2, Large "fat" (per Valentine) O; V-3, Medium O per Valentine, but it does seem to differ from the illustration of his Large O; V-4, Small O, is quite rare.

G-4	VG-8	F-12	VF-20	EF-40	AU-50	MS-60	MS-63	MS-65
$35	$40	$60	$100	$200	$275	$675	$1,500	$5,750

1851

Circulation-strike mintage: 781,000

Proof mintage: See comments under Proofs

Availability in Mint State: *MS-60 to 62:* 250 to 300. *MS-63:* 50 to 50. *MS-64:* 40 to 50. *MS-65 or better:* 30 to 40.

actual size: 15.5 mm

Availability in circulated grades: This issue is readily available.

Characteristics of striking: Characteristics vary, but they are usually sharp. Some are lightly defined on Liberty's head.

Proofs: Some coins of 1851 and 1853 have been called Proofs over a long period of years, but it is uncertain if they were actually struck as such or if they were from dies polished after relapping or for other reasons. No Proof sets of this year are known. V-1 has a high date: the 1 and 8 contact the base of the figure, and the 5 and 1 protrude within the base. There are artifacts at stars five and ten. The reverse has many die-finish lines at the rim above MERIC. The obverse die was also used for circulation strikes.

Notes: Seven obverse and five reverse dies (Blythe 1992).

G-4	VG-8	F-12	VF-20	EF-40	AU-50	MS-60	MS-63	MS-65
$30	$35	$40	$45	$75	$140	$225	$350	$1,000

1851-O

Circulation-strike mintage: 860,000

Availability in Mint State: In 2015 the Eugene H. Gardner Sale featured examples of this coin in MS-66 and MS-65. *MS-60 to 62:* 150 to 175. *MS-63:* 20 to 25. *MS-64:* 15 to 20. *MS-65 or better:* 10 to 12.

actual size: 15.5 mm

Availability in circulated grades: This issue is somewhat scarce in all grades in spite of the generous mintage.

Characteristics of striking: These usually have some lightness.

Notes: V-1 and 2, both with Large O mintmark. The Friesner Collection Sale (Frossard 1894) had a Mint State coin.

G-4	VG-8	F-12	VF-20	EF-40	AU-50	MS-60	MS-63	MS-65
$30	$35	$40	$50	$115	$235	$450	$925	$4,200

1852

Circulation-strike mintage: 1,000,500
Proof mintage: *10–15*

Availability in Mint State: *MS-60 to 62:* 300 to 400. *MS-63:* 60 to 75. *MS-64:* 45 to 60. *MS-65 or better:* 30 to 40.

actual size: 15.5 mm

Availability in circulated grades: Circulated grades of this issue are common.

Characteristics of striking: This issue is usually well struck.

Proofs: V-3. The obverse die was also used for circulation strikes. Approximately 11 examples have been certified.

Notes: Valentine lists four varieties. Many were melted with the result that this date is somewhat scarce.

G-4	VG-8	F-12	VF-20	EF-40	AU-50
$30	$35	$40	$45	$75	$145

MS-60	MS-63	MS-65	PF-60	PF-63	PF-65
$200	$325	$1,050	$8,000	$10,000	$22,500

1852-O

Circulation-strike mintage: 260,000

Availability in Mint State: In 2014 the Eugene H. Gardner Sale featured an example of this coin in MS-66. *MS-60 to 62:* 30 to 45. *MS-63:* 10 to 13. *MS-64:* 6 to 9. *MS-65 or better:* 2 or 3.

actual size: 15.5 mm

Availability in circulated grades: This issue is fairly scarce, especially at the EF and AU levels.

Characteristics of striking: There is usually some lightness on the head for this issue.

Notes: V-1 and 2. A rare new discovery, the V-2 date slopes downward to the right.[31] The Large O mintmark reverse die is used on both.

G-4	VG-8	F-12	VF-20	EF-40	AU-50	MS-60	MS-63	MS-65
$35	$40	$80	$150	$275	$500	$1,000	$2,500	$7,500

1853, No Arrows

Circulation-strike mintage: 135,000

Availability in Mint State: This issue is slightly scarce but is easily enough obtained in grades from MS-60 to 64, which is surprising as this variety is elusive overall. In 2014 the Eugene H. Gardner Sale featured an example of

actual size: 15.5 mm

this coin in MS-68. *MS-60 to 62:* 45 to 60. *MS-63:* 15 to 20. *MS-64:* 10 to 13. *MS-65 or better:* 8 to 10.

Availability in circulated grades: These are long regarded as a key issue among Philadelphia dates, although enough exist to supply the demand for them.

Characteristics of striking: This issue is usually well struck.

Notes: V-1. Of the 135,000 struck, 50,000 were coined on February 19 and 85,000 on February 22, the last a day after the Act of February 21, 1853. Most probably the 85,000 went directly to the melting pot, and it is highly likely that the majority of the 50,000 met the same fate. At the time the coins were worth more in melt-down value than face value, and most available pieces went into the hands of speculators and bullion dealers. Breen mentions, but does not substantiate, that in the 1800s a small hoard was found by Harold P. Newlin.

G-4	VG-8	F-12	VF-20	EF-40	AU-50	MS-60	MS-63	MS-65
$60	$85	$140	$225	$325	$525	$750	$1,200	$2,000

1853-O, No Arrows

Circulation-strike mintage: 160,000

Availability in Mint State: In 2014 the Eugene H. Gardner Sale featured an example of this coin in MS-65. *MS-60 to 62:* 15 to 20. *MS-63:* 5 to 7. *MS-64:* 4 to 6. *MS-65 or better:* 1 or 2.

actual size: 15.5 mm

Availability in circulated grades: This famous key New Orleans half dime is quite scarce.

Characteristics of striking: This issue has areas of lightness.

Notes: V-1, Large O mintmark. This is one of the top key issues in the Liberty Seated half dime series. Date high, sloping down to the right, with 1 touching the base of Liberty; date figures are very lightly impressed into die—a characteristic of all authentic specimens. The New Orleans Mint called in and/or did not distribute much of its coinage struck prior to the Act of February 21, 1853, and in autumn of 1853 shipped more than $1 million of silver coins of various denominations to Philadelphia to be melted and recoined into lighter-weight issues under the new standard. $100 worth of old-style silver coins yielded $108.33 worth of the new, lighter coins (with arrows at date).

G-4	VG-8	F-12	VF-20	EF-40	AU-50	MS-60	MS-63	MS-65
$350	$600	$800	$1,375	$2,800	$3,850	$8,750	$13,500	$32,500

1853–1855, Arrows at Date (Variety 3)

Arrows were placed at the sides of the date for a brief period starting in 1853. They were placed there to denote the reduction of weight under the terms of the Act of February 21, 1853.

Designer: Christian Gobrecht. Arrows were added by James B. Longacre or someone else on the Mint staff.

Specifications: *Composition:* 90 percent silver, 10 percent copper. *Diameter:* 15.5 mm. *Weight:* 19.2 grains (1.24 grams). *Edge:* Reeded.

1853, With Arrows

Circulation-strike mintage: 13,210,020

Proof mintage: See comments under Proofs

actual size: 15.5 mm

Availability in Mint State: This issue is very common in grades from MS-60 to 64, and is one of the most easily found coins in the series. The market price is strong, however, due to the demand for the 1853 in type sets. Other issues of this type are scarcer. *MS-60 to 62:* 2,500 to 3,000. *MS-63:* 600 to 800. *MS-64:* 400 to 500. *MS-65 or better:* 150 to 200.

Availability in circulated grades: This issue is extremely common, and tens of thousands are known.

Characteristics of striking: Striking varies for this issue, but many are sharp.

Proofs: Some coins of 1851 and 1853 have been called Proofs over a long period of years, but it is uncertain if they were actually struck as such or if they were from dies polished after relapping or for other reasons. No Proof sets of this year are known. Half dimes of 1853 certified as Proof have the date high and adjacent to the base, and arrowheads are free of the base but with tips barely touching the denticles. Two examples have been certified.

Notes: Certainly there are not 78 obverse and 80 reverse dies known as published in available literature, this originating with Walter Breen. At times it might seem like there may be that many, but due to the use of the hubbing process in the manufacture of working dies, very few *different* dies have been identified.[32] In 1853 and 1854 the Mint was playing catch-up as silver coins had disappeared from circulation and record numbers needed to be minted to supply the demand following the Coinage Act of February 21, 1853. This act reduced the weight and permitted the coins to again circulate.

Kevin Flynn describes "1853 with Arrows and Dot," a variety which has a prominent raised round dot centered above a denticle below the 5. This seems to have been intentional, for a reason not known today.[33]

G-4	VG-8	F-12	VF-20	EF-40	AU-50
$30	$35	$40	$45	$75	$150
MS-60	MS-63	MS-65	PF-60	PF-63	PF-65
$200	$350	$950		$60,000	

1853-O, With Arrows

Circulation-strike mintage: 2,200,000

Availability in Mint State: These are surprisingly scarce in MS-60 to 64, especially in comparison proportionately to its Philadelphia Mint counterpart, but are easily enough found with patience. Gems are rare. In 2014 and

actual size: 15.5 mm

2015 the Eugene H. Gardner Sale featured examples of this coin in MS-67, MS-66, and MS-61. *MS-60 to 62:* 125 to 150. *MS-63:* 30 to 40. *MS-64:* 20 to 25. *MS-65 or better:* 10 to 15.

Availability in circulated grades: This issue is slightly scarce in higher grades, but there are more than enough to go around among specialists.

Characteristics of striking: The striking of this issue varies, but usually has some lightness.

Notes: Large O mintmark. In 1992 Al Blythe knew of eighteen obverse and eight reverse dies. Only three examples of the "1853/1853"-O, V-6, half dime were reported in the 2005 LSCC census survey.

G-4	VG-8	F-12	VF-20	EF-40	AU-50	MS-60	MS-63	MS-65
$30	$35	$45	$65	$100	$240	$350	$1,250	$3,750

1854, With Arrows

Circulation-strike mintage: 5,740,000
Proof mintage: *15–25*

Availability in Mint State: *MS-60 to 62:* 1,250 to 1,500. *MS-63:* 400 to 550. *MS-64:* 200 to 250. *MS-65 or better:* 75 to 100.

actual size: 15.5 mm

Availability in circulated grades: This issue is very common.

Characteristics of striking: This issue is usually fairly good.

Proofs: In 2015 the Eugene H. Gardner Sale featured an example of this coin graded PF-64 (ex Eliasberg). Approximately 11 examples have been certified.

Notes: There are many varieties, although Valentine describes only six combinations. The V-1 "Date Overlaps Base" variety is particularly interesting, but is not difficult to find.

G-4	VG-8	F-12	VF-20	EF-40	AU-50
$30	$35	$40	$45	$75	$150
MS-60	MS-63	MS-65	PF-60	PF-63	PF-65
$200	$325	$1,100	$4,000	$7,500	$10,000

1854-O, With Arrows

Circulation-strike mintage: 1,560,000

Availability in Mint State: *MS-60 to 62:* 200 to 250. *MS-63:* 45 to 60. *MS-64:* 25 to 32. *MS-65 or better:* 20 to 25.

Availability in circulated grades: In circulated grades these are scarcer than its Philadelphia cousin, but are common overall.

actual size: 15.5 mm

Characteristics of striking: This issue varies, but some are sharp.

Notes: The Medium O mintmark of this issue is sometimes called Large O. Valentine lists four combinations, but more are known.

G-4	VG-8	F-12	VF-20	EF-40	AU-50	MS-60	MS-63	MS-65
$30	$35	$40	$45	$100	$200	$350	$900	$3,750

1855, With Arrows

Circulation-strike mintage: 1,750,000

Proof mintage: *15–25*

Availability in Mint State: *MS-60 to 62:* 1,100 to 1,600. *MS-63:* 140 to 170. *MS-64:* 110 to 130. *MS-65 or better:* 90 to 110.

Availability in circulated grades: This issue is readily available in any grade desired.

actual size: 15.5 mm

Characteristics of striking: This issue is usually well struck.

Proofs: The figure of Liberty, the date numerals, and the arrowheads are all very finely granular, almost as if they were sandblasted in the die to give them an especially frosty effect—a very unusual situation. The fields are deep-mirror Proof. While the date is nearly centered, the arrowheads are high and touch the base. Approximately 20 examples have been certified.

Notes: V-1 to 6, plus V-7, added by Al Blythe. The mintage figure suggests that more can be found by very patient specialists using a microscope.

G-4	VG-8	F-12	VF-20	EF-40	AU-50
$30	$35	$40	$45	$75	$150
MS-60	MS-63	MS-65	PF-60	PF-63	PF-65
$210	$375	$1,650	$4,000	$7,500	$11,500

1855-O, With Arrows

Circulation-strike mintage: 600,000

Availability in Mint State: *MS-60 to 62:* 125 to 150, *MS-63:* 35 to 50, *MS-64:* 20 to 25, *MS-65 or better:* 15 to 20.

Availability in circulated grades: This issue is slightly scarce in circulated grades.

actual size: 15.5 mm

Characteristics of striking: This issue is usually fairly well struck.

Notes: V-1 is the only one listed by Valentine. In November 1990 Stephen A. Crain discovered V-2, having the same obverse die as V-1 but with a Large O mintmark.[34]

G-4	VG-8	F-12	VF-20	EF-40	AU-50	MS-60	MS-63	MS-65
$30	$40	$55	$85	$200	$380	$850	$1,250	$5,250

1856–1859, Variety 2 Resumed, With Weight Standard of Variety 3

From all outward appearances half dimes of this type are the same as those made before 1853. The arrowheads have been removed, but the new, lower weight standard adopted by the Coinage Act of February 21, 1853, is used. Note that the obverse for coins struck in Philadelphia in 1859 were modified; see pages 114–115 for the separate listing of those issues.

Designer: Christian Gobrecht.

Specifications: *Composition:* 90 percent silver, 10 percent copper. *Diameter:* 15.5 mm. *Weight:* 19.2 grains (1.24 grams). *Edge:* Reeded.

1856

Circulation-strike mintage: 4,880,000

Proof mintage: *40–60*

Availability in Mint State: *MS-60 to 62:* 600 to 800. *MS-63:* 175 to 225. *MS-64:* 125 to 150. *MS-65 or better:* 45 to 55.

Availability in circulated grades: This issue is very common.

actual size: 15.5 mm

Characteristics of striking: It is very hard to find this issue with full, sharp denticles on the obverse.

Proofs: The date is in small numerals placed above the center, somewhat weak (this was in the die) at the upper right of the 8 and the 56. There is possible repunching on the last date numeral, which under magnification is slightly irregular. In the past some have been called 1856, 6 Over 4, although modern scholars do not agree. Approximately 34 examples have been certified.

Notes: V-1 to 8, but more probably exists. As the years passed, the placement of date logotypes into working dies was more carefully done. Differences are usually minor, sometimes microscopic.

G-4	VG-8	F-12	VF-20	EF-40	AU-50
$30	$35	$40	$45	$70	$125
MS-60	**MS-63**	**MS-65**	**PF-60**	**PF-63**	**PF-65**
$185	$300	$750	$2,500	$4,000	$7,500

1856-O

Circulation-strike mintage: 1,100,000

Availability in Mint State: In 2014 and 2015 the Eugene H. Gardner Sale featured examples of this coin in MS-66 (2) and MS-65. *MS-60 to 62:* 50 to 65. *MS-63:* 20 to 25. *MS-64:* 12 to 15. *MS-65 or better:* 8 to 10.

actual size: 15.5 mm

Availability in circulated grades: These are plentiful in the context of the demand for them, but are not common in higher grades.

Characteristics of striking: Striking of this issue varies, but they are usually well struck.

Notes: V-1 to 7 with Large O mintmark. Walter Breen reported a variety with Small O mintmark, but Al Blythe could not verify it. John Zitz published a new muling for the 1856-O date (Obverse 4 with Reverse V-3) in the *Gobrecht Journal*, July 1994, now listed as V-8, also with Large O mintmark.

G-4	VG-8	F-12	VF-20	EF-40	AU-50	MS-60	MS-63	MS-65
$30	$35	$40	$55	$135	$285	$550	$1,000	$2,250

1857

Circulation-strike mintage: 7,280,000
Proof mintage: *40–60*

Availability in Mint State: *MS-60 to 62:* 1,250 to 1,500. *MS-63:* 450 to 600. *MS-64:* 300 to 400. *MS-65 or better:* 110 to 130.

actual size: 15.5 mm

Availability in circulated grades: This issue is very common in circulated grades.

Characteristics of striking: Striking of this issue is usually fairly sharp.

Proofs: V-3. The obverse die was also used to make circulation strikes. Approximately 55 examples have been certified.

Notes: V-1 to 9. V-1 is rare. A "V-10" has been described but is actually a rotated die striking of V-1.[35]

Valentine said: "Early in 1857 the hub, having become badly worn, was retouched. The most noticeable differences are in the drapery between the figure of Liberty and the flagpole, and a dent on the inside point of the third star. The coins struck from dies before these changes were made were No. 1 of the Philadelphia Mint and Nos. 1 to 3 of the New Orleans Mint."

G-4	VG-8	F-12	VF-20	EF-40	AU-50
$30	$35	$40	$45	$70	$125

MS-60	MS-63	MS-65	PF-60	PF-63	PF-65
$175	$300	$700	$2,000	$2,750	$4,000

1857-O

Circulation-strike mintage: 1,380,000

Availability in Mint State: *MS-60 to 62:* 500 to 700. *MS-63:* 80 to 100. *MS-64:* 45 to 60. *MS-65 or better:* 30 to 40.

actual size: 15.5 mm

Availability in circulated grades: These are easy to find, but far fewer exist than the Philadelphia half dime of this year.

Characteristics of striking: This issue varies, but is usually fairly sharp.

Notes: V-1 to 6. V-1 and 2 are Medium O (1.0 mm). V-3 is a Large O (1.1 mm). V-4, 5, and 6 are also Medium O (1.0 mm).[36] V-1 to 3 are from an earlier hub (see preceding Notes). These are scarcer than V-4 to 6.

G-4	VG-8	F-12	VF-20	EF-40	AU-50	MS-60	MS-63	MS-65
$30	$35	$40	$45	$85	$185	$325	$550	$1,250

1858

Circulation-strike mintage: 3,500,000
Proof mintage: *300*

Availability in Mint State: *MS-60 to 62:* 1,000 to 1,250. *MS-63:* 300 to 400. *MS-64:* 250 to 350. *MS-65 or better:* 150 to 200.

actual size: 15.5 mm

Availability in circulated grades: This issue is very common in circulated grades.

Characteristics of striking: Striking varies, but some are sharp.

Proofs: 210 were made for inclusion in the silver Proof sets. Additional pieces were possibly made. Many seeking a run of Proof Liberty Seated half dimes start their sets with this year. *PF-60 to 62:* 25 to 32. *PF-63:* 35 to 45. *PF-64:* 35 to 45. *PF-65 or better:* 30 to 40.

Notes: V-1 to 9 are recorded, but more exist. V-5 is a relapped die with light definition of the pole to cap. V-9, the Doubled Date, exhibits all four digits first struck too high, into the base, and then corrected in the proper position. Evidence of the under digits is seen *inside* of the final digits. Much rarer than the Inverted Date.[37]

1858, Over Inverted Date: The 1858 logotype was first punched upside-down into the die. The blunder was realized, the error was partially effaced, and the logotype was re-entered, now with the correct orientation. The tops of the inverted digits show a little above the middle of the date. Extensive traces of the earlier date can be seen between the digits.[38] *Cherrypickers' Guide to Rare Die Varieties* lists this as FS-H10-1858-302. This variety was not known to Valentine. The population in various grades is probably three percent to five percent of the above. In 2014 the Eugene H. Gardner Sale featured an example of this coin in MS-66.

G-4	VG-8	F-12	VF-20	EF-40	AU-50
$30	$35	$40	$45	$70	$125
MS-60	MS-63	MS-65	PF-60	PF-63	PF-65
$175	$325	$700	$750	$1,200	$3,000

1858-O

Circulation-strike mintage: 1,660,000

Availability in Mint State: *MS-60 to 62:* 200 to 250. *MS-63:* 60 to 75. *MS-64:* 35 to 45. *MS-65 or better:* 20 to 25.

Availability in circulated grades: This is one of the most plentiful New Orleans half dimes.

actual size: 15.5 mm

Characteristics of striking: These are often lightly struck, but there are exceptions. In many instances the Blythe text gives strike information in relation to various Valentine numbers.

Notes: V-1 to 4, described by Valentine, have Medium O mintmark; V-5 and 6, described by Blythe, have Large O mintmark. There are two known major reverse cud varieties for V-3 and 6, the latter much rarer.

According to Walter H. Breen, a hoard of about 20 Uncirculateds surfaced in late 1982.

G-4	VG-8	F-12	VF-20	EF-40	AU-50	MS-60	MS-63	MS-65
$30	$35	$40	$50	$80	$155	$250	$480	$1,150

For the 1859 Philadelphia half dime, see page 114.

1859-O

Circulation-strike mintage: 560,000

Availability in Mint State: In 2014 and 2015 the Eugene H. Gardner Sale featured examples of this coin in MS-66 (2) and MS-64. *MS-60 to 62:* 125 to 140. *MS-63:* 35 to 50. *MS-64:* 25 to 30. *MS-65 or better:* 8 to 10.

actual size: 15.5 mm

Availability in circulated grades: These are scarce, but are some of the more available New Orleans half dimes in higher grades.

Characteristics of striking: This issue is light in areas.

Notes: V-1 to 3. The 1859-O half dime has the traditional seated Liberty figure instead of the Paquet obverse of the Philadelphia half dimes (see listings that follow).

G-4	VG-8	F-12	VF-20	EF-40	AU-50	MS-60	MS-63	MS-65
$30	$35	$65	$90	$165	$225	$325	$525	$1,750

1859 and 1860, Paquet Obverse (Philadelphia Only)

In 1859, for reasons unknown, Anthony C. Paquet, an assistant engraver at the Mint, redesigned many obverse details. The head of Liberty is slightly farther from the border. The liberty cap is larger, slightly closer to the border, and Liberty's finger is tucked down with the rest of her hand, creating the illusion that her hand is farther down the pole. The stars have hollow centers (called "mullets" or "molets"), a style unique on American federal coinage. The rock at the lower left has different details. LIBERTY in the shield is in much larger letters. The same seated figure was used on the transitional pattern half dimes of 1860. This style was also used on the 1859 with reverse of 1860 transitional half dimes. In contrast, the 1859-O half dimes had the traditional seated figure as used in earlier years. The differences on the Paquet die are significant enough that it merits being collected as a separate type.

Designer: Christian Gobrecht. Obverse modified by Anthony C. Paquet.

Specifications: *Composition:* 90 percent silver, 10 percent copper. *Diameter:* 15.5 mm. *Weight:* 19.2 grains (1.24 grams). *Edge:* Reeded.

1859

Circulation-strike mintage: 340,000
Proof mintage: 800

Availability in Mint State: *MS-60 to 62:* 1,000 to 1,500. *MS-63:* 130 to 160. *MS-64:* 100 to 125. *MS-65 or better:* 80 to 100.

actual size: 15.5 mm

Availability in circulated grades: This issue is slightly scarce in circulated grades.

Characteristics of striking: This issue is usually sharp.

Proofs: V-1. The obverse die was also used for circulation strikes. *PF-60 to 62:* 80 to 100. *PF-63:* 200 to 275. *PF-64:* 175 to 250. *PF-65 or better:* 40 to 55.

Notes: V-1 and 2 described by Valentine, V-3 and 4 by Blythe.

As described in detail in the design introduction, the figure of Liberty was modified by Anthony C. Paquet, an assistant engraver on the Mint staff. Among the most noticeable differences are the hollow centers of the stars (known as molets or mullets) and Liberty's finger is tucked down with the rest of her hand. This new style was used only at Philadelphia in 1859 (and not at New Orleans). It was also used on the 1860 transitional pattern issue made for sale to collectors. The revised half dime motif had no counterpart among dimes or other Liberty Seated denominations.

Detail of the regular Liberty Seated die used on other issues.

Detail of the Paquet modification used only on 1859 Philadelphia and 1860 transitional half dimes. Note Liberty's tucked finger as well as the hollow center of the star.

G-4	VG-8	F-12	VF-20	EF-40	AU-50
$30	$35	$40	$45	$80	$145
MS-60	MS-63	MS-65	PF-60	PF-63	PF-65
$215	$425	$925	$550	$1,100	$2,500

1859, Obverse of 1859, Reverse of 1860, Transitional Issue

Proof mintage: *20*

actual size: 15.5 mm

Proofs: Approximately six examples have been certified.

Notes: This issue uses an 1859 obverse die with the Paquet modifications with hollow star centers, etc., as used on 1859 Philadelphia Mint half dimes, but not those of 1859-O (see page 114 and above). The 9 in the date is repunched. This issue is not from the Proof regular-issue Paquet die of this year used to coin the denomination for silver Proof sets. The reverse is the cereal-wreath type introduced for regular circulation in 1860. This is a "stateless" issue as UNITED STATES OF AMERICA does not appear anywhere on the coin. All are in Proof format. Also listed as a pattern, Judd-232.

PF-60	PF-63	PF-65
$20,000	$35,000	$75,000

1860, Obverse of 1859, Reverse of 1860, Transitional Issue

Circulation-strike mintage: 100

Availability in Mint State: *MS-60 to 62:* 5 to 8. *MS-63:* 10 to 13. *MS-64:* 20 to 25. *MS-65 or better:* 40 to 50.

actual size: 15.5 mm

Availability in circulated grades: Few examples of this issue are seen in circulated grades.

Characteristics of striking: These are nearly always seen with areas of light striking.

Notes: The obverse stars are from a mullet (or molet) punch and have holes at the center; style of the 1859 regular Philadelphia Mint issues, die by Anthony C. Paquet. This issue has the reverse-wreath style of 1860. Director James Ross Snowden had these pieces struck for the numismatic trade, all in Mint State. Listed as pattern Judd-267. This is also a "stateless" issue as there is no mention of UNITED STATES OF AMERICA.

In 1860 Director James Ross Snowden caused a transitional "pattern" to be made. The obverse was of the style in use the preceding year, with stars, but the reverse was of the 1860 type. Interestingly, this unusual combination of dies produced a coin which did not mention the country of origin. He announced that just 100 pieces had been struck. The number of specimens extant today suggests that this figure was publicized in order to help promote sales of the piece, but more may have been made. Veracity was not a Snowden attribute.

Die details: *Obverse:* There is a tiny spike from the right side of the 8 on the usually seen die; the 6 is somewhat misshapen on the lower right; the left serif of the 1 is thicker and larger than the right serif, and the lines of both are at an upward angle to the left (these features characterize the date logotype and are found on the regular-issue 1860 coins). There is a heavy die scratch from the left side of the base upward to the denticles. A second obverse die was discovered by Stephen A. Crain with different alignment of the date numerals and *sharply struck*. This was a surprise, considering the small mintage of only 100 or so coins.[39]

Reverse: The reverse has the "cereal wreath," but from a different die than the preceding 1859 pattern, and with somewhat different minute details (the H and D in HALF DIME are closer to the wreath on this issue; an acorn is on the outside right, and the wreath has a sharp outline instead of the rounded surface on the preceding, etc.).

G-4	VG-8	F-12	VF-20	EF-40	AU-50	MS-60	MS-63	MS-65
				$2,500	$2,750	$3,500	$5,500	$6,500

1860–1873, Legend on Obverse (Variety 4)

The obverse now has UNITED STATES OF AMERICA in place of the stars. The seated figure is slightly smaller, as is evidenced by wider spacing from the border. The brooch or clasp on Liberty's right shoulder has been modified slightly, and there are some minor changes in details.

The reverse is a "cereal wreath," as it has been called, composed of oak and maple leaves, wheat, and corn with HALF DIME in two lines in the center. The design was adapted from that used on a pattern half dollar in 1859. Mintmarks are below the bow from 1863 to 1869. In 1870 and 1871 it is above the bow. In 1872 varieties have both locations. In 1873 the mintmark is below the bow.

Designer: The obverse was modified by James B. Longacre. The reverse was designed by Longacre or Paquet, a cereal wreath reverse said by tradition to have been suggested by numismatist Harold P. Newlin and earlier used on pattern half dollars.[2]

Specifications: *Composition:* 90 percent silver, 10 percent copper. *Diameter:* 15.5 mm. *Weight:* 19.2 grains (1.24 grams). *Edge:* Reeded.

1860

Circulation-strike mintage: 798,000
Proof mintage: 1,000

actual size: 15.5 mm

Availability in Mint State: These are common in grades from MS-60 to 64, but are harder to find than the higher-mintage 1861. *MS-60 to 62:* 900 to 1,200. *MS-63:* 400 to 500. *MS-64:* 300 to 375. *MS-65 or better:* 200 to 250.

Availability in circulated grades: This issue is readily available.

Characteristics of striking: These are usually well struck.

Proofs: Proof mintage was 1,000 coins, but only 535 silver Proof sets plus a few extra pieces were sold. In 1859, 1860, and 1861 the Mint was overoptimistic about its Proof set sales, probably because the Mint was the focal point of much numismatic attention at the time (perhaps culminating in the dedication of the Washington Cabinet at the Mint on February 22, 1860, and certainly tapering off within the year as James Ross Snowden's Mint numismatically active directorship neared its close). After large numbers of unsold Proofs of 1859–1861 were spent, beginning in 1862 Proof mintages dropped precipitately, nearer to actual sales figures. For 1860 the number of surviving Proofs suggests that less than half were sold. *PF-60 to 62:* 100 to 150. *PF-63:* 80 to 95. *PF-64:* 70 to 90. *PF-65 or better:* 25 to 35.

Notes: This is the first year of the new style with UNITED STATES OF AMERICA on the obverse, no stars on either side, and a cereal wreath enclosing HALF / DIME on the reverse. The Liberty Seated figure is of the old style with LIBERTY in small letters on the shield, etc., now modified slightly. This motif was continued through the end of the series in 1873.

G-4	VG-8	F-12	VF-20	EF-40	AU-50
$30	$35	$40	$45	$55	$85

MS-60	MS-63	MS-65	PF-60	PF-63	PF-65
$175	$300	$600	$350	$550	$1,100

1860-O

Circulation-strike mintage: 1,060,000

Availability in Mint State: *MS-60 to 62:* 255 to 300. *MS-63:* 100 to 120. *MS-64:* 70 to 90. *MS-65 or better:* 50 to 60.

actual size: 15.5 mm

Availability in circulated grades: This is a plentiful New Orleans half dime.

Characteristics of striking: This issue is nearly always lightly struck in areas.

Notes: V-1 to 5. Small O mintmark. The V-2 exhibits perhaps the strongest obverse die clash seen, with the letters ME of the reverse denomination showing boldly across Liberty's abdomen and elbow, looking much like a counterstamp.

These are popular as the last half-dime variety from the New Orleans Mint, and have a record-high mintage for New Orleans.

On some, if not all, the 8 and 6 of the date logotype lack the irregularities seen on the Philadelphia Mint version, but are probably from the same punch, just in a different state.

G-4	VG-8	F-12	VF-20	EF-40	AU-50	MS-60	MS-63	MS-65
$30	$35	$40	$45	$80	$120	$175	$350	$1,000

1861

Circulation-strike mintage: 3,360,000

Proof mintage: 1,000

Availability in Mint State: *MS-60 to 62:* 400 to 500. *MS-63:* 300 to 375. *MS-64:* 200 to 275. *MS-65 or better:* 120 to 150.

actual size: 15.5 mm

Availability in circulated grades: This issue is very common.

Characteristics of striking: Striking of this issue is usually sharp.

Proofs: The Mint made 1,000 silver Proof sets, but many, seemingly more than half of the production, were unsold and later placed into circulation. There are at least two minor obverse die varieties. *PF-60 to 62:* 80 to 110. *PF-63:* 70 to 85. *PF-64:* 65 to 80. *PF-65 or better:* 20 to 30.

Notes: Al Blythe notes 42 obverse and 43 reverse dies are known. This equates to about 82,000 impressions per die (if no more are found, which is unlikely). This figure is useful when contemplating some of the early half-dime mintages for which relatively few Valentine varieties have been identified for large-production issues.

"1861/0": This so-called overdate is now discredited, but was previously listed in *Cherrypickers' Guide to Rare Die Varieties* as FS-H10-1861-301. "Without question the single most overrated Liberty Seated half dime is the so-called '1861/0' simply because it does not exist. Despite appearance, it is not an overdate or even a repunched date. Rather, it is simply the result of a defective numeral 1 punch. . . ."[40]

G-4	VG-8	F-12	VF-20	EF-40	AU-50
$30	$35	$40	$45	$70	$120
MS-60	MS-63	MS-65	PF-60	PF-63	PF-65
$175	$300	$650	$350	$550	$1,100

1862

Circulation-strike mintage: 1,492,000
Proof mintage: 550

Availability in Mint State: This is one of the most common half dimes in grades from MS-60 to 64. These were issued when public hoarding of silver coins was just getting underway and

actual size: 15.5 mm

many were saved. By early summer no silver coins were seen in circulation in the East or Midwest. *MS-60 to 62:* 1,000 to 1,250. *MS-63:* 500 to 650. *MS-64:* 300 to 375. *MS-65 or better:* 200 to 250.

Availability in circulated grades: This issue is very common.

Characteristics of striking: These vary, but are often sharp.

Proofs: R.W. Julian learned from archival material that some unsold Proofs were still at the Mint in 1877. *PF-60 to 62:* 100 to 125. *PF-63:* 80 to 100. *PF-64:* 60 to 70. *PF-65 or better:* 50 to 60.

Notes: Valentine and Blythe describe six varieties, but no doubt many more were made as 21 pairs of dies were produced.

Three pairs of dies were sent to the San Francisco Mint, but no coinage ensued.

G-4	VG-8	F-12	VF-20	EF-40	AU-50
$30	$35	$45	$55	$70	$100
MS-60	MS-63	MS-65	PF-60	PF-63	PF-65
$175	$300	$650	$350	$550	$1,100

1863

Circulation-strike mintage: 18,000
Proof mintage: 460

actual size: 15.5 mm

Availability in Mint State: These are plentiful in grades from MS-60 to 64 despite its low mintage. As noted below, these were not placed into circulation at the time. *MS-60 to 62:* 350 to 500. *MS-63:* 225 to 275. *MS-64:* 225 to 275. *MS-65 or better:* 90 to 120.

Availability in circulated grades: This issue is somewhat scarce, and when seen it is usually in EF or AU grades.

Characteristics of striking: This issue is usually well struck.

Proofs: Walter Breen breaks Proofs down to originals with a closed top of the D in UNITED, these being part of the 460 mintage, and restrikes with an open D using the Proof reverse die of 1870 and stated that only one was seen. The dies were polished for the Proof coinage, and then used again on high-speed presses, to create more coins for circulation. These prooflike circulation strikes can confuse modern numismatists, though they were never for sale to collectors. This was the case for many Philadelphia Mint Proof dies. *PF-60 to 62:* 80 to 100. *PF-63:* 65 to 90. *PF-64:* 60 to 80. *PF-65 or better:* 50 to 70.

Notes: V-1 with repunching at 18 is the only variety described by Valentine, to which can be added the open D die described above. In 1863 the Mint supplied silver coins only to banks, brokers, and others who paid a premium for them in terms of Legal Tender Notes. This situation extended until the end of Philadelphia coinage in 1873.

G-4	VG-8	F-12	VF-20	EF-40	AU-50
$200	$280	$340	$425	$600	$750
MS-60	**MS-63**	**MS-65**	**PF-60**	**PF-63**	**PF-65**
$835	$975	$1,650	$350	$550	$1,100

1863-S

Circulation-strike mintage: 100,000

actual size: 15.5 mm

Availability in Mint State: In 2015 the Eugene H. Gardner Sale featured examples of this coin in MS-67, MS-66, MS-65, and MS-64. *MS-60 to 62:* 65 to 80. *MS-63:* 40 to 50. *MS-64:* 30 to 40. *MS-65 or better:* 12 to 15.

Availability in circulated grades: This issue is scarce all around and is usually well-worn.

Characteristics of striking: This issue is usually sharp.

Notes: V-1. The date is low in the field, with Small S mintmark as on all San Francisco issues, but the vertical and horizontal dimensions varied slightly over the years. Most vertical dimensions are 7 mm give or take; 1863-S is 8 mm.

This is the first half-dime issue from the San Francisco Mint. In 1853 (the year *prior* to the San Francisco Mint officially opening for business), 1854, and 1855, two pairs of half-dime dies were sent each year from Philadelphia (where all dies were made) to San Francisco, but no half-dime coinage materialized until 1863. Why this was is not clear today, as there are numerous accounts of a need for small change, which at the time was typically filled by small Spanish-American silver coins. This and subsequent half dimes circulated actively in the American West, but most were probably shipped to China and melted there.

G-4	VG-8	F-12	VF-20	EF-40	AU-50	MS-60	MS-63	MS-65
$45	$65	$105	$200	$300	$425	$800	$1,175	$4,000

1864

Circulation-strike mintage: 48,000
Proof mintage: 470

actual size: 15.5 mm

Availability in Mint State: These are scarcer than the much-lower mintage of 1863. In 2014 the Eugene H. Gardner Sale featured an example of this coin in MS-67. *MS-60 to 62:* 20 to 25. *MS-63:* 30 to 40. *MS-64:* 30 to 40. *MS-65 or better:* 15 to 20.

Availability in circulated grades: This issue is very scarce. When seen, usually it is in EF or AU grades.

Characteristics of striking: This issue is usually sharp.

Proofs: In the date the 8 is repunched, and the bottom serifs of 1 and 4 are lopsided. The D in UNITED is closed at the top (on some others it is open—the latter called restrikes by Walter Breen, but the jury is still out as to whether they really are). *PF-60 to 62:* 110 to 135. *PF-63:* 90 to 110. *PF-64:* 60 to 70. *PF-65 or better:* 50 to 65.

Notes: V-1. This die is used for Proofs and circulation strikes.

G-4	VG-8	F-12	VF-20	EF-40	AU-50
$350	$475	$700	$875	$1,200	$1,250

MS-60	MS-63	MS-65	PF-60	PF-63	PF-65
$1,300	$1,475	$2,800	$350	$550	$1,100

1864-S

Circulation-strike mintage: 90,000

actual size: 15.5 mm

Availability in Mint State: This issue is much rarer at the gem level than is generally realized. In 2014 and 2015 the Eugene H. Gardner Sale featured examples of this coin in MS-67, MS-66, and MS-64. *MS-60 to 62:* 90 to 110. *MS-63:* 40 to 50. *MS-64:* 25 to 32. *MS-65 or better:* 10 to 12.

Availability in circulated grades: These are scarce, but enough survive to satisfy specialists.

Characteristics of striking: This issue typically has light weakness on the obverse.

Notes: V-1 has a Small S mintmark.

G-4	VG-8	F-12	VF-20	EF-40	AU-50	MS-60	MS-63	MS-65
$85	$115	$185	$275	$450	$750	$1,100	$1,750	$3,750

1865

Circulation-strike mintage: 13,000

Proof mintage: 500

Availability in Mint State: *MS-60 to 62:* 50 to 65. *MS-63:* 55 to 70. *MS-64:* 40 to 50. *MS-65 or better:* 30 to 40.

actual size: 15.5 mm

Availability in circulated grades: In worn grades this is considered to be the scarcest of the half dimes minted during the Civil War (1861–1865).

Characteristics of striking: This issue is usually sharp.

Proofs: V-1. The die was also used to make circulation strikes. *PF-60 to 62:* 100 to 125. *PF-63:* 80 to 100. *PF-64:* 60 to 70. *PF-65 or better:* 50 to 65.

Notes: V-1. Some circulation strikes are known with the reverse die rotated 10 to 45 degrees clockwise from the normal position.

G-4	VG-8	F-12	VF-20	EF-40	AU-50
$375	$475	$600	$750	$925	$1,200
MS-60	**MS-63**	**MS-65**	**PF-60**	**PF-63**	**PF-65**
$1,300	$1,650	$2,250	$350	$550	$1,100

1865-S

Circulation-strike mintage: 120,000

Availability in Mint State: In 2015 the Eugene H. Gardner Sale featured examples of this coin in MS-66 and MS-65 (2). *MS-60 to 62:* 10 to 14. *MS-63:* 5 to 7. *MS-64:* 3 or 4. *MS-65 or better:* 3 or 4.[41]

actual size: 15.5 mm

Availability in circulated grades: This issue is scarce, especially at the EF and AU levels.

Characteristics of striking: These usually have some areas of light striking.

Notes: Valentine describes V-1 and 2; Blythe, V-3 and 4. Small S mintmark.

The Friesner Collection Sale (Frossard 1894) included lot 794, "1865 San Francisco (5 Over 3). Fine; scarce." It sold for $2.00, as compared with a regular 1865-S in the same grade that brought $1.25. Apparently, it passed inspection by those who bid on it. This is probably what is known today as V-4, a repunched date.[42]

G-4	VG-8	F-12	VF-20	EF-40	AU-50	MS-60	MS-63	MS-65
$50	$80	$125	$200	$350	$550	$1,100	$2,450	$7,500

1866

Circulation-strike mintage: 10,000
Proof mintage: 725

actual size: 15.5 mm

Availability in Mint State: *MS-60 to 62:* 30 to 40. *MS-63:* 25 to 30. *MS-64:* 25 to 30. *MS-65 or better:* 18 to 22.

Availability in circulated grades: This issue is somewhat scarce. When seen, it is usually in EF or AU grades.

Characteristics of striking: These are usually sharp.

Proofs: V-1. This die was also used to make circulation strikes. *PF-60 to 62:* 100 to 125. *PF-63:* 90 to 110. *PF-64:* 60 to 70. *PF-65 or better:* 60 to 70.

Notes: V-1.

G-4	VG-8	F-12	VF-20	EF-40	AU-50
$325	$425	$550	$700	$850	$1,000
MS-60	**MS-63**	**MS-65**	**PF-60**	**PF-63**	**PF-65**
$1,100	$1,225	$2,650	$350	$550	$1,100

1866-S

Circulation-strike mintage: 120,000

actual size: 15.5 mm

Availability in Mint State: These are much rarer at the gem level than generally realized. In 2015 the Eugene H. Gardner Sale featured examples of this coin in MS-66 and MS-65. *MS-60 to 62:* 40 to 50. *MS-63:* 25 to 30. *MS-64:* 15 to 18. *MS-65 or better:* 6 to 9.

Availability in circulated grades: This issue is scarce.

Characteristics of striking: These have areas of weakness.

Notes: V-1 has a small, wide S mintmark; small and "chunky" per Valentine. The obverse exhibits a spectacular misplaced date. An errant 1 and 8 were first punched into the skirt between the shield banner and the pendant.[43]

G-4	VG-8	F-12	VF-20	EF-40	AU-50	MS-60	MS-63	MS-65
$45	$60	$90	$150	$225	$335	$500	$950	$4,500

1867

Circulation-strike mintage: 8,000
Proof mintage: 625

actual size: 15.5 mm

Availability in Mint State: This issue is readily available in Mint State notwithstanding its low mintage. *MS-60 to 62:* 20 to 25. *MS-63:* 35 to 45. *MS-64:* 30 to 40. *MS-65 or better:* 30 to 40.

Availability in circulated grades: When seen, these are usually in EF or AU grades, but are overall rare.

Characteristics of striking: Most but not all areas are usually sharply struck. Circulation strikes almost always have a die crack from the rim through the first S in STATES.

Proofs: V-1 was the only die used for Proofs. *PF-60 to 62:* 100 to 120. *PF-63:* 110 to 130. *PF-64:* 110 to 130. *PF-65 or better:* 60 to 70.

Notes: V-2 was used for circulation strikes. This has the lowest circulation-strike mintage of any half dime. Many were saved by numismatists at the time. Rare, early strikes are from perfect dies. Usually seen are later states with an obverse die crack from the rim at 11 o'clock through the second S in STATES to Liberty's shoulder. [44]

G-4	VG-8	F-12	VF-20	EF-40	AU-50
$475	$550	$675	$800	$875	$1,050

MS-60	MS-63	MS-65	PF-60	PF-63	PF-65
$1,200	$1,500	$2,500	$350	$550	$1,100

1867-S

Circulation-strike mintage: 120,000

actual size: 15.5 mm

Availability in Mint State: This is one of the harder to find San Francisco half dimes in Mint State. In 2014 and 2015 the Eugene H. Gardner Sale featured examples of this coin in MS-66 and MS-65. *MS-60 to 62:* 80 to 100. *MS-63:* 30 to 40. *MS-64:* 20 to 25. *MS-65 or better:* 4 to 6.[45]

Availability in circulated grades: This issue is slightly scarce.

Characteristics of striking: These are usually sharp.

Notes: V-1 and 1a, the last with a repunched 1 and a Small S mintmark on the reverse.

G-4	VG-8	F-12	VF-20	EF-40	AU-50	MS-60	MS-63	MS-65
$45	$65	$85	$115	$250	$345	$600	$1,150	$3,250

1868

Circulation-strike mintage: 88,600
Proof mintage: 600

Availability in Mint State: *MS-60 to 62:* 100 to 130. *MS-63:* 60 to 70. *MS-64:* 40 to 50. *MS-65 or better:* 25 to 35.

actual size: 15.5 mm

Availability in circulated grades: This issue is very scarce. Usually in higher grades VF upward, this being true of other half dimes of the era.

Characteristics of striking: This issue varies, but is usually sharp.

Proofs: V-1 and 2. The obverse die was also used for circulation strikes. *PF-60 to 62:* 100 to 120. *PF-63:* 110 to 130. *PF-64:* 110 to 130. *PF-65 or better:* 60 to 70.

Notes: V-1 and 2.

G-4	VG-8	F-12	VF-20	EF-40	AU-50
$55	$85	$120	$190	$325	$475
MS-60	**MS-63**	**MS-65**	**PF-60**	**PF-63**	**PF-65**
$675	$875	$1,500	$350	$550	$1,100

1868-S

Circulation-strike mintage: 280,000

Availability in Mint State: *MS-60 to 62:* 130 to 150. *MS-63:* 70 to 90. *MS-64:* 45 to 60. *MS-65 or better:* 30 to 40.

Availability in circulated grades: This issue is readily available in circulated grades.

actual size: 15.5 mm

Characteristics of striking: These vary, but they are usually sharp.

Notes: V-1 in various die states. V-2, a new die marriage, combines a new obverse with the reverse of V-1.[46]

G-4	VG-8	F-12	VF-20	EF-40	AU-50	MS-60	MS-63	MS-65
$30	$35	$40	$50	$85	$145	$325	$700	$1,650

1869

Circulation-strike mintage: 208,000
Proof mintage: 600

Availability in Mint State: Although the 1869 Philadelphia Mint half dime has a mintage well over double that of 1868, Mint State coins are scarcer than might be expected. *MS-60 to 62:* 65 to 80. *MS-63:* 35 to 45. *MS-64:* 30 to 35. *MS-65 or better:* 20 to 28.

actual size: 15.5 mm

Availability in circulated grades: This issue is plentiful, and can usually be found in high grades.

Characteristics of striking: This issue varies, but is usually sharp.

Proofs: V-1 and 2. The obverse die was also used for circulation strikes. *PF-60 to 62:* 100 to 120. *PF-63:* 110 to 130. *PF-64:* 110 to 130. *PF-65 or better:* 60 to 70.

Notes: V-1 to 4.

G-4	VG-8	F-12	VF-20	EF-40	AU-50
$30	$40	$50	$70	$110	$165
MS-60	**MS-63**	**MS-65**	**PF-60**	**PF-63**	**PF-65**
$275	$450	$1,000	$350	$550	$1,100

1869-S

Circulation-strike mintage: 230,000

Availability in Mint State: This is one of the rarest San Francisco Mint half dimes in Mint State. In 2015 the Eugene H. Gardner Sale featured examples of this coin in MS-67 and MS-65. *MS-60 to 62:* 25 to 32. *MS-63:* 12 to 15. *MS-64:* 7 to 9. *MS-65 or better:* 2 or 3.[47]

actual size: 15.5 mm

Availability in circulated grades: This issue is slightly scarce.

Characteristics of striking: Striking of this issue varies.

Notes: V-1 and 2 listed by Valentine; V-3 and 4 described by Blythe. There is a Small S mintmark on the reverse.

G-4	VG-8	F-12	VF-20	EF-40	AU-50	MS-60	MS-63	MS-65
$30	$40	$50	$90	$150	$250	$335	$500	$3,500

1870

Circulation-strike mintage: 535,000
Proof mintage: 1,000

Availability in Mint State: *MS-60 to 62:* 900 to 1,300. *MS-63:* 120 to 150. *MS-64:* 90 to 120. *MS-65 or better:* 70 to 95.

actual size: 15.5 mm

Availability in circulated grades: This issue is plentiful and can usually be found in high grades.

Characteristics of striking: Striking of this issue varies, but they are usually sharp.

Proofs: V-1. The obverse die was also used for circulation strikes. *PF-60 to 62:* 100 to 120. *PF-63:* 110 to 130. *PF-64:* 110 to 130. *PF-65 or better:* 60 to 70.

Notes: V-1 to 6.

G-4	VG-8	F-12	VF-20	EF-40	AU-50
$30	$35	$40	$45	$55	$85
MS-60	**MS-63**	**MS-65**	**PF-60**	**PF-63**	**PF-65**
$175	$400	$900	$350	$550	$1,100

1870-S

Circulation-strike mintage: Unknown

Availability in Mint State: This issue is unique. It was first graded AU, then MS-63 by NGC, and is presently MS-64 by PCGS.

Characteristics of striking: This issue is sharply struck.

actual size: 15.5 mm

Notes: The reverse die of this coin was also used on 1871-S half dimes. There is a Small S mintmark on the reverse. On December 15, 1869, six pairs of dies for the anticipated 1870-S coinage were shipped from Philadelphia to San Francisco. An 1870-S half dime was set aside for inclusion in the cornerstone of the new mint building. Records do not show a quantity made for general circulation.[48]

The 1870-S was unknown to modern scholars until 1978 when a visitor to RARCOA (Rare Coin Company of America) in Chicago brought one in to the shop and showed it to owner Ed Milas and associate Dennis Forgue. It was recognized for what it was and was purchased. The coin was exhibited at the 1978 ANA convention and created a lot of attention. What was its value? It was decided to sell it for whatever the 1804 silver dollar coming up in the autumn in the Bowers and Ruddy Galleries sale of the Garrett Collection Part I sold for, plus $25,000. The total amount under discussion turned out to be $425,000, but the coin was said to have been sold to dealer John Abbott for an undisclosed figure. On September 9, 1985, it was graded AU-55 and sold at auction by Bowers and Merena Galleries for $176,000, the buyer being B. Martin Paul of the Rarities Group.[49] In 1986 it was sold by Superior Galleries as part of Auction 1986, lot 1053, for $253,000. In 1991 it was offered by Jay Parrino, trading as The Mint, for $1,500,000. In October 2000 it was sold by Ira and Larry Goldberg as lot 1629 for $575,000.

G-4	VG-8	F-12	VF-20	EF-40	AU-50	MS-60	MS-63	MS-65
							$2,000,000	

1871

Circulation-strike mintage: 1,873,000
Proof mintage: 960

Availability in Mint State: *MS-60 to 62:* 300 to 400. *MS-63:* 130 to 150. *MS-64:* 100 to 120. *MS-65 or better:* 70 to 90.

actual size: 15.5 mm

Availability in circulated grades: This issue is plentiful, and can usually be found in high grades.

Characteristics of striking: This issue is usually well struck.

Proofs: The figure of Liberty is stippled, or etched—an unusual situation. The mintage of 1871 Proof half dimes was 960, but many unsold pieces were melted at the Mint on July 10, 1873, per several accounts. However, research in National Archives records by John Dannreuther demonstrates many "melted" Proofs were actually sold to coin dealers.[50] *PF-60 to 62:* 110 to 130. *PF-63:* 120 to 140. *PF-64:* 120 to 140. *PF-65 or better:* 70 to 80.

Notes: V-1 to 5. The Valentine descriptions of the 1860–1873 are often skimpy, not permitting identification in some instances. Al Blythe's descriptions are far more comprehensive, and are therefore of more use for these years. From this time forward the top of the D in UNITED is open, due to a defect in the hub. An obverse with a repunched 1 is new.[51]

G-4	VG-8	F-12	VF-20	EF-40	AU-50
$30	$35	$40	$45	$60	$85

MS-60	MS-63	MS-65	PF-60	PF-63	PF-65
$165	$300	$650	$350	$550	$1,100

1871-S

Circulation-strike mintage: 161,000

Availability in Mint State: In 2014 and 2015 the Eugene H. Gardner Sale featured examples of this coin in MS-66 and MS-65. *MS-60 to 62:* 100 to 125. *MS-63:* 35 to 45. *MS-64:* 30 to 40. *MS-65 or better:* 8 to 11.

actual size: 15.5 mm

Availability in circulated grades: These are easily enough found.

Characteristics of striking: This issue usually has lightness in some areas.[52]

Notes: Al Blythe mentions four die pairs; Valentine lists just V-1. There is a Small S mintmark on the reverse. The same die was used to strike 1870-S half dimes.

It is believed by the author that most of the 1871-S half dimes were sent to China and melted, although some were made into jewelry, and still others were subjected to scraping of the Liberty Seated figure to remove small amounts of silver (a clever spot to do so without attracting attention from casual observers).

Over the years there been scattered rumors of an 1871-S with mintmark below the bow, but none have been reported by a specialist.

G-4	VG-8	F-12	VF-20	EF-40	AU-50	MS-60	MS-63	MS-65
$30	$35	$40	$65	$80	$180	$250	$450	$1,400

1872

Circulation-strike mintage: 2,947,000
Proof mintage: 950

Availability in Mint State: *MS-60 to 62:* 300 to 400. *MS-63:* 130 to 150. *MS-64:* 100 to 120. *MS-65 or better:* 70 to 90.

actual size: 15.5 mm

Availability in circulated grades: These are plentiful, but not as common as the high mintage might suggest; usually seen in high grades.

Characteristics of striking: This issue varies, and some are from rusty dies.

Proofs: V-2. The mintage of 1872 Proof half dimes was 950, but many unsold pieces are said to have been melted at the Mint on July 10, 1873; however, they may have been sold to coin dealers.[53] *PF-60 to 62:* 100 to 125. *PF-63:* 90 to 110. *PF-64:* 60 to 70. *PF-65 or better:* 60 to 70.

Notes: V-1 to 7. The high mintage indicates that many more exist, but have not been described.

G-4	VG-8	F-12	VF-20	EF-40	AU-50
$30	$35	$40	$45	$55	$85

MS-60	MS-63	MS-65	PF-60	PF-63	PF-65
$165	$300	$675	$350	$550	$1,100

1872-S, Mintmark Above Bow

Circulation-strike mintage: Portion of 837,000

Availability in Mint State: *MS-60 to 62:* 50 to 65. *MS-63:* 50 to 65. *MS-64:* 30 to 35. *MS-65 or better:* 20 to 25.

actual size: 15.5 mm

Availability in circulated grades: These are easy to find.

Characteristics of striking: This issue is usually sharp.

Notes: V-1 and 2. There is a Small S mintmark on the reverse.

Detail of Mintmark Above Bow.

G-4	VG-8	F-12	VF-20	EF-40	AU-50	MS-60	MS-63	MS-65
$30	$35	$40	$45	$55	$100	$180	$300	$750

1872-S, Mintmark Below Bow

Circulation-strike mintage: Portion of 837,000

actual size: 15.5 mm

Availability in Mint State: In Mint State this is the most common half dime of the 1860–1873 type as reflected in market offerings. *MS-60 to 62:* 300 to 350. *MS-63:* 450 to 550. *MS-64:* 300 to 375. *MS-65 or better:* 225 to 275.

Availability in circulated grades: These are very common.

Detail of Mintmark Below Bow.

Characteristics of striking: This issue is usually sharp.

Notes: The V-4 has a Micro S mintmark (0.6 mm). The Micro S variety was first rumored by Stewart Jones in volume 17, issue 49, of the *Gobrecht Journal*, and was later published in volume 21, issue 62, by Bill Fivaz. It is listed as the "Blundered Die" MPD, Micro S, variety, with misplaced date numerals in the gown. The top of a misplaced 1 can be seen to the left of the *bulla*, or pendant, and a misplaced 8 to the right of the bulla. The 1 in the date is triple punched. This is properly the V-4; listed as V-6 by Blythe, and is assigned FS-H10-1872s-301 by Fivaz and Stanton.[54]

G-4	VG-8	F-12	VF-20	EF-40	AU-50	MS-60	MS-63	MS-65
$30	$35	$40	$45	$55	$120	$165	$300	$675

1873, Close 3

Circulation-strike mintage: 712,000
Proof mintage: 600

Availability in Mint State: *MS-60 to 62:* 250 to 300. *MS-63:* 120 to 140. *MS-64:* 90 to 110. *MS-65 or better:* 50 to 60.

actual size: 15.5 mm

Availability in circulated grades: This issue is slightly scarce despite the high mintage.

Characteristics of striking: The striking of this issue varies. Some have a light area on the wreath.

Proofs: V-2. *PF-60 to 62:* 60 to 75. *PF-63:* 90 to 110. *PF-64:* 120 to 150. *PF-65 or better:* 90 to 120.

Notes: V-1 and 2. This issue was coined in the first two months of the year. Many were melted later in July 1873 per conventional wisdom, but they may have been sold to coin dealers.[55] Unlike the Liberty Seated, No Arrows, dimes, quarters, and half dollars of 1873, which were struck with both an Open 3 and Close 3 logotype, half dimes of the year (as well as silver dollars) are found only in the Close 3 version.

G-4	VG-8	F-12	VF-20	EF-40	AU-50
$30	$35	$40	$45	$55	$85
MS-60	MS-63	MS-65	PF-60	PF-63	PF-65
$165	$350	$1,100	$350	$550	$1,100

1873-S, Close 3

Circulation-strike mintage: 324,000

Availability in Mint State: *MS-60 to 62:* 50 to 65. *MS-63:* 85 to 100. *MS-64:* 85 to 100. *MS-65 or better:* 50 to 65.

Availability in circulated grades: This

actual size: 15.5 mm

issue is scarce, but is available in all grades including EF and AU. A few numismatic hoards exist, including one with more than 500 pieces.[56]

Characteristics of striking: The striking of this issue varies.

Notes: Four varieties exist, each with a Small S mintmark, and were all struck early in the year. As discussed above, 1873 half dimes use the Close 3 logotype only.

G-4	VG-8	F-12	VF-20	EF-40	AU-50	MS-60	MS-63	MS-65
$30	$35	$40	$45	$65	$125	$165	$300	$675

5

LIBERTY SEATED DIMES (1837–1891)

Introduction

Dimes were first minted in 1796. By this time other silver dominations, except the quarter dollar, had been made in 1794 and 1795 using the Flowing Hair design. In 1795 the Draped Bust Obverse, Small Eagle Reverse, motif was created by engraver Robert Scot, and that autumn was used on two silver dollar obverse dies and one half dime die. In 1796 the Draped Bust Obverse, Small Eagle Reverse, became standard, including on the new quarter. In 1798 the reverse was changed to the Heraldic Eagle type. Dimes with this motif were produced through 1807. The next coinage of the denomination was in 1809. The Capped Bust Obverse, Perched Eagle Reverse, was created by assistant engraver John Reich in 1807 for use on the half dollar. This motif was produced intermittently from 1809 to early 1837, after which the Liberty Seated design became standard.

Liberty Seated dimes were made continuously at the Philadelphia Mint through 1891. The branch mint at New Orleans struck dimes with an O mintmark from 1838 intermittently to 1860 and again in 1891; the San Francisco Mint made dimes with an S mintmark from 1856 intermittently to 1877 and again in 1891; and the Carson City Mint produced dimes with a CC mintmark from 1871 to 1878. The weight of dimes was changed under the coinage acts of 1853 and 1873.

The Design of the Liberty Seated Dime

Christian Gobrecht's design on the 1837 and 1838-O dimes depicts Liberty seated on a rock, her left hand holding a liberty cap on a pole, and her right hand holding a shield inscribed LIBERTY. There is no drapery at her elbow, and there are no stars in the field. The result is a cameo-like appearance of rare beauty. The date is at the bottom border. The obverse design was inspired by the Gobrecht silver dollars of 1836. The reverse consists of an open wreath tied with a ribbon, enclosing ONE / DIME, with UNITED STATES OF AMERICA surrounding.

In 1838 stars were added to the obverse of the Liberty Seated dime. In 1840 drapery was added to Liberty's elbow, and the shield was adjusted to tilt slightly to the right, giving it an almost upright appearance. Through the 1840s and 1850s many different varieties were produced. In 1853 the Liberty Seated design was modified by the addition of tiny arrowheads to the left and right of the date to signify a decrease in the authorized weight from 41.2 grains to 38.4 grains. These arrows remained in place through 1855, after which they were discontinued, although the reduced weight remained in effect for later years as well until after February 1873.

In 1860 the obverse was modified by removing the stars and adding UNITED STATES OF AMERICA around the border. The reverse was changed as well, now with ONE / DIME in two lines within a cereal wreath. This style was continued through 1891, after which time the Liberty Seated design was replaced by Charles E. Barber's Liberty Head.

Edge Reed Counts on Liberty Seated Dimes

The subject of counting the vertical ribs, or reeds, on the edges of Liberty Seated dimes was detailed by John W. McCloskey, with findings as follows, lightly edited:[1]

Gauge 1: 89 reeds. This gauge reeding appears only on early Carson City dimes, 1871-CC to 1874-CC.

Gauge 2: 103 reeds. This is the basic reeding of the New Orleans Mint, continuing well into the Barber series to 1899. This characteristic makes it possible to detect altered coins to create the 1843-O, 1845-O, and 1860-O rarities.

Gauge 3: 113 reeds. This is the most common reeding type of the Liberty Seated dime series, and is used for all Philadelphia pieces except for a short period from 1855 to 1860. Early San Francisco dimes from 1856-S through 1869-S also have this gauge, as does an 1875-CC.[2]

Gauge 4: 121 reeds. Philadelphia dimes from 1855 to 1860 have this gauge reeding, as do later dimes from the San Francisco Mint.

Gauge 5: 141 reeds. This very narrow reeding is on all 1877-S dimes I have seen and on some 1876-S dimes. It is easily verified at sight and is an interesting variation from the other more common reedings.

Pattern Coins

There were no pattern quarters made for changing or modifying Gobrecht's design. In 1859 a transitional coin designated as a pattern was made for the numismatic trade and not to test the designs. It is listed in *A Guide Book of United States Coins*, and is listed separately on page 175. Related transitional patterns were made for half dimes.

Additionally, many different Proof strikings from original dies in off metals such as copper and aluminum were made from 1863 to 1876, and again in 1885. Particularly noteworthy is the 1876-CC pattern, J-1453a and b, struck from dies intended for Carson City but likely struck in Philadelphia. Popularly but incorrectly called "trial pieces," they were made for sale to collectors and are described in detail in *United States Pattern Coins* by J. Hewitt Judd. All are rare. A pairing with Longacre's Indian Princess "seated figure" motif was also struck, in 1871.

Also worth noting are experiments with different compositions from 1869, which paired a dateless Liberty Seated with Motto obverse with a reverse indicating the alloy's composition. Two versions were struck, one reading SIL. 9 / NIC. 1 / 1869 (J-714 and 715), the other reading SIL. / NIC. / COP. / 1869 (J-716 to 717a).

Aspects of Striking

Circulation-strike dimes were produced for use in commerce and little attention was given to the sharpness of details. As a general rule, most early issues, including the 1837 and 1838-O, Without Stars, and the issues through the early 1840s, are fairly well struck. After that time there are many variables. Weakness, when it does occur, is usually most noticeable on the head of Liberty and on the stars. Sometimes the higher-relief leaves in the laurel branches on the reverse show lightness.

The 1860 to 1873 coins with UNITED STATES OF AMERICA on the obverse are often lightly struck, most noticeably on the head of Liberty. Denticles are often soft as well. San Francisco issues are apt to be less well struck than those of Philadelphia or Carson City. Many Proofs have light striking on the highest-relief area of Liberty's head.

Release and Distribution

Excepting Proofs made for presentation and for collectors, all Liberty Seated dimes were intended for circulation. The *Niles' Weekly Register*, July 29, 1837, included this:

> *New dime.* The United States Gazette says: "A friend showed to us on Saturday a ten cent piece of the new coinage; it is smaller in circumference than those formerly emitted; on one side are the words ONE DIME, encircled with a wreath, on the other is a finely cut figure of liberty not the old head and trunk, that once looked so flaring out from our coin—but a neat, tidy female figure, sufficiently dressed, holding in one hand a staff, surmounted with a liberty cap; the other hand sustains a shield, inscribed with the word LIBERTY. The figure is in a sitting posture, and resembles, generally, the representation of Britannia on the English coins."

Liberty Seated dimes were made in quantity in most later years and served in commerce widely with the result that most became well-worn in time. The Civil War was declared on April 15, 1861. In the North it was envisioned as an easy win, and President Abraham Lincoln called for men to enlist for 90 days, after which time it surely would be over. That did not happen. The first major clash, the Battle of Bull Run in late July, resulted in a Confederate victory. Union troops scattered and fled. By late 1861 the outcome remained uncertain. In late December, gold coins began to be hoarded as "hard money" offered security. In March 1862 the Treasury Department began issuing Legal Tender Notes. These could be exchanged only for other paper notes and were not redeemable at par in federal silver or gold coins. Fear increased, and by late spring all silver coins were gone from circulation in the East and in the Midwest. In the meantime, on the West Coast there were no legal-tender bills in circulation. The Constitution of the State of California, adopted in 1850, forbid the use of paper money there. Silver coins continued to circulate at par, and any paper money brought into the state was accepted by merchants only at a deep discount.

When the San Francisco Mint began producing dimes in 1856, these readily went into circulation. Similar to the situation with half dimes (first minted in California in 1863) these were very popular with Chinese immigrants who sent many back to their homeland. Today, the average grade of a surviving San Francisco Mint dime of the 1850s or 1860s is much lower than one made in Philadelphia.

In the East, dimes were still made after the spring of 1862, but they were not seen in commerce. The Mint sold them only at a stiff premium if bought with Legal Tender Notes. Bullion brokers and banks maintained supplies for citizens who wanted to acquire them, again at a premium. It was anticipated that after the Civil War ended in April 1865 silver coins would reappear in circulation. The public remained wary of the solidity of the Treasury Department, and it was not until after April 20, 1876, that silver and paper were on a par, and silver coins, including long-hoarded dimes, were again seen in circulation. The Treasury Department did not anticipate this flood of old coins, and to be sure that enough coins were on hand increased mintages sharply from 1875 through 1878. This produced a glut, after which from 1879 through 1881 the mintage of dimes was very small.

Liberty Seated dimes remained in circulation for many years and were familiar sights into the 1920s. By the end of the 1930s, during which decade coin collecting became very popular, they were gone.

Proof Liberty Seated Dimes

Proofs were struck at the Philadelphia Mint for all years from 1837 through 1891, although no sets are known for 1851 and 1853. Some dimes of these years are highly mirror-like and have been called Proofs, but whether they were intended as such is a matter of debate.

From 1837 to 1858 Proofs were available as single coins and as part of silver sets for face value upon request to the Mint. In the latter year it seems that slightly more than 200 sets were made plus single coins. In 1859 the Mint anticipated great demand and made 800 silver sets, followed by 1,000 each in 1860 and 1861. Proofs of the 1860 and 1861 dimes are far and away the rarest of the 1860s as many collectors ignored them at the new retail price of $3 per set. It is likely that more than half of the coins were placed into circulation. Among later sets the figures reached lows of 460 and 470 in 1863 and 1864, although most survive today. Ordering Proofs from the Mint involved either paying in gold coins (only available at a premium in the marketplace), or by paying a strong premium in paper money. The Mint would not accept federal paper money at par.

Today, a complete run of Proof dates from 1858 to 1891 can be formed without difficulty. Typical grades are PF-63 and PF-64. Gems, or PF-65, and finer coins are in the minority.

Grading Liberty Seated Dimes

1876-CC, Variety 1. Graded MS-64.

MS-60 to 70 (Mint State). *Obverse:* At MS-60, some abrasion and contact marks are evident, most noticeably on the bosom and thighs and knees. Luster is present, but may be dull or lifeless, and interrupted in patches in the large open field. At MS-63, contact marks are very few, and abrasion is hard to detect except under magnification. An MS-65 coin has no abrasion, and contact marks are so minute as to require magnification. Luster should be full and rich, except for Philadelphia (but not San Francisco) dimes of the early and mid-1860s. Most Mint State coins of the 1861 to 1865 years, Philadelphia issues, have extensive die striae (from not completely finishing the die). Some low-mintage Philadelphia issues may be prooflike. Clashmarks are common in this era. This is true of contemporary half dimes as well. Half dimes of this type can be very beautiful at this level. Grades above MS-65 are seen with regularity, more so than for the related No Stars dimes. *Reverse:* Comments apply as for the obverse, except that in lower Mint State grades, abrasion and contact marks are most noticeable on the highest parts of the leaves and the ribbon, less so on ONE DIME. At MS-65 or higher there are no marks visible to the unaided eye. The field is mainly protected by design elements and does not show abrasion as much as does the open-field obverse on a given coin.

Illustrated coin: Note the blend of pink, lilac, and gold tones.

1838-O, No Stars; F-101. Graded AU-58.

AU-50, 53, 55, 58 (About Uncirculated). *Obverse:* Light wear is seen on the thighs and knees, bosom, and head. At AU-58, the luster is extensive, but incomplete. Friction is seen in the large open field. At AU-50 and 53, luster is less. *Reverse:* Wear is evident on the leaves (especially at the top of the wreath) and ribbon. An AU-58 coin has nearly full luster, more so than on the obverse, as the design elements protect the small field areas. At AU-50 and 53, there still is significant luster, more than on the obverse.

Illustrated coin: Lustrous and lightly toned, this is an exceptional example of this scarce New Orleans dime.

1838-O, No Stars; F-102. Graded EF-45.

EF-40, 45 (Extremely Fine). *Obverse:* Further wear is seen on all areas, especially the thighs and knees, bosom, and head. Little or no luster is seen. *Reverse:* Further wear is seen on all areas, most noticeably at the leaves to each side of the wreath apex and on the ribbon bow knot. Leaves retain details except on the higher areas.

1872-CC; F-101. Graded VF-30.

VF-20, 30 (Very Fine). *Obverse:* Further wear is seen. Most details of the gown are worn away, except in the lower-relief areas above and to the right of the shield. Hair detail is mostly or completely gone. *Reverse:* Wear is more extensive. The highest leaves are flat.

1874-CC. Graded F-12.

F-12, 15 (Fine). *Obverse:* The seated figure is well worn, with little detail remaining. LIBERTY on the shield is fully readable but weak in areas. On the 1838–1840 sub-type Without Drapery, LIBERTY is in higher relief and will wear more quickly; ER may be missing, but other details are at the Fine level. *Reverse:* Most detail of the leaves is gone. The rim is worn but bold, and most if not all denticles are visible.

Illustrated coin: The word LIBERTY is full but is weak at ER.

1843-O; F-101. Graded VG-8.

VG-8, 10 (Very Good). *Obverse:* The seated figure is more worn, but some detail can be seen above and to the right of the shield. The shield is discernible. In LIBERTY at least three letters are readable but very weak at VG-8; a few more visible at VG-10. On the 1838–1840 subtype Without Drapery, LIBERTY is in higher relief, and at Very Good only one or two letters may be readable. However, LIBERTY is not an infallible way to grade this type, as some varieties have the word in low relief on the die, so it wore away slowly. *Reverse:* Further wear has combined the details of most leaves. The rim is complete, but weak in areas. The reverse appears to be in a slightly higher grade than the obverse.

1873-CC. Graded G-4.

G-4, 6 (Good). *Obverse:* The seated figure is worn smooth. At G-4 there are no letters in LIBERTY remaining on most (but not all) coins. At G-6, traces of one or two can be seen (except on the early No Drapery coins). *Reverse:* Wear is more extensive. The leaves are all combined and in outline form. The rim is well worn and missing in some areas, causing the outer parts of the peripheral letters to be worn away in some instances. On most coins the reverse appears to be in a slightly higher grade than the obverse.

1874-CC. Graded AG-3.

AG-3 (About Good). *Obverse:* The seated figure is mostly visible in outline form, with no detail. The rim is worn away. The date remains clear. *Reverse:* Many if not most letters are worn away, at least in part. The wreath and interior letters are discernible. The rim is weak.

1886. Graded PF-67.

PF-60 to 70 (Proof). *Obverse and Reverse:* Proofs that are extensively cleaned and have many hairlines, or that are dull and grainy, are lower level, such as PF-60 to 62. These command less attention than more visually appealing pieces, save for the scarce (in any grade) dates of 1844 and 1846, and 1863 through 1867. Both the half dime and dime Proofs of 1837 were often cleaned, resulting in coins that have lost much of their mirror surface. With medium hairlines and good reflectivity, an assigned grade of PF-64 is indicated, and with relatively few hairlines, Gem PF-65. In various grades hairlines are most easily seen in the obverse field. PF-66 should have hairlines so delicate that magnification is needed to see them. Above that, a Proof should be free of such lines.

Collecting Liberty Seated Dimes

Apart from Proof coins, called "Master Coins" in the early days, there was not much interest in Liberty Seated dimes during the years they were issued. Circulation strikes were ignored, including New Orleans and San Francisco branch-mint issues and the later coins of Carson City. The curators of the Mint Cabinet, organized in June 1838, had no interest in them. As a result many dimes made in large quantities range from scarce to very rare in Mint State today. Most of the New Orleans issues range from very rare to nearly impossible to find in Mint State, and for certain Philadelphia dimes before 1853, some such as 1844 and 1846, are seen more often with Proof finish than in Choice or Gem Mint State.

Liberty Seated dimes were mentioned now and again in the two leading periodicals of the late 1800s and early 1900s—the *American Journal of Numismatics* and *The Numismatist*. An awakening happened in 1893 with the publication of *Mint Marks, A Treatise on the Coinage of United States Branch Mints*. In 1894 the William M. Friesner Collection was auctioned by Édouard Frossard and drew bids from many directions. Interest in mint-marked coins increased, and in ensuing years the issues of New Orleans and San Francisco gained a following. By that time most coins in numismatic hands showed extensive wear.

In the early and mid-1900s Liberty Seated dimes were collected by date and mint. Every now and again articles about the series were published in *The Numismatist, Hobbies, The Numismatic Scrapbook Magazine*, and elsewhere. As an example, the June 1912 issue of *The Numismatist* included this commentary by Howard R. Newcomb in "Unappreciated Silver Mint Rarities—Dimes":

> Everyone knows the 1894 San Francisco dime is the rarest in the dime series and one of the greatest rarities of all the United States coins. There are many others that are worth careful consideration in any state of preservation, but that which stands out next in point of rarity is the Carson City dime of 1874. Although the records give 10,817 pieces coined, I have met with less than a half dozen specimens, and all from circulation. 1871-CC, 1872-CC, and 1873-CC, with arrows [the 1873-CC without-arrows variety was unknown to Newcomb and would not emerge until the American Numismatic Society exhibit two years later in 1914], follow next, and of these three, only the 1871 have I heard of existing in Uncirculated condition. They are all of excessive rarity. I think I am safe in saying that a more recent coin now follows, the 1885-S dime. This piece is more likely to be passed by unnoticed than any other in the series. It recently brought a very low price at auction ($22.10 Uncirculated) if its rarity is taken into consideration with other well-known rarities of the United States series, such as a half cent of 1796.
>
> The 1860-O, 1870-S, 1858-S, 1859-S, and 1856-S are next in the order named; and those possessing these, especially in Uncirculated condition, have some very nice prizes. All the above mentioned pieces, together with a few others not noted, are vastly rarer than the so-called very rare 1860-S dime with stars. . . .

Listings of varieties, mintage figures, and prices in multiple grades were offered in *The Standard Catalogue of United States Coins* beginning in 1934 and *A Guide Book of United States Coins* from 1946 (cover date 1947) onward.

Numismatic interest moved forward dramatically in the 1970s when Kamal Ahwash, a well-known figure at conventions and other gatherings, began extolling the virtues of Liberty Seated coins in general and dimes in particular. In 1977 he self-published the *Encyclopedia of U.S. Liberty Seated Dimes, 1837–91* essential picture book, which enjoyed a wide sale and created a lot of attention. By that time certain earlier silver series, such as half dimes, quarters, half dollars, and silver dollars from the 1790s through the 1930s, had been studied by minute die differences. Ahwash's book on Liberty Seated dimes catalyzed the entire Liberty Seated field, resulting in specialized books being published in the 1990s by DLRC Press. These included *The Complete Guide to Liberty Seated Dimes* by Brian Greer in 1992. In the early 2000s the series went viral along with Gerry Fortin's *The Definitive Resource for Liberty Seated Dime Variety Collectors*, published only on the Internet at seateddimevarieties.com. In time the numbers assigned by Greer were supplanted, then largely replaced by new Fortin numbers that remain in wide use today. In the meantime the Liberty Seated Collectors Club along with their publications, the *Gobrecht Journal* and *E-Gobrecht*, added more interest.

Recently, Frank Trask, an Oregon dealer who travels the coin show circuit in the West, will have attended more than two dozen events this year, and reviewed the manuscript for this book, sent a commentary on his perspective on Liberty Seated coins at shows, with this on dimes:[3]

> [Liberty Seated is] a series that I know to be in demand, yet one that I never really pursued as a dealer because of the scarcity, cost, and limited market. Many Liberty Seated coins—especially the dimes—are in demand in circulated condition. Probably because of their reasonable pricing. I am a "retail" coin seller . . .
>
> In my experience Liberty Seated coins are more desired in circulated grades. Those in the greatest demands are probably Fine to Very Fine. They should be "clean," have even wear, no rim dings, no scratches. Ideally the high points will be lighter with darker coloring elsewhere. The date should be prominent and definitely without defects. This is a coin that "looks like it *should* look." Those are the most desirable.
>
> The "CC" Liberty Seated coins, dimes especially, are very rarely found at dealers' tables. The simple reason is because in the setup hours prior to a show, the "vest pocket" traders and others are out searching for all Liberty Seated material, especially the Carson City coins. Because of the pricing guides, a dealer like myself will readily market these coins to dealers instead of waiting for the public, because the dealers often pay about the same as collectors . . .

Today the collecting of Liberty Seated dimes is a popular pursuit all across the art and science of numismatics (as I like to call it). As several varieties are impossible or nearly so to find in Choice Mint State or finer, most enthusiasts content themselves with forming sets in circulated grades, typically from Very Fine upward. With Gerry Fortin's website as a meeting place (www.seateddimevarieties.com), there is a lot of interest in die varieties, including the attainment of a complete "Top 100 Varieties" set defined by Fortin and the Liberty Seated Collectors Club during 2005. The offering of many Liberty Seated coins on eBay has also helped the specialty.

Being a Smart Buyer

Repeating advice first given under half dimes, first and foremost—and this is true of all Liberty Seated denominations—do not be a slave to grading numbers. There are *two more* factors that can be equally or even more important. Sharpness of strike is very important, and there are many dimes within a certain certified grade that can have a needle-sharp strike or can be weak in areas. Eye appeal is equally important. Coins can be beautiful to view or they can be dark, stained, or otherwise ugly. I would rather have an MS-63 coin that is sharply struck and has good eye appeal than an MS-66 with lightly struck areas and is not very attractive. Even better, the MS-63 is apt to cost but a fraction of the MS-66!

As is true of all Liberty Seated denominations, cherrypicking Liberty Seated dimes for quality can pay dividends. The grading services pay little or no attention to strike or eye appeal. This provides the opportunity to acquire sharp coins, for varieties for which such exist, without paying any more for them. You can join Gerry Fortin's Internet "club" and report new discoveries as others have done. In addition there are many interesting varieties of which the public is not aware—such as repunched and misplaced dates—that often cost no more. The *Cherrypickers' Guide to Die Varieties of United States Coins* describes many such pieces.

For circulated coins, avoid those with nicks or scratches. Proofs are usually quite good, but some have light striking on Liberty's head and quite a few have scattered lint marks from residue on the dies. Eye appeal can vary.

1837 and 1838-O,
No Stars on Obverse (Variety 1)

There are no stars on the obverse. A wreath is on the reverse. This design is of the Small Letters variety. The mintmark is above the bow on the reverse for 1838-O.

Designer: Christian Gobrecht.

Specifications: *Composition:* 90 percent silver, 10 percent copper. *Diameter:* 17.9 mm. *Weight:* 41.25 grains (2.67 grams). *Edge:* Reeded.

1837, *Large Date*
Circulation-strike mintage: Portion of 682,500

Proof mintage: *25–35*

Availability in Mint State: Large Date 1837 dimes are the variety most often seen for this year. Brian Greer considered this to be among the four most available dimes before 1854. *MS-60 to 62:* 500 to 750. *MS-63:* 160 to 200. *MS-64:* 140 to 170. *MS-65 or better:* 70 to 90.

actual size: 17.9 mm

Detail of Large Date.

Availability in circulated grades:
This issue is readily available in all grades, the prevalent levels being VG through VF. Many were saved because they were the first year of issue.

Characteristics of striking: This issue is usually fairly well struck.[4]

Proofs: Fortin-101. This die combination was also used for circulation strikes. On June 30, 1837, 30 or a few more Proofs were struck for presentation purposes (not for inclusion in silver Proof sets). Apparently, nearly all of these went to non-numismatic recipients, for very few unimpaired specimens exist today. Approximately 26 examples have been certified.

Notes: The Large Date coins were the first produced, as evidenced by the fact that numerous Mint State pieces were saved due to their novelty. For many years these have been in great demand for inclusion in type sets. As a date, specimens are plentiful in most grades. Late die states show severe cracks and clash marks. F-101.

G-4	F-12	VF-20	EF-40	AU-50	MS-60
$65	$145	$275	$525	$800	$1,200
MS-63	**MS-64**	**MS-65**	**PF-60**	**PF-63**	**PF-65**
$2,000	$3,750	$6,750	$6,500	$12,500	$35,000

1837, Small Date

Circulation-strike mintage:
Portion of 682,500

actual size: 17.9 mm

Availability in Mint State: In
1992 Brian Greer considered
this to be among the four most
available dimes before 1854, but
this opinion probably would not
hold today. Among Mint State
dimes of this date, fewer than
20 percent are of the Small Date
variety.[5] The Eliasberg coin was
only AU-55. Very few Mint State
coins have been offered in major
collections over the years. This

Detail of Small Date.

relative rarity is not reflected in current market prices. In 2014 the Eugene H. Gardner Sale featured an example of this coin in MS-66. *MS-60 to 62:* 100 to 130. *MS-63:*
30 to 40. *MS-64:* 25 to 325. *MS-65 or better:* 15 to 20.

Availability in circulated grades: The Small Date variety is slightly scarcer than the
Large Date, but is easily available in all grades, mostly VG through VF. *AG-3 to AU-58:*
3,000 to 4,000.

Characteristics of striking: This issue is usually fairly well struck.

Notes: F-102 to 104.

G-4	F-12	VF-20	EF-40	AU-50	MS-60	MS-63	MS-64	MS-65
$65	$150	$325	$525	$800	$1,200	$2,000	$4,000	$8,500

1838-O

Circulation-strike mintage:
489,034

actual size: 17.9 mm

Availability in Mint State: At
gem level, the 1838-O in Mint
State is exceedingly rare, and often
a span of many years will lapse
between offerings. Lower-range
Mint State coins are available but
scarce. It has been my experience over the years that the majority of the specimens
described as Mint State would be more properly described as AU. The Eliasberg coin
(1996) was MS-64. Brian Greer noted the rumor of a small hoard of Mint State pieces,
a grouping of which I am not aware. In 2015 the Eugene H. Gardner Sale featured
examples of this coin in MS-65 and MS-64. *MS-60 to 62:* 35 to 45. *MS-63:* 17 to 22.
MS-64: 14 to 18. *MS-65 or better:* 7 to 10.

Availability in circulated grades: These are readily available, but are significantly scarcer than the 1837 of the same type. Several thousand exist. The attrition rate of New Orleans dimes was much greater than for Philadelphia.[6]

Characteristics of striking: This issue is usually fairly well struck. Some examples of the 1838-O show die rust. Some have light striking at the top part of the obverse. Some show significant obverse die erosion since only a single die was employed.

Notes: On May 12, the New Orleans Mint Superintendent wrote to Mint Director Robert M. Patterson: "I have the pleasure of enclosing a specimen of our coinage, a dime, one of the thirty pieces struck on the 8th inst. Mr. [Rufus] Tyler found the press required readjusting and that there was danger of breaking it and only struck a few pieces, ten of which were deposited in the cornerstone of the New American Theatre which was laid the same day, the remainder distributed as mementos of the event."[7]

Based on records in the National Archives, R.W. Julian found that 367,434 were struck in June and July 1838 and 121,600 additional 1838-O dimes were made in January 1839, suggesting a total mintage far in excess of the 406,034 *Guide Book* figure. Notwithstanding this, the 1838-O remains a rarity in high grades today.

In 1893, Augustus G. Heaton described mintmarks on New Orleans coins as follows: "The O Mint dime coinage has several sizes of the indicative letter which may be classified in three, *large*, which is about the height of the letters of the legend UNITED STATES OF AMERICA on the coin, *the medium*, about two-thirds and *small*, about one-half or less." Mintmark sizes on New Orleans issues are found on various dimes of the next quarter century.

F-101 (repunched mintmark) and 102.

G-4	F-12	VF-20	EF-40	AU-50	MS-60	MS-63	MS-64	MS-65
$100	$185	$425	$800	$1,100	$3,750	$6,000	$8,500	$22,500

1838–1841, Stars on Obverse (Variety 2—No Drapery)

Liberty, seated on a rock, has her head turned to the viewer's left. Her left hand holds a pole surmounted by a liberty cap, and her right hand rests on the corner of a shield inscribed LIBERTY. The shield is tilted sharply to the left, and there is no extra drapery at the elbow. Stars on the obverse were punched individually into each working die. The reverse is the same as on the preceding variety. Mintmarks are above the bow on the reverse.

Designer: Christian Gobrecht.

Specifications: *Composition:* 90 percent silver, 10 percent copper. *Diameter:* 17.9 mm. *Weight:* 41.25 grains (2.67 grams). *Edge:* Reeded.

1838, Small Stars

Circulation-strike mintage:
Portion of 1,992,500

Proof mintage: 2–3

actual size: 17.9 mm

Availability in Mint State: The Small Stars variety is exceedingly rare in Mint State. In 2014 and 2015 the Eugene H. Gardner Sale featured examples of this coin in MS-68 and MS-67. *MS-60 to 62:* 50 to 75. *MS-63:* 25 to 32. *MS-64:* 15 to 20. *MS-65 or better:* 12 to 15.

Availability in circulated grades: Many exist of this issue, mostly in lower grades. Nice EF and AU coins can be found by searching.

Characteristics of striking: This issue is usually well struck.

Proofs: The obverse die has stars one, five, eight, nine, and twelve repunched. Star twelve was originally punched too low in the die.[8] In 2014 the Eugene H. Gardner Sale featured examples of this coin in PF-67 (ex Kaufman), described as "likely unique" in Proof format.

Notes: It is believed that punches intended for use on the half dime were employed to create the stars on this variety. See pages 89–90 for close-up imagery of the two types. Based on the small sample of seven obverse dies for the Large Stars and one for the Small Stars the estimated mintage for the Small Stars might be in the 250,000 range. This seems to square with the Small Stars dimes being readily available today. The stars were individually punched into the working die. The first delivery by the coiner was 30,000 pieces on March 31, 1838. The star size is not known, although some have speculated they were all of the Small Stars style. F-101.

G-4	F-12	VF-20	EF-40	AU-50	MS-60
$30	$70	$125	$200	$425	$700
MS-63	**MS-64**	**MS-65**	**PF-60**	**PF-63**	**PF-65**
$1,350	$2,000	$4,000			

1838, Large Stars

Circulation-strike mintage:
Portion of 1,992,500

Availability in Mint State: Brian Greer considered this to be among the four most available dimes before 1854. *MS-60 to 62:* 200 to 250. *MS-63:* 125 to 150. *MS-64:* 100 to 125. *MS-65 or better:* 60 to 80.

actual size: 17.9 mm

Availability in circulated grades: This issue is common in all circulated grades.

Characteristics of striking: This issue is usually well struck.

Notes: This dime exists in two well-known varieties, Small Stars and Large Stars, with the preceding being by far the rarer. See pages 89–90 for close-up imagery.

One variety of the 1838 is known as having "partial drapery" from Liberty's left elbow. In actuality, this is simply a clash mark. It appears in the drapery position. All 1838 Liberty Seated Dimes were designed without drapery (called No Drapery in this book).

The stars were individually punched into the working dies. F-102 to 114. There are eight obverse dies and seven reverse dies in various combinations. Three boldly cracked obverse die varieties (F-106, 110a, and 111a) are popular among die variety collectors.

G-4	F-12	VF-20	EF-40	AU-50	MS-60	MS-63	MS-64	MS-65
$30	$40	$65	$180	$300	$500	$900	$1,250	$3,000

1838-O

Circulation-strike mintage: Unknown, if any

APOCRYPHAL

In 1893 in *Mint Marks* Augustus G. Heaton said: "1838 (of which the mintage is not recorded in the Mint Report) is without stars, with a Large O in the wreath on the reverse, and is rare. There is also a variety with stars and a Small O, which is very rare."

The 1838-O, With Stars, at present is unsubstantiated—unknown to any later researchers, and no further mention of it has been found. Heaton was a careful observer, and his comment indicates that he had either seen one or had received what he considered to be a reliable report of the same.

1839

Circulation-strike mintage: 1,053,115

Proof mintage: *4–5*

actual size: 17.9 mm

Availability in Mint State: Brian Greer considered this to be among the four most available dimes before 1854. These are relatively available in Mint State, including high grade examples, some of which are beyond MS-65. They are typically lustrous and frosty. *MS-60 to 62:* 120 to 160. *MS-63:* 60 to 80. *MS-64:* 40 to 55. *MS-65 or better:* 30 to 40.

Availability in circulated grades: There are probably more than 5,000 surviving today, mostly in lower grades.

Characteristics of striking: This issue is usually seen well struck. According to Fortin, there are two popular varieties from shattered obverse dies.

Proofs: Two die pairs, F-105 and 106, were also used for circulation strikes. It is estimated that the Eliasberg PF-63 (1996) had stars eight and ten repunched. In 2015 the Eugene H. Gardner Sale featured an example of this coin in PF-64. Approximately five examples have been certified.

Notes: F-101 to 109, with three obverse dies combined with eight reverses. The F-105c shattered obverse die variety is the most popular Liberty Seated dime variety among advanced variety collectors. The variety is scarce with perhaps a dozen or so known.[9] The mintage figure suggests more varieties remain to be discovered.

G-4	F-12	VF-20	EF-40	AU-50	MS-60
$25	$35	$65	$165	$300	$500

MS-63	MS-64	MS-65	PF-60	PF-63	PF-65
$900	$1,200	$3,000	$10,000	$22,500	$50,000

1839-O

Circulation-strike mintage: 1,291,600

Proof mintage: *2–3*

actual size: 17.9 mm

Availability in Mint State: This issue is fairly scarce, certainly much scarcer than its Philadelphia Mint counterpart, but it is available with patience. Most specimens tend to be at lower Mint State levels. In 2015 the Eugene H. Gardner Sale featured examples of this coin in MS-67 and MS-66. *MS-60 to 62:* 25 to 30. *MS-63:* 12 to 15. *MS-64:* 8 to 10. *MS-65 or better:* 5 to 7.[10]

Availability in circulated grades: There are thousands of this issue in existence, mostly in lower grades.

Characteristics of striking: This issue is usually well struck, but some have slight weakness on the horizontal shield lines.

Proofs: Proofs of this year and mintmark are extremely rare.

Notes: These exist with Small O and Large O varieties, not widely collected except by specialists. Brian Greer notes that the Small O is slightly scarcer. It is believed that some proportion of the 1,323,000 calendar year mintage at New Orleans consisted of 1838-O dimes (see earlier listing). F-101 to 110. F-105 with Large O is by far the most available in all grades. F-108 is the Huge O reverse variety, those being struck with a leftover reverse from 1838. This is usually seen in grades from AG to VG and is the rarest of the mintmark sizes.[11]

G-4	F-12	VF-20	EF-40	AU-50	MS-60
$30	$85	$150	$250	$450	$850
MS-63	MS-64	MS-65	PF-60	PF-63	PF-65
$1,950	$3,000	$7,500		$25,000	$70,000

1840, No Drapery

Circulation-strike mintage: 981,500

Proof mintage: *4–5*

actual size: 17.9 mm

Availability in Mint State: In Mint State this issue is fairly scarce, although obtainable. In 2014 the Eugene H. Gardner Sale featured an example of this coin in MS-67. *MS-60 to 62:* 75 to 100. *MS-63:* 35 to 50. *MS-64:* 25 to 32. *MS-65 or better*: 15 to 20.

Availability in circulated grades: These are readily available in any grade desired.

Characteristics of striking: This issue is usually fairly well struck.

Proofs: The Louis E. Eliasberg Sale in 1997 featured an example of this coin in PF-63 with star two dramatically repunched. There are die lines from the denticles over the space between OF and A. In 2014 the Eugene H. Gardner Sale featured an example of this coin in PF-65 (ex Kaufman). Approximately five examples have been certified.

Notes: F-101 to 108, combining eight obverse dies and eight reverse dies. F-103 is the popular "Chin Whiskers" variety, named as such due to some parallel vertical die scratches extending downward from Liberty's chin.

G-4	F-12	VF-20	EF-40	AU-50	MS-60
$25	$35	$65	$200	$300	$450

MS-63	MS-64	MS-65	PF-60	PF-63	PF-65
$850	$1,300	$3,500	$15,000	$20,000	$45,000

1840-O, No Drapery

Circulation-strike mintage: 1,175,000

actual size: 17.9 mm

Availability in Mint State: This issue is very rare in Mint State, as collecting dimes (and other coins) by mintmark was not followed, to my knowledge, by even a single numismatist in the 1840s decade, and all specimens slipped casually into circulation. By chance some were saved, but the number surviving is very small. In 2014 and 2015 the Eugene H. Gardner Sale featured examples of this coin in MS-65, MS-64, and MS-60. *MS-60 to 62:* 8 to 11. *MS-63:* 1 or 2. *MS-64:* 1. *MS-65 or better:* 1.

Availability in circulated grades: In circulated grades this issue is scarce, but no difficulty will be encountered in finding one. They are mostly found in lower grades as is true of all dimes of this era. According to Fortin, locating choice examples in EF and AU will be very challenging as variety collectors have hoarded most that come to market.

Characteristics of striking: Striking of this issue varies, but most have some light weakness. Many were struck from severely eroded dies leading to weakness, particularly on the obverse.

Notes: Three mintmark sizes are known. There were no 1840-O dies made with drapery. F-101 to 111, combining seven obverse dies with eight reverse dies.

G-4	F-12	VF-20	EF-40	AU-50	MS-60	MS-63	MS-64	MS-65
$60	$125	$185	$500	$1,025	$7,000	$14,500	$22,500	$45,000

1841, No Drapery

Proof mintage: 2–3

actual size: 17.9 mm

Proofs: There are only two verified examples of this issue. The Eric P. Newman Collection includes an example of this coin in PF-67 (NGC) that is valued at $305,000.

Notes: F-101. These lack drapery and were made from a die created from a No-Drapery hub of a modified style not used anywhere else in the series, per the research of John McCloskey in "The 1841 No Drapery Proof Dime" in the *Gobrecht Journal*, March 2000. As such, this constitutes a distinctly different and highly important variety.

A second and seemingly more likely theory was developed in 2015 by John Dannreuther.[12] After discussion with Andy Lustig, who had an 1840 splasher dime with the drapery scraped away from the left and right sides of Liberty, he did overlays of the 1841, No Drapery, dime with an 1842 dime. These matched with the only differences noted in the rocky base, which was altered on the 1841, No Drapery, die. The No-Drapery die was created by removing the drapery from a With-Drapery die, or more likely the drapery was removed from a With-Drapery hub.

Research is ongoing, but it is likely that the drapery was removed from a With-Drapery hub by Christian Gobrecht, then a new die was created, the rocky base altered, the die polished, and a few 1841, No Drapery, dimes were struck in Proof format. The rocky base had to be in the No-Drapery die, as the lines are raised on the coins, indicating a graver was used in the die.

Of course, it is impossible to prove whether the drapery was removed from a With-Drapery die or the drapery was added to the No-Drapery die, as John McCloskey concluded, but the 1840, With Drapery, dimes had already been struck. If the No Drapery had been first and then had drapery added, it would mean that the 1841, No Drapery, Proof dimes were struck before the 1840, With Drapery, regular issue dimes. This seems unlikely, so John Dannreuther has concluded that the No Drapery 1841 die was created from a With-Drapery hub. The 1840 splasher from Andy Lustig reinforces this conclusion.

One example of this coin was sold by Kagin's in the 1973 Middle Atlantic Numismatic Association Sale and was once described as a Proof, now VF to EF. The other, a gem Proof, was in the Eric P. Newman Collection and was sold by Heritage Auctions. Heritage stated that the worn piece is now graded AU-53 (NGC) and may be from the F.C.C. Boyd Collection (1945). It was also stated that the Newman coin is probably that described in Stack's December 1943 issue of the *Numismatic Review*, as part of an 1841 Proof set once owned by Colonel E.H.R. Green.

PF-60	PF-63	PF-65
	$75,000	

1840–1853, Stars on Obverse (Variety 2—With Drapery)

The obverse has been redesigned slightly. The most obvious change is the drapery added below the left elbow of Liberty. The seated figure is slightly smaller, as evidenced by there being larger spaces between the border and the lower left and right of the figure. The liberty cap is smaller and more distant from the border, and Liberty's hand is closer to the cap. The shield has been rotated slightly to the right and is closer to being upright. The drapery to the right of the shield has been redesigned. The stars are now part of the hub, and henceforth there are no variations in their positions.

The reverse is of the same design, but the wreath is heavier and the letters are larger, Large Letters style. Some of the buds in the laurel wreath have split ends, widely called "split buds." See page 92 for imagery. Mintmarks are above the bow through 1860.

Designer: Christian Gobrecht.

Specifications: *Composition:* 90 percent silver; 10 percent copper. *Diameter:* 17.9 mm. *Weight:* 41.2 grains (2.67 grams). *Edge:* Reeded.

1840, With Drapery

Circulation-strike mintage: 377,500

Availability in Mint State:
These are quite rare in Mint State, certainly in the top 15 or 20 percent. Most Mint State pieces tend to be in lower grades. The Louis E. Eliasberg Sale featured a

actual size: 17.9 mm

split-grade example of this coin in MS-65/66. In 2015 the Eugene H. Gardner Sale featured examples of this coin in MS-67, MS-64 (2), MS-63, and MS-61. *MS-60 to 62:* 3 to 5. *MS-63:* 2 or 3. *MS-64:* 2 or 3. *MS-65 or better:* 1 or 2.

Availability in circulated grades: This date is challenging in all circulated grades and is substantially more difficult to find than the 1840, No Drapery.

Characteristics of striking: This issue is often lightly struck on Liberty's head and the corresponding part of the reverse, though well struck specimens can be found.

Notes: The seated figure was redesigned slightly. The shield was moved upright from its formerly tilted appearance, and other minor changes were made to the obverse. On the reverse the letters are slightly larger. Buds on the laurel wreath have split ends, a style continuing until this style of wreath was replaced by the "cereal" wreath in 1860. See page 92 for imagery.

In all grades the 1840 Liberty Seated dime with drapery is considerably scarcer than its predecessor without. It is believed that the first examples were delivered in December of the year. F-101.

G-4	F-12	VF-20	EF-40	AU-50	MS-60	MS-63	MS-64	MS-65
$100	$185	$325	$825	$1,300	$3,250	$12,000	$20,000	$30,000

1841, With Drapery

Circulation-strike mintage: 1,622,500

Proof mintage: *2–3*

actual size: 17.9 mm

Availability in Mint State: In 2014 and 2015 the Eugene H. Gardner Sale featured examples of this coin in MS-67, MS-66 (2), and MS-65. *MS-60 to 62:* 70 to 100. *MS-63:* 30 to 40. *MS-64:* 20 to 25. *MS-65 or better:* 8 to 11.

Availability in circulated grades: This date is readily available in all grades, but is more challenging than its New Orleans counterpart.

Characteristics of striking: This issue is usually seen fairly well struck. Some are weak at the head of Liberty and the corresponding part of the reverse (the same can be said of most other dimes of this type).

Proofs: Only one example has been confirmed—Heritage Auction's sale of the Eugene H. Gardner Collection in 2014 featured an example in PF-63. It was seen earlier in the 1994 ANA, 1997 Halpern and Warner Collections Sale, 2005 Richmond Collection, and 2008 Kaufman Collection sales.

Notes: This issue is readily available in all grades. F-102 to 110. Eight obverse dies combined with eight reverse dies. Several obverse dies (F-103, 104, and 105) have bold-date repunching.

G-4	F-12	VF-20	EF-40	AU-50	MS-60
$20	$30	$40	$65	$150	$425

MS-63	MS-64	MS-65	PF-60	PF-63	PF-65
$775	$1,200	$4,000		$50,000	

1841-O

Circulation-strike mintage: 2,007,500

actual size: 17.9 mm

Availability in Mint State: The 1841-O is one of the more readily available Mint State New Orleans dimes of the era, although on an absolute basis it is fairly elusive. The reason for the availability of these is not known. They are not from the October 28, 1982, discovery of buried New Orleans coins, a find consisting mostly of half dollars. In 2014 the Eugene H. Gardner Sale featured examples of this coin in MS-65 (ex Eliasberg), MS-64, and MS-62. *MS-60 to 62:* 25 to 32. *MS-63:* 12 to 15. *MS-64:* 6 to 9. *MS-65 or better:* 3 or 4.

Availability in circulated grades: Thousands exist, but it is probably less than one percent of the original mintage, a comment appropriate to all New Orleans dimes.

Characteristics of striking: This issue is sometimes seen lightly struck at Liberty's head and the corresponding area of the reverse, in common with other dimes of the era, often due to relapping, removing many details.

Notes: With drapery at the elbow, as are all from this point forward. There are two distinctive reverses for this issue. Brian Greer devotes several pages to discussing both of them, calling the earlier the "Closed-Bud Reverse" and the later, or regular style, the "Open-Bud Reverse." This has to do with little slits or lines at the end of the buds on the laurel wreath creating an "open bud." Elsewhere in numismatics the additions to the wreath are called "berries." In nature the laurel is a flowering plant.

Gerry Fortin states on his website: "There is also an open question as to whether the stated mintage for 1841-O dimes is accurate. Variety 105 with a shattered reverse from use in 1842 and Variety 116 with a reverse die previously known from limited 1842 coinage suggest that 1841 New Orleans dimes could have been struck in 1842 and included in the 1842-O mintage report." F-101 to 115. 10 obverse dies combined with 13 reverse dies.

The 1841-O dimes have Transitional Reverses with Large O and Small O mintmarks, and leftover reverses from 1840. F-101 and 102. Regular reverses have Medium O and Small O mintmarks.

G-4	F-12	VF-20	EF-40	AU-50	MS-60	MS-63	MS-64	MS-65
$30	$50	$100	$150	$325	$850	$1,400	$5,500	$10,000

1842

Circulation-strike mintage: 1,887,500

Proof mintage: 6–10

Availability in Mint State: In 2015 the Eugene H. Gardner Sale featured an example of this coin in MS-66. *MS-60 to 62:* 70 to 90. *MS-63:* 40 to 50. *MS-64:* 25 to 30. *MS-65 or better:* 15 to 20.

actual size: 17.9 mm

Availability in circulated grades: This date is plentiful in all grades, but is not seen as often as its New Orleans Mint counterpart.

Characteristics of striking: This issue is usually well struck.

Proofs: There are two die pairs.[13] The Eugene H. Gardner Sale in 2015 also featured an example of this coin in PF-65 (ex Norweb). Approximately four examples have been certified.

Notes: This is one of the more plentiful dimes of the era and is easily obtainable in virtually any business-state grade desired. F-101 to 108. Seven obverse dies and seven reverse dies.

G-4	F-12	VF-20	EF-40	AU-50	MS-60
$20	$30	$40	$70	$150	$400

MS-63	MS-64	MS-65	PF-60	PF-63	PF-65
$650	$1,250	$3,000	$10,000	$20,000	$50,000

1842-O

**Circulation-strike mintage:
2,020,000**

Availability in Mint State: These
are very rare and are certainly one
of the most elusive varieties in the
series. It almost strains credulity
that a coin with a mintage on the

actual size: 17.9 mm

long side of two million would be
an ultra-rarity in Mint State. Gerry Fortin reports that known Mint State coins are all
of the Large O style. In 2015 the Eugene H. Gardner Sale featured examples of this
coin in MS-65 and MS-62. *MS-60 to 62:* 10 to 13. *MS-63:* 5 to 7. *MS-64:* 1 or 2.
MS-65 or better: 1 or 2.[14]

Availability in circulated grades: It is estimated that 4,000 to 8,000 survive—a tiny
fraction of the mintage.

Characteristics of striking: This issue is not as well struck as the Philadelphia Mint
version of the same date. They are typically weak at the "check points" for a dime of
this era—Liberty's head and the corresponding part of the wreath on the reverse.
These are occasionally seen with poor reverse details due to excessively relapped dies.[15]

Notes: The 1842-O dime is one of those curious pieces in American numismatics
which is readily enough available, indeed common, in low grades, but emerges as a
major rarity in Mint State. The reason is that the pieces attracted no numismatic interest at the time of issue. Thus, the survival of Mint State coins is strictly a matter of
chance. The Small O is scarcer than the Medium O mintmark. It has been questioned
as to whether the published mintage figure is accurate. F-101 to 107. Four obverse
dies and five reverse dies.

G-4	F-12	VF-20	EF-40	AU-50	MS-60	MS-63	MS-64	MS-65
$45	$100	$200	$500	$1,500	$2,750	$5,000	$7,500	$20,000

1843

**Circulation-strike mintage:
1,370,000**

Proof mintage: *10–15*

Availability in Mint State:
Higher-level Mint State pieces
are rare, as most in the Mint State
category hover in the MS-60 to 63

actual size: 17.9 mm

range. In 2014 the Eugene H. Gardner Sale featured an example of this coin in MS-66.
MS-60 to 62: 35 to 45. *MS-63:* 18 to 22. *MS-64:* 12 to 15. *MS-65 or better:* 4 to 6.[16]

Availability in circulated grades: These are easy to find in any desired grade.

Characteristics of striking: This issue is usually well struck, but there are some
exceptions.

Proofs: F-103. Approximately 15 examples have been certified.

Notes: F-101 to 106. Five obverse dies and six reverse dies.

G-4	F-12	VF-20	EF-40	AU-50	MS-60
$20	$30	$40	$70	$150	$475

MS-63	MS-64	MS-65	PF-60	PF-63	PF-65
$850	$1,850	$3,500	$5,000	$10,000	$22,500

1843-O

Circulation-strike mintage: 150,000

actual size: 17.9 mm

Availability in Mint State: This issue is exceedingly rare in Mint State, and only a few exist. From the Eliasberg Collection Sale, lot 1129: "MS-66. Deeply lustrous and frosty, extraordinarily so. Just a few tiny marks away from absolute perfection. Reverse lightly struck on the wreath, as always on authentic specimens." In 2014 the Eugene H. Gardner Sale featured an example of this coin in MS-62. *MS-60 to 62:* 1. *MS-63:* 0. *MS-64:* 0. *MS-65 or better:* 1.

Availability in circulated grades: This issue is fairly scarce in all grades, and is particularly elusive in EF and AU. The population is probably only in the mid-hundreds, less than one half of one percent of the mintage.

Characteristics of striking: These are often lightly struck on the head of Liberty. On the reverse the striking of the laurel leaves varies.

Notes: The 1843-O is one of the key issues of its era, and in just AU preservation an offering would be truly memorable, in MS-60 extraordinary. F-101.

G-4	F-12	VF-20	EF-40	AU-50	MS-60	MS-63	MS-64	MS-65
$200	$600	$1,350	$3,500	$11,000	$75,000			

1844

Circulation-strike mintage: 72,500

Proof mintage: 4–8

actual size: 17.9 mm

Availability in Mint State: This issue is very rare, more so than realized. Over the years, the author has handled more Proofs than Mint State coins! However, the 1846 is rarer yet. In 2014 the Eugene H. Gardner sale featured an example of this coin in MS-64. *MS-60 to 62:* 3 to 5. *MS-63:* 1 or 2. *MS-64:* 1 or 2. *MS-65 or better:* 1.

Availability in circulated grades: This is a well-known scarcity, indeed perhaps the best known among Liberty Seated dimes of this era due to its low mintage. However, the interested collector will have no difficulty obtaining one, with the typical grade being Good, Very Good, or Fine. EF and AU pieces, particularly the latter, are rare. Beginning in 2003, Heritage Auctions offered a hoard of 612 coins in various circulated grades assembled by Terry Brand, a Los Angeles collector who accumulated more than 900 coins, including purchasing more than 450 from Larry Briggs.[17] Most of these were later sold by Heritage Auctions. While he was buying, other examples were available in the marketplace.

Characteristics of striking: This issue is usually fairly well struck.

Proofs: F-101. In 2014 the Eugene H. Gardner Sale featured examples of this coin in PF-65 (ex Pittman) and PF-64 (ex Richmond). Approximately seven examples have been certified.

Notes: The 1844 dime, the famous "Orphan Annie" variety, is the best-known Liberty Seated dime of the era, although in high grades a number of the New Orleans pieces are rarer (although a high grade 1844 Philadelphia Mint dime is nothing to be sneezed at). The "Orphan Annie" nickname was first used by Frank C. Ross in the April 1931 issue of *Hobbies Magazine*. Ross held a monthly column into the 1950s and periodically offered suggestions as to the coin's supposed rarity. Ross also enlisted others to hype the 1844 dime, and in October 1935 William Brimelow of Elkhart, Indiana, published an article in *The Numismatist*. The gist was that with a mintage of 72,500 they should be common. Instead, according to Brimelow, they are much rarer than the 1846 with a mintage of 31,200. Were they melted at the Mint? Did some speculator buy most of them? Or . . .? As a result the 1844 is an orphan, so to speak, all by itself figuratively. Today this makes interesting reading. In actuality, the 1846 *is* rarer.

The first edition of *A Guide Book of United States Coins*, 1946, had the following:

> Orphan Annie Dime. The record shows that 72,500 dimes were minted in 1844. For some mysterious reason very few of these dimes are still available, and old collectors state that they have been a scarce item back as far as can be remembered. The dimes of 1846, for instance, are much more plentiful though less than half as many were struck. Many explanations have been advanced, but none has been proved. Among the most popular theories and legends are the following: melted by the government; melted by speculators, because their bullion value exceeded their monetary value; 50,000 of the dimes were lost at sea en route to New Orleans; a great quantity were destroyed in the great Chicago fire, or the Johnstown Flood; during the Mexican War our soldiers were paid off in 1844 dimes, and the coins remained in Mexico; 70,000 dimes of 1844 were sent overland to the forty-niners in California, but before reaching the destination by the Santa Fe Trail they were seized by bandits who cached them. The bandits who were later killed carried the secret of the hiding place to their shallow graves.

This romantic notation was dropped from later *Guide Book* issues, presumably due to lack of space.

F-101 and 102. Two obverse dies and two reverse dies.

G-4	F-12	VF-20	EF-40	AU-50	MS-60
$200	$375	$600	$1,000	$1,750	$4,000
MS-63	**MS-64**	**MS-65**	**PF-60**	**PF-63**	**PF-65**
$11,500	$15,000	$27,500	$12,500	$27,500	$50,000

1845

Circulation-strike mintage: 1,755,000

Proof mintage: 6–10

Availability in Mint State:
MS-60 to 62: 120 to 140.
MS-63: 50 to 65. *MS-64:* 40 to
50. *MS-65 or better:* 30 to 40.

actual size: 17.9 mm

Availability in circulated grades: This issue is readily available in all grades.

Characteristics of striking: These are usually seen well struck.

Proofs: The 8 and 4 are heavily double-punched, while the 5 is less so. There are artifacts near stars one through six and twelve through thirteen. The reverse has a die line through the TE, continuing to the rim above the S in STATES. The Louis E. Eliasberg Sale in 1997 featured an example of this coin in PF-65. In 2015 the Eugene H. Gardner Sale featured an example of this coin in PF-66 (ex Pittman). Approximately six examples have been certified.

Notes: F-101 to 110. Six obverse dies and nine reverse dies.

G-4	F-12	VF-20	EF-40	AU-50	MS-60
$20	$30	$40	$65	$155	$425

MS-63	MS-64	MS-65	PF-60	PF-63	PF-65
$800	$1,250	$3,000	$5,000	$10,000	$20,000

1845-O

Circulation-strike mintage: 230,000

Availability in Mint State: In 1977, the Eliasberg Sale featured an example of this coin in lot 1132: "MS-67. Brilliant, lustrous, and frosty, just about as nice as it was on the day of coining. . . ." This

actual size: 17.9 mm

was graded as MS-69 by PCGS when it appeared in the Gardner Collection in 2015. Today this stands as the finest example of this issue. Low ranges of Mint State examples only appear over a wide span of years, and we would not want to take bets that most such pieces really are Uncirculated. *MS-60 to 62:* 1 or 2. *MS-63:* 0. *MS-64:* 0. *MS-65 or better:* 1.

Availability in circulated grades: This issue is fairly scarce, though not as scarce as 1843-O (as comparison in mintages indicates). They are rare in EF or finer, and are quite rare in AU with mint luster.

Characteristics of striking: These are usually fairly well struck, but there are exceptions.

Notes: F-101.

G-4	F-12	VF-20	EF-40	AU-50	MS-60	MS-63	MS-64	MS-65
$100	$250	$600	$1,100	$3,000	$12,000	$25,000		

1846

Circulation-strike mintage: 31,300

Proof mintage: 8–12

actual size: 17.9 mm

Availability in Mint State: This issue is exceedingly rare; probably just two or three exist. In 2014 the Eugene H. Gardner Sale featured an example of this coin in MS-63. *MS-60 to 62:* 1 or 2. *MS-63:* 1. *MS-64:* 0. *MS-65 or better:* 0.

Availability in circulated grades: These are quite scarce in circulated grades. When usually seen, coins are apt to be Good to Fine. VF pieces are scarcer yet, EF examples are rare, and AU coins with luster are extremely rare.

Characteristics of striking: Sometimes this issue is lightly struck at the head of Liberty along with her neckline and lower leg, resulting in a flat obverse appearance on full VF or EF specimens.

Proofs: There are some minor die flaws and/or repunching at the 46 of the date. There are artifacts at stars two through six, less so at star seven but still visible, and stars 12 through 13, most being cusp-shaped as on half dimes of this year. From this point on, cusps appear with regularity as part of the artifacts mentioned. Approximately 18 examples have been certified.

Notes: The 1846 dime, with its low mintage, is even rarer than the famous 1844 "Orphan Annie." F-101 and 102. Two obverse dies and two reverse dies.

G-4	F-12	VF-20	EF-40	AU-50	MS-60
$400	$800	$1,500	$2,500	$7,000	$25,000
MS-63	**MS-64**	**MS-65**	**PF-60**	**PF-63**	**PF-65**
$50,000			$7,500	$15,000	$35,000

1847

Circulation-strike mintage: 245,000

Proof mintage: 3–5

actual size: 17.9 mm

Availability in Mint State: This issue is rare, with most examples seen being in the MS-60 to 63 category. Gerry Fortin considers such coins to be unappreciated and undervalued.[18] In 2014 the Eugene H. Gardner Sale featured an example of this coin in MS-64. *MS-60 to 62:* 10 to 13. *MS-63:* 3 or 4. *MS-64:* 1 or 2. *MS-65 or better:* 1.

Availability in circulated grades: This issue is fairly scarce, as the mintage suggests, but is not widely sought after. There are enough to supply the demand, particularly in lower grades.

Characteristics of striking: These are usually seen well struck.

Proofs: F-104. The date is high and impacting the base. There is a raised die line under the 47. In 2014 the Eugene H. Gardner Sale featured an example of this coin in PF-66 (ex Eliasberg). Approximately three examples have been certified.

Notes: While the 1847 is not in the class of the 1844 or 1846 Philadelphia Mint dimes, it handily out-distances the 1842, 1843, and 1845 in all grades. One interesting variety, illustrated by Breen and Greer, shows the date numerals overlapping the base of Liberty. Numerals of this date were too large for the space provided, giving it a crowded effect. F-101 to 104.

G-4	F-12	VF-20	EF-40	AU-50	MS-60
$35	$55	$85	$180	$425	$1,550

MS-63	MS-64	MS-65	PF-60	PF-63	PF-65
$4,000	$6,000	$10,000	$8,500	$15,000	$30,000

1848

Circulation-strike mintage: 451,500

Proof mintage: *10–15*

Availability in Mint State: This issue is scarce in Mint State, but on an absolute basis enough are available to satisfy the specialist. As

actual size: 17.9 mm

is the norm, most are in lower Mint State echelons. In 2015 the Eugene H. Gardner Sale featured an example of this coin in MS-65. *MS-60 to 62:* 30 to 40. *MS-63:* 15 to 20. *MS-64:* 12 to 15. *MS-65 or better:* 6 to 8.[19]

Availability in circulated grades: This issue is fairly plentiful in low grades, although not among the commonest issues of the era. EF and AU coins are slightly scarce.

Characteristics of striking: These are sometimes seen lightly struck at the head and corresponding areas of the reverse.

Proofs: The date is high with 18 touching the base, and there are traces of artifacts at stars two through six. In 2015 the Eugene H. Gardner Sale featured an example of this coin in PF-65 (ex Eliasberg). Approximately 16 examples have been certified.

Notes: The dates on the various 1848 dimes seem overly large for the space beneath Liberty, giving the numerals a crowded appearance. F-101 to 103. Three obverse dies and three reverse dies.

G-4	F-12	VF-20	EF-40	AU-50	MS-60
$30	$50	$75	$100	$225	$725

MS-63	MS-64	MS-65	PF-60	PF-63	PF-65
$1,000	$2,500	$6,500	$8,500	$15,000	$20,000

1849

Circulation-strike mintage: 839,000

Proof mintage: 4–6

actual size: 17.9 mm

Availability in Mint State: These are rare in Mint State, although enough exist that specialists will not run short. Again, most pieces are in lower levels of Mint State, say MS-60 through MS-63. In 2014 and 2015 the Eugene H. Gardner Sale featured two examples of this coin in MS-66. *MS-60 to 62:* 25 to 32. *MS-63:* 10 to 13. *MS-64:* 5 to 7. *MS-65 or better:* 7 to 9.[20]

Availability in circulated grades: This issue is plentiful in circulated grades.

Characteristics of striking: These are occasionally seen lightly struck on Liberty's head and on the corresponding part of the reverse.

Proofs: Greer-103: "9 Over 8. An obvious overdate is listed by Breen. Proof only." Today this is known as F-104 as "prior 1849/8," and presently as "Repunched 89." In 1997, the Louis E. Eliasberg Sale contained an example of this coin in lot 1137: G-103, PF-65. Approximately six examples have been certified.

Notes: In this year the Mint finally gave up on trying to squeeze large date numbers into small spaces, and the date logotype is much smaller than on 1847–1848, thus giving ample surrounding area. F-101 to 107. Five obverse dies and five reverse dies.

G-4	F-12	VF-20	EF-40	AU-50	MS-60
$25	$35	$50	$100	$225	$500
MS-63	**MS-64**	**MS-65**	**PF-60**	**PF-63**	**PF-65**
$900	$1,500	$3,500	$10,000	$15,000	$45,000

1849-O

Circulation-strike mintage: 300,000

actual size: 17.9 mm

Availability in Mint State: In Mint State the 1849-O was considered to be a nearly impossible rarity. Today a number of them have been certified, but it is still a key to the series. In 2014 the Eugene H. Gardner Sale featured an example of this coin in MS-64. *MS-60 to 62:* 7 to 9. *MS-63:* 5 to 7. *MS-64:* 1 or 2. *MS-65 or better:* 0.

Availability in circulated grades: This is a well-known, semi-key date. Perhaps a couple of thousand exist, mostly in worn grades.

Characteristics of striking: A light strike at the top of the obverse and corresponding part of the reverse is the rule, not the exception.

Notes: Four die combinations are known, including the Large O (F-101) and the Small O (F-102 to 104) mintmarks which differ dramatically in appearance. In 1893 Heaton described the 1849-O as "somewhat scarce." According to Fortin, the 1849-O date is also well-known for having been struck with rotated die alignment; the most of any date in the series. F-101 to 104. Three obverse dies and two reverse dies.

Large O Mintmark

Small O Mintmark

G-4	F-12	VF-20	EF-40	AU-50	MS-60	MS-63	MS-64	MS-65
$35	$80	$165	$400	$950	$2,500	$5,500	$13,500	$50,000

1850

Circulation-strike mintage: 1,931,500

Proof mintage: *4–6*

actual size: 17.9 mm

Availability in Mint State: This issue is readily available within context of this general era, although far scarcer than the common issues of the 1880s. Walter Breen noted that most Mint State pieces are from a hoard of about 30 coins discovered circa 1977. MS-65 or finer coins are challenging to find. In 2014 the Eugene H. Gardner Sale featured an example of this coin in MS-64. *MS-60 to 62:* 80 to 100. *MS-63:* 30 to 40. *MS-64:* 20 to 25. *MS-65 or better:* 8 to 10.[21]

Availability in circulated grades: This issue is common in circulated grades.

Characteristics of striking: These are usually well struck.

Proofs: In Proof format this was considered to be rarer in the 1950s and 1960s than it is today. Most of the known examples have appeared since then. Still, on an absolute basis it is a first-class rarity. In 2015 the Eugene H. Gardner Sale featured examples of this coin in PF-67 (ex Kaufman) and PF-64 (ex Pittman). Approximately seven examples have been certified.

Notes: Except as Proof strikes, the 1850 dime is readily available in all grades. F-101 to 112. There are 9 obverse dies and 11 reverse dies.

G-4	F-12	VF-20	EF-40	AU-50	MS-60
$20	$35	$45	$65	$165	$325

MS-63	MS-64	MS-65	PF-60	PF-63	PF-65
$700	$1,500	$5,000	$10,000	$15,000	$40,000

1850-O

Circulation-strike mintage: 510,000

Availability in Mint State: The 1850-O is rare in Mint State but is available to the patient collector. Possibly 20 or more are known, some of which are gems (but data may represent resubmissions). In

actual size: 17.9 mm

2015 the Eugene H. Gardner Sale featured an example of this coin in MS-67, MS-66, and MS-65. *MS-60 to 62:* 4 to 6. *MS-63:* 4 to 6. *MS-64:* 4 or 5. *MS-65 or better:* 2 or 3.

Availability in circulated grades: These are somewhat scarce, but are hardly rare. Most are in low grades.

Characteristics of striking: This issue is often seen with Liberty's head lightly struck and with light striking on the corresponding part of the reverse.

Notes: Three sizes of mintmarks occur and are nicely illustrated in the Greer text and Fortin website, the Small O having perhaps 30 percent of the total area of the Large O, with the Medium O being closer to the latter than to the former. PCGS and NGC take no note of mintmark sizes, thus the Large O, which in high grades is rarer than the Small O, would probably cost little if any more to purchase. In Mint State the Medium O is the rarest. F-101 to 107. Four obverse dies and five reverse dies.

G-4	F-12	VF-20	EF-40	AU-50	MS-60	MS-63	MS-64	MS-65
$40	$100	$125	$325	$900	$2,250	$5,000	$6,500	$8,500

1851

Circulation-strike mintage: 1,026,500

Proof mintage: See below

Availability in Mint State: This issue is scarce in the context of an early Liberty Seated Philadelphia Mint dime, but in absolute terms

actual size: 17.9 mm

this issue is readily available to specialists. Most examples are at lower Mint State levels. In 2015 the Eugene H. Gardner Sale featured an example of this coin in MS-67. *MS-60 to 62:* 40 to 50. *MS-63:* 15 to 20. *MS-64:* 10 to 13. *MS-65 or better:* 4 to 6.

Availability in circulated grades: This issue is easy to find in circulated grades.

Characteristics of striking: These are usually seen well struck, but are sometimes weak on the head of Liberty and/or ribbon bow area.

Proofs: Some coins of 1851 and 1853 have been called Proofs over a long period of years, but it is uncertain if they were actually struck as such or they were from dies polished after relapping or for other reasons. No Proof sets of this year or of 1853 are known.

Notes: The 1851 is a readily available date in all grades from well-worn up through lower Mint State levels. Date placement differences are very slight for this year. F-101 to 108. Six obverse dies and seven reverse dies.

G-4	F-12	VF-20	EF-40	AU-50	MS-60	MS-63	MS-64	MS-65
$20	$30	$45	$80	$200	$450	$850	$2,000	$5,000

1851-O

Circulation-strike mintage: 400,000

Availability in Mint State: This issue is very rare in Mint State, and is one of the scarcer issues of the series. Many are colorfully toned. In 2015 the Eugene H. Gardner Sale featured an example of this coin in MS-65. *MS-60 to 62:* 3 to 5. *MS-63:* 1. *MS-64:* 1. *MS-65 or better:* 1.

actual size: 17.9 mm

Availability in circulated grades: This issue is fairly scarce in lower circulated grades, as the mintage would tend to indicate. EF and, in particular, lustrous AU coins are very elusive.

Characteristics of striking: These are sometimes lightly struck on Liberty's head on the obverse and on the corresponding part of the reverse. According to Fortin, the dies were relapped at some point during usage leading to weak drapery and overall obverse device details.

Notes: In keeping with most other New Orleans issues of the era, the 1851-O is very elusive in higher states of preservation, as there is no numismatic interest in coins from this mint at the time of issue. Large O mintmark. F-101 with just one die combination. The large mintage suggests that others may exist. Walter Breen lists a Small O mintmark, but this variety has not been confirmed by Gerry Fortin and those who contribute to his website.

G-4	F-12	VF-20	EF-40	AU-50	MS-60	MS-63	MS-64	MS-65
$35	$75	$125	$325	$1,100	$2,500	$3,750	$6,500	$17,500

1852

Circulation-strike mintage: 1,535,000

Proof mintage: *5–10*

Availability in Mint State: These are readily available in Mint State. *MS-60 to 62:* 150 to 250. *MS-63:* 75 to 100. *MS-64:* 50 to 65. *MS-65 or better:* 30 to 40.

actual size: 17.9 mm

Availability in circulated grades: This issue is common in circulated grades.

Characteristics of striking: These are usually well struck.

Proofs: From the Louis E. Eliasberg Collection Sale: "Proof-66. No repunching at date, thus not listed by Brian Greer. Minor vestiges of artifacts at stars two through six. On reverse under magnification diagonal die lines can be seen at the bow." In 2015 the Eugene H. Gardner Sale featured an example of this coin in PF-65 (ex Pittman). Approximately 13 examples have been certified.

Notes: F-101 to 118. There are 14 obverse dies and 18 reverse dies, a record up to this point in time. F-105b, 110b, and 112b are late die states with partial or retained cud die breaks.

G-4	F-12	VF-20	EF-40	AU-50	MS-60
$20	$30	$45	$65	$150	$325

MS-63	MS-64	MS-65	PF-60	PF-63	PF-65
$650	$1,000	$2,500	$6,500	$12,500	$25,000

1852-O

Circulation-strike mintage: 430,000

actual size: 17.9 mm

Availability in Mint State: This issue is quite scarce in Mint State, particularly in higher levels. The Louis E. Eliasberg Sale in 1997 featured an example of this coin in MS-66. In 2014 and 2015 the Eugene H. Gardner Sale featured examples of this coin in MS-65 and MS-63. *MS-60 to 62:* 20 to 25. *MS-63:* 7 to 10. *MS-64:* 5 to 7. *MS-65 or better:* 2 or 3.

Availability in circulated grades: This issue is scarce, as the mintage suggests. It was probably the instance that this issue saw more melting than usual due to the high price of silver on the international markets.

Characteristics of striking: Some light areas are typical of this issue.

Notes: F-101 and 102 share the same obverse with high date sloping down to the right, in combination with two reverse dies.

G-4	F-12	VF-20	EF-40	AU-50	MS-60	MS-63	MS-64	MS-65
$35	$100	$225	$350	$550	$1,800	$3,600	$5,000	$12,500

1853, No Arrows

Circulation-strike mintage: 95,000

actual size: 17.9 mm

Availability in Mint State: Mint State specimens come on the market with some regularity, including at the gem level. This suggests that a group of high-grade coins may have existed at one time. Indeed, Walter Breen noted that a "batch" was rescued by numismatist Harold P. Newlin before 1883, but no specific information has been found relating to this. As is seen, extant Mint State coins are clustered at the top end, an unusual situation.

The Louis E. Eliasberg Sale in 1997 featured an example of this coin in MS-66. In 2014 and 2015 the Eugene H. Gardner Sale featured two examples of this coin in MS-68. *MS-60 to 62:* 10 to 13. *MS-63:* 15 to 20. *MS-64:* 40 to 50. *MS-65 or better:* 20 to 30.

Availability in circulated grades: This issue is very scarce in circulated grades. They are usually seen in grades of About Good to Very Good or, interestingly, in higher grades such as VF and EF.[22]

Characteristics of striking: These are usually seen well struck.

Notes: The 1853, No Arrows, dime is an anomaly, struck to the early (before February 21, 1853), heavier weight standard. Conventional wisdom is that many of these were melted by the Treasury and were not released, thereby resulting in effective distribution far lower than the 95,000 mintage. This thought echoes throughout numismatic writings for many years. Whatever the case may be, this variety is well-known as a dime that is scarce in an absolute sense when the entire population is considered, but in Mint State survivors are more plentiful than logic suggests—indicating a special circumstance of saving as noted above. F-101 and 102 share a common reverse die.

G-4	F-12	VF-20	EF-40	AU-50	MS-60	MS-63	MS-64	MS-65
$175	$350	$500	$700	$850	$1,000	$1,650	$2,500	$3,000

1853–1855, Arrows at Date (Variety 3)

Arrows were placed at the sides of the date for a brief period starting in 1853. They were placed there to denote the reduction of weight under the terms of the Act of February 21, 1853.

Designer: Christian Gobrecht. Arrows were added by someone on the Mint staff.

Specifications: *Composition:* 90 percent silver, 10 percent copper. *Diameter:* 17.9 mm. *Weight:* 38.4 grains (2.49 grams). *Edge:* Reeded.

1853, With Arrows

Circulation-strike mintage: 12,173,000

Proof mintage: See below

Availability in Mint State: These are readily available in Mint State, although on an absolute basis they are scarcer than certification

actual size: 17.9 mm

service data suggests. The reason for this is that dimes of the With-Arrows style have significantly higher value than, for example, more common issues of the late 1880s, and because of this value more have been sent to the certification services. Regardless, specimen examples can easily be obtained in Mint State. *MS-60 to 62:* 800 to 1,000. *MS-63:* 300 to 400. *MS-64:* 200 to 250. *MS-65 or better:* 125 to 150.

Availability in circulated grades: This issue is extremely common. Take your pick of any grade you want. From this year forward the survival ratio of dimes is higher than earlier years (for which many coins were melted).

Characteristics of striking: These are usually well struck. A few are highly prooflike, especially on the obverse.

Proofs: See comments under the 1851 Liberty Seated dime. Opinion is divided, and as of June 2015, NGC and PCGS each listed five Proofs in their reports. This raises the old question: Is a coin a Proof if it looks like one? This can be argued *ad infinitum*. On the other side of the question, the Mint issued 2,350 Proofs and no circulation strikes of the 1878 Shield nickel, but many of the coins are frosty without a hint of mirror surface.

Notes: On many dies the position of the arrowheads varied in relation to the date logotype. Other dies were hubbed—with the date and arrows in the master die. A detailed explanation of this can be found on Gerry Fortin's website, including descriptions of more than two dozen unhubbed varieties.

For unhubbed dies F-101 to 125. There are 23 obverse dies and 25 reverse dies.

G-4	F-12	VF-20	EF-40	AU-50	MS-60
$20	$25	$35	$55	$165	$350

MS-63	MS-64	MS-65	PF-60	PF-63	PF-65
$650	$1,000	$1,550	$10,000	$20,000	$35,000

1853-O

Circulation-strike mintage: 1,100,000

actual size: 17.9 mm

Availability in Mint State: This issue is quite scarce in Mint State. Logic would dictate that this piece should be about 10 or 11 times scarcer in Mint State than the 1853 Philadelphia version, but in actuality far fewer were saved proportionally, and it is far rarer. As the market differential doesn't reflect this, the 1853-O represents an excellent value if a Mint State piece can be located. In 2014 the Eugene H. Gardner Sale featured an example of this coin in MS-65. *MS-60 to 62:* 5 to 8. *MS-63:* 2 or 3. *MS-64:* 2 or 3. *MS-65 or better:* 1 or 2.[23]

Availability in circulated grades: These are common in well-worn grades, with more than enough to go around, although it is not as plentiful as its Philadelphia Mint cousin. AU coins are very scarce.

Characteristics of striking: This issue is often lightly struck on the head of Liberty and the corresponding part of the reverse, endemic with most New Orleans issues of this era.

Notes: Fortin states that all 1853-O obverse dies were hubbed from a die containing date and arrows. Accordingly, there are no date or arrow placement variations on 1853 New Orleans dimes. Several obverse dies were poorly hubbed leading to weak dates. F-101 to 108. Four obverse dies and three reverse dies.

G-4	F-12	VF-20	EF-40	AU-50	MS-60	MS-63	MS-64	MS-65
$25	$85	$125	$300	$650	$2,250	$5,000	$6,750	$12,000

1854

Circulation-strike mintage: 4,470,000

Proof mintage: *8–12*

actual size: 17.9 mm

Availability in Mint State: The 1854 dime is readily available in Mint State, but markedly less so than the 1853 of the same type. *MS-60 to 62:* 250 to 325. *MS-63:* 140 to 160. *MS-64:* 100 to 125. *MS-65 or better:* 50 to 80.

Availability in circulated grades: This issue is common in circulated grades.

Characteristics of striking: These are usually seen well struck, but there are exceptions.

Proofs: From the Louis E. Eliasberg Sale in 1997: "Proof-66. Date and arrows high, barely touching base. Tiny die defect at star 6." In 2014 the Eugene H. Gardner Sale featured an example of this coin in PF-65. Approximately nine examples have been certified.

Notes: A readily available dime, second only—and a distant second—to the 1853, With Arrows, among issues of this type. F-101 to 112. All dies were hubbed, and there are no positional variations.

G-4	F-12	VF-20	EF-40	AU-50	MS-60
$20	$25	$35	$65	$175	$350

MS-63	MS-64	MS-65	PF-60	PF-63	PF-65
$700	$950	$1,750	$6,000	$10,000	$20,000

1854-O

Circulation-strike mintage: 1,770,000

actual size: 17.9 mm

Availability in Mint State: The 1854-O is decidedly elusive in Mint State, but is not a rarity; there are enough around that specialists can find one without difficulty. Most are at lower Mint State levels. In 2015 the Eugene H. Gardner Sale featured examples of this coin in MS-67 and MS-66. *MS-60 to 62:* 70 to 90. *MS-63:* 30 to 40. *MS-64:* 20 to 25. *MS-65 or better:* 12 to 15.

Availability in circulated grades: This issue is easy to obtain, mostly in lower grades. However, the number of EF and AU coins is more than adequate to supply the number of dime specialists.

Characteristics of striking: These can sometimes be seen lightly struck at Liberty's head and the corresponding part of the reverse.

Notes: All dies were hubbed and there are no positional variations. F-101 to 112.

G-4	F-12	VF-20	EF-40	AU-50	MS-60	MS-63	MS-64	MS-65
$40	$85	$115	$150	$250	$450	$1,000	$1,650	$4,500

1855

Circulation-strike mintage: 2,075,000

Proof mintage: 8–12

actual size: 17.9 mm

Availability in Mint State: These are quite scarce in the author's experience, although certification numbers do not necessarily reflect this. In 2014 the Eugene H. Gardner Sale featured an example of this coin in MS-67. *MS-60 to 62:* 100 to 125. *MS-63:* 40 to 55. *MS-64:* 25 to 32. *MS-65 or better:* 16 to 20.

Availability in circulated grades: This issue is common in circulated grades.

Characteristics of striking: These are usually with areas of light striking.

Proofs: From the Louis E. Eliasberg Sale in 1997: "Proof-65. Date numerals and arrowheads slightly double-punched in the die. Some raised die finish lines are seen, particularly within the wreath on the reverse, indicating this was a very early striking from new Proof dies. After repeated strikings, die finish lines wear away." Approximately 15 examples have been certified.

Notes: All dies were hubbed, and there are no positional variations. F-101 to 108. Several obverse dies are seen with weakly hubbed dates and arrows, especially F-105 and 106.

G-4	F-12	VF-20	EF-40	AU-50	MS-60
$20	$25	$35	$65	$185	$350
MS-63	**MS-64**	**MS-65**	**PF-60**	**PF-63**	**PF-65**
$850	$1,100	$3,000	$6,000	$10,000	$20,000

1856–1860, Variety 2 Resumed, With Weight Standard of Variety 3

The design is the same as that used before 1853, but with the new weight adopted by the Coinage Act of February 21, 1853. The arrows indicating the change in weight were removed. Accordingly, many collectors building type sets ignore this sub-type.

Designer: Christian Gobrecht.

Specifications: *Composition:* 90 percent silver, 10 percent copper. *Diameter:* 17.9 mm. *Weight:* 38.4 grains (2.49 grams). *Edge:* Reeded.

1856, Small Date

Circulation-strike mintage: 5,057,500

Proof mintage: 40–60

actual size: 17.9 mm

Availability in Mint State: These are readily available, often with nice luster. *MS-60 to 62:* 150 to 200. *MS-63:* 80 to 100. *MS-64:* 50 to 70. *MS-65 or better:* 30 to 40.

Availability in circulated grades: This issue is easy to find in any and all grades.

Characteristics of striking: This issue is sometimes seen with light

Detail of Small Date.

striking on the top of the obverse and on the corresponding part of the reverse. On some, the denticles are flattened or missing.[24]

Proofs: F-101. Three obverse denticles at about the 4:30 position are flattened. Approximately 26 examples have been certified.

Notes: Small-date numerals fit comfortably into the space allotted with room to spare. The same logotype punch was used to make quarter-eagle dies. F-101 to 123 from 21 different obverse dies and 23 reverse dies. For the Large Date (see following entry) there are four varieties from four obverse and four reverse dies. The total mintage for both varieties is 5,780,000. From this it would seem that seven-eighths of the mintage was of the Small Date style and one-eighth of the Large Date, leading to the mintage estimates given here.

G-4	F-12	VF-20	EF-40	AU-50	MS-60
$17	$20	$30	$60	$150	$325
MS-63	MS-64	MS-65	PF-60	PF-63	PF-65
$550	$1,000	$2,250	$2,500	$3,500	$8,000

1856, Large Date

Circulation-strike mintage: 722,500

actual size: 17.9 mm

Detail of Large Date.

Availability in Mint State: This issue is extremely rare and is one of the key Philadelphia Mint issues of the series. In 2014 and 2015 the Eugene H. Gardner Sale featured examples of this coin in MS-67 and MS-65. *MS-60 to 62:* 20 to 25. *MS-63:* 12 to 15. *MS-64:* 5 to 8. *MS-65 or better:* 3 to 5.

Availability in circulated grades: Circulated grades of this issue are somewhat scarce, and most are in very low grades.[25]

Characteristics of striking: This issue is usually well struck, but there is sometimes weakness on Liberty's head.

Notes: The Large Date is dramatically different from the Small Date. The latter has a slanting, or italic, 5 and very small numerals, while the former has an upright 5 and digits much greater in size. In fact, the Large Date is *oversized* for the space allotted, and at first glance seems incongruous. The Large Date is from the same logotype punch to make dies for half cents and $3 gold pieces. F-101 to 104, from four obverse dies and four reverse dies. F-103a has a severely relapped obverse die with considerable loss of device details.

G-4	F-12	VF-20	EF-40	AU-50	MS-60	MS-63	MS-64	MS-65
$40	$95	$125	$185	$300	$650	$2,250	$3,750	$9,500

1856-O

Circulation-strike mintage: 1,180,000

actual size: 17.9 mm

Availability in Mint State: These are quite rare in Mint State, as relatively few were saved at the time of issue. The same is generally true of other New Orleans varieties of the era. In 2014 and 2015 the Eugene H. Gardner Sale featured two examples of this coin in MS-65. *MS-60 to 62:* 40 to 55. *MS-63:* 18 to 22. *MS-64:* 10 to 14. *MS-65 or better:* 4 to 6.

Availability in circulated grades: This issue is slightly scarce, but is certainly available enough that any specialist can find one. They are rarer in EF or AU grades.

Characteristics of striking: These are often lightly struck at the top of the obverse and the corresponding part of the reverse.

Notes: The Medium O mintmark is scarce, and the Large O mintmark is seen much more often. A Small O (Breen-3299) has not been verified. F-101 to 109. F-104 and 105 have bold repunching on the date, and are pursued by variety specialists. Fivaz and Stanton list the Repunched Date as FS-10-1856o-2301. Six obverse dies and six reverse dies.

G-4	F-12	VF-20	EF-40	AU-50	MS-60	MS-63	MS-64	MS-65
$25	$70	$100	$155	$400	$850	$1,350	$2,650	$6,500

1856-S

Circulation-strike mintage: 70,000

Availability in Mint State: This issue is extremely rare in Mint State and only a few exist. As is true for so many rare Liberty Seated coins, grading numbers shift around and make it impossible to be precise. In

actual size: 17.9 mm

2015 the Eugene H. Gardner Sale featured examples of this coin in MS-64 (ex Norweb) and MS-63. *MS-60 to 62:* 3 to 5. *MS-63:* 1 or 2. *MS-64:* 2. *MS-65 or better:* 1.

Availability in circulated grades: This issue is very scarce overall, as the low mintage suggests. Most are in low grades with problems. EF coins are in the rare category, and an AU piece with luster is of notable numismatic significance.

Characteristics of striking: These are usually well struck.

Notes: 1856-S is important as it is the first San Francisco Mint coin of this denomination. At the time of issue, not a single numismatist desired to acquire San Francisco Mint pieces (ditto New Orleans coins), as emphasis was on "date only," and a readily available Philadelphia coin would fill the bill.

A large amount of all San Francisco Mint silver coinage was shipped to China, often by merchants and individuals sending money to their families back home.

Heaton commented as follows in 1893: "The mint mark letter S identifying this series [referring to all years] may also be divided into three sizes: the *large*, being somewhat larger than the letters of the legend, the *medium*, somewhat smaller, and the *small*, about half their height and quite minute." In the same text, Heaton noted that the 1856-S "is rare." F-101.

G-4	F-12	VF-20	EF-40	AU-50	MS-60	MS-63	MS-64	MS-65
$345	$800	$1,250	$1,800	$2,500	$7,250	$15,000	$25,000	$45,000

1857

Circulation-strike mintage: 5,580,000

Proof mintage: *45–60*

Availability in Mint State: This issue is readily available in Mint State. *MS-60 to 62:* 150 to 225. *MS-63:* 80 to 100. *MS-64:* 50 to 65. *MS-65 or better:* 20 to 30.

actual size: 17.9 mm

Availability in circulated grades: This is one of the most common dimes of the era.

Characteristics of striking: This issue is usually seen well struck, but there are exceptions.

Proofs: Approximately 70 examples have been certified.

Notes: This date is readily available in all grades. Proofs seem to be a bit scarcer than those for 1856, so the mintage may have been a bit less. F-101 to 115. There are 15 obverse dies and 15 reverse dies paired in sequence, suggesting that each pair was replaced in one action, rather than replacing individual dies as they became worn or unserviceable.

G-4	F-12	VF-20	EF-40	AU-50	MS-60
$17	$20	$30	$55	$150	$300

MS-63	MS-64	MS-65	PF-60	PF-63	PF-65
$550	$850	$2,000	$2,000	$3,000	$5,000

1857-O

Circulation-strike mintage: 1,540,000

actual size: 17.9 mm

Availability in Mint State: This issue is fairly scarce, but enough are around that the specialist will not go unsatisfied. *MS-60 to 62:* 110 to 130. *MS-63:* 50 to 65. *MS-64:* 30 to 40. *MS-65 or better:* 20 to 25.

Availability in circulated grades: These are common in proportion to the mintage—but are not as available as its Philadelphia Mint counterpart.

Characteristics of striking: This issue is usually seen well struck, but there are exceptions.

Notes: These are readily available as a New Orleans Mint issue, one of the few New Orleans dimes for which this comment can be made for Mint State examples. F-101 to 107. Six obverse dies and seven reverse dies.

G-4	F-12	VF-20	EF-40	AU-50	MS-60	MS-63	MS-64	MS-65
$20	$30	$40	$75	$200	$425	$750	$1,000	$2,000

1858

Circulation-strike mintage: 1,540,000

Proof mintage: unknown

actual size: 17.9 mm

Availability in Mint State: This issue is readily available, but is not common. Most have areas of light striking. *MS-60 to 62:* 120 to 140. *MS-63:* 55 to 70. *MS-64:* 35 to 45. *MS-65 or better:* 20 to 30.

Availability in circulated grades: In circulated grades this issue is easy to find.

Characteristics of striking: These are sometimes lightly struck at the top of the obverse and the corresponding part of the reverse. Cherrypicking is advised.

Proofs: Approximately 210 were made for inclusion in silver-Proof sets. Many seeking a run of Proof Liberty Seated dimes start their sets with this year. *PF-60 to 62:* 20 to 25. *PF-63:* 55 to 65. *PF-64:* 55 to 65. *PF-65 or better:* 20 to 25.

Notes: Ten obverse dies and ten reverse dies paired in sequence.

G-4	F-12	VF-20	EF-40	AU-50	MS-60
$17	$20	$30	$55	$150	$325
MS-63	MS-64	MS-65	PF-60	PF-63	PF-65
$550	$850	$2,000	$1,000	$1,750	$4,000

1858-O

Circulation-strike mintage: 290,000

Availability in Mint State: This issue is very rare in Mint State. In 2014 the Eugene H. Gardner Sale featured an example of this coin in MS-66. *MS-60 to 62:* 11 to 15. *MS-63:* 5 to 7. *MS-64:* 4 to 6. *MS-65 or better:* 4 to 6.[26]

actual size: 17.9 mm

Availability in circulated grades: These are scarce, but are available with searching. They are particularly elusive at the EF and AU levels.

Characteristics of striking: This issue is often lightly struck at the top of the obverse and on certain areas of the reverse.

Notes: Although 1858-O is not recognized as a key date, in Mint State it is a notable rarity simply because numismatists did not search for them until most had long since disappeared into circulation. F-101.

G-4	F-12	VF-20	EF-40	AU-50	MS-60	MS-63	MS-64	MS-65
$25	$55	$120	$200	$375	$950	$2,250	$4,250	$8,000

1858-S

Circulation-strike mintage: 60,000

Availability in Mint State: In Mint State this issue is exceedingly rare; virtually unobtainable. The Louis E. Eliasberg Sale in 1997 featured an example of this coin in MS-64. In 2014 and 2015 the

actual size: 17.9 mm

Eugene H. Gardner Sale featured examples of this coin in MS-66, MS-65, and MS-62. *MS-60 to 62:* 2 or 3. *MS-63:* 1 or 2. *MS-64:* 1 or 2. *MS-65 or better:* 2.

Availability in circulated grades: This issue is notably scarce and is a well-known key date. Most are in low grades and have problems, which is generally true for all San Francisco Liberty Seated coins of this decade. They are rarer still at higher levels such as EF and AU.

Characteristics of striking: These are usually seen fairly well struck.

Notes: In 1893 Heaton called this issue "rare." F-101 to 103. Two obverse dies and three reverse dies.

G-4	F-12	VF-20	EF-40	AU-50	MS-60	MS-63	MS-64	MS-65
$250	$450	$950	$1,700	$2,000	$8,000	$15,000	$25,000	$35,000

1859

**Circulation-strike mintage:
429,200**

Proof mintage: unknown

Availability in Mint State: A Mint
State coin of this issue can easily
be found with average sharpness,
but it can be challenging to find

actual size: 17.9 mm

one sharply struck. *MS-60 to 62:* 200 to 250. *MS-63:* 110 to 130. *MS-64:* 75 to 95.
MS-65 or better: 50 to 65.

Availability in circulated grades: This issue is scarce compared to higher-mintage issues of the year, but there are enough still around that no problem will be experienced in tracking down a decent specimen.

Characteristics of striking: These are sometimes, perhaps often, seen lightly struck on the head and corresponding part of the reverse.

Proofs: F-101 and 102. It is thought that hundreds of unsold Proofs were placed into circulation. *PF-60 to 62:* 130 to 160. *PF-63:* 155 to 175. *PF-64:* 150 to 170. *PF-65 or better:* 80 to 110.

Notes: F-101 to 107. Seven obverse dies and seven reverse dies paired in sequence, the first two only for Proofs.

G-4	F-12	VF-20	EF-40	AU-50	MS-60
$20	$22	$35	$65	$150	$325
MS-63	**MS-64**	**MS-65**	**PF-60**	**PF-63**	**PF-65**
$650	$850	$2,000	$900	$1,250	$2,000

1859-O

**Circulation-strike mintage:
480,000**

Availability in Mint State: This
issue is readily available in relation
to the number of specialists
desiring Mint State coins, but
is slightly scarce overall. The
mintage of the 1859-O is slightly

actual size: 17.9 mm

larger than that of its Philadelphia cousin. True to form, New Orleans dimes had a higher-proportional attrition rate. *MS-60 to 62:* 100 to 130. *MS-63:* 40 to 50. *MS-64:* 25 to 32. *MS-65 or better:* 20 to 25.

Availability in circulated grades: In circulated grades this issue is common, but is not the most plentiful issue of its era.

Characteristics of striking: These are usually seen decently struck.

Notes: The Eliasberg gem with Large O mintmark was described as: "Seated figure of Liberty from rusted or etched die, giving it a satiny *Lalique* appearance in contrast with the polished fields. On the reverse there are similar characteristics. The writer conjectures that this die was rusted, but at the New Orleans Mint was given a highly polished finish in order to remove the rust from the fields, thus giving it a beautiful prooflike character. In the process, certain low-relief details were removed."

F-101 to 105. Three obverse dies and three reverse dies in various combinations.

G-4	F-12	VF-20	EF-40	AU-50	MS-60	MS-63	MS-64	MS-65
$25	$35	$65	$100	$275	$400	$750	$1,150	$2,250

1859-S

Circulation-strike mintage: 60,000

Availability in Mint State: These are exceedingly rare. In 2014 the Eugene H. Gardner Sale featured an example of this coin in MS-63. *MS-60 to 62:* 1 or 2. *MS-63:* 1. *MS-64:* 0 or 1. *MS-65 or better:* 1.

actual size: 17.9 mm

Availability in circulated grades: This issue is scarce, as the mintage suggests. The population is probably in the low hundreds. It is considered to be the rarest San Francisco dime of the decade. Coins in EF and AU grades are seldom encountered. Brian Greer calls this rare above the VF grade level. Many have surface problems.

Characteristics of striking: These are typically well struck.

Notes: In 1893 Heaton called this issue "rare."[27]

G-4	F-12	VF-20	EF-40	AU-50	MS-60	MS-63	MS-64	MS-65
$275	$500	$1,200	$3,000	$5,750	$18,000	$30,000	$50,000	$90,000

1860-S

Circulation-strike mintage: 140,000

Availability in Mint State: In Mint State this issue is extremely rare, and probably fewer than a dozen exist. From the Louis E. Eliasberg Sale in 1997: "MS-63 to 64. From die on hand at the San

actual size: 17.9 mm

Francisco Mint since 1858." In 2014 and 2015 the Eugene H. Gardner Sale featured examples of this coin in MS-65, MS-64, and MS-62. *MS-60 to 62:* 4 to 6. *MS-63:* 2 or 3. *MS-64:* 2 or 3. *MS-65 or better:* 2 or 3.

Availability in circulated grades: These are quite scarce, but more are available than the mintage might suggest.

Characteristics of striking: These are sometimes seen lightly struck on the top of the obverse and corresponding part of the reverse.

Notes: The 1860-S dime has always been a favorite of collectors as it is an anachronism, the With-Stars style used 1859 and earlier. By contrast, Philadelphia and New Orleans Mint dimes of this date have the legend UNITED STATES OF AMERICA on the obverse. F-101 and 102. Two obverse dies and two reverse dies.

G-4	F-12	VF-20	EF-40	AU-50	MS-60	MS-63	MS-64	MS-65
$85	$200	$350	$550	$1,000	$2,500	$8,500	$12,500	$42,500

1859, Obverse of 1859, Reverse of 1860, Transitional Issue

Proof mintage: *20–25*

Characteristics of striking: These are usually well struck.

actual size: 17.9 mm

Proofs: Proofs of this issue are very rare.

Notes: The 1859 issue is a transitional pattern with stars on the obverse, in keeping with the standard design of the period, but with the reverse displaying a so-called "cereal" wreath enclosing the inscription ONE / DIME. Nowhere does the identification UNITED STATES OF AMERICA appear, making this a "stateless" coin. Indeed, the only inscriptions on the issue are the denomination as stated, plus the word LIBERTY emblazoned on the shield. Listed as J-233.

Although this is strictly a pattern issue made for the numismatic trade it has been "adopted" into the regular series of listings in *A Guide Book to United States Coins* and other places. As such, it is highly desired.

PF-60	PF-63	PF-65
$10,000	$15,000	$22,500

1860–1873, Legend on Obverse (Variety 4)

The obverse now has UNITED STATES OF AMERICA in place of the stars. The seated figure is slightly smaller, as evidenced by wider spacing from the border. The brooch or clasp on Liberty's right shoulder has been modified slightly, and there are some minor changes in details.

Brian Greer has divided this into two obverse types:

Type 1 (1860–1861): Five vertical lines are seen on the shield above the ribbon inscribed LIBERTY.

Type 2 (1861–1891): Six vertical lines are seen on the shield above the ribbon inscribed LIBERTY. Liberty is slightly more slender in appearance.

Detail of Type 1 Obverse   Detail of Type 2 Obverse

The reverse is a "cereal wreath," as it has been called, composed of oak and maple leaves, wheat, and corn with ONE DIME in two lines in the center. The design was adapted from that used on a pattern half dollar in 1859. Mintmarks are below the bow from 1860 to 1891. An exception is 1875 when varieties were made with mintmarks above and below the bow.

Brian Greer has divided this into two reverse types:

Type 1 (1860–1878): The left ribbon end is split, and the E in ONE is close to the wreath.

Type 2 (1876–1891): The left ribbon end is pointed, and the E in ONE is slightly farther from the wreath.

Detail of Type 1 Reverse   Detail of Type 2 Reverse

Designer: Christian Gobrecht.

Specifications: *Composition:* 90 percent silver, 10 percent copper. *Diameter:* 17.9 mm. *Weight:* 38.4 grains (2.49 grams). *Edge:* Reeded.

1860

Circulation-strike mintage: 606,000

Proof mintage: 1,000

actual size: 17.9 mm

Availability in Mint State: This issue is somewhat surprisingly scarce. *MS-60 to 62:* 110 to 130. *MS-63:* 55 to 70. *MS-64:* 40 to 50. *MS-65 or better:* 25 to 35.

Availability in circulated grades: These are much scarcer than the mintage suggests, although enough exist in various grades to supply the demand for them.[28]

Characteristics of striking: This issue is usually seen sharply struck, but the delicate Type 1 design was prone to rapid wear and loss of device details. In general, dimes of the 1860–1891 type, when lightly struck, show this on the head of Liberty, the wreath detail at the bottom of the reverse, and the upper left–wheat sheaf.

Proofs: F-101. Breen lists a Type 2 Proof, presently unconfirmed. It seems that many unsold Proofs of this year were placed into circulation, as was also done with Proofs of 1859 and 1861. *PF-60 to 62:* 225 to 275. *PF-63:* 100 to 135. *PF-64:* 90 to 120. *PF-65 or better:* 50 to 70.

Notes: Among dimes of the era, 1860 (as here) and 1860-O have a Type 1 shield, while 1861 comes with both Type 1 and Type 2 shields, 1861-S with Type 1, and 1862 and later with Type 2. F-101 to 113. There are 13 obverse dies and 13 reverse dies in sequential pairs.

G-4	F-12	VF-20	EF-40	AU-50	MS-60
$17	$20	$30	$55	$100	$250

MS-63	MS-64	MS-65	PF-60	PF-63	PF-65
$400	$600	$1,000	$425	$700	$1,350

1860-O

Circulation-strike mintage: 40,000

actual size: 17.9 mm

Availability in Mint State: This issue is very rare and only a few exist. The finest is the Allen Lovejoy coin (Stack's 1990) now MS-65 (NGC). The Eliasberg coin (1996) graded MS-62/65 is now MS-64 (NGC), sold with the Gardner Collection in 2015. *MS-60 to 62:* 1 or 2. *MS-63:* 1. *MS-64:* 2. *MS-65 or better:* 1.

Availability in circulated grades: Even in circulated grades this issue is very elusive. It is decidedly rare in EF and AU levels. Fortin states that most circulated examples will have varying degrees of surface issues as many were recovered from Civil War sites. The late Jim Johnson, popular *Coin World* staffer and writer in the 1960s and 1970s, believed that there were only a dozen or so known based on his spending a long time searching and not being able to buy a single coin![29] The population is in the multiple dozens, most with problems as noted.

Characteristics of striking: This issue is usually well struck.

Notes: These have the Type 1 shield. The fame of the 1860-O dime, perhaps somewhat under-served by today's standards, traces its genesis to this comment made by Augustus G. Heaton in 1893: "The 1860-O dime is a very small issue, exceedingly rare, and a great prize." This is the last Liberty Seated dime issue from the New Orleans Mint until the 1891-O. F-101.

G-4	F-12	VF-20	EF-40	AU-50	MS-60	MS-63	MS-64	MS-65
$775	$1,550	$2,500	$5,000	$9,500	$18,000	$35,000	$75,000	

1861

Circulation-strike mintage: 1,883,000

Proof mintage: 1,000

Availability in Mint State: These are plentiful in relation to the demand. *MS-60 to 62:* 140 to 170. *MS-63:* 70 to 90. *MS-64:* 45 to 60. *MS-65 or better:* 30 to 40.

actual size: 17.9 mm

Availability in circulated grades: In circulated grades this issue is common.

Characteristics of striking: This issue is usually well struck.

Proofs: F-101 has the Type 2 shield. Some were carelessly made with lint adhering to the dies. On the reverse there is a raised dot on the upper right of the M in DIME. Many unsold Proofs were placed into circulation. Proofs of 1861 are significantly rarer than are those of 1860 with the same official mintage figure. *PF-60 to 62:* 190 to 220. *PF-63:* 90 to 110. *PF-64:* 65 to 80. *PF-65 or better:* 20 to 30.

Notes: These have the Type 1 and 2 shields on circulation strikes. The Type 1 is slightly scarcer. Reliable data is not available as little note has been made of the distinction. Gerry Fortin lists these separately:

 Type 1: F-101 to 107.

 Type 2: F-101 to 113.

G-4	F-12	VF-20	EF-40	AU-50	MS-60
$17	$22	$30	$40	$100	$200

MS-63	MS-64	MS-65	PF-60	PF-63	PF-65
$325	$500	$1,150	$425	$750	$1,350

1861-S

**Circulation-strike mintage:
172,500**

Availability in Mint State: This
issue is very rare and probably
fewer than a half dozen are known.
In 2014 the Eugene H. Gardner
Sale featured an example of this
coin in MS-66. *MS-60 to 62:* 3 to
5. *MS-63:* 0 or 1. *MS-64:* 0 or 1. *MS-65 or better:* 1.

actual size: 17.9 mm

Availability in circulated grades: These are fairly scarce, but are not a prime rarity.
In AU levels this issue is particularly elusive.

Characteristics of striking: This issue is sometimes lightly struck at the top of the
obverse and the corresponding part of the reverse.

Notes: These have the Type 1 shield, a type subject to rapid wear.
The various San Francisco Mint dates of this era are all prime rarities in Mint State.
The author suspects, but does not know, that quantities of these were sent to China;
at least, this is true for contemporary half dimes. F-101 and 102. Two obverse dies
and one reverse die.

G-4	F-12	VF-20	EF-40	AU-50	MS-60	MS-63	MS-64	MS-65
$185	$450	$700	$950	$1,250	$5,500	$18,000	$35,000	$45,000

1862

**Circulation-strike mintage:
847,000**

Proof mintage: 550

Availability in Mint State: These
are slightly scarce. *MS-60 to 62:*
120 to 160. *MS-63:* 60 to 80.
MS-64: 40 to 55. *MS-65 or
better:* 25 to 35.

actual size: 17.9 mm

Availability in circulated grades: This issue is common in circulated grades.

Characteristics of striking: These are usually seen well struck. Many are prooflike.

Proofs: Some were carelessly made with lint adhering to the dies. PF-65 and finer coins
are inexplicably rare. *PF-60 to 62:* 190 to 225. *PF-63:* 110 to 140. *PF-64:* 70 to 90.
PF-65 or better: 8 to 12.

Notes: The Type 2 shield is solely employed from this year onward. F-101 to 110.
Ten obverse dies and ten reverse dies in consecutive pairs.

G-4	F-12	VF-20	EF-40	AU-50	MS-60
$17	$25	$30	$45	$100	$185

MS-63	MS-64	MS-65	PF-60	PF-63	PF-65
$375	$550	$1,150	$425	$750	$1,350

1862-S

Circulation-strike mintage: 180,750

Availability in Mint State: These are very rare; probably fewer than ten exist, and anyone would be hard pressed to specifically account for even that many. In 2014 the Eugene

actual size: 17.9 mm

H. Gardner Sale featured an example of this coin in MS-65 (ex Eliasberg). *MS-60 to 62:* 2 or 3. *MS-63:* 2 or 3. *MS-64:* 2 or 3. *MS-65 or better:* 1.

Availability in circulated grades: This issue is quite scarce, but there are enough around to satisfy the population of specialists. Sharp EF or lustrous AU pieces are rare.

Characteristics of striking: Most of these are well struck.

Notes: F-101 and 102. One obverse die and two reverse dies. Brian Greer mentions a second obverse die, but Gerry Fortin has not seen one and does not list it.

G-4	F-12	VF-20	EF-40	AU-50	MS-60	MS-63	MS-64	MS-65
$165	$325	$600	$1,100	$2,500	$4,500	$10,000	$16,500	$40,000

1863

Circulation-strike mintage: 14,000

Proof mintage: 460

Availability in Mint State: This issue in Mint State is quite rare, but is a bit more plentiful than its lower mintages indicate due to

actual size: 17.9 mm

retention by the Treasury at the time of mintage. Rich Uhrich considers this to be the rarest Philadelphia Mint dime of the decade.[30] For this decade Proofs are far more available in the marketplace than are Mint State coins. *MS-60 to 62:* 20 to 25. *MS-63:* 20 to 25. *MS-64:* 15 to 20. *MS-65 or better:* 15 to 20.

Availability in circulated grades: This issue is very rare in worn grades, existing today in approximate proportion to the mintage. Most are VF to AU. It is a highly important and key issue.

Characteristics of striking: These are usually well struck. Die striae or finish lines are seen on high-grade coins.

Proofs: Some have obverse die striae or finish lines. The mintage for 1863 was the lowest of the era. *PF-60 to 62:* 75 to 90. *PF-63:* 65 to 85. *PF-64:* 55 to 67. *PF-65 or better:* 25 to 32.

Notes: Walter Breen makes the observation that only one pair of dies was used to strike 1863 dimes, the circulation strikes being coined in March 1863 and Proofs in three batches from March 5 through May 26. F-101 was used for Proofs and circulation strikes.

G-4	F-12	VF-20	EF-40	AU-50	MS-60
$925	$1,500	$1,750	$2,250	$2,750	$3,250
MS-63	**MS-64**	**MS-65**	**PF-60**	**PF-63**	**PF-65**
$4,000	$5,000	$5,500	$425	$750	$1,350

1863-S

Circulation-strike mintage: 157,500

actual size: 17.9 mm

Availability in Mint State: In Mint State this issue is very rare; probably fewer than a dozen or so exist, and even this estimate may be on the high side. In 2015 the Eugene H. Gardner Sale featured an example of this coin in MS-66. *MS-60 to 62:* 4 to 6. *MS-63:* 3 or 4. *MS-64:* 1. *MS-65 or better:* 1.

Availability in circulated grades: This issue is quite scarce, particularly in EF or finer.

Characteristics of striking: These typically have weak impressions on the head of Liberty, the lower part of her figure, the letters STATES OF AMER in the legend, and on the lower part of the reverse. There are some notable exceptions, however.

Notes: At the time of issue, the 1863-S dime was placed into circulation on the West Coast and, as were other silver coins of the year, some were shipped to China by Chinese immigrants. This was also true of half dimes. F-101.

G-4	F-12	VF-20	EF-40	AU-50	MS-60	MS-63	MS-64	MS-65
$155	$350	$525	$1,000	$1,250	$3,750	$9,500	$12,500	$35,000

1864

Circulation-strike mintage: 11,000

Proof mintage: 470

actual size: 17.9 mm

Availability in Mint State: In 2014 and 2015 the Eugene H. Gardner Sale featured examples of this coin in MS-66 and MS-65 (2). *MS-60 to 62:* 10 to 13. *MS-63:* 20 to 25. *MS-64:* 20 to 25. *MS-65 or better:* 18 to 22.

Availability in circulated grades: In worn grades, the 1864 is a key issue. Most are VF to AU.

Characteristics of striking: This issue is usually sharp.

Proofs: *PF-60 to 62:* 110 to 130. *PF-63:* 100 to 125. *PF-64:* 75 to 95. *PF-65 or better:* 40 to 50.

Notes: F-101 and 102. Two obverse dies and two reverse dies. Both pairs were used for circulation strikes and Proofs.

G-4	F-12	VF-20	EF-40	AU-50	MS-60
$650	$1,200	$1,500	$2,000	$2,350	$3,000
MS-63	**MS-64**	**MS-65**	**PF-60**	**PF-63**	**PF-65**
$3,750	$4,500	$5,500	$425	$700	$1,350

1864-S

Circulation-strike mintage: 230,000

Availability in Mint State: This issue is rare in Mint State. Many have unsatisfactory surfaces from an aesthetic viewpoint. In 2014 and 2015 the Eugene H. Gardner Sale featured examples of this coin in

actual size: 17.9 mm

MS-67 and MS-64. *MS-60 to 62:* 2 or 3. *MS-63:* 2 or 3. *MS-64:* 0 or 1. *MS-65 or better:* 1 or 2.

Availability in circulated grades: They are scarce in circulated grades but in sufficient supply that no specialist has ever gone without one.

Characteristics of striking: These are nearly always lightly struck on the head of Liberty and the corresponding part of the reverse. Fortin says locating a fully struck example will take years of searching.[31]

Notes: The obverse of one circulation-strike variety is from a deeply basined die, polished to give it a prooflike surface.[32] F-101 to 105. Three obverse dies and three reverse dies in various combinations.

G-4	F-12	VF-20	EF-40	AU-50	MS-60	MS-63	MS-64	MS-65
$130	$275	$450	$900	$1,100	$1,500	$2,250	$5,500	$13,000

1865

Circulation-strike mintage: 10,000

Proof mintage: 500

Availability in Mint State: These are very scarce. Most are in high grades and many are somewhat prooflike. In 2014 the Eugene H.

actual size: 17.9 mm

Gardner Sale featured an example of this coin in MS-67. *MS-60 to 62:* 16 to 20. *MS-63:* 8 to 12. *MS-64:* 12 to 16. *MS-65 or better:* 10 to 14.

Availability in circulated grades: This issue is rare and a key issue. Most are VF to AU.

Characteristics of striking: These are usually seen well struck.

Proofs: A few Proofs have the reverse misaligned 180 degrees. *PF-60 to 62:* 60 to 90. *PF-63:* 95 to 110. *PF-64:* 60 to 75. *PF-65 or better:* 22 to 28.

Notes: F-101 and 102. Two obverse dies and two reverse dies. Both pairs were used for circulation strikes and Proofs.

G-4	F-12	VF-20	EF-40	AU-50	MS-60
$675	$1,250	$1,650	$2,250	$2,500	$3,500

MS-63	MS-64	MS-65	PF-60	PF-63	PF-65
$4,000	$4,500	$5,500	$425	$700	$1,350

1865-S

Circulation-strike mintage: 175,000

Availability in Mint State: These are exceedingly rare. In 2014 and 2015 the Eugene H. Gardner Sale featured examples of this coin in MS-65 and MS-63. *MS-60 to 62:* 5 to 8. *MS-63:* 3 to 5. *MS-64:* 1. *MS-65 or better:* 1.

actual size: 17.9 mm

Availability in circulated grades: This issue is scarce in circulated grades, but is in sufficient supply. No specialist has ever been forced to go without one. Many examples in low grades show no mintmark or only faint traces, and are sometimes offered as rarer Philadelphia Mint coins.[33]

Characteristics of striking: These are nearly always lightly struck on the head of Liberty and the corresponding part of the reverse. Fortin states that locating a fully struck example will take years of searching, especially for the F-101 or 102 die pairings.[34]

Notes: F-101 to 105. Three obverse dies and three reverse dies in various combinations.

G-4	F-12	VF-20	EF-40	AU-50	MS-60	MS-63	MS-64	MS-65
$125	$375	$750	$1,250	$3,000	$7,500	$16,500	$25,000	$40,000

1866

Circulation-strike mintage: 8,000
Proof mintage: 725

Availability in Mint State: This issue is quite rare. In 2015 the Eugene H. Gardner Sale featured an example of this coin in MS-66. *MS-60 to 62:* 15 to 20. *MS-63:* 14 to 18. *MS-64:* 14 to 18. *MS-65 or better:* 12 to 15.

actual size: 17.9 mm

Availability in circulated grades: These are very elusive and most seen are VF to AU. *Proofs* are easier to find than circulated coins.

Characteristics of striking: This issue is usually well struck.

Proofs: The base of the 1 is dramatically repunched, the bases of the 8 and 7 are less so. Proofs of this issue usually have some lightness on the head. Obverse die-polish lines are visible. *PF-60 to 62:* 100 to 125. *PF-63:* 150 to 180. *PF-64:* 75 to 95. *PF-65 or better:* 45 to 55.

Notes: F-101 and 102. Two obverse dies and two reverse dies. Both pairs were used for circulation strikes and Proofs.

G-4	F-12	VF-20	EF-40	AU-50	MS-60
$800	$1,350	$1,500	$2,000	$2,350	$3,000

MS-63	MS-64	MS-65	PF-60	PF-63	PF-65
$3,500	$3,750	$4,500	$400	$625	$1,350

1866-S

Circulation-strike mintage: 135,000

Availability in Mint State: Probably fewer than 20 exist of this issue in Mint State. In 2015 the Eugene H. Gardner Sale featured an example of this coin in MS-66. *MS-60 to 62:* 7 to 12. *MS-63:* 1 or 2. *MS-64:* 1 or 2. *MS-65 or better:* 1 or 2.[35]

actual size: 17.9 mm

Availability in circulated grades: This issue is scarce in worn grades, commensurate with the mintage.

Characteristics of striking: These are usually weak in areas. The mintmark is very light on one reverse die, sometimes causing coins to be mistaken for a Philadelphia issue.

Notes: F-101 to 103. Two obverse dies and two reverse dies.[36]

G-4	F-12	VF-20	EF-40	AU-50	MS-60	MS-63	MS-64	MS-65
$125	$300	$450	$700	$1,500	$3,750	$7,000	$9,500	$11,500

1867

Circulation-strike mintage: 6,000
Proof mintage: 625

Availability in Mint State: This issue is quite rare. Probably somewhere between 50 and 100 exist, mostly in higher grades. *MS-60 to 62:* 15 to 20. *MS-63:* 10 to 13. *MS-64:* 25 to 30. *MS-65 or better:* 25 to 30.

actual size: 17.9 mm

Availability in circulated grades: These are very scarce, as the low mintage tends to indicate. Most are VF to AU.

Characteristics of striking: This issue is usually seen well struck.

Proofs: A few have some lightness on the hair and wreath. F-101 and 103. *PF-60 to 62:* 100 to 125. *PF-63:* 150 to 180. *PF-64:* 80 to 95. *PF-65 or better:* 30 to 40.

Notes: As a general rule, very few Philadelphia Mint dimes from 1863 through the end of the decade reached circulation. Surviving Mint State coins tend to be in higher grades. Well-worn coins are extremely rare.[37] F-101 to 103. Three obverse dies and three reverse dies.

G-4	F-12	VF-20	EF-40	AU-50	MS-60
$950	$1,650	$1,800	$2,000	$2,250	$3,500

MS-63	MS-64	MS-65	PF-60	PF-63	PF-65
$4,000	$4,500	$5,500	$400	$625	$1,100

1867-S

Circulation-strike mintage: 140,000

Availability in Mint State: These are exceedingly rare and probably fewer than ten exist. In 2014 the Eugene H. Gardner Sale featured an example of this coin in MS-65. *MS-60 to 62:* 4 or 5. *MS-63:* 2. *MS-64:* 2. *MS-65 or better:* 1 or 2.[38]

actual size: 17.9 mm

Availability in circulated grades: These are scarce and exist in proportion to their mintage.

Characteristics of striking: This issue often has light areas on the obverse with a small, thin mintmark.

Notes: F-101 and 102. Two obverse dies and two reverse dies.

G-4	F-12	VF-20	EF-40	AU-50	MS-60	MS-63	MS-64	MS-65
$130	$250	$425	$750	$1,650	$3,000	$5,000	$7,500	$10,000

1868

Circulation-strike mintage: 464,000

Proof mintage: 600

Availability in Mint State: These are scarcer than the mintage indicates. Probably fewer than 50 Mint State pieces are known,

actual size: 17.9 mm

mostly in higher grades. The 1868 is not typically considered to be a rare date. However, the facts indicate that in Mint State it indeed is. Market prices of this and all other low-mintage Philadelphia Mint coins of the era are held down by the ready availability of Proofs. In 2015 the Eugene H. Gardner Sale featured two examples of this coin in MS-65. *MS-60 to 62:* 10 to 13. *MS-63:* 10 to 13. *MS-64:* 15 to 20. *MS-65 or better:* 10 to 12.[39]

Availability in circulated grades: These are scarcer than the mintage would suggest, but there are still enough to satisfy specialists. In 1993, a group of 500 or so circulated pieces were located in, of all places, Czechoslovakia. Many were distributed by Heritage.

Characteristics of striking: This issue is usually well struck due to limited usage of multiple die pairs.

Proofs: The description of the Eliasberg Proof (F-104), adapted: "Some raised die lines are visible on both sides from die preparation; this must have been one of the first impressions from the Proof dies. On obverse top curve of first S in STATES nearly missing. Seated figure somewhat stippled (deliberately to create a cameo effect?); very interesting—actually dramatic under magnification. Concentric arcs are visible at the base of the seated figure, and, especially, at Liberty's neck and bosom, another fascinating characteristic rarely seen elsewhere."[40] F-101 and 104. **PF-60 to 62:** 100 to 125. **PF-63:** 150 to 180. **PF-64:** 80 to 95. **PF-65 or better:** 40 to 55.

Notes: Beginning about this time the Engraving Department of the Mint had difficulty with the obverse of the Liberty Seated dime. The first S in STATES occurs in these styles from now until the end of the series in 1891:

1. Perfect S.
2. Top curve of S mostly missing (appears as a very thin line). Cited as "broken top to first S."
3. Top curve of S completely missing; serif is isolated as an "island." Cited as "missing top to first S."
4. Top curve of S patched with small "dash." Cited as "dash-patch to top of first S."
5. Top curve of S patched with wavy line. Cited as "wavy patch to top of first S."
6. Top curve of first S thin, but nearly complete.

F-101 to 112. There are 12 dies in consecutive pairs, an exceptionally high number of dies in relation to the total mintage figure.

G-4	F-12	VF-20	EF-40	AU-50	MS-60
$20	$30	$45	$75	$150	$300

MS-63	MS-64	MS-65	PF-60	PF-63	PF-65
$850	$1,500	$4,000	$400	$625	$1,000

1868-S

Circulation-strike mintage: 260,000

Availability in Mint State: This issue is very rare in Mint State, although this is generally overlooked and catalog values do not reflect this. The Louis E. Eliasberg Sale in 1997 featured an

actual size: 17.9 mm

example of this coin in MS-67. The mintmark filled, as usual. In 2014 and 2015 the Eugene H. Gardner Sale featured examples of this coin in MS-67 and MS-66. **MS-60 to 62:** 12 to 16. **MS-63:** 7 to 9. **MS-64:** 4 to 6. **MS-65 or better:** 3 or 4.[41]

Availability in circulated grades: These are scarce. They are traditionally believed to exist in approximate proportion to its mintage, but are very rare at the AU level.

Characteristics of striking: Many of this issue have light striking on the obverse.

Notes: It is evident that a number of these were shipped to China where some had metal carefully shaved from the features of the Liberty Seated figure (a clever way to obtain small amounts of silver without being obvious), and others were made into buttons. Breen references a Doubled-Die reverse, today thought to be the result of strike doubling (die chatter). F-101.

G-4	F-12	VF-20	EF-40	AU-50	MS-60	MS-63	MS-64	MS-65
$65	$165	$275	$575	$700	$1,450	$2,500	$4,000	$5,500

1869

Circulation-strike mintage: 256,000

Proof mintage: 600

Availability in Mint State: This issue is quite rare in Mint State. Fortin says essentially all Mint State examples are struck with Long Flag 1

actual size: 17.9 mm

dies. The author is aware of two Mint State examples struck with the Short Flag 1 die.[42] In 2015 the Eugene H. Gardner Sale featured examples of this coin in MS-67 and MS-66. *MS-60 to 62:* 5 to 8. *MS-63:* 8 to 12. *MS-64:* 8 to 12. *MS-65 or better:* 10 to 15.

Availability in circulated grades: These are scarce in proportion to the relatively low mintage. Quite scarce in EF or AU.

Characteristics of striking: Fortin states the Long Flag 1 examples come well struck as a rule. Short Flag 1 examples will show weakness at the upper obverse and lower reverse.

Proofs: F-104, 105, and 106. *PF-60 to 62:* 100 to 125. *PF-63:* 150 to 180. *PF-64:* 100 to 130. *PF-65 or better:* 70 to 90.

Notes: The serif or "flag" at the upper left of the 1 is short on most dies, but is long on F-105 and 106. F-101 to 107. Seven obverse dies and seven reverse dies in consecutive pairs.

G-4	F-12	VF-20	EF-40	AU-50	MS-60
$30	$45	$100	$200	$250	$550

MS-63	MS-64	MS-65	PF-60	PF-63	PF-65
$1,000	$1,750	$3,250	$400	$625	$1,000

1869-S

**Circulation-strike mintage:
450,000**

Availability in Mint State: These
are quite rare, but generally more are
available than earlier San Francisco
dimes. In 2014 and 2015 the Eugene
H. Gardner Sale featured examples
of this coin in MS-66 and MS-65.

actual size: 17.9 mm

MS-60 to 62: 24 to 28. *MS-63:* 14 to 18. *MS-64:* 12 to 16. *MS-65 or better:* 10 to 14.

Availability in circulated grades: These are scarce, but exist in proportion to the
mintage.

Characteristics of striking: This issue is often weak on the head and the corresponding part of the reverse. The tiny S mintmark on the reverse typically appears as a blob.

Notes: There are wo different mintmark styles—a small, thin S that appears as a
blob, and small, weak S with delicate serifs. F-101 and 102. Two obverse dies and two
reverse dies.

G-4	F-12	VF-20	EF-40	AU-50	MS-60	MS-63	MS-64	MS-65
$30	$65	$100	$250	$325	$800	$1,200	$1,500	$3,500

1870

**Circulation-strike mintage:
470,500**

Proof mintage: 1,000

Availability in Mint State: This
issue is quite scarce in Mint State.
In 2014 the Eugene H. Gardner
Sale featured an example of this
coin in MS-66. *MS-60 to 62:* 70 to

actual size: 17.9 mm

90. *MS-63:* 30 to 40. *MS-64:* 16 to 20. *MS-65 or better:* 10 to 14.

Availability in circulated grades: These exist in proportion to the mintage, but are
slightly scarce.

Characteristics of striking: This issue is typically weakly struck on the head and
other features of Liberty, and on the corresponding parts of the reverse.

Proofs: F-101 and 102. Some Proofs were carelessly made and are weak on the obverse.
The high mintage of this year does not translate into a proportionally large number of
Proofs existing today. Proofs of this year are rarer today than are those of 1869, which
has a lower mintage. *PF-60 to 62:* 100 to 125. *PF-63:* 140 to 170. *PF-64:* 90 to 120.
PF-65 or better: 50 to 65.

Notes: F-101 to 107. Seven obverse dies and seven reverse dies in consecutive pairs.

G-4	F-12	VF-20	EF-40	AU-50	MS-60
$25	$30	$40	$75	$125	$300
MS-63	**MS-64**	**MS-65**	**PF-60**	**PF-63**	**PF-65**
$500	$1,000	$1,650	$400	$625	$1,000

1870-S

Circulation-strike mintage: 50,000

actual size: 17.9 mm

Availability in Mint State: Walter Breen writes that in 1977 a hoard of about 15 pieces turned up in England, constituting what probably comprises most of the known pieces. Absent this hoard and, seemingly, at least one other small group of high-grade pieces, the 1870-S would be a major rarity. As it is, probably somewhere around two dozen, more or less, exist. In 2014 and 2015 the Eugene H. Gardner Sale featured examples of this coin in MS-66 and MS-65. *MS-60 to 62:* 7 to 10. *MS-63:* 6 to 8. *MS-64:* 12 to 14. *MS-65 or better:* 12 to 14.

Availability in circulated grades: These are fairly scarce, as the mintage indicates, and are quite rare in EF or better grade, especially so if AU with luster. Most have rough surfaces.[43]

Characteristics of striking: This issue is often weak at the head of Liberty, and is typically weak at the IM of DIME.

Notes: Although the San Francisco Mint had six pairs of dies on hand for the 1870-S coinage, apparently only one pair was employed, that in November of the year. "A small coinage makes it very rare," noted Augustus G. Heaton in his 1893 treatise, *Mint Marks.*

Although 50,000 specimens were struck, it is probably the case that nearly all were exported for use in the China trade (a common fate of San Francisco silver coins in the era before the trade dollar). F-101.

G-4	F-12	VF-20	EF-40	AU-50	MS-60	MS-63	MS-64	MS-65
$350	$650	$850	$1,100	$1,250	$2,350	$3,000	$4,000	$8,500

1871

Circulation-strike mintage: 906,750

Proof mintage: 960

actual size: 17.9 mm

Availability in Mint State: These are quite scarce, but that is not important in the marketplace as enough Proofs exist to satisfy the demand for the date. In 2014 the Eugene H. Gardner Sale featured an example of this coin in MS-66. *MS-60 to 62:* 15 to 20. *MS-63:* 20 to 25. *MS-64:* 20 to 25. *MS-65 or better:* 9 to 12.

Availability in circulated grades: This issue is plentiful in circulated grades.

Characteristics of striking: These are often weak at the centers.

Proofs: F-101 to 103. *PF-60 to 62:* 125 to 160. *PF-63:* 130 to 160. *PF-64:* 90 to 110. *PF-65 or better:* 40 to 55.

Notes: F-101 to 114. There are 14 obverse dies and 13 reverse dies. F-101 and 102 shared a reverse die.

G-4	F-12	VF-20	EF-40	AU-50	MS-60
$17	$25	$35	$55	$150	$350

MS-63	MS-64	MS-65	PF-60	PF-63	PF-65
$550	$850	$1,600	$400	$625	$1,000

1871-CC

Circulation-strike mintage: 20,100

Availability in Mint State: These are exceedingly rare in Mint State; just a few exist. An example of this coin was featured in the Battle Born Collection Sale in 2013 in MS-63 (ex Norweb). In 2014 the

actual size: 17.9 mm

Eugene H. Gardner Sale featured an example of this coin in MS-65 (ex Stack). *MS-60 to 62:* 1 or 2. *MS-63:* 1. *MS-64:* 1. *MS-65 or better:* 1.[44]

Availability in circulated grades: These are rare and are highly prized in any preservation. The vast majority are quite worn with Fine and VF being about par. Most have problems of one sort or another, often with a porous or etched surface (this also being characteristic of Carson City dimes of the next two years).[45]

Characteristics of striking: This issue is usually seen with slight weakness on the head of Liberty.

Notes: There are only 89 reeds on the edges of 1871-CC to 1874-CC dimes. F-101.

G-4	F-12	VF-20	EF-40	AU-50	MS-60	MS-63	MS-64	MS-65
$3,500	$6,500	$9,500	$17,500	$25,000	$52,500	$150,000	$200,000	$325,000

1871-S

Circulation-strike mintage: 320,000

Availability in Mint State: These are extremely rare; probably fewer than 50 exist. However, catalogs pay scant notice of this, due to the relatively high overall mintage. The Louis E. Eliasberg Sale in

actual size: 17.9 mm

1997 featured an example of this coin in MS-65. In 2014 and 2015 the Eugene H. Gardner Sale featured examples of this coin in MS-65 and MS-64. *MS-60 to 62:* 16 to 20. *MS-63:* 8 to 12. *MS-64:* 6 to 8. *MS-65 or better:* 3 to 5.

Availability in circulated grades: This issue is fairly scarce.

Characteristics of striking: These are often seen weak at the reverse center. Fortin says one variety (F-102) employs leftover reverse dies from 1869 and 1870 with very weak denominations and devices.

Notes: The 1871-S is scarce but is still quite available in circulated grades, but emerges as a rarity in Mint State. In 1893, Heaton wrote that the 1871-S was "abundant." Presumably, generous quantities of worn coins were still found in circulation. F-101 to 103. Two obverse dies and two reverse dies.

G-4	F-12	VF-20	EF-40	AU-50	MS-60	MS-63	MS-64	MS-65
$40	$125	$185	$400	$850	$1,650	$3,750	$5,500	$12,500

1872

Circulation-strike mintage: 2,395,500

Proof mintage: 950

Availability in Mint State: This issue is fairly scarce in Mint State, at least in comparison to issues of the past decade. However, in Mint

actual size: 17.9 mm

State this falls into the "who cares?" category, as Proofs are readily available. The issue has a sufficiently large mintage, so few have been attracted to it. In 2015 the Eugene H. Gardner Sale featured an example of this coin in MS-68. *MS-60 to 62:* 100 to 130. *MS-63:* 30 to 40. *MS-64:* 16 to 20. *MS-65 or better:* 12 to 15.

Availability in circulated grades: This issue is common in circulated grades.

Characteristics of striking: These are often lightly struck at the head of Liberty and the corresponding part of the reverse.

Proofs: F-103 and 109. The dies were poorly prepared and show many striations. Walter Breen's *Proof Coins Encyclopedia* addresses the indifferent quality of Proof dimes of this era and notes: "This sort of carelessness is seen on various denominations during the 1870s; possibly inexperienced employees were on duty making Proofs, possibly there was enough haste and chaos in the Mint that nobody really cared a whistle in a high wind about quality control." *PF-60 to 62:* 100 to 125. *PF-63:* 150 to 180. *PF-64:* 100 to 130. *PF-65 or better:* 50 to 65.

Notes: F-101 to 116. There are 16 obverse dies and 14 reverse dies.

Doubled-Die Reverse: This is one of the most numismatically significant Doubled Dies in the entire American series. At the same time, its diagnostics are subtle for this reason: During the preparation of a working die for a reverse the working hub was either lightly impressed into the working die or it was deeply impressed and then mostly ground away. Remaining were just a few traces of the  design. The working hub was then rotated 175 degrees and the master die was deeply impressed into it. Only slight traces remain of the first impression, most notably a line within the O, a claw-shaped fragment above the right of the N in DIME, a curved fragment within the lower part of the interior of the D, and the ghost of a leaf to the right of the E in DIME. Scattered other elements can be seen as well. F-105. *Cherrypickers' Guide to Rare Die Varieties* lists this as FS-10-1872-801. It was discovered by Lee Day and was attributed as such by Tom DeLorey.[46] This variety is very rare. Larry Briggs has seen only five coins. Probably fewer than 20 are known.[47]

G-4	F-12	VF-20	EF-40	AU-50	MS-60
$18	$25	$30	$40	$90	$175
MS-63	MS-64	MS-65	PF-60	PF-63	PF-65
$300	$650	$1,250	$400	$625	$1,000

1872-CC

Circulation-strike mintage: 35,480

Availability in Mint State: These are exceedingly rare. The Battle Born Collection Sale in 2013 featured an example of this coin in MS-63 (PCGS), which was later featured in the Gardner Collection Sale in 2015. *MS-60 to 62:* 0 or 1. *MS-63:* 2. *MS-64:* 0. *MS-65 or better:* 0.

actual size: 17.9 mm

Availability in circulated grades: This issue is rare, but is the most available of the 1871-CC to 1874-CC dimes. Most have rough surfaces.[48]

Characteristics of striking: These are usually well struck, but are sometimes seen with typical weakness at the head of Liberty.

Notes: F-101.

G-4	F-12	VF-20	EF-40	AU-50	MS-60	MS-63	MS-64	MS-65
$1,850	$3,500	$5,000	$13,500	$25,000	$85,000	$225,000	$300,000	$500,000

1872-S

Circulation-strike mintage: 190,000

Availability in Mint State: These are very rare, with probably fewer than two dozen extant. The Louis E. Eliasberg Sale in 1997 featured an example of this coin in MS-66. In 2015 the Eugene H. Gardner

actual size: 17.9 mm

Sale featured an example of this coin in MS-65. *MS-60 to 62:* 7 to 9. *MS-63:* 5 to 7. *MS-64:* 5 to 7. *MS-65 or better:* 3 to 4.

Availability in circulated grades: These are fairly scarce, as the mintage indicates. However, there are enough to satisfy specialists. For a long time the 1872-S was unappreciated in the marketplace. The turning point may have come from John W. McCloskey's study, "Availability of Liberty Seated Dimes by Grade," in the *Gobrecht Journal*, July 1981.

Characteristics of striking: This issue is often lightly struck at the head as well as certain parts of the wreath features on the reverse.

Notes: This is another issue that probably saw shipment in quantity to Eastern Asia, although this is not documented. F-101.

G-4	F-12	VF-20	EF-40	AU-50	MS-60	MS-63	MS-64	MS-65
$45	$135	$185	$350	$550	$2,000	$3,500	$8,500	$27,500

1873, Close 3

Circulation-strike mintage:
1,506,800

Proof mintage: 600

Availability in Mint State:
These are quite rare, but are not recognized as such due to the availability of Proofs. In 2014 and 2015 the Eugene H. Gardner Sale featured examples of this coin in MS-67 and MS-66. *MS-60 to 62:* 50 to 70. *MS-63:* 25 to 32. *MS-64:* 15 to 20. *MS-65 or better:* 12 to 15.

actual size: 17.9 mm

Detail of Close 3.

Availability in circulated grades:
This issue is relatively common, but is scarcer in higher grades such as EF and AU.

Characteristics of striking: This issue is often lightly struck at the central portions of the obverse and reverse, sometimes in other areas as well.

Proofs: F-101. Kam Ahwash has reported a second die, not yet confirmed. *PF-60 to 62:* 100 to 125. *PF-63:* 130 to 160. *PF-64:* 120 to 150. *PF-65 or better:* 50 to 65.

Notes: The majority of 1873 Philadelphia dimes are of this style. F-101 to 108. Eight obverse dies and eight reverse dies of consecutive pairs. At least one variety was struck after Open 3 coins were made.

G-4	F-12	VF-20	EF-40	AU-50	MS-60
$17	$35	$50	$75	$125	$250

MS-63	MS-64	MS-65	PF-60	PF-63	PF-65
$500	$1,000	$1,650	$400	$625	$1,000

1873, Open 3

Circulation-strike mintage:
60,000

Availability in Mint State: This issue is rarer than its previous Closed 3 counterpart. In 2014 and 2015 the Eugene H. Gardner Sale featured examples of this coin in MS-64, MS-63, and MS-62. *MS-60 to 62:* 20 to 25. *MS-63:* 12 to 15. *MS-64:* 9 to 12. *MS-65 or better:* 4 or 5.

actual size: 17.9 mm

Detail of Open 3.

Availability in circulated grades: This issue is much scarcer than the Close 3 design, and is particularly elusive in higher grades such as EF and AU.

Characteristics of striking: These are often lightly struck at the central portions of the obverse and reverse.

Notes: Mintage figures of 1,508,000 for the 1873, Close 3, dimes as opposed to 60,000 for the circulation-strike Open 3 dimes are estimates by Walter Breen and R.W. Julian, and have been widely accepted in the numismatic literature. However, the generous supply of the Open 3 dimes and the Fortin die data suggests that the mintage was probably at least several hundred-thousand.

Separate numbering system. F-101 to 106, with six obverse dies and four reverse dies.

G-4	F-12	VF-20	EF-40	AU-50	MS-60	MS-63	MS-64	MS-65
$20	$55	$75	$130	$250	$750	$1,500	$3,500	$15,000

1873-CC, No Arrows

Circulation-strike mintage: 12,400

Availability in Mint State: There is only one known to exist in Mint State, graded MS-65 (PCGS).

Characteristics of striking: This unique Mint State specimen is well struck.

actual size: 17.9 mm

Notes: This is one of the most famous of all U.S. rarities. It was probably saved from the 1873 coins sent to the Assay Commission, although facts are scarce. It first appeared in Edward Cogan's sale of the John Swan Randall Collection, May 1878. It was later owned by William H. Woodin, who displayed the coin at the 1914 ANS Exhibit in New York City and consigned it to the following: Wayte Raymond's "Collection of a Prominent American" Sale, May 1915, where it realized $170; New York numismatist Rudolph "Rud" Kohler; Waldo C. Newcomer, acquired in 1915; Charles M. Williams acquired it in 1933 from Newcomer via Texas dealer B. Max Mehl, who then consigned it to Abe Kosoff's Adolphe Menjou Collection Sale, June 15, 1950, where it sold for $3,650; James C. Kelly and Sol Kaplan, who outbid Louis E. Eliasberg Sr. at the Menjou Collection sale, causing ill feelings on the part of their good customer(!); Louis E. Eliasberg Sr. acquired it November 7, 1950, while biting his tongue from Kelly and Kaplan for $4,000, allowing him to complete his collection of every U.S. coin minted to date; Bowers and Merena Galleries' sale of the Louis E. Eliasberg Collection, May 1996, lot 1198, where it realized $550,000; Waldo E. "Pat" Bolen Jr.; Heritage's sale of the Waldo E. Bolen Jr. Collection of 1873-CC Coinage, April 1999, lot 5928, where it realized $632,500; Jay Parrino, who consigned the coin to sell alongside Bowers and Merena Galleries' sale of Jim Gray's North Carolina Collection, July 2004, lot 2149, where it was acquired for $891,250 by Carson City Mint specialist Rusty Goe; and finally, it sold privately into the Battle Born Collection for an undisclosed sum. PCGS #4661. It was later sold by Stack's Bowers Galleries in August 2012 for $1,840,000.

As the 1873-CC, No Arrows, Liberty Seated dime is a superb satiny gem and shows no evidence of circulation, it seems likely that it was reserved for inspection by the Assay Commission, which met in Philadelphia on Wednesday, February 11, 1874, to review the prior year's gold and silver production from all mints. Parcels of coins from the various mints were opened, and random representative pieces were selected by Assay Commission members and were destructively tested in the Mint laboratory for weight and precious metal content. Only a few coins reserved for the Commission were actually tested; most were later melted or placed into circulation.

An interesting sideline concerning this coin is that in 1893 in his study, *Mint Marks*, Augustus, G. Heaton stated that the only 1873-CC dime he knew of was "without the arrowheads." Apparently, he did not know of the 1873-CC *with* arrows! This was an experimental era in American numismatic research. Apart from Heaton, relatively little study had been done in the field of mintmarks, and many discoveries were yet to be made. The order of rarities had not yet been sorted out. In fact, among the four issues of the early 1870s known to Heaton (1871-CC; 1872-CC; 1873-CC, No Arrows; and 1874-CC), he considered the 1874 to be "the highest rarity of the four."

G-4	F-12	VF-20	EF-40	AU-50	MS-60	MS-63	MS-64	MS-65
								$3,500,000

1873–1874, Arrows at Date (Variety 5)

Following the Mint Act of February 12, 1873, arrowheads were added to each side of the date and were retained there into 1874. These denoted a slight change in weight. From 1875 to 1891 the arrowheads were discontinued, but the new weight remained the same.

Designer: Christian Gobrecht.

Specifications: *Composition:* 90 percent silver, 10 percent copper. *Diameter:* 17.9 mm. *Weight:* 38.58 grains (2.50 grams). *Edge:* Reeded.

1873, With Arrows

Circulation-strike mintage: 2,377,700

Proof mintage: 500

Availability in Mint State: This issue is fairly plentiful, but is always in strong demand due to its status as a type coin. *MS-60 to 62:*

actual size: 17.9 mm

120 to 150. *MS-63:* 65 to 85. *MS-64:* 45 to 60. *MS-65 or better:* 25 to 30.

Availability in circulated grades: This issue is common in circulated grades.

Characteristics of striking: These are often seen with lightness at the head of Liberty and at the upper left of the wreath on the reverse.

Proofs: *PF-60 to 62:* 125 to 160. *PF-63:* 130 to 160. *PF-64:* 90 to 115. *PF-65 or better:* 40 to 50.

Notes: F-101 to 124. There are 23 obverse dies and 23 reverse dies. F-111 and 124 have the same obverse die.

Doubled-Die Obverse: This is the most dramatically obvious Doubled Die in the Liberty Seated dime series. The doubling is most noticeable in the shield at the upper right, with extra horizontal lines (on a slight slant) and the outline of the right border of the earlier-impressed shield. F-103. *Cherrypickers' Guide to Rare Die Varieties* lists this as FS-10-1873-101. Probably fewer than two dozen are known today. In 2014 the Eugene H. Gardner Sale featured an example of this coin in AU-58.

G-4	F-12	VF-20	EF-40	AU-50	MS-60
$20	$30	$60	$155	$325	$550
MS-63	MS-64	MS-65	PF-60	PF-63	PF-65
$900	$1,500	$3,500	$650	$850	$3,500

1873-CC, With Arrows

Circulation-strike mintage:
18,791

Availability in Mint State: These are exceedingly rare. The Battle Born Collection Sale in 2013 featured an example of this coin in

actual size: 17.9 mm

MS-65. In 2014 the Eugene H. Gardner Sale featured an example of this coin in MS-65. *MS-60 to 62:* 0 or 1. *MS-63:* 0 or 1. *MS-64:* 0 or 1. *MS-65 or better:* 2.

Availability in circulated grades: Traditionally, this is one of the key issues of the series. Most are well-worn, AG-3 to VG-8, and with rough surfaces. VF and finer coins are prizes if they have nice, problem-free surfaces, but such coins are in the distinct minority. It remains a mystery why so many early Carson City coins, especially dimes, are porous.[49]

Characteristics of striking: This issue is usually well struck. Of all the dimes in the Liberty Seated series, the 1873-CC, With Arrows, is nearly always seen with a porous or granular surface. The reason for this is not known. Walter Breen says that the issue is "often on porous or rough planchets," implying that before striking, rough planchets were used. However, the author doubts this is the case. Dozens exist. Here is a minor numismatic mystery. F-101.

G-4	F-12	VF-20	EF-40	AU-50	MS-60	MS-63	MS-64	MS-65
$3,500	$6,500	$9,500	$22,500	$55,000	$87,500			$500,000

1873-S

Circulation-strike mintage:
455,000

Availability in Mint State: This issue is fairly rare, but specimens appear on the market frequently enough that no advanced specialist need be without one. The

actual size: 17.9 mm

population is probably on the order of 50 to 100 pieces. In 2014 and 2015 the Eugene H. Gardner Sale featured examples of this coin in MS-67 (ex Eliasberg) and MS-66. *MS-60 to 62:* 15 to 20. *MS-63:* 15 to 20. *MS-64:* 11 to 14. *MS-65 or better:* 3 or 4.

Availability in circulated grades: In circulated grades this issue is scarce and is often with rough surfaces.

Characteristics of striking: These are often lightly struck on the head and on the upper left of the reverse wreath.

Notes: 1873-S is a scarce issue and is in strong demand due to the arrows feature. They are multiples rarer than its Philadelphia Mint counterpart.[50] F-101 and 102. Two obverse dies and two reverse dies.

G-4	F-12	VF-20	EF-40	AU-50	MS-60	MS-63	MS-64	MS-65
$25	$40	$65	$200	$500	$1,000	$2,000	$3,500	$8,500

1874

Circulation-strike mintage: 2,940,000

Proof mintage: 700

Availability in Mint State: This issue is readily available in Mint State, though scarcer than certification service reports

actual size: 17.9 mm

indicate as a disproportionately high number of these have been submitted for certification due to their relatively high value as a type coin. *MS-60 to 62:* 150 to 200. *MS-63:* 125 to 150. *MS-64:* 80 to 110. *MS-65 or better:* 60 to 80.

Availability in circulated grades: In circulated grades this issue is plentiful.

Characteristics of striking: These are sometimes seen lightly struck at the head on the obverse and the upper left of the wreath on the reverse.

Proofs: F-101. *PF-60 to 62:* 150 to 200. *PF-63:* 150 to 200. *PF-64:* 120 to 150. *PF-65 or better:* 40 to 50.

Notes: Several 1874 dimes without one or both arrows have been reported and are very rare. F-106. These were struck from highly polished dies. Experimentation with a combination date and arrows logotype is plausible based on evidence. Normal die preparation required separate date and arrows die sinking.[51] An AU example sold for $10,000 on eBay in January 2009.[52] The arrowheads to the left and right of the date are slanted upward on the 1874, unlike the 1873. F-101 to 115. There are 14 obverse dies and 15 reverse dies.

G-4	F-12	VF-20	EF-40	AU-50	MS-60
$20	$25	$65	$165	$325	$600

MS-63	MS-64	MS-65	PF-60	PF-63	PF-65
$1,000	$1,400	$3,500	$650	$850	$3,500

1874-CC

Circulation-strike mintage:
10,817

actual size: 17.9 mm

Availability in Mint State: It is thought that only five exist. The Battle Born Collection Sale in 2013 featured an example of this coin in MS-62. In 2014 the Eugene H. Gardner Sale featured an example of this coin in MS-63 (ex Buddy Ebsen). *MS-60 to 62:* 1. *MS-63:* 1. *MS-64:* 0. *MS-65 or better:* 0.

Availability in circulated grades: More so than generally realized, this issue is very scarce and is most often seen with rough surfaces. It handily outdistances the 1873-CC, With Arrows, in terms of rarity.

Characteristics of striking: These are usually fairly well struck.

Notes: As noted in the previous entry, the arrowheads were punched separately into working dies, sometimes causing misalignment as on the 1874-CC.

Without question the 1874-CC is one of the most highly prized issues in the entire dime denomination. F-101.[53]

G-4	F-12	VF-20	EF-40	AU-50	MS-60	MS-63	MS-64	MS-65
$10,000	$18,500	$22,500	$37,500	$57,500	$125,000	$265,000	$375,000	

1874-S

Circulation-strike mintage:
240,000

actual size: 17.9 mm

Availability in Mint State: The 1874-S is very rare in Mint State, with a population on the order of 25 to 50 pieces. A disproportionately high number of these have been certified due to the fame of the variety and the popularity of the arrows feature. In 2014 and 2015 the Eugene H. Gardner Sale featured two examples of this coin in MS-66. *MS-60 to 62:* 15 to 20. *MS-63:* 10 to 14. *MS-64:* 9 to 12. *MS-65 or better:* 7 to 9.

Availability in circulated grades: These are quite scarce in circulated grades.

Characteristics of striking: This issue is usually lightly struck at the head of Liberty and the upper left of the reverse. The mintmark is often a blob.

Notes: F-101 and 102. Two obverse dies and two reverse dies.[54]

G-4	F-12	VF-20	EF-40	AU-50	MS-60	MS-63	MS-64	MS-65
$50	$125	$150	$350	$800	$1,250	$2,250	$3,500	$7,500

1875–1891, Variety 4 Resumed, With Weight Standard of Variety 5

The design is the same used from 1860 to 1873, without arrows at the date. The weight, however, is slightly lighter, conforming to the Coinage Act of February 12, 1873.

Designer: Christian Gobrecht.

Specifications: *Composition:* 90 percent silver, 10 percent copper. *Diameter:* 17.9 mm. *Weight:* 38.58 grains (2.50 grams). *Edge:* Reeded.

1875

Circulation-strike mintage: 10,350,000

Proof mintage: 700

Availability in Mint State: This issue is common in Mint State. Here begins the era of really common Mint State dimes, a few

actual size: 17.9 mm

issues excepted. These issues are much more available than population reports suggest, as the vast majority have never been certified. *MS-60 to 62:* 350 to 500. *MS-63:* 175 to 210. *MS-64:* 125 to 160. *MS-65 or better:* 75 to 100.

Availability in circulated grades: In circulated grades this issue is very common.

Characteristics of striking: These are usually seen well struck.

Proofs: *PF-60 to 62:* 125 to 160. *PF-63:* 130 to 160. *PF-64:* 90 to 115. *PF-65 or better:* 40 to 50.

Notes: The immense mintage of the 1875 was in anticipation of the resumption of specie (coin) payments which took place in a big way the following year, 1876. This happened, and in the next two years a flood of long-hoarded dimes came back on the market. With new mintages there was a glut of the denomination that resulted in low mintages for 1879 to 1881, after which time more were needed. F-101 to 124. There are 21 obverse dies and 20 reverse dies.

G-4	F-12	VF-20	EF-40	AU-50	MS-60
$15	$20	$25	$35	$85	$155

MS-63	MS-64	MS-65	PF-60	PF-63	PF-65
$250	$450	$700	$400	$625	$1,000

1875-CC, Mintmark Above Bow

**Circulation-strike mintage:
Portion of 4,645,000**

Availability in Mint State: These
are common in Mint State. They
are not as plentiful as certain
Philadelphia Mint issues of the late

actual size: 17.9 mm

1880s, but are very plentiful in the context of the Carson City series. The Battle Born
Collection Sale in 2013 featured an example of this coin in MS-67. *MS-60 to 62:* 250
to 325. *MS-63:* 160 to 190. *MS-64:* 120 to 150. *MS-65 or better:* 90 to 120.

Availability in circulated grades: In circulated grades the 1875-CC, Mintmark Above
Bow, is common.

Characteristics of striking: This issue is sometimes lightly struck at Liberty's head
and the upper-left side of the wreath.

Notes: Today collectors recognize these as what may have been the earliest 1875-CC
dime variety struck, with mintmark CC widely spaced, and with wide reeding (as with
Carson City dimes earlier in the decade); the same variety exists with narrow reeding.

The widely spaced CC mintmark with tiny letters was used only on selected dies of the
era. The most famous use of this style is on the 1873-CC and certain other trade dollars.

In 1893, Heaton wrote: "We have 1875-CC in three varieties: the first has a close CC
below the wreath, the second has a close CC within the wreath, and the third has a wide
CC within the wreath, the latter two very scarce." Years ago the varieties within the
wreath cataloged for less than those below the wreath. Today they are about the same.

For an in-depth study see Gerry Fortin's "An Analysis of Dies for 1875-CC Dimes,"
the *Gobrecht Journal*, November 2010.

F-101 to 119. There are 13 obverse dies and 18 reverse dies.

G-4	F-12	VF-20	EF-40	AU-50	MS-60	MS-63	MS-64	MS-65
$45	$75	$95	$145	$250	$425	$950	$1,500	$3,250

1875-CC, Mintmark Below Bow

**Circulation-strike mintage:
Portion of 4,645,000**

Availability in Mint State: The
1875-CC with mintmark below
wreath (below bow) represents the
second major variety of this year.

actual size: 17.9 mm

It is estimated that of the production of 4,645,000, fewer than 15 percent were of this
variety, making it scarce in comparison to the style with mintmark within the wreath.
However, enough exist across various grades that finding a choice example will not be
difficult. Even in Mint State they cross the auction block with some frequency. The
Battle Born Collection Sale in 2013 featured an example of this coin in MS-66, as are
the two Gardner coins sold in 2015. *MS-60 to 62:* 25 to 32. *MS-63:* 16 to 19. *MS-64:*
12 to 15. *MS-65 or better:* 9 to 12.

Availability in circulated grades: This issue is scarce in circulated grades.

Characteristics of striking: These are sometimes seen weak at the head of Liberty and on the upper left of the reverse wreath.

Notes: This variety was probably struck second of the two Carson City issues. The edge reeding on this is closely spaced as was the standard for the era, unlike the Carson City Mint dimes earlier in this decade. F-101 to 104. Three obverse dies and four reverse dies.

G-4	F-12	VF-20	EF-40	AU-50	MS-60	MS-63	MS-64	MS-65
$60	$95	$145	$200	$315	$550	$1,550	$2,000	$4,500

1875-S, Mintmark Above Bow

Circulation-strike mintage: Portion of 9,070,000

Availability in Mint State: This issue is rare and was not in the Eugene H. Gardner Collection. *MS-60 to 62:* 25 to 32. *MS-63:* 12 to 15. *MS-64:* 5 to 7. *MS-65 or better:* 2 to 4.[55]

actual size: 17.9 mm

Availability in circulated grades: This issue is scarce in circulated grades.

Characteristics of striking: These are often seen lightly struck on the head and on the upper left of the wreath on the reverse, often due to the use of cracked or eroded dies.

Notes: So-called "Medium S" mintmark. F-101 to 106. Two obverse dies and five reverse dies, an unusual ratio.

G-4	F-12	VF-20	EF-40	AU-50	MS-60	MS-63	MS-64	MS-65
$15	$20	$25	$35	$85	$165	$275	$500	$1,750

1875-S, Mintmark Below Bow

Circulation-strike mintage: Portion of 9,070,000

Availability in Mint State: These are somewhat scarcer than expected given the large mintage. *MS-60 to 62:* 225 to 275. *MS-63:* 130 to 160. *MS-64:* 80 to 110. *MS-65 or better:* 45 to 60.

actual size: 17.9 mm

Availability in circulated grades: This issue is common in circulated grades.

Characteristics of striking: These are sometimes seen weakly struck on Liberty's head and the upper-left part of the wreath on the reverse. Commonly seen struck from fresh obverse dies paired with weak or eroded reverse dies.[56] Sharp strikes exist and are rare.

Notes: Gerry Fortin gives separate numbers to Micro S and Small S varieties:

> **Micro S:** F-101 to 104. Three obverse dies and four reverse dies.
>
> **Small S:** F-101 to 122. There are 18 obverse dies and 20 reverse dies.

G-4	F-12	VF-20	EF-40	AU-50	MS-60	MS-63	MS-64	MS-65
$15	$20	$25	$40	$100	$175	$285	$475	$1,350

1876

Circulation-strike mintage: 11,460,000

Proof mintage: 1,250

Availability in Mint State: This issue is common in Mint State. *MS-60 to 62:* 250 to 325. *MS-63:* 130 to 160. *MS-64:* 90 to 120. *MS-65 or better:* 50 to 70.

actual size: 17.9 mm

Availability in circulated grades: These are plentiful in any and all grades.

Characteristics of striking: The 1876 Philadelphia issue is usually seen well struck.

Proofs: These have the Type 1 reverse. F-101 to 103. The large mintage does not translate to the number of coins known today. Many were spent or carelessly handled, perhaps by non-numismatists who bought Proof sets during the centennial year. *PF-60 to 62:* 250 to 400. *PF-63:* 140 to 170. *PF-64:* 80 to 110. *PF-65 or better:* 40 to 50.

Notes: There are two reverse varieties (known as types). The Type 1 reverse, generally used from 1860 through 1877, has two points at the left ribbon end. The new Type 2 has one point and was used from 1876 through 1891. Both Type 1 and Type 2 are known for certain issues of 1876 and 1877.

Gerry Fortin gives separate numbers to the two reverse styles (see page 176):

> **Type 1 Reverse:** F-101 to 122. There are 22 obverse dies and 21 reverse dies.
>
> **Type 2 Reverse:** F-101 to 105. Five obverse dies and five reverse dies in sequence.

G-4	F-12	VF-20	EF-40	AU-50	MS-60
$15	$20	$25	$35	$80	$165

MS-63	MS-64	MS-65	PF-60	PF-63	PF-65
$250	$450	$850	$400	$625	$1,000

1876-CC

Circulation-strike mintage: 8,270,000

Availability in Mint State: Common, although the Type 2 reverse is very rare within the date. *MS-60 to 62:* 200 to 275. *MS-63:* 120 to 150. *MS-64:* 90 to 120. *MS-65 or better:* 40 to 60.

actual size: 17.9 mm

Availability in circulated grades: Common, but with the Type 2 reverse the 1876-CC is very rare and worth much more if sold with proper attribution.

Characteristics of striking: This issue is usually seen well struck. A few are highly prooflike, perhaps branch-mint Proofs or presentation strikes.[57]

Notes: Many were struck from corroded or pitted dies, resulting in microscopic bumps on the surface.[58]

The 1876-CC exists with Type 1 and Type 2 reverses, the latter being rare. Rare it may be, but dedicated numismatists seeking examples are also few in number so that they can be cherrypicked at the regular price.

Gerry Fortin gives separate numbers to the two reverse styles (see page 176):

Type 1 Reverse: F-101 to 135. There are 27 obverse dies and 26 reverse dies.

Type 2 Reverse: F-101.

Doubled-Die Obverse: FS-10-1876CC-102 has a doubled-die obverse with the doubling visible on the peripheral letters and a few other features. Nearly all are struck from heavily oxidized dies, giving the pieces a very granular or porous appearance. A few have a rotated reverse. Additionally, the right C in the mint-mark is raised.

G-4	F-12	VF-20	EF-40	AU-50	MS-60	MS-63	MS-64	MS-65
$35	$50	$70	$110	$180	$375	$750	$1,150	$2,250

1876-S

Circulation-strike mintage: 10,420,000

Availability in Mint State: This issue is slightly scarce in Mint State. In 2014 the Eugene H. Gardner Sale featured an example of this coin in MS-66. *MS-60 to 62:* 100 to 130. *MS-63:* 40 to 55. *MS-64:* 25 to 32. *MS-65 or better:* 15 to 20.

actual size: 17.9 mm

Availability in circulated grades: These are very common.

Characteristics of striking: The 1876-S is sometimes seen with weak striking at the head of Liberty and on the upper part of the reverse wreath, but is also found well struck. A few are highly prooflike (illustrated).

Notes: As with the Philadelphia and the Carson City issues of this date, the 1876-S exists with Type 1 and Type 2 reverses. The Type 2 is the scarcer of the two, but is not in the rarity league with the 1876-CC, Type 2. A number of date and mintmark varieties exist and are sought by specialists.

Gerry Fortin gives separate numbers to the two reverse styles (see page 176):

Type 1 Reverse: F-101 to 121. There are 21 obverse dies and 19 reverse dies.

Type 2 Reverse: F-101 to 105. Four obverse dies and three reverse dies.

G-4	F-12	VF-20	EF-40	AU-50	MS-60	MS-63	MS-64	MS-65
$15	$20	$25	$40	$80	$165	$250	$500	$1,500

1877

Circulation-strike mintage:
7,310,000

Proof mintage: 510

Availability in Mint State: These
are readily available in Mint State.
MS-60 to 62: 400 to 550. *MS-63:*
200 to 250. *MS-64:* 120 to 150.
MS-65 or better: 80 to 110.

actual size: 17.9 mm

Availability in circulated grades: This issue is very common in circulated grades.

Characteristics of striking: The 1877 dime is usually well struck.

Proofs: All coins of this issue are with the Type 2 reverse. F-101. *PF-60 to 62:* 80 to
120. *PF-63:* 120 to 150. *PF-64:* 90 to 120. *PF-65 or better:* 60 to 80.

Notes: Gerry Fortin gives separate numbers to the two reverse styles (see page 176):

   Type 1 Reverse: F-101 to 109. Nine obverse dies and eight reverse dies.

   Type 2 Reverse: F-101 to 115. There are 15 obverse dies and 14 reverse dies.

G-4	F-12	VF-20	EF-40	AU-50	MS-60
$15	$20	$25	$35	$80	$165
MS-63	MS-64	MS-65	PF-60	PF-63	PF-65
$250	$450	$850	$400	$625	$1,000

1877-CC

Circulation-strike mintage:
7,700,000

Availability in Mint State: These
are common. Population data for
Carson City issues is higher
proportionally to the number
known than such information
is for high-mintage Philadelphia

actual size: 17.9 mm

coins. *MS-60 to 62:* 150 to 250. *MS-63:* 110 to 130. *MS-64:* 80 to 100. *MS-65 or*
better: 40 to 60.

Availability in circulated grades: This issue is common and is very popular, as are
all Carson City dimes.

Characteristics of striking: These are usually seen well struck.

Notes: Gerry Fortin gives separate numbers to the two reverse styles (see page 176;
also see the listing for 1877-CC, 7 Over 6, which follows):

   Type 1 Reverse: F-101 to 110. Six obverse dies and nine reverse dies.

   Type 2 Reverse: F-101 to 106 and 109 to 121. There are 13 obverse dies
   and 14 reverse dies.

G-4	F-12	VF-20	EF-40	AU-50	MS-60	MS-63	MS-64	MS-65
$30	$45	$75	$150	$200	$325	$750	$1,300	$2,250

1877-CC, 7 Over 6

Circulation-strike mintage:
Portion of 1877 mintage

Availability in Mint State:
MS-60 to 62: 50 to 65. *MS-63:* 20
to 25. *MS-64:* 12 to 15. *MS-65 or*
better: 8 to 11.

Availability in circulated grades:
EF and AU coins are common. The
overdate is not identifiable on well-
worn coins.

actual size: 17.9 mm

Characteristics of striking: These
are typically fairly well struck. Some
trivial lightness can be seen on Liberty's head.

Detail of Overdate.

Notes: This overdate is *very subtle* and is apt to be overlooked except on the closest
examination. This variety can be identified another way: The obverse shield stripes
have a long diagonal die scratch through the vertical lines.[59] The second 7 has tiny
traces of an earlier 6 in the wide top of the digit. The first overdate was discovered by
dealer Rick DeSanctis of Numismatic Classics in Fort Myers, Florida. DeSanctis discovered the overdate in March 2010 while examining a group of previously purchased
coins and sent the coin to Gerry Fortin. The find was announced by Paul Gilkes in
Coin World, April 26, 2010.[60] Searches ensued, and another die combination was
found. Today the overdate is very collectible.

F-107 and 108. Two obverse dies and two reverse dies. Many are known of each,
mostly in circulated grades.

G-4	F-12	VF-20	EF-40	AU-50	MS-60	MS-63	MS-64	MS-65

1877-S

Circulation-strike mintage:
2,340,000

Availability in Mint State: This
issue is easy enough to find in
Mint State. *MS-60 to 62:* 200
to 300. *MS-63:* 100 to 130.
MS-64: 60 to 80. *MS-65 or*
better: 30 to 40.

actual size: 17.9 mm

Availability in circulated grades: This issue is common on an absolute basis, but is
slightly scarcer than certain other issues of the era; the 1877-S exists in proportion to
the mintage.

Characteristics of striking: These are sometimes seen weak at the head of Liberty
and the upper part of the reverse.

Notes: Examples seen by specialists are all of the Type 2 reverse, although Walter Breen reports that a Type 1 dime has been "reported untraced." Here is a searching opportunity for the alert specialist. F-101 to 115. There are 10 obverse dies and 11 reverse dies.[61]

G-4	F-12	VF-20	EF-40	AU-50	MS-60	MS-63	MS-64	MS-65
$20	$25	$35	$55	$100	$165	$300	$1,000	$3,500

1878

Circulation-strike mintage: 1,677,200

Proof mintage: 800

Availability in Mint State: These are somewhat scarce. *MS-60 to 62:* 160 to 190. *MS-63:* 90 to 120. *MS-64:* 50 to 70. *MS-65 or better:* 35 to 45.

actual size: 17.9 mm

Availability in circulated grades: The 1878 dime is common on an absolute basis, scarcer than the context of the era.

Characteristics of striking: This issue is usually seen well struck.

Proofs: Type 2 reverse. F-101. *PF-60 to 62:* 140 to 180. *PF-63:* 175 to 210. *PF-64:* 120 to 150. *PF-65 or better:* 30 to 40.

Notes: The mintage dropped this year and would continue to do so, as a large glut of previously hoarded coins entered commerce, and the high mintages of recent years (the Treasury Department thought there would be a scarcity) contributed to a record supply.

This variety exists with Type 1 and Type 2 reverses, most circulation strikes and all Proofs being the latter. Gerry Fortin gives separate numbers to the two reverse styles (see page 176):

> **Type 1 Reverse:** F-101 to 104. Four obverse dies and four reverse dies in sequence.

> **Type 2 Reverse:** F-101 to 110. Ten obverse dies and nine reverse dies.

G-4	F-12	VF-20	EF-40	AU-50	MS-60
$15	$20	$25	$35	$80	$165

MS-63	MS-64	MS-65	PF-60	PF-63	PF-65
$250	$450	$1,100	$400	$625	$1,000

1878-CC

Circulation-strike mintage: 200,000

Availability in Mint State: These are scarce but are more available than the low mintage indicates. Apparently, quite a few were saved. The Louis E. Eliasberg Sale in

actual size: 17.9 mm

1997 featured an example of this coin in MS-66/67 (split grade). The Battle Born Collection Sale in 2013 featured an example of this coin in MS-66. In 2014 the Eugene H. Gardner Sale featured an example of this coin in MS-67. *MS-60 to 62:* 50 to 65. *MS-63:* 20 to 25. *MS-64:* 20 to 25. *MS-65 or better:* 15 to 20.

Availability in circulated grades: This issue is very scarce in circulated grades, and most seen are in very low grades. When found with the Type 2 reverse (see below) the coins have a very unsatisfactory appearance.[62]

Characteristics of striking: These are usually seen well struck. Fortin states F-101 examples produced with the Type 1 reverse are seen well struck and are often found prooflike. Type 2 reverse examples were struck with relapsed reverse dies resulting in one to two grade differences between obverse and reverse. Many Type 2 dimes will grade fully Fine on obverse and Good on the reverse with partial mintmark.

Notes: Heaton called this issue "somewhat scarce" when he wrote of it in 1893 in his treatise *Mint Marks.* Gerry Fortin combines numbers to the two reverse styles (see page 176):

  Type 1 Reverse: F-101.

  Type 2 Reverse: F-102 to 104. One obverse die and three reverse dies.

G-4	F-12	VF-20	EF-40	AU-50	MS-60	MS-63	MS-64	MS-65
$250	$350	$400	$550	$1,200	$1,650	$2,750	$3,250	$5,500

1879

Circulation-strike mintage: 14,000

Proof mintage: 1,100

actual size: 17.9 mm

Availability in Mint State: At one time this issue was considered to be quite scarce, but certification service data indicates that it is one of the most plentiful varieties of the era. A hoard of more than 200 of these was once owned by Tatham Stamp and Coin Company of Springfield, Massachusetts, and was bought by the author in the 1950s. These had been kept together since the year of issue. Beginning with the low-mintage silver dimes, quarters, and half dollars of 1879 there was a great numismatic awareness that they might someday become rare, and all from this time forward were saved in appreciable quantities in comparison to the production figures. *MS-60 to 62:* 100 to 130. *MS-63:* 100 to 130. *MS-64:* 225 to 350. *MS-65 or better:* 200 to 300.

Availability in circulated grades: These are very scarce in circulated grades. Most are AG to VF. Mint State and Proof coins are easier to find for this and the next two years.

Characteristics of striking: This issue is sometimes seen lightly struck on the head of Liberty.

Proofs: F-101 to 104. These dies were also used to make circulation strikes. M.H. Bolender liquidated many coins from the Mason estate. His mail-bid sales of May 22 and October 15, 1935, included 145 1879 Proof dimes. *PF-60 to 62:* 180 to 220. *PF-63:* 200 to 275. *PF-64:* 200 to 275. *PF-65 or better:* 140 to 180.

Notes: The 1879 is one of the most famous dates among the Liberty Seated dimes due to its low mintage (Proofs and circulation strikes combined). To an extent, 1880 and 1881 share the limelight for the same reasons.

For many years the 1879 has basked in the glow of publicity as a highly favored date, and this will undoubtedly continue, as there is nothing more magical than a low-mintage figure to entice buyers. This is as it should be in this instance. Worn specimens are considerably rarer than either Mint State or Proof examples.

From *Mason's Coin Collectors' Herald*, March 1880: "1879 Halves, Quarters, and Dimes for sale. U.S. silver half dollars (Uncirculated) $1.10. U.S. silver quarter dollars (Uncirculated) 40¢. U.S. silver dimes, (Uncirculated) 25¢. Complete set of three pieces, $1.60. Mason & Co. 143 N. Tenth St, Phila., Pa."

Then this curious news from June 1880, *Mason's Coin Collectors' Herald*: "Parties who have been busy the past six months in putting away the Proof sets of 1879, and the Uncirculated fifty, twenty-five and ten-cent pieces of the same year, have had but little profit for their pains. Recently one of the corners broke, unexpectedly and Proof sets of 1879 were offered at $5.50, half dollars at 70¢, quarter dollars at 35¢, and dimes at 20¢, while the former prices were respectively $7.00, $1.00, 50¢, and 30¢. It is better to get a reasonable profit on scarce coins and sell rather than to be compelled to unload at an unprofitable season."

All dimes have Type 2 reverses from this year forward. F-101 to 105. Five obverse dies and five reverse dies in sequence.

G-4	F-12	VF-20	EF-40	AU-50	MS-60
$200	$325	$400	$525	$600	$650
MS-63	MS-64	MS-65	PF-60	PF-63	PF-65
$700	$800	$1,200	$400	$625	$1,000

1880

Circulation-strike mintage: 36,000

Proof mintage: 1,355

Availability in Mint State: These are readily available, as many (but far fewer than for 1879) were sold to collectors at the time of issue.

actual size: 17.9 mm

MS-60 to 62: 70 to 90. *MS-63:* 90 to 120. *MS-64:* 120 to 160. *MS-65 or better:* 100 to 150.

Availability in circulated grades: This issue is very scarce, as the mintage indicates. Most show extensive wear.

Characteristics of striking: The 1880 dime is sometimes lightly struck on the head of Liberty and the upper left part of the wreath on the reverse.

Proofs: F-101 and 102; also used to coin circulation strikes. The high mintage of this issue is explained by a penchant for coin investment which arose in 1879 and then suddenly faded. At the time, numerous numbers of the public were attracted by gold dollars, $3 pieces, dimes, quarters, half dollars, and trade dollars, and sought to buy Proofs primarily. By 1881, the sentiment had faded considerably. Also see the comments under the 1879 trade dollar listing. *PF-60 to 62:* 180 to 220. *PF-63:* 200 to 275. *PF-64:* 200 to 275. *PF-65 or better:* 150 to 190.

Notes: From *Mason's Coin Collectors' Herald,* June 1880: "Trade dollars of this year are still in demand, in Proof condition, at $2. While Proof sets remain at Mint prices the half dollars, quarters and dimes of this year, for general circulation, have not yet been coined, and we shall probably have a repetition of the speculative excitement which attended the distribution of the halves, quarters and dimes of 1879, in the latter part of the present year."

Then from January 1881, *Mason's Coin & Stamp Collector's Magazine:* "1880 halves, quarters, and dimes. We have the official statement from the Mint that all *bona fide* coin collectors can procure the subsidiary coins as above, by applying to the U.S. Mint in this city. All those who fail to procure a set of the 1880 pieces can be supplied at $1.50 per set, postage paid, by writing to this office before the 15th inst. *G.W.M., Baltimore.* Although the report was current, when 1880 sets of halves, quarters and dimes were struck that '100 sets were to be given out and dies destroyed,' we learn that 1,000 sets have been struck at Mint."[63]

Dealer S.K. Harzfeld printed the following in his sale of January 24–25, 1881:

> Lot 1081a: 1880 Half Dollar, Quarter, Dime. Uncirculated: Bright. 3 pieces. The Superintendent of the U.S. Mint, Colonel A.L. Snowden, has authorized me to state that he will furnish on application, to every bona fide collector, two sets of these Uncirculated coins, at face value. As was done in 1879, speculators (not the legitimate coin dealers) tried to secure these coins and to sell them at fancy prices, claiming that only 100 sets were struck. Colonel Snowden, however, stopped at once the sale to these speculators, and had a sufficient number struck ($1,000 worth of each denomination) to supply all bona fide collectors. It is particularly just on my part, to state that Superintendent Snowden shows an earnest effort to suppress the abuses and acts of favoritism I complained of, and to assist the legitimate efforts of legitimate coin sellers. I regret that I cannot say the same of the director of the Mint. Notwithstanding all remonstrances, and the resolution passed by the Numismatic and Antiquarian Society of Philadelphia, the name of whose president—the venerable Eli K. Price—should alone be sufficient to secure respectful consideration on the part of a "public servant," at the hour of writing, the Director has ordered the 150 Goloid Metric Sets, still at the Mint, to be forwarded to Washington, "subject to the order of the Coinage Committee." In other words, we may again have to apply for those sets to some speculator, or some political bummer, or to people who are neither "the wives, the sisters, the cousins, nor the aunts" of congressmen. There certainly seems to be room here for the operation of the advocates of Civil Service Reform.

F-101 to 103. Three obverse dies and two reverse dies.

G-4	F-12	VF-20	EF-40	AU-50	MS-60
$150	$250	$350	$400	$500	$650

MS-63	MS-64	MS-65	PF-60	PF-63	PF-65
$700	$800	$1,200	$400	$625	$1,000

1881

Circulation-strike mintage: 24,000

Proof mintage: 975

actual size: 17.9 mm

Availability in Mint State: These are somewhat elusive. By 1881 the investment interest in low-mintage pieces wasn't what it was in 1879 or 1880. *MS-60 to 62:* 30 to 40. *MS-63:* 60 to 80. *MS-64:* 50 to 70. *MS-65 or better:* 25 to 35.

Availability in circulated grades: This issue is scarce in proportion to the low mintage. Most are in lower grades.

Characteristics of striking: Some 1881 dimes show lightness in strike at the head of Liberty and the corresponding part of the reverse.

Proofs: F-101 to 103. Three obverse dies and two reverse dies. The first two die pairs were used for circulation strikes as well, and F-103 only for Proofs. John Dannreuther commented: "The mintages for the Proofs are 675 and 460 for the first and fourth quarters, which are the F-101 and 102 varieties, used for Mint State and Proof issues, although we don't know which was used for these strikings. There were 50 coins struck in the second quarter, so Gerry and I believe that the F-103 is a Proof-only issue. I discovered this variety while working on my Proof book and neither of us could find a circulation strike. This adds up to 1,185 with 210 either melted, placed into circulation, or sold to dealers, so the net mintage is reported as 975. I doubt they melted these, of course, and the 'friends of the Mint' likely obtained them out the back door!"[64] *PF-60 to 62:* 180 to 220. *PF-63:* 200 to 250. *PF-64:* 180 to 230. *PF-65 or better:* 120 to 130.

Notes: F-101 to 103. Three obverse dies and two obverse dies.

G-4	F-12	VF-20	EF-40	AU-50	MS-60
$175	$260	$375	$425	$550	$725

MS-63	MS-64	MS-65	PF-60	PF-63	PF-65
$775	$1,100	$2,000	$400	$625	$1,000

1882

Circulation-strike mintage: 3,910,000

Proof mintage: 1,100

Availability in Mint State: These are very common. *MS-60 to 62:* 1,200 to 1,500. *MS-63:* 650 to 800. *MS-64:* 400 to 550. *MS-65 or better:* 250 to 325.

actual size: 17.9 mm

Availability in circulated grades: This issue is very common in all grades.

Characteristics of striking: These are sometimes lightly struck at the top of the obverse.

Proofs: F-101. Some remained unsold by January 1883 and were probably turned over to dealers. *PF-60 to 62:* 150 to 200. *PF-63:* 230 to 270. *PF-64:* 190 to 230. *PF-65 or better:* 180 to 220.

Notes: Beginning with this year, Philadelphia Mint Liberty Seated dimes are very common. These were saved in large quantities and today are readily available. Taken from the June 1882 issue of *Mason's Coin Collectors' Herald:* "Forewarned. Forearmed. The year 1882 is creeping on towards the end, and yet there are no U.S. silver half dollars, quarters, or dimes coined for general circulation this year, and it is not likely there will be, and but a few thousand struck off for collectors in December; hence, the reflective collector will perceive the necessity of keeping the matter in mind, else he will pay twice the intrinsic value of the coins in January 1883, when they can be had at par in December, 1882."

F-101 to 112. There are 12 obverse dies and 12 reverse dies used in sequence.

G-4	F-12	VF-20	EF-40	AU-50	MS-60
$15	$20	$25	$35	$85	$165
MS-63	MS-64	MS-65	PF-60	PF-63	PF-65
$265	$450	$650	$400	$625	$1,000

1883

Circulation-strike mintage: 7,674,673

Proof mintage: 1,039

actual size: 17.9 mm

Availability in Mint State: Brian Greer considered this to be among the six most common dimes in Mint State. *MS-60 to 62:* 1,600 to 2,000. *MS-63:* 900 to 1,200. *MS-64:* 550 to 700. *MS-65 or better:* 350 to 500.

Availability in circulated grades: These are very common in all grades.

Characteristics of striking: This issue is sometimes seen lightly struck in the upper part of the obverse.

Proofs: F-103 and 119. Many were unsold and were later spent or wholesaled to dealers. *PF-60 to 62:* 150 to 200. *PF-63:* 225 to 260. *PF-64:* 180 to 220. *PF-65 or better:* 150 to 190.

Notes: F-101 to 121. There are 21 obverse dies and 21 reverse dies used in sequence.

G-4	F-12	VF-20	EF-40	AU-50	MS-60
$15	$20	$25	$35	$85	$165
MS-63	MS-64	MS-65	PF-60	PF-63	PF-65
$265	$450	$650	$400	$625	$1,000

1884

Circulation-strike mintage: 3,365,505

Proof mintage: 875

actual size: 17.9 mm

Availability in Mint State: The 1884 dime is very common. *MS-60 to 62:* 1,200 to 1,500. *MS-63:* 650 to 800. *MS-64:* 350 to 500. *MS-65 or better:* 200 to 250.

Availability in circulated grades: This issue is very common in all grades.

Characteristics of striking: Liberty's head is usually weakly struck.

Proofs: F-101. *PF-60 to 62:* 140 to 190. *PF-63:* 210 to 250. *PF-64:* 180 to 220. *PF-65 or better:* 165 to 195.

Notes: F-101 to 111. There are 11 obverse dies and 10 reverse dies.

G-4	F-12	VF-20	EF-40	AU-50	MS-60
$15	$20	$25	$35	$85	$165

MS-63	MS-64	MS-65	PF-60	PF-63	PF-65
$265	$450	$650	$400	$625	$1,000

1884-S

Circulation-strike mintage: 564,969

Availability in Mint State: These are rare. Most were placed into circulation at the time of issue, in an era in which numismatists were not interested in mintmarks. In 2015 the Eugene H. Gardner sale

actual size: 17.9 mm

featured examples of this coin in MS-68 and MS-66. *MS-60 to 62:* 35 to 45. *MS-63:* 15 to 20. *MS-64:* 12 to 15. *MS-65 or better:* 3 or 4.[65]

Availability in circulated grades: This issue is scarce in proportion to the mintage, and most are extensively worn.

Characteristics of striking: These are usually well struck but are occasionally seen weak at the characteristic points—the top of the head of Liberty and at the top of the reverse.

Notes: Small S mintmark. This is the first branch-mint dime since 1878, and the first San Francisco Mint dime since 1877. In comparison to the Philadelphia version of the same year, the 1884-S is elusive in all grades. F-101 to 105. Three obverse dies and three reverse dies in various combinations.

G-4	F-12	VF-20	EF-40	AU-50	MS-60	MS-63	MS-64	MS-65
$25	$40	$75	$125	$325	$750	$1,100	$1,500	$5,500

1885

Circulation-strike mintage: 2,532,497

Proof mintage: 930

Availability in Mint State: These are common. *MS-60 to 62:* 1,200 to 1,500. *MS-63:* 650 to 800. *MS-64:* 350 to 500. *MS-65 or better:* 200 to 250.

actual size: 17.9 mm

Availability in circulated grades: This issue is very common in circulated grades.

Characteristics of striking: These are often seen with some lightness on Liberty's head and on the top of the reverse.

Proofs: F-101. *PF-60 to 62:* 140 to 190. *PF-63:* 220 to 260. *PF-64:* 180 to 220. *PF-65 or better:* 165 to 195.

Notes: F-101 to 111. There are 11 obverse dies and 11 reverse dies in sequence.

G-4	F-12	VF-20	EF-40	AU-50	MS-60
$15	$20	$25	$35	$85	$165

MS-63	MS-64	MS-65	PF-60	PF-63	PF-65
$265	$450	$650	$400	$625	$1,000

1885-S

**Circulation-strike mintage:
43,690**

actual size: 17.9 mm

Availability in Mint State:
These are very rare. The Louis E. Eliasberg Sale in 1997 featured a prooflike example of this coin in MS-65. In 2014 the Eugene H. Gardner Sale featured an example of this coin in MS-66. *MS-60 to 62:* 6 to 9. *MS-63:* 1 or 2. *MS-64:* 1 or 2. *MS-65 or better:* 1 or 2.[66]

Availability in circulated grades: A key issue in any grade and rare. Lower-grade coins up to F-12 will usually have the reverse a full grade less than the obverse.[67] Circulated coins are notorious for having rough surfaces, the cause of which is unknown.[68]

Characteristics of striking: This issue is usually seen well struck, but there are exceptions.

Notes: Augustus G. Heaton noted: "The smallest issue of the whole series makes that piece very rare." At the time he noted that in order of descending importance, rarity among San Francisco Liberty Seated dimes from 1885-S, 1870-S, 1858-S, 1859-S, and 1856-S. After that, 1866-S, 1860-S, 1867-S, and 1863-S were considered "rather scarce." F-101, the only die pair.

G-4	F-12	VF-20	EF-40	AU-50	MS-60	MS-63	MS-64	MS-65
$800	$1,200	$1,750	$2,750	$4,500	$6,500	$9,500	$16,500	$30,000

1886

**Circulation-strike mintage:
6,376,684**

Proof mintage: 886

actual size: 17.9 mm

Availability in Mint State: Brian Greer considered this to be among the six most common dimes in Mint State. *MS-60 to 62:* 1,200 to 1,500. *MS-63:* 650 to 800. *MS-64:* 350 to 500. *MS-65 or better:* 200 to 335.

Availability in circulated grades: These are very common in all grades.

Characteristics of striking: This issue is usually well struck.

Proofs: F-103 and 104. Many are poorly struck. *PF-60 to 62:* 140 to 190. *PF-63:* 210 to 250. *PF-64:* 140 to 180. *PF-65 or better:* 130 to 145.

Notes: F-101 to 119. There are 19 obverse dies and 19 reverse dies in sequence.

G-4	F-12	VF-20	EF-40	AU-50	MS-60
$15	$20	$25	$35	$85	$165

MS-63	MS-64	MS-65	PF-60	PF-63	PF-65
$265	$450	$650	$400	$625	$1,000

1886-S

Circulation-strike mintage: 206,524

Availability in Mint State: This issue is elusive in Mint State, although traditionally this has not been considered a key issue. The Louis E. Eliasberg Sale in 1997 featured an example of this

actual size: 17.9 mm

coin in MS-66. In 2014 and 2015 the Eugene H. Gardner Sale featured an example of this coin in MS-67. *MS-60 to 62:* 45 to 65. *MS-63:* 30 to 40. *MS-64:* 20 to 25. *MS-65 or better:* 20 to 25.

Availability in circulated grades: These are scarce, but enough exist that the specialist will not go unsatisfied for very long. Most are in lower grades.

Characteristics of striking: The top of the obverse is often seen lightly struck.

Notes: F-101 and 102. Two obverse dies and two reverse dies. The F-102 die pairing is many times rarer than F-101.

G-4	F-12	VF-20	EF-40	AU-50	MS-60	MS-63	MS-64	MS-65
$35	$65	$100	$150	$225	$550	$1,100	$2,000	$3,250

1887

Circulation-strike mintage: 11,283,229

Proof mintage: 710

Availability in Mint State: Brian Greer considered this to be among the six most common dimes in Mint State. *MS-60 to 62:* 1,200 to

actual size: 17.9 mm

1,500. *MS-63:* 650 to 800. *MS-64:* 375 to 500. *MS-65 or better:* 150 to 200.

Availability in circulated grades: This issue is very common in all grades.

Characteristics of striking: These are sometimes seen lightly struck at the top of the obverse and the upper left of the reverse. These pieces were struck at high speed with little attention paid to quality.

Proofs: F-101 and 117. *PF-60 to 62:* 130 to 180. *PF-63:* 200 to 230. *PF-64:* 120 to 160. *PF-65 or better:* 75 to 85.

Notes: F-101 to 117. There are 17 obverse dies and 17 reverse dies in sequence.

G-4	F-12	VF-20	EF-40	AU-50	MS-60
$15	$20	$25	$35	$85	$165

MS-63	MS-64	MS-65	PF-60	PF-63	PF-65
$265	$450	$650	$400	$625	$1,000

1887-S

Circulation-strike mintage: 4,454,450

Availability in Mint State: These are common. *MS-60 to 62:* 200 to 260. *MS-63:* 120 to 140. *MS-64:* 80 to 100. *MS-65 or better:* 50 to 65.

actual size: 17.9 mm

Availability in circulated grades: This issue is common in circulated grades.

Characteristics of striking: These are often lightly struck at the high part of the obverse and the upper left of the wreath on the reverse.

Notes: Perhaps a hoard of these survived well into the present century, but no documentation has been found. F-101 to 121. There are 19 obverse dies and 18 reverse dies.

G-4	F-12	VF-20	EF-40	AU-50	MS-60	MS-63	MS-64	MS-65
$15	$20	$25	$35	$85	$165	$300	$475	$1,000

1888

Circulation-strike mintage: 5,495,655

Proof mintage: 832

Availability in Mint State: These are very common. *MS-60 to 62:* 1,200 to 1,500. *MS-63:* 650 to 800. *MS-64:* 350 to 500. *MS-65 or better:* 200 to 250.

actual size: 17.9 mm

Availability in circulated grades: This issue is very common in all grades.

Characteristics of striking: These are often lightly struck at the top of the obverse and corresponding part of the reverse.

Proofs: F-101 to 103. *PF-60 to 62:* 130 to 180. *PF-63:* 200 to 230. *PF-64:* 130 to 170. *PF-65 or better:* 85 to 105.

Notes: F-101 to 121. There are 21 obverse dies and 19 reverse dies.

G-4	F-12	VF-20	EF-40	AU-50	MS-60
$15	$20	$25	$35	$85	$165

MS-63	MS-64	MS-65	PF-60	PF-63	PF-65
$265	$475	$750	$400	$625	$1,000

1888-S

Circulation-strike mintage: 1,720,000

Availability in Mint State: These are very scarce in Mint State, although this issue is not usually recognized as such, due to the overall mintage. *MS-60 to 62:* 50 to 65. *MS-63:* 30 to 40. *MS-64:* 30 to 40. *MS-65 or better:* 20 to 25.

actual size: 17.9 mm

Availability in circulated grades: This issue is slightly scarce.

Characteristics of striking: These are often seen with light striking on the high part of the obverse and the corresponding part of the reverse

Notes: The *Report of the Director of the Mint*, 1888, told why the San Francisco Mint struck dimes and quarters during the period indicated, precedence having been given at the Mint at Philadelphia to the mandatory coinage of silver dollars, and the latter institution was unable to meet the demand for dimes. The Mint at San Francisco was therefore called upon to execute a coinage in dimes, of which $395,284.80 was coined. It was also found that the stock of quarter dollars held by the sub-treasury at San Francisco was likely to be soon absorbed. The same Mint therefore coined during the fiscal year from trade-dollar bullion on hand $192,000 in this denomination of subsidiary coin. This coinage was increased to $250,000 in August 1888.

F-101 to 112. Nine obverse dies and nine reverse dies in various combinations.[69]

G-4	F-12	VF-20	EF-40	AU-50	MS-60	MS-63	MS-64	MS-65
$20	$25	$30	$55	$100	$300	$875	$1,250	$3,500

1889

Circulation-strike mintage: 7,380,000

Proof mintage: 711

Availability in Mint State: These are very common. *MS-60 to 62:* 1,200 to 1,500. *MS-63:* 650 to 800. *MS-64:* 350 to 500. *MS-65 or better:* 200 to 250.

actual size: 17.9 mm

Availability in circulated grades: This issue is very common in all grades.

Characteristics of striking: These are often lightly struck on the top of the obverse.

Proofs: F-101 and 102. *PF-60 to 62:* 130 to 180. *PF-63:* 145 to 190. *PF-64:* 140 to 180. *PF-65 or better:* 105 to 130.

Notes: F-101 to 129. There are 28 obverse dies and 29 reverse dies.

G-4	F-12	VF-20	EF-40	AU-50	MS-60
$15	$20	$25	$40	$85	$165
MS-63	**MS-64**	**MS-65**	**PF-60**	**PF-63**	**PF-65**
$265	$450	$650	$400	$625	$1,000

1889-S

Circulation-strike mintage: 972,678

Availability in Mint State: This issue is rare in Mint State. In 2014 and 2015 the Eugene H. Gardner Sale featured examples of this coin in MS-66 (ex Eliasberg) and

actual size: 17.9 mm

MS-65 (2). *MS-60 to 62:* 40 to 55. *MS-63:* 20 to 25. *MS-64:* 6 to 9. *MS-65 or better:* 5 to 7.[70]

Availability in circulated grades: These are somewhat scarce, but enough exist that specialists can easily find one.

Characteristics of striking: This issue has weakness on Liberty's head as a rule.

Notes: This issue has Small S (more available) and Medium S varieties. F-101 to 110. Seven obverse dies and seven reverse dies in various combinations.

G-4	F-12	VF-20	EF-40	AU-50	MS-60	MS-63	MS-64	MS-65
$25	$30	$55	$85	$150	$450	$1,000	$1,650	$4,750

1890

Circulation-strike mintage: 9,910,951

Proof mintage: 590

Availability in Mint State: Brian Greer considered this to be among the six most common dimes in Mint State. *MS-60 to 62:* 1,400 to

actual size: 17.9 mm

1,700. *MS-63:* 800 to 1,100. *MS-64:* 425 to 575. *MS-65 or better:* 250 to 325.

Availability in circulated grades: This issue is very common in all grades.

Characteristics of striking: These are usually seen sharply struck.

Proofs: F-101 to 104; also used to coin circulation strikes. *PF-60 to 62:* 130 to 180. *PF-63:* 150 to 200. *PF-64:* 150 to 190. *PF-65 or better:* 105 to 130.

Notes: F-101 to 122. There are 22 obverse dies and 22 reverse dies in sequence.

Misplaced Date: The tops of several date numerals are seen in the lower part of Liberty's gown. F-106. *Cherrypickers' Guide to Rare Die Varieties* lists this as FS-10-1890-302. Discovered by Chris Pilliod.

G-4	F-12	VF-20	EF-40	AU-50	MS-60
$15	$20	$25	$35	$85	$165
MS-63	MS-64	MS-65	PF-60	PF-63	PF-65
$265	$450	$650	$400	$625	$1,000

1890-S

Circulation-strike mintage: 1,423,076

Availability in Mint State: These are scarce but available. In 2015 the Eugene H. Gardner Sale featured three examples of this coin in MS-66. *MS-60 to 62:* 60 to 80. *MS-63:* 30 to 40. *MS-64:* 20 to 25. *MS-65 or better:* 16 to 20.

actual size: 17.9 mm

Availability in circulated grades: This issue is slightly scarce despite the high mintage.[71]

Characteristics of striking: These are sometimes seen lightly struck on the head of Liberty.

Notes: This issue has Small S and Medium S varieties. F-101 to 119. There are 13 obverse dies and 14 reverse dies.

G-4	F-12	VF-20	EF-40	AU-50	MS-60	MS-63	MS-64	MS-65
$18	$25	$55	$85	$150	$350	$700	$1,000	$1,500

1891

Circulation-strike mintage: 15,310,000

Proof mintage: 600

Availability in Mint State: Apparently, this is the most common of all Mint State Liberty Seated dimes. *MS-60 to 62:* 2,500 to 3,250. *MS-63:* 1,200 to 1,500. *MS-64:* 800 to 1,100. *MS-65 or better:* 500 to 700.

actual size: 17.9 mm

Availability in circulated grades: This issue is extremely common in all grades.

Characteristics of striking: These are frequently seen with weakness at the top of the obverse and the corresponding part of the reverse.

Proofs: F-101, 130, and 131. *PF-60 to 62:* 120 to 160. *PF-63:* 150 to 200. *PF-64:* 160 to 200. *PF-65 or better:* 115 to 140.

Notes: From the *American Journal of Numismatics*, July 1891: "The demand for dimes continues unabated, and most of the recoinage for the present at the U.S. Mint in Philadelphia, will be of that denomination. The coinage of dimes during the last three years has been $3,156,476, or 31,564,762 pieces, the principal part of which was executed at Philadelphia, taxing that mint, with its cramped space, to its utmost capacity. It is proposed to distribute this recoinage between the mints at San Francisco, Philadelphia, and New Orleans . . ."

F-101 to 135. There are 35 obverse dies and 35 reverse dies in sequence; the longest such run of pairs in the series.

G-4	F-12	VF-20	EF-40	AU-50	MS-60
$15	$20	$25	$35	$85	$165

MS-63	MS-64	MS-65	PF-60	PF-63	PF-65
$265	$450	$650	$400	$625	$1,000

1891-O

Circulation-strike mintage: 4,540,000

Availability in Mint State: The 1891-O is common in Mint State. *MS-60 to 62:* 160 to 200. *MS-63:* 100 to 125. *MS-64:* 70 to 90. *MS-65 or better:* 50 to 60.

actual size: 17.9 mm

Availability in circulated grades: This issue is common in circulated grades.

Characteristics of striking: Most are well struck with many exhibiting heavy die clashing. The 1891-O date is a playground for shattered dies and die cuds. Excessive striking pressure for a smaller denomination may have been the cause for rapid die failure.

Notes: The 1891-O dime is desirable as the only New Orleans Mint issue of this denomination after 1860-O, and one of just two of this design type. Enough were preserved that there will be no difficulty in obtaining a specimen in just about any grade desired.

F-101 to 132. There are 29 obverse dies and 31 reverse dies.

O Over Horizontal O: Traces of the earlier O are readily visible at the center. *Cherrypickers' Guide to Rare Die Varieties* lists this as FS-10-1891o-501. This is a rare variety.

G-4	F-12	VF-20	EF-40	AU-50	MS-60	MS-63	MS-64	MS-65
$20	$30	$35	$50	$100	$185	$350	$550	$1,100

1891-S

Circulation-strike mintage:
3,196,116

Availability in Mint State: These are very common, indeed possibly the most common of all Liberty Seated dimes. *MS-60 to 62:* 140 to 180. *MS-63:* 90 to 120. *MS-64:* 70 to 90. *MS-65 or better:* 50 to 60.

actual size: 17.9 mm

Availability in circulated grades: This issue is common in circulated grades.

Characteristics of striking: These are often seen lightly struck in Liberty's head.

Notes: This issue has Small S and Medium S varieties. F-101 to 119. There are 12 obverse dies and 14 reverse dies.

Medium S Over Small S Mintmark: The under-mintmark is sharp and clear. *Cherrypickers' Guide to Rare Die Varieties* lists this as FS-10-1891S-501.

G-4	F-12	VF-20	EF-40	AU-50	MS-60	MS-63	MS-64	MS-65
$15	$20	$25	$35	$85	$185	$300	$450	$1,000

LIBERTY SEATED TWENTY-CENT PIECES (1875–1878)

Introduction

Produced for circulation only in 1875 and 1876 and in Proof finish from 1875 to 1878, the twenty-cent piece is the shortest-lived of all regular-issue federal coin denominations. In original listings these were sometimes called double dimes. These coins have a unique connection to the state of Nevada. Although a twenty-cent piece had been suggested in the United States as early as 1791, and in neighboring Canada the twenty-cent piece had been distributed in quantity in 1858, it was not until February 1874 that the notion of this denomination was translated into reality this side of the border.

The scenario in 1874 was centered on the West Coast. Small-denomination minor coins, including Indian cents, two-cent pieces, nickel three-cent pieces, and Shield nickel five-cent pieces, had never circulated there to any extent, nor was the silver three-cent piece used in commerce. For this reason, the San Francisco Mint produced none of these denominations. Half dimes were made in San Francisco from 1863 through 1873. When half dimes were discontinued by the Coinage Act of February 12, 1873, the smallest denomination regularly seen in circulation was the dime, or ten-cent piece. If someone wanted to buy an item priced at 10¢ and offered 25¢ in payment, he received a Spanish-American silver one-real "bit" (worth 12-1/2¢; such coins were still in circulation, but were not as plentiful as they had been earlier) in change. Or, he might receive what was called a "short bit," or dime, as there was no way of giving 15¢ back, absent a circulating five-cent piece. If an item was priced at 5¢ retail, a buyer would have to pick up two of them as there were no coins to effect a solo 5¢ purchase.

By rather complicated reasoning, if the twenty-cent piece became a reality, someone could make a 5¢ purchase, tender a 25-cent piece in payment, and receive a twenty-cent piece as change. Or, for a 10¢ purchase a twenty-cent piece could be offered, and a dime would be given in change.

In February 1874, Senator John P. Jones of Nevada introduced a bill for the twenty-cent piece. At the time, Nevada was America's leading silver-producing state. While fortunes from the Comstock Lode in Virginia City, Nevada, had been at a high crest in the 1860s and had prompted the establishment of the Carson City Mint a few miles away from Virginia City, by the 1870s the price of the metal had fallen, and times were difficult. New markets were needed. Certainly, a new silver denomination such as the twenty-cent piece would help. Many different patterns were made in 1874 and 1875, some of them quite beautiful.

Senator J.P. Jones lent his name to a popular cigar.

The *Annual Report of the Director of the Mint*, 1874, covering the fiscal year from July 1, 1874, to June 30, 1875, included this:

> A bill authorizing the coinage of a twenty-cent silver piece passed the Senate at the last session of Congress, but was not considered in the House of Representatives for want of time. The issue of a coin of that denomination will not only be in accordance with our decimal system of money, but will remove a difficulty in making change which now exists upon the Pacific coast and in Texas, where the five-cent copper-nickel coins do not circulate, and where it was formerly the practice to apply the term "bits," "two bits," and "four bits," respectively, to the fractions of the Spanish dollar which circulated there. The custom appears to continue, notwithstanding those coins have disappeared from circulation. Accordingly, if a payment of one bit is to be made, and a twenty-five cent coin be used for the purpose, a ten-cent coin (one bit) is returned as the proper change, five cents being lost in the transaction by the purchaser. The issue of a twenty-cent coin will no doubt remove this difficulty. It may be added that, although this "bit" system appears to be quite an unimportant matter, few visitors to the Pacific coast fail to suffer some vexation at least from its existence. . . .

The market for the twenty-cent piece was necessarily limited to the American West, as silver coins in the East and Midwest had not been in circulation since widespread hoarding took place beginning in the spring of 1862. It would not be until after April 20, 1876, that they would be seen again in the channels of commerce east of the Rocky Mountains.

In his proposal, Senator Jones suggested that the twenty-cent piece would facilitate change-making and help eliminate the use of Spanish-American coins, although these had not been legal tender since 1859.[1] On March 3, 1875, the twenty-cent piece became a reality. The first coinage took place in Philadelphia in mid-June followed by production at the two Western mints in July.

In the first year 1,155,000 pieces were struck at the San Francisco Mint, 133,290 at Carson City, but only 36,910 (plus 2,790 Proofs) in Philadelphia, as the coins were not needed for circulation in the East.

Circulation coinage for the second year of the coin's existence, 1876, fell to just 10,000 at Carson City (most of which were later melted) and 14,640 at Philadelphia (most probably melted as well). None were made in San Francisco. Proofs were produced for collectors in 1875 and 1876 and also for two later years, 1877 and 1878, when no circulation strikes were made.

The twenty-cent piece might have been successful had there been no quarters in circulation, however, quarters were firmly ensconced in commerce, and soon the twenty-cent coins were forgotten.

On March 11, 1878, Senator John Sherman testified before the House Committee on Coinage, Weights, and Measures about the twenty-cent piece and said:

> I don't see any use for it. It was adopted at the urgent request of Senator Jones of Nevada, who said that in California it would be a convenient coin. It was adopted at his request, but in practice it is a rather inconvenient coin here, because it is confounded with the twenty-five cent piece.

On May 2, 1878, authorization for the twenty-cent piece was repealed.

In his book *Money and Legal Tender*, Dr. Henry R. Linderman said it was a mistake to introduce the piece, but that it was a proper denomination between a dime and a half dollar and should have been used instead of a quarter dollar. It will be recalled that there is no $25 bill. Linderman conveniently forgot that he was enthusiastic about the denomination when it was first coined in 1875.

The Design of the Liberty Seated Twenty-Cent Piece

In 1875 a number of different patterns were made, most of them quite different from the quarter dollar, including having the head (rather than the full figure) of Liberty on the obverse and having a shield on the reverse. However, it seems this diversity was not wanted. The adopted obverse design features Christian Gobrecht's motif of Liberty in a seated position, stars surrounding, and the date below. The reverse is a new motif by William Barber and depicts a perched eagle, somewhat similar in configuration to that used on the trade dollar, surrounded by UNITED STATES OF AMERICA and the denomination expressed as TWENTY CENTS. The edge is plain, unlike other silver denominations of the era, except the silver three-cent piece, which had reeded edges.

From *The New York Times*, April 16, 1875:

> *California Gets Her Twenty-Cent Piece:* To satisfy those queer people, the Californians, the government has ordered the issue of twenty-cent pieces. In the happy land beyond the Sierra Nevada the smallest available coin is a "bit"—an imaginary issue of the Mint valued at 12 and a half cents. But a silver dime, worth ten cents, is also a bit, and two dimes are two bits, and a silver coin is a "two-bit piece."
>
> Therefore, when the silver dime becomes indefinitely multiplied, five cents drop off every two bits, to the great profit of sharp fellows who can bring their minds to consider so small a matter. The twenty-cent coin, of which we have an elaborate description, will be the first common multiple of the California bit; and the moral people of that region will regret to learn that the piece is so small that we cannot say on it, as on half dollars, "In God We Trust."

From *Banker's Magazine*, June 1875:

> *The Twenty-Cent Coin:* The designs of the twenty-cent silver piece were selected in April by Dr. Linderman, Director of the Mint. The obverse contains a sitting figure of Liberty with the word "Liberty" inscribed on the shield, the whole surrounded by thirteen stars, and beneath the figure the date "1875." On the reverse the figure of an eagle surrounded by the inscription, "United States of America," and beneath the eagle the words "twenty cents." The edge of the coin is perfectly smooth, in order to distinguish it more readily from the twenty-five-cent coin, which bears a milled, fluted edge. The new piece is mainly designed for circulation on the Pacific Coast.

From the *San Francisco Chronicle*, November 28, 1875:

> There has been a great deal of inquiry from various quarters elicited by the non-appearance in actual circulation of the much-talked-of twenty-cent pieces. Numerous and curious are the surmises that have been indulged in on this interesting subject. One theory which has been widely accepted is to the effect that the saloon-keepers and the corner-grocery men had entered into a mysterious conspiracy to keep these double-decimal coins out of circulation, in order to prevent too clear a line of demarcation from being drawn between fifteen cents and the "short bit," which, according to California custom where of the memory of man runneth not to the contrary, is the legitimate change for a quarter, where ten cents have been invested in the purchase.
>
> It is now stated that the reason why we seen none of the new twenty-cent pieces in circulation is that the people do not appear to want them. They are issued from the Mint in exchange for gold coin at par, and no one wants them on those terms. We are told that the Mint has turned out over $200,000 worth of these pieces, of which five or six thousand dollars' worth have been paid out in the institution, which the rest, with the exception of $22,000 remaining on hand, has been shipped East. The $22,000 still in the Mint can be obtained for gold by any parties desiring them. If no one wants them it is not the fault of the Government or the Mint. Hence there seems to be no foundation to the "conspiracy" theory.

From the *Cincinnati Commercial* (reprinted in the *Atlanta Constitution*), July 16, 1876:

> The new silver twenty-cent piece is the most unpopular coin ever struck from the mint. It so closely resembles the silver quarter of a dollar in size and appearance that a person handling subsidiary silver coin is liable to be deceived, and to take and give it as a twenty-five-cent piece. Moreover, it is not needed in making change. With the dime and "nickel" for change there is no requirement which calls for a twenty-cent piece. The coinage of this coin should be stopped.

Pattern Coins

In 1874 many patterns, including special pieces for the numismatic trade, were made. From a historical viewpoint, the most important are those associated with the new denomination, the twenty-cent piece, these being Judd–1354 through 1358. The obverse design by J.A. Bailly was borrowed from his unprepossessing motif created for certain trade dollars of 1873 (J-1315 to 1319). It features a Seated Liberty holding a pole with a Liberty cap in her right hand; her left hand rests on a globe inscribed LIBERTY. Bales of cotton and a cotton plant are at her feet; a sheaf of wheat rests behind her. Whether there was serious consideration for this motif for regular circulation of the twenty-cent piece is not known.

A design combining elements of Bailly's Liberty Seated and the adopted trade dollar design was also developed and struck in 1875. Referred to as Liberty at the Seashore, it shows Liberty by the sea holding an olive branch in her right hand, as on the trade dollar design, with her left hand resting on a globe inscribed LIBERTY, as on the Bailly design. Two flags join the sheaf of wheat; an illogical ship with steam and sails blowing in opposite directions is placed on the seas.

Additionally, off-metal strikes from original dies were made in 1875 and 1876.

1874 Twenty cents (J-1354 to 1356a): *Obverse:* J.A. Bailly's design was adopted from the 1873 pattern trade dollar J-1315 with Liberty seated, facing left, stars around, and date below. *Reverse:* Similar to the die adopted in 1875, but with minor differences (terminal leaves of the laurel branch overlap). J-1354 is struck

J-1355. (actual size: 22 mm)

in silver and has a plain edge. J-1355 is struck in copper and has a plain edge. J-1356 is struck in aluminum and has a plain edge. J-1356a² is struck in nickel and also has a plain edge.

1874 Twenty cents (J-1357 and 1358): *Obverse:* Bailly's design, same as preceding. *Reverse:* Open wreath enclosing 20 / CENTS with UNITED STATES OF AMERICA at the border. J-1357 is struck in silver and has a plain edge. J-1358 is struck in nickel and has a plain edge.

J-1358. (actual size: 22 mm)

1875 Twenty cents (J-1392 to 1395): *Obverse:* Liberty head designed by William Barber, sometimes nicknamed the *Sailor Head*, facing left, with coronet inscribed LIBERTY, and hair tied back with ribbon. *Reverse:* Spade-type shield with 20 incuse, rays above shield, with two arrows and laurel branch at lower border

J-1392. (actual size: 22 mm)

of shield. UNITED STATES OF AMERICA / CENTS is around the border. J-1392 is struck in silver and has a plain edge. J-1393 is struck in copper and has a plain edge. J-1394 is struck in aluminum and has a plain edge. J-1395 is struck in nickel and also has a plain edge.

1875 Twenty cents (J-1396 to 1398): *Obverse:* Liberty Seated at the seashore, laurel branch in right hand, and left hand resting on globe inscribed LIBERTY. There are two flags and a wheat sheaf behind her. A steamship is in the distance with sails and smoke going in opposite directions. *Reverse:* An open wreath enclosing 1/5 / OF A

J-1396. (actual size: 22 mm)

/ DOLLAR with UNITED STATES OF AMERICA / TWENTY CENTS around the border. J-1396 is struck in silver and has a plain edge. J-1397 is struck in copper and has a plain edge. J-1398 is struck in aluminum and also has a plain edge.

The obverse shares a common motif with some trade-dollar patterns, showing a ship at sea in the distance, its auxiliary sails billowing *forward*, while smoke from its stack drifts *to the rear*—in defiance of the laws of physics, creating one of the most egregious gaffes in American coinage.

1875 Twenty cents (J-1399 to 1402): *Obverse:* Liberty Seated at the seashore, as preceding, with illogical ship depiction. *Reverse:* Similar to the die adopted in 1875, but with minor differences, such as terminal leaves of the laurel branch overlap. This die was earlier used to strike J-1354 in 1874. J-1399 is struck in silver

J-1402. (actual size: 22 mm)

and has a plain edge. J-1400 is struck in copper and has a plain edge. J-1401 is struck in aluminum and has a plain edge. J-1402 is struck in nickel and also has a plain edge.

1875 Twenty cents (J-1403 to 1406): *Obverse:* Liberty Seated at the seashore, as preceding, with illogical ship depiction. *Reverse:* An open wreath enclosing 20 / CENTS with UNITED STATES OF AMERICA at the border (first used on J-1357 in 1874). J-1403 is struck in silver and has a plain edge. J-1404 is

J-1404. (actual size: 22 mm)

struck in copper and has a plain edge. J-1405 is struck in aluminum and has a plain edge. J-1406 is struck in white metal and also has a plain edge.

1875 Twenty cents (J-1407 to 1410): *Obverse:* Liberty Seated die similar in appearance to the regular die, but the date is in smaller numerals, with LIBERTY incuse in the shield instead of raised as on circulation strikes. *Reverse:* Open wreath enclosing 1/5 / OF A / DOLLAR. Around the border is UNITED STATES

J-1407. (actual size: 22 mm)

OF AMERICA / TWENTY CENTS; die of J-1396. J-1407 is struck in silver and has a plain edge. J-1408 is struck in copper and has a plain edge. J-1409 is struck in aluminum and has a plain edge. J-1410 is struck in nickel and also has a plain edge.

1875 Twenty cents (J-1411 to 1413): *Obverse:* Liberty Seated die as preceding. *Reverse:* Similar to the design adopted in 1875, but with minor differences such as terminal leaves of the laurel branch overlap. J-1411 is struck in silver and has a plain edge. J-1412 is struck in copper and has a plain edge. J-1413 is struck in aluminum and has a plain edge.

J-1411. (actual size: 22 mm)

1875 Twenty cents, regular dies (J-1414 and 1415): On the regular die the word LIBERTY is raised, rather than incuse. It is the only circulating Liberty Seated issue to have the word raised except for the 1836 Gobrecht dollar (J-60). J-1414 is struck in copper and has a reeded edge. J-1415 is struck in aluminum and has a reeded edge.

J-1414. (actual size: 22 mm)

In 1876 there was one "pattern" made, an off-metal striking for sale to collectors. In addition, an 1876-S in copper was made, probably at a later date.

1876 Twenty cents, regular dies (J-1454): J-1454 is struck in copper and has a plain edge.

J-1454. (actual size: 22 mm)

1876-S Twenty cents, regular dies (J-unlisted): *Obverse:* Regular twenty-cent die of the year. *Reverse:* Regular die of the era, such as the San Francisco die of 1875 (no regular issue 1876-S coins are known). An example from slightly rusted dies was carefully studied by the author in the 1960s, the coin being a part of the collection of a famous eastern numismatist. It is presumed this was made at a later date, possibly at the Philadelphia Mint using dies stored there. It was struck in copper and has a plain edge.

These patterns were made privately and were not available to numismatists except those who had secret connections with Mint officers. Edward Cogan, a leading Philadelphia dealer, had petitioned the Mint for many years in an effort to be included among favorite buyers, but most patterns were funneled out through John W. Haseltine of the same city and pharmacist-collector Robert Coulton Davis. In his catalog for his sale of April 11–12, 1877, Cogan revealed his unfamiliarity with such patterns:

> 683. Pattern twenty-cent piece. *Silver.* Proof. The first one I have ever seen or heard of. Rare.[3]

Aspects of Striking

Taken as a whole, the striking sharpness of twenty-cent pieces is excellent. On the issues of 1875-CC and 1875-S there is often some lightness on Liberty's head on the obverse and on the top of the eagle's wing on the reverse. Some 1878 Proofs have incomplete details on the head. As certification services take no notice of this, and as sharply struck examples can be found without difficulty, it is easy enough to acquire sharp coins.

Release and Distribution

Philadelphia Mint coins of 1875 and 1876 were available only by paying a slight premium for them. No twenty-cent pieces circulated in commerce in the East and Midwest until silver coins achieved par with Legal Tender Notes after April 20, 1876.

Most twenty-cent pieces were released in the greater San Francisco area starting in the early summer of 1875. The *San Francisco Evening Bulletin* printed on June 4:

> Samples of the new 20-cent coin were received in this city this morning from the Carson Mint. The officers of that Mint were anxious to make the first coin of this description on the Pacific Coast, and, accordingly, had everything in readiness upon the arrival of the dies from Washington. The first coins were struck on the 1st of June.
>
> The new coin has heretofore been minutely described. It is of course a little smaller than the Quarter Dollar, and has the words "Twenty Cents" in place of the words "Quar. Dol."; otherwise there is but little difference in the general appearance of the two coins. Some care will be necessary in receiving change not to take them for more than their face value. The new coin has a clean look, and was probably made from Consolidated Virginia bullion.[4]

Almost immediately, the public confused the new coin with the Liberty Seated quarter dollar of nearly similar size. Moreover, the coins were strange to merchants, and few wanted to change their habits. It was a caper for riders on the Oakland Ferry and other public transportation to offer a twenty-cent piece which, in the haste to collect fares, the cashier or conductor could mistake for a quarter. Some twenty-cent pieces had grooving or reeding applied to their edges to make them more like a quarter.[5] As to whether the coins served to easily make change, as per the original intent, is not known, as no specific accounts have been found.

The coin was redundant by 1876. None were struck in San Francisco that year. At the Carson City Mint 10,000 were made, but most were melted (see 1876-CC listing on page 237). The 14,400 struck in Philadelphia were likely mostly offered or sold as souvenirs at the Centennial Exhibition in that city.[6] By that time they circulated at par with paper money, a moot point as the denomination never gained traction.

Twenty-cent pieces were reviewed in *The Coin Collector's Journal*, the *American Journal of Numismatics*, and elsewhere, usually unfavorably.

Proof Liberty Seated Twenty-Cent Pieces

Proofs were struck of all years from 1875 to 1878. The generous mintage of 1,200 coins for 1875 included many distributed as the first year of issue among non-numismatists. The production of 1,500 Proofs in 1876—among the most generous nineteenth century Proof mintages—was in anticipation of additional sales in the centennial year of American independence.

In 1877 and 1878 Proofs were made for collectors, but no circulating coins were made. Quite a few Proofs of these two years were lightly polished in later times, a situation sometimes masked today by toning. Such coins have many hairlines when viewed under high magnification. A few Proofs were later spent by their owners.

Grading Liberty Seated Twenty-Cent Pieces

1875. Graded MS-64.

MS-60 to 70 (Mint State). *Obverse:* At MS-60, some abrasion and contact marks are evident, most noticeably on the bosom and thighs and knees. Luster is present, but may be dull or lifeless. At MS-63, contact marks are very few, and abrasion is hard to detect except under magnification. An MS-65 coin has no abrasion, and contact marks are sufficiently minute as to require magnification. Check the knees of Liberty and the right field. Luster should be full and rich. *Reverse:* Comments apply as for the obverse, except that in lower–Mint State grades abrasion and contact marks are most noticeable on the eagle's breast and the top of the wing to the left. At MS-65 or higher, there are no marks visible to the unaided eye. The field is mainly protected by design elements and does not show abrasion as much as does the obverse on a given coin.

Illustrated coin: Semi-Proof surfaces contrast nicely against the frosted devices of this well-struck piece.

1875-CC. Graded AU-55.

AU-50, 53, 55, 58 (About Uncirculated). *Obverse:* Light wear is seen on the thighs and knees, bosom, and head. At AU-58, the luster is extensive but incomplete, especially in the right field. At AU-50 and 53, luster is less. *Reverse:* Wear is evident on the eagle's breast (the prime focal point) and the top of the wings. An AU-58 coin will have nearly full luster, more so than on the obverse, as the design elements protect the small field areas. At AU-50 and 53, there still are traces of luster.

1875-S. Graded EF-45.

EF-40, 45 (Extremely Fine). *Obverse:* Further wear is seen on all areas, especially the thighs and knees, bosom, and head. Little or no luster is seen on most coins. From this grade downward, sharpness of strike of the stars and the head does not matter to connoisseurs. *Reverse:* Further wear is evident on the eagle's breast and wings. Some feathers may be blended together.

1875-S. Graded VF-25.

VF-20, 30 (Very Fine). *Obverse:* Further wear is seen. Most details of the gown are worn away, except in the lower-relief areas above and to the right of the shield. Hair detail is mostly or completely gone. As to whether LIBERTY should be completely readable, this seems to be a matter of debate. On many coins in the marketplace the word is weak or missing on one to several letters. ANA grading standards and PCGS require full LIBERTY. *Reverse:* Wear is more extensive, with more feathers blended together, especially in the right wing. The area below the shield shows more wear.

1875-S. Graded F-15.

F-12, 15 (Fine). *Obverse:* The seated figure is well worn, but with some detail above and to the right of the shield. LIBERTY has no more than two and a half letters missing (per ANA grading standards) or can have three letters missing (per PCGS). In the marketplace, some have four or five letters missing. *Reverse:* Wear is extensive, with about half of the feathers flat or blended with others.

1875-S. Graded VG-10.

VG-8, 10 (Very Good). *Obverse:* The seated figure is more worn, but some detail can be seen above and to the right of the shield. The shield is discernible. In LIBERTY at least a letter or two should be visible per ANA grading standards and PCGS. In the marketplace, many have no letters. *Reverse:* Further wear has flattened about half of the feathers. Those remaining are on the inside of the wings. The rim is full and shows many if not most dentils.

1875-CC. Graded G-6.

G-4, 6 (Good). *Obverse:* The seated figure is worn nearly smooth, but with some slight detail above and to the right of the shield. At G-4, there are no letters in LIBERTY remaining. On some at the G-6 level, there may be a trace of letters. *Reverse:* Most feathers in the eagle are gone. The border lettering is weak. The rim is visible partially or completely (depending on the strike).

1875-CC. Graded AG-3.

AG-3 (About Good). *Obverse:* The seated figure is mostly visible in outline form, with only a hint of detail. Much of the rim is worn away. The date remains clear. *Reverse:* The border letters are partially worn away. The eagle is mostly in outline form, but with a few details discernible. The rim is weak or missing.

1877. Graded PF-61.

PF-60 to 70 (Proof). *Obverse and Reverse:* Proofs that are extensively cleaned and have many hairlines, or that are dull and grainy, are lower level, such as PF-60 to 62. These are not widely desired. With medium hairlines and good reflectivity, an assigned grade of PF-64 is indicated, and with relatively few hairlines, Gem PF-65. In various grades hairlines are most easily seen in the obverse field. PF-66 should have hairlines so delicate that magnification is needed to see them. Above that, a Proof should be free of such lines.

Illustrated coin: Lovely frosted devices are complemented by indigo toning in the peripheries of the fields.

Collecting Liberty Seated Twenty-Cent Pieces

With so few dates and mintmarks, not many numismatists have made a specialty of this denomination. Most buyers seek a single example to illustrate in a type set. Most easily obtained in Mint State and all grades by far is the 1875-S. The 1875-CC is considerably scarcer, but enough are around that finding a nice one will be no problem.

To learn more about this series and its history acquire copies of these two books: Lane J. Brunner and John M. Frost's *Double Dimes—The United States Twenty-Cent Piece* (2014) and Kevin Flynn's, *The Authoritative Reference on Liberty Seated Twenty Cents* (2013). The former lists many die varieties and is available free online at www.doubledimes.com.

Being a Smart Buyer

Twenty-cent pieces are the simplest of the Liberty Seated denominations to analyze numismatically as the series is so short. As I have mentioned before under half dimes and dimes, do not be a slave to grading numbers. There are two more factors that can be equally or even more important. Sharpness of strike is very important, and some cherrypicking will yield sharp examples of the sometimes-weak 1875-CC and 1875-S. Eye appeal is the final key element in connoisseurship.

1875–1878, Liberty Seated

Liberty Seated with 13 stars to the left and right, and the date below. The reverse has an eagle similar to that found on the trade dollar.

Designer: Christian Gobrecht (obverse) and William Barber (reverse).

Specifications: *Composition:* 90 percent silver, 10 percent copper. *Diameter:* 22 mm. *Weight:* 77.16 grains (5 grams). *Edge:* Plain.

1875

Circulation-strike mintage: 38,500

Proof mintage: 1,200

Availability in Mint State: Mint State coins are far rarer than Proofs and, when seen, typically have a somewhat

actual size: 22 mm

prooflike (rather than deeply frosty) surface. *MS-60 to 62:* 250 to 300. *MS-63:* 125 to 150. *MS-64:* 100 to 125. *MS-65 or better:* 50 to 60.

Availability in circulated grades: This is far and away the scarcest of the three issues of this year, and most show extensive wear.[7]

Characteristics of striking: This issue is usually well struck.

Proofs: It is likely that some Proofs were placed into circulation or sold to coin dealers. *PF-60 to 62:* 400 to 500. *PF-63:* 200 to 250. *PF-65 or better:* 90 to 110.

Notes: The first twenty-cent pieces were struck on May 18, 1875, in Philadelphia. Proofs were also first struck about this time. On May 20 four Proofs were sold to a collector for 30¢ each.

All obverse dies for 1875 twenty-cent pieces are from the same four-digit logotype punch. The figures are somewhat curiously formed, the 7 having a particularly large top, the top or "flag" part of the 5 also being large, and the ball of the 5 being quite small.

G-4	VG-8	F-12	VF-20	EF-40	AU-50
$225	$250	$300	$325	$425	$600
MS-60	**MS-63**	**MS-65**	**PF-60**	**PF-63**	**PF-65**
$925	$1,450	$4,500	$1,450	$2,750	$6,500

1875-CC

Circulation-strike mintage:
133,290

Availability in Mint State:
In 2013 the Battle Born
Collection Sale featured an
example of this coin in MS-67.
MS-60 to 62: 150 to 175.
MS-63: 120 to 140. *MS-64:*
100 to 125. *MS-65 or better:* 25 to 35.

actual size: 22 mm

Availability in circulated grades: This issue is available, but is slightly scarce in circulated grades. Typical grades are VG to VF, but EF and AU coins are readily available. Beginning in about 2010, a large numismatic hoard began to be dispersed. Once there were 227 listings on eBay at the same time![8]

Characteristics of striking: The majority are lightly struck, a feature that is quickly ascertainable by checking the highest part of the eagle's right (on the observer's left) wing.

G-4	VG-8	F-12	VF-20	EF-40	AU-50	MS-60	MS-63	MS-65
$250	$300	$450	$500	$850	$1,050	$1,850	$2,850	$11,500

1875-S

Circulation-strike mintage:
1,155,000

Availability in Mint State:
The easy winner in the availability category. *MS-60 to 62:*
2,000 to 2,500. *MS-63:* 1,300
to 1,600. *MS-64:* 1,000 to
1,250. *MS-65 or better:* 350
to 450.

actual size: 22 mm

Availability in circulated grades: This issue is very common. Typical grades are VG to VF, but EF and AU coins are plentiful.

Characteristics of striking: Some of this issue have a repunched S mintmark, giving it the fanciful (some imagination is needed) appearance of a dollar sign ($). Still others are somewhat prooflike, some of which have been called branch-mint Proofs. Walter Breen, who often invented "facts," stated that in June of 1875 at a special ceremony in San Francisco 12 Proofs were struck, but no documentation of such an event has been found.

John Frost, co-author of the *Double Dimes* book, commented that anyone studying a particular 1875-S graded as PF-64 Cameo (PCGS) would become a believer that Proofs were made in San Francisco. The situation is controversial, however. Per Frost:

> Making the entire mess worse, the Breen plate coin for the branch-mint Proof (the Roy Rauch coin) is clearly not a Proof or Specimen strike at all, but in my opinion is merely a proof-like circulation strike. I studied it. I think there were a few (but an undocumented number of) special pieces struck (call them Proofs or specimen strikes). Only a couple of them are equal to Philadelphia Proofs, but a few more are Specimens struck from the same dies, but the planchets not quite as polished on reverse as obverse. Even my slightly impaired Specimen is far and away superior

to the proof-like circulation strikes, including the Rauch coin. The actual branch mint Proofs or Specimen strikes speak for themselves. They remain controversial to be sure, but I do not believe they are merely proof-like circulation strikes.

The Proof discussion is taken up in detail by Len Augsburger in "Branch Mint Proofs in the Liberty Seated Series: Twenty Cent Pieces" in the *E-Gobrecht*, January 2007. Whether the 1875-S coins were deliberately struck as Proofs is unknown, and the story that 12 were made in a special ceremony has no foundation. "In any case, highly prooflike examples of the 1875-S clearly exist, and this coin has been one of the more accepted branch-mint Proofs in the Liberty Seated series, with three pieces currently certified by PCGS and two by NGC."

An extensive study of so-called branch Proofs will be found in Kevin Flynn's *The Authoritative Reference on Liberty Seated Twenty Cents*. Flynn believes they are prooflike circulation strikes.

Notes: The 1875-S is popular with variety collectors, and there are numerous misplaced dates (MPD) and several repunched mintmarks. These can be cherrypicked without paying a premium.

G-4	VG-8	F-12	VF-20	EF-40	AU-50	MS-60	MS-63	MS-65
$125	$145	$150	$175	$250	$350	$750	$1,050	$2,500

1876

Circulation-strike mintage: 14,750

Proof mintage: 1,150

Availability in Mint State: In Mint State, this issue is elusive overall, but there are enough around to satisfy the needs of specialists. *MS-60 to 62:* 150 to 170. *MS-63:* 130 to 150. *MS-64:* 110 to 130. *MS-65 or better:* 70 to 90.

actual size: 22 mm

Availability in circulated grades: This issue is very scarce. Typical grades are EF and AU.

Characteristics of striking: These are usually well struck, but all have slight doubling on the reverse.[9]

Proofs: In this year, the Mint officials were invited to relocate the Mint Collection from the Philadelphia Mint to nearby Fairmount Park where the Centennial Exhibition was being held. The curator declined, but suggested that the Mint's doors would be open to anyone who cared to visit the permanent display. Presumably, additional quantities of Proof silver sets were made in anticipation of the demand. However, customers seem to have stayed away in the proverbial droves, and today Proofs of 1876 are considered scarce, about in keeping with other dates of the era. It is believed that unsold Proofs were simply put into circulation, as certain silver Proofs are seen today with extensive handling marks (this being particularly true of 1876 twenty-cent pieces. *PF-60 to 62:* 400 to 500. *PF-63:* 200 to 250. *PF-65 or better:* 100 to 130.

G-4	VG-8	F-12	VF-20	EF-40	AU-50
$250	$300	$400	$500	$600	$700
MS-60	**MS-63**	**MS-65**	**PF-60**	**PF-63**	**PF-65**
$925	$1,600	$4,500	$1,300	$2,800	$6,500

1876-CC

Circulation-strike mintage: 10,000

Availability in Mint State: There are 18 to 20 or so estimated to exist. The grades per the certification services have bounced around in recent years due to resubmissions, but MS-63 and 64 are usual grades, with a few MS-65.

Availability in circulated grades: Four are known to specialist John Frost.

Characteristics of striking: This issue is well struck.

actual size: 17.9 mm

Detail of doubling.

Notes: All authentic 1876-CC twenty-cent pieces have the word LIBERTY doubled on the shield—a doubled die. The obverse stars and certain other features are doubled as well.

As of January 6, 1876, there were 4,261 1875-CC coins on hand at the Mint, necessitating a call for more. At the time such coins circulated in Nevada and California for the most part, with few going elsewhere. Records reveal that 10,000 1876-CC twenty-cent pieces were struck in March.[10] However, by the time they were produced by the Carson City Mint, the denomination was rendered effectively obsolete, and it appears that nearly all were melted. On May 8 and May 15, 1876, there were 13,315 twenty-cent pieces in the vault at Carson City, presumably representing 3,315 left over 1875-CC coins, plus the new 1876-CC production. From May 8, 1876, through May 11, 1877, only 954 twenty-cent pieces were paid out. It is not known what dates these were, but they quite possibly could have been 1875-CC, while the coinage of 1876-CC remained intact in cloth bags.

On May 19, 1877, Mint Director Dr. Henry R. Linderman wrote to James Crawford, superintendent of the Carson City Mint, directing him: "You are hereby authorized and directed to melt all the twenty-cent pieces you have on hand and you will debit Silver Profit Fund with any loss hereon." Thus, it would seem that nearly all of the 1876-CC twenty-cent pieces that were minted, plus the remaining 1875-CC pieces, went to the melting pot.[11]

Perhaps the first specimen of the 1876-CC twenty-cent piece to attract notice in a catalog was that sold for $7 in the R. Coulton Davis Collection auction by New York Coin & Stamp Company, January 20–24, 1890. Davis was very close to Mint officials, and it may be that he obtained it from the five 1876-CC twenty-cent pieces in the possession of the 1877 Assay Commission that reviewed the previous year's coinage. Two coins for a special assay were also sent to the office of the director of the Mint in Washington. Of the total seven coins, two were destroyed, leaving net five in the possession of Mint authorities in the East. At that time only a few numismatists collected coins by mintmark varieties, and virtually nothing was known of the 1876-CC.

In his 1893 text, Heaton mentioned the 1876-CC twenty-cent piece in two places, noting in the preface that it was "excessively rare in any condition," and in the main text the following: "The pieces of 1876-CC have become very rare, as we have mentioned in our preface, from the negligence of western collectors, or the indifference involved in mintmark rarities."

The June 1894 issue of *The Numismatist* included this: "Three of the rare twenty-cent pieces of 1876 from the Carson City Mint have lately turned up in Uncirculated condition. It was not two days before they were incorporated into three of our leading collections where their presence is highly appreciated."

The Maryland estate hoard is one of the most remarkable finds in the American series. In the late 1950s, Baltimore dealer Tom Warfield found a group of seven, eight, or possibly nine, splendid Mint State coins in his hometown. Each piece was a lustrous gem, delicately toned and virtual perfection. Perhaps a few of these may have come from the Assay Commission. The genesis of this cache was never revealed. The author bought four of them, and John J. Ford Jr. bought at least three (which he sold to Morton Stack).

G-4	VG-8	F-12	VF-20	EF-40	AU-50	MS-60	MS-63	MS-65
					$225,000	$325,000	$425,000	$750,000

1877

Proof mintage: 510

Impaired Proofs: 10 or so.
PF-60 to 62: 200 to 250.
PF-63: 125 to 175. *PF-65 or better:* 75 to 85.

Characteristics of striking:
This issue is always sharp.

actual size: 22 mm

Notes: By 1877 the twenty-cent piece had been discontinued for circulation purposes, but the denomination lingered on in the form of specimens made with Proof finish for collectors.

PF-60	PF-63	PF-65
$5,500	$8,500	$12,500

1878

Proof mintage: 600

Impaired Proofs: 8 to 12.
PF-60 to 62: 250 to 300.
PF-63: 150 to 200. *PF-65 or better:* 50 to 70.

Characteristics of striking:
Some of these have the head of Liberty lightly struck.

actual size: 22 mm

Notes: This is the final issue in the short-lived twenty-cent series. Only Proofs were struck and only to the extent of 600 pieces.

PF-60	PF-63	PF-65
$3,500	$4,500	$8,000

LIBERTY SEATED QUARTERS (1838–1891)

Introduction

Quarter-dollar coins, usually referred to simply as quarters, were first coined in 1796, combining the Draped Bust obverse design with the Small Eagle reverse. After that year no coins of this denomination were made until 1804, when the Draped Bust obverse was continued, now with the new Heraldic Eagle reverse. These designs were used through 1807. Production of quarters was suspended, to be resumed in 1815 with the Capped Bust obverse in combination with a reverse showing a perched eagle. These were made intermittently through 1828, then in slightly smaller diameter and with E PLURIBUS UNUM omitted from 1831 continuously into 1838.

The Liberty Seated quarter-dollar series commenced with the year 1838. By then the Liberty Seated design had been standard for the half dime and dime for a year, and the motif had appeared first on the silver dollars of 1836. In 1838 Christian Gobrecht prepared models, hubs, and dies for Liberty Seated quarters. The first samples of the new quarter were sent from Philadelphia to Secretary of the Treasury Levi Woodbury in Washington on September 14, 1838:

> I have the honor to send you by this mail $5 worth of quarter dollars of a new coinage, which I hope will meet your approbation.[1]

This general obverse and reverse motif, with changes as described below, was continued through 1891. Although there were many exceptions, in general fewer quarters were produced in a given year than were dimes or half dollars. Production was continuous at the Philadelphia Mint. The New Orleans Mint struck Liberty Seated quarters for most years from 1840 to 1860 and again in 1891. In San Francisco quarters were struck from 1855 to 1878, except for 1863, and again in 1888 and 1891. In Carson City they were made continuously from 1870 through 1878.

The Design of the Liberty Seated Quarter

The obverse motif, no drapery at the elbow, is adapted from Christian Gobrecht's illustrious silver dollar design of 1836 as modified by adding stars in 1838. Matching other new silver designs of the time, the quarter dollar depicts Liberty seated on a rock, her left hand holding a liberty cap on a pole and her right holding a shield inscribed LIBERTY. Thirteen stars are around the border, and the date is below.

The reverse depicts an eagle perched on a laurel branch and holding three arrows. UNITED STATES OF AMERICA is above and the denomination QUAR. DOL. is below. There is no motto on the reverse, E PLURIBUS UNUM having been absent from the series since 1828 (and not to reappear until the Barber coinage of 1892).

Edge Reed Counts on Liberty Seated Quarters

The subject of counting the vertical ribs or reeds on the edges of Liberty Seated quarters was detailed by John W. McCloskey, with findings as follows, lightly edited:[2]

Gauge 1: 110 reeds. This gauge reeding was used in striking the New Orleans quarters from 1849-O through to the 1891-O and the San Francisco quarters from 1859-S to 1873-S. This gauge was never used at the Philadelphia Mint to my knowledge, so that the edge reeding can help in identifying some of the rare branch mint pieces.

Gauge 2: 113 reeds. This is the most common reeding gauge used in the quarter series and was used extensively at the Philadelphia Mint. Used for all Philadelphia quarters from 1838 to 1860, some dated from 1871 to 1875, and all from 1880 to 1890. Also used at the San Francisco Mint from 1855-S to 1858-S and at the Carson City Mint for pieces from 1876-CC to 1878-CC. This reeding is very similar to Gauge 1 but can be distinguished by careful examination.

Gauge 3: 122 reeds. Used at the Philadelphia Mint to strike pieces dated 1861 to 1879, and also used in 1891. Used in Carson City to strike pieces from 1870-CC to 1878-CC. Thus the rare early Carson City pieces cannot be distinguished from the Philadelphia pieces of the same year by edge reeding.

Gauge 4: 137 reeds. The finest reeding used at the San Francisco Mint and found on pieces from 1874-S to 1891-S. To my knowledge this reeding was not used at any other mint and can therefore be used to identify the late San Francisco pieces.

Gauge 5: 145 reeds. Used in the early years at the New Orleans Mint and found on pieces from 1840-O to 1847-O. This fine reeding thus characterizes all early New Orleans pieces and was not used at any other mint to my knowledge. This information could be used to detect any attempt to remove the mintmark from an 1842-O Small Date quarter to create the very rare 1842, Small Date Philadelphia issue.

Gauge 6: 153 reeds. Used only on the 1876-CC quarter and reported as the "fine reeding" variety in the literature.

John McCloskey reported that both Gauges 2 and 3 were used at the Philadelphia Mint from 1871 to 1875. Both gauges were used for the 1873, No Arrows, Close 3, coins. For 1876-CC he reported Gauges 2, 3, and 6.

Pattern Coins

There were no pattern quarters made for changing or modifying Gobrecht's design. Other patterns using a "seated figure" motif were struck in 1870–1872, namely William Barber's Seated Liberty design, James Longacre's Indian Princess design, and Barber's Amazonian design. Quarters in copper, aluminum, and silver dated 1863, 1864, and 1865 are known with the IN GOD WE TRUST motto adopted in

1866, but these were made after 1866 for private sale to numismatists. Related half dollars and silver dollars were made.

Additionally, many different Proof strikings from original dies in off metals such as copper and aluminum were made in 1860–1861, 1864–1876, 1879, and 1884–1885. Popularly but incorrectly called "trial pieces," they were made for sale to collectors and are described in detail in *United States Pattern Coins* by J. Hewitt Judd. All are rare.

Aspects of Striking

The striking quality of Liberty Seated quarters varies widely. Nearly all New Orleans coins have weakness in areas, and the quarters struck at the mints in Philadelphia, San Francisco, and Carson City vary.

Details of an 1838 quarter certified as MS-64. The holder makes no mention of the very weakly struck head and stars.

Proofs are usually sharply struck, but some are weak in areas, such as the star centers at the upper left on this 1886 quarter certified as PF-68. Again, there was no mention of the weakness.

Weak areas on coins were caused by spacing the dies slightly too far apart, so as to extend die life and minimize damage such as cracks. Most areas of light striking are on the obverse, particularly on the head of Liberty and on the stars. The reverses are usually sharp, but sometimes show lightness at the tops of the eagle's wings, particularly on the right. The denticles on either side can be weak or even mushy.

As the certification services make no mention of sharpness or lack thereof, and as auction listings usually recite just the information on holders, the field is wide open for cherrypicking sharp coins for no extra cost—a reward for your knowledge!

Release and Distribution

On September 13, 1838, 20 of the new Liberty Seated quarter dollars were sent by Mint Director Robert Maskell Patterson to Secretary of the Treasury Levi Woodbury in Washington for his approval. This was granted, and minting in quantity for circulation commenced on September 29.

Quarters were readily accepted in commerce, but were not seen as often as dimes and half dollars. More plentiful in circulation in the early years through the end of the 1850s were Spanish-American two reales or "two bit" coins that circulated for the value of 25¢.

In 1849 the advent of large quantities of gold from California disturbed the traditional value ratio between silver and gold, and silver bullion rose slightly in value on international markets. This caused quarters and other Liberty Seated silver coins to be withdrawn from circulation to be hoarded or to be melted. In 1850 through early 1853 hardly any quarters were seen in commerce. The Spanish-American two-reales coins were not affected and remained plentiful in circulation.

To remedy the situation the Act of February 21, 1853, lowered the amount of silver in Liberty Seated coins from the half dime to the half dollar (but not the dollar). The first quarters under the new weight standard were released on Friday, April 1,

1853. Within a month the coins were familiar sights throughout the East and were widely reported upon in the newspapers.

By early 1862 the outcome of the Civil War was uncertain. To help fund government operations the Treasury Department authorized Legal Tender Notes—paper money with face values from $1 to $1,000 that were not redeemable at par in gold or silver coins. Concerned about the economy, the public hoarded these coins. By early summer 1862 all silver coins were gone from circulation. It was thought that after the Civil War ended in April 1865 hoarded silver coins would come out of hiding, but that did not happen. Citizens remained concerned about the finances of the government.

Finally, after April 20, 1876, silver coins and Legal Tender Notes were exchangeable at par. A flood of long-stored silver coins came on the market. This was not anticipated by the Treasury, which in 1875 and 1876 had been coining large quantities of dimes, quarters, and half dollars. The result was a glut of silver that reduced new mintages of circulating coins of these denominations beginning in 1879. Production of circulation-strike quarters remained low through the 1880s.

After Barber quarters were introduced in 1892, Liberty Seated quarters remained in circulation for many years. By the time collecting coins became widely popular in the 1930s, such pieces remaining in commerce were worn down to very low grades.

Proof Liberty Seated Quarters

Proofs were struck at the Philadelphia Mint for all years from 1837 through 1891, although no silver Proof sets are known for 1851 and 1853. Certain "Proofs" of these two years may be inadvertent—from relapped dies or dies polished to remove surface irregularities, not prepared especially to create coins for collectors. This has been a point of discussion among specialists for many years.

Proofs in the years 1837 to 1858 were supplied to collectors at face value as a currency. There was a warm relationship between the Mint Cabinet (authorized in June 1838) and numismatists, and trades and exchanges were frequent. Proof quarters were availably singly and in sets. Those of the late 1830s through the 1840s are very rare, some being extremely so. Beginning in 1859, silver Proofs were sold only in sets, with a few scattered exceptions. Production that year was 800 sets, not all of which found buyers. Beginning in 1860 a set of silver Proofs could be purchased for $3. In that year, 1,000 sets were made, and an equal number in 1861. The production proved to be far in excess of the demand, with the result that most coins were melted or spent. Today, high-grade Proofs of these two years are rarer than later years in the decade with lower published mintages.

In 1873 the first Proof sets of the year were of the design and specification of those used since 1866 (when the motto IN GOD WE TRUST was added). After the Coinage Act of February 12, 1873, was implemented, arrows were added to the side of the date and a new type was created. Proofs were struck and were available in sets as well as singly.

The philosophy that "brilliant is best" pervaded numismatics from the 19th century into the modern era. As silver is active chemically, Proofs oxidized and became toned— easily enough remedied by the unfortunate use of silver polish or by dipping. Repeated dipping, toning, and dipping again caused the vast majority of Liberty Seated silver Proofs to acquire hairlines, ranging from microscopic to severe. Were this not true, all would survive today in perfect condition. As it is, typical grades average PF-63 and 64, with PF-65 and better grades being in the minority. Ever since about 1979, nicely toned Proofs have been "acceptable," now even desired by collectors. Accordingly, cleaning is less frequent. A new art, that of adding artificial toning, is widely practiced.

Grading Liberty Seated Quarters

**1853, Repunched Date, No Arrows or Rays;
FS-301. Graded MS-67.**

MS-60 to 70 (Mint State). *Obverse:* At MS-60, some abrasion and contact marks are evident, most noticeably on the bosom and thighs and knees. Luster is present, but may be dull or lifeless. At MS-63, contact marks are very few, and abrasion is hard to detect except under magnification. An MS-65 coin has no abrasion, and contact marks are sufficiently minute as to require magnification. Check the knees of Liberty and the right field. Luster should be full and rich. Most Mint State coins of the 1861 to 1865 years, Philadelphia issues, have extensive die striae (from not completely finishing the die). *Reverse:* Comments apply as for the obverse, except that in lower Mint State grades abrasion and contact marks are most noticeable on the eagle's neck, the claws, and the top of the wings (harder to see there, however). At MS-65 or higher there are no marks visible to the unaided eye. The field is mainly protected by design elements and does not show abrasion as much as does the obverse on a given coin.

Illustrated coin: Note the delicate toning in the fields. In addition to hints of green, rose, and teal there is a good deal of luster as well.

1891. Graded AU-53.

AU-50, 53, 55, 58 (About Uncirculated). *Obverse:* Light wear is seen on the thighs and knees, bosom, and head. At AU-58, the luster is extensive, but incomplete, especially in the right field. At AU-50 and 53, luster is less. *Reverse:* Wear is evident on the eagle's neck, claws, and top of the wings. An AU-58 coin has nearly full luster, more so than on the obverse, as the design elements protect the small field areas. At AU-50 and 53, there still are traces of luster.

Illustrated coin: Light wear is evident, and faintly toned luster can be seen on both sides.

1843. Graded EF-40.

EF-40, 45 (Extremely Fine). *Obverse:* Further wear is seen on all areas, especially the thighs and knees, bosom, and head. Little or no luster is seen on most coins. From this grade downward, sharpness of strike of the stars and the head does not matter to connoisseurs. *Reverse:* Further wear is evident on the eagle's neck, claws, and wings. Some feathers in the right wing may be blended together.

1860-S. Graded VF-25.

VF-20, 30 (Very Fine). *Obverse:* Further wear is seen. Most details of the gown are worn away, except in the lower-relief areas above and to the right of the shield. Hair detail is mostly or completely gone. *Reverse:* Wear is more extensive, with more feathers blended together, especially in the right wing. The area below the shield shows more wear.

Illustrated coin: The surfaces of this coin are unusually smooth and problem free for the issue.

1854-O. Graded F-12.

F-12, 15 (Fine). *Obverse:* The seated figure is well-worn, but with some detail above and to the right of the shield. LIBERTY is readable but weak in areas. *Reverse:* Wear is extensive, with about half of the feathers flat or blended with others.

1872-CC. Graded VG-10.

VG-8, 10 (Very Good). *Obverse:* The seated figure is more worn, but some detail can be seen above and to the right of the shield. The shield is discernible. In LIBERTY at least the equivalent of two or three letters (can be a combination of partial letters) must be readable but can be very weak at VG-8, with a few more visible at VG-10. However, LIBERTY is not an infallible guide to grade this type, as some varieties had the word in low relief on the die, so it wore away slowly. *Reverse:* Further wear has flattened all but a few feathers, and the horizontal lines of the shield are indistinct. The leaves are only in outline form. The rim is visible all around, as are the ends of most denticles.

Illustrated coin: Note the faint red toning evident in areas of this otherwise pleasingly gray coin.

1872-CC. Graded G-6.

G-4, 6 (Good). *Obverse:* The seated figure is worn smooth. At G-4 there are no letters in LIBERTY remaining on most (but not all) coins; some coins, especially of the early 1870s, are exceptions. At G-6, traces of one or two can barely be seen. *Reverse:* The designs are only in outline form, although some vertical shield stripes can be seen on some. The rim is worn down, and tops of the border letters are weak or worn away, although the inscription can still be read.

1862-S. Graded AG-3.

AG-3 (About Good). *Obverse:* The seated figure is mostly visible in outline form, with only a hint of detail. Much of the rim is worn away. The date remains clear. *Reverse:* The border letters are partially worn away. The eagle is mostly in outline form, but with a few details discernible. The rim is weak or missing.

1860. Graded PF-65.

PF-60 to 70 (Proof). *Obverse and Reverse:* Proofs that are extensively cleaned and have many hairlines, or that are dull and grainy, are lower level, such as PF-60 to 62. These are not widely desired by connoisseurs. With medium hairlines and good reflectivity, an assigned grade of PF-64 is appropriate and with relatively few hairlines, Gem PF-65. In various grades hairlines are most easily seen in the obverse field. PF-66 should have hairlines so delicate that magnification is needed to see them. Above that, a Proof should be free of such lines.

Collecting Liberty Seated Quarters

As a class, year by year, type by type, Liberty Seated quarters from 1838 to 1891 are rarer than half dimes, dimes, or half dollars. Only the shorter-range 1840–1873 Liberty Seated dollars are more challenging.

As a rule of thumb, Mint State quarters dated before 1853 are quite scarce as most were melted when the metallic content of silver coins rose above the face value. (The authorized weight was reduced in 1853, solving the problem.) This is particularly true of New Orleans pieces, except a few issues of the early 1840s, which were discovered in quantity a few years ago when a hoard was excavated in the downtown section of the city, not far from the old New Orleans Mint. These coins, considerably blackened, had been hidden away for nearly a century and a half. Most other New Orleans quarters are major rarities in MS-63 or finer grade. Philadelphia quarters of the 1840s range from very scarce to rare if MS-63 or better, although their average grade is usually higher than are those from New Orleans. Proofs for the Philadelphia Mint years have often supplied the demand when choice and gem Mint State coins could not be found, this being especially true for the years after the late 1850s.

San Francisco quarters starting in 1855, and the early years of Carson City quarters starting in 1870, range from scarce to very rare in high grades. The 1870-CC quarter in particular is a landmark in this regard. The 1873-CC, No Arrows, is a great rarity, with only a handful known.

Liberty Seated quarters dated after 1874 are for the most part readily available through 1891, the last year in the series. A number of dates from 1879 onward have very low circulation strike mintages, adding to their popularity with collectors. These were well publicized at the time, with the result that Philadelphia Mint quarters from 1879 to 1891 are easily available in grades of MS-64 and higher.

The *Gobrecht Journal,* published by the Liberty Seated Collectors Club, forms a meeting place for specialists who submit articles, tell of new discoveries, and exchange information. The standard text on the series was published in 1991 by Larry Briggs, *The Comprehensive Encyclopedia of Liberty Seated Quarters.* For each date and mintmark, the book gives numbers such as 1, 2, 3, and onward for different obverses, and letters starting with A for different reverses. For example, 2-A of 1861 pairs the second obverse of the year with the first reverse. In proportion to certain large mintages, relatively few die pairs are given—furnishing many opportunities for new discoveries.

Over the years many articles about quarters have been published in the *Gobrecht Journal.* Information in earlier issues is often made obsolete in part by later studies as more information is obtained. An article by John W. McCloskey, "Availability of Liberty Seated Quarters By Grade," appeared in the *Gobrecht Journal,* March 1981, and surveyed public appearances of Liberty Seated quarters as reflected in advertisements in *Coin World* during that era. The study gives an interesting view of what was viewed as scarce at the time. These are the varieties that were *not* found in Mint State:

> 1840-O, No Drapery; 1840, With Drapery; 1842-O, Small Date; 1842-O, Large Date; 1843-O; 1844-O; 1847-O; 1849-O; 1850; 1850-O; 1851; 1851-O; 1852-O; 1853-O; 1855-O; 1856-S; 1857-O; 1858-O; 1858-S; 1859-O; 1859-S; 1860-S; 1861-S; 1862-S; 1863; 1864-S; 1866-S; 1868; 1868-S; 1869; 1869-S; 1870; 1870-CC; 1871-CC; 1871-S; 1872; 1872-CC; 1872-S; 1873-CC, No Arrows; 1873-CC, With Arrows; 1873-S; 1875-CC; and 1891-O.

The sample covered only a relatively short duration and, indeed, Mint State coins of some of the issues appeared in other venues (and were later noted in certification service population reports). However, the McCloskey data certainly indicate what dates and mintmarks were not and still are not *easily* available in Mint State, in some instances, not available at all.

Today the population reports issued by PCGS and NGC give expanded information. Such data requires careful interpretation, as low-grade common coins have few listings and can appear to be rare. Further complicating the scenario is gradeflation, which has raised many coins from AU to lower ranges of Mint State, and among rarities, the same coin can be resubmitted multiple times. Many MS-63 and 64 coins of the 1980s are now certified as MS-65 and higher. This makes scientific market analysis impossible. However, many dealers and collectors have studied this over the years, and general ranges of availability as given in the present text are useful.

In the winter of 1996–1997, when staff members and I were cataloging the quarters in the Louis E. Eliasberg Collection, we compiled all of the listings in the PCGS and NGC population reports. Our findings included these:

> No example of a Mint State coin graded by either service: 1854-O, Huge O; 1859-S; 1860-S; 1861-S; 1870-CC.
>
> No example of a coin finer than MS-64 graded by either service: 1840-O, No Drapery; 1842-O, Small Date; 1842-O, Large Date; 1843-O; 1847-O; 1849-O; 1850-O; 1851-O; 1852-O; 1853-O; 1854-O, Huge O; 1855-O; 1857-O; 1858-S; 1859-S; 1860-S; 1861-S; 1862-S; 1864-S; 1869; 1870-CC; 1872-CC; 1873, Close 3; 1877-S, S Over Horizontal S.

The preceding lists are very "tight" as they combine both services. If each individual service were to be considered alone, the lists would be much lengthier. The point is that among Liberty Seated quarters there are many rarities among high grade coins. Both PCGS and NGC make their population reports available on the Internet.

Being a Smart Buyer

My advice for being a smart buyer of Liberty Seated quarters parallels what I give for other series. Basically, use the number on a certified holder as a *starting point* then check the sharpness of strike. If light strikes are typical for a given variety, buy the sharpest you can, even if there is some weakness. If the issue is known for having sharply struck coins, find one. The third step is to find a coin with nice eye appeal. In any grade from G-4 to MS-65 and beyond, within the same level some coins are ugly, some are so-so, and others are attractive.

This formula will set you on the right course for a quality collection no matter what your budget or grade desires are. The secret is that 90 percent or more of *other* buyers simply look at the grade on a holder. In actuality, a sharply struck MS-63 coin with beautiful eye appeal can be far more desirable than a Gem MS-65 that is weakly struck and unattractive. Don't tell anyone!

1838–1840, No Motto above Eagle (Variety 1—No Drapery)

There is no drapery at Liberty's elbow for this design. This type encompasses the issues of 1838, 1839, and some of 1840-O. The first New Orleans quarter dollar made its appearance in 1840 within this type. The Small Date numerals on the obverse and Small Letters on the reverse give quarters of this date a particularly attractive appearance.

Designer: Christian Gobrecht.

Specifications: *Composition:* 90 percent silver, 10 percent copper. *Diameter:* 24.3 mm. *Weight:* 103.125 grains (6.68 grams). *Edge:* Reeded.

1838

Circulation-strike mintage: 466,000

Proof mintage: 2–3

Availability in Mint State: Per Larry Briggs, this is the most available Mint State Liberty Seated quarter prior to 1853. It is very popular

actual size: 24.3 mm

and is in everlasting demand as the first year of the type. The Louis E. Eliasberg Sale in 1997 featured an example of this coin in MS-65, as did the Eugene H. Gardner Sale in 2014. *MS-60 to 62:* 65 to 90. *MS-63:* 50 to 75. *MS-64:* 30 to 45. *MS-65 or better:* 7 to 9.

Availability in circulated grades: This issue is readily available in circulated grades. Most are in lower grade ranges, but enough EF and AU coins exist to satisfy the demand by specialists.

Characteristics of striking: Striking on this issue varies. They are nearly always weak in areas, especially the head and stars, but there are occasional exceptions.

Proofs: Proof 1838 quarters are apparently unique. An example appeared in Stack's Anderson-Dupont sale in 1954. In 2014 the Eugene H. Gardner Sale featured an example of this coin in PF-63.

Notes: Varieties with Open Claws (common) and Closed Claws, the last being perhaps eight to ten times rarer, were first reported by Larry Briggs in 1990.

G-4	VG-8	F-12	VF-20	EF-40	AU-50
$50	$65	$75	$225	$500	$1,050
MS-60	**MS-63**	**MS-65**	**PF-60**	**PF-63**	**PF-65**
$1,750	$4,500	$35,000		$300,000	

1839

Circulation-strike mintage: 491,146

Proof mintage: 2–3

Availability in Mint State: From the Louis E. Eliasberg Sale in 1997: "MS-66 or finer. Well struck in all areas." In 2014

actual size: 24.3 mm

the Eugene H. Gardner sale featured an example of this coin in MS-67. *MS-60 to 62:* 35 to 50. *MS-63:* 25 to 30. *MS-64:* 12 to 15. *MS-65 or better:* 4 to 6.

Availability in circulated grades: These are readily available in lower grades, but are scarce at the AU level.

Characteristics of striking: This issue is often weakly struck.

Proofs: Only one Proof has been confirmed to exist, the coin that was part of the F.C.C. Boyd Collection (1945), later in the Pittman and Gardner collections, PF-65.

Notes: There are varieties with Closed Claws, Open Claws, and Very Long Claws (only about 10 percent of survivors are of the last variety). The Long Claws reverse is mated with two obverses, one with the border denticles somewhat resembling beads or pellets.[3]

G-4	VG-8	F-12	VF-20	EF-40	AU-50
$50	$65	$75	$225	$500	$1,050

MS-60	MS-63	MS-65	PF-60	PF-63	PF-65
$1,750	$4,500	$37,500			$450,000

1840-O, No Drapery

Circulation-strike mintage: 382,200

actual size: 24.3 mm

Availability in Mint State: Most Mint State pieces seen are from the famous New Orleans Hoard (described below). These typically show what Larry W. Briggs called "dull and/or corroded surfaces," from burial in the ground. The Louis E. Eliasberg Sale in 1997 featured an example of this coin in MS-64. In 2014 and 2015 the Eugene H. Gardner Sale featured examples of this coin in MS-67 and MS-65. *MS-60 to 62:* 12 to 15. *MS-63:* 3 or 4. *MS-64:* 2 or 3. *MS-65 or better:* 2 or 3.

Availability in circulated grades: This issue is one of the most plentiful early quarters in worn grades from AG-3 up. Some etched pieces from the New Orleans Hoard are AU.

Characteristics of striking: These usually have areas of weakness.

Notes: Jack Marston's "The Transitional 1840-O No Drapery Quarter," the *Gobrecht Journal*, March 1992, noted: "On the obverse you will notice that the dentils are very small and in some places almost non-existent. This feature creates considerably more space around the figure of Liberty and around the stars and the dates. This feature is like no other Liberty Seated quarter before or after it."

The New Orleans hoard of Liberty Seated silver coins of various denominations and types, mostly quarter dollars of 1840-O (a few) and 1841-O (many), came to light around noon, October 29, 1982, when excavations for the new Meridien Hotel in the French Quarter of the city revealed three long-buried wooden boxes filled with coins![4]

G-4	VG-8	F-12	VF-20	EF-40	AU-50	MS-60	MS-63	MS-65
$65	$70	$100	$225	$500	$1,050	$1,850	$5,500	$35,000

1840–1853, No Motto Above Eagle (Variety 1—With Drapery)

The design is the same as the preceding, but drapery has been added to the elbow of Liberty. This era is replete with many repunched dates, cracked dies, and other interesting features and constitutes a particularly challenging area for numismatic specialists. The Type 1 reverse concluded with the elusive 1853 Philadelphia quarter dollar without arrows, of which relatively few were distributed.

Reverse Hub Changes of 1840

In 1840 a new reverse hub was introduced. The 1840 Type 1 reverse was changed out for the 1840 Type 2 reverse.

1840 Type 1: Used from 1838 to 1840, the eagle has a prominent tongue.

1840 Type 2: This reverse was used from 1840 to 1853 and again from 1856 to 1873. The eagle is without the previously prominent tongue. Many changes to the feathers have been made, most visibly on the eagle's neck.

Detail of Type 1 reverse.   Detail of Type 2 reverse.

Designer: Christian Gobrecht.

Specifications: *Composition:* 90 percent silver, 10 percent copper. *Diameter:* 24.3 mm. *Weight:* 103.125 grains (6.68 grams). *Edge:* Reeded.

1840

Circulation-strike mintage: 188,127

Proof mintage: *5–8*

Availability in Mint State: A small hoard of seven pieces turned up in Baltimore circa 1984, of which Larry Briggs

actual size: 24.3 mm

purchased the four best pieces.[5] In 2015 the Eugene H. Gardner Sale featured examples of this coin in MS-65 and MS-62. *MS-60 to 62:* 15 to 20. *MS-63:* 10 to 14. *MS-64:* 7 to 9. *MS-65 or better:* 4 to 6.

Availability in circulated grades: This issue is readily available in circulated grades through VF, though EF and AU coins are slightly scarce.

Characteristics of striking: The strike varies, but on average most are more strongly struck than are the quarters of the preceding two years.

Proofs: The Louis E. Eliasberg Sale in 1997 featured an example of this coin in PF-64. In 2015 the Eugene H. Gardner Sale featured an example of this coin in PF-65 (ex Pittman). Approximately three examples have been certified.

Notes: This issue has both hub Type 1 and 2 reverses, the latter being four or five times scarcer.[6]

G-4	VG-8	F-12	VF-20	EF-40	AU-50
$60	$65	$75	$175	$425	$700

MS-60	MS-63	MS-65	PF-60	PF-63	PF-65
$1,650	$5,000	$18,000			$100,000

1840-O, With Drapery

Circulation-strike mintage: 43,000

actual size: 24.3 mm

Availability in Mint State: The Louis E. Eliasberg Sale in 1997 featured an example of this coin in MS-65. In 2015 the Eugene H. Gardner Sale featured examples of this coin in MS-65 and MS-62. *MS-60 to 62:* 25 to 30. *MS-63:* 18 to 22. *MS-64:* 15 to 20. *MS-65 or better:* 4 to 6.

Availability in circulated grades: This issue is easily available in most lower grades, but AU coins are scarce.

Characteristics of striking: Striking of this issue varies, but well struck coins can be found.

Notes: More so than at the Philadelphia Mint, dies at the New Orleans Mint were kept in service for a prolonged period of time, even after they became broken or damaged. Due to the only ready access to New Orleans being by sea in 1840, replacement was not an easy matter.

Large-O Mintmark: This issue has varieties with Large O (about 50 to 75 are known[7]) and Small O mintmarks. The O appears approximately 25 percent larger on the Large O variety. It is listed as FS-25-1840o-501 in *Cherrypickers' Guide to Rare Die Varieties.* The Briggs Reverse 1-B, Large O, has denticles hand-entered in New Orleans to prolong the life of the dies.

G-4	VG-8	F-12	VF-20	EF-40	AU-50	MS-60	MS-63	MS-65
$45	$75	$115	$215	$450	$700	$1,400	$3,800	$22,500

1841

Circulation-strike mintage: 120,000

Proof mintage: 3–5

Availability in Mint State: In 2014 the Eugene H. Gardner Sale featured examples of this coin in MS-66, MS-65 (2), and MS-64. *MS-60 to 62:* 15 to 20. *MS-63:* 9 to 12. *MS-64:* 7 to 9. *MS-65 or better:* 3 or 4.[8]

actual size: 24.3 mm

Availability in circulated grades: Many 1841 Philadelphia Mint quarters exist, mostly in lower grades.

Characteristics of striking: This issue varies in striking.

Proofs: In 2014 the Eugene H. Gardner Sale featured an example of this coin in PF-66 (ex Pittman). Approximately three examples have been certified.

G-4	VG-8	F-12	VF-20	EF-40	AU-50
$65	$105	$135	$250	$500	$875

MS-60	MS-63	MS-65	PF-60	PF-63	PF-65
$1,350	$2,250	$8,000	$45,000	$65,000	

1841-O

Circulation-strike mintage: 452,000

Availability in Mint State: In 2014 the Eugene H. Gardner Sale featured examples of this coin in MS-67 and MS-64 (Doubled-Die obverse). *MS-60 to 62:* 60 to 80. *MS-63:* 12 to 15. *MS-64:* 7 to 9. *MS-65 or better:* 1 or 2.[9]

actual size: 24.3 mm

Availability in circulated grades: This issue is readily available in any grade desired. The number of extant coins can readily supply the relatively small population of numismatists seeking Liberty Seated quarters by date and mintmark varieties.

Characteristics of striking: Most coins of this issue are sharply struck, which is unusual (as a class) for a New Orleans quarter.

Notes: See the New Orleans hoard *Notes* under the 1840-O, No Drapery, listing.

Doubled-Die Obverse: This 1841-O quarter has doubling on the shield, ribbon, and on the first three stars. Prior to a number of them being found in the New Orleans hoard, this variety was very rare.[10] It is listed as FS-25-1841o-101 in *Cherrypickers' Guide to Rare Die Varieties.*

G-4	VG-8	F-12	VF-20	EF-40	AU-50	MS-60	MS-63	MS-65
$50	$65	$90	$165	$350	$425	$950	$2,000	$10,000

1842, Small Date

Proof mintage: *3–5*

Availability in circulated grades: No circulated Proofs have been seen.

Characteristics of striking: When seen these quarters are sharply struck.

Proofs: In 2014 the Eugene H. Gardner Sale featured an example of this coin in PF-65 (ex Eliasberg). Seven specimens have been identified.[11]

actual size: 24.3 mm

Detail of Small Date.

Notes: In 1842 a small number of Proofs, probably no more than 10 to 15, were produced for collectors, presentation to foreign dignitaries, use by government officials, and so on. The Proof obverse die was prepared by using a very small date logotype, thus creating the "Small Date." By contrast, dies used to produce circulation strikes had the date in larger numerals. The 1842, Small Date, quarters are believed to have been issued only as part of 1842 silver Proof sets (or, possibly, to separate requests for Proofs, but this is unlikely); no examples were made for general circulation or, so far as is known, for individual numismatic sale.

Apparently, the few Proofs made of the quarter dollar denomination in 1842 were of the Small Date type; none were made of the Large Date. Walter Breen reports a Proof 1842, Large Date in the collection of a "New York State specialist" (the late John Jay Pittman), but David W. Akers, who handled the Pittman numismatic estate, commented (letter, December 30, 1996): "The Pittman Collection does not contain the 1842, Small Date quarter and never did. In John's assembled 1842 'Proof set' the quarter was represented by a 'Proof' 1842, Large Date. In my opinion there is no such thing; all 1842 Proof quarters are Small Dates. John's coin is Uncirculated, proof-like."

In the *Gobrecht Journal*, April 1975, P. Scott Rubin presented an article, "Three Rare Quarters," which discussed the rarity of the 1842, Small Date; 1873-CC, No Arrows; and the 1873-CC, With Arrows.

Concerning the 1842, Small Date, quarter, Rubin noted that the first he could find offered for sale appeared in Charles Steigerwalt's June 1893 Fixed Price List #39.

Presumably, the 1842, Small Date, obverse dies in this and the half dollar series were made early in the year 1842, at which time it was thought that the logotype was too small, and the later circulation strike pieces, constituting the majority, were of the Large Date format. This would also explain the rarity of the 1842-O, Small Date, quarter and half dollar.

PF-60	PF-63	PF-65
	$65,000	$150,000

1842, Large Date

Circulation-strike mintage: 88,000

Availability in Mint State:
In 2014 the Eugene H. Gardner Sale featured examples of this coin in MS-65 (ex Pittman) and MS-64. *MS-60 to 62:* 12 to 15. *MS-63:* 2 or 3. *MS-64:* 1 or 2. *MS-65 or better:* 1 or 2.[12]

actual size: 24.3 mm

Availability in circulated grades:
This issue is scarce in any grade, and is rare in AU. Most are well worn.

Detail of Large Date.

Characteristics of striking: These usually have lightness on the head and a few stars, sometimes with slight weakness on the eagle.

Notes: All of the circulation (non-Proof) strikes of this date were made in the Large Date format, more appropriately called the Medium Date. The reputation of the 1842 Philadelphia Mint quarter dollar is long standing. In his *Mint Marks* treatise in 1893, Augustus G. Heaton remarked concerning this date: "The 1842 has a large date and a medium O [mintmark]. In the O Mint it is easy to get, but is very rare in the Philadelphia coinage, and most collectors will find themselves depending upon a mintmark for this date." The Heaton comment reflects not only the rarity of the Philadelphia Mint quarter of this year, but also the predilection of the typical collector to simply acquire one coin of each *date* for a collection.

G-4	VG-8	F-12	VF-20	EF-40	AU-50	MS-60	MS-63	MS-65
$65	$100	$150	$275	$450	$850	$1,600	$4,500	$12,500

1842-O, Small Date

Circulation-strike mintage: 769,000

Availability in Mint State:
This issue is exceedingly rare and any example is a landmark. In 2014 the Eugene H. Gardner Sale featured an example of this coin in MS-63 (ex Norweb 1988). *MS-60 to 62:* 1 or 2. *MS-63:* 1. *MS-64:* 0. *MS-65 or better:* 0.

actual size: 24.3 mm

Availability in circulated grades: These are usually seen well worn. They are extremely rare in EF and AU.

Detail of Small Date.

Characteristics of striking: This issue is struck better than average for a New Orleans coin. Late-die-state strikes show that the die came into contact with something which damaged the upper left corner of the shield and wing area.[13]

Notes: This is generally conceded to be the rarest New Orleans Seated Liberty quarter with the 1849-O a close competitor.

Although this issue has been described as a formidable rarity, Larry Briggs suggests that about 200 to 250 exist, including all grades. Most range from About Good to Fine.[14]

G-4	VG-8	F-12	VF-20	EF-40	AU-50	MS-60	MS-63	MS-65
$675	$1,250	$1,750	$3,000	$8,000	$12,500	$37,500	$70,000	

1842-O, Large Date

Circulation-strike mintage: Large portion of 1842-O, Small Date, mintage

Availability in Mint State: "Virtually unknown in Uncirculated," noted Larry Briggs in his reference book, which did not include the Louis E. Eliasberg (1997) MS-61 coin. In 2014 the Eugene H. Gardner Sale featured an example of this coin in MS-64 (ex Pittman). *MS-60 to 62:* 15 to 20. *MS-63:* 8 to 11. *MS-64:* 4 to 6. *MS-65 or better:* 0 or 1.

actual size: 24.3 mm

Detail of Large Date.

Availability in circulated grades: This issue is readily available in lower grades, but is quite scarce at the AU level.

Characteristics of striking: These quarters are usually sharp.

Notes: The 1842-O, Large Date, constituted the vast majority of the New Orleans quarter output of this year. They are sometimes called Medium Date.

G-4	VG-8	F-12	VF-20	EF-40	AU-50	MS-60	MS-63	MS-65
$55	$70	$85	$125	$275	$500	$1,750	$4,500	

1843

Circulation-strike mintage: 645,600

Proof mintage: 10–15

Availability in Mint State: In 2015 the Eugene H. Gardner Sale featured an example of this coin in MS-65. *MS-60 to 62:* 50 to 65. *MS-63:* 25 to 32. *MS-64:* 12 to 15. *MS-65 or better:* 2 or 3.[15]

actual size: 24.3 mm

Availability in circulated grades: This issue is common in all grades.

Characteristics of striking: Striking on these varies, but sharp coins can be found.

Proofs: In 2015 the Eugene H. Gardner Sale featured an example of this coin in PF-64 (ex Allenburger, Starr). Approximately seven examples have been certified.

Notes: The "Lightning Bolt reverse," Briggs Reverse C, has a zigzag die crack from the border to between the I and C in AMERICA to the eagle.

G-4	VG-8	F-12	VF-20	EF-40	AU-50
$50	$65	$85	$95	$200	$350
MS-60	MS-63	MS-65	PF-60	PF-63	PF-65
$750	$1,300	$4,500	$15,000	$30,000	$80,000

1843-O

Circulation-strike mintage: 968,000

Availability in Mint State: The 1843-O is very rare. The Norweb Collection Sale in 1988 featured an example of this coin in MS-63. The Louis E. Eliasberg Sale in 1997

actual size: 24.3 mm

featured an example of this coin in MS-63/65 (split grade) with Small O. "This probably will pass as full MS-65 to all but the most careful observer, as the few marks that can be seen are mostly hidden at Liberty's knee, along a skirt fold, and at the bottom of the first date digit." In 2015 the Eugene H. Gardner Sale featured an example of this coin in MS-64 with Small O. *MS-60 to 62:* 10 to 14. *MS-63:* 4 to 6. *MS-64:* 1 or 2. *MS-65 or better:* 1.

Availability in circulated grades: Most coins of this issue are well worn and have problems. EF and AU coins are rare. In well-worn grades the 1843-O is scarce but readily available in relation to the demand for it.

Characteristics of striking: This issue is usually fairly well struck but for some denticles.

Notes: These come with both Large (scarcer) and Small O mintmarks.

G-4	VG-8	F-12	VF-20	EF-40	AU-50	MS-60	MS-63	MS-65
$60	$85	$165	$400	$1,000	$1,750	$3,000	$6,500	$22,500

1844

Circulation-strike mintage: 421,200

Proof mintage: *3–5*

Availability in Mint State: In 2014 the Eugene H. Gardner Sale featured an example of this coin in MS-65. *MS-60 to 62:* 20 to 25. *MS-63:* 12 to 15. *MS-64:* 2 or 3. *MS-65 or better:* 1 or 2.

actual size: 24.3 mm

Availability in circulated grades: These are common across the board.

Characteristics of striking: This issue is usually sharp.

Proofs: The number of Proofs known has been a matter of debate for a long time. Larry Briggs and Walter Breen each suggested a population of five. David Akers, in his offering of the Pittman coin (later Gardner 2014, PF-66), said he knew of only three. Mark Borckardt says, "Two confirmed Proofs are the Pittman-Kaufman-Gardner coin and one in the National Numismatic Collection. One or two others may exist."[16]

G-4	VG-8	F-12	VF-20	EF-40	AU-50
$50	$65	$75	$80	$165	$325

MS-60	MS-63	MS-65	PF-60	PF-63	PF-65
$750	$2,000	$15,000			

1844-O

Circulation-strike mintage: 740,000

Availability in Mint State: Mint State coins of this issue are extremely rare. In 2014 the Eugene H. Gardner Sale featured an example of this coin in MS-65. *MS-60 to 62:* 14 to 18. *MS-63:* 6 to 9. *MS-64:* 5 to 7. *MS-65 or better:* 2 or 3.

actual size: 24.3 mm

Availability in circulated grades: Nearly all examples of this issue in circulated grades are well worn and are very common as such. AU coins are elusive.

Characteristics of striking: These usually have lightness on the obverse.

Notes: Some of this issue have the same reverse as the 1843-O, Large O, quarter. Of these, about two-thirds to three-quarters have the normal coin turn, and the remainder have medal turn, making the medal turn 1844-O with Reverse of 1843-O, Large O, a very scarce variety.[17]

G-4	VG-8	F-12	VF-20	EF-40	AU-50	MS-60	MS-63	MS-65
$55	$65	$85	$125	$275	$475	$1,500	$2,250	$10,000

1845

Circulation-strike mintage: 922,000

Proof mintage: 6–8

Availability in Mint State: This issue is very rare in Mint State. In 2014 the Eugene H. Gardner Sale featured an example of this coin in MS-65. *MS-60 to 62:* 22 to 25. *MS-63:* 15 to 20. *MS-64:* 8 to 10. *MS-65 or better:* 4 to 6.[18]

actual size: 24.3 mm

Availability in circulated grades: These are common in the context of the series.

Characteristics of striking: Striking in this issue varies, so cherrypicking is recommended.

Proofs: The obverse is not matched. The date, not described by Larry Briggs, is heavily repunched at 845 and is slightly repunched at the lower right of the 1. Indeed, the repunching is among the most dramatic seen on any Liberty Seated quarter dollar of this era. The reverse is similar to Briggs's Reverse D, but there may be some differences. Notably, the most prominent vertical stripes in the shield that pierce the horizontal stripes above seem to be on the present coin numbers one, two, five, ten, and eleven, with ten and eleven being the very most prominent. Several stripes pierce the bottom part of the shield as well, with the most outstanding in this regard being stripes seven and eight. The Louis E. Eliasberg Sale in 1997 featured an example of this coin in PF-65. In 2014 the Eugene H. Gardner Sale featured an example of this coin in PF-66. Approximately 13 examples have been certified.

G-4	VG-8	F-12	VF-20	EF-40	AU-50
$50	$65	$75	$80	$165	$250
MS-60	MS-63	MS-65	PF-60	PF-63	PF-65
$650	$1,250	$6,500		$20,000	$32,500

1846

Circulation-strike mintage: 510,000

Proof mintage: *15–20*

Availability in Mint State: In 2015 the Eugene H. Gardner Sale featured examples of this coin in MS-66 (2) and MS-65.

actual size: 24.3 mm

MS-60 to 62: 40 to 50. *MS-63:* 22 to 28. *MS-64:* 4 to 6. *MS-65 or better:* 3 to 5.

Availability in circulated grades: This issue is readily available in lower grades, but is elusive at the AU level.

Characteristics of striking: These quarters are usually sharply struck.

Proofs: The vertical shield stripes in all instances extend through the horizontal lines, but numerous shield stripes also extend below. This reverse die was used to strike Proof quarter dollars of 1846, 1847, and 1848. In 2015 the Eugene H. Gardner Sale featured an example of this coin in PF-64 (ex Eliasberg). Approximately 21 examples have been certified.

Note: The repunched date variety, "46/46," is readily available.

G-4	VG-8	F-12	VF-20	EF-40	AU-50
$55	$80	$115	$135	$275	$450
MS-60	MS-63	MS-65	PF-60	PF-63	PF-65
$1,000	$2,000	$12,500	$6,500	$15,000	$30,000

1847

Circulation-strike mintage: 734,000

Proof mintage: 6–8

Availability in Mint State: In 2014 and 2015 the Eugene H. Gardner Sale featured examples of this coin in MS-65 (2) and MS-64. *MS-60 to 62:* 22 to 28. *MS-63:* 10 to 14. *MS-64:* 4 to 5. *MS-65 or better:* 3.

actual size: 24.3 mm

Availability in circulated grades: This issue is readily available in circulated grades.

Characteristics of striking: This issue is usually sharp.

Proofs: The final date digit has a flat or truncated bottom, apparently from a defective punch. This was used on other dies as well and is clearly illustrated in the Briggs reference. The identical reverse die was used to strike Proof quarter dollars of 1846, 1847, and 1848. The Louis E. Eliasberg Sale in 1997 featured an example of this coin in PF-65. In 2014 the Eugene H. Gardner Sale featured an example of this coin in PF-66. Approximately four examples have been certified.

Notes: The following years of Philadelphia Mint quarters have a "compass point" reverse with a circular mark at the top of the leftmost vertical stripe in the shield, thought to have been a centering mark: 1847, 1848, 1849, 1854, 1855, 1856, 1857, and 1858.[19] The 1847 can be found in many different minute varieties; see Larry Briggs's *Comprehensive Encyclopedia of United States Liberty Seated Quarters*.

G-4	VG-8	F-12	VF-20	EF-40	AU-50
$50	$65	$75	$95	$160	$275
MS-60	**MS-63**	**MS-65**	**PF-60**	**PF-63**	**PF-65**
$750	$1,750	$5,500	$5,000	$10,000	$25,000

1847-O

Circulation-strike mintage: 368,000

Availability in Mint State: This issue is extremely rare. In 2014 and 2015 the Eugene H. Gardner Sale featured examples of this coin in MS-63 and MS-62. *MS-60 to 62:* 1 or 2. *MS-63:* 1. *MS-64:* 0 or 1. *MS-65 or better:* 0 or 1.

actual size: 24.3 mm

Availability in circulated grades: This issue is scarce in all lower grades, very scarce EF, and rare AU.[20]

Characteristics of striking: These usually have lightness on the obverse.

Notes: The vast majority of coins in all grades have die cracks on the reverse.[21] There are three mintmark placements for the 1847-O: left, centered, and right. All are available, but the centered is the most challenging.[22]

G-4	VG-8	F-12	VF-20	EF-40	AU-50	MS-60	MS-63	MS-65
$115	$175	$350	$600	$1,000	$1,750	$8,000	$15,000	

1848

Circulation-strike mintage: 146,000

Proof mintage: 5–8

actual size: 24.3 mm

Availability in Mint State: Among Philadelphia quarters of this era, the 1848 is in-credibly rare in Mint State. In 2014 and 2015 the Eugene H. Gardner Sale featured examples of this coin in MS-64 and MS-65. *MS-60 to 62:* 2 to 4. *MS-63:* 1 or 2. *MS-64:* 1 or 2. *MS-65 or better:* 1 or 2.[23]

Availability in circulated grades: This issue is quite scarce.

Characteristics of striking: Striking on this issue varies, and sharp pieces can be found.

Proofs: Under high magnification, star nine shows some "artifacts" around the point, to a lesser extent these are seen on star ten, and then become prominent on star eleven. The explanation for these extra-raised pieces of metal is not known to the writer, but must involve the hubbing or die-making process (not individual repunching of stars). Briggs Reverse C. The identical reverse die was used to strike Proof quarter dollars of 1846, 1847, and 1848. The Louis E. Eliasberg Sale in 1997 featured an example of this coin in PF-64. In 2014 the Eugene H. Gardner Sale featured an example of this coin in PF-66 (ex Pittman). Approximately six examples have been certified.

Doubled Date: Briggs 1-A. The first impact of the four-digit logotype was light and slightly above and to the left of the finished product. Interestingly, the early undertype digit 4 had a pointed left end, very sharply so, whereas the final, heavy digit 4 in the date has the left side trimmed off so as to avoid impacting the neighboring 8. One can theorize that this was a die made early in the year and upon inspection of the test imprint the digits 8 and 4 touched each other. The logotype was then corrected, and additional dies were made. Larry Briggs knows of two of these with the reverse rotated 90 degrees.[24]

G-4	VG-8	F-12	VF-20	EF-40	AU-50
$55	$95	$150	$200	$450	$650
MS-60	**MS-63**	**MS-65**	**PF-60**	**PF-63**	**PF-65**
$1,250	$4,750	$12,000	$5,000	$10,000	$30,000

1849

Circulation-strike mintage: 340,000

Proof mintage: 5–8

Availability in Mint State: In 2015 the Eugene H. Gardner Sale featured examples of this coin in MS-65 and MS-62. *MS-60 to 62:* 15 to 20. *MS-63:* 6 to 8. *MS-64:* 4 or 5. *MS-65 or better:* 1 or 2.

actual size: 24.3 mm

Availability in circulated grades: This issue is common, well worn, and slightly scarce in AU.

Characteristics of striking: These are usually sharply struck.

Proofs: The Louis E. Eliasberg Sale in 1997 featured an example of this coin in PF-64. In 2015 the Eugene H. Gardner Sale featured an example of this coin in PF-66 (ex Pittman). Approximately eight examples have been certified.

G-4	VG-8	F-12	VF-20	EF-40	AU-50
$50	$75	$95	$100	$250	$400
MS-60	**MS-63**	**MS-65**	**PF-60**	**PF-63**	**PF-65**
$1,000	$1,650	$10,000	$5,000	$10,000	$27,500

1849-O

Circulation-strike mintage: *16,000*

Availability in Mint State: In Mint State this issue is extremely rare. One certified MS coin appeared to the writer to be a recolored AU-50. The Louis E. Eliasberg Sale in 1997 featured an example of this coin in MS-62. In 2015 the Eugene H. Gardner Sale featured an example of this coin in MS-64. *MS-60 to 62:* 4 or 5. *MS-63:* 2 or 3. *MS-64:* 2 or 3. *MS-65 or better:* 0.

actual size: 24.3 mm

Availability in circulated grades: Most coins of this issue show extensive wear and have problems. This is one of the rarer issues among early Liberty Seated quarters.

Characteristics of striking: These usually have lightness on the obverse and some are sharper than others.

Notes: The mintage is not in *The Annual Report of the Director of the Mint*, but it should probably be deducted from the mintage of 1850-O. Walter Breen and Larry Briggs have both estimated 16,000.[25]

G-4	VG-8	F-12	VF-20	EF-40	AU-50	MS-60	MS-63	MS-65
$1,500	$2,150	$3,250	$3,750	$7,500	$8,500	$17,500	$22,500	

1850

Circulation-strike mintage: 190,800

Proof mintage: *5–8*

Availability in Mint State: In 2014 and 2015 the Eugene H. Gardner Sale featured examples of this coin in MS-67 and MS-65. *MS-60 to 62:* 9 to 12. *MS-63:* 4 to 6. *MS-64:* 2 or 3. *MS-65 or better:* 2 or 3.[26]

actual size: 24.3 mm

Availability in circulated grades: This issue is slightly scarce and most are well worn.

Characteristics of striking: These are usually well struck.

Proofs: In Proof format the 1850 quarter is very rare and takes its place as one of the most elusive of the denomination. Approximately six examples have been certified.

Notes: One die has the base of an extra 1 spectacularly punched on the raised rim, a very deep detail in the die. Many were probably melted for their bullion content.

G-4	VG-8	F-12	VF-20	EF-40	AU-50
$45	$95	$135	$225	$400	$650
MS-60	**MS-63**	**MS-65**	**PF-60**	**PF-63**	**PF-65**
$2,000	$3,500	$12,500			$85,000

1850-O

Circulation-strike mintage: 412,000

Availability in Mint State: This issue is elusive. Larry Briggs states, "A small hoard of five or six Uncirculated pieces surfaced around 1986."[27] In 2014 and 2015 the

actual size: 24.3 mm

Eugene H. Gardner Sale featured examples of this coin in MS-65 and MS-64 (ex Eliasberg). *MS-60 to 62:* 9 to 12. *MS-63:* 4 to 6. *MS-64:* 1 or 2. *MS-65 or better:* 1 or 2.[8]

Availability in circulated grades: These are available in any grade desired through EF and AU coins are scarce.

Characteristics of striking: This issue is usually poorly struck, especially at the rims, but there are exceptions.

Notes: The damp climate of New Orleans often caused dies to rust, as is evident on this detail from the obverse of an 1850-O quarter.

Detail of die rust.

G-4	VG-8	F-12	VF-20	EF-40	AU-50	MS-60	MS-63	MS-65
$65	$125	$165	$225	$750	$850	$2,000	$5,500	$13,500

1851

Circulation-strike mintage: 160,000

Proof mintage: See below

actual size: 24.3 mm

Availability in Mint State: The Louis E. Eliasberg Sale in 1997 featured an example of this coin in MS-65. In 2014 and 2015 the Eugene H. Gardner Sale featured two examples of this coin in MS-65. *MS-60 to 62:* 20 to 25. *MS-63:* 15 to 20. *MS-64:* 12 to 15. *MS-65 or better:* 6 to 9.

Availability in circulated grades: This issue is very scarce in circulated grades, but enough are available that any desired grade through VF can be found. Greg Johnson states: "In my studies I have found it far easier to locate a Mint State coin than a choice EF or AU."[29] In recent years studies have shown that the 1851 is slightly scarcer than the 1851-O with a much lower mintage. Probably, many were melted in the East, while most of the New Orleans coins remained in circulation.[30]

Characteristics of striking: These are usually sharply struck.

Proofs: Some coins of 1851 and 1853 have been called Proofs over a long period of years, but it is uncertain if they were actually struck as such or they were from dies polished after relapping or for other reasons. No Proof sets of this year are known.

G-4	VG-8	F-12	VF-20	EF-40	AU-50	MS-60	MS-63	MS-65
$115	$175	$275	$400	$700	$1,000	$1,450	$2,500	$6,500

1851-O

Circulation-strike mintage: 88,000

actual size: 24.3 mm

Availability in Mint State: In 2014 the Eugene H. Gardner Sale featured an example of this coin in MS-63 (ex Eliasberg). *MS-60 to 62:* 5 to 7. *MS-63:* 1 or 2. *MS-64:* 0. *MS-65 or better:* 0.

Availability in circulated grades: This is one of the key issues of the decade, but most show extensive wear and/or damage.

Characteristics of striking: These usually have very weak head detail and overall lightness on the obverse.

G-4	VG-8	F-12	VF-20	EF-40	AU-50	MS-60	MS-63	MS-65
$525	$750	$1,000	$1,250	$2,500	$3,350	$10,000	$35,000	

1852

**Circulation-strike
mintage: 177,060**

Proof mintage: 5–8

actual size: 24.3 mm

Availability in Mint State:
The Louis E. Eliasberg Sale
in 1997 featured an example
of this coin in MS-65. In
2015 the Eugene H.
Gardner Sale featured examples of this coin in MS-68 and MS-66. *MS-60 to 62:* 18
to 22. *MS-63:* 12 to 15. *MS-64:* 12 to 15. *MS-65 or better:* 4 to 6.

Availability in circulated grades: This issue is available in any grade desired.

Characteristics of striking: These are usually sharp.

Proofs: This die with double-punched 52 in the date was also used to make circulation strikes.[31] Proofs are in the National Numismatic Collection and the American
Numismatic Society. In 2014 the Eugene H. Gardner Sale featured an example of this
coin in PF-66 (ex Pittman). Approximately one example has been certified.

Notes: The Mint outdid itself this year with the date logotype, and the digit 2 is more
ornate than seen on any coin of this design denomination up to this point in time.
Briggs 1-A is a repunched date oriented horizontally. 2-A is a normal date that slopes
slightly down to the right; two are known with the reverse rotated 90 degrees.[32]

G-4	VG-8	F-12	VF-20	EF-40	AU-50
$125	$225	$325	$350	$600	$750
MS-60	**MS-63**	**MS-65**	**PF-60**	**PF-63**	**PF-65**
$1,250	$2,000	$5,500			$75,000

1852-O

**Circulation-strike
mintage: 96,000**

actual size: 24.3 mm

Availability in Mint State:
This issue is exceedingly
rare. A group of seven etched
sea-salvaged Mint State pieces
came to light in 1988.[33] In
2015 the Eugene H. Gardner
Sale featured two examples of
this coin in MS-62. *MS-60 to 62:* 2 or 3. *MS-63:* 0. *MS-64:* 0. *MS-65 or better:* 0.

Availability in circulated grades: These coins are mostly well circulated. EF and AU
coins are rarities. This is one of the key issues among early Liberty Seated quarters.

Characteristics of striking: This issue is usually struck with weak areas. These have
a rather curious beveled rim that seems to have accelerated the effects of wear in
circulation.

G-4	VG-8	F-12	VF-20	EF-40	AU-50	MS-60	MS-63	MS-65
$375	$525	$850	$1,500	$2,250	$6,750	$10,000	$35,000	

1853,
Repunched Date,
No Arrows
or Rays

Circulation-strike mintage: 44,200

actual size: 24.3 mm

Detail of the Repunched Date.

Availability in Mint State:
The Louis E. Eliasberg Sale in 1997 featured an example of this coin in MS-66. A hoard distributed under unrecorded circumstances accounts for coins graded MS-64 and higher. In 2014 and 2015 the Eugene H. Gardner Sale featured examples of this coin in MS-68, MS-66, and MS-65. *MS-60 to 62:* 5 to 7. *MS-63:* 6 to 8. *MS-64:* 15 to 18. *MS-65 or better:* 12 to 15.

Availability in circulated grades: *AG-3 to AU-58:* 100 to 150 are known. These are quite rare, and most are in higher grades such as EF and AU.

Characteristics of striking: This issue is usually sharply struck.

Notes: The last two date numerals are repunched on genuine coins. Alterations have been made by removing the arrows on 1853, With Arrows quarters, or by altering the last 8 to a 3 on an 1858 quarter. Most were melted. The net mintage representing the quantity actually released is not known. It has been estimated at various levels from several thousand coins on up. In any event, the issue is a major rarity today, and has been recognized as such for generations.

From *Ballou's Pictorial Drawing-Room Companion*, January 1855: "The silver coins most prized by jewelers for melting, are those bearing the stamp of the United States Mint prior to the late revision of the standard. The quarter and half dollars of the old standard command a premium of four percent, and French five franc pieces and Spanish milled dollars are the only other coins regarded with equal favor by the melters."

In his offering of an 1853-O *half dollar* without arrows and rays in the 1885 sale of the J. Colvin Randall Collection, W. Elliot Woodward reflected upon the *quarter dollar* without arrows and rays: "The discovery of the quarter dollar is due to an interesting incident which occurred in this way; a broker was weighing a quantity of silver coins; the weight was found to surpass, by a number of grains, the value of the coins by count. After repeatedly weighing and counting, critical examination revealed the fact that one of the quarters weighed several grains more than any of the others, and gave to collectors a variety hitherto unknown. Diligent search, carefully continued for many years, has added to the piece first discovered possibly a dozen examples,—I think not more."

Years ago this was sometimes called 1853, 3 Over 2. It is listed as FS-25-1853-301 in the *Cherrypickers' Guide to Rare Die Varieties*.

G-4	VG-8	F-12	VF-20	EF-40	AU-50	MS-60	MS-63	MS-65
$1,250	$2,000	$2,650	$3,500	$4,500	$6,000	$6,500	$7,500	$12,000

1853, Arrows at Date, Rays Around Eagle (Variety 2)

This design is the same as the preceding, but with the addition of arrows at the date on the obverse and a glory of rays around the eagle on the reverse. This variety was only made from spring 1853 until the end of the year. The Coinage Act of 1853 made these coins lighter in weight than the preceding.

Designer: Christian Gobrecht. Arrows and rays added by someone on the Mint staff.

Specifications: *Composition:* 90 percent silver, 10 percent copper. *Diameter:* 24.3 mm. *Weight:* 96 grains (6.22 grams). *Edge:* Reeded.

1853, With Arrows and Rays

actual size: 24.3 mm

Circulation-strike mintage: 15,210,020

Proof mintage: See below

Availability in Mint State: According to Larry Briggs, this and the 1876 are tied for being the most common Mint State Liberty Seated quarters. *MS-60 to 62:* 500 to 700. *MS-63:* 250 to 325. *MS-64:* 200 to 250. *MS-65 or better:* 40 to 50.

Availability in circulated grades: These are extremely common and are available in any grade desired. This is the most common issue in the Liberty Seated series up to this point in time.

Characteristics of striking: Striking on this issue varies.

Proofs: See comments under 1851. The Louis E. Eliasberg Sale in 1997 featured an example of this coin in MS-64, prooflike or finer. In 2014 and 2015 the Eugene H. Gardner Sale featured examples of this coin in PF-65 and PF-64 (ex Pittman). In the date, the numerals are repunched, particularly the last two. Both arrowheads are lightly repunched, particularly the one on the right. Diagonal die finish lines are seen prominently over stars 11 and 12. In a letter dated December 30, 1996, David W. Akers handled the John J. Pittman estate and commented that he is calling the Pittman 1853 quarter dollar a Proof, and that it is Proof on the obverse, but not within the reverse shield. He continued by saying this after examining the description of the Eliasberg coin: "I will say that, in my experience, a proof-like 1853 arrows and rays quarter is *most* unusual; they are always frosty. So, the coin you describe may well be a Proof, at least as that term applies to anything dated 1853. All 1853 'Proofs' are questionable, in my opinion, except for the restrike Proof dollars." The same die was also used to make circulation strikes without proof-like surfaces.[34] Pittman 1853 is from a different obverse die without repunching. Approximately five examples have been certified.

Notes: This is a very common issue. The market price strength is derived in large part from it being a one-year type needed in sets. For the with-arrows coinages from 1853 to 1855 the arrowheads were part of the master die and were not added individually. Accordingly, there are no positional variations.

1853, 3 Over 4 Overdate: This curious variety shows clear traces of 854 under the final 1853 date. Part of the earlier right-side arrow shaft is also visible. The likely scenario is that late in the 1853 year, dies were being made in advance for use in 1854. There was a call for an 1853-dated die to  be used toward the end of the 1853 year, and an 1854 die was overdated.[35] *Cherrypickers' Guide to Rare Die Varieties* lists this as FS-25-1853-301. Several dozen are known, mostly in circulated grades. As this variety is not widely known, finding one listed as a regular variety is a strong possibility. In 2014 the Eugene H. Gardner Sale featured an example of this coin in MS-64.

G-4	VG-8	F-12	VF-20	EF-40	AU-50
$35	$40	$50	$60	$200	$350
MS-60	MS-63	MS-65	PF-60	PF-63	PF-65
$1,000	$1,750	$10,000	$30,000	$55,000	$150,000

1853-O

Circulation-strike mintage: 1,332,000

actual size: 24.3 mm

Availability in Mint State: This issue is very rare, surprisingly so. The Louis E. Eliasberg Sale in 1997 featured an example of this coin in MS-65 or finer. It was highly prooflike and sharply struck—a breathtaking gem! It is believed to be by far the finest known. In 2014 and 2015 the Eugene H. Gardner Sale featured two examples of this coin in MS-64. *MS-60 to 62:* 15 to 20. *MS-63:* 5 to 8. *MS-64:* 2 or 3. *MS-65 or better:* 1.[36]

Availability in circulated grades: This issue is easily obtainable, but is seen far less often than its Philadelphia Mint counterpart.

Characteristics of striking: There is usually some flatness at the obverse center.

Notes: One variety has concentric circular marks in the obverse shield, an unusual feature caused from an incompletely machined die face.[37] This obverse was combined with two different reverses.[38]

O Over Horizontal O: The mintmark was first punched horizontally, and then corrected. Traces of the first O are visible, primarily at the top of the central opening. Perhaps 40 to 60 are known, all reported examples of which are in circulated grades. The finest seen by Larry Briggs is  AU-55.[39] *Cherrypickers' Guide to Rare Die Varieties* lists this as FS-25-1853o-501.

G-4	VG-8	F-12	VF-20	EF-40	AU-50	MS-60	MS-63	MS-65
$55	$75	$100	$150	$400	$1,100	$4,250	$10,000	$25,000

1854–1855, Arrows at Date, No Rays (Variety 3)

This variety has the same design as the preceding variety with arrows at the date, but now the rays are omitted from the reverse.

Designer: Christian Gobrecht. Arrows added by someone on the Mint staff.

Specifications: *Composition:* 90 percent silver, 10 percent copper. *Diameter:* 24.3 mm. *Weight:* 96 grains (6.22 grams). *Edge:* Reeded.

1854

Circulation-strike mintage: 12,380,000

Proof mintage: 20–30

Availability in Mint State: According to Larry Briggs, it is among the most available Liberty Seated quarters in Mint State.

actual size: 24.3 mm

MS-60 to 62: 400 to 600. *MS-63:* 140 to 140. *MS-64:* 80 to 100. *MS-65 or better:* 30 to 40.

Availability in circulated grades: This issue is easily available in any grade desired.

Characteristics of striking: Striking of this issue varies as is true of nearly all large-mintage issues.

Proofs: On the obverse the left arrowhead is slightly repunched at its bottom. The date is perfect (without repunching). Approximately 24 examples have been certified.

Notes: Some coins of this issue have the reverse rotated 90 degrees clockwise and also medal-wise. Briggs Obverse-1, the "Thin Date," is from relapping or impressing the logotype lightly into the die.

G-4	VG-8	F-12	VF-20	EF-40	AU-50
$35	$40	$45	$75	$85	$250

MS-60	MS-63	MS-65	PF-60	PF-63	PF-65
$725	$1,150	$5,500	$8,500	$12,500	$30,000

1854-O

Circulation-strike mintage: 1,484,000

actual size: 24.3 mm

Availability in Mint State: The Louis E. Eliasberg Sale in 1997 featured an example of this coin in MS-66 or finer. In 2015 the Eugene H. Gardner Sale featured an example of this coin in MS-65. *MS-60 to 62:* 30 to 40. *MS-63:* 14 to 18. *MS-64:* 9 to 12. *MS-65 or better:* 2 or 3.[40]

Availability in circulated grades: This issue is common in circulated grades. It is one of the more available New Orleans quarters.

Characteristics of striking: These are usually weakly struck in areas.

Notes: The Briggs Obverse-2 can be found in various states of deterioration.

Huge O Mintmark: The mintmark is large and some-what misshapen, for reasons unknown. It might be die damage according to one theory, or overly aggressive polishing according to another. Or perhaps the die was shipped into New Orleans from Philadelphia (where all dies were made) without the mintmark, the error was realized, and an improvised mintmark was added at New Orleans by some inexpert tooling. The bottom of the lau-

rel branch and the tops of the R and D in QUAR. DOL. show damage. Dozens are known, all in circulated grades except a single example sold as a regular coin in 1976 at an Indiana coin show.[41] *Cherrypickers' Guide to Rare Die Varieties* lists this as FS-25-1854o-501. In 2014 the Eugene H. Gardner Sale featured an example of this coin in EF-40.

G-4	VG-8	F-12	VF-20	EF-40	AU-50	MS-60	MS-63	MS-65
$50	$55	$65	$100	$125	$350	$1,100	$1,750	$16,500

1855

Circulation-strike mintage: 2,857,000

Proof mintage: 20–30

actual size: 24.3 mm

Availability in Mint State: According to Larry Briggs, it is among the most available Liberty Seated quarters in Mint State. In 2014 and 2015 the Eugene H. Gardner Sale featured examples of this coin in MS-67 and MS-66. *MS-60 to 62:* 80 to 100. *MS-63:* 40 to 50. *MS-64:* 25 to 32. *MS-65 or better:* 9 to 12.

Availability in circulated grades: This issue is common in circulated grades.

Characteristics of striking: The striking of coins of this issue varies widely. The denticles under the date are weak on coins of just about every grade and on well-worn coins are usually absent. Sharp pieces can be found by looking. There is usually no premium when they are found, as the certification services do not take note of whether a coin is weak or sharp.

Proofs: This issue is extremely rare in Proof format, rarer in the author's experience than either the date before (1854) or the date after. The obverse has the date punched very shallowly into the die. The arrowheads are significantly lower than on 1854, just above the center of the date, with the left arrowhead tilting upward. In 2014 the Eugene H. Gardner Sale featured an example of this coin in PF-66 (ex Eliasberg). Approximately 13 examples have been certified.

Notes: A minor Doubled-Die obverse is known with the vertical lines in the shield doubled. It is scarce, but not rare.[42]

G-4	VG-8	F-12	VF-20	EF-40	AU-50
$35	$40	$45	$50	$125	$275

MS-60	MS-63	MS-65	PF-60	PF-63	PF-65
$675	$1,250	$6,500	$8,500	$15,000	$30,000

1855-O

Circulation-strike mintage: 176,000

Availability in Mint State: These are very rare, even at lower levels in the Mint State range. The Louis E. Eliasberg Sale in 1997 featured an example of this coin in MS-66 or finer. In

actual size: 24.3 mm

2014 and 2015 the Eugene H. Gardner Sale featured examples of this coin in MS-67 and MS-63. *MS-60 to 62:* 6 to 8. *MS-63:* 3 or 4. *MS-64:* 2 or 3. *MS-65 or better:* 2 or 3.

Availability in circulated grades: Coins of this issue are mostly found well worn and with problems. AU coins are very rare.

Characteristics of striking: For this issue, weak striking is the norm.

Notes: The mintmark O is often light as it was punched shallowly into the die.

G-4	VG-8	F-12	VF-20	EF-40	AU-50	MS-60	MS-63	MS-65
$150	$225	$350	$750	$1,500	$3,500	$6,000	$15,000	

1855-S

Circulation-strike mintage: 396,400

Proof mintage: *1–2*

actual size: 24.3 mm

Availability in Mint State: The Louis E. Eliasberg Sale in 1997 featured an example of this coin in MS-63. In 2014 and 2015 the Eugene H. Gardner Sale featured examples of this coin in MS-64 and MS-63. *MS-60 to 62:* 8 to 13. *MS-63:* 3 or 4. *MS-64:* 2 or 3. *MS-65 or better:* 1.

Availability in circulated grades: These are very elusive in all grades, with most showing extensive circulation. Many show traces of solder or tooling from having been used as buttons.[43] Many of the much rarer, higher grade EF and AU coins have been purchased by Liberty Seated Coin Club members, thus skewing survey data published in the *Gobrecht Journal*, as previously noted in chapter 2.

Characteristics of striking: This issue is weak in areas.

Proofs: One has been reported; this coin was in the Richmond Collection (DLRC 2005) graded as PF-63 by NGC, which upgraded it to PF-64 when it was offered again by Heritage Auctions in August 2011 and August 2013. It may have been created to the order of San Francisco Mint Superintendent Robert Aiken Birdsall.[44]

Notes: In his 1893 treatise, *Mint Marks*, Augustus G. Heaton called attention to the large size of the S mintmark on the earlier dates in the San Francisco quarter dollar coinage, continuing to state: "There are at least three other sizes on later dates, which may be called *medium, small*, and *very small*, ranging from within the highlight of letters of the [surrounding] legend to hardly more than a dot."

A large amount of all San Francisco Mint silver coinage was shipped to China, often by merchants and individuals sending to their families back home.

Liberty Seated silver coins struck in San Francisco (and later in Carson City) circulated widely in the West and in the Mountain States with the result that the typical coin surviving today shows extensive wear. In contrast, in the East and Midwest silver coins were hoarded by the public beginning in the spring of 1862 and did not reappear in circulation until after April 20, 1876. Due to this, the average grade of surviving Philadelphia coins is significantly higher, and Mint State coins are seen with frequency.[45]

G-4	VG-8	F-12	VF-20	EF-40	AU-50
$175	$300	$400	$700	$1,000	$1,850

MS-60	MS-63	MS-65	PF-60	PF-63	PF-65
$3,500	$8,500	$27,500		—	

1856–1866, Variety 1 Resumed, With Weight Standard of Variety 2

These have the basic design as used from 1840 to 1853 with no arrows or rays, but now have the reduced weight introduced in 1853.

Designer: Christian Gobrecht.

Specifications: *Composition:* 90 percent silver, 10 percent copper. *Diameter:* 24.3 mm. *Weight:* 96 grains (6.22 grams). *Edge:* Reeded.

1856

Circulation-strike mintage: 7,264,000

Proof mintage: *40–50*

Availability in Mint State: According to Larry Briggs, this coin is among the most available Liberty Seated quarters in Mint State. In

actual size: 24.3 mm

2014 and 2015 the Eugene H. Gardner Sale featured two examples of this coin in MS-66. *MS-60 to 62:* 200 to 300. *MS-63:* 90 to 120. *MS-64:* 60 to 80. *MS-65 or better:* 25 to 35.

Availability in circulated grades: This issue is common in circulated grades.

Characteristics of striking: These vary from slightly weak to needle sharp.

Proofs: The reverse die is bulged at the right. The same die was used in 1857 for all Proofs and for some Proofs in 1858. In 2015 the Eugene H. Gardner Sale featured an example of this coin in PF-66 (ex Eliasberg). Approximately 46 examples have been certified.

G-4	VG-8	F-12	VF-20	EF-40	AU-50
$35	$40	$45	$50	$85	$200
MS-60	MS-63	MS-65	PF-60	PF-63	PF-65
$350	$650	$2,750	$3,500	$4,500	$12,500

1856-O

Circulation-strike mintage: 968,000

actual size: 24.3 mm

Availability in Mint State: These are extremely rare. The Louis E. Eliasberg Sale in 1997 featured an example of this coin in MS-66. In 2014 and 2015 the Eugene H. Gardner Sale featured an example of this coin in MS-65 and MS-64. *MS-60 to 62:* 5 to 7. *MS-63:* 2 or 3. *MS-64:* 2 or 3. *MS-65 or better:* 2 or 3.

Availability in circulated grades: This issue is mostly well circulated, and AU coins are scarce.

Characteristics of striking: These usually have weakness on the head and obverse stars.

G-4	VG-8	F-12	VF-20	EF-40	AU-50	MS-60	MS-63	MS-65
$50	$60	$85	$125	$250	$600	$1,250	$2,500	$12,500

1856-S

Circulation-strike mintage: 286,000

actual size: 24.3 mm

Availability in Mint State: These are extremely rare. In 2014 the Eugene H. Gardner Sale featured an example of this coin in MS-64. *MS-60 to 62:* 4. *MS-63:* 2 or 3. *MS-64:* 1 or 2. *MS-65 or better:* 1.

Availability in circulated grades: This issue is rare in circulated grades and most are well worn. The Louis E. Eliasberg Sale in 1997 featured an example of this coin in AU-58.

Characteristics of striking: This issue is usually sharply struck.

Large S Over Small S: The regular S is punched over an earlier S mintmark possibly intended for a dime. *Cherrypickers' Guide to Rare Die Varieties* lists this as FS-25-1856S-501. This is a rare variety, especially in VF or higher grades, and many have problems. In 2014 the Eugene H. Gardner Sale featured an example of this coin in AU-58; probably the finest known.

G-4	VG-8	F-12	VF-20	EF-40	AU-50	MS-60	MS-63	MS-65
$425	$575	$750	$850	$2,000	$3,750	$9,500	$13,500	$45,000

1857

**Circulation-strike
mintage: 9,644,000**

Proof mintage: *40–50*

Availability in Mint State:
According to Larry Briggs,
this coin is among the most
available Liberty Seated
quarters in Mint State. In

actual size: 24.3 mm

2014 and 2015 the Eugene
H. Gardner Sale featured examples of this coin in MS-67 (2) and MS-66. *MS-60 to
62:* 200 to 275. *MS-63:* 130 to 150. *MS-64:* 80 to 110. *MS-65 or better:* 50 to 70.

Availability in circulated grades: This issue is very common in circulated grades.

Characteristics of striking: Striking on this issue varies.

Proofs: The reverse die, bulged at the right, was also used to strike all 1856 Proof
quarters and some of 1858. Approximately 70 examples have been certified.

Notes: One very scarce and popular variety, the "Smoking Liberty," has a die line or
die crack at Liberty's lower hand, giving the illusion that she is holding a cigarette!

1857 Quarter with Clash Marks from an 1857 cent:
During the production of 1857 Flying Eagle cents, a
coining press was inadvertently fitted with an 1857 cent
reverse die and an 1857 quarter reverse die. The two dies
came together without an intervening planchet, and
each die left clash marks on the other. A number of cents
are known today with the outline in mirror image of the
quarter dollar die, this being most prominent above

Detail of clash marks.

ONE. A detail of such a cent is shown above the eagle's head. Snow variety eight;
Fivaz-Stanton FND-002. Quarters with clash marks from the cent die are known and
are slightly scarce. This feature is most prominent above the eagle's wing to the left.
Nearly all are in circulated grades. *Cherrypickers' Guide to Rare Die Varieties* lists this
as FS-25-1857-901.

G-4	VG-8	F-12	VF-20	EF-40	AU-50
$35	$40	$45	$50	$85	$200
MS-60	**MS-63**	**MS-65**	**PF-60**	**PF-63**	**PF-65**
$375	$650	$2,750	$3,000	$4,000	$10,000

1857-O

Circulation-strike mintage: 1,180,000

actual size: 24.3 mm

Availability in Mint State: These are very rare. The Louis E. Eliasberg Sale in 1997 featured an example of this coin in MS-66, prooflike, possibly a branch-mint Proof. It has full Proof surfaces, including within the shield stripes. *It is possibly a presentation coin.* In 2014 and 2015 the Eugene H. Gardner Sale featured examples of this coin in MS-64 (3) and MS-63. *MS-60 to 62:* 20 to 25. *MS-63:* 8 to 12. *MS-64:* 4 to 6. *MS-65 or better:* 0 or 1.

Availability in circulated grades: Most coins of this issue are well worn and AU coins are rare.

Characteristics of striking: There are often areas of weakness on these coins. The detail at right is from a coin that is weak at the top and bottom of the obverse and the top of the reverse.

G-4	VG-8	F-12	VF-20	EF-40	AU-50	MS-60	MS-63	MS-65
$50	$65	$100	$165	$300	$500	$1,300	$2,750	

1857-S

Circulation-strike mintage: 82,000

actual size: 24.3 mm

Availability in Mint State: These are extremely rare. The Louis E. Eliasberg Sale in 1997 featured an example of this coin in MS-66, prooflike, with full, deeply mirrored fields, now a Gardner MS-64 ("although now certified as MS-64 by PCGS, this coin does command generous eye appeal with a small dark spot in the right obverse field, the only flaw of note").[46] In 2014 and 2015 the Eugene H. Gardner Sale featured three examples of this coin in MS-64. *MS-60 to 62:* 11 to 15. *MS-63:* 5 to 7. *MS-64:* 5 to 7. *MS-65 or better:* 1.

Availability in circulated grades: These are very scarce, even more so than 1855-S, 1856-S, or 1858-S. As an anomaly, the 1857-S in AU grade is the most often seen San Francisco quarter of the 1850s.[47] Most show extensive wear and have corrosion or other problems.

Characteristics of striking: This issue is usually quite well struck.

G-4	VG-8	F-12	VF-20	EF-40	AU-50	MS-60	MS-63	MS-65
$300	$525	$650	$850	$1,200	$2,250	$4,500	$8,500	

1858

Circulation-strike mintage: 7,368,000

Proof mintage: *300*

Availability in Mint State: According to Larry Briggs, it is among the most available Liberty Seated quarters in Mint State. In 2014 and

actual size: 24.3 mm

2015 the Eugene H. Gardner Sale featured examples of this coin in MS-67, MS-66 (2), and MS-65. *MS-60 to 62:* 400 to 600. *MS-63:* 170 to 300. *MS-64:* 120 to 150. *MS-65 or better:* 50 to 70.

Availability in circulated grades: These are readily available in any grade desired.

Characteristics of striking: This issue is usually well struck, but some have areas of weakness.

Proofs: Approximately 210 were made for inclusion in silver Proof sets. Additional pieces were possibly made. Some but not all Proofs are from the die used to strike Proof quarters in 1856 and 1857, with a distinctive bulge at the right. Many seeking a run of Proof Liberty Seated quarters start their sets with this year. In general, the earlier issues are scarcer. Quality varies among the issues and eras. Some quarter dollars circa 1860 have quite a few lint marks on them (due to debris in the dies; this is primarily peculiar to quarters; it has not been observed on silver dollars, for example), while some Proof silver coins of the 1870s have other problems—sloppy striking and handling at the Mint and incomplete polishing of the dies. Most Proof quarters of 1858 and the years extending into the 1860s are in lower grades from repeated cleaning over a long period of time. *PF-60 to 62:* 90 to 120. *PF-63:* 35 to 45. *PF-64:* 20 to 25. *PF-65 or better:* 6 to 9.

G-4	VG-8	F-12	VF-20	EF-40	AU-50
$35	$40	$45	$50	$85	$200

MS-60	MS-63	MS-65	PF-60	PF-63	PF-65
$375	$650	$2,500	$1,500	$2,000	$5,500

1858-O

Circulation-strike mintage: 520,000

Availability in Mint State: These are extremely rare and most are at lower levels. The Louis E. Eliasberg Sale in 1997 featured an example of this coin in MS-64/65. In 2015 the Eugene H. Gardner

actual size: 24.3 mm

Sale featured examples of this coin in MS-65, MS-64, and MS-62. *MS-60 to 62:* 15 to 20. *MS-63:* 7 to 10. *MS-64:* 4 to 6. *MS-65 or better:* 2 or 3.

Availability in circulated grades: Most coins of the issue are well worn. AU coins are hard to find.

Characteristics of striking: Liberty's head is usually weak.

G-4	VG-8	F-12	VF-20	EF-40	AU-50	MS-60	MS-63	MS-65
$50	$55	$85	$125	$300	$650	$4,500	$10,000	$25,000

1858-S

Circulation-strike mintage: 121,000

Availability in Mint State: These are exceedingly rare. In 2015 the Eugene H. Gardner Sale featured an example of this coin in MS-62. *MS-60 to 62:* 1 or 2. *MS-63:* 0 or 1. *MS-64:* 0 or 1. *MS-65 or better:* 1.

actual size: 24.3 mm

Availability in circulated grades: This issue is scarce at all levels and is rare at the AU level (illustrated). An example of this coin in AU-58 was featured in the Louis E. Eliasberg Sale in 1997.

Characteristics of striking: Coins of this issue are usually sharp.

Notes: Mintmark positions include centered (normal), slightly to the left, and tilted to the right.

G-4	VG-8	F-12	VF-20	EF-40	AU-50	MS-60	MS-63	MS-65
$275	$450	$650	$1,000	$3,000	$5,000	$20,000	—	

Hub Changes of 1859

Within any given type the hubs were usually standard, however there are some differences. In 1859 new hubs were introduced, called Type 2 by specialists. This became the new standard, but for several years at the Philadelphia Mint both types were used. The differences between the two sets of hubs are minute.

1859 Type 1 Obverse: There is one tiny vertical fragment of a stripe over the E in LIBERTY in the shield.

1859 Type 1 Reverse: The eagle's eye is recessed (concave).

Details of Type 1 obverse and reverse.

1859 Type 2 Obverse: There are two more prominent vertical stripes over the E.

1859 Type 2 Reverse: The eagle's eye is raised (convex) and there are other slight differences in the eye treatment.

Details of Type 2 obverse and reverse.

1859

**Circulation-strike
mintage: 1,343,200**

Proof mintage: 800

Availability in Mint State:
These are fairly scarce.
There are enough higher
grades, MS-64 and above, to
supply the limited number of
collectors building sets. In 2014 the Eugene H. Gardner Sale featured an example of
this coin in MS-65. *MS-60 to 62:* 50 to 70. *MS-63:* 25 to 32. *MS-64:* 22 to 28. *MS-65
or better:* 7 to 10.

actual size: 24.3 mm

Availability in circulated grades: This issue is common in circulated grades, though
most are in lower grades.

Characteristics of striking: Coins of this issue vary in striking. The stars are weak
on some.

Proofs: *PF-60 to 62:* 150 to 200. *PF-63:* 100 to 130. *PF-64:* 90 to 120. *PF-65 or better:*
30 to 40.

Notes: Dies for all mints have a small 1859 logotype. This trend continued for the
next several years.

Type 1 Obverse, Type 1 Reverse: The most often seen.

Type 1 Obverse, Type 2 Reverse: About twice as rare as the previous.

Type 2 Obverse, Type 2 Reverse: Not often seen; perhaps 10 percent or so of the
population.

G-4	VG-8	F-12	VF-20	EF-40	AU-50
$35	$40	$45	$65	$100	$200
MS-60	**MS-63**	**MS-65**	**PF-60**	**PF-63**	**PF-65**
$450	$900	$4,000	$1,000	$1,500	$4,500

1859-O

**Circulation-strike
mintage: 260,000**

Availability in Mint State:
These are very rare. Prior
to late 1900s research, the
1859-O was considered
common. The Louis E.
Eliasberg Sale in 1997
featured an example of this

actual size: 24.3 mm

coin in MS-65. In 2014 the Eugene H. Gardner Sale featured an example of this coin
in MS-65. *MS-60 to 62:* 12 to 15. *MS-63:* 4 to 6. *MS-64:* 2 or 3. *MS-65 or better:* 2
or 3.[48]

Availability in circulated grades: These are available easily enough, mostly in well-worn grades.

Characteristics of striking: This issue is usually seen with some weakness on the head.

G-4	VG-8	F-12	VF-20	EF-40	AU-50	MS-60	MS-63	MS-65
$65	$100	$115	$165	$300	$1,200	$2,500	$7,500	$22,500

1859-S

Circulation-strike mintage: 80,000

Availability in Mint State: None have been reported.

Availability in circulated grades: This issue is rare in all grades. Most are in low grades and have problems,

actual size: 24.3 mm

some with etching or corrosion, suggesting they may have been unearthed.[49] The Louis E. Eliasberg Sale in 1997 featured an example of this coin in AU-55. In 2014 the Eugene H. Gardner Sale featured an example of this coin in AU-58.

Characteristics of striking: This issue is usually sharp.

G-4	VG-8	F-12	VF-20	EF-40	AU-50	MS-60	MS-63	MS-65
$475	$625	$1,000	$1,450	$4,500	$11,000		—	

1860

Circulation-strike mintage: 804,400

Proof mintage: 1,000

Availability in Mint State: In 2014 the Eugene H. Gardner Sale featured an example of this coin in MS-66. *MS-60 to 62:* 30 to 40. *MS-63:* 18 to 25. *MS-64:* 25 to 32. *MS-65 or better:* 8 to 10.

actual size: 24.3 mm

Availability in circulated grades: These are slightly scarce and most are well worn.

Characteristics of striking: This issue is usually seen with light areas on the obverse.

Proofs: Although 1,000 Proofs were struck, it is likely not more than 600 or so were actually sold. Many have lightness at the star centers. *PF-60 to 62:* 150 to 200. *PF-63:* 100 to 130. *PF-64:* 90 to 120. *PF-65 or better:* 35 to 45.

Type 2 Obverse, Type 1 Reverse: The most often seen.

Type 2 Obverse, Type 2 Reverse: Somewhat scarcer than the preceding.

G-4	VG-8	F-12	VF-20	EF-40	AU-50
$35	$40	$45	$65	$125	$200
MS-60	MS-63	MS-65	PF-60	PF-63	PF-65
$550	$1,000	$5,000	$700	$1,200	$4,000

1860-O

Circulation-strike mintage: 388,000

Availability in Mint State:
In Mint State this is the most plentiful New Orleans quarter. The Louis E. Eliasberg Sale in 1997 featured an example of this coin in MS-66. In 2014 the

actual size: 24.3 mm

Eugene H. Gardner Sale featured an example of this coin in MS-65. *MS-60 to 62:* 60 to 75. *MS-63:* 25 to 32. *MS-64:* 7 to 10. *MS-65 or better:* 3 to 5.

Availability in circulated grades: These are slightly scarce.

Characteristics of striking: This issue is usually seen with some lightness on the obverse. Briggs Reverse B has the mintmark lightly impressed into the die.

Notes: This is the last New Orleans Mint quarter until 1891.

G-4	VG-8	F-12	VF-20	EF-40	AU-50	MS-60	MS-63	MS-65
$55	$65	$85	$110	$250	$500	$1,250	$1,850	$12,500

1860-S

Circulation-strike mintage: 56,000

Availability in Mint State:
None were reported in early times. The Gardner MS-61 (NGC) has friction on the higher points, typical for silver coins in this grade (illustrated). *MS-60 to 62:* 1. *MS-63:* 0. *MS-64:* 0. *MS-65 or better:* 0.

actual size: 24.3 mm

Availability in circulated grades: These are very rare, the most elusive of all San Francisco Mint quarters of this type.[50] They are usually seen in low grades and with problems.[51]

Characteristics of striking: This issue is usually seen with some weak obverse details. On the reverse the rim is often weak from seven o'clock to nine o'clock.

G-4	VG-8	F-12	VF-20	EF-40	AU-50	MS-60	MS-63	MS-65
$1,150	$1,650	$3,000	$5,750	$9,000	$16,500	$45,000	—	

1861

Circulation-strike mintage: 4,853,600

Proof mintage: 1,000

Availability in Mint State: According to Larry Briggs, it is among the most available Liberty Seated quarters in Mint State.

actual size: 24.3 mm

MS-60 to 62: 300 to 375. *MS-63:* 175 to 225. *MS-64:* 120 to 150. *MS-65 or better:* 80 to 110.

Availability in circulated grades: These coins are common in circulated grades, mostly in lower grades.

Characteristics of striking: This issue is usually sharp.

Proofs: Although 1,000 Proofs were struck, it is likely no more than 500 or so were actually sold, perhaps even fewer. The 1861 is significantly rarer than the 1860 of similar mintage. *PF-60 to 62:* 85 to 115. *PF-63:* 70 to 85. *PF-64:* 65 to 80. *PF-65 or better:* 15 to 20.

Type 2 Obverse, Type 1 Reverse: Very scarce; perhaps 10 percent of the population.

Type 2 Obverse, Type 2 Reverse: The variety most often seen.

G-4	VG-8	F-12	VF-20	EF-40	AU-50
$35	$45	$50	$65	$100	$200

MS-60	MS-63	MS-65	PF-60	PF-63	PF-65
$400	$725	$2,500	$700	$1,200	$4,000

1861-S

Circulation-strike mintage: 96,000

Availability in Mint State: None have been reported, one of very few Liberty Seated coins for which this can be said.

Availability in circulated

actual size: 24.3 mm

grades: These are at any level. Most show extensive wear and have problems. An evenly worn coin without problems is especially rare. In 2015 the Eugene H. Gardner Sale featured an example of this coin in AU-58.

Characteristics of striking: This issue is usually seen with some lightness on the obverse and at five to nine o'clock on the reverse.

G-4	VG-8	F-12	VF-20	EF-40	AU-50	MS-60	MS-63	MS-65
$750	$1,000	$1,250	$2,750	$4,750	$10,000			—

1862

**Circulation-strike
mintage: 932,000**

Proof mintage: 550

Availability in Mint State:
According to Larry Briggs,
this coin is among the most
available Liberty Seated
quarters in Mint State.

actual size: 24.3 mm

MS-60 to 62: 200 to 300. *MS-63:* 90 to 120. *MS-64:* 60 to 80. *MS-65 or better:* 40
to 50.

Availability in circulated grades: These are more elusive than the high mintage
might suggest.

Characteristics of striking: This issue is usually sharp.

Proofs: *PF-60 to 62:* 150 to 200. *PF-63:* 75 to 95. *PF-64:* 60 to 75. *PF-65 or better:*
30 to 40.

G-4	VG-8	F-12	VF-20	EF-40	AU-50
$35	$40	$50	$75	$150	$250
MS-60	MS-63	MS-65	PF-60	PF-63	PF-65
$500	$750	$2,750	$700	$1,200	$4,000

1862-S

**Circulation-strike
mintage: 67,000**

Availability in Mint State:
These are very rare. The
Louis E. Eliasberg Sale in
1997 featured an example of
this coin in MS-64. In 2014
and 2015 the Eugene H.
Gardner Sale featured

actual size: 24.3 mm

examples of this coin in MS-64 and MS-62. *MS-60 to 62:* 10 to 14. *MS-63:* 7 to 9.
MS-64: 2 or 3. *MS-65 or better:* 0.

Availability in circulated grades: This issue is rare in circulated grades, especially so
in higher levels.

Characteristics of striking: Coins of this issue are usually seen with some lightness
on the obverse and at five to nine o'clock on the reverse.

G-4	VG-8	F-12	VF-20	EF-40	AU-50	MS-60	MS-63	MS-65
$225	$350	$450	$675	$1,500	$2,500	$4,500	$8,500	

1863

Circulation-strike mintage: 191,600

Proof mintage: 460

Availability in Mint State:
MS-60 to 62: 55 to 70.
MS-63: 55 to 70. *MS-64:*
40 to 55. *MS-65 or better:*
25 to 35.

actual size: 24.3 mm

Availability in circulated grades: These are scarce. From this point forward through the decade many Philadelphia coins are in higher grades such as EF and AU.

Characteristics of striking: This issue is usually sharp.

Proofs: *PF-60 to 62:* 120 to 150. *PF-63:* 90 to 120. *PF-64:* 60 to 80. *PF-65 or better:* 25 to 35.

G-4	VG-8	F-12	VF-20	EF-40	AU-50
$65	$85	$115	$275	$500	$700
MS-60	**MS-63**	**MS-65**	**PF-60**	**PF-63**	**PF-65**
$1,000	$1,500	$5,500	$700	$1,200	$4,000

1864

Circulation-strike mintage: 93,600

Proof mintage: 470

Availability in Mint State:
Mint State Philadelphia quarters of the Civil War years and extending into the early 1870s are mostly in

actual size: 24.3 mm

higher levels. In 2015 the Eugene H. Gardner Sale featured examples of this coin in MS-67 and MS-66. *MS-60 to 62:* 20 to 25. *MS-63:* 25 to 32. *MS-64:* 25 to 32. *MS-65 or better:* 18 to 22.

Availability in circulated grades: These are rare in any grade.

Characteristics of striking: This issue is usually sharp.

Proofs: *PF-60 to 62:* 120 to 150. *PF-63:* 90 to 110. *PF-64:* 70 to 90. *PF-65 or better:* 35 to 50.

G-4	VG-8	F-12	VF-20	EF-40	AU-50
$175	$275	$325	$500	$575	$875
MS-60	**MS-63**	**MS-65**	**PF-60**	**PF-63**	**PF-65**
$1,350	$2,500	$5,500	$700	$1,200	$4,000

1864-S

**Circulation-strike
mintage: 20,000**

Availability in Mint State:
These are exceptionally
rare. The finest may be
the Louis E. Eliasberg
MS-66 (1997), ex Friesner
Collection. Before this the
finest seen by NGC was

actual size: 24.3 mm

EF-40 and the finest by PCGS was MS-63. In 2014 the Eugene H. Gardner Sale featured two examples of this coin in MS-64. *MS-60 to 62:* 1 or 2. *MS-63:* 1 or 2. *MS-64:* 2. *MS-65 or better:* 1.

Availability in circulated grades: These are very rare and most show extensive wear. In contrast to Philadelphia coins of this era San Francisco quarters are usually seen well worn.

Characteristics of striking: This issue is usually seen with slight lightness on the obverse stars and at five to nine o'clock on the reverse, this being a characterization of many San Francisco quarters of the era.[52]

G-4	VG-8	F-12	VF-20	EF-40	AU-50	MS-60	MS-63	MS-65
$1,100	$1,250	$1,500	$2,250	$5,500	$7,500	$15,000	$22,500	

1865

**Circulation-strike
mintage: 58,800**

Proof mintage: 500

Availability in Mint State:
In 2014 the Eugene H.
Gardner Sale featured
an example of this coin in
MS-66. *MS-60 to 62:* 12 to

actual size: 24.3 mm

16. *MS-63:* 15 to 20. *MS-64:* 9 to 12. *MS-65 or better:* 9 to 12.

Availability in circulated grades: These are rare and most are in higher ranges.

Characteristics of striking: This issue us usually sharp.

Proofs: *PF-60 to 62:* 150 to 200. *PF-63:* 80 to 100. *PF-64:* 45 to 60. *PF-65 or better:* 30 to 40.

G-4	VG-8	F-12	VF-20	EF-40	AU-50
$100	$165	$250	$400	$500	$850
MS-60	**MS-63**	**MS-65**	**PF-60**	**PF-63**	**PF-65**
$1,500	$1,850	$10,000	$700	$1,200	$4,000

1865-S

Circulation-strike mintage: 41,000

actual size: 24.3 mm

Availability in Mint State: These are very rare. The Louis E. Eliasberg Sale in 1997 featured an example of this coin in MS-63 to 64. In 2014 the Eugene H. Gardner Sale featured an example of this coin in MS-66. *MS-60 to 62:* 16 to 22. *MS-63:* 9 to 12. *MS-64:* 1. *MS-65 or better:* 1 or 2.[53]

Availability in circulated grades: These are rare and most are well worn.

Characteristics of striking: This issue is typically seen with some very slight weakness at the star centers, the tops of the date digits, and five to nine o'clock on the reverse.

G-4	VG-8	F-12	VF-20	EF-40	AU-50	MS-60	MS-63	MS-65
$275	$350	$475	$900	$1,100	$1,600	$4,000	$6,000	$25,000

1866, No Motto

Proof mintage: 1

actual size: 24.3 mm

Proof: One is known.

Notes: The 1866, No Motto, quarter (one known), half dollar (one known), and dollar (two known) were secretly made at the Mint at a later date, possibly under the aegis of A. Loudon Snowden in the late 1870s or early 1880s, and sold through John W. Haseltine. A set of three was acquired from Abe Kosoff by Willis Harrington DuPont. These and other coins were stolen from him by five masked armed intruders in his Coconut Grove, Florida, home on October 5, 1967. In 1999 the quarter was identified in a group of miscellaneous coins brought to the Los Angeles Coin Company. It was recognized by Paul Wojdak and was returned to the DuPont family. Not long afterward, in September 1999, the half dollar was brought to the Superior Stamp & Coin Co. in Beverly Hills by a person who did not seem to be aware of its value. It was identified by staff expert Steve Deeds, recovered, and given to the DuPont family. The quarter and half dollar were placed on loan with the American Numismatic Association museum in Colorado Springs. The silver dollar surfaced in Maine and on February 26, 2004, was identified by John Kraljevich and John Pack, experts on the staff of American Numismatic Rarities, and was returned to the family, who placed it with the other two coins at the ANA. In November 2014 the DuPont family donated the trio to the National Numismatic Collection at the Smithsonian Institution in Washington, D.C., where they are carefully kept today.[54]

1866–1873, Motto Above Eagle
(Variety 4)

The design for this variety is the same as the preceding, but now IN GOD WE TRUST is on a ribbon above the eagle on the reverse.

Designer: Christian Gobrecht. Motto added by someone on the Mint staff.

Specifications: *Composition:* 90 percent silver, 10 percent copper. *Diameter:* 24.3 mm. *Weight:* 96 grains (6.22 grams). *Edge:* Reeded.

1866,
With Motto

Circulation-strike mintage: 16,800

Proof mintage: 725

actual size: 24.3 mm

Availability in Mint State: In 2014 the Eugene H. Gardner Sale featured an example of this coin in MS-66. *MS-60 to 62:* 14 to 18. *MS-63:* 10 to 14. *MS-64:* 15 to 20. *MS-65 or better:* 7 to 10.

Availability in circulated grades: These are rare, but most have relatively little wear.

Characteristics of striking: These are nearly always seen with lightness at the star centers and at the obverse shield area. "I've only seen two or three sharp circulation strikes in my life," Larry Briggs commented.[55]

Proofs: *PF-60 to 62:* 225 to 300. *PF-63:* 150 to 200. *PF-64:* 90 to 120. *PF-65 or better:* 35 to 45.

Notes: In keeping with certain other denominations of this year (notably the 1866 Shield nickel five-cent piece), the fourth digit in the date logotype appears to be significantly larger than the third. The exact reason for this is not obvious. A couple of theories have surfaced, including the fourth digit being punched separately and more deeply when the logotype was made, or the fourth digit being from a different punch. There is some difference in the punches, notable in several areas, particularly the space between the top knob and the bottom curve of the 6.

G-4	VG-8	F-12	VF-20	EF-40	AU-50
$775	$1,000	$1,250	$1,500	$1,850	$2,450
MS-60	MS-63	MS-65	PF-60	PF-63	PF-65
$2,800	$3,150	$10,000	$500	$875	$2,500

1866-S

Circulation-strike mintage: 28,000

Availability in Mint State: In 2014 the Eugene H. Gardner Sale featured an example of this coin in MS-65. *MS-60 to 62:* 3 or 4. *MS-63:* 1 or 2. *MS-64:* 1 or 2. *MS-65 or better:* 1 or 2.

actual size: 24.3 mm

Availability in circulated grades: These are rare and are mostly well worn. The Louis E. Eliasberg Sale in 1997 featured an example of this coin in AU-55.

Characteristics of striking: The star centers are usually incomplete, although the hair details are sharp. They are typically seen with weakness on the reverse from five to nine o'clock.

Notes: In his *Mint Marks* monograph in 1893, Augustus G. Heaton commented: "The 1866-S is the first of the series with the motto IN GOD WE TRUST. It is also the first to dismiss the large S mint mark and show a very small S that continues with little change through the rest of the San Francisco Mint quarters." The reverse die was also used to strike 1868-S and 1869-S quarters according to Larry Briggs.

For further reading see the *Gobrecht Journal*, March 1983, "The 1866-S Quarter," by Bill Cregan. He illustrates a worn piece, comments that it is very underrated even in relation to its sparse 28,000 mintage, and that the 1864-S has appeared at public sale five times more often than the 1866-S. "Stretching rarity even further, the 1866-S might rank in rarity with the Carson City quarters minted 1870–1873, which were all scarce," the same writer concluded. Moreover, he was not aware that a coin existed even in as high as the AU level.

G-4	VG-8	F-12	VF-20	EF-40	AU-50	MS-60	MS-63	MS-65
$600	$1,000	$1,500	$1,650	$2,300	$3,500	$6,500	$13,500	$35,000

1867

Circulation-strike mintage: 20,000

Proof mintage: 625

Availability in Mint State: In 2014 and 2015 the Eugene H. Gardner Sale featured examples of this coin in MS-64 (2) and MS-63 (3). *MS-60 to 62:* 7 to 10. *MS-63:* 4 to 6. *MS-64:* 3 or 4. *MS-65 or better:* 1 or 2.

actual size: 24.3 mm

Availability in circulated grades: These are rare and most are in higher grades.

Characteristics of striking: This issue is usually seen weak in areas on circulation strikes. LIBERTY often looks sharp at casual glance, but under magnification it is revealed that the die has been polished to weaken these letters.[56]

Proofs: *PF-60 to 62:* 190 to 250. *PF-63:* 140 to 175. *PF-64:* 100 to 130. *PF-65 or better:* 30 to 40.

G-4	VG-8	F-12	VF-20	EF-40	AU-50
$425	$650	$900	$1,000	$1,500	$1,850
MS-60	MS-63	MS-65	PF-60	PF-63	PF-65
$2,500	$4,500	$15,000	$500	$875	$2,250

1867-S

Circulation-strike mintage: 48,000

Availability in Mint State: These are very rare. The Louis E. Eliasberg Sale in 1997 featured an example of this coin in MS-64. In 2015 the Eugene H. Gardner Sale featured an example of this coin in MS-67. *MS-60 to 62:* 1 or 2. *MS-63:* 1. *MS-64:* 1. *MS-65 or better:* 1.

actual size: 24.3 mm

Availability in circulated grades: These are rare and most are well worn.

Characteristics of striking: This issue is usually seen with weakness on the stars and head on the obverse and some weakness on the reverse.

G-4	VG-8	F-12	VF-20	EF-40	AU-50	MS-60	MS-63	MS-65
$675	$1,000	$1,350	$1,650	$3,500	$8,750	$12,500	$15,000	

1868

Circulation-strike mintage: 29,400

Proof mintage: 600

Availability in Mint State: State: In 2014 and 2015 the Eugene H. Gardner Sale featured examples of this coin in MS-66 and MS-65. *MS-60 to 62:* 70 to 90. *MS-63:* 30 to 40. *MS-64:* 20 to 25. *MS-65 or better:* 7 to 9.

actual size: 24.3 mm

Availability in circulated grades: These are seldom seen, and when they are most are in higher grades.

Characteristics of striking: This issue is usually sharp.

Proofs: *PF-60 to 62:* 200 to 260. *PF-63:* 120 to 150. *PF-64:* 70 to 90. *PF-65 or better:* 20 to 30.

G-4	VG-8	F-12	VF-20	EF-40	AU-50
$250	$350	$500	$575	$750	$1,000
MS-60	MS-63	MS-65	PF-60	PF-63	PF-65
$2,000	$4,000	$9,000	$500	$875	$2,250

1868-S

Circulation-strike mintage: 96,000

Availability in Mint State: Rare. The Louis E. Eliasberg Sale in 1997 featured an example of this coin in MS-66. In 2014 and 2015 the Eugene H. Gardner Sale featured

actual size: 24.3 mm

examples of this coin in MS-66 and MS-64. *MS-60 to 62:* 1. *MS-63:* 0. *MS-64:* 1. *MS-65 or better:* 2.[57]

Availability in circulated grades: These are rare and most have extensive wear and problems.

Characteristics of striking: This issue is usually seen with weakness on the obverse.

G-4	VG-8	F-12	VF-20	EF-40	AU-50	MS-60	MS-63	MS-65
$125	$200	$375	$750	$1,000	$2,000	$5,500	$10,000	$17,500

1869

Circulation-strike mintage: 16,000

Proof mintage: 600

Availability in Mint State: In 2014 the Eugene H. Gardner Sale featured an example of this coin in MS-66. *MS-60 to 62:* 6 to 9.

actual size: 24.3 mm

MS-63: 6 to 9. *MS-64:* 3 or 4. *MS-65 or better:* 2 or 3.[58]

Availability in circulated grades: These are rare and survivors are mainly in grades from AG-3 to Fine-12, or EF and AU—an interesting distribution.[59]

Characteristics of striking: This issue is usually sharp.

Proofs: *PF-60 to 62:* 200 to 250. *PF-63:* 90 to 120. *PF-64:* 70 to 90. *PF-65 or better:* 25 to 35.

G-4	VG-8	F-12	VF-20	EF-40	AU-50
$500	$650	$850	$1,000	$1,250	$1,500
MS-60	MS-63	MS-65	PF-60	PF-63	PF-65
$2,250	$5,500	$10,000	$500	$875	$2,250

1869-S

Circulation-strike mintage: 76,000

Availability in Mint State: This issue is very rare. The Louis E. Eliasberg Sale in 1997 featured an example of this coin in MS-64 with "creamy" luster, as is typical for San Francisco Mint coins

actual size: 24.3 mm

of this era. In 2014 and 2015 the Eugene H. Gardner Sale featured two examples of this coin in MS-64. *MS-60 to 62:* 1 or 2. *MS-63:* 2. *MS-64:* 2. *MS-65 or better:* 1.

Availability in circulated grades: These are scarce, but are seen on the market with some frequency. Most are well worn.

Characteristics of striking: This issue is usually seen with lightness in areas. A die crack connects many of the stars.

Notes: 1869 Philadelphia Mint coins have the date high in the field and on 1869-S coins it is low.

G-4	VG-8	F-12	VF-20	EF-40	AU-50	MS-60	MS-63	MS-65
$175	$275	$475	$675	$1,250	$1,650	$5,500	$8,000	$17,500

1870

Circulation-strike mintage: 86,400

Proof mintage: 1,000

Availability in Mint State: In 2015 the Eugene H. Gardner Sale featured an example of this coin in MS-66. *MS-60 to 62:* 40 to 65. *MS-63:* 16 to 20. *MS-64:* 10 to 14. *MS-65 or better:* 9 to 12.

actual size: 24.3 mm

Availability in circulated grades: These are very scarce, but are more available than are any Philadelphia quarters of recent earlier years.

Characteristics of striking: This issue is usually sharp.

Proofs: There were 1,000 pieces minted for reasons not explained. This is a sharp increase from the 600 for the year preceding, and might be explained by production problems for Proofs. Quite a few of the silver Proofs of this year (present coin excepted) are sloppily made. One can imagine that certain others were produced, discarded, and replaced by better pieces. In any event, today the higher-mintage 1870 is no more plentiful than the lower mintage 1869. *PF-60 to 62:* 200 to 250. *PF-63:* 90 to 120. *PF-64:* 70 to 90. *PF-65 or better:* 25 to 35.

G-4	VG-8	F-12	VF-20	EF-40	AU-50
$65	$100	$175	$275	$450	$650

MS-60	MS-63	MS-65	PF-60	PF-63	PF-65
$1,000	$2,500	$6,500	$500	$875	$2,250

1870-CC

Circulation-strike mintage: 8,340

actual size: 24.3 mm

Availability in Mint State: This issue is unique. The Louis E. Eliasberg Sale in 1997 featured an example of this coin in MS-64, prooflike, a spectacular piece.[60] *MS-60 to 62:* 0. *MS-63:* 0. *MS-64:* 1. *MS-65 or better:* 0.

Availability in circulated grades: These are very rare and are a key issue. Many coins have problems, which can be said of all Carson City quarters through 1873. The Battle Born Collection coin (2013) is AU-55. In 2015 the Eugene H. Gardner Sale featured an example of this coin in AU-55.

Characteristics of striking: This issue has lightness seen at most star centers. There is often weakness on the lower part of the reverse as well.

Notes: The dies used to strike the 1870-CC quarter dollars arrived at the Carson City Mint on December 31, 1869, as part of the shipment dispatched from the Engraving Department of the Philadelphia Mint on October 29 of the same year. Just one obverse and one reverse die were employed, although two pairs had been sent. Apparently the other pair was discarded, for the 1870 obverse has not been seen on any known examples of the quarter, and the identical reverse die was continued in use afterward for 1871-CC; 1872-CC; 1873-CC, With Arrows; and 1876-CC. The 1873-CC, No Arrows, reverse die is different and was used for that short run and again for a short time in combination with one obverse in 1876.[61] The first delivery of 1870-CC quarters occurred on April 20, 1870, when 3,540 were struck. The second delivery of 1,400 pieces occurred on May 24, followed by the third and final delivery of 3,400 on August 15. This is the rarest of the Carson City quarters excepting the 1873-CC, No Arrows.

All were circulated regionally. There was no numismatic interest in them at the time, nor was there until the early 1890s. In 1893, when the 1870-CC was scarcely 23 years old, Augustus G. Heaton reflected that, "It has the smallest coinage of the CC series and is exceedingly rare."

The 1870-CC; 1871-CC; 1872-CC; and the 1873-CC, With Arrows, quarters were all struck from the same reverse die. No Carson City coins were minted in 1874. The next piece, 1875-CC, is from a different reverse die and has the mintmark in an entirely different position with relation to the bottom arrow feather.[62]

G-4	VG-8	F-12	VF-20	EF-40	AU-50	MS-60	MS-63	MS-65
$11,500	$15,000	$22,500	$27,500	$55,000	$150,000		—	

1870-S

Mintage: 1 or more

Notes: Six pairs of quarter dies were sent from Philadelphia to San Francisco on January 15, 1870, but there is no record of any quarters having been struck for circulation. At least one was made to be placed in the cornerstone of the second San Francisco Mint, however, as evidenced by the receipt shown here. The 1870-S half dime (see listing in chapter 4) is also on the receipt, although there is no record of the coinage for circulation.[63] There is also no record of 1870-S Liberty Seated dollars (see listing in chapter 9) having been struck, but a number of examples exist today.

1871

Circulation-strike mintage: 118,200

Proof mintage: 960

Availability in Mint State: In 2014 and 2015 the Eugene H. Gardner Sale featured examples of this coin in MS-67 and MS-65.

actual size: 24.3 mm

MS-60 to 62: 10 to 14. *MS-63:* 12 to 15. *MS-64:* 12 to 15. *MS-65 or better:* 2 or 3.

Availability in circulated grades: These are very scarce, but are usually seen VF or finer.

Characteristics of striking: This issue is usually sharp at first glance. Two obverse dies had LIBERTY over-polished, creating lightness that can be seen under magnification.[64]

Proofs: *PF-60 to 62:* 200 to 250. *PF-63:* 90 to 120. *PF-64:* 70 to 90. *PF-65 or better:* 25 to 35.

G-4	VG-8	F-12	VF-20	EF-40	AU-50
$60	$85	$125	$175	$325	$500
MS-60	MS-63	MS-65	PF-60	PF-63	PF-65
$750	$1,500	$7,000	$500	$875	$2,250

1871-CC

Circulation-strike mintage: 10,890

actual size: 24.3 mm

Availability in Mint State: These are exceedingly rare. There are only three Mint State 1871-CC Liberty Seated quarters known:

1. PCGS, MS-65. Stack's Giacomo Pezzo Sale, August 1941, lot 1865; Stack's sale of the James A. Stack Collection, March 1975, lot 130; Stack's sale of the Reed Hawn Collection, March 1977, lot 365; unknown intermediaries; the Battle Born Collection, Stack's Bowers Galleries, August 2013; and the Eugene H. Gardner Sale in 2014 and 2015.

2. MS-65. Numismatic Gallery's "World's Greatest Collection," March 1945; and Louis E. Eliasberg, Bowers and Merena Galleries' sale of the Louis E. Eliasberg Collection, April 1997, lot 1497. This coin might be the MS-65 currently listed in the NGC census.

3. PCGS, MS-64. Ambassador and Mrs. R. Henry Norweb; Bowers and Merena's sale of the Norweb Collection, Part II, March 1988, lot 1640; William Greene; Superior's sale of the William Greene Collection, February 1998, lot 2033; Heritage's sale of the Nevada Collection, August 1999, lot 6279; and American Numismatic Rarities' Kennywood Collection sale, January 2005, lot 443.

Availability in circulated grades: This issue is rare across the board, the second rarest of the early Carson City quarters (excepting the 1870-CC and the exceedingly rare 1873-CC, No Arrows). AU coins are especially rare, and many coins have problems. In 2014 the Eugene H. Gardner Sale featured an example of this coin in AU-55.

Characteristics of striking: These have some slight weakness on both sides, but it is not important as this is typical of all Carson City quarters.

Notes: Dies for the coinage of the 1871-CC quarter dollar were received at the Carson City Mint on December 15, 1870, having been ordered from Philadelphia (where all dies are made and mintmarks applied) during the preceding month. The first delivery of 1871-CC quarters amounted to 3,490 pieces and took place on February 2, 1871, followed by 2,400 on August 11, and 5,000 on September 30. Although four obverse dies were ordered from Philadelphia, apparently only one obverse was actually used—one with both 1 digits very slightly doubled.[65]

G-4	VG-8	F-12	VF-20	EF-40	AU-50	MS-60	MS-63	MS-65
$10,000	$15,000	$22,500	$35,000	$55,000	$75,000			$500,000

1871-S

Circulation-strike mintage: 30,900

Availability in Mint State: These are very rare. The Louis E. Eliasberg Sale in 1997 featured an example of this coin in MS-66. It is sharply struck and very attractive. In 2014 and 2015

actual size: 24.3 mm

the Eugene H. Gardner Sale featured examples of this coin in MS-66 and MS-65. *MS-60 to 62:* 12 to 15. *MS-63:* 8 to 11. *MS-64:* 7 to 9. *MS-65 or better:* 3 or 4.

Availability in circulated grades: These are rare and most show extensive wear

Characteristics of striking: Within this issue most coins are sharp, but some have obverse lightness, and lower-grade coins show weakness from five to nine o'clock.

Notes: In 1893 Augustus G. Heaton observed, somewhat presciently, as the elusive quality of the 1871-S was not generally recognized until much later: "The piece is very rare."[66]

G-4	VG-8	F-12	VF-20	EF-40	AU-50	MS-60	MS-63	MS-65
$950	$1,500	$2,250	$3,200	$4,000	$5,500	$7,500	$10,000	$20,000

1872

Circulation-strike mintage: 182,000

Proof mintage: 950

Availability in Mint State: In 2014 the Eugene H. Gardner Sale featured an example of this coin in MS-67. *MS-60 to 62:* 8 to 11. *MS-63:* 4 or 5. *MS-64:* 4 or 5. *MS-65 or better:* 4 or 5.[67]

actual size: 24.3 mm

Availability in circulated grades: These are scarce in circulated grades.

Characteristics of striking: This issue is usually sharp.

Proofs: The same reverse die was used to coin Proofs of 1873, Close 3; 1873, With Arrows; 1874; 1875; 1876; 1877; 1878; 1879; and 1880; after which it was used to make circulation strikes. For some of the preceding years other dies were also used.[68] *PF-60 to 62:* 275 to 350. *PF-63:* 150 to 200. *PF-64:* 90 to 120. *PF-65 or better:* 50 to 65.

Notes: Numismatists of this era who collected by date sequence usually bought Proofs. Mint State coins were not desired. And, if they had been, they would have been very difficult to find, as no Philadelphia silver coins were released into circulation for face value after the spring of 1862. This continued until after April 20, 1876, although there were a few occasional releases several years earlier.

G-4	VG-8	F-12	VF-20	EF-40	AU-50
$65	$100	$175	$250	$400	$600

MS-60	MS-63	MS-65	PF-60	PF-63	PF-65
$1,250	$2,250	$7,500	$500	$875	$1,850

1872-CC

Circulation-strike mintage: 22,850

actual size: 24.3 mm

Availability in Mint State: These are exceedingly rare— they outrank and outflank the famous 1871-CC in this regard, and *in gem Mint State it is even rarer than the legendary 1873-CC, No Arrows!* The Louis E. Eliasberg Sale in 1997 featured an example of this coin in MS-66 or finer. In 2014 the Eugene H. Gardner Sale featured an example of this coin in MS-62 (ex Norweb 1988; Battle Born 2013). *MS-60 to 62:* 1. *MS-63:* 0. *MS-64:* 0. *MS-65 or better:* 1.

Availability in circulated grades: These are in any grade and are very rare at the EF and AU levels, but many coins have problems. Counterfeits are seen now and again. Buying NGC or PCGS coins is recommended.

Characteristics of striking: This issue has some areas of slight weakness seen on both sides.

Notes: Only one obverse was used and is identifiable by having a long diagonal die gouge through the rock and shield, almost reaching the RT in LIBERTY.[69] The first delivery of 1872-CC quarters was 8,000 pieces on February 29 of that year; followed by 5,750 on March 30; 5,100 on September 27; and the final delivery of 4,000 on December 31, totaling 22,850.

G-4	VG-8	F-12	VF-20	EF-40	AU-50	MS-60	MS-63	MS-65
$2,500	$2,800	$5,500	$12,500	$17,500	$22,500	$100,000		

1872-S

Circulation-strike mintage: 83,000

actual size: 24.3 mm

Availability in Mint State: These are extremely rare. The Louis E. Eliasberg Sale in 1997 featured an example of this coin in MS-62. In 2014 the Eugene H. Gardner Sale featured an example of this coin in MS-66. *MS-60 to 62:* 1. *MS-63:* 0. *MS-64:* 0. *MS-65 or better:* 1.[70]

Availability in circulated grades: This issue is very rare in all grades

Characteristics of striking: These are usually seen with lightly struck star centers, sometimes with slight weakness at LIBERTY, and with reverse weakness from five to nine o'clock. Across the board, this common reverse weakness is most noticeable on well-worn coins.

Notes: These are far, far rarer than the mintage would indicate. Perhaps some were not distributed by the time of the Coinage Act of 1873 and were melted.

Writing in the *Gobrecht Journal*, March 1987, Roy D. Ash, under the title "Liberty Seated Quarter Dollars Survey," noted that among San Francisco Mint issues, far fewer had been seen of the 1872-S than any other studied, with only 12 examples reported in a survey he conducted. Runner-up in rarity was the 1871-S with 21 examples, closely followed by the 1866-S with 22, 1864-S with 23, and 1860-S and 1867-S tied at 25. Most plentiful was the 1888-S. Bill Cregan in "The Rare 1872-S Quarter," the *Gobrecht Journal*, July 1990 stated: "Some specialists even believe the 1872-S quarter is as difficult to obtain as some of the rarest date Carson City quarters."

G-4	VG-8	F-12	VF-20	EF-40	AU-50	MS-60	MS-63	MS-65
$2,500	$2,750	$3,500	$5,500	$8,500	$10,000	$15,000	$20,000	$40,000

1873, No Arrows, Close 3

Circulation-strike mintage: 40,000

Proof mintage: 600

actual size: 24.3 mm

Availability in Mint State: These are rare. Fewer than two dozen are estimated to exist. *MS-60 to 62:* 3 or 4. *MS-63:* 0. *MS-64:* 0. *MS-65 or better:* 0.

Availability in circulated grades: A Liberty Seated Coin Club survey found 28 in members' hands. Probably 100 or so exist.

Characteristics of striking: This issue is usually sharp.

Proofs: *PF-60 to 62:* 275 to 350. *PF-63:* 180 to 220. *PF-64:* 80 to 110. *PF-65 or better:* 30 to 40.

Notes: Two obverse dies were used.[71]

G-4	VG-8	F-12	VF-20	EF-40	AU-50
$550	$700	$1,000	$1,300	$3,000	$4,500

MS-60	MS-63	MS-65	PF-60	PF-63	PF-65
$20,000	$35,000		$500	$850	$2,000

1873, No Arrows, Open 3

Circulation-strike mintage: 172,000

actual size: 24.3 mm

Availability in Mint State: In 2015 the Eugene H. Gardner Sale featured an example of this coin in MS-66. *MS-60 to 62:* 20 to 25. *MS-63:* 15 to 20. *MS-64:* 11 to 15. *MS-65 or better:* 8 to 11.

Availability in circulated grades: These are readily available in circulated grades.

Characteristics of striking: Striking of this issue varies, but sharp coins can be found.

G-4	VG-8	F-12	VF-20	EF-40	AU-50	MS-60	MS-63	MS-65
$65	$75	$150	$250	$300	$425	$675	$2,000	$6,500

1873-CC, No Arrows

Circulation-strike mintage: 4,000

Availability in Mint State: There are three examples of this coin in Mint State: the Battle Born Collection (2014) coin is MS-64, the second finest (illustrated); in 2015 the Eugene H. Gardner Sale featured an example of this coin in MS-63, (ex Eliasberg); and the James A. Stack coin is the third in MS-66.

actual size: 24.3 mm

Availability in circulated grades: There are two coins in circulated grades. One has VG details and the other is VF.[72]

Characteristics of striking: This issue is well struck except for star centers at the right side of the obverse.

Notes: The mintage of the 1873-CC, No Arrows, quarter dollar is believed to have been only 4,000 coins. Apparently, most were melted (between April 1, 1873, and July 10, 1873) for being obsolete; the Coinage Act of 1873 had specified a slightly increased authorized weight, and later 1873-CC, With Arrows, quarters were made under this new standard.

This is one of the most famous, most heralded rarities in the Liberty Seated series. A detailed history and registry is given in the Louis E. Eliasberg Collection catalog, 1997.

The reverse die used for these quarters was also used for a short run of 1876-CC quarters.[73]

G-4	VG-8	F-12	VF-20	EF-40	AU-50	MS-60	MS-63	MS-65
				$250,000			$500,000	$850,000

1873–1874, Arrows at Date (Variety 5)

The design for this variety is the same as the preceding variety, With Motto, but now arrows have been added at the date to indicate a slightly increased weight.

Designer: Christian Gobrecht. Motto and arrows added by someone on the Mint staff.

Specifications: *Composition:* 90 percent silver, 10 percent copper. *Diameter:* 24.3 mm. *Weight:* 96.45 grains (6.25 grams). *Edge:* Reeded.

1873, With Arrows

Circulation-strike mintage: 1,271,200

Proof mintage: 540

actual size: 24.3 mm

Availability in Mint State: According to Larry Briggs, it is among the most available Liberty Seated quarters in Mint State. The Louis E. Eliasberg Sale in 1997 featured an example of this coin in MS-66. It is sharply struck and very attractive. In 2014 and 2015 the Eugene H. Gardner Sale featured examples of this coin in MS-67 and MS-64. *MS-60 to 62:* 110 to 130. *MS-63:* 70 to 90. *MS-64:* 55 to 70. *MS-65 or better:* 22 to 24.

Availability in circulated grades: These are fairly plentiful in relation to the demand.

Characteristics of striking: This issue varies, but most have some slight weakness.

Proofs: There are two reverse dies, one of which had been used in 1872. The 1873, With Arrows is very scarce in higher grades, causing considerable effort for those wanting the first year of issue for a type set. *PF-60 to 62:* 240 to 300. *PF-63:* 90 to 120. *PF-64:* 60 to 75. *PF-65 or better:* 30 to 40.

G-4	VG-8	F-12	VF-20	EF-40	AU-50
$35	$40	$55	$65	$225	$425

MS-60	MS-63	MS-65	PF-60	PF-63	PF-65
$1,000	$1,650	$4,000	$900	$1,350	$5,500

1873-CC, With Arrows

Circulation-strike mintage: 12,462

actual size: 24.3 mm

Availability in Mint State: These are exceedingly rare. The Louis E. Eliasberg Sale in 1997 featured examples of this coin in MS-66 and MS-63/65, prooflike. It is sharply struck and very attractive. In 2015 the Eugene H. Gardner Sale featured an example of this coin in MS-64. *MS-60 to 62:* 0 or 1. *MS-63:* 0 or 1. *MS-64:* 1. *MS-65 or better:* 1.

Availability in circulated grades: This issue is rare and most show extensive wear. Many coins have problems. The Eugene H. Gardner Collection features an example of this coin in AU-55.

Characteristics of striking: There is some lightness on coins of this issue, but this varies from coin to coin. Cherrypicking is advised, but you can't be too picky as there are not many in the marketplace.

Notes: The first delivery was made on June 23, 1873, and amounted to 3,500 pieces. On July 31, a further 8,962 were made.

G-4	VG-8	F-12	VF-20	EF-40	AU-50	MS-60	MS-63	MS-65
$6,500	$10,000	$13,500	$20,000	$27,500	$50,000	$125,000	$200,000	$375,000

1873-S

Circulation-strike mintage: 156,000

Availability in Mint State: These are very rare. The Louis E. Eliasberg Sale in 1997 featured an example of this coin in MS-66. It is sharply struck and very attractive. In 2014 and 2015

actual size: 24.3 mm

the Eugene H. Gardner Sale featured examples of this coin in MS-65 (2) and MS-64. *MS-60 to 62:* 2 or 3. *MS-63:* 1 or 2. *MS-64:* 1 or 2. *MS-65 or better:* 2 or 3.

Availability in circulated grades: "Scarce, but there are enough around to fill the collector demand for them."[74]

Characteristics of striking: This issue usually has some lightness.

Notes: Concerning the 1873-S, *No Arrows,* quarter: Today numismatists believe that no example of the 1873-S, No Arrows quarter dollar exists, and not a single piece has ever been reliably reported. However, J.M. Clapp in his notebook in the 1890s wrote that DeWitt S. Smith had informed him that an 1873-S, No Arrows, quarter dollar was in the Heaton Collection, having been bought from Harlan P. Smith, but upon checking, Clapp found that neither Heaton nor H.P. Smith ever owned such a coin.

G-4	VG-8	F-12	VF-20	EF-40	AU-50	MS-60	MS-63	MS-65
$100	$125	$185	$275	$450	$650	$1,750	$4,500	$16,500

1874

Circulation-strike mintage: 471,200

Proof mintage: 700

Availability in Mint State: In 2014 the Eugene H. Gardner Sale featured an example of this coin in MS-66. *MS-60 to 62:* 50 to

actual size: 24.3 mm

65. *MS-63:* 35 to 45. *MS-64:* 35 to 45. *MS-65 or better:* 14 to 18.

Availability in circulated grades: These are readily available, including in higher grades.

Characteristics of striking: This issue is often seen with some lightness on Liberty's head.

Proofs: *PF-60 to 62:* 300 to 400. *PF-63:* 120 to 150. *PF-64:* 60 to 75. *PF-65 or better:* 30 to 40.

Notes: In this year a number of quarters, half dollars, and trade dollars were counterstamped with the advertisement, SAGE'S / CANDY / COIN. Today these are known in VF and EF grades and are very rare. See page 393 for an example on a half dollar.

G-4	VG-8	F-12	VF-20	EF-40	AU-50
$35	$40	$45	$75	$200	$450

MS-60	MS-63	MS-65	PF-60	PF-63	PF-65
$850	$1,150	$3,000	$900	$1,350	$5,500

1874-S

Circulation-strike mintage: 392,000

actual size: 24.3 mm

Availability in Mint State: The 1874-S is available mostly from a hoard of choice and gem coins dispersed by Lester Merkin in the 1960s. For details see Q. David Bowers, *Lost and Found Coin Hoards and Treasures.* Were it not for this marvelous find, high-grade coins would probably be great rarities today, although in 1997 the unrelated Louis E. Eliasberg coin from the David S. Wilson Collection (1906) was cataloged as MS-66. The author can recall the time that the hoard was of mysterious origin and comprised at least several-dozen coins. Walter Breen gave the number as 80 to 100 from a "West Coast bank" in 1949. The Eugene H. Gardner Collection features an example of this coin in MS-67. *MS-60 to 62:* 18 to 22. *MS-63:* 20 to 25. *MS-64:* 75 to 90. *MS-65 or better:* 90 to 120.

Availability in circulated grades: Most coins of this issue show extensive circulation; scarce.

Characteristics of striking: These are usually seen with some lightness on the obverse.

G-4	VG-8	F-12	VF-20	EF-40	AU-50	MS-60	MS-63	MS-65
$35	$45	$65	$100	$265	$485	$850	$1,150	$3,000

1875–1891, Variety 4 Resumed, With Weight Standard of Variety 5

The design is the same as the preceding, but without arrows at the date. The slightly increased weight is maintained through this variety. Coins of this design are similar in appearance to the 1866–1873 type with the only difference being the weight.

Reverse Hub Changes of 1875

In 1875 a new reverse hub was introduced that was subsequently used at all mints. This is called the 1875 Type 2 Reverse.

1875 Type 1: The bases of TAT in STATES are so close they seem nearly connected. This type was used earlier.

1875 Type 2: The bases of the TAT letters are distinctly separated.

Detail of Type 1 reverse.   Detail of Type 2 reverse.

Designer: Christian Gobrecht. Motto added by someone on the Mint staff.

Specifications: *Composition:* 90 percent silver, 10 percent copper. *Diameter:* 24.3 mm. *Weight:* 96.45 grains (6.25 grams). *Edge:* Reeded.

1875

Circulation-strike mintage: 4,292,800

Proof mintage: 700

Availability in Mint State: According to Larry Briggs this coin is among the most available Liberty Seated quarters in Mint State.

actual size: 24.3 mm

MS-60 to 62: 225 to 300. *MS-63:* 125 to 150. *MS-64:* 100 to 125. *MS-65 or better:* 70 to 90.

Availability in circulated grades: These are common in circulated grades.

Characteristics of striking: This issue is usually sharp.

Proofs: *PF-60 to 62:* 225 to 300. *PF-63:* 190 to 250. *PF-64:* 80 to 100. *PF-65 or better:* 25 to 35.

Type 1 Reverse: Readily available.

Type 2 Reverse: Readily available. Slightly scarcer than the preceding.

G-4	VG-8	F-12	VF-20	EF-40	AU-50
$35	$40	$45	$50	$75	$160
MS-60	MS-63	MS-65	PF-60	PF-63	PF-65
$275	$550	$1,750	$500	$800	$1,500

1875-CC

actual size: 24.3 mm

Circulation-strike mintage: 140,000

Availability in Mint State: Many 1875-CC quarter dollars are prooflike. In 2014 the Eugene H. Gardner Sale featured an example of this coin in MS-65. *MS-60 to 62:* 13 to 17. *MS-63:* 10 to 14. *MS-64:* 10 to 14. *MS-65 or better:* 5 to 7.[75]

Availability in circulated grades: These are fairly scarce.

Characteristics of striking: The obverse of some pieces is highly prooflike, but some weakness is usual. Many have four or five letters of LIBERTY visible, but a Fair to About Good reverse![76]

Notes: These coins have the Type 2 Reverse.

In the July 1977 issue of the *Gobrecht Journal*, Eddie Randell's article, "An Auction Comparison Between the 1875-CC and 1878-S Quarters," pointed out that the 1875-CC was much rarer than realized. Interestingly, Randell said that his first notice of the variety was when he ordered the *Empire Investors Report* in 1963. Surprisingly, a survey of auction catalogs of the 1960s and 1970s yielded 21 auction appearances for the famous and rare 1878-S, but just nine for the somewhat overlooked 1875-CC.

The March 1981 issue of the *Gobrecht Journal* contained an article by John W. McCloskey, "The 1875-CC Quarter," which paid tribute to its rarity, noting that "the listed mintage of 140,000 pieces doesn't stand out as anything unusual in a series that has 45 other dates with lower figures given. Yet in terms of availability is one of the most difficult dates in the series to find. Please note that I do not mean to imply that the 1875-CC quarter is prohibitively rare, but only wish to indicate that it is just not available in today's market." Additional comments on the 1875-CC by the same author appeared in the subsequent July and November issues.

G-4	VG-8	F-12	VF-20	EF-40	AU-50	MS-60	MS-63	MS-65
$300	$425	$600	$950	$1,750	$2,750	$5,500	$8,500	$25,000

1875-S

actual size: 24.3 mm

Circulation-strike mintage: 680,000

Availability in Mint State: These are very rare despite the generous mintage. The Louis E. Eliasberg Sale in 1997 featured examples of this coin in MS-64, MS-64/65, and MS-60. In 2014 the Eugene H. Gardner Sale featured an example of this coin in MS-65. *MS-60 to 62:* 60 to 80. *MS-63:* 30 to 40. *MS-64:* 25 to 32. *MS-65 or better:* 15 to 20.

Availability in circulated grades: These are quite scarce in circulated grades.

Characteristics of striking: This issue is usually weak in areas.

Type 1 Reverse: Slightly scarce.

Type 2 Reverse: Slightly scarce. The most often seen variety.

G-4	VG-8	F-12	VF-20	EF-40	AU-50	MS-60	MS-63	MS-65
$45	$60	$95	$130	$250	$325	$650	$1,000	$3,000

1876

Circulation-strike mintage: 17,816,000

Proof mintage: 1,150

Availability in Mint State: According to Larry Briggs, this and the 1853, With Arrows, are tied for being the most common Mint

actual size: 24.3 mm

State Liberty Seated quarters. *MS-60 to 62:* 400 to 550. *MS-63:* 225 to 350. *MS-64:* 200 to 275. *MS-65 or better:* 130 to 160.

Availability in circulated grades: These are extremely common.

Characteristics of striking: This issue varies widely, but sharp coins can be found.

Proofs: It is thought that many Proofs were spent by Centennial Exhibition visitors who were not numismatists and later tired of their novelty. *PF-60 to 62:* 325 to 400. *PF-63:* 200 to 275. *PF-64:* 120 to 150. *PF-65 or better:* 60 to 90.

Notes: There are two general reverse types, so-called Type 1 with the TAT in STATES closely spaced, and Type 2 with the same letters spaced slightly farther apart.

Type 1 Reverse: Common, but fewer exist than of the following.

Type 2 Reverse: Common.

G-4	VG-8	F-12	VF-20	EF-40	AU-50
$35	$40	$45	$50	$75	$160
MS-60	**MS-63**	**MS-65**	**PF-60**	**PF-63**	**PF-65**
$300	$550	$1,600	$500	$800	$1,500

1876-CC

Circulation-strike mintage: 4,944,000

Availability in Mint State: According to Larry Briggs, this coin is among the most available Liberty Seated quarters in Mint State. *MS-60 to 62:* 120 to 140. *MS-63:* 80 to 95. *MS-64:* 75 to 90. *MS-65 or better:* 16 to 22.

actual size: 24.3 mm

Availability in circulated grades: This is one of the most available of all Carson City coins of the era.

Characteristics of striking: This issue varies widely. Take your time until you find a sharp one!

Notes: The reeding on the edges is most unusual with three different counts noted: 113 or coarse reeding, 122, and 153 or fine reeding, the last being the highest in the entire series. The ones with fine-reeded edges are the most common, although a number of accounts list them as the rarest.[77]

For some 1876-CC quarters, the reverse of 1870-CC, also used on certain other early quarters, was employed.[78]

Type 1 Reverse: Plentiful.

Type 2 Reverse: Plentiful.

G-4	VG-8	F-12	VF-20	EF-40	AU-50	MS-60	MS-63	MS-65
$65	$100	$125	$150	$225	$350	$650	$1,250	$4,500

1876-S

Circulation-strike mintage: 8,596,000

Availability in Mint State: According to Larry Briggs, it is among the most available Liberty Seated quarters in Mint State. *MS-60 to 62:* 220 to 275. *MS-63:* 125 to 150. *MS-64:* 100 to 125. *MS-65 or better:* 22 to 26.

actual size: 24.3 mm

Availability in circulated grades: These are common in circulated grades.

Characteristics of striking: This issue varies, but sharp coins can be found.

Type 1 Reverse: Slightly scarce.

Type 2 Reverse: Common.

G-4	VG-8	F-12	VF-20	EF-40	AU-50	MS-60	MS-63	MS-65
$35	$40	$45	$50	$75	$160	$275	$550	$1,800

1877

Circulation-strike mintage: 10,911,200

Proof mintage: 510

Availability in Mint State: According to Larry Briggs, it is among the most available Liberty Seated quarters in Mint State. *MS-60 to 62:* 500 to 650. *MS-63:* 175 to 250. *MS-64:* 150 to 225. *MS-65 or better:* 100 to 150.

actual size: 24.3 mm

Availability in circulated grades: These are common. Many are very low grades and must have been taken from circulation well into the 20th century.

Characteristics of striking: This issue varies as is nearly always the case with high-mintage issues. You can find a sharp one.

Proofs: *PF-60 to 62:* 120 to 150. *PF-63:* 100 to 130. *PF-64:* 70 to 90. *PF-65 or better:* 50 to 60.

G-4	VG-8	F-12	VF-20	EF-40	AU-50
$35	$40	$45	$50	$75	$160
MS-60	**MS-63**	**MS-65**	**PF-60**	**PF-63**	**PF-65**
$275	$550	$1,300	$500	$800	$1,500

1877-CC

Circulation-strike mintage: 4,192,000

Availability in Mint State: According to Larry Briggs, this coin is among the most available Liberty Seated quarters in Mint State. In the 1950s a small hoard of these came on the market. *MS-60*

actual size: 24.3 mm

to 62: 160 to 230. *MS-63:* 150 to 225. *MS-64:* 120 to 150. *MS-65 or better:* 60 to 80.

Availability in circulated grades: These are common and most are well worn.

Characteristics of striking: This issue varies, so shop around.

G-4	VG-8	F-12	VF-20	EF-40	AU-50	MS-60	MS-63	MS-65
$65	$90	$120	$150	$225	$325	$600	$1,450	$3,000

1877-S

Circulation-strike mintage: 8,996,000

Availability in Mint State: According to Larry Briggs, it is among the most available Liberty Seated quarters in Mint State. *MS-60 to 62:* 300 to 400. *MS-63:* 150 to 180.

actual size: 24.3 mm

MS-64: 120 to 150. *MS-65 or better:* 60 to 80.

Availability in circulated grades: These are common in circulated grades.

Characteristics of striking: This issue is usually seen with some weakness, but there are many exceptions to be found.

1877-S, S Over Horizontal S: The die sinker in the Engraving Department at the Philadelphia Mint first punched the S mintmark in a "lazy" or horizontal position, recognized his blunder, and corrected it by overpunching the S in the correct position. However, even under low magnification the error is dramatically visible.

This famous variety lends a bit of spice to the sunset era of the Liberty Seated quarter dollar series and is scarce. In the 1950s the author handled a small group of Mint State pieces. Today this variety is encountered with frequency and most are in circulated grades. *Cherrypickers' Guide to Rare Die Varieties* lists this as FS-25-1877S-501. The Eugene H. Gardner Collection features an example of this coin in MS-65. Approximately 30 to 40 Mint State coins are known, most in ranges up to MS-64. Some of these are from a group of 13 that appeared at an Indiana coin show in 1986.[79]

G-4	VG-8	F-12	VF-20	EF-40	AU-50	MS-60	MS-63	MS-65
$35	$40	$45	$50	$75	$160	$275	$550	$1,300

1878

Circulation-strike mintage: 2,260,000

Proof mintage: 800

Availability in Mint State: According to Larry Briggs, it is among the most available Liberty Seated quarters in Mint State. *MS-60 to 62:*

actual size: 24.3 mm

100 to 125. *MS-63:* 50 to 65. *MS-64:* 25 to 32. *MS-65 or better:* 15 to 20.

Availability in circulated grades: These are common and many are in higher grades.

Characteristics of striking: The striking of this issue varies.

Proofs: *PF-60 to 62:* 250 to 325. *PF-63:* 180 to 220. *PF-64:* 90 to 120. *PF-65 or better:* 40 to 50.

G-4	VG-8	F-12	VF-20	EF-40	AU-50
$35	$40	$45	$50	$75	$160

MS-60	MS-63	MS-65	PF-60	PF-63	PF-65
$300	$550	$2,250	$500	$800	$1,500

1878-CC

Circulation-strike mintage: 996,000

Availability in Mint State: The Battle Born Collection (2014) featured an example of this coin in MS-67. The Louis E. Eliasberg Sale in 1997 featured an example of this coin in MS-66. It is sharply struck and very attractive.

actual size: 24.3 mm

In 2014 the Eugene H. Gardner Sale featured an example of this coin in MS-66. *MS-60 to 62:* 95 to 120. *MS-63:* 65 to 85. *MS-64:* 60 to 80. *MS-65 or better:* 28 to 35.

Availability in circulated grades: These are readily available, although are not common. Many are in very low grades.

Characteristics of striking: This issue is usually weak in areas.

Notes: Briggs Obverse-1 accounts for approximately one third of extant 1878-CC quarters, and it is the most interesting variety of the issue. A long, thin die gouge diagonally bisects Liberty's midsection, and is crossed by a second, much shorter die gouge that originates at Liberty's left (facing) forearm. A detail of the cancellation is

Detail of the die gouge.

shown at right (running from upper left to lower right). This is the so-called "cancelled obverse" variety of the issue, the physical evidence on coins such as this suggesting that employees at the Carson City Mint partially cancelled this die before it was used to strike some portion of the 1878-CC quarter issue. Considerable die rust is also evident throughout Liberty's portrait, suggesting that the die was set aside for a period of time and not properly stored before being retrieved for production. Examples of this variety are plentiful among 1878-CC quarters and are mostly in circulated grades.

G-4	VG-8	F-12	VF-20	EF-40	AU-50	MS-60	MS-63	MS-65
$75	$100	$130	$175	$325	$425	$1,000	$1,700	$4,250

1878-S

Circulation-strike mintage: 140,000

Availability in Mint State: These are exceedingly rare despite their large mintage. The Louis E. Eliasberg Sale in 1997 featured an example of this coin in MS-66, as did

actual size: 24.3 mm

the Eugene H. Gardner Sale in 2014. *MS-60 to 62:* 12 to 16. *MS-63:* 11 to 15. *MS-64:* 11 to 15. *MS-65 or better:* 2 or 3.[80]

Availability in circulated grades: Among the consultants for this book there was divided opinion as to the present-day rarity of this issue. Larry Briggs, who wrote *the* book on Liberty Seated quarters, weighed in with this: "I consider this coin to be one of the key coins of the series. I travel to 40+ shows a year and very seldom see this coin at all in any grade. I have had only five coins in the past two years, but have turned down others with surface problems. When I find one it does not stay in stock very long."[81]

Characteristics of striking: This issue is usually well struck.

Notes: Larry Briggs suggests that substantial quantities of the 1878-S were melted at the San Francisco Mint to be converted into Morgan silver dollars. Further, he comments that a number of coins that come on the market have been altered with added mintmarks. One has been certified as genuine by a leading grading service.[82]

G-4	VG-8	F-12	VF-20	EF-40	AU-50	MS-60	MS-63	MS-65
$350	$500	$650	$900	$1,250	$1,700	$3,000	$5,500	$12,000

1879

Circulation-strike mintage: 13,600

Proof mintage: 1,100

actual size: 24.3 mm

Availability in Mint State: According to Larry Briggs, it is among the most available Liberty Seated quarters in Mint State. They are readily available as many were saved at the time by numismatists. *MS-60 to 62:* 75 to 100. *MS-63:* 100 to 125. *MS-64:* 125 to 165. *MS-65 or better:* 120 to 160.

Availability in circulated grades: These are rare and most are in higher grades.

Characteristics of striking: This issue is usually weak in areas.

Proofs: Beginning with this year and continuing to the end of the series, a fairly high proportion of surviving Proofs are in grades of PF-64 and higher. *PF-60 to 62:* 325 to 400. *PF-63:* 250 to 325. *PF-64:* 120 to 160. *PF-65 or better:* 75 to 90.

Notes: Mint State coins were heavily promoted at one time; see *Notes* under the 1879 dime for details.

G-4	VG-8	F-12	VF-20	EF-40	AU-50
$200	$275	$350	$425	$550	$600
MS-60	**MS-63**	**MS-65**	**PF-60**	**PF-63**	**PF-65**
$700	$850	$2,000	$500	$800	$1,500

1880

Circulation-strike mintage: 13,600

Proof mintage: 1,355

actual size: 24.3 mm

Availability in Mint State: According to Larry Briggs, this coin is among the most available Liberty Seated quarters in Mint State. They are readily available as many were saved at the time by numismatists. *MS-60 to 62:* 60 to 80. *MS-63:* 100 to 125. *MS-64:* 125 to 165. *MS-65 or better:* 120 to 160.

Availability in circulated grades: These are rare and most are in higher grades.

Characteristics of striking: Striking on this issue varies.

Proofs: In this year a Proof reverse die that had been in use since 1872 (see information under 1872) was retired from Proof duty and was then used to make circulation strikes.[83] *PF-60 to 62:* 325 to 450. *PF-63:* 275 to 350. *PF-64:* 150 to 180. *PF-65 or better:* 80 to 100.

Notes: Mint State coins were heavily promoted at one time; see *Notes* under the 1880 dime for details.

Type 1 Reverse: Used on Proofs.

Type 2 Reverse: Scarce. Used on circulation strikes.

G-4	VG-8	F-12	VF-20	EF-40	AU-50
$200	$275	$350	$425	$550	$600
MS-60	**MS-63**	**MS-65**	**PF-60**	**PF-63**	**PF-65**
$700	$850	$2,250	$500	$800	$1,500

1881

Circulation-strike mintage: 12,000

Proof mintage: 975

Availability in Mint State: These are readily available as many were saved at the time by numismatists, but not as many as for 1879 and

actual size: 24.3 mm

1880 as most dealer promotions had stopped. *MS-60 to 62:* 30 to 40. *MS-63:* 45 to 60. *MS-64:* 35 to 45. *MS-65 or better:* 25 to 32.

Availability in circulated grades: These are rare and most are in higher grades.

Characteristics of striking: This issue is usually weak in areas.

Proofs: *PF-60 to 62:* 200 to 250. *PF-63:* 200 to 250. *PF-64:* 160 to 190. *PF-65 or better:* 120 to 160.

Notes: This issue has the Type 2 Reverse.

G-4	VG-8	F-12	VF-20	EF-40	AU-50
$200	$275	$350	$425	$550	$600
MS-60	**MS-63**	**MS-65**	**PF-60**	**PF-63**	**PF-65**
$700	$850	$2,100	$500	$800	$1,500

1882

Circulation-strike mintage: 15,200

Proof mintage: 1,100

Availability in Mint State: These are readily available as many were saved at the time by numismatists, but not as many as for 1879 and 1880.

actual size: 24.3 mm

MS-60 to 62: 20 to 25. *MS-63:* 50 to 65. *MS-64:* 50 to 65. *MS-65 or better:* 45 to 50.

Availability in circulated grades: These are rare and most are in higher grades.

Characteristics of striking: This issue is usually well struck, but careful selection is advised.

Proofs: *PF-60 to 62:* 225 to 275. *PF-63:* 200 to 250. *PF-64:* 160 to 190. *PF-65 or better:* 100 to 140.

Notes: For speculative comments on this coinage see the item from *Mason's Coin Collectors' Herald* under *Notes* for the 1882 dime.

G-4	VG-8	F-12	VF-20	EF-40	AU-50
$200	$275	$350	$425	$550	$600

MS-60	MS-63	MS-65	PF-60	PF-63	PF-65
$700	$850	$2,100	$500	$800	$1,500

1883

Circulation-strike mintage: 14,400

Proof mintage: 1,039

Availability in Mint State: These are available but are slightly scarce. *MS-60 to 62:* 25 to 32. *MS-63:* 30 to 40. *MS-64:* 30 to 40. *MS-65 or better:* 25 to 32.

actual size: 24.3 mm

Availability in circulated grades: These are rare and most are in higher grades.

Characteristics of striking: Striking on this issue varies.

Proofs: *PF-60 to 62:* 200 to 250. *PF-63:* 200 to 250. *PF-64:* 160 to 190. *PF-65 or better:* 120 to 160.

G-4	VG-8	F-12	VF-20	EF-40	AU-50
$200	$275	$350	$425	$550	$600

MS-60	MS-63	MS-65	PF-60	PF-63	PF-65
$700	$850	$2,400	$500	$800	$1,500

1884

Circulation-strike mintage: 8,000

Proof mintage: 875

Availability in Mint State: These are scarce but are still available. *MS-60 to 62:* 25 to 32. *MS-63:* 30 to 40. *MS-64:* 30 to 40. *MS-65 or better:* 25 to 32.

actual size: 24.3 mm

Availability in circulated grades: These are rare and most are in higher grades. Well-worn coins are very rare, not that it makes a difference.

Characteristics of striking: This issue is usually well struck.

Proofs: Proofs were very carelessly made this year. *PF-60 to 62:* 150 to 250. *PF-63:* 200 to 250. *PF-64:* 160 to 190. *PF-65 or better:* 120 to 160.

G-4	VG-8	F-12	VF-20	EF-40	AU-50
$300	$400	$500	$575	$650	$800

MS-60	MS-63	MS-65	PF-60	PF-63	PF-65
$900	$1,150	$2,100	$500	$800	$1,500

1885

Circulation-strike
mintage: 13,600

Proof mintage: 930

actual size: 24.3 mm

Availability in Mint State:
These are scarce but are
still available. *MS-60 to 62:*
50 to 70. *MS-63:* 60 to 80.
MS-64: 35 to 45. *MS-65
or better:* 30 to 40.

Availability in circulated grades: These are rare and most are in higher grades.

Characteristics of striking: This issue is usually well struck.

Proofs: *PF-60 to 62:* 210 to 260. *PF-63:* 170 to 210. *PF-64:* 110 to 150. *PF-65 or better:* 110 to 140.

G-4	VG-8	F-12	VF-20	EF-40	AU-50
$200	$250	$350	$500	$575	$700
MS-60	**MS-63**	**MS-65**	**PF-60**	**PF-63**	**PF-65**
$850	$1,100	$2,400	$500	$800	$1,500

1886

Circulation-strike
mintage: 5,000

Proof mintage: 886

actual size: 24.3 mm

Availability in Mint State:
These are rare because
apparently relatively few
were saved. All Mint State
coins are prooflike, without
exception.[84] *MS-60 to 62:* 15 to 20. *MS-63:* 25 to 32. *MS-64:* 45 to 60. *MS-65 or better:* 18 to 24.

Availability in circulated grades: This is the rarest Philadelphia Mint Liberty Seated quarter. Nearly all are in higher grades.

Characteristics of striking: All circulation strikes are weak at the tops of both 8s and at LIBERTY on the shield.

Proofs: Some have flat-star centers. In the 1940s and early 1950s, Charles E. Green and his wife, Ruth Green, of Skokie, Illinois, took a fancy to Proof quarter dollars of this date and endeavored to hoard as many as possible. Eventually they succeeded in obtaining several hundred coins. The author helped sell some of these in later years, when Ruth Green was handling Charlie's estate. Most were in grades that would be called below PF-64 today. *PF-60 to 62:* 150 to 200. *PF-63:* 180 to 210. *PF-64:* 90 to 120. *PF-65 or better:* 110 to 130.

G-4	VG-8	F-12	VF-20	EF-40	AU-50
$350	$450	$650	$750	$850	$975
MS-60	**MS-63**	**MS-65**	**PF-60**	**PF-63**	**PF-65**
$1,250	$1,650	$2,600	$500	$800	$1,500

1887

Circulation-strike mintage: 10,000

Proof mintage: 710

actual size: 24.3 mm

Availability in Mint State: These are rare because apparently relatively few were saved. *MS-60 to 62:* 18 to 25. *MS-63:* 55 to 70. *MS-64:* 50 to 65. *MS-65 or better:* 50 to 65.

Availability in circulated grades: These are very scarce and most are in higher grades.

Characteristics of striking: This issue is usually weak in areas. Circulation strikes have a raised line from a scratch in the die below LIBERTY on the shield.

Proofs: Some have many or most stars with flat centers. Beginning with this year, many Proofs were unsold at the Mint and spent, or something else happened, as the survival ratio of Proofs dropped. The coin hobby was entering a slump. *PF-60 to 62:* 150 to 200. *PF-63:* 130 to 170. *PF-64:* 90 to 120. *PF-65 or better:* 80 to 100.

G-4	VG-8	F-12	VF-20	EF-40	AU-50
$250	$350	$425	$500	$600	$625
MS-60	**MS-63**	**MS-65**	**PF-60**	**PF-63**	**PF-65**
$850	$1,150	$2,500	$500	$800	$1,500

1888

Circulation-strike mintage: 10,001

Proof mintage: 832

actual size: 24.3 mm

Availability in Mint State: These are rare on an absolute basis. Most are in higher grades. *MS-60 to 62:* 18 to 25. *MS-63:* 40 to 50. *MS-64:* 70 to 85. *MS-65 or better:* 60 to 75.

Availability in circulated grades: These are rare and most are in higher grades.

Characteristics of striking: This issue is often seen with lightly struck star centers.

Proofs: *PF-60 to 62:* 225 to 300. *PF-63:* 110 to 140. *PF-64:* 70 to 100. *PF-65 or better:* 60 to 75.

G-4	VG-8	F-12	VF-20	EF-40	AU-50
$250	$350	$425	$500	$550	$600
MS-60	**MS-63**	**MS-65**	**PF-60**	**PF-63**	**PF-65**
$700	$900	$1,600	$500	$800	$1,500

1888-S

Circulation-strike mintage: 1,216,000

actual size: 24.3 mm

Availability in Mint State: These are elusive despite the very large mintage. The Louis E. Eliasberg Sale in 1997 featured an example of this coin in MS-66. It is sharply struck and very attractive. In 2015 the Eugene H. Gardner Sale featured examples of this coin in MS-66 (2) and MS-63. *MS-60 to 62:* 50 to 65. *MS-63:* 35 to 45. *MS-64:* 30 to 40. *MS-65 or better:* 10 to 14.[85]

Availability in circulated grades: These are very scarce in circulated grades.

Characteristics of striking: This issue is usually very sharp except for LIBERTY polished to create weakness on two obverse dies.

Notes: The *Report of the Director of the Mint*, 1888, told why the San Francisco Mint struck dimes and quarters during the period indicated:

> Precedence having been given at the Mint at Philadelphia to the mandatory coinage of silver dollars, that institution was unable to meet the demand for dimes. The mint at San Francisco was therefore called upon to execute a coinage in dimes, of which $395,284.80 was coined. It was also found that the stock of quarter dollars held by the Sub-Treasury at San Francisco was likely to be soon absorbed. The same mint therefore coined during the fiscal year from trade-dollar bullion on hand $192,000 in this denomination of subsidiary coin. This coinage was increased to $250,000 in August 1888.[86]

G-4	VG-8	F-12	VF-20	EF-40	AU-50	MS-60	MS-63	MS-65
$35	$40	$45	$50	$75	$200	$400	$750	$3,000

1889

Circulation-strike mintage: 12,000

Proof mintage: 711

actual size: 24.3 mm

Availability in Mint State: These are rare on an absolute basis. Most Mint State coins are at higher levels. *MS-60 to 62:* 18 to 25. *MS-63:* 130 to 160. *MS-64:* 120 to 150. *MS-65 or better:* 120 to 150.

Availability in circulated grades: These are rare and most are in higher grades.

Characteristics of striking: This issue varies, so cherrypicking is advised.

Proofs: *PF-60 to 62:* 225 to 300. *PF-63:* 100 to 120. *PF-64:* 60 to 90. *PF-65 or better:* 50 to 60.

G-4	VG-8	F-12	VF-20	EF-40	AU-50
$200	$275	$375	$500	$550	$600

MS-60	MS-63	MS-65	PF-60	PF-63	PF-65
$700	$900	$1,950	$500	$800	$1,500

1890

Circulation-strike mintage: 80,000

Proof mintage: 590

Availability in Mint State: These are rare despite the high mintage because apparently relatively few were saved. *MS-60 to 62:*

actual size: 24.3 mm

55 to 60. *MS-63:* 70 to 90. *MS-64:* 70 to 90. *MS-65 or better:* 60 to 80.

Availability in circulated grades: These are scarce and most are in higher grades.

Characteristics of striking: This issue is usually seen with flat-star centers. A few are highly prooflike on the obverse and have been called one-sided Proofs.[87]

Proofs: *PF-60 to 62:* 275 to 350. *PF-63:* 110 to 150. *PF-64:* 80 to 100. *PF-65 or better:* 90 to 120.

G-4	VG-8	F-12	VF-20	EF-40	AU-50
$95	$135	$200	$275	$325	$375
MS-60	**MS-63**	**MS-65**	**PF-60**	**PF-63**	**PF-65**
$650	$900	$1,400	$500	$800	$1,500

1891

Circulation-strike mintage: 3,920,000

Proof mintage: 600

Availability in Mint State: According to Larry Briggs, it is among the most available Liberty Seated quarters in Mint State. *MS-60 to 62:*

actual size: 24.3 mm

250 to 325. *MS-63:* 250 to 325. *MS-64:* 200 to 250. *MS-65 or better:* 110 to 130.

Availability in circulated grades: These are common and most are in higher grades.

Characteristics of striking: This issue is usually weak in areas.

Proofs: The coin market continued to be in a slump. Many Proof coins either were unsold by the Mint or disappeared in other ways. A later generation would find the Proof 1890 quarter to be the rarest since the 1870s. *PF-60 to 62:* 250 to 300. *PF-63:* 100 to 130. *PF-64:* 80 to 100. *PF-65 or better:* 70 to 90.

G-4	VG-8	F-12	VF-20	EF-40	AU-50
$35	$40	$45	$50	$75	$160
MS-60	**MS-63**	**MS-65**	**PF-60**	**PF-63**	**PF-65**
$275	$550	$1,800	$500	$800	$1,500

1891-O

Circulation-strike mintage: 68,000

Availability in Mint State: These are very rare. The Louis E. Eliasberg Sale in 1997 featured an example of this coin in MS-66. In 2015 the Eugene H. Gardner Sale featured an example of this coin in MS-65. *MS-60 to 62:* 5 to 7. *MS-63:* 3 or 4. *MS-64:* 3 or 4. *MS-65 or better:* 3 or 4.

actual size: 24.3 mm

Availability in circulated grades: These are scarce in lower grades. Some Fair to About Good coins have nearly all details worn smooth, but four or five letters in LIBERTY are readable.[88] Rare at the VF and EF levels and even more so in AU grade.[89]

Characteristics of striking: This issue varies, but some are highly prooflike and have been certified as Proofs. At the very least they are special strikings.[90]

Notes: This is the first and only New Orleans Mint quarter dollar struck after 1860, and the only New Orleans Mint Liberty Seated quarter dollar with the motto IN GOD WE TRUST on the reverse.

G-4	VG-8	F-12	VF-20	EF-40	AU-50	MS-60	MS-63	MS-65
$375	$700	$1,000	$1,650	$2,850	$3,350	$7,500	$13,500	$30,000

1891-S

Circulation-strike mintage: 2,216,000

Availability in Mint State: According to Larry Briggs, it is among the most available Liberty Seated quarters in Mint State, and is often prooflike. *MS-60 to 62:* 90 to 120. *MS-63:* 45 to 60. *MS-64:* 40 to 55. *MS-65 or better:* 20 to 25.

actual size: 24.3 mm

Availability in circulated grades: These are common and most are in higher grades.

Characteristics of striking: This issue varies, but they are usually fairly sharp.

G-4	VG-8	F-12	VF-20	EF-40	AU-50	MS-60	MS-63	MS-65
$35	$40	$45	$50	$75	$175	$350	$550	$2,000

LIBERTY SEATED HALF DOLLARS (1839–1891)

Introduction

In many ways the history and numismatic aspects of Liberty Seated half dollars parallel those of the quarters. Half dollars are different, however, in that as a class they are much more plentiful in the marketplace, have been offered more frequently at auction, and have been the objects of more numismatic study than have quarter dollars. These are the most plentiful of the regular Liberty Seated denominations and include many relatively inexpensive varieties.

The obverse of the 1839–1891 Liberty Seated half dollar type depicts Liberty seated on a rock, holding in her left hand a pole with a Liberty cap on top, and in her right hand a shield inscribed LIBERTY. Thirteen stars are located to the left and right of the seated figure, and the date is displayed below. This is an adaptation of the obverse motif, but now with stars, used on the famous 1836 Gobrecht silver dollars.

The reverse illustrates an eagle perched on a laurel branch and holding three arrows, with UNITED STATES OF AMERICA above and HALF DOL. below, similar to the motif introduced on Liberty Seated quarters in 1838.

The half dollars minted in 1839 were made with and without drapery at Liberty's elbow. Mint Director Robert M. Patterson sent the first samples of the new half dollar to Secretary of the Treasury Levi Woodbury on August 13, 1839:

> I have the honor to send you herewith a half dollar of a new impression, which I respectfully submit to you for your approbation. I will complete the new series for silver coins, all of which, if you consent to this coinage of half dollars, will have a full-length figure of Liberty on the obverse. It is intended to retain the bust of Liberty for the gold coinage.
>
> PS: You will remark that one of the figures is bright and the other frosted.[1]

The With-Drapery variety was made a short time later and shows modifications made by Gobrecht. During this era various alterations to obverse designs were made as well on Liberty Seated half dimes, dimes, quarters, and silver dollars.

Liberty Seated half dollars were struck at the Philadelphia Mint continuously from 1839 onward and at the New Orleans Mint from 1840 until the facility was seized by secessionists early in 1861 (who continued coinage for a short time using bullion on hand).

From 1839 through the end of the 1840s there are many interesting die characteristics among Liberty Seated half dollars. Most prominent are variations in the date logotype and letter sizes and, occasionally, repunched numerals, errors, and the inevitable die cracks. All of these variations make a very fertile field for the numismatist with a magnifying glass and a sense of curiosity. The issues from 1839 through the 1840s are mostly inexpensive in circulated grades and range from rare to very rare in Mint State. At the time they were made there was hardly any numismatic interest in them.

The circulation strikes of the early 1850s are elusive. Interestingly, when seen most are in higher circulated grades. Well-worn coins are in the minority.[2] By this time the price of silver had risen dramatically on domestic and international markets, and freshly minted coins could be sold at a profit above face value to bullion dealers. Help came with the passage of the Coinage Act of February 21, 1853, which lowered the authorized weights of the silver three-cent piece, half dime, dime, quarter dollar, and half dollar. This permitted the pieces struck from that point onward to effectively reach the channels of general commerce. To alert the public to the new weight standards, arrowheads were added alongside the date on the obverse, and a glory of rays was added to the reverse. In 1854 the rays were eliminated, but the arrows were continued, again in 1855, after which the arrows also were dropped, although the authorized weight remained the same. Presumably, by this time the public was acquainted with the new standard. In 1855 the San Francisco Mint struck half dollars for the first time, starting a run that would extend through 1878.

In 1866 the motto IN GOD WE TRUST was added to the reverse of the half dollar, constituting another type. In 1870 half dollars were struck at the Carson City Mint for the first time. Production would be continuous at the Nevada facility through 1878. In 1873 the authorized weight was increased slightly, and again arrowheads were placed alongside the date of certain issues of this year, continuing through all issues of 1874, after which they were discontinued, although the new increased weight remained the same through the end of the Liberty Seated series.

Distribution of Liberty Seated Half Dollars

For all practical purposes the Liberty Seated half dollar was the largest circulating coin of the realm from its inception in 1839 until Morgan-design dollars made their debut in 1878. Liberty Seated silver dollars were struck continuously from 1840 onward, but as detailed in the next chapter, the 1840s saw few dollars in circulation, and after 1849 nearly all were exported.

Half dollars were made in quantity and were popular in commerce in the 1840s, circulating alongside Spanish-American silver coins, the most prominent being two-reales coins valued at 25¢, but also four-reales and other denominations. The advent of large quantities of California-mined gold in 1849, followed the next year by gold strikes in Australia, disturbed the traditional ratio of silver prices in relation to gold prices on the international market (where the values were often reckoned in London). Silver rose to the point at which by 1850 it cost more than silver value to mint new coins. By 1851 it cost an average of 50.017¢ in silver to mint a half dollar. Bullion dealers and exchange houses dealt in such coins, often in large wholesale quantities. $100 in face value of silver coins was worth $103.40 on average that year. Liberty Seated coins continued to be minted, but they traded at a slight premium in relation to face value. Nearly all coins in circulation disappeared as they were gathered up by speculators.

As noted earlier, the Coinage Act of February 21, 1853, reduced the silver content of Liberty Seated coins from the half dime to the half dollar (but not the dollar, which continued to trade at a premium and was used nearly entirely in the export trade). Beginning in April 1853, newly minted coins of the other denominations appeared in circulation and soon became common. The Civil War began with the bombardment of Fort Sumter on April 12, 1861, and was officially declared on April 15. By early 1862 the outcome was uncertain, and citizens hoarded gold coins, which thereafter were available only at a premium from banks and brokers. In March 1862 Congress authorized Legal Tender Notes that were not redeemable in gold or silver. Concern spread, and by early summer all silver coins were gone from circulation in the East and Midwest. In the West they remained in circulation (as explained in chapter 10). This situation continued through until April 1876, when, at last, specie payments were resumed, and silver coins were again seen in circulation.

Meanwhile, ordering Proof coins was rather difficult for the typical numismatist. In the 1860s, during the Civil War, the Mint would not accept federal paper money *at par* for Proof coins, and to order Proofs one had to pay a significantly larger sum in paper or go to a bullion dealer, buy ordinary silver coins at a premium, and remit them in a package to the Mint! Because of this, Proof mintages tended to be low during the early 1860s, and were to remain that way for a number of years thereafter.

In anticipation of the resumption of use of silver coins in circulation the Treasury Department ordered the striking of large quantities of coins from dimes to half dollars (the half dime denomination having been discontinued in 1873). Unexpectedly, at least to Treasury officials, a flood of long-hoarded old silver coins flooded the market, resulting in a glut of such pieces. This oversupply reduced the need for new half dollars, and mintages were low from 1879 to 1891.

The SS *Republic* Treasure

One of the greatest treasures ever found has a direct connection to Liberty Seated half dollars.

On October 18, 1865, the SS *Republic* left New York City bound for New Orleans with a reported $400,000 (1865 value) in gold coins and an undisclosed amount in silver.[3] This was in a very uncertain financial era, with gold and silver coins of all denominations being hoarded by the public, as they had been for several years. Federal bills in circulation such as Legal Tender and National Bank Notes traded at a sharp discount to gold and silver. Specie brokers, exchange houses, and banks were well stocked with gold and silver coins and did a lively trade dealing in them. Traders and others expecting to do business in New Orleans necessarily bought such coins to take with them.

On October 22 the *Republic* passed Cape Hatteras, well known as a graveyard for passing ships. The following morning the sidewheel steamer was off the Carolina coast when an east-northeasterly gale blew in. By evening, the storm had become a raging hurricane. The scenario was all too familiar to ship captains of the era, and in the vast majority of instances the successful challenge was to maintain forward speed and control until the storm was over.

The SS *Republic.*

On October 24 matters worsened, and the ship's paddlewheels stalled and couldn't carry the engine past dead center. Without power, the *Republic* was adrift and at the mercy of the elements. At 9 o'clock in the morning steam was raised on the donkey boiler to run the pumps, but the next morning the donkey boiler failed and water began to pour into the hold. With little time left to spare, the crew began preparing the four lifeboats. They also built a makeshift raft from the ship's spars and boards. By 1:30, the water was above the engine room floor. All hands were called to help launch the safety vessels.

At 4:00 in the afternoon on October 25, after two days of valiant struggle to keep the vessel afloat, the *Republic* went down. Most of the passengers and crew were stowed safely on the four boats and the makeshift raft. The remaining survivors then jumped into the sea. Swimming for their lives, most found safety aboard passing craft. Two are believed to have drowned while swimming through the ship's floating debris.

Days later, all of the survivors aboard the four lifeboats were rescued by passing ships. Of the passengers who fled on the hastily constructed raft, only two remained when it was finally spotted seven days later by a U.S. Navy steamship near Cape Hatteras Light. Among newspaper accounts, the Charleston *Daily Herald* on October 30 reported, "Her cargo was valuable, and in addition she had on board some $400,000 in treasure, which went down with the ship."

In July 2003 Odyssey Marine Exploration, Inc. found the wreck off the coast of Georgia in about 1,700 feet of water. Strewn on the sea floor was an array of gold and silver coins along with bottles and other artifacts. Recovery with the ROV (Remotely Operated Vehicle) *ZEUS*, a tethered underwater vehicle configured for deep-sea excavation, commenced with vigor in late 2003, and continued through early 2004.

A primary objective of the excavation of the shipwreck was to locate and study the historically attested cargo of specie. Almost as soon as the intrusive phase of the project commenced, extensive coin deposits were uncovered in the stern hold.

In time about 31,000 silver coins and 3,425 gold pieces had been brought up from the depths, amounting in face value to slightly less than 18 percent of the estimated coins lost. By late 2004 the count had crossed the 50,000 mark, mostly augmented by a cascade of silver half dollars eventually numbering 47,263 coins. The coins were all recovered individually, one by one, and handled carefully. Significantly, the only other silver coins were two Liberty Seated quarters and four British silver florins. This verified that, at the time, the half dollar was the largest silver coin of the realm used in general commerce. As the inventory of coins was very heavily weighted toward New Orleans coins—not at all what might have been in the hands of bullion dealers and exchange brokers in New York City at the time—it seems likely that most of the half dollars were gathered in New Orleans, shipped to New York for safekeeping (Union troops reoccupied New Orleans in May 1862, but with no assurance that they would remain), then sent back to New Orleans after the war ended. Or, perhaps there is another explanation. Treasures hold their secrets well!

After the discovery I was given an early view of the coins by Odyssey curator Ellen Gerth and company co-founder Gregory Stemm. You can imagine my delight when, upon examining an "ordinary" 1861-O half dollar in exceptional Mint State condition shown to me, I discerned that it had a tiny die crack at Miss Liberty's nose. Here, certainly, was an 1861-O half dollar that could be positively attributed to the Confederacy and minted after control was taken from the U.S. government. Later, many of the half dollars were viewed by Randall E. Wiley and attributed to 17 different die varieties, including early coins minted under federal auspices, later coins struck by the Louisiana State government, and the final mintage by the Confederate States of America.

There were 4,765 half dollars that could not be identified, and some others were dated before 1839. They were turned over to the Numismatic Conservation Services (NCS), which used non-destructive methods to remove accumulated dirt, encrustations, and other matter. The result was a marvelous group of coins. Many showed the effects of sea immersion etching the surfaces, usually lightly, but with most design details sharp. These were put in holders marked "Shipwreck Effect." Some coins, especially of later dates, were certified by the Numismatic Guaranty Corporation (NGC) as Mint State and had no problems resulting from their years of immersion.[4] An inventory of the Liberty Seated issues follows. Within each listing the number of Mint State coins (graded by NGC) is given. These were only a tiny percentage of the treasure:

Silver half dollars on the ocean floor prior to recovery.

A group of half dollars after processing by the Numismatic Conservation Services.

1839: 3	1848-O 68	1856-O: 1,424	1860-S: 12
1840: 2	1849: 1	(MS-60, MS-61	1861: 599
1840-O: 5	1849-O: 55	(5), MS-62,	1861-O: 13,532
1841-O: 6	1850-O: 59	MS-63)	(MS-61 [7],
1842: 10	1851-O: 3	1856-S: 7	MS-62 [6],
1842-O: 17	1852-O: 4	1857: 257	MS-63 [3]; plus
1843: 11	1853: 403	1857-O: 747	MS-61 [2] with
1843-O: 34	1853-O, With	1857-S: 5	CSA obverse)
1844: 1	Arrows: 829	1858: 481	1861-S: 27
1844-O: 32	(MS-61, MS-64)	1858-O: 9,085	1862: 137 (MS-62)
1845: 2	1854: 338	1858-S: 21	1862-S: 48
1845-O: 33	1854-O: 3,434	1859: 101	1863: 82
1846: 7	1854, 4 Over 5: 20	1859-O: 4,502	1863-S: 9
1846-O: 56	1855: 67	1859-S: 30	1864: 8
1847: 3	1855-O: 1,864	1860: 31	1864-S: 9
1847-O: 64	1855-S: 7	1860-O: 3,746	1865: 39
1848: 1	1856: 102	(MS-62 [2])	1865-S: 6

Pattern Pieces

It is likely that the half dollar was selected as the primary denomination for patterns of 1838, as the design of the dollar (struck for circulation in 1836) may have been considered to be complete. Now it was time to turn attention to the second-highest-value silver coin. Whether most patterns of 1838 were made as proposals for circulating coinage is uncertain. Starting in 1859, many restrikes and new die combinations were made. The Mint and its designers experimented widely with the "seated figure" motif, different from the pattern half dollars that were also struck in a multitude of metals and reverse pairings using the Seated Liberty design by Barber, as was used on trade dollars. Additionally, patterns featuring a Longacre-designed Seated Indian Princess, a Seated Liberty designed by Paquet, and Barber's Amazonian design were struck— other patterns, using various bust and portrait motifs followed. Many later patterns, off-metal strikes, and other issues were made through the mid-1880s, nearly all for private sale to numismatists. These can be found in *United States Pattern Coins* (tenth edition) by Dr. J. Hewitt Judd (from which the 1838 and 1839 listings below are adopted. See that text for illustrations of the following pieces). This listing includes pattern half dollars of 1838 and 1839 only.

Half Dollar Obverse Dies of 1838

Basically, the obverse dies for the 1838 half dollar pattern coinage are three, numbered here for convenience, probably in the order that the dies were made:

Obverse 1: "Liberty Head." Gobrecht's head of Liberty is facing left, with luxuriant tresses falling to her shoulder, and with the word LIBERTY on the ribbon in her hair. There are seven stars to the right, six stars to the left, and the date 1838 below. This is the die that Snowden attributed to Kneass, but it was probably by Gobrecht. Used with Judd-72 to Judd-75b.

Obverse 2: "Liberty Seated, raised letters." The Liberty Seated motif as was employed on the 1836 Gobrecht silver dollar, with the word LIBERTY in raised rather than incuse letters. There are 13 stars to the left and right and the date 1838 below. The date is in a gentle curve. All strikings from this die have been *original* issues. Used with J-76b, 76c, 79, 82, 83.

Obverse 3: "Liberty Seated, incuse letters." The Liberty Seated motif and details as foregoing, except with the word LIBERTY in incuse letters. The date is straight (not gently curved). Used with J-76 to 78 (restrikes), 79a (originals), and 80, 81 (restrikes).

| 1838 Half Dollar, Obverse 1 | 1838 Half Dollar, Obverse 2 (actual size: 30.6 mm) | 1838 Half Dollar, Obverse 3 |

Half Dollar Reverse Dies of 1838

The reverse motifs employed for the 1838 pattern half dollar coinage are several in number, including one (on J-82) from 1836 and another possibly created in *1858* (J-222 of 1858, and used extensively in 1859).

Reverse A: "Perched eagle holding four arrows." The perched eagle is holding a laurel branch and *four arrows* with its head turned towards the viewer's right. UNITED STATES OF AMERICA is above and HALF DOLLAR is below. Used with J-72, 76–78.

Reverse B: "Flying eagle in plain field." The eagle is flying to the left, mouth open, and its neck feathers are somewhat ruffled, similar but not identical to the 1836 dollar reverse (in which the eagle's mouth is closed and the outline of the neck feathers are smooth). UNITED STATES OF AMERICA is above and HALF DOLLAR is below. In 1849 (no day or month date) George J. Eckfeldt entered this in his private diary: "The flying eagle [die] for half dollars cracked and is good for nothing."[6] Used with J-73, 74, 79, 79a.

Reverse C: "Regular reverse of 1838." The perched upright eagle is holding a laurel branch and three arrows with UNITED STATES OF AMERICA above and the denomination as HALF DOL. is below. This is similar to the style used to coin Large Letters regular-issue Draped Bust reeded-edge half dollars of 1838 and 1839. Used with J-75, 83.

Reverse D: "Paquet's perched eagle, broken ribbon." This reverse is primarily used on pattern half dollars dated 1859. The perched eagle has a ribbon across the shield continuing to the eagle's beak. The eagle's head is facing to the viewer's left with a laurel branch and arrows below. The legends are in tall letters, UNITED STATES OF AMERICA / HALF DOLLAR. The ribbon is broken; there are groups of three vertical lines on the shield; there are six tail feathers on the eagle; a split wingtip is at the right; and a stem or half-leaf is above the A in HALF. This reverse was created by engraver Anthony C. Paquet. It is listed in the present text as J-75a and b (listed in Judd under *1859* as J-255 and 256, these being out of order in Judd). This is the same as Reverse B of 1859 in the 1838-dated die combination extensively relapped with some details ground off the die. Used with J-75a, 75b.

Reverse E: "Perched eagle, side view, facing left, holding arrows and branch." The eagle is perched, viewed from the side, facing left in the manner of a flying eagle, but with tail downward and with a laurel branch and arrows below. The inscription UNITED STATES OF AMERICA / HALF DOL is around. Used with J-80, 81.

Reverse F: "Regular reverse of 1836." The perched eagle is facing the viewer with shield on breast, its head is turned to the observer's left, and the talons are holding a laurel branch and three arrows. UNITED STATES OF AMERICA is above and 50 CENTS is below. This style was used on regular-issue, reeded-edge Capped Bust half dollars of 1836 and 1837. Used with J-82.

1838 Half Dollar, Reverse A   1838 Half Dollar, Reverse B   1838 Half Dollar, Reverse C

1838 Half Dollar, Reverse D   1838 Half Dollar, Reverse E   1838 Half Dollar, Reverse F
                                (actual size: 30.6 mm)

Pattern Half Dollars of 1838

The preceding dies occur in several combinations in both original (contemporary with 1838) and restrikes (1859 and later) productions. Likely, the originals are of approximately 206-1/4 grains weight, this being the standard for a half-dollar planchet prior to the Act of February 21, 1853, at which time the weight was reduced to 192 grains (6.22 grams). When restrikes were made at the Mint in 1859 and later, the current planchets were used, these being of the lighter weight. Often, actual specimens do not neatly fit into either weight category but are close to them.

1838 Half dollar (J-72): Dies 1-A. *Obverse:* Liberty Head. *Reverse:* Flying eagle in plain field with ruffled feathers. Silver examples exist of approximately 206 grains weight (originals) and 192 grains (restrikes), the last coined 1859 and later. Anomalous-weight silver pieces exist.[7] J-72 is struck in silver and has a reeded edge.

1838 Half dollar (J-73 and 74): Dies 1-B. *Obverse:* Liberty Head. *Reverse:* Flying eagle in plain field. Silver pieces of 206-1/4 grains weight are believed to be originals; pieces of 192 grains, dies cracked, exhibit different states from light cracks to heavy cracks, the variety most often seen. The copper striking is believed unique. From cracked reverse die. J-73 is struck in silver and has a reeded edge. J-74 is struck in copper and has a reeded edge.

1838 Half dollar (J-75): Dies 1-C. *Obverse:* Liberty Head. *Reverse:* Regular reverse of 1838. An example is in the Smithsonian Institution.[8] J-75 is struck in silver and has a reeded edge.

1838 Half dollar (J-75a and b): Dies 1-D. *Obverse:* Liberty Head. *Reverse:* Paquet die of 1858. Listed in Judd under *1859* as J-254 and 255, relocated to 1838 in the present text as that is the date on the coin. Restrikes made 1859 or later, probably to the mid-1870s. Reverse die extensively relapped, the "broken ribbon reverse." J-75a (J-254 in earlier editions) is struck in silver and has a reeded edge. J-75b (J-255 in earlier editions) is struck in copper and has a reeded edge.

1838 Half dollar (J-76b): Dies 2-A. *Obverse:* Liberty Seated, raised letters. *Reverse:* Perched eagle holding four arrows. J-76b is the Eliasberg coin (possibly ex Mickley and Col. Cohen) and is in the Smithsonian Institution. Originals only. J-76b is struck in silver and has a reeded edge.

1838 Half dollar (J-76 to 78): Dies 3-A. *Obverse:* Liberty Seated, incuse letters. *Reverse:* Perched eagle holding four arrows. Restrikes made at a later date, possibly to the mid-1870s. J-76 is struck in silver and has a plain edge. J-76a is struck in silver and has a reeded edge. J-77 is struck in copper and has a plain edge. J-78 is struck in copper and has a reeded edge.

1838 Half dollar (J-79): Dies 2-B. *Obverse:* Liberty Seated, raised letters. *Reverse:* Flying eagle in plain field. All are believed to be original strikings. J-79 is struck in silver and has a reeded edge.

1838 Half dollar (J-79a): Dies 3-B. *Obverse:* Liberty Seated, incuse letters. *Reverse:* Flying eagle in plain field. An example in an auction in 1981 weighed 206 grains. Original striking. J-79a is struck in silver and has a reeded edge.

1838 Half dollar (J-80 and 81): Dies 3-E. *Obverse:* Liberty Seated, incuse letters. *Reverse:* Perched eagle, side view, facing left, holding arrows and branch. All believed to be restrikes. J-80 is struck in silver and has a reeded edge. J-81 is struck in copper and has a reeded edge.

1838 Half dollar (J-82): Dies 2-F. *Obverse:* Liberty Seated, raised letters. *Reverse:* Regular reverse of 1836. Originals. J-82 is struck in silver and has a reeded edge.

1838 Half dollar (J-83): Dies 2-C. *Obverse:* Liberty Seated, raised letters. *Reverse:* Regular reverse of 1838. Originals. J-83 is struck in silver and has a reeded edge.

Half Dollar Obverse Dies of 1839

1839 half dollar pattern coinage were produced from three dies, utilizing multiple motifs:

Obverse 1: "Coronet Head facing right." Gobrecht's Coronet or Braided Hair head, facing right, with the word LIBERTY beginning above the ear and ending with the Y above the forehead, an arrangement much different from any Liberty Head ever used on any coinage. 13 stars around, date below. Used with J-91 to 98.

Obverse 2: "Regular Capped Bust die." Regular Capped Bust die of the year as employed on circulating coinage. Used with J-99 and 100.

Obverse 3: "Regular Liberty Seated with-drapery die." Regular Liberty Seated half dollar die as used later in the year for circulating coinage, style *with drapery at the elbow*. Used with J-101 to 103.

1839 Half Dollar, Obverse 1	1839 Half Dollar, Obverse 2	1839 Half Dollar, Obverse 3
	(actual size: 30.6 mm)	

Half Dollar Reverse Dies of 1839

The reverse motifs employed for the 1839 pattern half dollar coinage are several, a mixture of those used in 1838 with certain regular-issue dies. Those dies used in 1838 are listed first, Reverse A and B, with the same letter designations as employed in 1838.

Reverse A: "Perched eagle holding four arrows." The perched eagle is holding a laurel branch and *four arrows* and its head is turned towards the viewer's right. UNITED STATES OF AMERICA is above and HALF DOLLAR is below. *Same as Reverse A of 1838.* Used for restrikes J-99, 101.

Reverse B: "Flying eagle in plain field." The eagle is flying to the left, mouth open, and its neck feathers are somewhat ruffled, similar but not identical to the 1836 dollar reverse (in which the eagle's mouth is closed and the outline of the neck feathers are smooth). UNITED STATES OF AMERICA is above and HALF DOLLAR is below. *Same as Reverse B of 1838.* Used for restrikes J-91, 92, 100, 102.

Reverse C: "Regular reverse die, Small Letters." The regular reverse die used on Liberty Seated half dollars made for circulation, Small Letters. Used for originals J-93, 94.

Reverse D: "Regular reverse die, Medium Letters." The regular reverse die used in this era with Medium Letters. Used for restrikes J-95, 96, 103.

Reverse E: "Regular reverse die, Large Letters." The regular reverse die used in 1842 and later, with Large Letters. Used for restrikes J-97, 98.

1839 Half Dollar, Reverse A   1839 Half Dollar, Reverse B   1839 Half Dollar, Reverse C

1839 Half Dollar, Reverse D   1839 Half Dollar, Reverse E
(actual size: 30.6 mm)

Pattern Half Dollars of 1839

The preceding dies occur in several combinations in both original (contemporary with 1838, these limited to J-93 and 94) and restrike (1859 or later, most likely in the 1870s[9]) productions. Likely, the originals are of approximately 206-1/4 grains weight, this being the standard for a half dollar planchet prior to the Act of February 21, 1853, at which time the weight was reduced to 192 grains (6.22 grams). When restrikes were made at the Mint, current planchets were used, these being of the lighter weight.

1839 Half dollar (J-91 and 92): Dies 1-B. *Obverse:* Coronet Head facing right. *Reverse:* Flying eagle in plain field. Restrike. J-91 is struck in silver and has a reeded edge. J-92 is struck in copper and has a reeded edge.

1839 Half dollar (J-93 and 94): Dies 1-C. *Obverse:* Coronet Head facing right. *Reverse:* Regular reverse die, Small Letters. Original. J-93 is struck in silver and has a reeded edge. J-94 is struck in copper and has a reeded edge.

1839 Half dollar (J-95 and 96): Dies 1-D. *Obverse:* Coronet Head facing right. *Reverse:* Regular reverse die, Medium Letters. Restrike. J-95 is struck in silver and has a reeded edge. J-96 is struck in copper and has a reeded edge.

1839 Half dollar (J-97 and 98): Dies 1-E. *Obverse:* Coronet Head facing right. *Reverse:* Regular reverse die, Large Letters. *De facto* a restrike, as this reverse style was not made until 1842. J-97 is struck in silver and has a reeded edge. J-98 is struck in copper and has a reeded edge.

1839 Half dollar (J-99): Dies 2-A. *Obverse:* Regular Capped Bust die. *Reverse:* Perched eagle holding four arrows. Restrike. J-99 is struck in silver and has a reeded edge.

1839 Half dollar (J-100): Dies 2-B. *Obverse:* Regular Capped Bust die. *Reverse:* Flying eagle in plain field. Restrike.[10] J-100 is struck in silver and has a reeded edge.

1839 Half dollar (J-101): Dies 3-A. *Obverse:* Regular Liberty Seated with-drapery die. *Reverse:* Perched eagle holding four arrows. Restrike. J-101 is struck in silver and has a plain edge.

1839 Half dollar (J-102): Dies 3-B. *Obverse:* Regular Liberty Seated with-drapery die. *Reverse:* Flying eagle in plain field. Restrike. J-102 is struck in silver and has a reeded edge.

1839 Half dollar (J-103): Dies 3-D. *Obverse:* Regular Liberty Seated with-drapery die. *Reverse:* Regular reverse die, Medium Letters. Restrike. J-103 is struck in copper and has a reeded edge.

Aspects of Striking

With so many varieties, four different mints, and large production quantities for some issues, striking is bound to vary, and it does. Generally, on the obverse the places to look for weakness are on the head and the centers of the stars. On the reverse the eagle's leg to the right is often lightly defined. Individual comments are given under the variety listings.

Proof Liberty Seated Half Dollars

Proof half dollars were made at the Philadelphia Mint for all years from 1839 to 1891. Early issues through 1858 could be bought singly at face value from the Mint as a courtesy to collectors and others, or could be ordered in sets. Most were sold separately, resulting in widely differing populations of early Proofs known today for any given year for various denominations. No official mintage figures exist for early Proofs. Production seems to have been fewer than two dozen half dollars for issues prior to 1854, with many below an estimated 15 or so. It is thought that in 1858 about 210 or so sets were sold (see more information under half dimes). Many collectors start their sets with this date. In 1859 there were 800 silver sets made, followed by 1,000 each in 1860 and 1861. Many of these were unsold and seem to have been melted or put into circulation. For 1861 in particular, likely more than half the mintage did not find buyers.

Among later Proofs the mintage figures do not have a proportional correlation to the numbers of coins surviving today. For example, Proof 1870 half dollars of which 1,000 were minted are rarer today than are those of 1869 with a mintage of 600. As a general rule surviving Proof half dollars of the earlier dates continuing through the 1860s are mostly in lower levels from PF-60 to 63. PF-65 or better coins are elusive. Choice and gem coins can be found from the 1870s onward, particularly among the issues of 1879 and later.

A Proof coin that has never been cleaned with an abrasive since the time of minting would survive today in perfect or as-struck condition, Proof-70. However, the "brilliant is best" philosophy endured from the 1800s through the late 20th century with the result that more than 99 percent of existing Liberty Seated Proof coins have from a few to many tiny hairlines.

Grading Liberty Seated Half Dollars

1856-O. Graded MS-63.

MS-60 to 70 (Mint State). *Obverse:* At MS-60, some abrasion and contact marks are evident, most noticeably on the bosom and thighs and knees. Luster is present, but may be dull or lifeless. At MS-63, contact marks are very few, and abrasion is hard to detect except under magnification. An MS-65 coin has no abrasion, and contact marks are sufficiently minute as to require magnification. Check the knees of Liberty and the right field. Luster should be full and rich. Most Mint State coins of the 1861 to 1865 years, Philadelphia issues, have extensive die striae (from dies not being completely finished); note that these are *raised* (whereas cleaning hairlines are incuse). *Reverse:* Comments as preceding, except that in lower Mint State grades abrasion and contact marks are most noticeable on the eagle's head, neck, and claws, and the top of the wings (harder to see there, however). At MS-65 or higher there are no marks visible to the unaided eye. The field is mainly protected by design elements and does not show abrasion as much as does the obverse on a given coin.

Illustrated coin: This lightly toned coin has nice eye appeal.

1841-O. Graded AU-55.

AU-50, 53, 55, 58 (About Uncirculated). *Obverse:* Light wear is seen on the thighs and knees, bosom, and head. At AU-58, the luster is extensive, but incomplete, especially in the right field. At AU-50 and 53, luster is less. *Reverse:* Wear is evident on the eagle's neck, the claws, and the top of the wings. An AU-58 coin has nearly full luster, more so than on the obverse, as the design elements protect the small field areas. At AU-50 and 53, there still are traces of luster.

Illustrated coin: Gray toning is evident on this coin. The reverse is lightly struck, a characteristic that should not be mistaken for wear.

1839, No Drapery From Elbow. Graded EF-40.

EF-40, 45 (Extremely Fine). *Obverse:* Further wear is seen on all areas, especially the thighs and knees, bosom, and head. Little or no luster is seen on most coins. From this grade downward, sharpness of strike of stars and the head does not matter to connoisseurs. *Reverse:* Further wear is evident on the eagle's neck, claws, and wings.

1839, No Drapery From Elbow. Graded VF-20.

VF-20, 30 (Very Fine). *Obverse:* Further wear is seen. Most details of the gown are worn away, except in the lower-relief areas above and to the right of the shield. Hair detail is mostly or completely gone. *Reverse:* Wear is more extensive, with some of the feathers blended together.

1842-O, Small Date. Graded F-12.

F-12, 15 (Fine). *Obverse:* The seated figure is well-worn, but with some detail above and to the right of the shield. LIBERTY is readable but weak in areas, perhaps with a letter missing (a slightly looser interpretation than the demand for full LIBERTY a generation ago). *Reverse:* Wear is extensive, with about a third to half of the feathers flat or blended with others.

1873-CC, Arrows at Date. Graded VG-8.

VG-8, 10 (Very Good). *Obverse:* The seated figure is more worn, but some detail can be seen above and to the right of the shield. The shield is discernible, but the upper-right section may be flat and blended into the seated figure. In LIBERTY at least the equivalent of two or three letters (can be a combination of partial letters) must be readable, possibly very weak at VG-8, with a few more visible at VG-10. In the marketplace and among certified coins, parts of *two* letters seem to be allowed. Per PCGS, "localized weakness may obscure some letters." *However*, LIBERTY is not an infallible way to grade this type, as some varieties have the word in low relief on the die, so it wore away slowly. *Reverse:* Further wear has flattened all but a few feathers, and many if not most horizontal lines of the shield are indistinct. The leaves are only in outline form. The rim is visible all around, as are the ends of most denticles.

1873, Open 3. Graded G-6.

G-4, 6 (Good). *Obverse:* The seated figure is worn nearly smooth. At G-4 there are no letters in LIBERTY remaining on most (but not all) coins; some coins, especially of the early 1870s, are exceptions. At G-6, traces of one or two can barely be seen and more details can be seen in the figure. *Reverse:* The eagle shows only a few details of the shield and feathers. The rim is worn down, and the tops of the border letters are weak or worn away, although the inscription can still be read.

1873, Open 3. Graded AG-3.

AG-3 (About Good). *Obverse:* The seated figure is visible in outline form. Much or all of the rim is worn away. The date remains clear. *Reverse:* The border letters are partially worn away. The eagle is mostly in outline form, but with a few details discernible. The rim is weak or missing.

1889. Graded PF-65.

PF-60 to 70 (Proof). *Obverse and Reverse:* Proofs that are extensively cleaned and have many hairlines, or that are dull and grainy, are lower level, such as PF-60 to 62. These are not widely desired, save for the low mintage (in circulation-strike format) years from 1879 to 1891. With medium hairlines and good reflectivity, an assigned grade of PF-64 is appropriate, and with relatively few hairlines, Gem PF-65. In various grades hairlines are most easily seen in the obverse field. PF-66 should have hairlines so delicate that magnification is needed to see them. Above that, a Proof should be free of such lines.

Illustrated coin: This lovely gem has cameo contrast against mirrored fields.

Collecting Liberty Seated Half Dollars

Nearly all half dollars of this type are readily available and quite affordable in circulated grades. Although newspaper headlines are given to Mint State rarities and ultragrade coins, a survey of past issues of the *Gobrecht Journal* quickly reveals that the vast majority of collectors seek, and are very content with, such grades as Fine, Very Fine, and Extremely Fine. Among Philadelphia half dollars there are no great rarities for circulated grades, but rarities can be found among Mint State issues.

Throughout the New Orleans series from 1840-O through 1849-O, most issues are plentiful enough in worn grades, but are extremely rare at the gem level. New Orleans issues in the 1850s continue the trend, but are somewhat more readily available in higher grades, the 1853-O, Without Arrows and Rays being a notable exception as the several known examples show extensive wear. The 1854-O and 1855-O are among the most common of all Liberty Seated half dollars in Mint State.

In contrast, San Francisco Mint half dollars, struck from 1855 onward, offer many elusive issues. Early dates from 1855-S through 1859-S are rarities in all grades. The issues in the 1860s are relatively plentiful in circulated grades but are rare in Mint State. San Francisco Mint coins of the 1870s include some notable rarities (the 1878-S being particularly important) and many readily obtainable issues as well.

Carson City half dollars are rarities for the first several years, 1870-CC through 1874-CC, after which they are relatively plentiful for a brief period, closing with the rare 1878-CC. As a general rule the earlier issues are nearly often seen with extensive wear and are landmark rarities in Mint State. Among the later dates 1875-CC to 1877-CC are available readily enough in Mint State, and 1878-CC is rare at that level.

Robert Spangler's contribution of "Results of the Liberty Seated Half Dollar Survey" to the March 1992 number of the *Gobrecht Journal* brought dramatically to the fore the fact that most specimens of various issues in cabinets are in the VF to EF range. This was based on a survey sent to the Liberty Seated Collectors Club. For Philadelphia coins, Proofs were not included:

Philadelphia: 1873, No Arrows, Open 3; 1840, Large Date; 1852; 1886; 1851; 1850; 1887; 1884; 1889; and 1890; these being the top 10.

New Orleans: 1853-O, No Arrows and Rays (of which not a single piece was reported as being owned by Liberty Seated Collectors Club members); 1842-O, Small Date; 1852-O; 1842-O, Large Date; 1851-O; 1857-O; 1858-O; 1843-O; 1850-O; and 1849-O.

San Francisco: 1878-S (rarest by far, just eight reported); 1855-S (34 reported); 1866-S, Without Motto; 1873-S, With Arrows; 1856-S; 1857-S; 1872-S; 1874-S; 1870-S; and 1869-S.

Carson City: 1874-CC (the rarest on the list, just 31 reported, median grade F-18); 1878-CC (32, VG-10); 1870-CC (37, VG-10); 1873-CC, No Arrows (37, VF-22); 1871-CC (38, F-18); 1873-CC, With Arrows (40, VF-25); 1872-CC (55, VF-22); 1875-CC (60, VF-32); 1876-CC (71, EF-42); and 1877-CC (72, EF-42).

For the series the standard reference is *The Complete Guide to Liberty Seated Half Dollars* by Randy Wiley and Bill Bugert (1993). The authors present a remarkable, indeed incredible selection of historical material, technical notes (edge reed counts, for example), and more. Another valuable source of data is the *Gobrecht Journal* periodical of the Liberty Seated Collectors Club. John W. McCloskey has carefully edited and shepherded the progress of the publication for many years. Since 2004 LSCC has published the *E-Gobrecht* on the Internet. Also important, but with much if not most of the information rendered obsolete by later studies, is *Walter Breen's Complete Encyclopedia of U.S. and Colonial Coins* (1988). As useful cross-references, I also recommend the catalogs of the James Bennett Pryor Collection (January 1996), the Louis E. Eliasberg Collection (1997), the George Byers Collection (October 2006), the Eric P. Newman Collection (2013, 2014), and the especially comprehensive Eugene H. Gardner Collection (2014, 2015).

Being a Smart Buyer

Cherrypicking can pay rich dividends. As is the case for other Liberty Seated denominations, the grading services pay little or no attention to whether a Liberty Seated half dollar has areas of weak striking or if it has good eye appeal. This provides the opportunity to acquire sharp coins, for varieties for which such exist, without paying any more for them.

Coins with poor or low eye appeal, including deep toning, should be avoided entirely. Cherrypick for quality. For circulated coins, avoid those with nicks or scratches. For Mint State coins opt for brilliant to delicately or medium-toned pieces with rich luster. If you prefer deeply toned coins be careful as much toning masks friction or wear. For Proofs do the same. Some Proofs have lint marks from residue on the dies and a few have light striking. Generally, however, most Proofs are problem-free.

As I have mentioned under other denominations, today nearly all buyers make their purchase decisions based on the numerical grade given on a holder. The zeal to complete Registry Sets at PCGS and NGC has added a great dynamism to the market, buoying the prices for coins that are among the finest of their kind, *as solely determined by the grade number*. This is fine, and all owners and sellers of coins can be grateful that this provides buyers for many coins that a connoisseur would reject.

In my opinion, numerical grade is just one of three major factors in determining the desirability of a coin, and not necessarily the most important. The other two are sharpness of strike and eye appeal. For my money I would without question prefer a sharply struck MS-63 Liberty Seated half dollar with good eye appeal to a certified MS-65 that is weakly struck and unattractive. Many of the latter coins exist and can be easily enough studied on Internet sites.

1839, No Motto Above Eagle (Variety 1—No Drapery)

There is no drapery at Liberty's elbow on this variety. This type was used only in 1839 and only for part of that year. The small-date numerals on the obverse and small letters on the reverse give half dollars of this date a particularly attractive appearance.

Designed by: Christian Gobrecht.

Specifications: *Composition:* 90 percent silver, 10 percent copper. *Diameter:* 30.6 mm. *Weight:* 206.25 grains (13.36 grams). *Edge:* Reeded.

1839, No Drapery

Circulation-strike mintage: Portion of 1,972,400

Proof mintage: 4–6

actual size: 30.6 mm

Availability in Mint State: In 2014 the Eugene H. Gardner Sale featured examples of this coin in MS-65 and MS-64. *MS-60 to 62:* 30 to 40. *MS-63:* 10 to 13. *MS-64:* 6 to 9. *MS-65 or better:* 3 or 4.[11]

Availability in circulated grades: *AG-3 to AU-58:* These are slightly scarce in circulated grades. Many are in grades such as VF and EF.

Characteristics of striking: This issue is usually fairly well struck, although sometimes stars four and five are light.

Proofs: Approximately nine examples have been certified.

Notes: This is the only true "No Drapery" design type from Christian Gobrecht's original motif as used on his illustrious silver dollar of 1836. Many specialists consider this issue to be the most beautiful in the Liberty Seated half dollar series. All later issues without drapery at Liberty's elbow were inadvertently created as the result of polished or relapped dies or, alternatively, from insufficient depth of impression of the working hub into the working die. One No-Drapery die clashed with its reverse die, creating a raised clash mark that looks like partial drapery in that position.[12] Wiley-Bugert-1 through 4 are die marriages with two obverse and four reverse dies.

Harry Salyards, who enjoys the series, commented: "Unlike the other four denominations, in which Miss Liberty was more or less *engulfed* in anatomy-hiding drapery, the half dollar retained the closest appearance to Gobrecht's original 1836 design— even though that meant that (gasp!) you could actually see the curve of her leg under that flimsy gown, and a hint of a little tummy bulge below her breasts! In other words, unlike her fate on the other Liberty Seated denominations, she was somehow spared the worst of the Victorians' enshrouding of the natural female form."[13]

G-4	VG-8	F-12	VF-20	EF-40	AU-50
$300	$425	$625	$950	$2,150	$3,000

MS-60	MS-63	MS-65	PF-60	PF-63	PF-65
$7,500	$27,500	$185,000	$125,000	$175,000	$275,000

1839–1853, No Motto Above Eagle
(Variety 1—With Drapery)

Drapery was added during 1839 to Liberty's left elbow. Other, more subtle changes were made, including slightly reducing the size of the rock to the left. The drapery varies in strength, and on some coins struck from relapped dies the drapery can be thin or missing; this is not a design change and adds no value. During the rise of silver prices in the early 1850s large quantities were melted.

Designed by: Christian Gobrecht.

Specifications: *Composition:* 90 percent silver, 10 percent copper. *Diameter:* 30.6 mm. *Weight:* 206.25 grains (13.36 grams). *Edge:* Reeded.

1839, With Drapery

Circulation-strike mintage: Portion of 1,972,400

Proof mintage: *1–2*

Availability in Mint State: In 2014 the Eugene H. Gardner Sale

actual size: 30.6 mm

featured an example of this coin in MS-65. *MS-60 to 62:* 60 to 100. *MS-63:* 30 to 45. *MS-64:* 20 to 25. *MS-65 or better:* 6 to 10.

Availability in circulated grades: *AG-3 to AU-58:* This issue is often seen but is hardly common. It is more available than the No-Drapery issue, but is mostly found in lower grades.

Characteristics of striking: This issue usually has light striking in areas, especially on the obverse stars. On the reverse check the eagle's talons on the right.

Proofs: In 2014 the Eugene H. Gardner Sale featured examples of this coin in PF-64 (ex Pittman). These are apparently unique.

Notes: This is the most often seen variety of 1839. WB-5 through 7 with three obverse and three reverse dies. The With-Drapery issue has star one farther from the rock than on the No-Drapery coins.

G-4	VG-8	F-12	VF-20	EF-40	AU-50
$55	$80	$105	$200	$375	$700
MS-60	**MS-63**	**MS-65**	**PF-60**	**PF-63**	**PF-65**
$1,450	$3,500	$17,500		$95,000	$200,000

1840, Small Letters

Circulation-strike mintage: 1,435,008

Proof mintage: *4–8*

actual size: 30.6 mm

Availability in Mint State: In 2014 and 2015 the Eugene H. Gardner Sale featured examples of this coin in MS-66 (2), MS-65, and MS-63. *MS-60 to 62:* 100 to 200. *MS-63:* 8 to 12. *MS-64:* 2 or 3. *MS-65 or better:* 3.[14]

Availability in circulated grades: *AG-3 to AU-58:* These are common, mostly in lower grades.

Characteristics of striking: This issue is usually well struck, but sometimes has weakness on the stars.

Proofs: In 2015 the Eugene H. Gardner Sale featured an example of this coin in PF-65 (ex Pittman). Approximately seven examples have been certified.

Notes: On February 17, 1840, Mint Director R.M. Patterson wrote to Treasury Secretary Levi Woodbury: "Being pleased with the half dollars which are now striking at the Mint and which I think are creditable specimens of ordinary coinage, I send ten to you by this present mail. You will please return to me a half eagle for them."[15]

WB-1 through 11 are die marriages with seven obverse and ten reverse dies.

G-4	VG-8	F-12	VF-20	EF-40	AU-50
$75	$95	$105	$165	$375	$525
MS-60	**MS-63**	**MS-65**	**PF-60**	**PF-63**	**PF-65**
$950	$2,000	$10,000			$65,000

1840, Medium Letters

Circulation-strike mintage: Portion of 1840, Small Letters, mintage

actual size: 30.6 mm

Availability in Mint State: In 2014 the Eugene H. Gardner Sale featured an example of this coin in MS-64. *MS-60 to 62:* 12 to 15. *MS-63:* 5 to 8. *MS-64:* 2 or 3. *MS-65 or better:* 0.

Availability in circulated grades: *AG-3 to AU-58:* These are very scarce and are mostly in lower grades.

Characteristics of striking: This issue is usually well struck.

Notes: This variety was called Large Letters years ago. It is a classic rarity, a transitional issue with the reverse of 1838 Capped Bust coinage. It was struck at the *New Orleans Mint*, but without a mintmark as this reverse was earlier paired with an 1839-O Capped Bust half dollar which had the mintmark on the obverse.[16] It has a slightly smaller diameter than the 1840, Small-Letters reverse.

The possibility that this particular variety may have been struck at the New Orleans Mint was raised by Harlan P. Smith in his 1886 sale of the Charles White Collection, lot 246. An 1840 half dollar lacking an O mintmark was described as follows: "This appears to be the same die used in the New Orleans Mint in 1839, and re-engraved, this variety is seldom seen."

WB-4 and 12 are die marriages with two obverse and one reverse dies.

G-4	VG-8	F-12	VF-20	EF-40	AU-50	MS-60	MS-63	MS-65
$285	$425	$650	$1,000	$1,850	$2,500	$5,750	$10,000	$50,000

1840-O

Circulation-strike mintage: 855,100

Availability in Mint State: In 2014 the Eugene H. Gardner Sale featured an example of this coin in MS-66. *MS-60 to 62:* 8 to 12. *MS-63:* 7 to 10. *MS-64:* 1 or 2. *MS-65 or better:* 1.

actual size: 30.6 mm

Availability in circulated grades: *AG-3 to AU-58:* These are scarce in circulated grades.

Characteristics of striking: This issue is sometimes lightly struck on the obverse, such as at the tip of the foot and the end of the rock.

Notes: The long denticles or short denticles on various dies are caused by die wear, not by any changes in the hubs.

WB-1 through 14 (WB-4 and 12 are Medium-Letters reverse) with six obverse and ten reverse dies.

One 1840-O reverse die and a different reverse used on 1841-O half dollars has what Wiley and Bugert describe as "a heavy baseball die crack pattern similar to the seams on a baseball" and sells for a premium.[17]

G-4	VG-8	F-12	VF-20	EF-40	AU-50	MS-60	MS-63	MS-65
$65	$80	$105	$200	$350	$600	$2,350	$5,000	

1841

Circulation-strike mintage: 310,000

Proof mintage: *4–8*

actual size: 30.6 mm

Availability in Mint State: In his 1988 *Encyclopedia* Walter H. Breen stated that a hoard of possibly 40 Mint State coins turned up in Clearwater, Florida, sometime before 1957, but no other information has been obtained about these. Writing in the *Gobrecht Journal*, November 2008, Ken Cable-Camilleis in "A Market Analysis for Mint State Pre-1853 Philadelphia Seated Half Dollars" commented: "This is a date that I would classify as a *major rarity* in Mint State, even more so than the 1839, No-Drapery issue."[18] In 2015 the Eugene H. Gardner Sale featured an example of this coin in MS-65. *MS-60 to 62:* 12 to 15. *MS-63:* 8 to 12. *MS-64:* 4 to 6. *MS-65 or better:* 2 or 3.[19]

Availability in circulated grades: *AG-3 to AU-58:* These are scarce and are mostly in lower grades.

Characteristics of striking: Striking of this issue varies. Some are lightly struck on Liberty's head and on parts of the eagle, but sharp examples can be found.

Proofs: In 2015 the Eugene H. Gardner Sale featured an example of this coin in PF-64. Approximately 12 examples have been certified.

Notes: WB-1 through 5 are die marriages with three obverse and three reverse dies. For the "baseball" reverse see the previous 1840-O.

G-4	VG-8	F-12	VF-20	EF-40	AU-50
$70	$115	$145	$225	$425	$650

MS-60	MS-63	MS-65	PF-60	PF-63	PF-65
$1,450	$2,750	$10,000	$15,000	$20,000	$37,500

1841-O

Circulation-strike mintage: 401,000

actual size: 30.6 mm

Availability in Mint State: Wiley and Bugert mention the Clearwater hoard as being found "on the site of the former Fort Harrison; they were presumably buried by a soldier stationed there at the time of issue." No specific information of numismatic use has been learned. In 2015 the Eugene H. Gardner Sale featured examples of this coin in MS-66 and MS-65. *MS-60 to 62:* 20 to 25. *MS-63:* 7 to 10. *MS-64:* 3 to 5. *MS-65 or better:* 2 or 3.[20]

Availability in circulated grades: *AG-3 to AU-58:* These are quite scarce and are mostly in lower grades. EF and AU coins are elusive.

Characteristics of striking: This issue is usually well struck.

Notes: During this period the New Orleans Mint employed shattered dies on a number of different issues, commencing with the 1839-O. Whereas, apparently, the Philadelphia shattered dies were discarded at an early time and replaced with readily available new dies, those in charge of dies in New Orleans kept them in use for a longer period of time. Receiving new dies from Philadelphia in the early 1840s was not an easy matter, and involved a delay of weeks. Because of this, dies were sometimes relapped.

WB-1 to 11 are die marriages with seven obverse and eight reverse dies.

G-4	VG-8	F-12	VF-20	EF-40	AU-50	MS-60	MS-63	MS-65
$60	$85	$155	$225	$425	$775	$1,450	$3,500	$12,500

Reverse Hub Change of 1842

In 1842 the reverse hub was changed from small letters to large letters for reasons unknown, although it has been suggested that this would improve the flow of metal during the striking process. From a numismatic viewpoint most collectors consider the earlier Small-Letters style to be especially attractive, giving the coins a cameo-like aspect.

Detail of Small Letters.   Detail of Large Letters.

1842, Small Date, Small Letters

Circulation-strike mintage: Portion of 1842, Medium Date, mintage

Availability in Mint State: In 2014 the Eugene H. Gardner Sale featured an example of this coin in MS-64.

actual size: 30.6 mm

Availability in circulated grades: Three are known: G-6, VF-20 (the discovery coin), and AU, once cleaned.[21]

Characteristics of striking: This issue is usually lightly struck.

Notes: This variety was discovered by Brian Greer in early 1998 and was first publicized in an article by Stuart Segan in *Coin World* on April 6 of that year.[22] The owner was reported to be Sheridan Downey, a California dealer. The piece had been certified by the American Numismatic Association Authentication Bureau.

The *Gobrecht Journal*, Volume 24, Issue 72, 1998, "An 1842 Half Dollar with a Small Letters Reverse Discovered," included this (excerpted):

This coin has been identified as a new variety in the series by Brian Greer. . . . The reverse is easily identified. This reverse has several vertical lines in the reverse shield extending up into the horizontal shield stripes, with one of these lines in the last set of vertical stripes on the right extending up to the top of the shield. These vertical line extensions are almost like fingerprints for Small Letters reverses, with the extension pattern distinctive for each Small Letters reverse in the series. The Small Letters reverse for the 1842 Small Date half does not match the two known reverses used to strike 1842-O, Small Date half dollars. This information, along with edge reeding characteristics and other die scratches and marks, has indicated that the 1842 Small date half with the small letters reverse is a genuine mint issue struck in Philadelphia.

They are all from the same pair of dies, WB-1.

G-4	VG-8	F-12	VF-20	EF-40	AU-50	MS-60	MS-63	MS-65
$17,000			$32,500		$40,000			

1842, Small Date, Large Letters

Circulation-strike mintage: Portion of 1842, Medium Date, mintage

Proof mintage: *4–8*

actual size: 30.6 mm

Availability in Mint State: The Eliasberg coin (1997) is MS-62. In 2014 and 2015 the Eugene H. Gardner Sale featured examples of this coin in MS-64 (now upgraded to MS-65), MS-63 (2), and MS-62. *MS-60 to 62:* 30 to 40. *MS-63:* 18 to 22. *MS-64:* 10 to 14. *MS-65 or better:* 2.[23]

Availability in circulated grades: *AG-3 to AU-58:* These are scarce and are mostly in lower grades.

Characteristics of striking: This issue is sometimes weakly struck on the obverse, such as on the stars to the left. Cherrypicking is advised.

Proofs: Approximately seven examples have been certified.

Notes: Beginning with this issue, the reverse was modified with large letters in the legend. WB-2 through 7 are die marriages with two obverse and five reverse dies.

G-4	VG-8	F-12	VF-20	EF-40	AU-50
$65	$115	$145	$225	$350	$450
MS-60	MS-63	MS-65	PF-60	PF-63	PF-65
$1,300	$3,750	$15,000	$15,000	$25,000	$45,000

1842, Medium Date

Circulation-strike mintage: 2,012,764

Availability in Mint State: In 2014 the Eugene H. Gardner Sale featured an example of this coin in MS-66.
MS-60 to 62: 55 to 70.

actual size: 30.6 mm

MS-63: 35 to 45. **MS-64:** 25 to 32. **MS-65 or better:** 2 or 3.

Availability in circulated grades: *AG-3 to AU-58:* These are common, mostly in lower grades.

Characteristics of striking: This issue is often seen with some lightness, but better struck than the Small-Date varieties.

Notes: To quickly differentiate between the Small and Medium-Date varieties just look at the 4. The Small Date has a plain, straight crossbar to the 4. The Medium Date has a crosslet (vertical serif) at the right end of the crossbar. WB-8 through 14 are die marriages with five obverse and six reverse dies.

G-4	VG-8	F-12	VF-20	EF-40	AU-50	MS-60	MS-63	MS-65
$65	$95	$105	$165	$235	$350	$1,000	$2,000	$7,000

1842-O, Small Date, Small Letters

Circulation-strike mintage: 203,000

Availability in Mint State: In 2014 the Eugene H. Gardner Sale featured an example of this coin in MS-63.

actual size: 30.6 mm

MS-60 to 62: 1 or 2. **MS-63:** 1. **MS-64:** 0. **MS-65 or better:** 0.

Availability in circulated grades: *AG-3 to AU-58:* These are very scarce and are usually seen well worn.

Characteristics of striking: This issue is usually lightly struck in areas, including on the reverse.

Notes: The estimated circulation-strike mintage is from the *Guide Book* and seems far too generous in light of the rarity of the variety. The illustrated coin was recovered from the wreck of the SS *New York* lost in the Gulf of Mexico in 1846. WB-1 and 2 are die marriages with one obverse and two reverse dies.

G-4	VG-8	F-12	VF-20	EF-40	AU-50	MS-60	MS-63	MS-65
$800	$1,100	$1,550	$2,250	$3,650	$7,000	$16,500	$35,000	

1842-O, Medium Date, Large Letters

Circulation-strike mintage: 754,000

Availability in Mint State: *MS-60 to 62:* 5 to 7. *MS-63:* 4 to 6. *MS-64:* 4 to 6. *MS-65 or better:* 1 or 2.

actual size: 30.6 mm

Availability in circulated grades: *AG-3 to AU-58:* These are common, mostly in lower grades.

Characteristics of striking: Striking of this issue varies, but they are sharper than the Small Date.

Notes: In general, New Orleans Mint half dollars of this era are very elusive in gem Mint State, although they are quite available in lower grades. WB-3 through 13 are die marriages with seven obverse and nine reverse dies.

G-4	VG-8	F-12	VF-20	EF-40	AU-50	MS-60	MS-63	MS-65
$70	$75	$175	$250	$400	$675	$2,250	$5,500	$20,000

1843

Circulation-strike mintage: 3,844,000

Proof mintage: *4–8*

Availability in Mint State: In 2014 and 2015 the Eugene H. Gardner Sale featured examples of this coin in MS-67, MS-66, and MS-65. *MS-60 to 62:* 50 to 65. *MS-63:* 18 to 22. *MS-64:* 6 to 8. *MS-65 or better:* 4 or 5.

actual size: 30.6 mm

Availability in circulated grades: *AG-3 to AU-58:* These are very common, mostly in lower grades.

Characteristics of striking: This issue sometimes sees light weakness on Liberty's head, on some stars, and on the eagle's talons on the right. There is much variation, as might be expected from the large mintage. "Nearly every 1843 reverse die is extensively and uniquely cracked. This date is therefore popular and widely collected for these cracks."[24]

Proofs: One example was graded PF-65 by PCGS, and is now PF-66 by NGC. In 2014 the Eugene H. Gardner Sale featured an example of this coin in PF-64 (ex Pittman). Approximately four examples have been certified.

Notes: WB-1 through 37 are die marriages with 18 obverse and 29 reverse dies, far and away the largest number of pairs up to this point in time.

G-4	VG-8	F-12	VF-20	EF-40	AU-50
$55	$75	$125	$150	$350	$400

MS-60	MS-63	MS-65	PF-60	PF-63	PF-65
$1,000	$2,250	$8,500	$15,000	$27,500	$60,000

1843-O

Circulation-strike mintage: 2,268,000

actual size: 30.6 mm

Availability in Mint State: A small hoard of a dozen to 20 of these was found in Florida in the 1950s. In 2014 and 2015 the Eugene H. Gardner Sale featured examples of this coin in MS-65 and MS-66. *MS-60 to 62:* 18 to 25. *MS-63:* 10 to 14. *MS-64:* 6 to 9. *MS-65 or better:* 4 to 5.

Availability in circulated grades: *AG-3 to AU-58:* These are easy to find, mostly in lower grades.

Characteristics of striking: This issue is sometimes seen with light weakness on the eagle's talons on the right.

Notes: According to Wiley and Bugert: "With few exceptions, New Orleans half dollars dated 1843 and later have noticeably larger diameters than those dated 1840–1842." Among 1843-O half dollars, diameters vary from 1.186 inches to 1.210 inches. See the WB text for more information. WB-1 through 18 are die marriages with ten obverse and eight reverse dies.

G-4	VG-8	F-12	VF-20	EF-40	AU-50	MS-60	MS-63	MS-65
$55	$80	$125	$150	$350	$450	$1,550	$3,750	$25,000

1844

Circulation-strike mintage: 1,766,000

Proof mintage: 3–6

actual size: 30.6 mm

Availability in Mint State: In 2014 and 2015 the Eugene H. Gardner Sale featured examples of this coin in MS-65 and MS-64 (2). *MS-60 to 62:* 40 to 55. *MS-63:* 18 to 25. *MS-64:* 4 to 6. *MS-65 or better:* 2.[25]

Availability in circulated grades: *AG-3 to AU-58:* These are common, mostly in lower grades.

Characteristics of striking: This issue is usually well struck, but some have slight weakness. Many are from cracked reverse dies, adding to their numismatic appeal.

Proofs: Approximately three examples have been certified.

Notes: WB-1 through 15 are die marriages with 10 obverse and 12 reverse dies.

G-4	VG-8	F-12	VF-20	EF-40	AU-50
$55	$75	$100	$150	$250	$400
MS-60	**MS-63**	**MS-65**	**PF-60**	**PF-63**	**PF-65**
$750	$1,700	$10,000			$80,000

1844-O

Circulation-strike mintage: 2,005,000

Availability in Mint State: In 2015 the Eugene H. Gardner Sale featured examples of this coin in MS-65 (ex Eliasberg) and MS-64. *MS-60 to 62:* 18 to 25. *MS-63:* 10 to 14. *MS-64:* 3 or 4. *MS-65 or better:* 3.[26]

actual size: 30.6 mm

Availability in circulated grades: *AG-3 to AU-58:* These are common, mostly in lower grades.

Characteristics of striking: This issue is usually well struck.

Notes: WB-1 through 2 are die marriages with 10 obverse and 14 reverse dies.

1844-O, Doubled Date: This is a spectacular die blunder which ranks as one of the most egregious of an era in which there were many mistakes made at the Mint. On the 1844-O, Doubled Date the date, consisting of a four-digit punch, was first placed in the die approximately 60 percent too high and was repunched in its

normal position. In his 1893 treatise, *Mint Marks,* Augustus G. Heaton referred to this in the following manner: "There is also a curious restrike of this O-mint date." In 2015 the Eugene H. Gardner Sale featured an example of this coin in MS-64. Three or four are known in Mint State. WB-103; *Cherrypickers' Guide to Rare Die Varieties* lists this as FS-50-1844o-301.

G-4	VG-8	F-12	VF-20	EF-40	AU-50	MS-60	MS-63	MS-65
$55	$80	$100	$175	$275	$450	$1,450	$3,500	$13,500

1845

Circulation-strike mintage: 589,000

Proof mintage: 3–6

Availability in Mint State: The 1845 is one of the rarest Philadelphia Mint coins of the era, and relatively few exist in high grades. In 2014 and 2015

actual size: 30.6 mm

the Eugene H. Gardner Sale featured two examples of this coin in MS-64. *MS-60 to 62:* 10 to 13. *MS-63:* 5 to 7. *MS-64:* 2 or 3. *MS-65 or better:* 0.

Availability in circulated grades: *AG-3 to AU-58:* These are slightly scarce and are usually well worn.

Characteristics of striking: This issue is often seen with some slight lightness on Liberty's head and the lower right of the reverse. On nearly all there is slight weakness on the eagle. Sharp examples can be easily found.

Proofs: Earlier estimates placed this as rarer than is thought today. Approximately five examples have been certified.

Notes: WB-1 through 5 are die marriages with three obverse and three reverse dies.

G-4	VG-8	F-12	VF-20	EF-40	AU-50
$65	$100	$125	$200	$300	$675

MS-60	MS-63	MS-65	PF-60	PF-63	PF-65
$1,100	$3,500		$15,000	$30,000	$65,000

1845-O

Circulation-strike mintage: 2,094,000

Availability in Mint State: In 2014 the Eugene H. Gardner Sale featured examples of this coin in MS-65, MS-63, and MS-62. *MS-60 to 62:* 22 to 28. *MS-63:* 9 to 12. *MS-64:* 7 to 9. *MS-65 or better:* 2 or 3.[27]

actual size: 30.6 mm

Availability in circulated grades: *AG-3 to AU-58:* These are common, mostly in lower grades.

Characteristics of striking: This issue is usually seen with some light weakness, but sharp coins can be found.

Notes: Coins struck from one of two relapped obverse dies lack drapery. One obverse also has the date dramatically doubled and is very common; *Cherrypickers' Guide to Rare Die Varieties* lists this as FS-50-1845o-303.

Notes: WB-1 through 20 are die marriages with 13 obverse and 11 reverse dies.

O Over Horizontal O: The first mintmark was punched in a horizontal position and then corrected. WB-103; *Cherrypickers' Guide to Rare Die Varieties* lists this as FS-50-1845o-501. Examples are easy to find.

G-4	VG-8	F-12	VF-20	EF-40	AU-50	MS-60	MS-63	MS-65
$55	$80	$100	$200	$250	$500	$1,000	$3,000	$9,000

1846, Medium Date

actual size: 30.6 mm

Circulation-strike mintage: 2,210,000

Proof mintage: *15–20*

Availability in Mint State: This is one of the Philadelphia Mint half dollars of the era seen in Mint State with some frequency in the marketplace. In 2014 and 2015 the Eugene H. Gardner Sale featured examples of this coin in MS-64 and MS-62. *MS-60 to 62:* 35 to 45. *MS-63:* 16 to 22. *MS-64:* 5 to 7. *MS-65 or better:* 2 or 3.

Availability in circulated grades: *AG-3 to AU-58:* These are common, mostly in lower grades.

Characteristics of striking: This issue is usually well struck.

Proofs: Approximately 23 examples have been certified.

Notes: WB-1 through 10 are die marriages with nine obverse and eight reverse dies.

1846, 6 Over Horizontal 6: This is one of the most memorable varieties in the entire Liberty Seated half dollar series and is a notable rarity as well. The Mint employee preparing this die first placed the digits "184" in the die, most likely with a three digit date punch containing these numerals. Next he picked up the punch for

the final digit and placed the "6" in the die sideways! After his error was discovered, the digit was repunched in the die in the proper upright alignment. During this era it was standard to use four-digit logotypes, but scattered exceptions occur. WB-104; *Cherrypickers' Guide to Rare Die Varieties* lists this as FS-50-1846-301. Several dozen circulated coins are known, and about a half dozen Mint State coins exist, mostly at lower levels. In 2014 the Eugene H. Gardner Sale featured an example of this coin in MS-65.

The J.M. Clapp notebook lists the purchase of an 1846 half dollar "Over 44?" from the Ropes Collection sale, 1899. Apparently, the coin was deaccessioned later and was not sold into the Louis E. Eliasberg Collection.

G-4	VG-8	F-12	VF-20	EF-40	AU-50
$55	$75	$100	$155	$250	$500

MS-60	MS-63	MS-65	PF-60	PF-63	PF-65
$1,000	$2,000	$12,500	$11,000	$21,000	$50,000

1846, Tall Date

Circulation-strike mintage: Portion of 1846, Medium Date, mintage

Availability in Mint State: In 2014 the Eugene H. Gardner Sale featured an example of this coin in MS-63.

actual size: 30.6 mm

MS-60 to 62: 5 to 7. *MS-63:* 1 or 2. *MS-64:* 1 or 2. *MS-65 or better:* 1 or 2.[28]

Availability in circulated grades: *AG-3 to AU-58:* These are common, but are not as plentiful as the foregoing, and are mostly in lower grades.

Characteristics of striking: This issue is usually well struck.

Notes: The date numerals, also called Large Date in the past, are a bit more vertically extended than on the "Medium Date" of this issue.[29] WB-11 through 17 are die marriages with six obverse and seven reverse dies.

G-4	VG-8	F-12	VF-20	EF-40	AU-50	MS-60	MS-63	MS-65
$85	$135	$185	$275	$375	$500	$1,350	$2,750	$20,000

1846-O, Medium Date

Circulation-strike mintage: 2,304,000

Availability in Mint State: In 2015 the Eugene H. Gardner Sale featured examples of this coin in MS-65, MS-64, and MS-62 (2). *MS-60 to 62:* 7 to 10. *MS-63:* 1 or 2. *MS-64:* 1 or 2. *MS-65 or better:* 1 or 2.

actual size: 30.6 mm

Availability in circulated grades: *AG-3 to AU-58:* These are common, mostly in lower grades.

Characteristics of striking: This issue is usually well struck.

Notes: Some coins of this issue lack drapery at the elbow from relapping. Writing in *The Numismatist* in May 1894, "Mint Mark" said: "1846. Scott mentions error 1846 [over sidewise 6] for Philadelphia. I have it from both the Philadelphia and New Orleans mints; strange that the same error should be on two dies of the same year." No 1846-O with this feature has been confirmed.

WB-1 through 27 are die marriages with 9 obverse and 20 reverse dies, with Medium Date (nearly all) and Tall Date (see the following).

G-4	VG-8	F-12	VF-20	EF-40	AU-50	MS-60	MS-63	MS-65
$55	$90	$175	$250	$350	$575	$1,650	$3,600	$20,000

1846-O, Tall Date

Circulation-strike mintage: Portion of 1846-O, Medium Date, mintage

Availability in Mint State: In 2015 the Eugene H. Gardner Sale featured an example of this coin in MS-63. *MS-60 to 62:* 1 or 2. *MS-63:* 1. *MS-64:* 0. *MS-65 or better:* 0.

actual size: 30.6 mm

Availability in circulated grades: *AG-3 to AU-58:* These are very scarce and most are well worn. They are a key to the series.

Characteristics of striking: This issue is usually well struck, but sometimes has slight weakness on the reverse.

Notes: The 1846-O Tall Date is a classic rarity of long standing.

G-4	VG-8	F-12	VF-20	EF-40	AU-50	MS-60	MS-63	MS-65
$255	$450	$600	$900	$2,000	$2,500	$9,500	$17,500	

1847, 7 Over 6

Circulation-strike mintage: Portion of 1847 mintage

Availability in Mint State: *MS-60 to 62:* 1 or 2. *MS-63:* 1. *MS-64:* 1. *MS-65 or better:* 1.

Availability in circulated grades: *AG-3 to AU-58:* These are very rare— probably about 60 exist in all circulated grades combined.[30] In 2015 the Eugene H. Gardner Sale featured an example of this coin in AU-55.

actual size: 30.6 mm

Detail of the Overdate.

Characteristics of striking: This issue is usually well struck. Early strikes show the overdate much more clearly than do later strikes. When buying, take note of this difference as it is hardly ever described. There are three distinct die states:

Early: Shows part of 1, 4, and 6 undertypes. The most desirable.

Middle: Shows part of the 6, but no trace of the 1 and 4.

Late: Shows *none* of the undertype and is verified as the overdate die only by slight doubling on the obverse shield. Thus, it is not a desirable substitute for an overdate.[31]

Notes: WB-11. The 1847, 7 Over 6, is so rare that only a few of the "name" collections offered in the past have included a specimen in any grade. The overdate is somewhat subtle and consists of small traces of the bottom of the 4 and 6 of the earlier 1846 in the field near the denticles, below the 4 (1847). Close examination is required. *Cherrypickers' Guide to Rare Die Varieties* lists this as FS-50-1847-301. The obverse die is also slightly doubled.

G-4	VG-8	F-12	VF-20	EF-40	AU-50	MS-60	MS-63	MS-65
$2,250	$3,000	$4,000	$5,000	$10,000	$13,500	$25,000		

1847

Circulation-strike mintage: 1,156,000

Proof mintage: 15–20

Availability in Mint State: Per Ken Cable-Camilleis: "This issue begins a six-year run of very scarce Philadelphia Mint half dollars."[32] In

actual size: 30.6 mm

2015 the Eugene H. Gardner Sale featured an example of this coin in MS-65. *MS-60 to 62:* 20 to 25. *MS-63:* 9 to 13. *MS-64:* 5 to 7. *MS-65 or better:* 2 or 3.[33]

Availability in circulated grades: *AG-3 to AU-58:* These are common, mostly in lower grades.

Characteristics of striking: This issue is often seen with some light weakness on Liberty's head.

Proofs: The same Proof reverse die was used to strike the 1847, 1848, and 1849 Proof half dollars in the Louis E. Eliasberg Collection. In 2015 the Eugene H. Gardner Sale featured an example of this coin in PF-64 (ex F.C.C. Boyd). Approximately 17 examples have been certified.

Notes: WB-1 through 12 are die marriages with seven obverse and seven reverse dies, including WB-11, the overdate discussed above.

G-4	VG-8	F-12	VF-20	EF-40	AU-50
$55	$75	$100	$175	$350	$450

MS-60	MS-63	MS-65	PF-60	PF-63	PF-65
$850	$2,000	$7,000	$10,000	$20,000	$45,000

1847-O

Circulation-strike mintage: 2,584,000

Availability in Mint State: In 2015 the Eugene H. Gardner Sale featured examples of this coin in MS-65, MS-64, and MS-63. *MS-60 to 62:* 12 to 16. *MS-63:* 5 to 7. *MS-64:* 3 or 4. *MS-65 or better:* 2 or 3.[34]

actual size: 30.6 mm

Availability in circulated grades: *AG-3 to AU-58:* This is a scarce New Orleans issue and is mostly found in lower grades.

Characteristics of striking: Striking of this issue varies. They are sometimes slightly weak on the head, certain stars, on the eagle's left leg, and on the arrow feathers.

Notes: WB-1 through 28 are die marriages with 8 obverse and 12 reverse dies. This date is very popular for its doubled date, repunched date, and doubled-die varieties.

The J.M. Clapp notebook indicates that the collection at one time had an Uncirculated "1847/6-O" overdate, a coin not known to exist today.

G-4	VG-8	F-12	VF-20	EF-40	AU-50	MS-60	MS-63	MS-65
$55	$75	$100	$175	$250	$550	$1,250	$3,000	$15,000

1848

Circulation-strike mintage: 580,000

Proof mintage: 4–8

Availability in Mint State: In 2015 the Eugene H. Gardner Sale featured an example of this coin in MS-65. *MS-60 to 62:* 30 to 40. *MS-63:* 12 to 16. *MS-64:* 10 to 14. *MS-65 or better:* 2 or 3.

actual size: 30.6 mm

Availability in circulated grades: *AG-3 to AU-58:* These are slightly scarce and are usually seen with extensive circulation. For any of the issues in this era sharp EF and AU coins are in the minority.

Characteristics of striking: This issue is often seen with some slight weakness.

Proofs: Approximately five examples have been certified.

Notes: WB-1 through 17 are die marriages with 12 obverse and 9 reverse dies.

G-4	VG-8	F-12	VF-20	EF-40	AU-50
$75	$125	$175	$250	$450	$750

MS-60	MS-63	MS-65	PF-60	PF-63	PF-65
$1,250	$3,000	$15,000	$10,000	$20,000	$45,000

1848-O

Circulation-strike mintage: 3,180,000

Availability in Mint State: In 2014 and 2015 the Eugene H. Gardner Sale featured examples of this coin in MS-66, MS-65, and MS-64. *MS-60 to 62:* 18 to 22. *MS-63:* 6 to 9. *MS-64:* 4 to 6. *MS-65 or better:* 3 or 4.

actual size: 30.6 mm

Availability in circulated grades: *AG-3 to AU-58:* These are common, mostly in low and medium grades.

Characteristics of striking: This issue varies from very sharp to with some weakness. Cherrypicking will pay.

Notes: WB-1 through 26 are die marriages with 13 obverse and 15 reverse dies.

G-4	VG-8	F-12	VF-20	EF-40	AU-50	MS-60	MS-63	MS-65
$55	$75	$100	$150	$255	$550	$1,350	$2,250	$27,500

1849

Circulation-strike mintage: 1,252,000

Proof mintage: 4–8

Availability in Mint State: In 2014 and 2015 the Eugene H. Gardner Sale featured examples of this coin in MS-64 (2), and MS-62. *MS-60 to*

actual size: 30.6 mm

62: 35 to 45. *MS-63:* 15 to 20. *MS-64:* 12 to 16. *MS-65 or better:* 2 or 3.

Availability in circulated grades: *AG-3 to AU-58:* These are common, mostly in medium grades.

Characteristics of striking: This issue is often seen with slight weakness, but sharp examples are plentiful.

Proofs: In 2014 the Eugene H. Gardner Sale featured an example of this coin in PF-66 (ex Eliasberg). Approximately seven examples have been certified.

Notes: One rare variety has a significantly doubled date and an extraneous digit protruding from the rock. WB-1 through 15 are die marriages with 11 obverse and 11 reverse dies.

G-4	VG-8	F-12	VF-20	EF-40	AU-50
$75	$100	$150	$200	$255	$500
MS-60	**MS-63**	**MS-65**	**PF-60**	**PF-63**	**PF-65**
$1,050	$2,250	$13,500	$10,000	$20,000	$45,000

1849-O

Circulation-strike mintage: 2,310,000

Availability in Mint State: In 2014 the Eugene H. Gardner Sale featured an example of this coin in MS-65. *MS-60 to 62:* 35 to 45. *MS-63:* 15 to 20. *MS-64:* 8 to 12. *MS-65 or better:* 2 or 3.

actual size: 30.6 mm

Availability in circulated grades: *AG-3 to AU-58:* These are common, mostly in low and medium grades.

Characteristics of striking: This issue is often weak on the obverse and many show extensive die rust in the form of tiny raised dots.

Notes: WB-1 through 16 are die marriages with 11 obverse and 12 reverse dies. Many have rotated reverses to varying degrees. The entire field of rotated reverses across the various Liberty Seated series is detailed in the specialized books on each denomination.

G-4	VG-8	F-12	VF-20	EF-40	AU-50	MS-60	MS-63	MS-65
$55	$75	$100	$155	$375	$750	$1,600	$2,700	$20,000

1850

Circulation-strike mintage: 227,000

Proof mintage: *4–8*

Availability in Mint State: These are rare and sometimes prooflike. In 2015 the Eugene H. Gardner Sale featured an example of this coin in

actual size: 30.6 mm

MS-67. *MS-60 to 62:* 15 to 20. *MS-63:* 4 to 6. *MS-64:* 1 or 2. *MS-65 or better:* 1.

Availability in circulated grades: *AG-3 to AU-58:* These coins are rare. Low-grade coins are very rare.

Characteristics of striking: This issue is usually well struck.

Proofs: In 2015 the Eugene H. Gardner Sale featured an example of this coin in PF-64 (ex Anderson-Dupont). Approximately seven examples have been certified.

Notes: WB-1 through 4 are die marriages with three obverse and three reverse dies.

G-4	VG-8	F-12	VF-20	EF-40	AU-50
$350	$500	$750	$900	$1,200	$1,500
MS-60	**MS-63**	**MS-65**	**PF-60**	**PF-63**	**PF-65**
$2,250	$3,750	$27,500	$13,000	$27,500	$60,000

1850-O

Circulation-strike mintage: 2,456,000

Availability in Mint State: In 2015 the Eugene H. Gardner Sale featured an example of this coin in MS-66. *MS-60 to 62:* 35 to 45. *MS-63:* 15 to 20. *MS-64:* 12 to 16. *MS-65 or better:* 3 to 5.

actual size: 30.6 mm

Availability in circulated grades: *AG-3 to AU-58:* These are common, mostly in medium grades.

Characteristics of striking: This issue is usually seen with some areas of lightness.

Notes: WB-1 through 17 are die marriages with 12 obverse and 12 reverse dies. One with a repunched mintmark is desired by specialists and is scarce.

G-4	VG-8	F-12	VF-20	EF-40	AU-50	MS-60	MS-63	MS-65
$55	$75	$100	$175	$300	$450	$1,000	$2,000	$12,500

1851

Circulation-strike mintage: 200,750

Proof mintage: See below

Availability in Mint State: In 2015 the Eugene H. Gardner Sale featured an example of this coin in MS-66.

actual size: 30.6 mm

MS-60 to 62: 8 to 11. *MS-63:* 6 to 8. *MS-64:* 4 or 5. *MS-65 or better:* 2.[35]

Availability in circulated grades: *AG-3 to AU-58:* These coins are rare, as are low-grade coins (not that it makes a difference).

Characteristics of striking: This issue is usually sharply struck.

Proofs: Some coins of 1851 and 1853 have been called Proofs over a long period of years, but it is uncertain if they were actually struck as such or if they were from dies polished after relapping, or for other reasons. No Proof sets of this year are known.

Notes: WB-1 through 8 are die marriages with four obverse and four reverse dies. One with a misplaced eight (MPD) in the denticles is rare and eagerly sought.

G-4	VG-8	F-12	VF-20	EF-40	AU-50	MS-60	MS-63	MS-65
$850	$1,000	$1,500	$1,750	$2,350	$2,850	$3,500	$5,000	$12,500

1851-O

Circulation-strike mintage: 402,000

Availability in Mint State: In 2014 the Eugene H. Gardner Sale featured an example of this coin in MS-66.

MS-60 to 62: 35 to 45. *MS-63:* 18 to 22. *MS-64:* 15 to 20. *MS-65 or better:* 5 or 6.[36]

actual size: 30.6 mm

Availability in circulated grades: *AG-3 to AU-58:* These are scarce in circulated grades.

Characteristics of striking: This issue is sharply struck and well defined, which is unusual for a New Orleans issue.

Notes: WB-1 through 5 are die marriages with four obverse and four reverse dies.

G-4	VG-8	F-12	VF-20	EF-40	AU-50	MS-60	MS-63	MS-65
$70	$125	$175	$250	$500	$900	$2,000	$4,000	$10,000

1852

Circulation-strike mintage: 77,130

Proof mintage: 3–6

Availability in Mint State: In 2014 the Eugene H. Gardner Sale featured an example of this coin in MS-66. *MS-60 to 62:* 30 to 40. *MS-63:* 13 to 16. *MS-64:* 5 to 7. *MS-65 or better:* 3 to 5.[37]

actual size: 30.6 mm

Availability in circulated grades: *AG-3 to AU-58:* These are rare in circulated grades. Well-worn coins are seldom seen. These are a key issue.

Characteristics of striking: This issue is sometimes seen with slight weakness on the obverse, but most are quite sharp.

Proofs: Approximately four examples have been certified.

Notes: WB-1 through 3 are die marriages with one obverse and three reverse dies.

G-4	VG-8	F-12	VF-20	EF-40	AU-50
$550	$750	$1,000	$1,250	$2,000	$2,500

MS-60	MS-63	MS-65	PF-60	PF-63	PF-65
$3,250	$4,500	$13,500		$35,000	$55,000

1852-O

Circulation-strike mintage: 144,000

Availability in Mint State: These are extremely rare. In 2014 the Eugene H. Gardner Sale featured an example of this coin in MS-65 (ex Pryor, 1996). *MS-60 to 62:* 9 to 12. *MS-63:* 3 to 5. *MS-64:* 3 to 5. *MS-65 or better:* 1 or 2.

actual size: 30.6 mm

Availability in circulated grades: *AG-3 to AU-58:* These are very scarce, mostly in medium grades.

Characteristics of striking: This issue is often very sharp, which is not common among New Orleans half dollars. Some are prooflike.

Notes: In 1893 in his treatise, *Mint Marks*, Augustus G. Heaton noted that the 1852-O was the first coin of the New Orleans Mint in the Liberty Seated series which he considered to be scarce in all grades.

WB-1 and 2 are die marriages with two obverse and two reverse dies, indicating that both obverse and reverse dies were put in and taken out of the press at the same time, the earliest this is found in the half dollar series. One reverse was also used to coin the rare 1853-O, No Arrows, half dollars.

G-4	VG-8	F-12	VF-20	EF-40	AU-50	MS-60	MS-63	MS-65
$375	$575	$600	$875	$1,300	$1,800	$4,500	$12,500	$35,000

1853-O, No Arrows or Rays

Circulation-strike mintage: unknown

Availability in Mint State: None.

Availability in circulated grades: There are only

actual size: 30.6 mm

four known examples in circulated grades: G-6 (King 1892), VG-8 (Granberg 1911, later Eliasberg), VG-8 (discovered in 2012[38]), and VF-35 (Haseltine before 1881, Garrett, Queller, Byers).

Characteristics of striking: This issue is seemingly fairly well struck, but as all show extensive wear, the original state cannot be determined.

Notes: The 1853-O half dollar without arrows on the obverse or rays on the reverse is one of the legendary rarities of American numismatics. With only four specimens known, it has few peers anywhere in the American series. All but a few of the great specialized half dollar collections formed in past decades have lacked an example.

The New Orleans *Times-Picayune*, January 2, 1853, told of one of these on display:

> *New Coinage.* The officers of the Mint in our city marked the opening of the New Year by very appropriately making a new issue of American coin. How extensive that was we are unable to say but the twenty dollar gold piece and silver half dollar laid on our table for examination, as the product of the massive stamping machinery on the first day of the year 1853, were admirable specimens of elegant design and finish.[39]

From *Mason's Coin Collectors' Herald*, September 1880:

> B.T. Walton, of this city, called our attention recently to a new variety of our silver half dollars, viz: The 1853 half dollar, New Orleans mint, without arrow points at either side of date; and without rays on the reverse. There may have been other specimens of this rarity seen by collectors, but we confess that Mr. Walton's coin

is the first we ever saw, or noticed in a pretty large experience in handling coins. If any of our readers know of, or possess a similar half dollar, we will be thankful for an early notification of the same, and if anyone has a specimen for sale, we are prepared to offer a liberal sum for its possession. A rumor comes to our ears that another specimen of this peculiar coin is in existence in this city, but the rumor is not authenticated as yet. Mr. Walton sold his 1853 piece to a gentleman in this city.

In 1885, in his offering of J. Colvin Randall's specimen of the 1853-O half dollar without arrows and rays (now known as the Garrett specimen), W. Elliot Woodward described lot 421: "1853 No. 1; without arrows; Orleans [sic] Mint. I consider this coin the gem of Mr. Randall's whole collection. It belongs to the regular series of U.S. coins, and is undoubtedly unique. I am well aware that other specimens are claimed to exist, but one which has long passed unchallenged is now admitted by the owner to be an alteration . . ."

In his treatise, *Mint Marks*, 1893, Augustus G. Heaton commented: "If the judgment of several authorities is well-founded, there is a variety of the 1853-O, No Arrows and Rays similar to the quarter of the Philadelphia Mint, but never known in the half dollar coinage of that institution, which takes a bound at the highest place among mintmarked rarities. Such a piece has been purchased as genuine for considerably over $100. It was found in the West. We are disposed to recognize the possibility of such a variety."[40]

G-4	VG-8	F-12	VF-20	EF-40	AU-50	MS-60	MS-63	MS-65
$175,000	$200,000	$300,000	$500,000					

1853, Arrows at Date, Rays Around Eagle (Variety 2)

The Coinage Act of February 21, 1853, reduced the silver content of half dollars to the point which they were no longer profitable to hoard or melt. To signify the change, the new half dollars had arrowheads on each side of the date and a glory of rays around the eagle on the reverse. This was done in the hubs, so there are no differences in the placement of these features on the coins.

Designed by: Christian Gobrecht. The arrows and rays were added by someone on the Mint staff.

Specifications: *Composition:* 90 percent silver, 10 percent copper. *Diameter:* 30.6 mm. *Weight:* 192 grains (12.44 grams). *Edge:* Reeded.

1853

Circulation-strike mintage: 3,532,708

Proof mintage: See below

Availability in Mint State: *MS-60 to 62:* 250 to 325. *MS-63:* 120 to 140. *MS-64:* 110 to 130. *MS-65 or better:* 25 to 35.

actual size: 30.6 mm

Availability in circulated grades: *AG-3 to AU-58:* These are extremely common.

Characteristics of striking: Striking of this issue varies, but sharp examples can be found.

Proofs: See comments under the previous entry in 1851. The Eliasberg coin was cataloged as PF-63 with extensive die details furnished for research purposes. An estimated five or six have been cataloged as Proofs over the years.

Notes: One variety from a relapped obverse die lacks drapery. Such instances occur with frequency in the series and are simply late states of die, not changes in the design.[41] A number of Doubled-Die reverses are known for this year.

G-4	VG-8	F-12	VF-20	EF-40	AU-50
$65	$100	$115	$165	$325	$575
MS-60	**MS-63**	**MS-65**	**PF-60**	**PF-63**	**PF-65**
$1,500	$3,500	$22,000		$65,000	$225,000

1853-O, With Arrows and Rays

Circulation-strike mintage: 1,328,000

Availability in Mint State: In 2014 the Eugene H. Gardner Sale featured an example of this coin in MS-65. *MS-60 to 62:* 50

actual size: 30.6 mm

to 65. *MS-63:* 18 to 25. *MS-64:* 12 to 16. *MS-65 or better:* 3 to 5.

Availability in circulated grades: *AG-3 to AU-58:* These are common, but are several orders more elusive than its Philadelphia counterpart.

Characteristics of striking: Striking of this issue varies, but they are usually with some lightness.

Notes: There are some that lack drapery at the elbow due to either relapping of the die or shallow impressing of the master die into the working die. WB-1 through 22 with 15 obverse and 9 reverse dies.

G-4	VG-8	F-12	VF-20	EF-40	AU-50	MS-60	MS-63	MS-65
$65	$100	$115	$200	$425	$850	$2,750	$5,500	$40,000

1854–1855, Arrows at Date, No Rays (Variety 3)

The arrowheads were continued in 1854 and 1855, but the rays on the reverse were removed, constituting a new type. The arrowheads were part of the hub dies.

Designed by: Christian Gobrecht. The arrows were added by someone on the Mint staff.

Specifications: *Composition:* 90 percent silver, 10 percent copper. *Diameter:* 30.6 mm. *Weight:* 192 grains (12.44 grams). *Edge:* Reeded.

1854

Circulation-strike mintage: 2,982,000

Proof mintage: *15–20*

Availability in Mint State: *MS-60 to 62:* 160 to 200. *MS-63:* 70 to 90. *MS-64:* 45 to 60. *MS-65 or better:* 25 to 35.

actual size: 30.6 mm

Availability in circulated grades: *AG-3 to AU-58:* These are extremely common, mostly in medium grades.

Characteristics of striking: This issue is usually seen with some lightness.

Proofs: Approximately 28 examples have been certified.

G-4	VG-8	F-12	VF-20	EF-40	AU-50
$55	$75	$100	$145	$200	$350
MS-60	**MS-63**	**MS-65**	**PF-60**	**PF-63**	**PF-65**
$625	$1,350	$8,750	$8,500	$13,500	$30,000

1854-O

Circulation-strike mintage: 5,240,000

Availability in Mint State: This issue is among the most often seen Mint State Liberty Seated half dollars as ranked by Wiley and Bugert. *MS-60 to 62:* 140 to 174. *MS-63:* 75 to 90. *MS-64:* 50 to 65. *MS-65 or better:* 25 to 35.

actual size: 30.6 mm

Availability in circulated grades: *AG-3 to AU-58:* These are very common and are easily available in any grade desired.

Characteristics of striking: This issue is usually seen with some lightness.

Notes: From lot 1861 of the Louis E. Eliasberg Collection: "Under magnification this is one of the most curious Liberty Seated half dollar obverse dies we have ever seen. The date region below the base of Liberty has numerous raised and cross-hatched die finish lines, giving the entire area a virtually three-dimensional background rather than usual plane surface." In actuality, two obverse dies have this characteristic.[42]

Some were sent to China, as John Frost has seen two with chopmarks.[43]

WB-1 through 59 with 42 obverse and 29 reverse dies.

G-4	VG-8	F-12	VF-20	EF-40	AU-50	MS-60	MS-63	MS-65
$55	$75	$100	$145	$200	$350	$650	$1,350	$6,500

1855, 1855 Over 1854

Circulation-strike mintage: Portion of 1855 mintage

Proof mintage: *1–2*

Availability in Mint State: In 2014 the Eugene H. Gardner Sale featured examples of this coin in MS-66 and MS-65. *MS-60 to 62:* 5 to 7. *MS-63:* 3 to 5. *MS-64:* 2 or 3. *MS-65 or better:* 2 or 3.[44]

actual size: 30.6 mm

Detail of the Overdate.

Availability in circulated grades: *VF-20 to AU-58:* There are several dozen or more of these known.

Characteristics of striking: This issue is usually sharp. The overdate feature diminishes in sharpness with die wear; cherrypick for an early die state showing this feature clearly.

Proofs: 1855, 1855 Over 1854 Proofs were sold as 1855 Proofs. In 2014 the Eugene H. Gardner Sale featured an example of this coin in PF-65 (ex Norweb). No examples have been certified.

Notes: The overdate feature consists of the crossbar of the 4 being visible within the lower part of the 5, and with some traces of the vertical element as well. This same die was later used for circulation strikes. Randy Wiley and Bill Bugert report that three different circulation strike dies are known of the 1855, 1855 Over 1854. *Cherrypickers' Guide to Rare Die Varieties* lists this as FS-50-1855-301. Dozens are known in circulated grades, but only 10 to 15 Mint State coins exist.

G-4	VG-8	F-12	VF-20	EF-40	AU-50
$85	$125	$200	$375	$500	$1,200
MS-60	**MS-63**	**MS-65**	**PF-60**	**PF-63**	**PF-65**
$2,250	$4,000	$12,500	$10,000	$22,000	$60,000

1855

Circulation-strike mintage: 759,500

Proof mintage: *15–20*

Availability in Mint State: In 2014 the Eugene H. Gardner Sale featured an example of this coin in MS-66. *MS-60 to 62:* 50 to 65. *MS-63:* 20 to 25. *MS-64:* 10 to 14. *MS-65 or better:* 3 to 5.[45]

actual size: 30.6 mm

Availability in circulated grades: *AG-3 to AU-58:* 8,000 to 10,000.

Characteristics of striking: This issue is usually seen with some areas of lightness.

Proofs: At least one was struck in aluminum in an era in which this was a semi-precious metal. The coin has a reeded edge, and is now held by Princeton University.[46] Estimates of surviving pieces have varied widely. Approximately nine examples have been certified.

G-4	VG-8	F-12	VF-20	EF-40	AU-50
$55	$75	$100	$145	$250	$450

MS-60	MS-63	MS-65	PF-60	PF-63	PF-65
$950	$1,750	$10,000	$7,500	$12,500	$35,000

1855-O

Circulation-strike mintage: 3,688,000

Availability in Mint State: This issue is among the most often seen Mint State Liberty Seated half dollars as ranked by Wiley and Bugert. *MS-60 to 62:* 125 to 160. *MS-63:* 75 to 90. *MS-64:* 45 to 60. *MS-65 or better:* 35 to 45.

actual size: 30.6 mm

Availability in circulated grades: *AG-3 to AU-58:* These are common, mostly in medium grades.

Characteristics of striking: Striking of this issue varies, as might be expected from such a large mintage, but sharp coins can be found.

Notes: WB-1 through 19 with 18 obverse and 16 reverse dies.

O Over Horizontal O Mintmark: WB-102; *Cherrypickers' Guide to Rare Die Varieties* lists this as FS-50-1855o-501. This variety is fairly scarce.

G-4	VG-8	F-12	VF-20	EF-40	AU-50	MS-60	MS-63	MS-65
$55	$75	$100	$145	$250	$350	$650	$1,500	$6,500

1855-S

Circulation-strike mintage: 129,950

Proof mintage: _2–3_

actual size: 30.6 mm

Availability in Mint State: The Pryor MS-66 may be the finest example of this issue. In 2014 the Eugene H. Gardner Sale featured an example of this coin in MS-61. *MS-60 to 62:* 1. *MS-63:* 0 or 1. *MS-64:* 0 or 1. *MS-65 or better:* 1.

Availability in circulated grades: *AG-3 to AU-58:* These are rare in circulated grades. They are usually well-worn, and many have problems.

Characteristics of striking: This issue is usually well struck, though LIBERTY is weak up to and including the VF grade. Die states vary due to relapping.

Proofs: It seems that a die was extensively polished (to the extent that the elbow drapery was removed) and used to strike Proofs, one of which was sent to the Mint Cabinet in 1855.

Notes: The size of mintmarks on half dollars of the 1850s and 1860s was noticed at length by Augustus G. Heaton in his 1893 treatise, *Mint Marks*. Concerning the San Francisco coinage of the Liberty Seated type, Heaton noted the rare nature of the 1855-S, 1857-S, and, especially, the 1878-S.[47]

An article by David Helfer, "1855-S half dollars in the China Trade," *Gobrecht Journal*, July 1993, included this: "It is my opinion that in all probability a substantial number of these pieces were shipped to China to purchase goods in the China trade. In the Far East these coins would have been viewed as merely bullion and traded to the Chinese by American ship captains." Four examples of counterstamped 1855-S half dollars were illustrated.

WB-1 through 4 with four obverse and two reverse dies.

G-4	VG-8	F-12	VF-20	EF-40	AU-50
$525	$1,250	$1,500	$2,500	$4,000	$7,000

MS-60	MS-63	MS-65	PF-60	PF-63	PF-65
$35,000	$55,000			$175,000	$450,000

1856–1866, Variety 1 Resumed, With Weight Standard of Variety 2

The arrowheads were dropped in 1856, but the reduced weight remained the same. The general appearance of this Type 1s the same as the 1839–1853 with-drapery type; only the weight is different.

Designed by: Christian Gobrecht.

Specifications: *Composition:* 90 percent silver, 10 percent copper. *Diameter:* 30.6 mm. *Weight:* 192 grains (12.44 grams). *Edge:* Reeded.

1856

Circulation-strike mintage: 938,000

Proof mintage: *20–30*

Availability in Mint State: In 2015 the Eugene H. Gardner Sale featured examples of this coin in MS-68 and MS-65 (2). *MS-60 to 62:* 120 to 160. *MS-63:* 55 to 70. *MS-64:* 35 to 45. *MS-65 or better:* 10 to 14.

actual size: 30.6 mm

Availability in circulated grades: *AG-3 to AU-58:* These are common, mostly in medium grades.

Characteristics of striking: This issue is usually sharply struck.

Proofs: On the reverse the leftmost set of vertical stripes has been somewhat amateurishly adjusted in an effort to remove the center dot. This identical reverse die was used to coin 1857 Proof half dollars as well. Approximately 35 examples have been certified.

G-4	VG-8	F-12	VF-20	EF-40	AU-50
$55	$75	$100	$145	$200	$350
MS-60	MS-63	MS-65	PF-60	PF-63	PF-65
$675	$1,500	$6,000	$4,000	$8,500	$25,000

1856-O

Circulation-strike mintage: 2,658,000

Availability in Mint State: In 2015 the Eugene H. Gardner Sale featured examples of this coin in MS-66 and MS-61. *MS-60 to 62:* 80 to 110. *MS-63:* 35 to 45. *MS-64:* 30 to 40. *MS-65 or better:* 12 to 15.[48]

actual size: 30.6 mm

Availability in circulated grades: *AG-3 to AU-58:* These are common, mostly in medium grades.

Characteristics of striking: This issue is usually well struck, but there are many exceptions.

Notes: WB-1 through 19 with 12 obverse and 10 reverse dies.

G-4	VG-8	F-12	VF-20	EF-40	AU-50	MS-60	MS-63	MS-65
$55	$75	$100	$145	$200	$350	$675	$1,250	$5,500

1856-S

Circulation-strike mintage: 211,000

Availability in Mint State: In 2015 the Eugene H. Gardner Sale featured an example of this coin in MS-65. *MS-60 to 62:* 1 or 2. *MS-63:* 1. *MS-64:* 1. *MS-65 or better:* 1.

actual size: 30.6 mm

Availability in circulated grades: *AG-3 to AU-58:* These are scarce and are usually well worn. This is a key issue in the series.

Characteristics of striking: This issue is usually sharply struck.

Notes: One variety from a relapped obverse die lacks drapery and is rare. All have Large S mintmarks. At the time of coinage, virtually all 1856-S half dollars were placed into circulation, with many going to China where they were melted. WB-1 through 6 with three obverse and three reverse dies.

G-4	VG-8	F-12	VF-20	EF-40	AU-50	MS-60	MS-63	MS-65
$125	$200	$350	$500	$1,150	$2,250	$6,000	$13,000	

1857

Circulation-strike mintage: 1,988,000

Proof mintage: *30–50*

Availability in Mint State: In 2014 and 2015 the Eugene H. Gardner Sale featured examples of this coin in MS-66 and MS-65. *MS-60 to* *62:* 120 to 160. *MS-63:* 55 to 70. *MS-64:* 35 to 45. *MS-65 or better:* 8 to 12.

actual size: 30.6 mm

Availability in circulated grades: *AG-3 to AU-58:* These are very common, mostly in medium grades.

Characteristics of striking: Striking of this issue varies, but they are usually light in areas. Well-struck coins can be found.

Proofs: Approximately 80 examples have been certified.

G-4	VG-8	F-12	VF-20	EF-40	AU-50
$55	$75	$100	$145	$200	$350
MS-60	**MS-63**	**MS-65**	**PF-60**	**PF-63**	**PF-65**
$600	$1,250	$4,750	$3,000	$4,500	$20,000

1857-O

Circulation-strike mintage: 818,000

Availability in Mint State: Considering its fairly generous mintage, the 1856-O is surprisingly rare in Mint State. In 2014 the Eugene H. Gardner Sale featured an example of this coin in MS-64. *MS-60 to 62:* 20 to 25. *MS-63:* 8 to 12. *MS-64:* 6 to 8. *MS-65 or better:* 2 or 3.

actual size: 30.6 mm

Availability in circulated grades: *AG-3 to AU-58:* These are scarcer than their mintage might suggest. They are mostly found in medium grades.

Characteristics of striking: Striking of this issue ranges from sharp to with light areas.

Notes: WB-1 through 7 with six obverse and three reverse dies.

G-4	VG-8	F-12	VF-20	EF-40	AU-50	MS-60	MS-63	MS-65
$55	$75	$100	$175	$275	$525	$1,650	$4,000	$12,500

1857-S

Circulation-strike mintage: 158,000

Availability in Mint State: The James Bennett Pryor Sale in 1996 featured an example of this coin in MS-65. In 2014 the Eugene H. Gardner Sale featured an

actual size: 30.6 mm

example of this coin in MS-66. *MS-60 to 62:* 6 to 9. *MS-63:* 3 to 5. *MS-64:* 3 to 5. *MS-65 or better:* 2.

Availability in circulated grades: *AG-3 to AU-58:* These are scarce in all grades. They are usually seen in very low grades or EF and AU; an anomaly.[49]

Characteristics of striking: Striking of this issue varies, but they are usually sharp.

Notes: This issue has both Medium and Large S mintmarks. WB-1 through 4 with four obverse and three reverse dies.

G-4	VG-8	F-12	VF-20	EF-40	AU-50	MS-60	MS-63	MS-65
$185	$250	$350	$525	$1,350	$2,000	$4,500	$12,500	$35,000

Reverse Hub Change of 1858

In 1858 a minor change was made to the reverse hub. This was explained by David W. Lange in "The Transitional 1858 Half Dollar" in the *Gobrecht Journal*, March 1982. The easiest way to tell the difference between Type 1, used since 1842, and Type 2, introduced in 1858, is by examining the L in HALF. "The base of the L will extend only a short distance from the upright on Type 1 coins, while Type 2 pieces will show the base extending further from the upright and well beyond the top serif of the L."

1858 Type 1: Philadelphia Mint: 1858, 1859; New Orleans Mint: 1858–1860; San Francisco Mint: 1858–1862, 1864.

1858 Type 2: Philadelphia Mint: 1858–1865; New Orleans Mint: 1860, 1861; San Francisco Mint: 1862–1866.

Detail of the Type 1 Hub.   Detail of the Type 2 Hub.

1858

Circulation-strike mintage: 4,225,700

Proof mintage: *300+*

Availability in Mint State: *MS-60 to 62:* 170 to 200. *MS-63:* 90 to 120. *MS-64:* 60 to 80. *MS-65 or better:* 25 to 35.

actual size: 30.6 mm

Availability in circulated grades: *AG-3 to AU-58:* These are very common, mostly in medium grades.

Characteristics of striking: This issue is usually light in some areas, but sharp coins can be found.

Proofs: Approximately 210 coins were made for inclusion in silver Proof sets. Additional pieces were possibly made. Many seeking a run of Proof Liberty Seated half dollars start their sets with this year. *PF-60 to 62:* 75 to 90. *PF-63:* 40 to 50. *PF-64:* 25 to 30. *PF-65 or better:* 7 to 9.

Notes: One variety from a relapped obverse die lacks drapery. The 1858 with the Type 2 hub reverse was thought to be rare, but today is considered just slightly scarce as many collectors have searched for it. Not much attention has been given to it, however.[50]

G-4	VG-8	F-12	VF-20	EF-40	AU-50
$55	$75	$100	$145	$200	$350

MS-60	MS-63	MS-65	PF-60	PF-63	PF-65
$600	$1,250	$5,000	$1,400	$2,250	$6,500

1858-O

Circulation-strike mintage: 7,294,000

Availability in Mint State: In 2014 the Eugene H. Gardner Sale featured an example of this coin in MS-66. *MS-60 to 62:* 75 to 95. *MS-63:* 30 to 40. *MS-64:* 15 to 20. *MS-65 or better:* 3 or 4.[51]

actual size: 30.6 mm

Availability in circulated grades: *AG-3 to AU-58:* This is one of the most common issues of the era. They are mostly in medium grades.

Characteristics of striking: Striking of this issue ranges from sharp, which is usually the case, to with light areas.

Notes: One variety from a relapped obverse die lacks drapery. This issue has the Type 1 reverse hub. WB-1 through 41 with 24 obverse and 22 reverse dies. Many repunched and misplaced date varieties exist.

G-4	VG-8	F-12	VF-20	EF-40	AU-50	MS-60	MS-63	MS-65
$55	$75	$100	$145	$200	$350	$600	$1,250	$8,500

1858-S

Circulation-strike mintage: 476,000

Availability in Mint State: In 2015 the Eugene H. Gardner Sale featured examples of this coin in MS-66, MS-65, and MS-64. *MS-60 to 62:* 12 to 14.

actual size: 30.6 mm

MS-63: 8 to 10. *MS-64:* 4 to 6. *MS-65 or better:* 2 or 3.[52]

Availability in circulated grades: *AG-3 to AU-58:* These are scarce and are usually seen well worn.

Characteristics of striking: This issue is usually sharply struck.

Notes: This issue has both Large and Medium S mintmarks. WB-1 through 14 with ten obverse and two reverse dies.

G-4	VG-8	F-12	VF-20	EF-40	AU-50	MS-60	MS-63	MS-65
$75	$100	$150	$250	$400	$675	$2,250	$4,500	$13,500

1859

Circulation-strike mintage: 747,200

Proof mintage: 800

Availability in Mint State: In 2015 the Eugene H. Gardner Sale featured an example of this coin in MS-67. *MS-60 to 62:* 75 to 90.

actual size: 30.6 mm

MS-63: 30 to 40. *MS-64:* 20 to 25. *MS-65 or better:* 12 to 15.

Availability in circulated grades: *AG-3 to AU-58:* These are slightly scarce, mostly in medium grades.

Characteristics of striking: This issue is typically seen with light areas, but sharp coins can be found.

Proofs: Many of these coins were unsold and were probably spent. *PF-60 to 62:* 250 to 300. *PF-63:* 140 to 170. *PF-64:* 80 to 100. *PF-65 or better:* 50 to 65.

G-4	VG-8	F-12	VF-20	EF-40	AU-50
$55	$75	$100	$145	$200	$350

MS-60	MS-63	MS-65	PF-60	PF-63	PF-65
$600	$1,250	$5,000	$1,150	$1,600	$5,500

1859-O

**Circulation-strike
mintage: 2,834,000**

actual size: 30.6 mm

**Availability in Mint
State:** In 2015 the
Eugene H. Gardner
Sale featured an example
of this coin in MS-66.
MS-60 to 62: 70 to 90.
MS-63: 30 to 40. *MS-64:*
35 to 32. *MS-65 or better:* 10 to 14.

Availability in circulated grades: *AG-3 to AU-58:* These are very common, mostly in medium grades.

Characteristics of striking: This issue is often very sharp, but there are many exceptions.

Notes: Some coins of this issue have partial drapery due to relapping of the obverse die. WB-1 through 16 with 12 obverse and 13 reverse dies, including interesting repunched-date and misplaced-date varieties.

G-4	VG-8	F-12	VF-20	EF-40	AU-50	MS-60	MS-63	MS-65
$55	$75	$100	$165	$200	$350	$650	$2,000	$8,000

1859-S

**Circulation-strike
mintage: 566,000**

actual size: 30.6 mm

**Availability in Mint
State:** In 2015 the
Eugene H. Gardner
Sale featured an example
of this coin in MS-68.
MS-60 to 62: 40 to 50.
MS-63: 20 to 25. *MS-64:*
18 to 22. *MS-65 or better:* 12 to 16.

Availability in circulated grades: *AG-3 to AU-58:* These are quite scarce, however, they are the most available San Francisco half dollar up to this point in time.

Characteristics of striking: This issue is usually sharply struck.

Notes: This issue has both Large and Medium S mintmarks. It is probable that most San Francisco half dollars of this era including the 1859-S were used in the China trade. In this year the San Francisco Mint struck 20,000 Liberty Seated dollars for this purpose (see listing for the 1859-S silver dollar in chapter 9). WB-1 through 8 with six obverse and seven reverse dies.

G-4	VG-8	F-12	VF-20	EF-40	AU-50	MS-60	MS-63	MS-65
$60	$100	$150	$200	$325	$700	$1,350	$3,500	$7,500

1860

Circulation-strike mintage: 302,700

Proof mintage: 1,000

actual size: 30.6 mm

Availability in Mint State: In 2014 the Eugene H. Gardner Sale featured an example of this coin in MS-67. *MS-60 to 62:* 75 to 90. *MS-63:* 30 to 40. *MS-64:* 25 to 32. *MS-65 or better:* 10 to 14.

Availability in circulated grades: *AG-3 to AU-58:* These are scarce in circulated grades.

Characteristics of striking: This issue is usually sharply struck.

Proofs: Many Proofs of this year were placed into circulation. *PF-60 to 62:* 270 to 320. *PF-63:* 140 to 170. *PF-64:* 80 to 100. *PF-65 or better:* 30 to 40.

G-4	VG-8	F-12	VF-20	EF-40	AU-50
$60	$75	$100	$145	$225	$400
MS-60	**MS-63**	**MS-65**	**PF-60**	**PF-63**	**PF-65**
$725	$1,450	$5,000	$750	$1,600	$5,000

1860-O

Circulation-strike mintage: 1,290,000

actual size: 30.6 mm

Availability in Mint State: A few coins of this issue are highly prooflike. Christie's auctioned 15 Mint State coins in September 1991. In 2014 the Eugene H. Gardner Sale featured an example of this coin in MS-66. *MS-60 to 62:* 120 to 140. *MS-63:* 55 to 70. *MS-64:* 30 to 40. *MS-65 or better:* 9 to 12.

Availability in circulated grades: *AG-3 to AU-58:* These are common in circulated grades.

Characteristics of striking: Striking of this issue ranges from sharp to with some weakness.

Notes: WB-1 through 12 with seven obverse and seven reverse dies.

G-4	VG-8	F-12	VF-20	EF-40	AU-50	MS-60	MS-63	MS-65
$55	$75	$100	$150	$225	$350	$700	$1,300	$5,000

1860-S

Circulation-strike mintage: 472,000

Availability in Mint State: In 2014 and 2015 the Eugene H. Gardner Sale featured examples of this coin in MS-64 and MS-63. *MS-60 to 62:* 35 to 45. *MS-63:* 20 to 25. *MS-64:* 13 to 18. *MS-65 or better:* 2 or 3.

actual size: 30.6 mm

Availability in circulated grades: *AG-3 to AU-58:* These are scarce, usually seen in lower grades. As a rule, San Francisco coins are on average a grade level or two below Philadelphia coins.

Characteristics of striking: This issue is usually sharply struck.

Notes: This issue has both Large and Medium S mintmarks. WB-1 through 2 with two obverse and two reverse dies. These dies were used in two pairs in the press.

G-4	VG-8	F-12	VF-20	EF-40	AU-50	MS-60	MS-63	MS-65
$55	$100	$150	$200	$350	$550	$1,650	$5,000	

1861

Circulation-strike mintage: 2,887,400

Proof mintage: 1,000

Availability in Mint State: This issue is among the most often seen Mint State Liberty Seated half dollars as ranked by Wiley and Bugert. *MS-60 to 62:* 225 to 300. *MS-63:* 120 to 150. *MS-64:* 80 to 110. *MS-65 or better:* 50 to 65.

actual size: 30.6 mm

Availability in circulated grades: *AG-3 to AU-58:* These are very common in circulated grades.

Characteristics of striking: Striking of this issue varies, but most are sharp.

Proofs: Many Proofs were placed into circulation. Although 1,000 were minted, probably fewer than 500 were actually distributed. This is by far the rarest Proof of the decade. *PF-60 to 62:* 90 to 120. *PF-63:* 70 to 85. *PF-64:* 65 to 80. *PF-65 or better:* 10 to 15.

G-4	VG-8	F-12	VF-20	EF-40	AU-50
$55	$75	$100	$145	$250	$400
MS-60	**MS-63**	**MS-65**	**PF-60**	**PF-63**	**PF-65**
$600	$1,250	$5,000	$750	$1,600	$5,000

1861-O, Confederate States of America, Original

Mintage: Portion of 1861-O mintage

actual size: 30.6 mm

Availability in circulated grades: Four exist, VF and EF being the typical grades. Examples were offered by Heritage Auctions in January 2015 and Stack's Bowers Galleries in March 2015, each described with history. Tradition has it that four were struck—one went to an officer of the Confederacy, another to B.F. Taylor of the New Orleans Mint, another to Dr. Ames of New Orleans, and another to Professor Biddle of the University of Louisiana. However, Nancy Oliver and Richard Kelly discovered a document stating that another went to Augustas Heinrich Marcus Peterson, engraver of the Confederate reverse die.[53] Four are known today, one of them said to have been owned by CSA President Jefferson Davis. Once again, facts are scarce.

G-4	VG-8	F-12	VF-20	EF-40	AU-50	MS-60	MS-63	MS-65
			$1,500,000					

1861-O, Confederate States of America, Restrike

Circulation-strike mintage: Portion of 1861-O mintage

actual size: 30.6 mm

Availability in Mint State: Mint State coins are usually seen. Grading is done by the reverse as the obverse is always slightly flattened and shows wear. An estimated 400 to 450 exist, most of which have Mint State reverses. Five of these were made from the 1861-O half dollar, WB-102, with the die crack from the nose.[54]

Availability in circulated grades: Circulated grades are in the minority for these coins.

Characteristics of striking: This issue has light areas on the obverse.

Notes: These are also known as the "Scott Restrike." In 1879, J.W. Scott & Co. advertised for and subsequently purchased 500 genuine 1861-O half dollars. He then routed the center of the reverse of each and struck the coins with the original reverse CSA die.

G-4	VG-8	F-12	VF-20	EF-40	AU-50	MS-60	MS-63	MS-65
			$6,500	$7,500				

1861-O

Circulation-strike mintage: 2,532,633

Availability in Mint State: This issue is among the most often seen Mint State Liberty Seated half dollars as ranked by Wiley and Bugert. In 2014 the

actual size: 30.6 mm

Eugene H. Gardner Sale featured an example of this coin in MS-65. *MS-60 to 62:* 110 to 130. *MS-63:* 55 to 70. *MS-64:* 30 to 40. *MS-65 or better:* 15 to 20.

Availability in circulated grades: *AG-3 to AU-58:* These are very common in circulated grades.

Characteristics of striking: Striking of this issue varies.

Proofs: Over the years there have been dozens of auction listings for Proofs, these being special strikings with mirror-like surfaces.

Notes: The coinage of the 1861-O half dollar is historically interesting. In essence, 330,000 pieces were minted under Union auspices, 1,020,000 additional pieces when the facility was controlled by the State of Louisiana from February 1 to March 24, and a final production of 1,212,000 under control of the Confederate States of America starting on March 25 (some of the last issues have a distinctive die crack on the obverse to the bridge of Liberty's nose; see below).[55] One variety from a relapsed obverse die lacks drapery.

Cracked obverse die used on the CSA half dollar: WB-102; *Cherrypickers' Guide to Rare Die Varieties* lists this as FS-50-1861o-401. There is a die crack extending from Liberty's nose to the border; the same die used to coin 1861 Confederate States of America half dollars (with the distinctive CSA reverse). These are very plentiful in high-circulated grades and in low Mint State levels, but they are only a small minority of the overall population of surviving 1861-O half dollars. Many of these were found in the SS *Republic* treasure.

G-4	VG-8	F-12	VF-20	EF-40	AU-50	MS-60	MS-63	MS-65
$85	$90	$150	$225	$500	$900	$1,500	$3,500	$7,500

1861-S

Circulation-strike mintage: 939,500

Availability in Mint State: In 2014 the Eugene H. Gardner Sale featured an example of this coin in MS-66. *MS-60 to 62:* 30 to 40. *MS-63:* 18 to 22. *MS-64:* 15 to 20. *MS-65 or better:* 5 to 7.

actual size: 30.6 mm

Availability in circulated grades: *AG-3 to AU-58:* These are slightly scarce, usually in lower grades. John J. Ford Jr., gave this account:

> About 1942 the Stack's dealership [Joe and Morton Stack] in New York City bought a tremendous hoard of Liberty Seated half dollars. These were somewhat oxidized and were said to have been dug up in Guatemala. Perhaps they were buried during the Civil War. Dates ranged from 1853 to about 1864. I remember that there were a lot of San Francisco coins, especially 1861-S, but there was no 1855-S. I studied the lot carefully and was the first, I believe, to notice that the S mintmarks from this era came in three different sizes. These coins were retailed to customers, including in price lists I wrote in 1942.[56]

Characteristics of striking: This issue is usually seen with some touches of lightness but is generally good overall.

Notes: This issue has both Large and Medium S mintmarks. WB-1 through 11 with six obverse and five reverse dies.

G-4	VG-8	F-12	VF-20	EF-40	AU-50	MS-60	MS-63	MS-65
$65	$75	$125	$200	$450	$750	$1,200	$3,250	$25,000

1862

Circulation-strike mintage: 253,000

Proof mintage: 550

Availability in Mint State: In 2015 the Eugene H. Gardner Sale featured an example of this coin in MS-66. *MS-60 to 62:* 40 to 50. *MS-63:* 20 to 25. *MS-64:* 15 to 20. *MS-65 or better:* 8 to 12.

actual size: 30.6 mm

Availability in circulated grades: *AG-3 to AU-58:* These are scarce in circulated grades.

Characteristics of striking: This issue is usually sharply struck.

Proofs: *PF-60 to 62:* 160 to 180. *PF-63:* 90 to 120. *PF-64:* 65 to 80. *PF-65 or better:* 25 to 30.

G-4	VG-8	F-12	VF-20	EF-40	AU-50
$100	$150	$200	$285	$500	$650

MS-60	MS-63	MS-65	PF-60	PF-63	PF-65
$1,250	$2,000	$6,500	$750	$1,600	$5,000

1862-S

Circulation-strike mintage: 1,352,000

actual size: 30.6 mm

Availability in Mint State: In 2015 the Eugene H. Gardner Sale featured an example of this coin in MS-66. *MS-60 to 62:* 70 to 90. *MS-63:* 30 to 40. *MS-64:* 25 to 32. *MS-65 or better:* 2 or 3.

Availability in circulated grades: *AG-3 to AU-58:* These are slightly scarce in circulated grades.

Characteristics of striking: This issue is usually sharply struck; Wiley and Bugert reported no exceptions to this.

Notes: This issue has Large, Medium, and Small S mintmarks. WB-1 through 6 with five obverse and five reverse dies. The 6 in the date is often defective.

G-4	VG-8	F-12	VF-20	EF-40	AU-50	MS-60	MS-63	MS-65
$65	$90	$120	$200	$350	$500	$1,250	$2,700	$25,000

1863

Circulation-strike mintage: 503,200

Proof mintage: 460

actual size: 30.6 mm

Availability in Mint State: In 2014 the Eugene H. Gardner Sale featured an example of this coin in MS-67. *MS-60 to 62:* 100 to 125. *MS-63:* 50 to 65. *MS-64:* 32 to 38. *MS-65 or better:* 15 to 20.

Availability in circulated grades: *AG-3 to AU-58:* These are very scarce in circulated grades.

Characteristics of striking: Most coins of this issue are sharply struck.

Proofs: *PF-60 to 62:* 90 to 115. *PF-63:* 65 to 85. *PF-64:* 50 to 65. *PF-65 or better:* 35 to 50.

G-4	VG-8	F-12	VF-20	EF-40	AU-50
$100	$125	$165	$225	$350	$650

MS-60	MS-63	MS-65	PF-60	PF-63	PF-65
$1,250	$1,750	$8,000	$750	$1,600	$5,000

1863-S

Circulation-strike mintage: 916,000

Availability in Mint State: In 2014 and 2015 the Eugene H. Gardner Sale featured examples of this coin in MS-65 and MS-64. *MS-60 to 62:* 45 to 60. *MS-63:* 25 to 32. *MS-64:* 15 to 20. *MS-65 or better:* 2.[57]

actual size: 30.6 mm

Availability in circulated grades: *AG-3 to AU-58:* These are scarce in circulated grades.

Characteristics of striking: This issue is usually sharply struck.

Notes: This issue has the Small S mintmark. WB-1 through 4 with three obverse and three reverse dies.

G-4	VG-8	F-12	VF-20	EF-40	AU-50	MS-60	MS-63	MS-65
$65	$100	$125	$225	$400	$600	$1,300	$2,500	$12,500

1864

Circulation-strike mintage: 379,100

Proof mintage: 470

Availability in Mint State: In 2014 and 2015 the Eugene H. Gardner Sale featured examples of this coin in MS-67 and MS-66. *MS-60 to 62:* 55 to 70. *MS-63:* 28 to 35. *MS-64:* 20 to 25. *MS-65 or better:* 18 to 22.

actual size: 30.6 mm

Availability in circulated grades: *AG-3 to AU-58:* These are very scarce and are usually seen in higher grades.

Characteristics of striking: Most coins of this issue are sharply struck.

Proofs: *PF-60 to 62:* 115 to 130. *PF-63:* 70 to 85. *PF-64:* 50 to 65. *PF-65 or better:* 35 to 50.

Notes:

It will be recollected that at the time of the burning of the Winthrop House and Masonic Hall, the Freemasons lost many of their gold and silver jewels. In looking over the ruins a considerable amount of silver was found, the jewels having been melted and run together. The silver was sent to the United States Mint and a number of half dollar pieces coined from it, which have been sold to the members of the different lodges, encampments, etc., for one dollar each. These, we are informed, are the only fifty cent pieces coined this year.

Boston Journal of September 23, 1864.

These are sometimes found today with engraving in the obverse field.

G-4	VG-8	F-12	VF-20	EF-40	AU-50
$100	$125	$175	$350	$550	$850

MS-60	MS-63	MS-65	PF-60	PF-63	PF-65
$1,500	$2,000	$7,500	$750	$1,600	$5,000

1864-S

Circulation-strike mintage: 658,000

Availability in Mint State: In 2014 the Eugene H. Gardner Sale featured an example of this coin in MS-66. *MS-60 to 62:* 5 to 7. *MS-63:* 1 or 2. *MS-64:* 1 or 2. *MS-65 or better:* 2.[58]

actual size: 30.6 mm

Availability in circulated grades: *AG-3 to AU-58:* These are scarce in circulated grades.

Characteristics of striking: This issue is sharp as a rule.

Notes: This issue has both Large and Small S mintmarks. WB-1 through 5 with five obverse and two reverse dies.

G-4	VG-8	F-12	VF-20	EF-40	AU-50	MS-60	MS-63	MS-65
$100	$150	$200	$285	$550	$800	$2,000	$5,000	$15,000

1865

Circulation-strike mintage: 511,400

Proof mintage: 500

Availability in Mint State: *MS-60 to 62:* 50 to 65. *MS-63:* 50 to 65. *MS-64:* 30 to 40. *MS-65 or better:* 25 to 32.

actual size: 30.6 mm

Availability in circulated grades: *AG-3 to AU-58:* These are scarce and are usually seen in higher grades.

Characteristics of striking: This issue is usually sharply struck.

Proofs: *PF-60 to 62:* 200 to 235. *PF-63:* 80 to 100. *PF-64:* 60 to 70. *PF-65 or better:* 40 to 55.

Notes: Some coins of this issue have the drapery partially or completely missing due to die relapping.

Doubled Date: WB-102 shows traces of all four digits of the undertype. The first impression was punched slanting slightly down to the right and was then corrected. *Cherrypickers' Guide to Rare Die Varieties* lists this as FS-50-1865-301.

G-4	VG-8	F-12	VF-20	EF-40	AU-50
$125	$150	$175	$300	$650	$1,000

MS-60	MS-63	MS-65	PF-60	PF-63	PF-65
$2,000	$2,500	$5,500	$750	$1,600	$5,000

1865-S

Circulation-strike mintage: 675,000

Availability in Mint State: In 2015 the Eugene H. Gardner Sale featured an example of this coin in MS-66. *MS-60 to 62:* 8 to 11. *MS-63:* 5 to 8. *MS-64:* 4 to 6. *MS-65 or better:* 1 or 2.

actual size: 30.6 mm

Availability in circulated grades: *AG-3 to AU-58:* These are very scarce in circulated grades.

Characteristics of striking: This issue is generally well struck, though some are lightly struck on the eagle's left leg.

Notes: This issue has both the Small wide and Small thin S mintmarks. WB-1 through 9 with seven obverse and eight reverse dies.

G-4	VG-8	F-12	VF-20	EF-40	AU-50	MS-60	MS-63	MS-65
$125	$155	$200	$300	$600	$850	$2,500	$4,500	$30,000

1866,
No Motto

Proof mintage: 1

Proof: Only one is known.

Notes: This coin is housed in the National Numismatic Collection at the Smithsonian

actual size: 30.6 mm

Institution in Washington, D.C. For the story of this coin see *Notes* under the 1866, No Motto, quarter dollar in chapter 7.

1866-S,
No Motto

Circulation-strike mintage: 60,000

Availability in Mint State: In 2015 the Eugene H. Gardner Sale featured an example of this coin in MS-65. *MS-60 to 62:* 3 or 4.

actual size: 30.6 mm

MS-63: 1 or 2. *MS-64:* 1 or 2. *MS-65 or better:* 1 or 2.

Availability in circulated grades: *AG-3 to AU-58:* These are rare in any grade, though EF and AU coins are particularly elusive.

Characteristics of striking: This issue is usually sharply struck.

Notes: From 1866-S to 1870-S all issues have a Small S mintmark. Mintage figures for 1866 were not broken down, and attributions of San Francisco Mint silver and gold issues into with-motto and without-motto figures are guesswork.

WB-1 from a single pair of dies.

From the September 15–17, 1885, W. Elliot Woodward's Seventy-Eighth Sale of the Randall Collection, number two, Lot 664: "Without the motto. Condition much better than usual. Only one Uncirculated specimen known."

G-4	VG-8	F-12	VF-20	EF-40	AU-50	MS-60	MS-63	MS-65
$550	$750	$900	$1,250	$2,300	$3,500	$10,000	$17,500	$70,000

1866–1873, Motto
Above Eagle (Variety 4)

Part way through the year 1866 the motto IN GOD WE TRUST was added to the reverse above the eagle. Some other minor changes to the reverse were made as well. The weight was unchanged.

Designed by: Christian Gobrecht. The motto was added by someone on the Mint staff.

Specifications: *Composition:* 90 percent silver, 10 percent copper. *Diameter:* 30.6 mm. *Weight:* 192 grains (12.44 grams). *Edge:* Reeded.

1866, With Motto

Circulation-strike mintage: 744,900

Proof mintage: 725

Availability in Mint State: In 2014 and 2015 the Eugene H. Gardner Sale featured examples of this coin in MS-67 and

actual size: 30.6 mm

MS-66. *MS-60 to 62:* 50 to 65. *MS-63:* 25 to 32. *MS-64:* 20 to 25. *MS-65 or better:* 16 to 20.

Availability in circulated grades: *AG-3 to AU-58:* These are slightly scarce, mostly in higher grades.

Characteristics of striking: This issue is usually sharply struck.

Proofs: Despite the higher mintage, Proofs of this year are no more plentiful than those of 1865 when far fewer were struck. *PF-60 to 62:* 190 to 225. *PF-63:* 80 to 100. *PF-64:* 60 to 70. *PF-65 or better:* 25 to 35.

G-4	VG-8	F-12	VF-20	EF-40	AU-50
$100	$150	$165	$185	$250	$500
MS-60	**MS-63**	**MS-65**	**PF-60**	**PF-63**	**PF-65**
$1,000	$2,000	$6,000	$700	$1,350	$3,200

1866-S, With Motto

Circulation-strike mintage: 994,000

actual size: 30.6 mm

Availability in Mint State: In 2014 and 2015 the Eugene H. Gardner Sale featured examples of this coin in MS-66 and MS-65. *MS-60 to 62:* 30 to 40. *MS-63:* 18 to 22. *MS-64:* 12 to 16. *MS-65 or better:* 4 to 6.

Availability in circulated grades: *AG-3 to AU-58:* These are slightly scarce in circulated grades.

Characteristics of striking: This issue is usually very sharply struck.

Notes: WB-2 through 10 with five obverse and five reverse dies.

G-4	VG-8	F-12	VF-20	EF-40	AU-50	MS-60	MS-63	MS-65
$65	$100	$165	$225	$325	$600	$1,150	$2,500	$12,000

1867

Circulation-strike mintage: 449,300

Proof mintage: 625

actual size: 30.6 mm

Availability in Mint State: In 2014 and 2015 the Eugene H. Gardner Sale featured examples of this coin in MS-68, MS-66, and MS-67. *MS-60 to 62:* 30 to 40. *MS-63:* 18 to 22. *MS-64:* 13 to 16. *MS-65 or better:* 12 to 15.

Availability in circulated grades: *AG-3 to AU-58:* These are scarce and are usually seen in higher grades.

Characteristics of striking: This issue is usually sharply struck.

Proofs: *PF-60 to 62:* 190 to 225. *PF-63:* 90 to 110. *PF-64:* 60 to 70. *PF-65 or better:* 30 to 40.

Notes: Some coins of this issue have partial drapery at Liberty's elbow due to relapping.

G-4	VG-8	F-12	VF-20	EF-40	AU-50
$100	$125	$225	$285	$450	$650
MS-60	**MS-63**	**MS-65**	**PF-60**	**PF-63**	**PF-65**
$1,150	$1,750	$6,500	$700	$1,500	$3,200

1867-S

Circulation-strike mintage: 1,196,000

Availability in Mint State: In 2014 and 2015 the Eugene H. Gardner Sale featured examples of this coin in MS-66 and MS-64. *MS-60 to 62:* 20 to 25. *MS-63:* 4 to 6. *MS-64:* 4 or 5. *MS-65 or better:* 2 or 7.[59]

actual size: 30.6 mm

Availability in circulated grades: *AG-3 to AU-58:* These are common in the context of San Francisco half dollars.

Characteristics of striking: This issue is usually with some weakness, especially on the obverse.

Notes: This issue has both Large S and Small S mintmarks. WB-1 through 12 with ten obverse and six reverse dies.

G-4	VG-8	F-12	VF-20	EF-40	AU-50	MS-60	MS-63	MS-65
$65	$100	$150	$200	$325	$600	$1,250	$3,250	$12,500

1868

Circulation-strike mintage: 417,600

Proof mintage: 600

Availability in Mint State: In 2015 the Eugene H. Gardner Sale featured an example of this coin in MS-65. *MS-60 to 62:* 35 to 45. *MS-63:* 20 to 25. *MS-64:* 8 to 12. *MS-65 or better:* 5 to 7.

actual size: 30.6 mm

Availability in circulated grades: *AG-3 to AU-58:* These are scarce and are usually seen in higher grades.

Characteristics of striking: This issue is usually sharply struck.

Proofs: *PF-60 to 62:* 200 to 235. *PF-63:* 100 to 125. *PF-64:* 60 to 70. *PF-65 or better:* 30 to 40.

G-4	VG-8	F-12	VF-20	EF-40	AU-50
$100	$125	$165	$250	$425	$600
MS-60	**MS-63**	**MS-65**	**PF-60**	**PF-63**	**PF-65**
$1,100	$2,000	$7,500	$700	$1,250	$3,200

1868-S

Circulation-strike mintage: 1,160,000

Availability in Mint State: In 2015 the Eugene H. Gardner Sale featured an example of this coin in MS-66. *MS-60 to 62:* 22 to 28. *MS-63:* 12 to 15. *MS-64:* 4 to 6. *MS-65 or better:* 3 or 4.

actual size: 30.6 mm

Availability in circulated grades: *AG-3 to AU-58:* These are readily available in circulated grades.

Characteristics of striking: Striking of this issue varies, but most are fairly sharp.

Notes: WB-1 through 8 with seven obverse and six reverse dies.

G-4	VG-8	F-12	VF-20	EF-40	AU-50	MS-60	MS-63	MS-65
$75	$95	$165	$250	$350	$550	$1,250	$2,500	$12,500

1869

Circulation-strike mintage: 795,300

Proof mintage: 600

Availability in Mint State: In 2014 the Eugene H. Gardner Sale featured an example of this coin in MS-65. *MS-60 to 62:* 60 to 80. *MS-63:* 14 to 18. *MS-64:* 11 to 15. *MS-65 or better:* 9 to 12.

actual size: 30.6 mm

Availability in circulated grades: *AG-3 to AU-58:* These are common and are usually seen in higher grades.

Characteristics of striking: This issue is usually sharply struck.

Proofs: *PF-60 to 62:* 225 to 275. *PF-63:* 140 to 170. *PF-64:* 75 to 95. *PF-65 or better:* 35 to 45.

G-4	VG-8	F-12	VF-20	EF-40	AU-50
$75	$95	$165	$225	$350	$500

MS-60	MS-63	MS-65	PF-60	PF-63	PF-65
$850	$1,750	$15,000	$700	$1,250	$3,200

1869-S

Circulation-strike mintage: 656,000

Availability in Mint State: In 2014 the Eugene H. Gardner Sale featured an example of this coin in MS-66. *MS-60 to 62:* 7 to 10. *MS-63:* 3 or 4. *MS-64:* 3 or 4. *MS-65 or better:* 3 or 4.[60]

actual size: 30.6 mm

Availability in circulated grades: *AG-3 to AU-58:* These are slightly scarce in circulated grades.

Characteristics of striking: Most coins of this issue are sharp, but some show slight weakness on both sides.

Notes: Some of these coins have partial or no drapery due to relapping. WB-1 through 3 with three obverse and three reverse dies indicating the use of matched pairs. Rather than replacing only one die of a pair when it showed damage, both dies were replaced.

G-4	VG-8	F-12	VF-20	EF-40	AU-50	MS-60	MS-63	MS-65
$75	$95	$165	$225	$350	$525	$1,000	$3,000	$7,500

1870

Circulation-strike mintage: 633,900

Proof mintage: 1,000

Availability in Mint State: In 2014 and 2015 the Eugene H. Gardner Sale featured examples of this coin in MS-67 and MS-65 (2). *MS-60 to 62:* 30 to 40. *MS-63:* 15 to 18. *MS-64:* 13 to 16. *MS-65 or better:* 6 to 8.

actual size: 30.6 mm

Availability in circulated grades: *AG-3 to AU-58:* These are common and are usually seen in higher grades.

Characteristics of striking: This issue is usually sharply struck.

Proofs: Microscopic concentric, circular marks can be seen in the lower areas of the fold of Liberty's skirt. Proofs of 1870 with 1,000 coined are rarer today than are those of 1869 of which 600 were made. *PF-60 to 62:* 215 to 250. *PF-63:* 130 to 155. *PF-64:* 65 to 85. *PF-65 or better:* 35 to 45.

Notes: Some coins of this issue have partial drapery due to relapping.

G-4	VG-8	F-12	VF-20	EF-40	AU-50
$75	$100	$165	$185	$350	$450
MS-60	MS-63	MS-65	PF-60	PF-63	PF-65
$850	$1,750	$8,000	$700	$1,250	$2,500

1870-CC

Circulation-strike mintage: 54,617

Availability in Mint State: These are exceedingly rare. The Pryor No-Drapery coin is MS-63. The Battle Born Collection Sale in 2013 featured an example of this coin in MS-62. In 2014 the Eugene H. Gardner Sale featured an example of this coin in MS-62. *MS-60 to 62:* 3 to 5. *MS-63:* 2. *MS-64:* 0. *MS-65 or better:* 0.

actual size: 30.6 mm

Availability in circulated grades: *AG-3 to AU-58:* This issue is a popular rarity and is the rarest of the Carson City half dollars. Probably 200 to 275 exist, most with extensive wear.

Characteristics of striking: Coins of this issue always have some areas of weakness.

Notes: Some 1870-CC half dollars lack drapery due to relapping, and as such are prooflike. WB-1 through 5 with three obverse and three reverse dies.

The reverse of this issue has the Large CC mintmark, which is normally associated with coins from the middle years of the decade. The norm for this era seems to be small or very small mintmarks that are individually punched, as can be seen on numerous issues including the dime, quarter, silver dollar, and other issues, including the later trade dollars (beginning in 1873). Small mintmarks do appear on the reverse of Carson City half dollars but not until 1873.

This is the first of the Carson City half dollars. Larry Briggs and Brian Greer rate the CC coins in this order of *descending* rarity, with respect to all grades combined: 1870-CC; 1878-CC; 1874-CC; close and debatable 1871-CC for 3rd or 4th; 1873-CC, No Arrows; 1873-CC, With Arrows; 1872-CC; 1875-CC; 1877-CC; and lastly the most available 1876-CC.[61]

G-4	VG-8	F-12	VF-20	EF-40	AU-50	MS-60	MS-63	MS-65
$1,750	$3,500	$4,500	$6,000	$12,500	$30,000		$110,000	$275,000

1870-S

Circulation-strike mintage: 1,004,000

Availability in Mint State: These are very rare. The Louis E. Eliasberg Sale in 1997 featured a prooflike example of this coin in MS-65. In 2014 the Eugene H. Gardner Sale featured an example of this coin in MS-65. *MS-60 to 62:* 12 to 15. *MS-63:* 5 to 7. *MS-64:* 4 to 6. *MS-65 or better:* 4 to 6.

actual size: 30.6 mm

Availability in circulated grades: *AG-3 to AU-58:* These are scarce, especially in higher grades.

Characteristics of striking: This issue is usually sharply struck.

Notes: Some coins of this issue lack drapery due to relapping. From the Eliasberg Collection Sale, lot 2013: "Under high-powered magnification the figure of Liberty has some of the strangest raised die marks we have ever seen. They are so extensive as to appear, in effect, like a scattering of straw or hay all across her features. . . . The marks are oriented every which way, although sometimes parallel in groups, and pairs—almost like pick-up sticks when thrown on the floor."

WB-1 through 4 with two obverse and three reverse dies.

G-4	VG-8	F-12	VF-20	EF-40	AU-50	MS-60	MS-63	MS-65
$100	$125	$165	$225	$500	$750	$2,250	$4,500	$35,000

1871

Circulation-strike mintage: 1,203,600

Proof mintage: 960

Availability in Mint State: In 2015 the Eugene H. Gardner Sale featured an example of this coin in MS-64. *MS-60 to 62:* 40 to 55. *MS-63:* 20 to 25. *MS-64:* 15 to 20. *MS-65 or better:* 6 to 9.

actual size: 30.6 mm

Availability in circulated grades: *AG-3 to AU-58:* These are slightly scarce and are usually seen in higher grades.

Characteristics of striking: This issue is usually sharp, but some have slight weakness.

Proofs: The 1871 Philadelphia Mint half dollar is more difficult to find than the mintage figure might suggest. *PF-60 to 62:* 200 to 225. *PF-63:* 120 to 145. *PF-64:* 70 to 90. *PF-65 or better:* 30 to 40.

G-4	VG-8	F-12	VF-20	EF-40	AU-50
$65	$75	$100	$125	$225	$325

MS-60	MS-63	MS-65	PF-60	PF-63	PF-65
$750	$1,300	$5,000	$700	$1,250	$3,250

1871-CC

Circulation-strike mintage: 153,950

Availability in Mint State: These are extremely rare. The 1996 James Bennett Pryor Sale contained an example of this coin in MS-62 with a prooflike obverse. The

actual size: 30.6 mm

Louis E. Eliasberg Sale in 1997 featured an example of this coin in MS-65. In 1998 the Emery May Holden Norweb Sale contained an example of this coin in MS-64. The Battle Born Collection Sale in 2013 featured an example in MS-64. In 2014 the Eugene H. Gardner Sale featured examples of this coin in MS-65 and MS-62. *MS-60 to 62:* 1 or 2. *MS-63:* 1. *MS-64:* 1. *MS-65 or better:* 2.

Availability in circulated grades: *AG-3 to AU-58:* 375 to 450 are estimated to exist, mostly with extensive wear.

Characteristics of striking: This issue is usually sharply struck, this being in great contrast to the 1870-CC.

Notes: Some coins of this issue have prooflike obverses. WB-1 through 7 with three obverse and five reverse dies.

G-4	VG-8	F-12	VF-20	EF-40	AU-50	MS-60	MS-63	MS-65
$650	$950	$1,250	$2,000	$3,750	$6,000	$30,000	$75,000	

1871-S

Circulation-strike mintage: 2,178,000

Availability in Mint State: In 2015 the Eugene H. Gardner Sale featured an example of this coin in MS-64. *MS-60 to 62:* 30 to 40. *MS-63:* 15 to 20. *MS-64:* 4 to 6. *MS-65 or better:* 2 or 3.

actual size: 30.6 mm

Availability in circulated grades: *VF-20 to AU-58:* These are slightly scarce in circulated grades.

Characteristics of striking: Striking of this issue varies. WB-101 is usually light in areas, but WB-102 is often quite sharp.

Notes: WB-1 through 9 with eight obverse and six reverse dies.

G-4	VG-8	F-12	VF-20	EF-40	AU-50	MS-60	MS-63	MS-65
$60	$75	$100	$125	$250	$325	$1,000	$2,000	$8,000

1872

Circulation-strike mintage: 880,600

Proof mintage: 950

Availability in Mint State: In 2014 and 2015 the Eugene H. Gardner Sale featured two examples of this coin in MS-65. *MS-60 to 62:* 40 to 50. *MS-63:* 18 to 25. *MS-64:* 16 to 20. *MS-65 or better:* 14 to 18.

actual size: 30.6 mm

Availability in circulated grades: *AG-3 to AU-58:* These are common and are usually seen in higher grades.

Characteristics of striking: The very slight weakness on Liberty's head is normal.

Proofs: *PF-60 to 62:* 225 to 250. *PF-63:* 130 to 155. *PF-64:* 80 to 110. *PF-65 or better:* 35 to 50.

G-4	VG-8	F-12	VF-20	EF-40	AU-50
$60	$95	$115	$150	$250	$325
MS-60	**MS-63**	**MS-65**	**PF-60**	**PF-63**	**PF-65**
$800	$1,650	$6,500	$700	$1,250	$2,500

1872-CC

**Circulation-strike
mintage: 257,000**

**Availability in Mint
State:** These are
exceedingly rare.
The Eliasberg and
Battle Born coins,
different specimens, are
both MS-63. In 2014 the

actual size: 30.6 mm

Eugene H. Gardner Sale featured an example of this coin in MS-63. *MS-60 to 62:* 0. *MS-63:* 2. *MS-64:* 0. *MS-65 or better:* 0.

Availability in circulated grades: *AG-3 to AU-58:* These are a popular Carson City issue. Probably 1,200 or so exist, mostly with extensive wear and problems.

Characteristics of striking: This issue is usually seen with some slight weakness on Liberty's head and foot. Sharp coins exist, but they are rare.

Notes: WB-1 through 9 with four obverse and five reverse dies, all with Large CC mintmarks. These dies were also used in 1870, 1871, 1873, and 1876.

G-4	VG-8	F-12	VF-20	EF-40	AU-50	MS-60	MS-63	MS-65
$350	$650	$750	$1,300	$2,500	$4,000	$25,000	$75,000	

1872-S

**Circulation-strike
mintage: 580,000**

**Availability in Mint
State:** In 2014 and 2015
the Eugene H. Gardner
Sale featured an example
of this coin in MS-67
and MS-66. *MS-60 to
62:* 14 to 16. *MS-63:* 7 to
9. *MS-64:* 2 or 3. *MS-65 or better:* 2 or 3.[62]

actual size: 30.6 mm

Availability in circulated grades: *AG-3 to AU-58:* These are scarce in all grades, especially at the EF and AU levels.

Characteristics of striking: This issue is usually sharply struck.

Notes: This issue has both Small-wide and Medium-small mintmarks. WB-1 through 5 with four obverse and three reverse dies.

G-4	VG-8	F-12	VF-20	EF-40	AU-50	MS-60	MS-63	MS-65
$75	$100	$115	$250	$450	$700	$2,150	$3,500	$13,500

1873, No Arrows, Close 3

Circulation-strike mintage: 587,000

Proof mintage: 600

actual size: 30.6 mm

Availability in Mint State: In 2014 the Eugene H. Gardner Sale featured an example of this coin in MS-65. *MS-60 to 62:* 40 to 50. *MS-63:* 25 to 32. *MS-64:* 20 to 25. *MS-65 or better:* 3 or 4.[63]

Availability in circulated grades: *AG-3 to AU-58:* These are fairly scarce and are usually seen in higher grades.

Characteristics of striking: This issue is usually seen with some lightness.

Proofs: *PF-60 to 62:* 225 to 250. *PF-63:* 135 to 160. *PF-64:* 80 to 110. *PF-65 or better:* 45 to 60.

Notes: Mintage figures are estimated. It is unlikely that all Close 3 dies were trashed when the Open 3 dies were introduced. Also see *Notes* under the Open 3.

G-4	VG-8	F-12	VF-20	EF-40	AU-50
$75	$100	$200	$225	$450	$500
MS-60	**MS-63**	**MS-65**	**PF-60**	**PF-63**	**PF-65**
$1,000	$1,500	$6,500	$700	$1,250	$2,500

1873, No Arrows, Open 3

Circulation-strike mintage: 214,200

Availability in Mint State: In 2014 the Eugene H. Gardner Sale featured an example of this coin in MS-61.

actual size: 30.6 mm

MS-60 to 62: 1 or 2. *MS-63:* 1. *MS-64:* 0. *MS-65 or better:* 0.

Availability in circulated grades: *AG-3 to AU-58:* More than 100 exist, which is enough to fill the demand. On an absolute basis this variety is scarce.[64]

Characteristics of striking: This issue is usually seen with some lightness.

Notes: WB-101. Mintage figures were estimated years ago as 587,600 Close 3 coins and 214,200 Open 3 coins from the Philadelphia Mint before arrows were added beside the date. These figures seem to have been guesses and seem to have no validity. The coins are made from four Close 3 *known* obverse dies and one Open 3 obverse. This being the case, the Close 3 dies each produced an average of 146,900 coins while the Open 3 die produced almost 70,000 more coins than this average. With a collective total of 801,800 coins of both varieties produced from five total dies, one might speculate that the actual Open 3 mintage was lower, perhaps much lower than the estimates mentioned. Beyond that it is believed that many of these were melted upon institution of the new weight standard which took effect April 1, 1873, perhaps in part accounting for the rarity and high value assigned to the variety today.

G-4	VG-8	F-12	VF-20	EF-40	AU-50	MS-60	MS-63	MS-65
$3,500	$5,000	$5,500	$6,750	$8,500	$13,500	$50,000	$100,000	

1873-CC, No Arrows

Circulation-strike mintage: 122,500

Availability in Mint State: In 2014 the Eugene H. Gardner Sale featured an example of this coin in MS-65. *MS-60 to 62:* 5 to 7. *MS-63:* 3 or 4. *MS-64:* 2 or 3. *MS-65 or better:* 2 or 3.

actual size: 30.6 mm

Availability in circulated grades: These are scarce and when seen are usually well worn. There are probably about 500 to 700 in existence.

Characteristics of striking: This issue is usually seen with some lightness.

Notes: This issue has Small mintmark letters for the first time in the series. There are also coins of this issue with Large CC mintmarks. This die was also used on certain half dollars of 1871 and 1876. WB-1 and 2 with two obverse and one reverse dies.

G-4	VG-8	F-12	VF-20	EF-40	AU-50	MS-60	MS-63	MS-65
$425	$750	$1,250	$2,250	$3,750	$6,750	$12,000	$35,000	$100,000

1873-S, No Arrows

Circulation-strike mintage: 5,000

Availability in Mint State: None are known to exist.

Availability in circulated grades: None are known to exist.

Notes: It is believed that all were melted, including one reserved for the Assay Commission meeting held in early 1874. The commissioners agreed that it would not be weighed or tested. It is possible that they knew most had been melted.

1873–1874, Arrows at Date
(Variety 5)

The Coinage Act of February 12, 1873, increased the weight of the dime, quarter, and half dollar slightly. To signify this, arrowheads were placed on each side of the date. This was done individually in the working dies, so differences in placement exist.

Designed by: Christian Gobrecht. The motto and arrows were added by someone on the Mint staff.

Specifications: *Composition:* 90 percent silver, 10 percent copper. *Diameter:* 30.6 mm. *Weight:* 192.9 grains (12.50 grams). *Edge:* Reeded.

1873,
With Arrows

Circulation-strike mintage: 1,815,200

Proof mintage: 800

Availability in Mint State: *MS-60 to 62:* 110 to 130. *MS-63:* 55 to 70. *MS-64:* 50 to 65. *MS-65 or better:* 25 to 32.

actual size: 30.6 mm

Availability in circulated grades: *AG-3 to AU-58:* These are common and are usually seen in higher grades.

Characteristics of striking: Striking of this issue varies, but sharp coins can be found.

Proofs: *PF-60 to 62:* 190 to 225. *PF-63:* 110 to 140. *PF-64:* 70 to 100. *PF-65 or better:* 20 to 30.

Notes: This issue has both large and small arrowhead varieties, one style being slightly larger than the other. One variety from a relapped obverse die lacks drapery. The arrowheads for this type were punched into the dies individually, creating many positional variations.

Quad Stripes in Shield: The Doubled-Die obverse has four instead of the normal three elements to each vertical stripe in the shield. *Cherrypickers' Guide to Rare Die Varieties* lists this as FS-50-1873-101. This variety is moderately scarce, but is not widely noticed. A similar doubling is seen on circulation-strike silver dollars of 1844 (but not Proofs of that year).

G-4	VG-8	F-12	VF-20	EF-40	AU-50
$60	$75	$100	$155	$300	$475

MS-60	MS-63	MS-65	PF-60	PF-63	PF-65
$950	$1,800	$15,000	$1,000	$2,200	$8,500

1873-CC, With Arrows

Circulation-strike mintage: 214,560

actual size: 30.6 mm

Availability in Mint State: The Battle Born Collection Sale in 2013 featured an example of this coin in MS-64. In 2014 the Eugene H. Gardner Sale featured an example of this coin in MS-64. *MS-60 to 62:* 9 to 12. *MS-63:* 1 or 2. *MS-64:* 2 or 3. *MS-65 or better:* 1 or 2.[65]

Availability in circulated grades: These are slightly scarce. Probably 1,000 or so exist, plus or minus a few. As a Carson City half dollar this issue is very popular and in great demand. Years ago Larry Briggs helped a collector assemble a hoard of these that eventually numbered 200 with Large CC and 201 with Small CC mintmarks. This group is now widely dispersed in the marketplace.[66]

Characteristics of striking: This issue is usually seen with some slight lightness.

Notes: This issue has both Large and Small CC mintmark varieties. WB-3 through 8 with five obverse and two reverse dies.

From the *Carson Daily Appeal*, Carson City, July 23, 1873: "Dies for the stamping of half-dollars and a new set of test weights came to the Mint yesterday. The new regulation half-dollar is to be something heavier than the old one; and it is to have a device indicating its weight—reversed arrow heads on each side of the date."[67]

G-4	VG-8	F-12	VF-20	EF-40	AU-50	MS-60	MS-63	MS-65
$325	$600	$800	$1,250	$2,000	$3,500	$10,000	$18,500	$55,000

1873-S, With Arrows

Circulation-strike mintage: 228,000

actual size: 30.6 mm

Availability in Mint State: The James Bennett Pryor Sale in 1996 featured an example of this coin in MS-64. In 2014 the Eugene H. Gardner Sale featured an example of this coin in MS-65. *MS-60 to 62:* 6 to 8. *MS-63:* 3 or 4. *MS-64:* 3 or 4. *MS-65 or better:* 2 or 3.[68]

Availability in circulated grades: *AG-3 to AU-58:* These range from scarce to rare and most show extensive wear.

Characteristics of striking: This issue is usually seen with some light weakness.

Notes: WB-1 from a single pair of dies.

G-4	VG-8	F-12	VF-20	EF-40	AU-50	MS-60	MS-63	MS-65
$100	$165	$200	$275	$600	$1,000	$3,500	$8,000	$35,000

1874

Circulation-strike mintage: 2,359,600
Proof mintage: 700

Availability in Mint State: This issue is among the most often seen Mint State Liberty Seated half dollars as ranked by Wiley and Bugert. *MS-60 to 62:* 130 to 160. *MS-63:* 70 to 90. *MS-64:* 50 to 70. *MS-65 or better:* 22 to 28.

actual size: 30.6 mm

Availability in circulated grades: *AG-3 to AU-58:* These are common and are usually seen in higher grades.

Characteristics of striking: Striking of this issue varies, but sharp coins can be found.

Proofs: *PF-60 to 62:* 275 to 325. *PF-63:* 155 to 185. *PF-64:* 100 to 130. *PF-65 or better:* 30 to 40.

Notes: One variety has large arrowheads punched over smaller arrowheads.[69]

In this year a number of quarters, half dollars, and trade dollars were counterstamped with the advertisement, SAGE'S / CANDY / COIN. Today these are known in VF and EF grades and are rare.

A counterstamped 1874 half dollar.

G-4	VG-8	F-12	VF-20	EF-40	AU-50
$85	$125	$200	$250	$350	$600
MS-60	**MS-63**	**MS-65**	**PF-60**	**PF-63**	**PF-65**
$1,000	$2,000	$15,000	$1,000	$2,200	$8,500

1874-CC

Circulation-strike mintage: 59,000

Availability in Mint State: It is estimated that there are 10 to 15. The Louis E. Eliasberg Sale in 1997 featured an example of this coin in MS-63/64. The 2013 Battle Born

actual size: 30.6 mm

Collection Sale featured an example of this coin in MS-64. In 2015 the Eugene H. Gardner Sale featured an example of this coin in MS-65. *MS-60 to 62:* 6 to 8. *MS-63:* 2 or 3. *MS-64:* 2 or 3. *MS-65 or better:* 1.

Availability in circulated grades: An estimated 375 to 450 exist and most are well worn.[70]

Characteristics of striking: This issue is usually sharply struck.

Notes: The arrowheads are tilted up sharply on each side of the date. WB-1 through 3 with three obverse and one reverse dies. One reverse die in a late state has a "railroad track" appearance at TE in STATES and is popular with collectors.

The mintage of the 1874-CC amounted to only 59,000 pieces, a tiny fraction of the next lowest With-Arrows coin (1873-CC, With Arrows, at 214,560). The survival of high-grade pieces was strictly a matter of rare chance.

G-4	VG-8	F-12	VF-20	EF-40	AU-50	MS-60	MS-63	MS-65
$1,350	$1,750	$2,750	$4,000	$6,500	$8,750	$16,500	$35,000	$95,000

1874-S

Circulation-strike mintage: 394,000

Availability in Mint State: The Louis E. Eliasberg Sale in 1997 featured an example of this coin in MS-66. In 2015 the Eugene H. Gardner Sale featured an

actual size: 30.6 mm

example of this coin in MS-65. *MS-60 to 62:* 20 to 25. *MS-63:* 12 to 15. *MS-64:* 7 to 9. *MS-65 or better:* 5 to 7.

Availability in circulated grades: *AG-3 to AU-58:* These are scarce in circulated grades. The 1874-S half dollar is a very popular issue.

Characteristics of striking: This issue is sharply struck.

Notes: WB-1 through 5 with three obverse and four reverse dies.

G-4	VG-8	F-12	VF-20	EF-40	AU-50	MS-60	MS-63	MS-65
$125	$200	$250	$325	$450	$750	$1,750	$3,000	$25,000

1875–1891, Variety 4 Resumed, With Weight Standard of Variety 5

In 1875 the arrowheads were discontinued, but the weight change of 1873 remained in effect.

Designed by: Christian Gobrecht. The motto was added by someone on the Mint staff.

Specifications: *Composition:* 90 percent silver, 10 percent copper. *Diameter:* 30.6 mm. *Weight:* 192.9 grains (12.50 grams). *Edge:* Reeded.

1875

Circulation-strike mintage: 6,026,800

Proof mintage: 700

Availability in Mint State: This issue is among the most often seen Mint State Liberty Seated half dollars as ranked by Wiley and

actual size: 30.6 mm

Bugert. *MS-60 to 62:* 225 to 275. *MS-63:* 130 to 160. *MS-64:* 110 to 130. *MS-65 or better:* 55 to 70.

Availability in circulated grades: *AG-3 to AU-58:* These are extremely common and are usually seen in higher grades.

Characteristics of striking: Striking of this issue varies, but cherrypicking will yield a sharp coin for no extra cost.

Proofs: *PF-60 to 62:* 190 to 225. *PF-63:* 120 to 150. *PF-64:* 75 to 110. *PF-65 or better:* 30 to 40.

G-4	VG-8	F-12	VF-20	EF-40	AU-50
$55	$75	$100	$125	$175	$275
MS-60	**MS-63**	**MS-65**	**PF-60**	**PF-63**	**PF-65**
$475	$850	$3,000	$675	$1,200	$2,500

1875-CC

Circulation-strike mintage: 1,008,000

actual size: 30.6 mm

Availability in Mint State: In 2014 and 2015 the Eugene H. Gardner Sale featured examples of this coin in MS-66 and MS-64. *MS-60 to 62:* 70 to 90. *MS-63:* 35 to 45. *MS-64:* 30 to 40. *MS-65 or better:* 7 to 9.

Availability in circulated grades: These are plentiful, the first Carson City half dollar for which this can be said. Probably 1,500 or more are known.

Characteristics of striking: This issue is usually sharp.

Notes: WB-1 through 12 with nine obverse and five reverse dies. All coins of this issue have Medium CC mintmarks.

G-4	VG-8	F-12	VF-20	EF-40	AU-50	MS-60	MS-63	MS-65
$125	$165	$275	$500	$750	$1,250	$2,000	$4,000	$8,500

1875-S

Circulation-strike mintage: 3,200,000

actual size: 30.6 mm

Availability in Mint State: This issue is among the most often seen Mint State Liberty Seated half dollars as ranked by Wiley and Bugert. *MS-60 to 62:* 300 to 375. *MS-63:* 160 to 200. *MS-64:* 130 to 160. *MS-65 or better:* 90 to 120.

Availability in circulated grades: *AG-3 to AU-58:* These are common in circulated grades.

Characteristics of striking: Most, but hardly all, coins of this issue are well struck.

Notes: This issue has both the Very Small and Micro S mintmarks. The Micro S is rare, especially in higher grades. WB-1 through 21 with 16 obverse and 15 reverse dies, but it is likely that others exist.

The Eliasberg coin, lot 2034, "has concentric raised circular marks in the figure of Liberty, particularly in the top part of the shield stripes and in the lower folds of her gown, as well as the upper reaches of her gown, and near her elbow. These are fairly well-defined traces of an incompletely finished die face and are quite rare on American coinage in general, and have been seen only a few times in the Liberty Seated half dollar series."

G-4	VG-8	F-12	VF-20	EF-40	AU-50	MS-60	MS-63	MS-65
$55	$75	$100	$125	$175	$275	$475	$850	$3,000

Reverse Hub Change of 1876

A hub modification was made in 1876. This was noticed at an early date by "Mint Mark," writing in *The Numismatist*, May 1894. After listing a few subtle points this was stated: "There is one point of difference which can be readily seen and remembered: on the old die the lower berry on the branch is in two parts and slightly open, while on the new die this berry is slender, closed and pointed, and directed more to the left."

In *The Complete Guide to Liberty Seated Half Dollars* Randall Wiley and Bill Bugert call these "varieties." The attachments on the branch are laurel buds. In the text, the authors describe the issues from 1876 onward with the reverses used.

1876 Type 1: Used prior to 1876 and continued in service for some years afterward, concurrently with Type 2. Used on circulation strikes of all mints in 1876 and 1877. Used on Proofs of 1876–1879 and 1881.

1876 Type 2: Used beginning in 1876. Used on circulation strikes of: 1876 Philadelphia, Carson City, San Francisco; 1877–1878 all mints; and 1879–1891 Philadelphia. Used on Proofs of 1877–1891.

Detail of the Type 1 Hub.   Detail of the Type 2 Hub.

1876

Circulation-strike mintage: 8,418,000

Proof mintage: 1,150

Availability in Mint State: This issue is among the most often seen Mint State Liberty Seated half dollars as ranked by Wiley and Bugert. *MS-60 to 62:*

actual size: 30.6 mm

225 to 275. *MS-63:* 140 to 170. *MS-64:* 60 to 80. *MS-65 or better:* 15 to 18.

Availability in circulated grades: *AG-3 to AU-58:* These are extremely common, usually in higher grades. In their 1993 book, Randy Wiley and Bill Bugert ranked the 1876 as the most common of all Liberty Seated half dollars.

Characteristics of striking: This issue is often seen with some slight weakness, but sharp coins can be found.

Proofs: *PF-60 to 62:* 300 to 350. *PF-63:* 155 to 185. *PF-64:* 100 to 130. *PF-65 or better:* 35 to 45.

Large Date Over Small Date: A four-digit logotype intended for the quarter was first entered in the die and then corrected.[71] Tiny traces of the earlier date can be seen in the upper interior sections of the eight and six. *Cherrypickers' Guide to Rare Die Varieties* lists this as FS-50-1876-301.

G-4	VG-8	F-12	VF-20	EF-40	AU-50
$55	$75	$100	$140	$175	$275
MS-60	MS-63	MS-65	PF-60	PF-63	PF-65
$475	$850	$3,800	$675	$1,200	$2,500

1876-CC

Circulation-strike mintage: 1,956,000

Availability in Mint State: *MS-60 to 62:* 70 to 90. *MS-63:* 35 to 45. *MS-64:* 28 to 35. *MS-65 or better:* 20 to 25.

Availability in circulated grades: These are readily available in circulated grades. Experts are divided on how many exist, but the number seems to be several thousand or more.[72]

actual size: 30.6 mm

Characteristics of striking: This issue is usually sharply struck.

Notes: This issue has Large, Medium, and Small CC mintmarks. The reverse die was also used to coin certain half dollars in 1871 and 1872. In 1876, for the first time, there were variations in the edge reed count, including 144, 152, 153, and 154. WB-1 through 42 with 29 obverse and 29 reverse dies.

G-4	VG-8	F-12	VF-20	EF-40	AU-50	MS-60	MS-63	MS-65
$125	$150	$185	$285	$550	$1,000	$1,600	$2,750	$6,500

1876-S

Circulation-strike mintage: 4,528,000

Availability in Mint State: *MS-60 to 62:* 180 to 210. *MS-63:* 80 to 110. *MS-64:* 60 to 80. *MS-65 or better:* 20 to 28.

Availability in circulated grades: *AG-3 to AU-58:* These are common in circulated grades.

actual size: 30.6 mm

Characteristics of striking: Striking of this issue varies, but some are sharp. WB-103 coins are prooflike.

Notes: WB-1 through 43 with 37 obverse and 31 reverse dies, but it is likely that others exist.

G-4	VG-8	F-12	VF-20	EF-40	AU-50	MS-60	MS-63	MS-65
$55	$65	$100	$125	$200	$275	$450	$800	$3,600

1877, 7 Over 6

Circulation-strike mintage: Portion of 1877 mintage

Availability in Mint State: In 2015 the Eugene H. Gardner Sale featured an example of this coin in MS-64. *MS-60 to 62:* 10 to 130. *MS-63:* 45 to 60. *MS-64:* 25 to 32. *MS-65 or better:* 10 to 12.

actual size: 30.6 mm

Availability in circulated grades: *AG-3 to AU-58:* These are very scarce.

Detail of Overdate.

They are only desirable in higher grades that show the subtle overdate feature and as such are not widely collected.

Characteristics of striking: This issue is usually sharply struck.

Notes: This overdate is discernible only by the trace of a 6 on top of the second 7 of the date. Certain early overdates in the Morgan-dollar series are similar in that they show traces of an earlier digit on the final digit. In the 1990s the discovery of this by F. Michael Fazzari stirred up controversy in the pages of the *Gobrecht Journal* (March 1991, July 1994, November 1994, March 1995). Overlays later confirmed that it is an overdate. This variety is listed in *Cherrypickers' Guide to Rare Die Varieties* as FS-50-1877-301.

G-4	VG-8	F-12	VF-20	EF-40	AU-50	MS-60	MS-63	MS-65
				$1,200	$2,200	$3,750	$12,000	

1877

Circulation-strike mintage: 8,304,000

Proof mintage: 510

Availability in Mint State: This issue is among the most often seen Mint State Liberty Seated half dollars as ranked by Wiley and Bugert. *MS-60 to 62:* 225 to 275. *MS-63:* 120 to 150. *MS-64:* 90 to 120. *MS-65 or better:* 70 to 90.

actual size: 30.6 mm

Availability in circulated grades: *AG-3 to AU-58:* These are extremely common, usually in higher grades.

Characteristics of striking: This issue is usually sharply struck.

Proofs: *PF-60 to 62:* 170 to 200. *PF-63:* 115 to 135. *PF-64:* 80 to 100. *PF-65 or better:* 20 to 30.

Notes: One variety from a relapped obverse die lacks drapery.

G-4	VG-8	F-12	VF-20	EF-40	AU-50
$55	$65	$100	$125	$200	$275

MS-60	MS-63	MS-65	PF-60	PF-63	PF-65
$475	$800	$4,000	$700	$1,300	$3,200

1877-CC

Circulation-strike mintage: 1,420,000

Availability in Mint State: This issue is among the most often seen Mint State Liberty Seated half dollars as ranked by Wiley and Bugert. *MS-60 to 62:*

actual size: 30.6 mm

190 to 250. *MS-63:* 110 to 130. *MS-64:* 60 to 80. *MS-65 or better:* 35 to 42.

Availability in circulated grades: Probably 3,000 or so exist.[73] This number is plentiful for a Carson City half dollar.

Characteristics of striking: This issue is usually sharp, but there are exceptions.

Notes: Wiley and Bugert have found the reed count on all to be 143, a significant change from the long-time standard of 154 used from 1870 through 1875. Small and Medium mintmark varieties are known. WB-1 through 16 with 13 obverse and 13 reverse dies.

G-4	VG-8	F-12	VF-20	EF-40	AU-50	MS-60	MS-63	MS-65
$115	$140	$165	$250	$450	$650	$1,150	$2,350	$5,500

1877-S

Circulation-strike mintage: 5,356,000

Availability in Mint State: This issue is among the most often seen Mint State Liberty Seated half dollars as ranked by Wiley and Bugert. *MS-60 to 62:*

actual size: 30.6 mm

300 to 375. *MS-63:* 170 to 210. *MS-64:* 110 to 140. *MS-65 or better:* 55 to 70.

Availability in circulated grades: *AG-3 to AU-58:* Significantly more than 10,000 exist in circulated grades; by far the most plentiful San Francisco variety of the series.

Characteristics of striking: This issue is usually sharply struck.

Notes: About a third of those seen lack drapery due to relapping. WB-1 through 40 with 31 obverse and 31 reverse dies, but it is likely that others exist. One reverse die was later used to coin 1878-S half dollars and can be identified by a marker in the shield.[74]

G-4	VG-8	F-12	VF-20	EF-40	AU-50	MS-60	MS-63	MS-65
$55	$65	$100	$125	$200	$250	$475	$800	$3,000

1878

Circulation-strike mintage: 1,377,600

Proof mintage: 800

Availability in Mint State: *MS-60 to 62:* 100 to 130. *MS-63:* 45 to 60. *MS-64:* 30 to 40. *MS-65 or better:* 24 to 30.

actual size: 30.6 mm

Availability in circulated grades: *AG-3 to AU-58:* These are fairly scarce despite the high mintage. They are usually seen in higher grades.

Characteristics of striking: This issue is usually sharply struck.

Proofs: *PF-60 to 62:* 190 to 325. *PF-63:* 150 to 175. *PF-64:* 90 to 120. *PF-65 or better:* 40 to 50.

Notes: Wiley and Bugert relate that Philadelphia coins of 1878 come with 152, 153, or 156 reeds.

G-4	VG-8	F-12	VF-20	EF-40	AU-50
$55	$65	$125	$150	$200	$300
MS-60	**MS-63**	**MS-65**	**PF-60**	**PF-63**	**PF-65**
$500	$1,100	$5,200	$675	$1,200	$2,500

1878-CC

Circulation-strike mintage: 62,000

Availability in Mint State: The Louis E. Eliasberg Sale in 1997 featured an example of this coin in MS-65 or finer. The 2013 Battle Born Collection Sale

actual size: 30.6 mm

featured an example of this coin in MS-65. In 2014 the Eugene H. Gardner Sale featured an example of this coin in MS-65. *MS-60 to 62:* 10 to 14. *MS-63:* 7 to 9. *MS-64:* 6 to 8. *MS-65 or better:* 5 to 7.

Availability in circulated grades: These are quite scarce; only an estimated 325 to 400 are known, making it the second rarest Carson City half dollar.

Characteristics of striking: This issue is usually sharp.

G-4	VG-8	F-12	VF-20	EF-40	AU-50	MS-60	MS-63	MS-65
$1,350	$1,850	$2,750	$3,500	$5,000	$6,250	$13,500	$25,000	$55,000

1878-S

Circulation-strike mintage: 12,000

Availability in Mint State: In 2015 the Eugene H. Gardner Sale featured an example of this coin in MS-64. *MS-60 to 62:* 6 to 8. *MS-63:* 4 or 5. *MS-64:* 2 or 3. *MS-65 or better:* 3.[75]

actual size: 30.6 mm

Availability in circulated grades: *AG-3 to AU-58:* An estimated 50 to 60 survive. This is one of the most famous rarities in the Liberty Seated half dollar series.

Characteristics of striking: This issue is sharply struck.

Notes: The 1878-S is one of the most famous rarities in the Liberty Seated half dollar series. Indeed, even a specimen in just Good or VG grade would be worthy of special notice. This issue has 147 edge reeds.

Wiley and Bugert state: "Authentication of this rare variety can be readily verified by a die chip (a raised lump) high in the recessed area between the left edge of the reverse shield and the first set of vertical stripes. Because this lump is in a recessed area it can be seen on coins of very low grade."

Writing in 1893 in *Mint Marks*, Augustus G. Heaton commented that while the 1855-S and 1857-S were rare, in the "1878 we have the *great rarity* of the San Francisco half dollar coinage."

G-4	VG-8	F-12	VF-20	EF-40	AU-50	MS-60	MS-63	MS-65
$32,500	$45,000	$50,000	$55,000	$75,000	$85,000	$100,000	$120,000	$250,000

1879

Circulation-strike mintage: 4,800

Proof mintage: 1,100

Availability in Mint State: This issue is among the most often seen Mint State Liberty Seated half dollars as ranked by Wiley and Bugert. *MS-60 to 62:* 200 to 400. *MS-63:* 300 to 450. *MS-64:* 300 to 450. *MS-65 or better:* 200 to 300.

actual size: 30.6 mm

Availability in circulated grades: *AG-3 to AU-58:* It is estimated that 200 to 300 exist, mostly in VF or finer. This issue is far rarer in circulated grades than in Mint State, a comment that can be given for all of the Philadelphia Mint half dollars of the next decade.

Characteristics of striking: This issue is usually sharply struck.

Proofs: Beginning this year and continuing for the next decade, the preservation rate of Proofs was much higher than earlier. As such, coins were viewed as being basically rare as *dates* beyond their being in Proof format. Today Proofs of these years are seen in higher average quality than those earlier. Proof-65 coins are readily available. *PF-60 to 62:* 250 to 300. *PF-63:* 260 to 315. *PF-64:* 150 to 200. *PF-65 or better:* 90 to 120.

Notes: Mint State coins of this issue were heavily promoted at one time; see *Notes* under the 1879 dime in chapter 5 for details. Although the low mintages of later years were recognized by numismatists, and many of the later issues were saved, most seem to have been spent once it was realized that they had no premium value and the novelty passed. Half dollars of 1879 alone exist in large quantities in Mint State today.

From the September 15–17, 1885, W. Elliot Woodward's Seventy-Eighth Sale of the Randall Collection, number two, lot 700: "Brilliant Uncirculated; much rarer than Proof. The Mint struck only a few during the latter days of December; nearly all of these were bought on speculation and held for an advance." The "much rarer than Proof" comment is curious.

G-4	VG-8	F-12	VF-20	EF-40	AU-50
$350	$450	$550	$650	$800	$950
MS-60	**MS-63**	**MS-65**	**PF-60**	**PF-63**	**PF-65**
$1,050	$1,300	$3,250	$675	$1,200	$2,500

1880

Circulation-strike mintage: 8,400

Proof mintage: 1,355

Availability in Mint State: *MS-60 to 62:* 50 to 75. *MS-63:* 100 to 125. *MS-64:* 100 to 150. *MS-65 or better:* 80 to 110.

actual size: 30.6 mm

Availability in circulated grades: *AG-3 to AU-58:* It is estimated that 250 to 350 exist.[76] These are mostly seen in VF or finer.

Characteristics of striking: This issue is usually sharply struck.

Proofs: *PF-60 to 62:* 250 to 300. *PF-63:* 280 to 325. *PF-64:* 150 to 200. *PF-65 or better:* 95 to 125.

Notes: Mint State coins were heavily promoted at one time; see *Notes* under the 1880 dime in chapter 5 for details.

G-4	VG-8	F-12	VF-20	EF-40	AU-50
$350	$550	$600	$700	$900	$1,000
MS-60	**MS-63**	**MS-65**	**PF-60**	**PF-63**	**PF-65**
$1,050	$1,500	$4,000	$675	$1,200	$2,500

1881

Circulation-strike mintage: 10,000

Proof mintage: 975

Availability in Mint State: *MS-60 to 62:* 60 to 85. *MS-63:* 110 to 130. *MS-64:* 110 to 130. *MS-65 or better:* 60 to 80.

actual size: 30.6 mm

Availability in circulated grades: *AG-3 to AU-58:* It is estimated that 250 to 350 exist. These are mostly seen in VF or finer.

Characteristics of striking: This issue is usually sharply struck.

Proofs: *PF-60 to 62:* 250 to 300. *PF-63:* 250 to 300. *PF-64:* 140 to 180. *PF-65 or better:* 70 to 100.

G-4	VG-8	F-12	VF-20	EF-40	AU-50
$350	$450	$550	$650	$800	$900
MS-60	**MS-63**	**MS-65**	**PF-60**	**PF-63**	**PF-65**
$1,050	$1,500	$4,000	$675	$1,200	$2,500

1882

Circulation-strike mintage: 4,400

Proof mintage: 1,100

Availability in Mint State: *MS-60 to 62:* 40 to 55. *MS-63:* 70 to 100. *MS-64:* 80 to 120. *MS-65 or better:* 80 to 120.

actual size: 30.6 mm

Availability in circulated grades: *AG-3 to AU-58:* It is estimated that 250 to 350 exist. These are mostly seen in VF or finer.

Characteristics of striking: This issue is usually sharply struck.

Proofs: *PF-60 to 62:* 250 to 300. *PF-63:* 250 to 300. *PF-64:* 140 to 180. *PF-65 or better:* 80 to 120.

Notes: For speculative comments on the coinage see the item from *Mason's Coin Collectors' Herald* under *Notes* for the 1882 dime in chapter 5.

G-4	VG-8	F-12	VF-20	EF-40	AU-50
$350	$450	$550	$650	$800	$900
MS-60	**MS-63**	**MS-65**	**PF-60**	**PF-63**	**PF-65**
$1,050	$1,600	$4,750	$675	$1,200	$2,500

1883

Circulation-strike mintage: 8,000

Proof mintage: 1,039

Availability in Mint State: *MS-60 to 62:* 60 to 80. *MS-63:* 110 to 130. *MS-64:* 110 to 130. *MS-65 or better:* 80 to 100.

actual size: 30.6 mm

Availability in circulated grades: *AG-3 to AU-58:* It is estimated that 225 to 325 exist. These are mostly seen in VF or finer.

Characteristics of striking: This issue is usually sharply struck.

Proofs: *PF-60 to 62:* 250 to 300. *PF-63:* 250 to 300. *PF-64:* 140 to 180. *PF-65 or better:* 80 to 120.

G-4	VG-8	F-12	VF-20	EF-40	AU-50
$350	$450	$550	$650	$800	$900
MS-60	**MS-63**	**MS-65**	**PF-60**	**PF-63**	**PF-65**
$1,050	$1,500	$4,250	$675	$1,200	$2,500

1884

Circulation-strike mintage: 4,400

Proof mintage: 875

Availability in Mint State: *MS-60 to 62:* 40 to 55. *MS-63:* 70 to 100. *MS-64:* 80 to 120. *MS-65 or better:* 80 to 100.

actual size: 30.6 mm

Availability in circulated grades: *AG-3 to AU-58:* It is estimated that 200 to 300 exist. These are mostly seen in VF or finer. The wide availability of Mint State and, especially Proof coins, has lessened the demand.

Characteristics of striking: This issue is usually sharply struck.

Proofs: *PF-60 to 62:* 200 to 250. *PF-63:* 190 to 250. *PF-64:* 100 to 140. *PF-65 or better:* 60 to 90.

G-4	VG-8	F-12	VF-20	EF-40	AU-50
$425	$475	$550	$650	$800	$925
MS-60	**MS-63**	**MS-65**	**PF-60**	**PF-63**	**PF-65**
$1,100	$1,500	$4,500	$675	$1,200	$2,500

1885

Circulation-strike mintage: 5,200

Proof mintage: 930

Availability in Mint State: *MS-60 to 62:* 50 to 75. *MS-63:* 100 to 125. *MS-64:* 100 to 150. *MS-65 or better:* 60 to 80.

actual size: 30.6 mm

Availability in circulated grades: *AG-3 to AU-58:* It is estimated that 200 to 300 exist. These are mostly seen in VF or finer.

Characteristics of striking: This issue is usually sharply struck.

Proofs: *PF-60 to 62:* 250 to 300. *PF-63:* 240 to 300. *PF-64:* 150 to 180. *PF-65 or better:* 60 to 90.

G-4	VG-8	F-12	VF-20	EF-40	AU-50
$425	$525	$625	$750	$850	$925
MS-60	**MS-63**	**MS-65**	**PF-60**	**PF-63**	**PF-65**
$1,100	$1,500	$4,500	$675	$1,200	$2,500

1886

Circulation-strike mintage: 5,000

Proof mintage: 886

Availability in Mint State: *MS-60 to 62:* 40 to 55. *MS-63:* 70 to 100. *MS-64:* 80 to 120. *MS-65 or better:* 50 to 70.

actual size: 30.6 mm

Availability in circulated grades: *AG-3 to AU-58:* It is estimated that 200 to 250 exist, making them especially hard to find. These are mostly seen in VF or finer.

Characteristics of striking: This issue is sometimes weak on the hair and on star eight.

Proofs: *PF-60 to 62:* 230 to 275. *PF-63:* 230 to 275. *PF-64:* 130 to 160. *PF-65 or better:* 55 to 80.

G-4	VG-8	F-12	VF-20	EF-40	AU-50
$475	$550	$625	$750	$850	$900
MS-60	**MS-63**	**MS-65**	**PF-60**	**PF-63**	**PF-65**
$1,100	$1,500	$4,250	$675	$1,200	$2,500

1887

Circulation-strike mintage: 5,000

Proof mintage: 710

Availability in Mint State: *MS-60 to 62:* 60 to 85. *MS-63:* 110 to 130. *MS-64:* 110 to 130. *MS-65 or better:* 120 to 160.

actual size: 30.6 mm

Availability in circulated grades: *AG-3 to AU-58:* It is estimated that 175 to 250 exist; another rare issue. These are mostly seen in VF or finer.

Characteristics of striking: This issue is sometimes seen with weakness on Liberty's hair.

Proofs: *PF-60 to 62:* 150 to 200. *PF-63:* 190 to 225. *PF-64:* 110 to 140. *PF-65 or better:* 50 to 70.

G-4	VG-8	F-12	VF-20	EF-40	AU-50
$525	$575	$650	$750	$950	$1,000
MS-60	**MS-63**	**MS-65**	**PF-60**	**PF-63**	**PF-65**
$1,100	$1,400	$4,250	$675	$1,200	$2,500

1888

Circulation-strike mintage: 12,001

Proof mintage: 832

Availability in Mint State: *MS-60 to 62:* 60 to 85. *MS-63:* 110 to 130. *MS-64:* 110 to 130. *MS-65 or better:* 120 to 160.

actual size: 30.6 mm

Availability in circulated grades: *AG-3 to AU-58:* It is estimated that 225 to 300 exist. These are mostly seen in VF or finer.

Characteristics of striking: Some coins of this issue have lightness on the head.

Proofs: The obverse die has a misplaced 8 in the rock support below the shield edge. *PF-60 to 62:* 130 to 160. *PF-63:* 170 to 200. *PF-64:* 100 to 125. *PF-65 or better:* 45 to 60.

Notes: The date is very subtly repunched, it being most evident at the bottom of the last digit. Apparently, all circulation strikes were struck from a single pair of dies.

G-4	VG-8	F-12	VF-20	EF-40	AU-50
$350	$425	$550	$650	$800	$900
MS-60	**MS-63**	**MS-65**	**PF-60**	**PF-63**	**PF-65**
$1,000	$1,350	$4,000	$675	$1,200	$2,500

1889

Circulation-strike mintage: 12,000

Proof mintage: 711

Availability in Mint State: *MS-60 to 62:* 60 to 85. *MS-63:* 110 to 130. *MS-64:* 110 to 130. *MS-65 or better:* 120 to 160.

actual size: 30.6 mm

Availability in circulated grades: *AG-3 to AU-58:* It is estimated that 300 to 400 exist. These are mostly seen in VF or finer.

Characteristics of striking: This issue is usually sharply struck.

Proofs: Two obverse dies were used. In September 1944 *The Numismatist* included this: "The Numismatic Gallery reports the discovery, while cataloging a consignment for their next sale, of a half dollar of 1889 which shows distinct signs of the nine over eight." This news caused a small stir in coin-collecting circles, and subsequently Proof half dollars of 1889 were listed in catalogs in two varieties, 1889 and 1889, 9 Over 8. Then someone sought to compare the "perfect date" Proof half dollar variety with the overdate and found they were both from the same dies and that no overdate existed. The knob at the bottom of the 9 was close to the upper loop of the 9, giving the fanciful appearance of an overdate. Subsequently the "discovery" was forgotten. *PF-60 to 62:* 130 to 160. *PF-63:* 190 to 180. *PF-64:* 90 to 120. *PF-65 or better:* 45 to 60.

G-4	VG-8	F-12	VF-20	EF-40	AU-50
$325	$425	$550	$650	$850	$900
MS-60	**MS-63**	**MS-65**	**PF-60**	**PF-63**	**PF-65**
$1,000	$1,250	$4,250	$675	$1,200	$2,500

1890

Circulation-strike mintage: 12,000

Proof mintage: 590

Availability in Mint State: *MS-60 to 62:* 40 to 55. *MS-63:* 70 to 100. *MS-64:* 80 to 120. *MS-65 or better:* 80 to 120.

actual size: 30.6 mm

Availability in circulated grades: *AG-3 to AU-58:* It is estimated that 300 to 400 exist. This issue is very elusive and is mostly seen in VF or finer.

Characteristics of striking: This issue is usually sharply struck.

Proofs: Two different obverse dies have been confirmed; a third was earlier reported by Breen. *PF-60 to 62:* 230 to 275. *PF-63:* 230 to 275. *PF-64:* 130 to 160. *PF-65 or better:* 60 to 90.

G-4	VG-8	F-12	VF-20	EF-40	AU-50
$325	$425	$550	$650	$750	$900
MS-60	**MS-63**	**MS-65**	**PF-60**	**PF-63**	**PF-65**
$1,000	$1,150	$4,000	$675	$1,200	$2,500

1891

Circulation-strike mintage: 200,000

Proof mintage: 600

Availability in Mint State: *MS-60 to 62:* 65 to 90. *MS-63:* 120 to 140. *MS-64:* 120 to 140. *MS-65 or better:* 140 to 170.

actual size: 30.6 mm

Availability in circulated grades: *AG-3 to AU-58:* It is estimated that 500 to 700 exist. These are mostly seen in VF or finer.

Characteristics of striking: This issue is usually sharply struck.

Proofs: *PF-60 to 62:* 150 to 180. *PF-63:* 160 to 190. *PF-64:* 100 to 125. *PF-65 or better:* 50 to 70.

G-4	VG-8	F-12	VF-20	EF-40	AU-50
$100	$150	$175	$250	$300	$700
MS-60	**MS-63**	**MS-65**	**PF-60**	**PF-63**	**PF-65**
$800	$1,200	$3,800	$675	$1,200	$2,500

9

GOBRECHT AND LIBERTY SEATED DOLLARS (1836–1873)

Introduction

The series comprising Gobrecht silver dollars of 1836 to 1839 and Liberty Seated silver dollars of 1840 to 1873 is far and away the most complex among the different denominations of the design. In numismatic literature, facts are often scarce or absent with theories abound.

The present text is an effort to bring together the various aspects of design, coinage, distribution, and use of these dollars and the national and international financial conditions that were so important in this context.

Silver dollars were last coined in calendar year 1804 from dies of earlier dates. The mintage totaled 19,570 coins. Further production was halted as nearly all were exported, thus being of little use to the domestic economy. Secretary of State James Madison made it official on May 1, 1806, in a letter to Mint Director Robert Patterson:

> Sir:
>
> In consequence of a representation from the director of the Bank of the United States that considerable purchases have been made of dollars coined at the Mint for the purpose of exporting them, and as it is probable further purchases and exportations will be made, the president directs that all the silver coined at the Mint shall be of small denominations, so that the value of the largest pieces shall not exceed half a dollar.

The following pages tell of the new silver dollars minted beginning in 1836. See chapter 1 for more details on the origin of the Liberty Seated design.

Gobrecht Dollars (1836–1839)
SILVER DOLLARS MINTED

In autumn of 1836 all was set to commence the coinage of Liberty Seated dollars with Liberty on the obverse and a flying eagle on the reverse, called Gobrecht dollars by numismatists today.[1] In its final form for quantity coinage, the 1836-dated Gobrecht silver dollar appeared with a Liberty Seated figure on the obverse, name inconspicuously on the base, with the eagle flying onward and upward on the reverse amid a galaxy of 26 stars, 13 large and 13 small. At the time there were 25 states in the Union, but it was not long until Michigan became the 26th (in 1837). Striking began on a hand-operated screw press in December 1836, with 1,000 coins in mirror Proof format and with plain edge. Although a knuckle-action Uhlhorn-type steam press designed by Franklin Peale had struck cents, quarters, and half dollars in that year, it would not be until after March 1837 that one would be installed of sufficient capacity to strike silver dollars. Notices were sent to newspapers and were widely reproduced, such as this article in the New York *Evening Post* from December 16, 1836:

New Coin

A new dollar of our own Mint will soon make its appearance. No American dollars have been coined since 1805. The following is a description of the coin.

The design for the face was drawn by Mr. Sully, that for the reverse by Titian Peale, and both executed by Mr. Gobrecht, the die-sinker. It is intended to adopt the design in other coins. The face of the coin represents a full length figure of Liberty, seated on a rock, with the classic emblem of the *pileus* or liberty-cap surmounting a spear held in the left hand. The right hand rests on an American shield, with its thirteen stripes, crossed by a scroll, on which is the word Liberty.

The reverse represents the American eagle on the wing drawn accurately from nature; all the heraldic appendages of the old coin being discarded. Over the field are placed irregularly twenty-six stars, the entrance of Michigan, having been, it seems, anticipated.

The *New York Commercial Advertiser* printed this on December 20, 1836, soon after receiving a new dollar, apparently well before their official release into circulation:

The New Coins

We have been bribed this morning by one of the Pet Banks—"that's a fact!"[2] The Bank of American has presented us with one of the newly coined dollars and also one of the new half dollars—the first that were struck. They are classical and beautiful.

The principal figure on the dollar is a full length of Liberty, seated on a rock, emblematic of duration, with her shield at her side—clad in flowing robes, with hair unbound and eminently graceful. The reverse presents us with the eagle on the wing amidst the American galaxy of twenty-six stars. The eagle is a novel and delicate design—very beautiful.

The dollar is not milled and is the greatest coin we have ever seen. The half dollar presents us the female head and cap of Liberty—and we are gratified to perceive that if the goddess has not renewed her age she has her head—for it is very pretty and has a great expression. The eagle, too, is of an improved race of that noble bird.

N.B. Not bribed yet, as these two coins we learn are the only two in town, and others are to take delight in looking at them as well as ourselves.

To the previous, the New York *Evening Star* took great exception in its issue of December 21:

Doctors Differ

The *Commercial Advertiser* calls the new dollar emission from our Mint "classical and beautiful," "eminently graceful"—the eagle of "a novel and delicate design, very beautiful—an improved race of that noble bird."

Col. Stone! Col. Stone! What's the matter with you?[3]

The dollar looks like a Brummagen medal made of Britannia ware—a poor, shivering, half-dressed figure on one side, intended no doubt for the Goddess of Liberty, but looking like one of the nymphs of the five points[4]; on the other, a huge turkey buzzard surrounded by a shower of stars. The half dollar is well enough. The dies of neither are cut sufficiently deep. The dollar is a very poor concern indeed.

As to whether Liberty is seated on a rock to typify her endurance is open to question. One early sketch had her seated on an ornate bench. Perhaps the "rock" consists of folds of drapery?[5]

On December 31, 1836, the first mintage of 1,000 pieces intended for general distribution was delivered by the coiner, these in addition to some that were given to banks and others before then. At various later times they were distributed to officials (President Andrew Jackson received two), and a few no doubt went to the small community of collectors and dignitaries, but most were deposited in the recently chartered Bank of the United States of Pennsylvania, which had no connection with the Second Bank of the United States.[6] The coins reached the channels of commerce and circulated extensively.

The Gobrecht silver dollars delivered on December 31, 1836, were of the old standard of 416 grains total weight, dies oriented coin-turn (alignment 1, see patterns).

The new coin engendered a complaint that it was too "medallic" looking.[7] Accordingly, in 1838 pattern dollars were made with stars on the obverse (where they should be, perhaps!), a plain reverse, and with a reeded instead of a plain edge, but no coinage for circulation resulted. Gobrecht effaced his C. GOBRECHT F. signature from the hub before the master die was made, perhaps because medalists signed their work but in America coin engravers did not. We may never know the exact reason. In 1838 stars were added to the obverses of the half dime and dime as well.

In 1839 a design with Liberty Seated on the obverse with stars surrounding (hand-punched into the working die) and a flying eagle in a plain field on the reverse was struck to the extent of 300 coins, again with Proof finish and for circulation.

Years later, beginning in spring 1859, restrikes in silver were made of certain die combinations. Copper restrikes of 1836–1839 dollars may have been made significantly later, into the 1870s.[8] Restrikes have the eagle flying horizontally as the minter(s) thought that proper—based on the position of the current Flying Eagle cent of the same design. Nearly all 1838 and 1839 Gobrecht dollars in numismatic hands are restrikes or in many instances novodels (not restrikes, as no originals were made in certain combinations). These have had a large following for a long time, helped by the listing of certain of them in *A Guide Book of United States Coins*, details published on www.uspatterns.com, and a book edited by Mark Van Winkle, *Gobrecht Dollars: Illustrated by the Collection of Julius Korein, M.D.* The study of such pieces has generated much controversy over a long period of years, and there are still unanswered questions.[9]

DIE ALIGNMENTS

Gobrecht dollars can be divided into four die alignments:

Die Alignment 1: The reverse is aligned 180 degrees from the obverse. The eagle appears to fly upward and onward, and ONE DOLLAR is centered at the bottom. Most 1836-dated original strikings are of this format.

Die Alignment 2: The reverse is the same as the obverse, "medal turn." The eagle appears to fly upward and onward, and ONE DOLLAR centered at the bottom.

Die Alignment 3: The reverse is inverted, nearly coin turn, but with the eagle flying horizontally with the result that ONE DOLLAR is at the lower right. This format was introduced in 1859 for restrikes and novodels.

Die Alignment 4: The reverse was inverted, medal turn or nearly, with the eagle upside down. This alignment exists in several rotational variations, perhaps from one die not being tightly locked in place on the coining press.

Pattern Gobrecht Dollars

As noted, only two varieties of Gobrecht dollars were originally struck for circulation. By tradition these have been given Judd numbers 60 and 104. Many varieties of patterns, novodels, restrikes, and off metal strikes were made strictly for the numismatic trade, these being classified as follows:

1836 (J-58 and 59): *Obverse:* Liberty Seated design with no stars in field. C GOBRECHT. F. is in raised letters below base and above date. Made at a later date (see below). *Reverse:* Eagle flying to the left, onward and upward, in a starry field of 13 small and 13 large stars, a total of 26. A fantasy or novodel (not a *restrike* as there were no originals!) created at the Mint circa spring 1859. The first appeared in an Edward Cogan auction of that year and failed to sell.

1836 (J-60): 1836 regular issue. *Obverse:* Liberty Seated design with no stars in field. C GOBRECHT. F. is in recessed letters on base. Date in field below. Originals and restrikes. See separate listings in the catalog.

1836 (J-61 and 62): Dies as preceding. Restrikes. J-61 (die alignment 4, original 1837 striking) is struck in silver and has a reeded edge. J-62 (die alignment 3, circa 1876, with rust in field left of Liberty's face) is struck in copper and has a plain edge. All copper Gobrecht dollars are novodels as no originals were struck in this metal.

1836 (J-63 and 64): *Obverse:* Liberty Seated design with no stars in field. C GOBRECHT. F. is in raised letters below base and above date; obverse of J-58. Created at the Mint in later years. A novodel as no originals were made with a starless reverse fields. All other silver Gobrechts that have different die combinations from those originally used in 1836, 1838, and 1839 are novodels. *Reverse:* Eagle flying to the left, onward and upward in a *plain* field (die first regularly used in 1838). Later strikings with die alignment 3, struck circa 1876. J-63 is struck in silver and has a plain edge. J-64 is struck in copper and has a plain edge.

1836 (J-65 and 66): *Obverse:* As preceding. *Reverse:* As preceding, eagle flying to the left, onward and upward in a *plain* field (die first regularly used in 1838). Restrikes with die alignment 3, circa 1876, with rust in field left of Liberty's face. J-65 is struck in silver and has a plain edge. J-66 is struck in copper and has a plain edge.

1838 (J-84, 85, and 87): *Obverse:* Liberty Seated with stars. *Reverse:* Flying eagle in plain (starless) field. Silver issues with some originals (some J-84), others restrikes. One is struck over an 1859 Liberty Seated dollar, with the 1859 date still visible.[10] Copper issues are restrikes. J-84 (exists in both alignments 3 and 4 from both the perfect and the cracked state of the reverse die[11]) is struck in silver and has a reeded edge. J-85 (restrikes, alignment 3[12]) is struck in silver and has a plain edge. J-87 (restrikes, alignment 3[13]) is struck in copper and has a plain edge.

1838 (J-88 and 89): *Obverse:* Liberty Seated with stars, die as preceding. *Reverse:* Flying eagle in field of 26 stars (style of 1836). Restrikes, alignment 3. J-88 is silver and has a plain edge. J-89 is struck in copper and has a plain edge.[14]

1839 (J-104, 105, and 107): *Obverse:* Liberty Seated with stars. *Reverse:* Flying eagle in plain (starless) field (style of 1838). It seems reasonable that original strikings of J-104 in silver would have the dies oriented coin-turn, but no example has been found. PCGS has reserved a number for such if one is located and has never certified an original. NGC certifies both originals (alignment 4) and restrikes. Most silver strikings in Proof grades of 62 and higher and all copper strikings are restrikes circa 1859 (silver) to the 1870s (copper). J-104 (originals alignment 4,[15] restrikes 3 and 4[16]) is struck in silver and has a reeded edge. J-105 (restrikes, alignment 3) is struck in silver and has a plain edge. J-107 (restrikes, alignment 3) is struck in copper and has a plain edge.

1839 (J-108 and 109): *Obverse:* Liberty Seated with stars, die as preceding. *Reverse:* Flying eagle in field of 26 stars (style of 1836). Restrikes made with the die used to coin J-60 of 1836; the use of stars on both obverse and reverse is illogical.[17] J-108 (restrikes, alignment 3) is struck in silver and has a plain edge. J-109 (alignment 3) is struck in copper and has a plain edge.

Mint Shenanigans

Most of the above Gobrecht dollars and countless thousands of other rare coins were secretly made at the Mint in the period from 1859 through the 1870s and were sold to local dealer William K. Idler and, later, to his son-in-law John W. Haseltine. Archibald Loudon Snowden at the Mint also had a large holding of patterns, restrikes, and related pieces as related below. In the early 1900s Haseltine revealed the existence of many patterns not heretofore known.

After early 1859 a veil of secrecy had descended upon the Mint, to the dismay of dealers and collectors. In a letter dated November 12, 1861, members of the Boston Numismatic Society wrote to James Pollock, appointed as Mint director as the successor to James Ross Snowden, by Abraham Lincoln.[18]

> The undersigned…were instructed to call your attention to the abuses which have of late years been practiced at the Mint of the United States whereby a number of pattern pieces and coins from dies of former years have been freely struck and disposed of by employees of the Mint to dealers who have in turn disposed of them at great prices . . .
>
> Under these circumstances we respectfully urge the expedience of destroying the dies of the current coin, and also of pattern pieces, at the close of each year.

Director Pollock replied on November 21:

> The abuses to which you refer, if they have ever had an existence, can no longer be practiced in this Institution. The practice of striking pattern pieces and coins from dies of former years cannot be too strongly condemned, and great care is now taken to prevent the recurrence of any such abuse. All the dies of former years are secured in such a manner that it is impossible for anyone to obtain possession of them without the knowledge of the director.
>
> The dies of the current coins and of pattern pieces will be destroyed at the close of the year. The dies of the past few years have also been destroyed.

How dies "of former years are secured in such a manner," etc., reconciles with the statement that old dies had been destroyed is beyond logic. In a tangled web involving a changing roster of Mint directors and insiders, patently false information was disseminated for the next quarter century. In summation, Mint comments about patterns made from spring 1859 until management changed in the summer of 1885 are largely false.

Throughout the period from 1860s onward alarms were sounded by S.K. Harzfeld, W. Elliott Woodward, and others in their catalogs, but to no avail. In the 1870s the auction catalogs of J.W. Haseltine were laden with rarities, restrikes, and novodels which no one knew existed.

On March 14, 1878, *The Nation* printed this:

Notes

The law provides that specimens of all "patterns" struck at the Mint— the coins struck from dies different from those in use, as patterns for proposed new issues— should be presented to the various numismatic societies, but the Mint officials have always refused to execute it.

The patterns, for example, of this year, were all distributed amongst members of Congress and friends of Mint officials, and were refused to societies, although season-able application was made in at least one instance.[19] This whole business of Mint patterns has been very singularly managed, and, to some extent, is so still. It has been estimated that in 1859 and 1860 fifty thousand dollars' worth of patterns were struck and disposed of at the Mint, without any benefit to the government at whose expense they were coined. Copies were not even put into the government collection of its own coins, which is inferior, (except in Washington's) to the most ordinary collections, while the officials in whose charge it is, take no pains to fill its numerous gaps.

During Mr. Lincoln's administration these abuses stopped, but of late years they have begun again.[20] For example, numerous pattern dollars, struck between 1869 and 1874, have since then turned up and passed into the hands of collectors, none of which appear in the government collection or were distributed in a lawful manner to numismatic societies, while favored individuals collected at a trifling expense sets which sold at large sums. Over $100 apiece have been paid for some of these mysterious pieces. We notice in a late catalogue a medal described as a rarity which will no doubt bring a good price. The dies for it were made within two years at the government Mint, by the Mint workmen, with the Mint machine, but none of the medals are in the government collection, (or were a short time ago, and none have appeared in the Mint sale-list or for distribution to numismatic societies. All this seems to show that laws for the distribution of Government favors are one thing, and their enforcement quite another.[21]

In his October 1880 sale of the Ferguson Haines Collection, W. Elliot Woodward included this:

. . . What the lords of the Treasury will do next is "what no feller can find out." We will wait and see. In these days of investigation, an inquiry into past conduct of some of its officials, would, if properly conducted, be fruitful in results; and if properly reported, would furnish what Horace Greeley used to call "mighty interesting reading."

As the government is fond of illustrating its reports, as a frontispiece, is suggested a view of a son of a late official of the Mint,[22] as he appeared at the store of the writer, when, on a peddling expedition from Philadelphia to Boston, he drew from his pocket rolls of (1861) "God Our Trust" patterns, and urged their purchase at wholesale, after sundry sets had been disposed of at one hundred dollars each to collectors of rare coins, with the assurance that only a very few had been struck, and that the dies were destroyed. . . .

In June 1909 it was revealed that New York City industrialist and numismatist William H. Woodin had acquired two 1877 pattern $50 gold coins, each of a slightly different design. The price paid was $10,000 each—far more than any coin had ever sold for at auction. The sellers were John W. Haseltine and Stephen K. Nagy of Philadelphia. This caused a furor, and the government stated that as they had not been officially released, it wanted them back.

They had come from A. Loudon Snowden, who had been chief coiner at the Mint in the 1870s, then superintendent until his resignation in June 1885. No paper trail was left, and it is not known if the following account of his acquisition of them is correct. Details were given in a letter from Woodin's attorney to U.S. Attorney Henry W. Wise, June 7, 1910:

> Col. Snowden, who had originally purchased these coins from the Director of the Mint in Philadelphia by depositing the bullion value and the charge for pattern pieces to save them from being melted down, in the course of negotiations between himself and Dr. Andrew, director of the mints, came to an agreement with the latter over all matters in dispute between them, and proposed to Mr. Woodin to repay him the $20,000 he had paid for these pieces, in order that he might carry out his arrangement with Dr. Andrew.
>
> Mr. Woodin after numerous visits to Philadelphia and Washington and conference with Dr. Andrew, both there and in this city, decided to accept this offer, returned the 50's to Col. Snowden, and I thereupon notified Mr. Pratt, as did Mr. Woodin, that the incident was closed, and we requested a letter from your office confirming the same.
>
> In view of the trouble and expense to which Mr. Woodin was put to facilitate Dr. Andrew in the adjustment of a very difficult situation, your letter seems a little unfair, in that it would tend to create the appearance of a record sometime in the future that Mr. Woodin had been compelled to give up something of which he was improperly in possession.[23]

Instead of getting a refund, Woodin opted to obtain from Snowden two large trunks containing thousands of pattern coins.

In "The Gobrecht Dollars," in *The Numismatist*, April 1912, Edgar H. Adams wrote (excerpts):

> Even the old-time collectors paid large sums for the Gobrecht dollars at a period when other coins, some of which have since brought enormous premiums, scarcely brought more than their face value and were not much in demand even at the low figures.
>
> But high as were the old-time premiums paid for the Gobrecht dollars, they did not seem to cause the rarest specimens of the series to come into the market, for it has not been until the most recent years that the rarest pieces have come to public notice, and some of these were altogether unknown to most of the old-time collectors. . . . During the year of 1911 quite a number of rarities of this series came to light—some of them for the first time—at least to the knowledge of collectors.[24]

Based on the large holding of patterns Woodin owned, he and Edgar H. Adams wrote *United States Patterns, Trial, and Experimental Pieces*, which was published by the American Numismatic Society in 1913.

THE 1836 "NAME BELOW BASE" ILLUSION

An 1836 Gobrecht dollar with name below base and detail. (Judd-58.)

Edgar H. Adams, one of the most highly respected scholars and writers of his day, told of the illusion in "Beautiful Coin Types by a Calico Engraver" in *The Numismatist*, January 1909:

> In 1836 Christian Gobrecht, of Philadelphia, an engraver of calico printers' rolls, bank notes, &c., was appointed as assistant to William Kneass. The latter was the second man to hold the position of engraver at the government Mint. As the coinage of silver dollars was again agitated about this time, after a long lapse of years stretching from 1804, the last year of issue of coins of the denomination, the mint authorities arranged to issue a number of pattern coins from which a suitable design for the new dollar could be selected.
>
> The story goes that Mr. Gobrecht, a short time after his appointment, was directed by the Director of the Mint to prepare dies for silver dollars after his own original designs. The new engraver, it is said, was quite embarrassed temporarily by these instructions, and told his superior that he never had created a coin design in his life; that he was simply an engraver, and was prepared to execute any design that might be presented to him, but that the designing of a coin was something with which he had not the slightest experience. Nevertheless, he undertook the work, with the result that a number of pattern dollars of exquisite design, of a character never before nor since attempted, and numbering several varieties of combinations of obverse and reverse, soon made their appearance. They met the instantaneous favor of those who took an interest in the Mint issues, and it is doubtful, indeed, if these coin designs have ever been equaled.
>
> The first of the pattern dollars, dated 1836, bore the original representation of the seated figure of Liberty, which design afterward became so familiar to the public, having been used on silver coins of various denominations up to within comparatively recent years. Just under the figure of Liberty, and over the date. "1836," appeared the engraver's name, "C. Gobrecht."
>
> In the field on the reverse was a representation of a large eagle in full flight, scattered all around being twenty-six stars. About the border was inscribed, "UNITED STATES OF AMERICA—ONE DOLLAR." The edge of this coin was plain. This piece has sold for $100 in silver, and a specimen in copper brought $40 at the Gschwend sale.
>
> When this handsome coin made its appearance it created favorable comment so far as the design was concerned, but the engraver was criticized by certain persons for placing his name upon it in such a conspicuous position. Mr. Gobrecht, much

hurt, removed the name altogether from the die, after eighteen specimens had been struck in silver and a few in copper. The Director of the Mint, however, very well pleased with the engraver's work, directed that the name be replaced upon the die, which Mr. Gobrecht obeyed with considerable reluctance, but this time put it at the base of the figure of Liberty, where it can be detected only by careful scrutiny.

This story became fact and was repeated many times.

In reality, by careful examination of examples of Judd-58, the name below base coin, during a visit to the American Numismatic Society on May 18, 2015, John Dannreuther and Saul Teichman determined that it was struck using a master hub made in 1838 or later in which the name on the *base*, used to strike Judd-60, had been mostly tooled away, leaving just microscopic traces of it having been there. To create Judd-58 a die was made using the later version, but now with the tiny traces removed. Accordingly, the name below base dollars were made at a much later date, and the story of their being made and Gobrecht being criticized for the placement is fantasy.[25]

The first public offering of an 1836 dollar with name below base was in the offering of a consignment from Joseph N.T. Levick held at Bangs, Merwin & Co., New York City, on December 19, 1859. The coin did not find a buyer.[26] Saul Teichman estimates that about 35 to 40 can be accounted for today.[27]

DISTRIBUTION OF GOBRECHT DOLLARS

The vast majority of the Gobrecht dollars struck in December 1836 were placed into circulation at face value. Most of them, 600 in total, were delivered to the Bank of the United States of Pennsylvania. The remaining 400 were kept at the Mint and were distributed in various ways, including through Secretary of the Treasury Levi Woodbury.

Those in circulation traded among banks, bullion brokers, and exchange houses, but not for face value in circulation. Beginning in the 1850s numismatics became a widely popular pursuit in America. Silver dollars did not circulate at the time, as the value of silver had risen to more than their face value. Most new dollars were exported, as detailed in the next chapter. The Gobrecht dollars were recognized as having a premium value to collectors, and these dealers and agents rescued hundreds of them and sold them to numismatists, accounting for most of the coins known today.

GRADING GOBRECHT DOLLARS

1839. Graded PF-65.

PF-60 to 70 (Proof). *Obverse and Reverse:* Many Proofs have been extensively cleaned and have many hairlines and dull fields. This is more applicable to 1836 than to 1839. Grades are PF-60 to 61 or 62. With medium hairlines and good reflectivity, an assigned grade of PF-64 is appropriate, and with relatively few hairlines, Gem PF-65. In various grades hairlines are most easily seen in the obverse field. PF-66 should have hairlines so delicate that magnification is needed to see them. Above that, a Proof should be free of such lines.

Illustrated coin: This is a restrike made at the Mint in or after spring 1859.

1836. Graded PF-58.

PF-50, 53, 55, 58 (Proof). *Obverse:* Light wear is seen on the thighs and knees, bosom, and head. At PF-58, the Proof surface is extensive, but the open fields show abrasion. At PF-50 and 53, most if not all mirror surface is gone and there are scattered marks. *Reverse:* Wear is most evident on the eagle's breast and the top of the wings. Mirror surface ranges from perhaps 60 percent complete (at PF-58) to none (at PF-50).

Illustrated coin: This original 1836 Gobrecht dollar, of which 1,000 were coined in 1836, is nicely toned and has excellent eye appeal.

1836. Graded PF-45.

PF-40 to 45 (Proof). *Obverse:* Further wear is seen on all areas, especially the thighs and knees, bosom, and head. The center of LIBERTY, which is in relief, is weak. Most at this level and lower are the 1836 issues. *Reverse:* Further wear is evident on the eagle, including the back edge of the closest wing, the top of the farthest wing, and the tail.

1836. Graded PF-20.

PF-20, 25, 30, 35 (Proof). *Obverse:* Further wear is seen. Many details of the gown are worn away, but the lower-relief areas above and to the right of the shield remain well defined. Hair detail is mostly or completely gone. LIBERTY is weak at the center. *Reverse:* Even more wear is evident on the eagle, with only about 60 percent of the feathers visible.

1836, Name on Base

Proof mintage: 1,000+

Availability in circulated grades: As noted previously, by the 1850s these dollars were recognized as having value. Sharp-eyed bullion brokers, bankers, and others retrieved many for face value, with the result

actual size: 39–40 mm

that an estimated 600 to 750 exist today. Some of them are worn down to low grades, but most are EF or finer. These are often given Proof grades such as PF-40, as all were struck with Proof finish.

Characteristics of striking: This issue is sharply struck.

Proofs: Coins grading PF-60 or higher probably comprise fewer than 250 of the quantity of 600 to 750 mentioned above. Most of these are PF-60 to 62 and were probably retrieved by bullion dealers and others. PF-64 coins are rare and PF-65 coins are very rare.

Notes: Most of the dollars struck in 1836 are of Die Alignment 1, but some were of alignments 2 and 4. All are of the 416-grain standard. Several years ago Craig Sholley, Saul Teichman, and John Dannreuther studied the 61 Gobrecht dollars dated 1836 with name on base in the Dr. Julius Korein collection, and made note of the alignments.[28] The coins at the 416-grain standard showed progressive deterioration of the dies, generating "markers" that contributed to research (see following 1837 information). All coins with Die Alignment 3 are restrikes from 1859 or later.

Delivery figures: December 31, 1836: 400; December 31, 1836 (additional delivery same day): 600. In addition, some were given out earlier.

PF-20	PF-40	PF-50	PF-60	PF-62	PF-63	PF-64	PF-65
$13,500	$16,000	$18,500	$26,500	$27,500	$42,500	$75,000	$125,000

1836-DATED DOLLARS COINED IN 1837

One of the enduring mysteries about one of the most enigmatic American coins is the fate of the 600 Gobrecht dollars delivered on March 31, 1837. These were struck close to or at the new dollar standard of 412.5 grains versus the old standard of 416 grains.

In the May 2015 study of the Korein Collection coins previously mentioned it was found that only one coin seemed to fit the new lighter weight standard and also have the same die markers as the dollars struck to the old standard and delivered in December 1836.[29] Judd-61 has a *reeded* edge and weighs 414.36 grains.

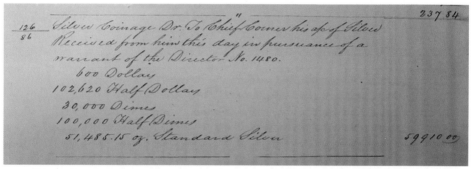

Detail from the Mint ledger showing 600 additional silver dollars delivered on March 31, 1836.

Page 325 in a Mint ledger shows Warrant 1480, dated March 31, 1836, that shows that 600 newly struck dollars were delivered. They could have been melted if overweight (see previously mentioned 414.36-grain dollars), as a delivery warrant is only an internal Mint document. No record exists that specifically shows this group was delivered to an outside source or returned to the melter and refiner to be recoined into other silver issues.[30]

1838 Gobrecht Dollar

actual size: 39–40 mm

Notes: Although all 1838 Gobrecht dollars are patterns, by tradition and by listing in *A Guide Book of United States Coins* they are collected by many numismatists who do not specialize in patterns.

Judd-84 is the variety most often seen, usually in grades of PF-60 to 64, occasionally higher. Up to about 100 are known. Worn PF-20 is known as is a PF-35, and there are a handful of impaired Proofs in the 50 to 58 range.[31] For more detailed information see www.uspatterns.com.

PF-20	PF-40	PF-50	PF-60	PF-62	PF-63	PF-64	PF-65
			$55,000	$65,000	$75,000	$85,000	$150,000

1839 Gobrecht Dollar

Proof mintage: 300

History: The obverse is with stars and the reverse has an eagle in a plain field. In 1860, James Ross Snowden noted this in his book, *The Cabinet Collection of the Mint of the United States:* "1839.

actual size: 39–40 mm
An 1839 J-104 Gobrecht dollar with stars on the obverse, plain reverse, struck in silver, and with a reeded edge. It has Die Alignment 4 with the eagle flying horizontally and upside-down.

A dollar, of the same type as the pattern dollar of the previous year, was struck. *The Director's Report* of that time states that 300 of these were coined, but we have been unable to find any memorandum to that effect on any of the Mint records, where it should properly appear, if such were the case. They are not as rare as the dollars of 1838, and the coinage was probably more extensive." Original coins have Die Alignment 4. In theory, to match the dollars of 1836, it would seem that Die Alignment 1 would be standard. However, no coin with that alignment has ever been reported. Restrikes were made in later years in Die Alignments 3 and 4. Most of the higher-grade Proofs in existence today are restrikes.

Availability in circulated grades: Many coins of this issue exist in grades from PF-30 to 58. Many if not most of these have problems and have not been certified. All are Die Alignment 4. Per Larry Briggs, "Back in the 1980s I searched for a so-called original with Die Alignment 1, only to encounter 44 coins that were impaired, spent, holed, and with other problems. I concluded that what many called restrikes at the time were in fact originals."[32] As of 2015 the matter of originals versus restrikes is still a matter of discussion and, in some instances, disagreement. The website www.uspatterns.com has discussions on this.

Characteristics of striking: This issue is well struck.

Proofs: These are in the minority, but 47 have been certified, mostly in lower Proof grades.

PF-20	PF-40	PF-50	PF-60	PF-62	PF-63	PF-64	PF-65
$20,000	$25,000	$37,500	$42,500	$50,000	$60,000	$70,000	$100,000

Liberty Seated Dollars (1840–1873)
THE NEW DESIGN

Before coinage of silver dollars commenced in 1840 Gobrecht modified the 1836 and 1839 designs. In the new version Liberty appears less delicate in form, has drapery (called by some a "chiton") extending from her left elbow, and the word LIBERTY, in relief on the Gobrecht dollars of 1836 to 1839, is now incuse. There is no indication of the engraver's name.

The reverse with a perched eagle was adapted from Gobrecht's motif used on quarters beginning in 1838 and half dollars in 1839 which, in turn, was taken from John Reich's half dollar reverse design of 1807.

SILVER DOLLARS IN COMMERCE

In 1840 the first Liberty Seated silver dollars were made in normal finish and were intended for circulation. The first coinage took place on July 21, 1840.[33] Sources differ as to whether these dollars and those of later dates ever circulated widely at face value.

From *Niles' National Register* November 21, 1840:

> *New Coin.* The United States Mint is engaged in coining a new dollar of a smaller diameter, and consequently more convenient, than the Spanish coin, and is altogether better executed.

Not even a full two months later, *Niles' National Register* introduced the new dollar on January 2, 1841:

> *New Dollars.* A few dollars have just been coined at the Mint in Philadelphia with new and very beautiful devices, resembling the latest halves and quarters. They have sold freely at three percent premium for New Year's presents.

Although in 1840 a dollar contained about its value in silver and other silver denominations were of full intrinsic value as well, only a few dollars circulated in commerce. In 1841 a silver dollar had a premium value of about 3 percent (as above) to 6 percent in terms of paper money, the last being bills of state-chartered banks in sound financial condition. One reason for this extra value is that while gold coins were exported in quantity to foreign banks and merchants (bank notes were not wanted) and took up most of the trade, there was a demand for silver dollars as well, these being more convenient to handle than coins of smaller denominations. Most were shipped to Europe, particularly to England and to a lesser extent France. China was also an important export destination beginning in 1842. The Chinese strongly preferred silver to gold, including in large transactions. Silver dollars sent to Europe were often returned to America to purchase goods. Dollars that went to China were nearly all melted.

Mintage quantities of silver dollars were modest in the 1840s with 1842 recording the largest production with 814,618. The low point of the decade was 1848 with just 15,000. In 1846 the first branch-mint coinage took place with 59,000 1846-O dollars. Most of the dollars in commerce at the time were Spanish-American eight-reales coins, of which there were millions. Unlike the U.S. dollar, the eight-reales were accepted in every port in the world and were instantly recognized as being full silver value. As an example, ships leaving New England ports for the "pepper trade" in the East Indies each took thousands of such Spanish-American dollars.[34] No account has been found of American silver dollars going there.

After 1849 when the international price of silver rose and gold became more "common" in ratio, all silver coins except some half dimes and dimes disappeared from circulation. For the smaller denominations the slight extra value was often not worth the effort. At that time it cost $1.013 in metal to make a dollar. This was not a deterrent to their coinage, as such pieces were made at the request of bullion depositors and circulated for slightly more than face value. After this point the price of silver rose further and dollars in circulation, not plentiful at the time, were bought up by exchange and bullion brokers, as were other silver denominations, especially quarters and half dollars. Production of silver dollars fell sharply, almost but not quite to the vanishing point in 1851 and 1852. In the meantime gold dollars, which made their debut in 1849, were produced in large quantities for the next several years and satisfied domestic demand for a dollar coin.

The Act of February 21, 1853, remedied the lack of silver coins in commerce by reducing the weight of silver coins from the half dime to the half dollar. The new lightweight coins circulated very effectively afterward. The weight of the silver dollar was unchanged as it was viewed as a bullion or trade coin used only for export. Beginning in that year, production of dollars increased. Nearly all were struck to the order of bullion depositors who used them in international commerce, especially to Liverpool (in large shipments during the decade, sometimes more than 100,000 dollars at a time) and to China (via clipper ships, the exciting mode of long-distance maritime trade at the time), this per newspaper accounts. Considering the large quantities involved *vis-à-vis* the mintages of Liberty Seated dollars it may be that some "American dollar" shipments included other coins. It also seems that many were returned to the United States and used again in the export trade, such as from England back to America to buy bales of cotton. This accounts for the circulation seen on many dollars, especially those dated in the 1840s. Such coins were exchanged for their bullion value at their destinations, and the face value did not matter.

Silver dollars continued to be made for commerce each year except for 1858 when the production was limited to about 210 or more for the numismatic trade.[35] In 1866 the motto IN GOD WE TRUST was added to the reverse of higher-denomination silver coins including the dollar.

BRANCH-MINT COINAGE OF DOLLARS

While the vast majority of Liberty Seated dollars were struck at the Philadelphia Mint, the branch mints at New Orleans, San Francisco, and Carson City each contributed a small share. The initial branch-mint issue of Liberty Seated dollars did not occur until 1846, when 59,000 coins were struck in New Orleans and used in the export trade from their port—the largest by far on the Gulf Coast. The next issue was the 1850-O dollar produced to the extent of 40,000 coins and distributed the same way. In 1859 and 1860 large quantities of silver dollars were minted in New Orleans. This was printed in the New Orleans *Times-Picayune*, April 22, 1859:

New Coinage at the Branch Mint

Correspondence has been recently published in this city by the superintendent of the Branch Mint stating that silver dollars are to be coined at that institution at an early period.

This is looked upon as a matter of much importance to the commerce of our city and to the American trade with China. These dollars are not needed at home, our half dollars, quarters, and dimes being the only silver coins required for convenient change, and the silver dollars will be coined only for exportation. . . .

The purpose now is to induce the Chinamen, if possible, to take the American dollars as they do the Mexican, the former having very nearly as much silver in them as the latter. If this can be done the great premium on Mexican dollars will be spared and the profits of the merchants being increased, the trade with China will increase . . .

At the Carson City Mint Liberty Seated dollars were produced from 1870 through 1873 inclusive, and bore distinguishing CC mintmarks. These were mostly distributed regionally. The 1870-CC dollars are seen with frequency today. The rarest variety is the 1873-CC.

The first San Francisco Mint Liberty Seated dollars were struck in 1859, the 1859-S, of which 20,000 were minted specifically for export to China. Examples are scarce today in all grades, and in Uncirculated preservation they are great rarities. The second San Francisco dollar is the 1870-S. No mintage figure for this issue was listed in official reports, but over the years nine specimens have surfaced, with reports of a tenth. The 1872-S, with a mintage of 9,000, is fairly scarce in all grades. In Uncirculated preservation it is extremely rare. The 1873-S Liberty Seated silver dollar has a reported mintage of 700 pieces, but with the exception of a single coin sent to Philadelphia for review by the Assay Commission, all were melted. The assay coin was probably melted as well.

OTHER ASPECTS OF MINTING AND CIRCULATION

Congressional testimony, newspaper accounts, and other narratives that tried to explain why silver dollars were not seen in circulation were usually inaccurate. Most people, including congressmen, did not understand that the coins cost more than face value to produce and thus were valued at bullion. Some thought that foreigners preferred dollars, and sharpers were buying them up at face value and shipping them at a profit. One congressional witness suggested that if the Mint stopped making silver dollars, the government would make huge profits if on its own it would ship half dollars overseas, never mind that the half dollars were lightweight.[36]

Beginning in the spring of 1862 when the Treasury Department began issuing a flood of Legal Tender Notes that were not redeemable in gold or silver coins, citizens, uncertain as to the outcome of the Civil War, began hoarding silver coins of all kinds from three-cent pieces to half dollars. Dollars were not a factor as they still cost more to produce ($1.041 in silver) than face value, had not been seen in circulation for years, and they continued to be used for export and for sale to bullion brokers and exchange houses. It was not until after April 20, 1876, that silver coins were at par with Legal Tender Notes, and long-stored coins began appearing in circulation. By that time the mintage of Liberty Seated dollars had been discontinued. In any event, few silver dollars had been among the coins hoarded.

ASPECTS OF STRIKING

Gobrecht dollars, the two circulating issues as well as various patterns, 1836 to 1839, are all in Proof format and are sharply struck. On circulating Liberty Seated dollars 1840 and later, the prominent relief of the shield caused the word LIBERTY to wear away much faster than on lower denominations in the Liberty Seated series, particularly the half dime and dime. These latter denominations can be worn considerably and still have LIBERTY showing, whereas on silver dollars the word begins to disappear after only slight wear.

On circulation strikes weakness can be present in several areas. On the obverse the prime places to look for weakness are the top of the head of Liberty and the stars. Weakness, when present, typically begins with stars eight and nine (counting from the left) and progresses gradually to the left and the right. There are some coins in which this varies, and stars to the left are sharply struck and stars to the right are weak, but in general the weakness begins or is centered around stars eight and nine.

On the reverse, typical areas of weakness are the top of the shield and the eagle's neck immediately above it, the top of the eagle's wing on the left, and the eagle's leg on the left. Striking can vary, even on coins made from the same die pairs. It was the practice to mount a pair of dies on a press, adjust them for separation (the distance between the dies determines how deep the metal will flow into the die recesses; the wider the distance, the poorer the strike, but the longer the dies will last), and strike coins. The dies were then removed, stored if they were still serviceable, and later put back on a press, adjusted again (perhaps differently from the first time), and used to strike additional coins.

PROOF LIBERTY SEATED DOLLARS

From 1840 through 1858 Proofs were issued to satisfy requests of collectors. Some were also issued as part of sets. The Mint was very accommodating to numismatists. Among enthusiastic numismatists of the early 1800s Robert Gilmor Jr. of Baltimore stood in the first rank.[37] Over a period of time he assembled a vast cabinet of treasures among which were such delicacies as virtually complete sets of U.S. coins by date sequence, two 1787 Brasher doubloons,[38] and many fine Greek, Roman, and classical issues. Beginning in the 1820s, Gilmor contacted Adam Eckfeldt at the Mint, presumably in connection with coins needed for his collection. In the 1830s he encouraged the institution to form a display of its own specimens, which became a reality when Adam Eckfeldt and W.E. Dubois set up the Mint Cabinet in June 1838. Eckfeldt had been with the Mint since its early years.

In 1841, Gilmor corresponded with former Secretary of War Joel Roberts Poinsett, who was involved in the establishment of the National Institute for the Promotion of Science to house American collections and other treasures. The National Cabinet of Curiosities owned by the government was given to the Institute's care, as were some other properties. Gilmor suggested that collections be formed to illustrate coinage of the Mint as well as the various states. In a letter dated April 14, 1841, Gilmor shared some thoughts with Poinsett and told of his own experiences with the Mint:

> The Mint has aided me considerably, and has even provided desiderata from the old dies, when I require it—Mr. Eckfeldt of the Mint has been of great service to me, and was stimulated by my attempt to commence one for the Mint itself, which really ought not to be without a specimen of every one of its coins—by timely attention to the subject by whoever has charge of the Department may soon make a considerable advance towards obtaining those in circulation, but no time should be lost, as the old gold coin is gradually disappearing by being coined into the new.[39] The Mint would no doubt aid you in this, and coin your deficiencies.

However, the National Institute did not flourish and in time was replaced by the Smithsonian Institution, which later acquired the Institute's collections.[40]

There have been various theories on whether the Mint restruck Proof dollars, and it seems likely that it did to accommodate collectors' needs. One obverse die is known for each of the Proof years of the 1840s. For 1840 there are two reverse dies. A single reverse die was used from 1841 to 1850, then discarded. This has a tiny "pimple" or projection on the right side of the final A in AMERICA. If restrikes were made the original die pairs were used.

Specialists know that in 1851 no original Proofs were made. At a later time the Mint provided restrikes for collectors that were privately sold by officials, mainly to Philadelphia dealer William K. Idler and, later, to his son-in-law John W. Haseltine. The 1851 restrikes have the date centered, rather than high as on the originals. As the date numerals are identical, it is not known if the restrike die was made in 1851 and not used at that time, or if it was made later.

No Proof silver dollars were coined in 1853. Years later restrikes were made and it was said to be 12 in number, but facts are scarce. These were made to satisfy numismatists who were building sets of Proofs. This may reflect that by the early 1860s this was more or less the number of active specialists in that area. The 1851 and 1852 restrikes were made to fill the need of many more collectors who were assembling date sets, mostly of circulation strikes.

Almost without exception numismatists of the 1800s and early 1900s who built high-grade sets of Liberty Seated dollars acquired Proofs. In most instances circulation strikes, preserved by chance, were simply unavailable in choice and gem grades.

GRADING LIBERTY SEATED SILVER DOLLARS

1864. Graded MS-65.

MS-60 to 70 (Mint State). *Obverse:* At MS-60, some abrasion and contact marks are evident, most noticeably on the bosom and thighs and knees. Luster is present, but may be dull or lifeless. At MS-63, contact marks are very few, and abrasion is minimal. An MS-65 coin has no abrasion in the fields (but may have a hint on the knees), and contact marks are trivial. Check the knees of Liberty and the right field. Luster should be full and rich on later issues, not necessarily so for dates in the 1840s. Most Mint State coins of the 1861 to 1865 years, Philadelphia issues, have extensive die striae (from not completely finishing the die). *Reverse:* Comments apply as for the obverse, except that in lower Mint State grades, abrasion and marks are most noticeable on the eagle's head, the neck, the claws, and the top of the wings (harder to see there, however). At MS-65 or higher, there are no marks visible to the unaided eye. The field is mainly protected by design elements and does not show abrasion as much as does the obverse on a given coin.

Illustrated coin: The fields show striations from incomplete polishing of the dies, but this does not affect the grade.

1842. Graded AU-58.

AU-50, 53, 55, 58 (About Uncirculated). *Obverse:* Light wear is seen on the thighs and knees, bosom, and head. At AU-58, the luster is extensive but incomplete, especially in the right field. At AU-50 and 53, luster is less. *Reverse:* Wear is visible on the eagle's neck, the claws, and the top of the wings. An AU-58 coin has nearly full luster. At AU-50 and 53, there still are traces of luster.

Illustrated coin: This is an attractive example with much of the original luster.

1846. Graded EF-40.

EF-40, 45 (Extremely Fine). *Obverse:* Further wear is seen on all areas, especially the thighs and knees, bosom, and head. Little or no luster is seen on most coins. From this grade downward, strike sharpness in the stars and the head does not matter to connoisseurs. *Reverse:* Further wear is evident on the eagle's neck, claws, and the wings, although on well-struck coins nearly all details are sharp.

1854. Graded VF-20.

VF-20, 30 (Very Fine). *Obverse:* Further wear is seen. Many details of the gown are worn away, but the lower-relief areas above and to the right of the shield remain well defined. Hair detail is mostly or completely gone. The word LIBERTY is weak at BE (PCGS allows BER to be missing "on some coins"). *Reverse:* Wear is more extensive, with some feathers blended together, especially on the neck for a typical coin. Detail remains quite good overall.

1872-CC. Graded F-12.

F-12, 15 (Fine). *Obverse:* The seated figure is well worn, but with some detail above and to the right of the shield. BER in LIBERTY is visible only in part or missing entirely. *Reverse:* Wear is extensive, with about a third to half of the feathers flat or blended with others.

    Illustrated coin: The reverse is stronger than the obverse on this coin.

1871-CC. Graded VG-8.

VG-8, 10 (Very Good). *Obverse:* The seated figure is more worn, but some detail can be seen above and to the right of the shield. The shield is discernible, but the upper-right section may be flat and blended into the seated figure. In LIBERTY two or three letters, or a combination totaling that, are readable. *Reverse.* Further wear has flattened half or slightly more of the feathers (depending on the strike). The rim is visible all around, as are the ends of the denticles. A Very Good Liberty Seated dollar usually has more detail overall than a lower-denomination coin of the same design.

1850-O. Graded G-6.

G-4, 6 (Good). *Obverse:* The seated figure is worn nearly smooth. The stars and date are complete, but may be weak toward the periphery. *Reverse:* The eagle shows only a few details of the shield and feathers. The rim is worn down. The tops of the border letters are weak or worn away, although the inscription can still be read.

1872. Graded AG-3.

AG-3 (About Good). *Obverse:* The seated figure is visible in outline form. Much or all of the rim is worn away. The stars are weak and some may be missing. The date remains clear. *Reverse:* The border letters are partially worn away. The eagle is mostly in outline form, but with a few details discernible. The rim is weak or missing.

1861. Graded PF-63.

PF-60 to 70 (Proof). *Obverse and Reverse:* Proofs that are extensively cleaned and have many hairlines, or that are dull and grainy, are lower level, such as PF-60 to 62. These are not widely desired, except for use as fillers for the dates (most circulation-strike dollars are rare after 1849 and before 1870). The rarities of 1851, 1852, and 1858 are in demand no matter what the grade. With medium hairlines and good reflectivity, an assigned grade of PF-64 is appropriate, and with relatively few hairlines, gem PF-65. In various grades hairlines are most easily seen in the obverse field. PF-66 should have hairlines so delicate that magnification is needed to see them. Above that, a Proof should be free of such lines.

Illustrated coin: The frosty cameo motifs on this example contrast with the deeply mirrored fields

Collecting Liberty Seated Dollars

In 1859 in the first widely circulated book published on the title subject, the *American Numismatical Manual* by Montroville Wilson Dickeson commented on the availability of silver dollars, including the Liberty Seated series. His remarks cover much of the first two decades of the issue and give an interesting view of how such coins were considered by numismatists of the era. The book was lightly researched at best, with the result that it was generally ignored by auction catalogers and other writers. However, the entries, of which many are off the mark of reality, make interesting reading today.

The 1840 dollar, the first year of issue of the Liberty Seated series, was called "scarce," while the issue of the following year, 1841, was designated as "plenty." Similarly, 1842 and 1843 were "plenty," but 1844 was "rare" and 1845 "scarce." Dollars of 1846 were likewise "scarce," but those of 1847 were "plenty." Followed by the "scarce" 1848 and "plenty" of the 1849 issue, the 1850 dollar was considered to be "scarce," and the 1851 dollar "extremely rare." The dollar of 1852 was considered "rare," while that of 1853 was "scarce" The 1854 Liberty Seated dollar, just five years old when Dickeson wrote his book in 1859, was already considered to be "rare," but 1855 for some reason was in the "plenty" category, followed by 1856 "rare" and 1857, the last year studied, "plenty."

Each of these issues is detailed in the present text. Today, probably most buyers of high-grade Liberty Seated dollars desire one of each type: 1840 to 1865, Without Motto and 1866 to 1873 with IN GOD WE TRUST to add to a type set. This is easily done.

Circulation strikes are readily available in such grades as VF to AU and in the upper ranges from MS-60 to 63. MS-64 coins are scarce and MS-65 examples are rare. Proofs are not hard to find with dates in the 1860s and 1870s, although gems are scarce.

Forming a complete collection by date and mintmarks is difficult to do and is limited by the 1870-S, of which only nine are confirmed to exist with a tenth reported. If this issue is ignored, then the most difficult in all grades are the 1851 and 1852 originals, the Proof-only 1858 among Philadelphia issues, and, among branch-mint coins, the 1873-CC. Next in rarity comes the 1871-CC, then 1872-CC. Other branch-mint issues such as 1846-O, 1850-O, 1859-S, 1870-CC, and 1872-S are somewhat elusive, particularly in higher grades. Among Carson City coins, 1870-CC is the most available and also is the best struck, often occurring (in better grades) with a prooflike surface. 1859-O and 1860-O are readily obtainable in Mint State, the typical piece being MS-60 with heavy scarring from coin-to-coin contact in bags. Unlike the situation for lower denominations in the Liberty Seated series, coins below the grade of Fine-12 are rarely encountered and thus are not studied here. Most circulated coins range from VF-20 upward.

After 1858, through the end of the series in 1873, Proofs were made in quantities averaging about 500 to 1,000 per year. Although these quantities in an absolute sense are small, still the remaining coins from the Proof mintages survive in larger numbers than do Mint State coins of certain of the same dates. In terms of auction appearances, for some dates in the early 1860s, more Proofs appear in catalogs than do VF, EF, AU, and Mint State coins combined! Impaired Proofs sell at a deep discount from attractive Proofs and provide the most feasible way to acquire high grade examples of dates in the early 1860s.

Most probably, the commonest date among without-motto Liberty Seated dollars 1840–1865 is the 1847 with competition furnished by 1842 and 1843. Among later Liberty Seated dollars, with IN GOD WE TRUST, 1866 through 1873, the 1871 is most often seen. However, for purposes of comparison, both of these dates are rare when viewed against Morgan and Peace silver dollars. Certainly there are more Mint State 1934-S Peace dollars (the key issue in that series) around than there are Mint State Liberty Seated dollars of all dates from in the 1840s combined! Such comparisons are not necessarily relevant, as many more people collect Peace dollars by date and mint than collect Liberty Seated dollars, and thus the demand for the 1934-S is higher. However, the comparison does point out that one can get "a lot of coin for the money" by going away from a popular series and buying pieces within an obscure specialty.

In general, Mint State Liberty Seated dollars are rare, exceptions being 1859-O and 1860-O, many of which came to light during the Treasury release of silver dollars in 1962. At the same time many thousands of circulated Liberty Seated coins were released. I recall purchasing large quantities of these, shipped to my company unsorted in cloth bags containing 1,000 each. Jim Ruddy, my business partner at the time, and I were so excited that we worked nonstop for a few days—not even going out for lunch—to arrange these dollars in poker-chip fashion in piles according to date, from 1840 onward. As I recall, we had more 1847-dated dollars than any other early issue.

BEING A SMART BUYER

First of all, if you intend to make Liberty Seated dollars a specialty, you need to adopt the mindset that most old-time collectors as well as members of the Liberty Seated Collectors Club have: Reality is nearly all existing circulation strikes are in grades below Mint State. This is quite different from the typical incoming collector or investor entering rare coins—who through advertising and promotion may be led to believe that the only coins worth owning are choice and gem Mint State and Proof pieces. Of course, this is silly when it comes to Liberty Seated coins of all denominations—as in the early series, worn coins are the rule for certain dates and mintmarks and not the exception. No one has ever completed a set of Mint State coins of the 1840s and 1850s.

When you determine what you would like, cherrypick for quality. Striking sharpness can vary, and a well-defined coin costs no more than one that is weakly struck. Avoid coins with dark or deep toning. Not only are they usually unattractive, but more than just a few have been recolored in order to mask friction or light wear. The most attractive coins are brilliant or are lightly toned. In all instances it is probably best to use PCGS or NGC certified coins as a *starting point*. Examine such pieces carefully. As mentioned for other Liberty Seated denominations, a sharply struck MS-63 coin with great eye appeal is more worthwhile, in my opinion, than is an MS-65 with areas of light striking and/or dark or unattractive toning.

Take your time when buying. No one ever built a fine collection of Liberty Seated dollars quickly. Enjoy the experience over a period of a year or two or three.[41]

1840–1866, No Motto (Variety 1)

The figure of Liberty has drapery at her elbow. The reverse has a perched eagle. This design is similar in general style to the quarters and half dollars of the time.

Designed by: Christian Gobrecht.

Specifications: *Composition:* 90 percent silver, 10 percent copper. *Diameter:* 38.1 mm. *Weight:* 412.5 grains (26.73 grams). *Edge:* Reeded.

1840

Circulation-strike mintage: 61,005

Proof mintage: 40–60

Availability in Mint State: Even though the 1840 is the first year of issue of this design, there seems to have been no

actual size: 38.1 mm

particular notice of it by the general public. By then the 1836 Gobrecht dollars were well known to those interested, and the 1840 dollars attracted little attention. Accordingly, surviving Mint State coins are those that were saved as a matter of chance, not intent. Among first-year-of-issue Liberty Seated denominations, dollars of 1840 are far and away rarer than any of the others. In 2014 and 2015 the Eugene H. Gardner

Sale featured two examples of this coin in MS-63. *MS-60 to 62:* 15 to 20. *MS-63:* 8 to 11. *MS-64:* 2 to 4. *MS-65 or better:* 0 or 1.

Availability in circulated grades: For some of the dollars in the 1840s an occasional example in lower grades is found, but most are Fine or better. *F-12 to AU-58:* 800 to 1,200.

Characteristics of striking: This issue is usually quite well struck with sharp stars and prominent, broad rims.

Proofs: The number of issued Proofs of the 1840 dollar exceeded that of any other Proofs of the decade. Those that survive are mostly at lower levels, suggesting that many may have been presented to various officials rather than to interested numismatists, although a few were included in sets. Two Proof reverse dies were created. The best known of these is the coin that was thereafter carefully preserved at the Mint, to be brought out on various occasions through 1850 to strike Proof dollars. This has a tiny raised area or "pimple" extending into the field from the final A in AMERICA. There is absolutely no evidence that the die was used at a later date for restriking. It is the opinion of the author, and also of the late David W. Akers (who was a consultant for certain early Proof listings over the years) that any Proof dollar 1840–1850 struck from this die is an original Proof made within the span indicated. This die was used on most of the single dollars as well as those in all of the rare Proof sets seen from this decade. Another die used for Proof 1840 dollars, and apparently not later, was first identified on a coin offered by Heritage Auctions in the 2002 Central States sale: (1) The first horizontal line in the shield extends to the left into the eagle's wing; (2) The final element of vertical stripe two and the first and third elements of stripe three penetrate the innermost shield border; (3) The final two elements of stripe one penetrate solidity to horizontal line five; (4) The first element of stripe two penetrates to horizontal line two. Approximately 27 examples have been certified.

Notes: Striking of dollars with the revised design began in July 1840, with 12,500 pieces being delivered by chief coiner Franklin Peale. This was a speculative coinage ordered by Mint Director Robert M. Patterson to acquaint silver bullion depositors with their new option. Little happened for some months, but finally enough bankers and bullion dealers became interested in the new coins to deposit the necessary silver and order them. Coinage resumed in November 1840 with 41,000 pieces. A further 7,505 were minted the following month.

In the year 1840, silver dollars amounted to 61,005 pieces, while half dollars came to 2,290,108 coins with a face value of $1,145,054, or 19 times greater than the value of silver dollars minted during the same 12-month period. While there is no doubt that the Liberty Seated dollar did limited duty in American commerce during the 1840s, the vast majority went into the hands of bullion dealers, banks, and exchange brokers, or where used in the export trade. As previously noted, such coins traded at a premium from the outset. All during the Liberty Seated dollar–era half dollars were the coins of choice for circulation at face value within the United States.[42]

The 1840 has always been in strong demand by type-set collectors seeking the first year of the design.

VG-8	F-12	VF-20	EF-40	AU-50	MS-60
$455	$500	$650	$1,000	$1,750	$5,500

MS-63	MS-65	PF-60	PF-63	PF-65
$18,500	—	$12,500	$25,000	$80,000

1841

Circulation-strike mintage: 173,000

Proof mintage: 10–15

actual size: 38.1 mm

Availability in Mint State: As is true of other silver dollars of the 1840s, there is no record of any numismatic interest in newly coined circulation strikes. The survival of Mint State coins is a matter of rare chance. In 2014 the Eugene H. Gardner Sale featured an example of this coin in MS-64. *MS-60 to 62:* 15 to 20. *MS-63:* 5 to 8. *MS-64:* 3 to 5. *MS-65 or better:* 1 or 2.

Availability in circulated grades: *F-12 to AU-58:* 1,000 to 1,500.

Characteristics of striking: Striking of this issue varies; some have flatness in areas, including stars and/or denticles.

Proofs: The 1841 Proof dollar is viewed today as one of the great Proof rarities in the series. Typically, a decade or more may elapse between auction offerings. Approximately four examples have been certified.

Notes: The 1841 *Annual Report of the Director of the Mint* showed the main sources of silver: bullion from North Carolina worth $4,198, foreign bullion worth $210,546, Mexican dollars worth $272,320, dollars of South America worth $14,292, European coins worth $55,692, and silver plate worth $5,398. The above figures totaled $562,446 in comparison to a total silver coinage (of all denominations from the half dime to the dollar) for the year of $577,750. However, the total supply of bullion had little to do with silver dollar coinage. The number struck depended solely on the bullion deposited by those specifically asking for dollars. Few depositors did as they were not useful for general circulation and sold at a slight premium.

VG-8	F-12	VF-20	EF-40	AU-50	MS-60
$450	$500	$600	$800	$1,250	$3,250

MS-63	MS-65	PF-60	PF-63	PF-65
$8,000	$90,000		$70,000	$250,000

1842

Circulation-strike mintage: 184,618

Proof mintage: 10–15

actual size: 38.1 mm

Availability in Mint State: Examples of the 1842 Liberty Seated dollar are occasionally available in grade levels of MS-60 to

MS-63, but in higher grades the issue is a rarity. This is the first Liberty Seated dollar variety that has any claim to general availability in Mint State, but, even so, in absolute terms Mint State specimens are rare. In 2015 the Eugene H. Gardner sale featured an example of this coin in MS-64. *MS-60 to 62:* 40 to 55. *MS-63:* 20 to 25. *MS-64:* 15 to 20. *MS-65 or better:* 0 or 1.

Availability in circulated grades: *F-12 to AU-58:* 3,500 to 5,000+.

Characteristics of striking: This issue is usually seen well struck, but there are exceptions, including some lightly struck on stars four through six on the obverse and at the top of the shield and on the eagle's neck on the reverse.

Proofs: In 2015 the Eugene H. Gardner Sale featured an example of this coin in PF-65 (years earlier ex Oscar G. Schilke as part of a silver Proof set of this year that also had a Small-Date quarter). Approximately eight examples have been certified.

VG-8	F-12	VF-20	EF-40	AU-50	MS-60
$405	$475	$525	$800	$1,000	$3,250

MS-63	MS-65	PF-60	PF-63	PF-65
$4,750		$15,000	$35,000	$80,000

1843

Circulation-strike mintage: 165,100

Proof mintage: 10–15

Availability in Mint State: In 2014 the Eugene H. Gardner Sale featured an example of this coin in MS-64. *MS-60 to 62:* 20 to 25. *MS-63:* 8 to 12. *MS-64:* 1 or 2. *MS-65 or better:* 0 or 1.

actual size: 38.1 mm

Availability in circulated grades: *F-12 to AU-58:* 3,500 to 5,000+.

Characteristics of striking: Striking of this issue varies, but the topmost stars and head of Liberty are often lightly struck.

Proofs: Approximately seven examples have been certified, of which one is lightly circulated.

VG-8	F-12	VF-20	EF-40	AU-50	MS-60
$405	$475	$525	$800	$1,000	$2,500

MS-63	MS-65	PF-60	PF-63	PF-65
$7,000		$15,000	$30,000	$110,000

1844

Circulation-strike mintage: 20,000

Proof mintage: 10–15

actual size: 38.1 mm

Availability in Mint State: What few Mint State coins the author has seen have all been very frosty, sometimes with prooflike reverse fields. In 2014 the Eugene H. Gardner Sale featured an example of this coin in MS-63. *MS-60 to 62:* 15 to 20. *MS-63:* 2 or 3. *MS-64:* 1 or 2. *MS-65 or better:* 0 or 1.

Availability in circulated grades: *F-12 to AU-58:* 700 to 1,000.

Characteristics of striking: This issue is usually well struck with smooth surfaces.

Proofs: Approximately eight examples have been certified, of which at least two are lightly circulated.

Notes: The year 1844 was notable as the first of low-mintage silver dollars of this design. As before, most depositors of silver bullion wanted lower denominations that could be placed in the channels of commerce for face value. Only one delivery of silver dollars was made this year, that of 20,000 pieces on December 31. The China trade in particular demanded silver after certain ports, mainly Canton, were opened for the first time to Westerners in 1842. Europe remained the primary destination for exported dollars.

Four stripes: This issue is also known as "quad stripes." Circulation strikes of the year 1844 have four tiny vertical stripes composing each large vertical stripe on the obverse shield, whereas all other circulation strikes in the Liberty Seated series from 1840 to 1873 have just three stripes, as do Proofs of all years (including 1844). The fourth or extra stripe, to the right side of the normal three, is in all cases more lightly defined than the other three and is

somewhat irregular. The feature is considered to be a doubled die. A few other elements of die doubling are present, including a doubling of the pointed top to the shield and the presence of three border lines (instead of the normal two) on the right edge of the shield. The feature of four elements to each stripe is unique in the series.

VG-8	F-12	VF-20	EF-40	AU-50	MS-60
$500	$600	$650	$900	$1,550	$4,750

MS-63	MS-65	PF-60	PF-63	PF-65
$13,500	$125,000	$17,500	$30,000	$90,000

1845

Circulation-strike mintage: 24,500

Proof mintage: 10–15

actual size: 38.1 mm

Availability in Mint State: In Mint State the 1845 is the rarest of all Liberty Seated dollars of the 1840s. In 2015 the Eugene H. Gardner Sale featured an example of this coin in MS-63. *MS-60 to 62:* 3 to 5. *MS-63:* 2 to 4. *MS-64:* 1 or 2. *MS-65 or better:* 0 or 1.

Availability in circulated grades: *F-12 to AU-58:* 900 to 1,400.

Characteristics of striking: This issue is usually well struck, but there are exceptions.

Proofs: The date is doubled. In 2015 the Eugene H. Gardner Sale featured an example of this coin in PF-66. Approximately 11 examples have been certified.

Notes: Depositor requests for dollars remained small. Only two deliveries of silver dollars were made during the year. Silver coins of all denominations were scarce in circulation (see "The Year 1845" in chapter 3).

VG-8	F-12	VF-20	EF-40	AU-50	MS-60
$525	$600	$750	$1,100	$1,750	$6,500

MS-63	MS-65	PF-60	PF-63	PF-65
$28,500		$12,500	$30,000	$70,000

1846

Circulation-strike mintage: 110,600

Proof mintage: 10–15

actual size: 38.1 mm

Availability in Mint State: In 2014 and 2015 the Eugene H. Gardner Sale featured examples of this coin in MS-65 and MS-64. *MS-60 to 62:* 25 to 32. *MS-63:* 9 to 12. *MS-64:* 5 to 7. *MS-65 or better:* 3 to 5.

Availability in circulated grades: *F-12 to AU-58:* 2,000+ to 3,000.

Characteristics of striking: This issue is usually very well struck and very pleasing in appearance.

Proofs: More Proofs than normal appear to have been made this year. The reason is unknown. The date is repunched over an earlier 1846 that was too low. This variety was formerly called 1846/1845 (per the Lorin G. Parmelee Collection Sale, 1890) and, more often, 1846/1844 (per the 1945 F.C.C. Boyd "World's Greatest Collection" Sale and others). Approximately 14 examples have been certified.

Detail of the repunched date.

VG-8	F-12	VF-20	EF-40	AU-50	MS-60
$430	$500	$600	$750	$1,000	$2,000

MS-63	MS-65	PF-60	PF-63	PF-65
$5,500	$90,000	$12,500	$30,000	$105,000

1846-O

Circulation-strike mintage: 59,000

actual size: 38.1 mm

Availability in Mint State: In Mint State the 1846-O is very rare; just how rare is not known with certainty. Some of the specimens seen have been so deeply toned that it is impossible for anyone (including a certification service) to determine, for example, whether they are AU-58 or Mint State.[43] The Eliasberg coin with prooflike fields was graded MS-65 prooflike in the sale, and MS-63 by PCGS in 1997; a downgrade in contrast to *many* Eliasberg coins being upgraded. In 2014 the Eugene H. Gardner Sale featured an example of this coin in MS-63. *MS-60 to 62:* 10 to 13. *MS-63:* 3 to 5. *MS-64:* 1 or 2. *MS-65 or better:* 1.

Availability in circulated grades: These were extensively circulated in the Mississippi River Basin. *VG-8 to AU-58:* 1,000 to 1,500, most of which are below EF.

Characteristics of striking: This issue has an average strike showing weakness, particularly on the obverse stars, head, and horizontal shield stripes and on the reverse the eagle's head and claws.

Notes: Although the New Orleans Mint opened for business in 1838 it struck no silver dollars until 1846. The mintage was accomplished in June. This was the first of only four dates of Liberty Seated dollars from this mint: 1846-O, 1850-O, 1859-O, and 1860-O.

Most 1846-O dollars were exported, serving the purpose for which they were made (see introductory material in this chapter). Some have the reverse die rotated about 45 degrees clockwise from the normal position.

VG-8	F-12	VF-20	EF-40	AU-50	MS-60	MS-63	MS-65
$455	$550	$675	$850	$1,350	$6,500	$20,000	$150,000

1847

Circulation-strike mintage: 140,750

Proof mintage: 10–15

actual size: 38.1 mm

Availability in Mint State: This issue is available in Mint State, and when seen is apt to be very frosty. From the beginning of the series to 1847, it is the date most often seen MS-60 or above. In 2014 and 2015 the Eugene H. Gardner Sale featured examples of this coin in MS-64 and MS-63. *MS-60 to 62:* 20 to 25. *MS-63:* 25 to 32. *MS-64:* 15 to 20. *MS-65 or better:* 3 to 5.

Availability in circulated grades: The 1847 is one of the most available of all Liberty Seated dollars of the 1840–1865 No-Motto type. In 1963 when the author was sorting through quantities of unattributed worn Liberty Seated dollars from the great Treasury release, he found more of this date than of any other early issue. *F-12 to AU-58:* 3,000 to 5,000.

Characteristics of striking: This issue is usually well struck.

Proofs: Approximately 16 examples have been certified.

Notes: The Philadelphia Mint was busy this year and turned out large numbers of silver coins of all denominations. However, as is true of other years, silver dollars were only struck to the order of bullion depositors specifically requesting them. Most were exported to England and the Chinese port of Canton.

VG-8	F-12	VF-20	EF-40	AU-50	MS-60
$430	$475	$550	$750	$1,000	$2,700

MS-63	MS-65	PF-60	PF-63	PF-65
$5,000	$75,000	$12,500	$22,000	$55,000

1848

Circulation-strike mintage: 15,000

Proof mintage: 10–15

actual size: 38.1 mm

Availability in Mint State: In 2015 the Eugene H. Gardner Sale featured an example of this coin in MS-64. *MS-60 to 62:* 15 to 20. *MS-63:* 4 to 6. *MS-64:* 2 or 3. *MS-65 or better:* 1 or 2.

Availability in circulated grades: *F-12 to AU-58:* 600 to 1,000.

Characteristics of striking: This issue is usually well struck.

Proofs: In 2015 the Eugene H. Gardner Sale featured an example of this coin in PF-66. Approximately ten examples have been certified. One of these shows light wear.

Notes: The Philadelphia Mint produced only 15,000 silver dollars, the lowest production of the 1840–1850 span.

Writing in *The History of Currency 1652–1896*, Second Edition, 1896, p. 259, W.A. Shaw told of the immediate benefits experienced by the Act of July 31, 1834, whereby gold coins began to circulate freely, but also noted this: "The panacea thus magnificently lauded soon proved itself worse than inefficient. The ratio was too high, and the silver dollars could not be maintained. They were unduly exported, especially between the years 1848 and 1851." Shaw knew only *part* of the story.

VG-8	F-12	VF-20	EF-40	AU-50	MS-60
$600	$800	$975	$1,700	$2,250	$5,500

MS-63	MS-65	PF-60	PF-63	PF-65
$13,000		$12,500	$30,000	$65,000

1849

Circulation-strike mintage: 62,600

Proof mintage: 10–15

Availability in Mint State: In 2014 the Eugene H. Gardner Sale featured an example of this coin in MS-64. *MS-60 to 62:* 30 to 40. *MS-63:* 10 to 15. *MS-64:* 5 to 7. *MS-65 or better:* 3 or 4.

actual size: 38.1 mm

Availability in circulated grades: *F-12 to AU-58:* 1,400 to 1,800.

Characteristics of striking: Striking of this issue varies; some are well struck and others show local weakness (particularly at the eagle's neck immediately above the shield, at the eagle's leg to the left, and/or at the stars on the right obverse). Some circulation strikes, even those with areas of light striking, have knife-rims, partial on the obverse, nearly full on the reverse and prooflike surface on both sides.

Proofs: The obverse has the date high and close to base. Extensive die finish marks can be seen under the chin of Liberty. Approximately 9 examples have been certified.

VG-8	F-12	VF-20	EF-40	AU-50	MS-60
$425	$500	$650	$950	$1,400	$2,750

MS-63	MS-65	PF-60	PF-63	PF-65
$6,000	$90,000	$13,500	$34,000	$65,000

1850

Circulation-strike mintage: 7,500

Proof mintage: 20–30

actual size: 38.1 mm

Availability in Mint State: Mint State coins, when seen, are apt to be nearly fully prooflike and are often mistaken for Proofs. Indeed, they were struck from dies also used to coin Proofs. Such coins are rare at all Mint State grade levels but are extremely so in MS-63 or better. In 2014 the Eugene H. Gardner Sale featured an example of this coin in MS-64. *MS-60 to 62:* 10 to 15. *MS-63:* 2 to 4. *MS-64:* 1 or 2. *MS-65 or better:* 0 or 1.

Availability in circulated grades: *F-12 to AU-58:* 350 to 500.

Characteristics of striking: This issue is usually well struck and is always prooflike.

Proofs: Approximately 16 examples have been certified.

Notes: The 1850 dollar begins a decade of rare Liberty Seated dollar issues with nearly all exported.

VG-8	F-12	VF-20	EF-40	AU-50	MS-60
$755	$975	$1,500	$2,100	$3,250	$6,500

MS-63	MS-65	PF-60	PF-63	PF-65
$17,500		$12,500	$25,000	$50,000

1850-O

Circulation-strike mintage: 40,000

actual size: 38.1 mm

Availability in Mint State: In 2014 the Eugene H. Gardner Sale featured an example of this coin in MS-65. *MS-60 to 62:* 7 to 10. *MS-63:* 1 or 2. *MS-64:* 1 or 2. *MS-65 or better:* 0 or 1.

Availability in circulated grades: *VG-8 to AU-58:* 800 to 1,200.

Worn examples of the 1850-O dollar are fairly plentiful today up through and including the Very Fine level. EF pieces are scarce, and AU specimens are fairly rare.

Characteristics of striking: This issue has an average strike for most, though some have weakness on Liberty's head and/or on the eagle's head and claws.

Notes: Most if not all of the metal for this coinage was from melted down Mexican dollars.[44]

VG-8	F-12	VF-20	EF-40	AU-50	MS-60	MS-63	MS-65
$550	$700	$950	$1,550	$3,200	$11,000	$30,000	$120,000

1851, Original, High Date

Circulation-strike mintage: 1,300

actual size: 38.1 mm

Availability in Mint State: In 2015 the Eugene H. Gardner Sale featured an example of this coin in MS-63. *MS-60 to 62:* 5 to 8. *MS-63:* 5 to 8. *MS-64:* 4 to 6. *MS-65 or better:* 2 or 3.

Availability in circulated grades: *VF-20 to AU-58:* 10 to 15, most of which are EF or AU. PCGS has graded a VG-8 and a VG-10.

Characteristics of striking: Stars on the right obverse are usually flat, otherwise, the coins are average strikes. Frosty circulation-strike coins have numerous die striae. The dies clashed at an early time, and to remove most traces the obverse die was relapped, giving it a highly prooflike surface. On all examples seen there is a clash mark in the field near Liberty's elbow drapery.

Notes: R.W. Julian was not able to determine from Mint records whether the 1851 silver dollars were coined for depositors or for the account of the government.

No originals are known in Proof format. Some called such have been prooflike circulation strikes.

VG-8	F-12	VF-20	EF-40	AU-50	MS-60	MS-63	MS-65
$15,000	$16,500	$18,500	$22,500	$30,000	$35,000	$55,000	$140,000

1851, Restrike, Date Centered

Proof-restrike mintage: 35–50

actual size: 38.1 mm

Proofs: Proofs of this issue were struck for the numismatic trade. The date is centered, making restrikes easily identifiable.

Notes: It is not known when restrikes first appeared on the market. Probably many if not most were sold through William K. Idler, the Philadelphia dealer who had close private connections with Mint officials. The terms "original" and "restrike" were not often used in catalogs. Among the exceptions was lot 422 in Edward D. Cogan's sale of June 29 and 30, 1864: "1851 Original Uncirculated impression, very rare."

The restrikes are believed to have been coined at the Philadelphia Mint on at least two occasions, one being 1859 and the other probably later, possibly circa 1867–1868. Two die pairs are known for restrikes.[45] The first public offering of the restrikes of 1851 and 1852 was in Edward Cogan's May 21, 1859, Simon Gratz Collection sale.[46] The catalog was in manuscript, and the sale was held in his art-goods store in Philadelphia.[47]

Restrikes are distinguished by having the date lower and better centered than on the originals. These may have been from a die made but not used in 1851, or a completely new die could have been made circa 1859. The date logotype is identical to that of the original obverse; Mint regulations did not even mention old logotypes, let alone mandate their destruction.[48]

One is struck over an 1846 dollar with the date still discernible under magnification.[49] Another is an "1851-O" dollar. A curious and interesting impression of the Proof restrike dies is overstruck on a previously made New Orleans Mint dollar, probably an 1859-O or 1860-O, but of a mintmark position variety not otherwise seen.[50] The O mintmark is still visible below the eagle on the reverse in the correct position.[51] This may indicate that at least during one restriking period those involved brought their own coins to be used as planchets. It has been suggested that in the 1860s certain unrelated pattern dies were loaned to and used by a private Philadelphia shop. Perhaps some of the dollars were struck off-premises.

Over a long period of years in the 1800s and early 1900s most auction offerings of Proof 1851 dollars omitted mentioning they were restrikes. There were exceptions of course.

PF-60	PF-63	PF-65
$20,000	$30,000	$75,000

1852

Circulation-strike mintage: 1,100

Proof original mintage: 20–30

Proof-restrike mintage: 20–30

Availability in Mint State: Mint State coins have satiny, lustrous surfaces with

Original; actual size: 38.1 mm

minute die striations (illustrated above). Perhaps the Mint saved a few of these for trading purposes at the time of issue. In high grades the 1852 seems to be slightly rarer than the 1851, but the population is so small that no unequivocal conclusions can be drawn. *MS-60 to 62:* 5 to 8. *MS-63:* 2 to 4. *MS-64:* 2 to 4. *MS-65 or better:* 1 or 2.

Availability in circulated grades: *F-12 to AU-58:* 30 to 40. In 2014 the Eugene H. Gardner Sale featured an example of this coin in AU-58.

Characteristics of striking: This issue is usually sharp except for weakness at several stars to the right, especially 9 through 13.

Proof originals: An estimated two to four are known.[52] These were coined using the reverse die used on Proofs of the 1840s.[53]

Proof restrikes: Approximately 15 examples have been certified.

The restrikes are thought to have been made beginning in 1859. All are sharply struck. These were sold privately by Mint officials. There are several minute differences on the reverse, indicating several periods of striking. The first public offering of the restrikes of 1851 and 1852 was in Edward Cogan's May 21, 1859, Simon Gratz Collection sale.[54]

Restrike; actual size: 38.1 mm

Notes: As is true for the 1851 dollar as well, R.W. Julian was not able to determine from Mint records whether the circulation strike 1852 silver dollars were coined for depositors or for the account of the government.

ORIGINAL STRIKES

VG-8	F-12	VF-20	EF-40	AU-50	MS-60
$8,500	$12,500	$15,000	$20,000	$27,500	$40,000

MS-63	MS-65	PF-60		PF-63	PF-65
$65,000	$140,000	$27,500		$43,500	$75,000

RESTRIKES

PF-60	PF-63	PF-65
$18,000	$30,000	$70,000

1853

Circulation-strike mintage: 46,110

Proof-restrike mintage: 15–20

Availability in Mint State: The author believes that somewhere a small hoard of Mint State pieces of this particular date

Original; actual size: 38.1 mm

came to light in the 1970s or early 1980s, but he has seen no notice of such in print. Prior to this, Uncirculated 1853 dollars were very rare. Most Mint State coins are brilliant or are lightly golden toned and are very frosty (rather than prooflike in areas), and seem to have come from a common source (in contrast to pieces from different sources, which have a wide variety of toning, handling marks, etc.). In any event, the 1853 is the only readily available Mint State Liberty Seated dollar of its immediate time frame. In 2014 the Eugene H. Gardner Sale featured an example of this coin in MS-64. *MS-60 to 62:* 100 to 200. *MS-63:* 35 to 50. *MS-64:* 10 to 13. *MS-65 or better:* 2 to 4.

Availability in circulated grades: *F-12 to AU-58:* 700 to 1,000. Most coins of this issue are in higher grades.

Characteristics of striking: This issue is usually well struck, however there are exceptions and some have weak stars, especially stars 9 through 13. "Chin whiskers" or die finish lines are seen below Liberty's chin on most circulation strikes.

Proof restrikes: It is thought that no Proofs were minted in 1853. As early as 1860, George F. Jones noted that no original Proof dollars were struck in 1853. This was rather frustrating, for a number of collectors desired to have complete sets of Proof

Restrike; actual size: 38.1 mm

dollars from 1840 onward. Accordingly, the traditional view held by numismatists for many years is that a number of Proof 1853 dollars were prepared at the Mint circa 1862. It has been repeated in numismatic literature that only 12 Proof 1853 pieces were made. The author does not quarrel with this figure, for over the years 1853 Proof dollars have appeared on the market at infrequent intervals. So far as is known, 1853 Proof dollars first came to the notice of collectors because of a listing in W. Elliot Woodward's catalog of the John F. McCoy Collection, which crossed the auction block May 17–21, 1864.[55] Approximately six examples have been certified.

Notes: Delivery figures for circulation strikes by day: April 21: 39,000; December 29: 7,110.

The Act of February 21, 1853, mandated a lowering of the weight of silver coins from the half dime through the half dollar but left the dollar untouched, a discrepancy frequently mentioned as an omission in various later annual Mint reports. In his memoirs, Senator John Sherman observed: [56] "No mention of the dollar was made in the Act of 1853. It had fallen into disuse and when coined was exported, being more valuable as bullion than coin."

In April 1853, *The Bankers' Magazine* noted the following: "The Mint will be abundantly supplied with silver for the creation of small coins contemplated by the late act of Congress. The Western banks have cut back their silver, awaiting the passage of the new Mint law. A shipment of $400,000 in silver was made by the several Louisville banks last week to the Philadelphia Mint. There are large sums, in dollars and half dollars, held by the banks of Indiana, Tennessee and other states, which will now be brought forward for recoinage." Whether such banks were holding Liberty Seated dollars is open to question. Neil Carothers, probably the most authoritative of writers on the subject, stated that the silver dollar had never circulated generally and had been *entirely unknown* since 1806.[57]

When Commodore Matthew C. Perry and his contingent arrived at Edo Bay in Japan in July 1853 in an effort to open trade, some sailors went ashore, some with Spanish-milled dollars and others with Liberty Seated dollars for barter purposes. The sailors with the U.S. coins complained that the sailors with the Spanish eight reales got "bigger and better" trinkets for their troubles. After that first day, all sailors were given the Spanish pieces to take ashore.[58]

VG-8	F-12	VF-20	EF-40	AU-50	MS-60
$600	$750	$1,000	$1,600	$2,000	$3,500
MS-63	MS-65	PF-60		PF-63	PF-65
$7,250	$85,000	$20,000		$37,000	$110,000

1854

Circulation-strike mintage: 33,140

Proof mintage: 40–60

actual size: 38.1 mm

Availability in Mint State: Some coins of this issue are from a group of five that surfaced in the 1970s.[59] Population data can be misleading due to resubmissions.[60] In 2015 the Eugene H. Gardner Sale featured an example of this coin in MS-64. *MS-60 to 62:* 8 to 12. *MS-63:* 5 to 8. *MS-64:* 12 to 18. *MS-65 or better:* 5 to 8.[61]

Availability in circulated grades: This may be the rarest Philadelphia Mint Liberty Seated dollar after 1851–1852. In fact, dollars of this date were considered *rare* by Montroville W. Dickeson in his *American Numismatical Manual* in 1859, just five years after they were minted! Writing in 1880, Ebenezer Locke Mason considered the 1854 to be the rarest circulation-strike silver dollar dated after 1852. (He did not consider mintmarks, as these were not collected at the time.) *VF-20 to AU-58:* 130 to 170.[62]

Characteristics of striking: Some coins of this issue are sharply struck, but others are lightly defined in areas, including the head of Liberty and the eagle's wings and claws. The top of the date is not bold in the die, a characteristic of all specimens, as the date logotype was punched more deeply into the die at the bottom.

Proofs: Beginning in this year, Proofs were issued with vigor, and apparently at least 60 to 80 Liberty Seated dollars reached collectors. The dollar, though rare, is considerably less rare than Proof three-cent pieces, half dimes, dimes, quarters, and half dollars of the same year. Approximately 17 examples have been certified.

Notes: All were delivered on one day, June 29, 1854.

These and other dollars of the era were made as bullion coins. Nearly all were exported to England and China and later melted. Walter H. Breen comments in his *Encyclopedia of U.S. and Colonial Coins* that 10,000 silver dollars dated 1854 were shipped from Philadelphia to San Francisco on November 11, 1854. Likely these were sent to China as well, as merchants of that city were in need of silver coins for export (see the 1859-S listing).

Banker's Magazine, February 1854, included this:

> *Dollars in Canton*. Since the publication of the proclamation of the Chinese authorities at Canton, permitting the circulation of dollars of the United States and South American Republics on an equal footing with the Spanish milled dollars, allowance being made for any ascertained difference of standard, we have received the overland *Friend of China*, of October 11, 1853, containing further information on this subject. Before the issue—of the proclamation— referred to, a document in Chinese had been circulated in Canton, recommending the adoption of a regulation by which all descriptions of dollars should be received on an equal footing, and arguing that it would be for the common benefit of the public. The *Friend of China* publishes a translation of this circular, together with the communication of the Imperial Commissioner, accompanied with the following remarks, from which it may be inferred that the ground on which the Spanish milled and Carolus dollars have sustained at times so high a premium in the American and European markets, is likely to be done away. The circular and proclamations together appear to have had the desired effect; the principal dissidents to the measure being the collectors and cashiers attached to the offices of the magistrates of the districts whence the proclamation emanated, who till recently (if they do not do so still) continued to exact a discount. Petitions, however, have been pouring in against them, and, from the fact of a change having suddenly occurred here in Hong Kong, there is hut little doubt but the admission of all dollars at par may now he considered as *un fait accompli*.

In London in 1854 Baring Bros. & Co., bankers, maintained a daily market in American silver dollars and gold eagles.

VG-8	F-12	VF-20	EF-40	AU-50	MS-60
$1,950	$2,500	$4,250	$5,250	$7,000	$12,500

MS-63	MS-65	PF-60	PF-63	PF-65
$20,000	$100,000	$12,500	$16,500	$45,000

1855

Circulation-strike mintage: 26,000

Proof mintage: 40–60

Availability in Mint State: The Mint State coins seen by the author all have somewhat dullish luster. The "fifty

actual size: 38.1 mm

scruffy Uncs" in a 1975 Superior Galleries auction, mentioned by John Dannreuther in John Highfill's *Comprehensive U.S. Silver Dollar Encyclopedia*, may represent a hoard, but it is not known if any would presently qualify as Mint State. Mint State 1855 dollars are extremely rare. The author has only seen a few of them in his experience over 60 years, and even large collections are apt to lack a Mint State example, or to have a Proof instead. The Dr. Arthur S. Weisel Collection, dispersed by Chris Napolitano in April 1992, had an MS-62 (PCGS) coin; in nine years of looking, this was the best circulation strike the owner could locate. (In May 1992, PCGS upgraded this coin to MS-63.) In 2014 the Eugene H. Gardner Sale featured an example of this coin in MS-64. *MS-60 to 62:* 8 to 12. *MS-63:* 2 or 3. *MS-64:* 1 or 2. *MS-65 or better:* 0 or 1.

Availability in circulated grades: Circulated examples of the 1855 Liberty Seated dollar are few and far between, and finding an acceptable specimen of this date has never been an easy task. However, in comparison to many other areas under the numismatic rainbow (Morgan dollars being an obvious instance), 1855 silver dollars are relatively inexpensive in proportion to their rarity. *F-12 to AU-58:* 175 to 250.

Characteristics of striking: Striking of this issue varies. They are sometimes seen with weakness on the head of Liberty and the stars (particularly 9 through 13) on the obverse and the top of the eagle's wings and on the leg on the left side of the reverse.

Proofs: 1855 Proofs are rarer than those dated 1854 for some unknown reason. These were made from a single 1855 obverse die combined with two reverses (one of them the same used for 1854 Proofs). Approximately 21 examples have been certified.

Notes: Delivery figures by day: May 4: 9,000; May 10: 3,000; May 15: 4,000; June 25: 10,000.

AU and better circulation strikes tend to be somewhat prooflike, and have often been cataloged as "Proofs" in the past, possibly causing a misconception of true Proof rarity in auction catalogs and other literature.

W. Elliot Woodward's Eightieth Sale, Coins and Medals: The Matthews Collection, December 16–19, 1885, included few Liberty Seated dollars. An example of an 1854, lot 281, graded Very Fine, was called *a rare dollar.* An 1855 was called "about as rare as 1854."

VG-8	F-12	VF-20	EF-40	AU-50	MS-60
$1,850	$2,750	$4,250	$6,000	$8,500	$10,500

MS-63	MS-65	PF-60	PF-63	PF-65
$35,000	–	$12,500	$16,000	$40,000

1856

Circulation-strike mintage: 63,500

Proof mintage: 40–60

Availability in Mint State: Although the 1856 dollar is an extreme rarity in Mint State, the appreciation of it by advanced

actual size: 38.1 mm

collectors, and, to an extent, its market price, have been dimmed slightly by the availability of Proofs of this date. Proofs, although rarities in their own right, have served to absorb some of the demand for top-grade coins. Mint State 1856 dollars are few and far between. In 2014 the Eugene H. Gardner Sale featured an example of this coin in MS-64. *MS-60 to 62:* 8 to 12. *MS-63:* 2 or 3. *MS-64:* 2 or 3. *MS-65 or better:* 0 or 1.

Availability in circulated grades: *F-12 to AU-58:* 200 to 300.

Characteristics of striking: This issue is usually weakly struck, typically with Liberty's head and stars eight through ten flat. On the reverse, the eagle's leg on the left is often weak.

Proofs: Approximately 37 examples have been certified.

Notes: Delivery figures by day: January 30: 10,000; January 31: 18,000; February 4: 17,000; February 9: 18,500.

The Bankers' Magazine and Statistical Register reported the following:

> Where Did the Gold and Silver Go? It is well-known that the silver coin held by the banks in the United States eight or ten years ago has almost entirely disappeared to this day. The remnants are composed of small coin, reserved for change. Gradually, from the years 1848 to 1855, all of the available silver coin of this country was exported to Europe; but there it did not remain. The exhaustion of silver noted in the banking and commercial history of the United States, for the past eight years, has also taken place in Europe...When we inquire further as to the causes and means of exhaustion of silver in Europe, we find that the preference felt for the metal in China and India demands a continued export of all that can be realized . . .[63]

The same publication, issue of September 1856, noted that in England much silver had been exported directly to China and the East Indies amounting to £1,716,100 in 1851, £2,630,238 in 1852, £4,710,665 in 1853, £3,132,003 in 1854, and £6,409,889 in 1855. "The main cause we opine lies in the enormous increase of Chinese exports of silk and tea to England and North America." Large amounts of American silver coins were sent from the United States to China during the same time for essentially the same purposes. Large quantities were exported to England as well.

A report in the *Financial and Commercial Money Market*, New York City, March 16, 1856, provides a sample of many notices of silver dollars (and other coins) being exported from that city: "Steamer *Asia* for Liverpool: U.S. gold bars $446,691.25; California gold bars $100,053.08; and silver dollars $13,000. Steamer *Etna* for Havre: U.S. gold bars and coin $178,146.21 and silver dollars $15,000."

In the last week of September the steamer *Atlantic* departed New York City for Liverpool carrying $150,000 in silver dollars, $150,059.73 in gold bars, $590,000 in U.S. gold coins, and $87.30 in British silver coins.

Although most silver dollars sent to China were melted, money brokers in Shanghai held quantities of them. According to accounts, the accuracy of which is questionable, at one particular time 150 American dollars could be exchanged for 100 Mexican dollars.[64]

VG-8	F-12	VF-20	EF-40	AU-50	MS-60
$1,100	$1,500	$2,000	$3,000	$4,200	$7,500

MS-63	MS-65	PF-60	PF-63	PF-65
$17,500		$12,500	$16,000	$40,000

1857

Circulation-strike mintage: 94,000

Proof mintage: 50–70

actual size: 38.1 mm

Availability in Mint State: At this level the 1857 dollar is quite rare, but is still one of the most available (with 1853) Philadelphia Mint issues of the 1850s up to this point. When seen, Mint State coins almost always have a prooflike surface and are nearly always lightly struck, particularly at the upper part of the obverse. In 2015 the Eugene H. Gardner Sale featured examples of this coin in MS-69 and MS-64. *MS-60 to 62:* 30 to 40. *MS-63:* 20 to 25. *MS-64:* 15 to 20. *MS-65 or better:* 2 to 4.

Availability in circulated grades: The 1857 is very rare, somewhat approaching the 1854 and 1855 in this regard, but not quite in the same league with them. *F-12 to AU-58:* 175 to 250.

Characteristics of striking: This issue is nearly always weakly struck at top of the obverse (Liberty's head and stars five through ten). Some coins are almost flat in this area and *very* flat on the eagle's wing to the left and on the eagle's head. Other coins are weak on the obverse but quite well struck on the reverse. Nearly all were made with prooflike surfaces. Only one needle-sharp example has been seen by the author, that with a frosty surface with no trace of being prooflike.

Proofs: The same reverse die was used to strike Proof silver dollars of 1856 and 1858. The Proof 1857 dollar is thought to be more available than the 1855 Proof but scarcer than the 1856 Proof. Approximately 28 examples have been certified.

Notes: Exports of silver dollars continued. On April 1 the steamer *Africa* bound for Liverpool departed from New York with $145,280 in California gold bars, $134,391 in U.S. Mint bars, California coins of $25,000 (presumably of private mintage), and 4,000 in silver dollars.

In the first week of July the steamer *North Star* sailed for Southampton and Bremen with $60,000 in American dollars (the Christy Minstrels were also aboard).

VG-8	F-12	VF-20	EF-40	AU-50	MS-60
$1,000	$1,350	$2,000	$3,000	$4,000	$5,500

MS-63	MS-65	PF-60	PF-63	PF-65
$8,500	$75,000	$5,500	$13,000	$30,000

1858

Proof mintage: 300

actual size: 38.1 mm

Proofs: This issue had 210 coins or so made for inclusion in silver Proof sets. Possibly others were struck as well. Many seeking a run of Proof Liberty Seated dollars start their sets with this year. Approximately 72 examples have been certified.

Notes: As the solitary Proof-only coin in the series the 1858 has been famous for a long time. The mintage was not recorded. Apparently, there was no call for export coins of this denomination. However, the Mint made large quantities of lower denomination silver coins throughout the year for circulation.

In the first week of January 1858 the steamer *Persia* bound for Liverpool left New York with $150,607 in U.S. silver dollars (of earlier dates) and $10,000 in Mexican silver plus other silver and gold.

PF-60	PF-63	PF-65
$10,000	$14,000	$35,000

1859

Circulation-strike mintage: 255,700

Proof mintage: 800

actual size: 38.1 mm

Availability in Mint State: In 2015 the Eugene H. Gardner Sale featured an example of this coin in MS-64. *MS-60 to 62:* 20 to 25. *MS-63:* 15 to 20. *MS-64:* 12 to 18. *MS-65 or better:* 2 to 4.

Availability in circulated grades: *F-12 to AU-58:* 350 to 500.

Characteristics of striking: Many coins of this issue are weakly struck at one or both of these areas: stars (irregularly weak striking, with stars one and four sharp and the others, especially eight and nine, weak) and the head of Liberty.

Proofs: These are readily available, mostly in lower-grade levels. Apparently, many Proofs were made this year in the hope that the public, which was becoming increasingly interested in numismatics, would buy them. Although 800 were struck, probably fewer than 450 were distributed. *PF-60 to 62:* 150 to 250. *PF-63:* 70 to 90. *PF-64:* 40 to 55. *PF-65 or better:* 35 to 50.

VG-8	F-12	VF-20	EF-40	AU-50	MS-60
$600	$700	$825	$1,200	$2,000	$3,500

MS-63	MS-65	PF-60	PF-63	PF-65
$6,000	$85,000	$7,000	$13,500	$30,000

1859-O

Circulation-strike mintage: 360,000

actual size: 38.1 mm

Availability in Mint State: During the 1962–1964 Treasury release of backdated silver dollars, it is believed that up to three mint-sealed bags of 1,000 Uncirculated coins were distributed. Almost without exception, the coins from these bags are heavily bagmarked and scarred, the result of careless storage, handling, and shipping procedures over the years. The average grade today is MS-60 or just slightly better. Mint State coins from other sources tend to be in higher grades. In 2014 the Eugene H. Gardner Sale featured an example of this coin in MS-65. *MS-60 to 62:* 2,250 to 2,750. *MS-63:* 40 to 80+. *MS-64:* 3 to 5. *MS-65 or better:* 2 to 4.

Availability in circulated grades: *F-12 to AU-58:* 2,000 to 3,000.

Characteristics of striking: Striking of this issue varies. The stars are often weak, beginning at stars eight and nine and, depending upon the coin, to the left or right as well. These are satiny rather than having a deeply frosty luster. The fields are usually prooflike.

Notes: Most of the 1859-O and 1860-O dollars were made for the China export trade. The first bullion deposit for this specific purpose was $7,000 on the morning of April 9, 1859.[65]

VG-8	F-12	VF-20	EF-40	AU-50	MS-60	MS-63	MS-65
$400	$450	$500	$750	$900	$2,000	$3,850	$40,000

1859-S

Circulation-strike mintage: 20,000

actual size: 38.1 mm

Availability in Mint State: In true Mint State the 1859-S is a formidable rarity. Many if not most offered at this level are darkly toned or overgraded. Very few lustrous pieces with beautiful eye appeal exist. In 2014 and 2015 the Eugene H. Gardner Sale featured examples of this coin in MS-63 and MS-62. *MS-60 to 62:* 5 to 8. *MS-63:* 1 or 2. *MS-64:* 0 or 1. *MS-65 or better:* 1.

Availability in circulated grades: *VG-8 to AU-58:* 500 to 750.

Characteristics of striking: This issue is usually well struck.

Notes: 15,000 silver dollars of 1859 struck at the San Francisco Mint were specifically minted for export on May 11 of that year. Of these, 8,985 of the dollars were obtained by Bolton, Barren & Co. (shipping merchants located at 92 Merchant Street, corner of Montgomery Street) for the China trade. A further 5,000 were coined in July.[66] Some were distributed on the West Coast where they remained in circulation for many years. Charles H. Hempstead, superintendent of the San Francisco Mint, in a letter dated November 18, 1858, wrote to Director James Ross Snowden that in San Francisco:

> We are now attracting to our shores large quantities of silver, in bars, from Mexico, for which we pay in silver coins. By reference to your letter of the fourth of August last, I find they you say that single 'silver deposits may be received, but they are only payable in *silver dollars* or in *fine silver* bars.' We have never received any dies for silver dollars, nor am I aware of the reason why this branch has never made that denomination of coin. I would, therefore, suggest that the coinage of silver dollars (if it be not contrary to the policy of government) would relieve us of just one-half of the labor now necessary in the coinage of large quantities of Mexican silver.

On February 19, 1859, Director Snowden sent this reply:

> As the facts stated by you indicate the propriety of coinage of silver dollars at your branch of the mint, I have caused four pairs of dies of that denomination to be prepared and forwarded to you per express. A weight for the adjustment of the coin (from which others can be made) will be found in the box containing the dies.[67]

VG-8	F-12	VF-20	EF-40	AU-50	MS-60	MS-63	MS-65
$825	$1,000	$1,500	$2,000	$3,500	$10,000	$22,500	

1860

Circulation-strike mintage: 217,600

Proof mintage: 1,330

Availability in Mint State: These are very scarce. When seen, examples often have a partially prooflike surface. The mint frost on typical

actual size: 38.1 mm

specimens is apt to be satiny rather than deeply coruscating and frosty. In 2014 the Eugene H. Gardner Sale featured an example of this coin in MS-64. *MS-60 to 62:* 40 to 75. *MS-63:* 20 to 25. *MS-64:* 20 to 25. *MS-65 or better:* 10 to 15.

Availability in circulated grades: *F-12 to AU-58:* 500 to 750.

Characteristics of striking: This issue is usually well struck. Many higher-grade coins show prooflike surfaces.

Proofs: This mintage is the largest Proof figure in the entire Liberty Seated series, all delivered on March 8. Only 527 were eventually sold, and the rest were consigned to the melting pot. It seems that among those sold, some were spent or lost. R.W. Julian has written:

> The 1860 Proof coinage of dollars is not the same as the coinage of the other denominations heretofore printed for 1860. The extra 330 pieces coined were produced because the Mint felt that there would be an extra demand for these over the other silver Proofs; this points out that in addition to Proofs being sold in sets, single pieces were sold very frequently. For example, in April 1860, there were 69 full silver sets sold (presumably including a copper-nickel cent in each set) plus 10 silver dollars, 3 half dollars, 16 dimes, 14 half dimes, 16 silver three-cent pieces, and 10 cents. It would appear that the Mint officials were wrong in believing that a large number of dollars would be sold beyond the regular set sales because after 1860 all silver coins were made in the same amounts for Proof sets.[68]

PF-60 to 62: 125 to 225. *PF-63:* 60 to 90. *PF-64:* 35 to 50. *PF-65 or better:* 30 to 45.

VG-8	F-12	VF-20	EF-40	AU-50	MS-60
$450	$525	$675	$1,000	$1,500	$2,800

MS-63	MS-65	PF-60	PF-63	PF-65
$5,000	$50,000	$2,500	$4,750	$12,000

1860-O

Circulation-strike mintage: 515,000

actual size: 38.1 mm

Availability in Mint State: An estimated 5,000 were released in the Treasury dispersal that began in November 1862. The 1860-O is the most plentiful Liberty Seated dollar in Mint State. In 2014 the Eugene H. Gardner Sale featured an example of this coin in MS-65. *MS-60 to 62:* 5,250 to 5,750; most are in the MS-60 category and are heavily bagmarked. *MS-63:* 90 to 120. *MS-64:* 20 to 25. *MS-65 or better:* 3 to 5.

Availability in circulated grades: *F-12 to AU-58:* 2,500 to 3,500.

Characteristics of striking: This issue is usually fairly well struck. Coins of this issue have a satiny rather than deeply frosty luster. The fields are usually prooflike, especially on non-hoard coins.

Notes: Most of these were made for export to China.

VG-8	F-12	VF-20	EF-40	AU-50	MS-60	MS-63	MS-65
$400	$450	$500	$750	$950	$2,000	$3,750	$35,000

1861

Circulation-strike mintage: 77,500

Proof mintage: 1,000

actual size: 38.1 mm

Availability in Mint State: High-grade coins typically show striations from incomplete polishing of the obverse die in particular. In 2015 the Eugene H. Gardner Sale featured an example of this coin in MS-65. *MS-60 to 62:* 15 to 20. *MS-63:* 15 to 20. *MS-64:* 15 to 20. *MS-65 or better:* 4 to 6.[69]

Availability in circulated grades: *F-12 to AU-58:* 200 to 300.

Characteristics of striking: Many 1861 circulation-strike dollars show areas of light striking, especially on Liberty's head. Indeed, this is a hallmark of this particular date.

Proofs: It is thought that only a few hundred were distributed. The others were melted in 1862, per printed comments, or were placed into circulation. This is the rarest Proof date in the 1860s by far. *PF-60 to 62:* 100 to 120. *PF-63:* 110 to 150. *PF-64:* 40 to 55. *PF-65 or better:* 30 to 40.

Notes: A new reverse die with claws and arrowheads slightly more delicate than earlier years was first employed in 1861, however the differences between the old and new dies are very subtle.

Dies were shipped to New Orleans for an 1861-O coinage of silver dollars, but they never went into use, so far as anyone knows. The 1861 *Mint Report* stated that the current price the Mint charged for silver dollars was $1.08. The buyers were agents of or those engaged in the export trade.

On March 19, 1878, Horace Davis, a representative to Congress from California, gave testimony regarding trade dollars and earlier transactions with regular silver dollars. Beginning in 1859 there was a glut of silver in the state from production in Nevada. Much of this was sent to Philadelphia and coined into dollars. In 1859, 1860, and 1861 more than 1,250,000 of these dollars were shipped to China, where they were received at bullion value.[70] They were not as popular as the slightly heavier Spanish-American dollars that took precedence there.

VG-8	F-12	VF-20	EF-40	AU-50	MS-60
$1,500	$2,000	$2,750	$4,250	$4,750	$6,500

MS-63	MS-65	PF-60	PF-63	PF-65
$9,500	$50,000	$2,500	$4,750	$12,000

1862

Circulation-strike mintage: 11,540

Proof mintage: 550

actual size: 38.1 mm

Availability in Mint State: High-grade coins typically have extensive die striae, as struck, on the obverse and reverse making it appear to the uninitiated as if the coin had been cleaned or brushed. This characteristic is similar to that seen on dollars of 1864. In 2014 the Eugene H. Gardner Sale featured an example of this coin in MS-64. *MS-60 to 62:* 25 to 40. *MS-63:* 10 to 13. *MS-64:* 5 to 8. *MS-65 or better:* 3 to 5.[71]

Availability in circulated grades: *F-12 to AU-58:* 200 to 300.

Characteristics of striking: Most coins of this issue are well struck.

Proofs: *PF-60 to 62:* 180 to 220. *PF-63:* 70 to 90. *PF-64:* 40 to 50. *PF-65 or better:* 20 to 30.

Notes: Delivery figures by day: February 4: 700; June 24: 500; July 30: 5,000; August 5: 5,340.

From the *Boston Traveler*, July 7, 1862: "New American Silver Dollars, 1859 and 1860, for sale by C.J. Russell, Specie Broker, No. 12 State Street."[72]

VG-8	F-12	VF-20	EF-40	AU-50	MS-60
$1,000	$1,500	$2,200	$4,000	$5,250	$6,500

MS-63	MS-65	PF-60	PF-63	PF-65
$9,000	$55,000	$2,500	$4,750	$11,500

1863

Circulation-strike mintage: 27,200

Proof mintage: 460

actual size: 38.1 mm

Availability in Mint State: In 2014 the Eugene H. Gardner Sale featured an example of this coin in MS-65. There are fewer than 75 of these, most of which are at lower levels. High-grade coins always show striations from incomplete polishing of the obverse die in particular, but not as strong as 1862 and 1864. *MS-60 to 62:* 15 to 20. *MS-63:* 7 to 10. *MS-64:* 20 to 25. *MS-65 or better:* 5 to 7.[73]

Availability in circulated grades: *F-12 to AU-58:* 125 to 175.

Characteristics of striking: Most coins of this issue are well struck.

Proofs: *PF-60 to 62:* 170 to 210. *PF-63:* 60 to 80. *PF-64:* 40 to 55. *PF-65 or better:* 18 to 25.

Notes: Delivery figures by day: March 9: 3,800; March 26: 1,400; April 10: 15,400; November 22: 6,600.

VG-8	F-12	VF-20	EF-40	AU-50	MS-60
$1,100	$1,500	$2,250	$3,000	$3,500	$5,500

MS-63	MS-65	PF-60	PF-63	PF-65
$7,000	$50,000	$2,500	$4,750	$11,500

1864

Circulation-strike mintage: 30,700

Proof mintage: 470

Availability in Mint State: Mint State 1864 dollars are very rare with fewer than 50 estimated to exist, but when they do appear they are apt to

actual size: 38.1 mm

be in higher levels, an unusual situation. High-grade coins typically have extensive die striae, as struck, on the obverse and reverse making it appear to the uninitiated as if the coin had been cleaned or brushed. This characteristic is similar to that seen on dollars of 1862. In 2014 and 2015 the Eugene H. Gardner Sale featured examples of this coin in MS-65 and MS-64. *MS-60 to 62:* 8 to 12. *MS-63:* 4 to 6. *MS-64:* 10 to 13. *MS-65 or better:* 8 to 12.[74]

Availability in circulated grades: *F-12 to AU-58:* 300 to 400.

Characteristics of striking: Most coins of this issue are very well struck.

Proofs: Three different obverse dies were used for the Proof coinage. *PF-60 to 62:* 200 to 230. *PF-63:* 80 to 100. *PF-64:* 45 to 60. *PF-65 or better:* 25 to 35.

Notes: Delivery figures by day: January 13: 5,700; April 30: 2,000; May 17: 8,500; July 29: 14,500.

VG-8	F-12	VF-20	EF-40	AU-50	MS-60
$650	$1,000	$1,500	$2,250	$3,250	$4,750

MS-63	MS-65	PF-60	PF-63	PF-65
$8,000	$60,000	$2,500	$4,750	$11,500

1865

Circulation-strike mintage: 46,500

Proof mintage: 500

actual size: 38.1 mm

Availability in Mint State: In 2014 the Eugene H. Gardner Sale featured an example of this coin in MS-64. *MS-60 to 62:* 20 to 25. *MS-63:* 7 to 10. *MS-64:* 20 to 25. *MS-65 or better:* 1 or 2.

Availability in circulated grades: *F-12 to AU-58:* 250 to 325.

Characteristics of striking: Many coins of this issue show areas of light striking, often including the head, stars, and the eagle's leg on the left.

Proofs: *PF-60 to 62:* 210 to 240. *PF-63:* 90 to 110. *PF-64:* 50 to 65. *PF-65 or better:* 30 to 40.

Notes: In 1865 Alfred S. Robinson, the Hartford, Connecticut, rare coin dealer, exchange broker, and banker, advertised in newspapers to buy and sell silver dollars in quantity.

VG-8	F-12	VF-20	EF-40	AU-50	MS-60
$800	$1,350	$2,000	$2,500	$3,000	$4,750

MS-63	MS-65	PF-60	PF-63	PF-65
$10,500	$80,000	$2,500	$4,750	$11,500

1866, No Motto

Proof mintage: 2

actual size: 38.1 mm

Proofs: Two are known to exist.

Notes: One is in the National Numismatic Collection at the Smithsonian Institution in Washington, D.C., the gift of the DuPont family. For the story of this coin see *Notes* under the 1866, No Motto, quarter dollar in chapter 7.

PF-60	PF-63	PF-65
	—	

1866–1873, With Motto
IN GOD WE TRUST (Variety 2)

Liberty still has drapery at her elbow and the reverse is still with perched eagle. The only addition to this design is the motto IN GOD WE TRUST added above the eagle.

Designed by: Christian Gobrecht. Motto added by someone on the Mint staff.

Specifications: *Composition:* 90 percent silver, 10 percent copper. *Diameter:* 38.1 mm. *Weight:* 412.5 grains (26.73 grams). *Edge:* Reeded.

1866, *With Motto*

Circulation-strike mintage: 48,900

Proof mintage: 725

Availability in Mint State: In 2014 the Eugene H. Gardner Sale featured an example of this coin in MS-65. *MS-60 to 62:* 20 to 25. *MS-63:* 20 to 25. *MS-64:* 15 to 20. *MS-65 or better:* 8 to 11.

actual size: 38.1 mm

Availability in circulated grades: *F-12 to AU-58:* 400 to 500.

Characteristics of striking: Striking of this issue varies, but there is often lightness on the head.

Proofs: Three different obverse dies were prepared for the Proof coinage. *PF-60 to 62:* 230 to 260. *PF-63:* 110 to 130. *PF-64:* 70 to 90. *PF-65 or better:* 45 to 60.

Notes: Delivery figures by day: January 30: 6,700; May 8: 15,900; June 21: 6,600; July 30: 13,900; August 24: 5,800.

VG-8	F-12	VF-20	EF-40	AU-50	MS-60
$500	$575	$800	$1,250	$1,750	$2,500

MS-63	MS-65	PF-60	PF-63	PF-65
$5,500	$65,000	$2,250	$3,800	$10,000

1867

Circulation-strike mintage: 46,900

Proof mintage: 625

actual size: 38.1 mm

Availability in Mint State: In 2015 the Eugene H. Gardner Sale featured examples of this coin in MS-65 and MS-64. *MS-60 to 62:* 20 to 25. *MS-63:* 10 to 13. *MS-64:* 7 to 10. *MS-65 or better:* 2 to 4.

Availability in circulated grades: *F-12 to AU-58:* 450 to 600.

Characteristics of striking: Striking of this issue varies, but some have slight weakness at stars eight and nine.

Proofs: *PF-60 to 62:* 100 to 150. *PF-63:* 200 to 250. *PF-64:* 80 to 125. *PF-65 or better:* 35 to 50.

Notes: Delivery figures by day: January 17: 6,000; March 20: 10,300; May 22: 6,600; June 18: 13,700; November 22: 10,300.

Large Date Over Small Date: Breen-5478. Apparently, a logotype for a half dollar was erroneously applied to the blank die, high and slanting down to the right, then the regular dollar logotype was punched in the correct position. The early state (rarest) shows much of the small date while later states (slightly less rare) show less, and finally only traces.

VG-8	F-12	VF-20	EF-40	AU-50	MS-60
$600	$650	$1,000	$1,350	$2,000	$3,500

MS-63	MS-65	PF-60	PF-63	PF-65
$7,500	$70,000	$2,250	$3,900	$10,000

1868

Circulation-strike mintage: 162,100

Proof mintage: 600

actual size: 38.1 mm

Availability in Mint State: Some high-grade pieces have unfinished areas within the lower right area of the shield. Most high-grade coins are prooflike. In 2014 the Eugene H. Gardner Sale featured an example of this coin in MS-64. *MS-60 to 62:* 30 to 40. *MS-63:* 4 to 6. *MS-64:* 3 to 5. *MS-65 or better:* 3 or 4.[75]

Availability in circulated grades: *F-12 to AU-58:* 300 to 400.

Characteristics of striking: Most coins of this issue are well struck.

Proofs: *PF-60 to 62:* 210 to 240. *PF-63:* 90 to 110. *PF-64:* 45 to 60. *PF-65 or better:* 30 to 40.

VG-8	F-12	VF-20	EF-40	AU-50	MS-60
$450	$650	$750	$1,100	$1,550	$2,750

MS-63	MS-65	PF-60	PF-63	PF-65
$7,500	$65,000	$2,250	$3,800	$10,000

1869

Circulation-strike mintage: 423,700

Proof mintage: 600

actual size: 38.1 mm

Availability in Mint State: Most high-grade coins are prooflike. In 2014 the Eugene H. Gardner Sale featured an example of this coin in MS-65. *MS-60 to 62:* 15 to 20. *MS-63:* 12 to 18. *MS-64:* 8 to 12. *MS-65 or better:* 4 to 6.[76]

Availability in circulated grades: *F-12 to AU-58:* 250 to 350.

Characteristics of striking: Striking of this issue varies, but the obverse is often sharp and the reverse often has slight weakness at top of the shield and top of the eagle's wing on the left.

Proofs: *PF-60 to 62:* 210 to 240. *PF-63:* 90 to 110. *PF-64:* 45 to 60. *PF-65 or better:* 30 to 40.

VG-8	F-12	VF-20	EF-40	AU-50	MS-60
$450	$550	$700	$1,000	$1,250	$2,750

MS-63	MS-65	PF-60	PF-63	PF-65
$5,250	$65,000	$2,250	$3,800	$10,000

1870

Circulation-strike mintage: 415,000

Proof mintage: 1,000

actual size: 38.1 mm

Availability in Mint State: In 2015 the Eugene H. Gardner Sale featured an example of this coin in MS-65. *MS-60 to 62:* 50 to 75. *MS-63:* 20 to 25. *MS-64:* 15 to 20. *MS-65 or better:* 3 or 4.[77]

Availability in circulated grades: Numerous worn coins came to light in the Treasury release of 1962–1964, but before that they were also easy to find. ***F-12 to AU-58:*** 1,200 to 1,800.

Characteristics of striking: Striking of this issue varies, but some have a curious pattern of weakness, with stars 10 through 13 weak, but eight, nine, and other stars more sharply defined. Many appear to have a reverse a grade or two sharper than the obverse.[78]

Proofs: Proofs were carelessly made and are often weak on the leg to the left and on the eagle's neck feathers. ***PF-60 to 62:*** 200 to 230. ***PF-63:*** 85 to 105. ***PF-64:*** 50 to 65. ***PF-65 or better:*** 25 to 35.

Notes: Exports continued apace in 1870, including to Bombay, India. For the first time since the 1840s, quantities of a Philadelphia Mint dollar remained within the borders of the United States. All coins were paid out to depositors at the time of coining and were worth a premium at the time. Any 1870 dollars found in Treasury vaults in later years were coins returned to the government, possibly in the mid-1870s.

VG-8	F-12	VF-20	EF-40	AU-50	MS-60
$425	$450	$600	$750	$950	$2,250

MS-63	MS-65	PF-60	PF-63	PF-65
$4,500	$55,000	$2,250	$3,800	$10,000

1870-CC

Circulation-strike mintage: 11,758

actual size: 38.1 mm

Availability in Mint State: The Battle Born Collection Sale in 2013 featured an example of this coin in MS-64 (variety 1-D). In 2014 the Eugene H. Gardner Sale featured an example of this coin in MS-64. ***MS-60 to 62:*** 10 to 15. ***MS-63:*** 7 to 10. ***MS-64:*** 2 to 4. ***MS-65 or better:*** 0 or 1.

Availability in circulated grades: ***VG-8 to F-15:*** 150-250. ***F-12 to AU-58:*** 260 to 350.

Characteristics of striking: This issue is usually well struck, a general characteristic of most varieties of Carson City dollars over the years; this is especially true of the reverse. However, as is the case with other Carson City Mint Liberty Seated dollars, the word LIBERTY on the shield is not as prominent as on Philadelphia coins and tended to wear away especially quickly once the coins saw circulation. Most if not all were struck with prooflike surfaces—visible today on coins in higher grades.

Notes: Delivery figures by day: February 10: 2,303; February 24: 1,444; March 5: 1,116; March 22: 1,175; March 24: 500; March 30: 1,300; April 7: 500; May 20: 600; June 11: 870; June 14: 550; June 30: 1,400.

Nine varieties are known. These consist of four obverse dies combined with six reverse dies.[79] All were struck using a press made in Philadelphia by Morgan & Orr.

VG-8	F-12	VF-20	EF-40	AU-50	MS-60	MS-63	MS-65
$2,150	$2,850	$4,000	$5,500	$8,500	$25,000	$45,000	—

1870-S

Circulation-strike mintage: *300 or fewer*

Availability in Mint State: Two or three are known in Mint State.

Availability in circulated grades: Nine are known in circulated grades.

actual size: 38.1 mm

Roster:[80]

1. Mint employee specimen: Mint State. San Francisco Mint employee, 1870; Family of the preceding; 1991: owned by a San Francisco area military officer. Said to be Mint State. An offer for $175,000 was made for it in 1991 by a San Francisco dealer, Sam E. Frudakis, who reported the situation to the author in 1992.
2. James A. Stack specimen: MS-62 (PCGS). Morton and Joseph Stack; James A. Stack (1944); James Stack Collection (Stack's, 1995); Rudolph Collection (Stack's, 2003), lot 2136, realized $1,092,500; Legend Collection.[81]
3. Emery May Holden Norweb specimen: AU-58 (PCGS). Colonel E.H.R. Green; Green estate until 1942; Burdette G. Johnson; Anderson-Dupont Sale (Stack's, November 1954); Arthur M. Kagin; Emery May Holden Norweb; Norweb Collection, Part III (Bowers and Merena, 1988); Jim Jessen Collection, offered as part of a silver dollar set in *Coin World*, January 1996.
4. Louis E. Eliasberg specimen: AU-53 (PCGS). Henry O. Granberg[82]; William H. Woodin; Waldo C. Newcomer; Col. E.H.R. Green via B. Max Mehl; Green estate; possibly George H. Hall Sale (Stack's, 1945); Will W. Neil Sale (Mehl, 1947); Stack's; Louis E. Eliasberg; Eliasberg Collection (Bowers and Merena, 1997); Stanford Coins and Bullion; Certified Acceptance Corporation (John Albanese, purchased for $1.3 million in February 2008).
5. Ostheimer-Gardner specimen: EF-40 (PCGS). Compton Collection; M.H. Bolender; Alfred and Jackie Ostheimer; Ostheimer Sale (Lester Merkin, 1968, not sold); Gilhousen Sale (Superior Galleries, 1973); ANA Sale (Superior, 1975); Julian M. Leidman; Gary Sturtridge; ANA Sale (Bowers and Ruddy Galleries, 1978); James E. Pohrer; ANA Sale (Kagin's, 1983); Leon Hendrickson and Sal Fusco; Private collection; Phoenix Rare Coin Galleries (1992); Richmond Sale (David Lawrence Rare Coins, 2004); Jack Lee III Collection (Heritage Auctions, 2005); Central States Signature Sale (Heritage Auctions, 2009); Boston Rarities (Bowers and Merena Galleries); FUN Sale (Heritage Auctions, 2014); Eugene H. Gardner; Gardner Sale (Heritage Auctions, May 2015).
6. David Queller specimen: EF-40 (NGC). Charles M. Williams; Sale outright to Numismatic Gallery; Adolphe Menjou Sale (Numismatic Gallery, 1950)[83]; Possibly Clinton Hester; Abe Kosoff price list 1955; Ben Koenig; Fairbanks Collection

(Stack's, 1960); Samuel Wolfson; Wolfson Sale (Stack's, 1963); R.L. Miles Jr.; Miles Sale (Stack's, 1969); Autumn Sale (Stack's, 1978); David Queller; Queller Family Collection (Heritage Auctions, 2008) realized $805,000; FUN Sale (Heritage, 2015).[84]

7. Amon Carter specimen: VF. B. Max Mehl; Col. E.H.R. Green; James F. Kelly; Jack V. Roe; James Kelly; Jerome Kern; Kern Sale (B. Max Mehl, 1950); Amon G. Carter Sr.; Amon G. Carter Jr.; Carter Family Sale (Stack's, 1984); L.R. French Sale (Stack's, 1989); James A. Stack Sr. Collection (Stack's, 1989).

8. Norman Shultz specimen: VF-25 PCGS. Norman Shultz Mail Bid Sale (1935); B. Max Mehl; King Farouk of Egypt; Palace Collections (Sotheby's, 1954); Hans M.F. Schulman; 1960 ANA Sale (Arthur Conn and Harold Whiteneck, 1960); Fall Festival Sale (Ben Dreiske, Ben's Coin Company, 1961); 10th Anniversary Sale (Abner Kreisberg and Hans M.F. Schulman, 1967). Herman Halpern Collection (Stack's, 1987); Private collection; 72nd Anniversary Sale (Stack's, 2007); Whitman Coin & Collectibles Expo Sale (Bowers and Merena Galleries).

9. F.C.C. Boyd Specimen: VF. Details PCGS, tooled to remove initials F.H.I. on obverse. Drake and Munroe Collections (William Hesslein, 1926); F.C.C. Boyd; World's Greatest Collection (Numismatic Gallery, 1945); Southern Sale (Hollinbeck Coin Co., 1951); Earl M. Skinner Collection (New Netherlands Coin Co., 1952); Charles A. Cass; Empire Collection (Stack's, 1957); Quarter Millennium Sale, Part III (Hollinbeck Coin Company, 1964); 274th Sale (Hollinbeck, 1967); Ancient, Foreign and U.S. Coins (Stack's, 1996); 73rd Anniversary Sale (Stack's, 2008); Whitman Coin & Collectibles Expo Sale (Bowers and Merena, November 2009).

10. Eureka Specimen, F/VF, nicked and scratched. Reportedly discovered by an 18-year-old man from Eureka, California, before 1922, who kept it until the 1970s; Donovan II Sale (Steve Ivy, 1978); Auction 1985 (Paramount, 1985); Manfra, Tordella, and Brookes fixed price list, spring 1987.

11. Long Beach specimen: Circulated, holed and polished, with ANACS certificate.[85]

12. Mint Cornerstone specimen: A coin was struck for inclusion in the cornerstone of the San Francisco Mint (see receipt illustrated under the 1870-S quarter). Whether it is one of the above or if it still exists today is not known. If still in the cornerstone it is probably Mint State.

Characteristics of striking: This issue had an average strike, but some have slight traces of prooflike surfaces.

Notes: Mint records omit this coinage. A reverse die with a Small S mintmark was shipped to San Francisco, but no record has been found for the obverse die. It could have been obtained from the Carson City Mint, or did Mint Superintendent O.H. LaGrange get one when he visited the Philadelphia Mint in December 1869?[86]

VG-8	F-12	VF-20	EF-40	AU-50	MS-60	MS-63	MS-65
$250,000	$300,000	$500,000	$550,000	$1,000,000	$1,750,000	–	–

1871

Circulation-strike mintage: 1,073,800

Proof mintage: 960

Availability in Mint State: This date is the most available Philadelphia Mint coin in the series. It is the author's opinion that several hundred Mint

actual size: 38.1 mm

State 1871 dollars were released by the Treasury from 1962 to 1964, probably mixed in with other coins. He has not been able to confirm the existence from the 1960s or know of any full bags, although Walter H. Breen in his *Encyclopedia* claimed to know of two bags. In 2014 the Eugene H. Gardner Sale featured an example of this coin in MS-65. *MS-60 to 62:* 250 to 350+. *MS-63:* 50 to 80. *MS-64:* 15 to 20. *MS-65 or better:* 5 to 7.

Availability in circulated grades: *F-12 to AU-58:* 4,000 to 6,000.

Characteristics of striking: Striking quality of this issue varies, but some show weakness. According to Larry Briggs: "Many coins have a two-grade difference between the obverse and reverse, such as a VF-35 obverse and an AU-50 reverse!"[87]

Proofs: *PF-60 to 62:* 210 to 240. *PF-63:* 90 to 110. *PF-64:* 40 to 55. *PF-65 or better:* 30 to 40.

VG-8	F-12	VF-20	EF-40	AU-50	MS-60
$400	$425	$475	$750	$900	$2,000

MS-63	MS-65	PF-60	PF-63	PF-65
$4,500	$50,000	$2,250	$3,800	$10,000

1871-CC

Circulation-strike mintage: 1,376

Availability in Mint State: The Battle Born Collection coin (2013) is MS-61. In 2014 the Eugene H. Gardner Sale featured an example of this coin in MS-61. *MS-60 to 62:* 3 or 4. *MS-63:* 0. *MS-64:* 1. *MS-65 or better:* 0 or 1.

actual size: 38.1 mm

Availability in circulated grades: *VG-8 to F-15:* 15 to 20. *F-12 to AU-58:* 60 to 100.

Characteristics of striking: This issue is usually sharply struck. Some have lightness at stars 12 and 13. As is the case with other Carson City Mint Liberty Seated dollars, the word LIBERTY on the shield is not as prominent as on Philadelphia coins, and it tended to wear away especially quickly once the coins saw circulation.

Notes: The 1871-CC has the lowest mintage of any Carson City Mint coin of this design. However, today specimens are more available than of the higher-mintage 1873-CC, for many of the latter presumably were melted.

VG-8	F-12	VF-20	EF-40	AU-50	MS-60	MS-63	MS-65
$5,500	$7,000	$10,500	$13,500	$22,500	$80,000	$225,000	–

1872

Circulation-strike mintage: 1,105,500

Proof mintage: 950

Availability in Mint State: Most of these are from the Treasury release of the 1960s. In 2014 the Eugene H. Gardner Sale featured an example of this coin in MS-65. *MS-60 to 62:* 75 to 125+. *MS-63:* 25 to 32. *MS-64:* 20 to 25. *MS-65 or better:* 3 to 5.

actual size: 38.1 mm

Availability in circulated grades: *F-12 to AU-58:* 3,000 to 5,000.

Characteristics of striking: Striking of this issue varies. Some are flat from star 4 through 13, or others. Liberty's head is often lightly struck. Check the reverse as well, but it is usually sharper than the obverse.

Proofs: *PF-60 to 62:* 200 to 230. *PF-63:* 80 to 100. *PF-64:* 40 to 55. *PF-65 or better:* 25 to 35.

Notes: The 1872 Liberty Seated dollar was coined in larger quantities than any other issue of the design. One interesting variety has an errant 2 punched into the rock on which Liberty is seated. Most were exported. This led to a call for a specific coin to be called a commercial trade dollar, name later changed to trade dollar. Such trade dollars were first made in 1873 and are the subject of the next chapter.

VG-8	F-12	VF-20	EF-40	AU-50	MS-60
$400	$450	$550	$675	$950	$2,200

MS-63	MS-65	PF-60	PF-63	PF-65
$4,700	$50,000	$2,250	$3,800	$10,000

1872-CC

Circulation-strike mintage: 3,150

actual size: 38.1 mm

Availability in Mint State: The Battle Born Collection Sale in 2013 featured an example of this coin in MS-64+. In 2014 the Eugene H. Gardner Sale featured an example of this coin in MS-64. ***MS-60 to 62:*** 5 to 8. ***MS-63:*** 1 or 2. ***MS-64:*** 2. ***MS-65 or better:*** 2.

Availability in circulated grades: ***VG-8 to F-15:*** 40 to 55. ***F-12 to AU-58:*** 100 to 150.

Characteristics of striking: This issue is usually seen well struck on the reverse with an average strike on the obverse. As is the case with other Carson City Mint Liberty Seated dollars, the word LIBERTY on the shield is not as prominent as on Philadelphia coins and tended to wear away especially quickly once the coins saw circulation.

Notes: Delivery figures by month: March: 2,150; July: 1,000.

VG-8	F-12	VF-20	EF-40	AU-50	MS-60	MS-63	MS-65
$2,750	$3,500	$4,250	$7,750	$12,500	$25,000	$135,000	$325,000

1872-S

Circulation-strike mintage: 9,000

actual size: 38.1 mm

Availability in Mint State: In 2014 the Eugene H. Gardner Sale featured an example of this coin in MS-63. ***MS-60 to 62:*** 1 to 4. ***MS-63:*** 1 or 2. ***MS-64:*** 1 or 2. ***MS-65 or better:*** 1.

Availability in circulated grades: ***F-12 to AU-58:*** 300 to 400.

Characteristics of striking: Striking of this issue varies. They often have slight weakness on Liberty's head and stars eight and nine on the obverse, and the leg to the right and on the talons of the eagle on the reverse. These often have semi-prooflike surface.

Notes: From *Banker's Magazine*, November 1872: "U.S. Coin in China. The new silver dollar recently struck in the San Francisco Mint is said to be adapted for general circulation in China, where the want of silver coin has been much felt. It is worth six percent more than the old dollar, and will be received in China on the same terms as the old Mexican dollar, which has hitherto been at a premium of five to eight percent." The dollars were sold at a premium for this purpose and were not placed into circulation.[88]

VG-8	F-12	VF-20	EF-40	AU-50	MS-60	MS-63	MS-65
$1,000	$1,250	$1,850	$2,250	$4,250	$12,000	$37,500	

1873

Circulation-strike mintage: 293,000

Proof mintage: 600

Availability in Mint State: In 2015 the Eugene H. Gardner Sale featured an example of this coin in MS-65. *MS-60 to 62:* 50 to 75. *MS-63:* 20 to 25. *MS-64:* 30 to 45. *MS-65 or better:* 4 to 6.[89]

actual size: 38.1 mm

Availability in circulated grades: *F-12 to AU-58:* 250 to 350. These are much scarcer than the mintage might suggest.[90,91]

Characteristics of striking: Striking of this issue varies, but some have lightly struck details on Liberty's head and light strike on stars, especially eight through ten. Some Mint State coins have satiny surfaces while others are partially prooflike.

Proofs: *PF-60 to 62:* 200 to 230. *PF-63:* 80 to 100. *PF-64:* 40 to 55. *PF-65 or better:* 25 to 35.

Notes: All 1873 Liberty Seated dollars have the Close 3 date logotype where the knobs of 3 are large and close together.

VG-8	F-12	VF-20	EF-40	AU-50	MS-60
$475	$500	$550	$650	$1,200	$3,000

MS-63	MS-65	PF-60	PF-63	PF-65
$5,500	$55,000	$2,250	$3,800	$10,000

1873-CC

Circulation-strike mintage: 2,300

Availability in Mint State: In 2015 the Eugene H. Gardner Sale featured an example of this coin in MS-61. *MS-60 to 62:* 1 or 2. *MS-63:* 0.[92] *MS-64:* 0. *MS-65 or better:* 1.

actual size: 38.1 mm

Availability in circulated grades: *VG-8 to F-15:* 10 to 15. *F-12 to AU-58:* 50 to 70.

Characteristics of striking: The 1873-CC is usually of above-average sharpness. However, some show weakness on Liberty's head and chest and/or on the reverse. As is the case with other Carson City Mint Liberty Seated dollars, the word LIBERTY on the shield is not as prominent as on Philadelphia coins, and tended to wear away especially quickly once the coins saw circulation.

VG-8	F-12	VF-20	EF-40	AU-50	MS-60	MS-63	MS-65
$17,500	$20,000	$22,500	$30,000	$50,000	$125,000		$650,000

1873-S

Circulation-strike mintage: 700

Notes: Although 700 coins were reported as minted, no example has ever been located. Six pairs of dies were shipped from Philadelphia in November 1872, indicating a possibility for a large mintage which never materialized. Probably the entire mintage of 700 coins was from a single pair.

In an article, "What Would An 1873-S Standard Dollar Look Like?" published in the *Gobrecht Journal*, July 1980, John W. McCloskey quoted Harry X. Boosel, who located a letter dated March 5, 1873, showing that a package of assay coins, including one standard silver dollar, was shipped from the San Francisco Mint by Wells Fargo to the superintendent of the U.S. Mint in Philadelphia. No further information is available today.

In early May of 1873 San Francisco Mint Superintendent Oscar LaGrange sent a telegram to newly appointed Mint Director Henry Linderman asking: "What is the mint to do with the silver coinage of the old standard?" On May 23, Linderman responded that it had not been decided as of yet what to do with the old standard silver coinage. On June 13, director Linderman sent a very interesting telegram to Superintendent LaGrange. In that message Linderman instructed LaGrange "to melt and recoin all silver coinage of 1873. If the recoinage of the old issue silver dollars in particular give a profit in the recoinage, then the difference is to be credited to the Silver Profit Fund."[93]

10

TRADE DOLLARS
(1873–1885)

Introduction

The father of the trade dollar was John Jay Knox, Comptroller of the Currency, who studied the matter in detail, and who did much of the work for what would become the Coinage Act of 1873.[1]

The idea for a commercial or trade dollar arose in 1870 when Knox was in San Francisco visiting Louis A. Garnett and others of influence. The port relied heavily on the China trade in which Mexican dollars were the coins of choice. Merchants had to pay a premium more than silver value to obtain them as the supply was nearly always short of the demand. If the San Francisco Mint, which started operations in 1854, could coin quantities of Liberty Seated dollars for the export trade this would be ideal, it was thought. In 1859 merchants in San Francisco suggested that the mint do this; silver dollars had not been struck there before. Some 20,000 1859-S Liberty Seated dollars were produced, were sent to Eastern Asia, and were very successful for their intended purpose. However, California was distant from the seat of government in Washington, D.C., and the needs of merchants there were not particularly important to most politicians.

John Jay Knox.

Despite the availability of Liberty Seated silver dollars minted in the United States and shipped in large quantities to Eastern Asia beginning in 1842, most Chinese merchants preferred the silver content of Mexican and other Spanish-American 8-reales coins, which were slightly heavier. Even accounts in inland China were often reckoned in this medium. Chinese bankers and other businessmen agreed to accept U.S. silver dollars only at a discount in comparison to the Spanish-American coins. In order to compete effectively, many commercial interests had to buy Mexican pesos at a premium of 10 to 15 percent in order to have a supply for trade with the Chinese. The Mexican coins weighed slightly more than 417 grains, were .902 fine silver, and had slightly more than 377 grains of pure silver, in comparison to the Liberty Seated dollar weighing 412.5 grains with 371.25 grains of silver. Thus, Congress, whose members were encouraged by silver-mining interests in the West, came to believe that a special "trade dollar," at first called a "commercial dollar," of slightly extra weight, would facilitate commerce on the other side of the Pacific Ocean. The California Legislature weighed in, literally, and requested that the federal government produce a new coin of 420 grains and .900 fine, which would about equal the Spanish-American dollar, and thus be competitive with it. Knox, following on this and his research, was in favor of the idea and envisioned it as a coin to be used strictly in the export trade and not domestically.

This set the scene for an extensive series of commercial dollar and trade dollar patterns produced from 1871 through 1873. In the latter year the denomination became official.

Trade Dollars Authorized

The Coinage Act of February 12, 1873, framed by John Jay Knox and the Treasury Department, and refined by much discussion in Congress, generally revised the coinage laws. Among many other provisions, the act created the trade dollar. One of the most relevant sections of the act is the following:

> Section 21: That any owner of silver bullion may deposit the same at any mint, to be formed into bars, or into dollars of the weight of 420 grains, troy, designated in this act as trade dollars, and no deposit of silver for other coinage shall be received; but silver bullion contained in gold deposits, and separated therefrom, may be paid for in silver coin, at such valuation as may be, from time to time, established by the director of the Mint.

In essence, the foregoing stated that owners of silver bullion could deposit the same at any mint and receive trade dollars in payment, but could not receive dimes, quarters, or half dollars for their deposits. If such silver had been obtained as a byproduct of gold refining, then subsidiary coins (dime to half dollar) could be paid out in exchange, at the discretion of the Mint director. Other provisions, including section 28, discussed subsidiary coins, but in practice few silver coins other than trade dollars were paid out in 1873.

The charge for converting silver bullion to trade dollars was to be set by the director of the Mint, with the concurrence of the secretary of the Treasury, so as to equal, but not to exceed, in their judgment, the actual average cost to each mint for labor, wastage, machinery, and other expenses.

A rider on the 1873 bill made trade dollars legal tender in the United States, this being against Knox's wishes. There was no problem for the bullion value of a trade dollar in 1873 as it averaged $1.02. At the time silver coins were not in circulation in the East and Midwest, but they were extensively used on the West Coast in lieu of paper money (which was forbidden to circulate at par under the California Constitution framed in 1850).

An Early Report

The *Annual Report of the Director of the Mint* for the fiscal year ending June 30, 1873, told of the trade dollar and its status, and that coinage of the new denomination had commenced after the fiscal year ended:

The trade dollar of silver authorized by the coinage act is designed expressly for export, and has no fixed value as compared with gold. It is in no proper sense a monetary standard or unit of account, and is not included or referred to when the silver coins for home use are spoken of; the latter being purposely overvalued, as before stated, to retain them in circulation. Having been made a legal tender in limited amounts, it may eventually, if the price of silver relative to gold falls sufficiently, to some extent enter into home circulation, but its export value will always be in excess of that of the subsidiary silver coin, its bullion value or quantity of pure metal being about 8-1/2% in excess.

The issue of the trade dollar was not commenced until nearly a month after the close of the fiscal year. It has been shipped to some extent to China and Japan,[2] but we have not, as yet, received any account of its reception in those empires. It will no doubt require a year or two for its successful introduction there.

Trade Dollars in Later Years

After 1873 the price of silver bullion went into a long decline, a situation not anticipated by the congressmen who passed the coinage act of that year. This was caused by two main factors. In Europe many countries that had issued silver coins of full weight and value altered their standards so that the silver content was less. As a result large quantities came on the market. In the United States new discoveries were made in Utah, Colorado, and elsewhere, mines were developed, and more metal was available than was needed for coinage.

As silver began its price decline, the Treasury desired to eliminate the profit that could be made by depositing silver bullion in a mint and receiving trade dollars in exchange. On July 22, 1876, Congress revoked the legal-tender provision. After 1876, trade dollars could not legally be spent at face value within the United States. Rather, their value in America fluctuated in the metal market. Nevertheless, many employers

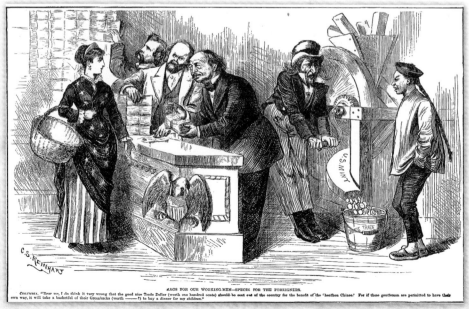

Cartoon protesting the trade dollar, reflecting that silver trade dollars of full weight and value were being shipped off to China while domestically no silver coins were in circulation and commerce was conducted in "rags" (paper money). (*Harper's Weekly*, April 25, 1874)

flouted the law, buying them at a discount and putting them into pay envelopes as full dollars. The effect was softened somewhat by merchants advertising to take trade dollars at par. This amounted to little more than giving a sale price or courtesy discount.

In the meantime in the 1870s the "Silver Question" dominated politics. Western mining interests wanted the government to produce more coins other than trade dollars to sustain the market. Standard silver dollars of 412.5 grains' weight had not been made since the Liberty Seated coins were discontinued by the Coinage Act of February 12, 1873. That particular legislation was hurriedly passed without study or awareness of its consequences, it was alleged. Thus arose a fiction that is widely seen today in lightly researched and historical accounts: Congressmen were hoodwinked and "the Crime of 1873" was the result.

The truth is completely different! There was no such "crime." In his memoirs, Senator John Sherman observed this concerning the Coinage Act of February 12, 1873:

> There was never a bill proposed in the Congress of the United States which was so publicly and openly presented and agitated. I know of no bill in my experience which was printed, as this was, 13 times, in order to invite attention to it. I know no bill which was freer from any immoral or wrong influence than this Act of 1873.[3]

Twilight of the Trade Dollar

The trade dollar was a great success. In 1877, the *Annual Report of the Director of the Mint* told of the export of San Francisco Mint trade dollars and of the general acceptance of the coins in China:

> The trade dollar continues to grow in favor in China, and the demand at San Francisco for the past fiscal year for export to that empire averaged over $687,000 per month, and in some months more than twice that amount was exported.
>
> On account of its superior mintage, it is difficult to counterfeit, and its close conformity to standard fineness and weight gives it some advantages over its principal competitor, the Mexican dollar, which it is likely to supplant to a still greater extent, notwithstanding the prestige the latter has long enjoyed as the successor of the Spanish dollar, and also some favoritism in its behalf by local customs authorities at certain Chinese ports. . . .
>
> The testimony of intelligent bankers, thoroughly familiar with the Chinese exchanges, (recently given before the United States Treasury commission in San Francisco), shows conclusively that the coinage of trade dollars has been attended with decided advantages both as respects our commercial and mining interests, and there can be no doubt but that it should be continued on a scale equal to the requirements for export to China. It may be added here, that the Japanese government, desiring to reap the benefits of a coinage manufactured exclusively for trade purposes, have followed the example of the United States, and are now coining a trade dollar of the same weight and fineness as our own, with the evident intention of exporting it to China, where it has been made a legal tender at one or two ports. Its general appearance is similar to the 'yen,' substituting, however, the English inscription "420 trade dollar 900," instead of "416 one yen 900."

By 1878 the price of silver had declined to such an extent that, if produced, a standard dollar would contain only 89 cents' worth of the metal. Two political factions squared off. The Silverites or Free Silver people, as they were called, wanted free and unlimited coinage of that metal. Those on the other side, mainly the Republicans, held that silver coinage should be limited to the quantities needed in commerce, and that gold was the most important coinage metal. At the time a $20 double eagle was of full weight and value.

The Silverites had their way, and Western mining interests and Midwestern agricultural interests combined to pass the Bland-Allison Act of February 28, 1878. This eliminated the trade dollar denomination and reinstituted the standard silver dollar. The government was mandated to purchase two to four million ounces of silver each month and to coin it into dollars. At the time a new standard dollar of 412.5 grains required only 89 cents worth of silver. Accordingly, the government made a profit on each one—a win-win situation for Westerners who found a market far in excess of the metal heretofore used for trade dollars and also for Uncle Sam.

On March 22, 1878, after the fact, the House Committee of Coinage, Weights, and Measures gave a report "relative to the continuance of the coinage of the trade dollar." The quoted testimony was positive, including the comment that at least $700,000 to $750,000 in trade dollars would be absorbed by China each month, and if they could be coined in response to the demand for them, rather than only for the requests of depositors, the quantity would be substantially higher.

This was to no avail.

Thus, production of trade dollars for export ceased, although logic suggests that they should have been continued parallel with the standard dollars as they were in strong demand by an entirely separate market. Proofs for collectors continued to be made through 1883. In 1884 and 1885 a very small number of Proofs was secretly made and sold to William K. Idler or to his son-in-law, John W. Haseltine. Their existence was not revealed until the early 1900s when Haseltine discovered them "by surprise" in the Idler estate.

In the *Annual Report of the Director of the Mint*, 1883, Horatio Burchard recommended that the coinage of trade dollars no longer be permitted and that older trade dollars held by the public be redeemed for face value:

An unwanted orphan trade dollar meets Uncle Sam. (*Frank Leslie's Illustrated Newspaper*, October 14, 1882)

"A Government Waif." (*Frank Leslie's Illustrated Newspaper*, July 14, 1883)

Although its coinage is now discretionary with the secretary of the Treasury and has been suspended by him, the issue of this coin in any contingency should no longer be authorized or permitted at any of the United States mints. Originally made in the coinage Act of 1873 a legal tender, to the same extent as the other designated silver coins, a considerable number had probably, before its demonetization in 1876, gone into circulation in this country. The statistics of coinage and exports show that at the latter date the number of pieces coined exceeded the exportations by over two million dollars. Probably from five to seven million of these coins are now held in the country, mostly in the mining and manufacturing regions of Pennsylvania and contiguous states, and in the vicinity of New York, where they have been paid to workmen and laborers, and by them paid to and received from tradesmen in those localities.

While the United States has incurred no legal liability, yet by the act of the government the coins were at first put into circulation and given compulsory currency, and have fallen into the hands of those who can ill afford to suffer from the depreciation, and it would seem but an act of justice that the United States should permit these coins to be sent to the mints and exchanged for other silver coins, into which they could be profitably recoined. I doubt not that action of this kind would have long since been taken, but for the apprehension that a large number of exported trade dollars would be returned to this country.

My own investigations and inquiries have satisfied me that the trade dollars sent to China have gone to the melting pots and become sycee silver or disappeared in the interior of that country, for, although their value as silver bullion would be only about eighty-seven cents, yet their commercial market value in New York City has, prior to the late movement to depress their price, fallen below ninety-eight cents but once, and that for a short period, and has usually ranged for several years above ninety-nine cents, and had it been possible to secure trade dollars for import from China to this country, the profits on the operation would have brought them here long since.

In the summer of 1886 trade dollars were worth about 75¢ in New York City, a value which continued through early 1887. Wholesale merchants in particular suffered, for trade dollars moved through the merchandising system from buyer to retailer and then to wholesaler, but the wholesaler could not pass them along except to bullion brokers at a discount.[4]

On February 19, 1887, legislation was passed which provided for the redemption of trade dollars that had not been mutilated. This redemption could only be done at the Sub-Treasury offices in New York and San Francisco, thus requiring most holders to sell them to brokers who could gather a quantity for shipment. In exchange any silver denomination could be requested. More than eight million pieces came back to the Treasury, including about two million that were returned from China. Redemption continued for several years.

The *Annual Report of the Director of the Mint*, 1891, prepared by Edward O. Leech, stated

Redeeming trade dollars at the Sub-Treasury in New York City.
(*Harper's Weekly*, June 4, 1887)

that to date 7,689,036 trade dollars had been redeemed. The report further noted that up to that point in time, the face value of silver dollars coined under the Act of March 3, 1891, providing for the recoinage of trade dollars into silver dollars, was 5,078,472. These were melted and the metal used to make Morgan-design silver dollars.

The Design of the Trade Dollar

Designed by Chief Engraver William Barber, the trade dollar incorporates motifs not used earlier on circulating coinage. Beginning in 1871, before the denomination was authorized, patterns were made and were called commercial dollars per the inscription on the reverse. The motifs for circulation were finalized in 1873.

The obverse portrays a female figure of Liberty holding a ribbon inscribed LIBERTY, seated on a bale of cotton tied with ropes.[5] On another ribbon below the bale is the motto IN GOD WE TRUST. She faces the Pacific Ocean, looking westward toward China. On her head is a beaded coronet reminiscent of that on the double eagle. In her extended right hand is a laurel branch symbolizing peace. Behind her is a sheaf of wheat. Around are 13 stars, spaced four, two, and seven, and the date is below. The overall configuration has been called the "Liberty Seated" type, as it is indeed, but the design is not related to that created by Christian Gobrecht for use on standard silver dollars.

The reverse of the trade dollar depicts an eagle perched, holding three arrows in his right (observer's left) talons and a laurel branch in his left (observer's right) talons, an error from a heraldic viewpoint. Above and around the border appears UNITED STATES OF AMERICA, with TRADE DOLLAR at the bottom border. In the field above the eagle is E PLURIBUS UNUM on a ribbon, and below the arrows and laurel branch is the inscription 420 GRAINS, 900 FINE.[6] A somewhat similar eagle was used later (1875–1878) on the 20-cent piece and on certain pattern coins.

The edge of the coin is reeded. The metallic composition is .900 silver and .100 copper. The weight of the trade dollar is 420 grains, which includes 378 troy grains of pure silver (the balance of the 420 grains' weight being copper, as noted). The standard diameter is 38.1 mm.

Pattern Coins

Patterns were first made in 1871 and were officially designated as COMMERCIAL DOLLAR on the reverse, with the weight given as 420 grains and fineness of .900. They were of use to merchants in China who valued silver coins by their metal value, not by country of origin or anything else. Soon thereafter, the designation *trade dollar* was adopted.

The first commercial dollar patterns made in 1871 employed the seated Indian princess design earlier engraved by James B. Longacre (who died on January 1, 1869). In 1872 additional patterns were made employing designs by Longacre, William Barber (who copied the Longacre motif), and Christian Gobrecht (the regular Liberty seated silver dollar obverse of the year). These and all other patterns are described in detail and illustrated in *United States Patterns and Related Issues*, by Andrew W. Pollock III and in *United States Pattern Coins*, by Dr. J. Hewitt Judd.

The following patterns are known from commercial dollar and trade dollar dies dated 1871 and 1872; a more detailed discussion of the dies produced in 1873 and struck in 1873–1876 follows.

1871 Commercial dollar (Judd-1154 to 1157): *Obverse:* Longacre's Indian Princess design with 13 stars around and 22 stars on the flag. *Reverse:* Commercial Dollar die. Large wreath enclosing COMMERCIAL / DOLLAR / 420 GRS. / 900 FINE. On wreath

An 1871 pattern commercial dollar. (Judd-1154.)

ribbon is GOD OUR TRUST.[7] At the top border is UNITED STATES OF AMERICA. The first appearance of the commercial dollar die; predecessor of the trade dollar. J-1154 is struck in silver and has a reeded edge. J-1155 is struck in silver and has a plain edge. J-1156 is struck in copper and has a reeded edge. J-1157 is struck in copper and has a plain edge.

1871 Commercial dollar (J-1158 and 1159): *Obverse:* Longacre's Indian Princess design with 13 stars around and 13 stars on the flag. *Reverse:* Commercial Dollar die. J-1158 is struck in silver and has a reeded edge. J-1159 is struck in copper and has a reeded edge.

1871 Commercial dollar (J-1160): *Obverse:* Regular Liberty Seated die of the year. *Reverse:* GOD OUR TRUST on ribbon below UNITED STATES OF AMERICA at top border. J-1160 is struck in silver and has a reeded edge.[8]

1872 Commercial dollar (J-1212 to 1213a): *Obverse:* Longacre's Indian Princess design with 13 stars around, 22 stars on the flag, without name below base, and was first used posthumously in 1870 (compare with J-1008). *Reverse:* Commercial Dollar die as first used in 1871. J-1212 is struck in silver and has a reeded edge. J-1213 is struck in silver and has a plain edge. J-1213a is struck in copper and has a reeded edge.

1872 Commercial dollar (J-1214 to 1218): *Obverse:* William Barber's adaptation of James B. Longacre's Indian Princess design, facing left, with 13 stars around, 13 stars on the flag, and date below. *Reverse:* Commercial Dollar die. J-1214 is

An 1872 pattern commercial dollar. (Judd-1214.)

struck in silver and has a reeded edge. J-1215 is struck in silver and has a plain edge. J-1216 is struck in copper and has a reeded edge. J-1217 is stuck in copper and has a plain edge. J-1218 is struck in aluminum and has a reeded edge.

1872 Commercial dollar (J-1219 and 1219a): *Obverse:* Regular Liberty Seated Die. *Reverse:* Commercial Dollar die. J-1219 is struck in silver and has a reeded edge. J-1219a is struck in copper and has a reeded edge.

1872 Trade dollar (J-1220 to 1222): *Obverse:* William Barber's adaptation of James B. Longacre's Indian Princess design, facing left, with 13 stars around, 13 stars on the flag, and date below. *Reverse:* Large open laurel wreath enclosing TRADE / DOLLAR / 420 GRAINS. / 900 FINE. On ribbon below is IN GOD WE TRUST. At the top border is UNITED STATES OF AMERICA. The reverse is the first trade dollar die, inspired by the commercial dollar die. J-1220 is struck in silver and has a reeded edge. J-1221 is struck in copper and has a reeded edge. J-1222 is stuck in aluminum and has a reeded edge.

1872 Trade dollar (J-1223): *Obverse:* William Barber's adaptation of James B. Longacre's Indian Princess design, as preceding. *Reverse:* Barber's standing eagle with shield, on which is a ribbon lettered IN GOD WE TRUST, and a scroll in its beak inscribed E PLURIBUS UNUM. In the field below the eagle is 420 GRAINS, 900 FINE. UNITED STATES OF AMERICA / TRADE DOLLAR around border. J-1223 is struck in silver and has a reeded edge.

Trade Dollar Obverse Dies of 1873–1876

In 1873 many more varieties of pattern trade dollars were made. Some of these were undoubtedly struck with the correct intent in mind, to eventually formulate a design for use in circulation. However, the majority seem to have been capricious combinations of dies struck to enrich privileged insiders at the Mint who quietly sold them to dealers and collectors in addition to a set of six different issues that was available to anyone interested.

Obverse 1: "Coronet Head facing left." The head of Liberty is facing left, wearing a coronet with LIBERTY in raised letters. Her hair is tied behind with a strand of pearls. 13 stars are around the border and 1873 is below. Used with J-1276 to 1280.

Obverse 2: "Bailly Head facing left." The head of Liberty is crowned with leaves, and her hair is braided and coiled behind, all compactly arranged. 13 stars are around the border and 1873 is below. The die is by Joseph Alexis Bailly (1825–1883) who worked as an occasional assistant to Charles E. Barber, son of the chief engraver, who was on the Mint staff. Used with J-1281 to 1286.

Obverse 3: "Coronet Head facing right." William Barber's head of Liberty is facing right and LIBERTY is on the coronet with Y at the front.[9] 13 stars are around the border and 1873 is below. Used with J-1287.

Obverse 4: "Double Eagle head." This is a close copy of the 1873 $20 gold die, here made as a trade dollar die, with Longacre's coronet head facing left. 13 stars are around the border and 1873 is below. Used with J-1288, 1289.

Obverse 5: "Liberty Seated on globe, short plow handles." Liberty Seated is facing left with her right hand holding a pole on which is a liberty cap and her left hand is resting on a globe. Behind her are a plow (with short handles) and a small sheaf of wheat. To the lower left are two bales of cotton. The sea is in the distance at the left. 13 stars are around the border and 1873 is below. Used with J-1290 to 1298.

Obverse 6: "Liberty Seated on globe, long plow handles." Liberty Seated is facing left with her right hand holding a pole on which is a liberty cap and her left hand is resting on a larger globe than on Obverse 6. Behind her are a plow (with long handles) and a larger sheaf of wheat than on Obverse 6. To the lower left are two bales of cotton, smaller than on Obverse 6. The sea is in the distance at the left. 13 stars are around the border and 1873 is below. Used with J-1299 to 1306.

Obverse 7: "Barber's Indian Princess." Barber's Indian Princess design, inspired by James B. Longacre. Indian Princess is seated facing left with her right hand holding a pole on which is a liberty cap and her left hand is resting on a globe. Two small flags are behind her, one with 13 stars. The sea is in the distance at the left. 13 stars are around the border and 1873 is below. Used with J-1307 to 1314.

Obverse 8: "Bailly's Liberty Seated die." J.A. Bailly's depiction of Liberty, seated and facing left. Her right hand is holding the pole on which is a liberty cap and her left hand rests on a globe inscribed LIBERTY, behind which is a wheat sheaf. In the front are two bales of cotton and a cotton plant. The design is such that to the viewer the figure of Liberty is overwhelmed by the items which are near her. 13 stars are around the border and 1873 is below. Used with J-1315 to 1319.

Obverse 9: "Similar to regular trade dollar die, but with wider sea." This obverse design is similar to the regular trade dollar die, but the sea extends farther to the left and nearly touches the denticles. Liberty is seated on bales with a sheaf of wheat to the right. Her left hand holds a branch extended to the left (toward China), while her right holds the top of a ribbon inscribed LIBERTY. Horizontally on base is IN GOD WE TRUST. 13 stars are around the border and 1873 is below. Used with J-1322 to 1326.

Obverse 10: "Regular trade dollar die." Liberty is seated on bales and a sheaf of wheat is to the right. Her left hand holds a branch extended to the left (toward China), while her right holds the top of a ribbon inscribed LIBERTY. Horizontally on base is IN GOD WE TRUST. Sea to the left is distant from the denticles. 13 stars are around the border and 1873 is below. Used with J-1327 to 1330.

Trade Dollar Reverse Dies of 1873–1876

Reverse A: "Trade Dollar inscription in laurel wreath die." A large open laurel wreath enclosing TRADE / DOLLAR / 420 GRAINS. / 900 FINE with a ribbon below inscribed IN GOD WE TRUST. At the top border is UNITED STATES OF AMERICA. This was first used in 1872 on J-1220. Used with J-1276 to 1280, 1287, 1304a to 1306.

Reverse B: "Barber's standing eagle holding shield, motto in field above eagle." Barber's standing eagle with a shield, on which is a ribbon lettered IN GOD WE TRUST. In the field above the eagle's head is E PLURIBUS UNUM. In the field below the eagle is 420 GRAINS, 900 FINE. UNITED STATES OF AMERICA / TRADE DOLLAR is around the border. Used with J-1281 to 1284, 1293 to 1298, 1299, 1307.

Reverse C: "Barber's standing eagle holding shield, motto on ribbon in eagle's beak." Barber's standing eagle with shield, on which is a ribbon lettered IN GOD WE TRUST, and a scroll in its beak inscribed E PLURIBUS UNUM. In the field below the eagle is 420 GRAINS, 900 FINE. UNITED STATES OF AMERICA / TRADE DOLLAR is around the border. It was first used in 1872 on J-1223. Used with J-1285, 1286, 1293 to 1298, 1300 to 1303, 1308, 1309.

Reverse D: "Small stocky eagle perched on shield, facing right." A small, stocky perched eagle is standing on a shield, wings raised with beak extending to the right. Three arrows are in the left talons and a laurel branch is in the right. E PLURIBUS UNUM is above the eagle. IN GOD WE TRUST is on a scroll below the shield, below which is 420 GRAINS / 900 FINE. Around the border is UNITED STATES OF AMERICA / TRADE DOLLAR. Used with J-1288, 1315 to 1319.

Reverse E: "Small eagle with raised wings, very wide ribbon above head and both wings." A small perched eagle is holding three arrows and a laurel branch. Above, on a very wide ribbon, is E PLURIBUS UNUM. In the field below the eagle is 420 GRAINS / 900 FINE / (and on a ribbon) IN GOD WE TRUST. Around the border is UNITED STATES OF AMERICA / TRADE DOLLAR. Used with J-1304, 1310 to 1314.

Reverse F: "Small perched eagle with ribbon in beak; ribbon in nearly a closed loop." A small perched eagle is holding in its beak a ribbon inscribed E PLURIBUS UNUM, three arrows and a laurel branch in its talons. Below in the field is 420 GRAINS, 900 FINE. Around the border is UNITED STATES OF AMERICA / TRADE DOL-LAR. Used with J-1322 to 1326.

Reverse G: "Regular trade dollar die." An eagle is perched, holding three arrows and a laurel branch. E PLURIBUS is on the ribbon above. In the field below is 420 GRAINS, 900 FINE. Around the border is UNITED STATES OF AMERICA / TRADE DOLLAR. Used on J-1327 to 1330.

Pattern Trade Dollars of 1873–1876

The preceding dies were used in a wide array of combinations, listed below.

1873 Trade dollar (J-1276 to 1280): Dies 1-A. *Obverse:* Coronet Head facing left. *Reverse:* Trade Dollar inscription in laurel wreath die. Both dies by William Barber. J-1276 is struck in silver and has a reeded edge. J-1277 is struck in silver and has a plain edge. J-1278 is struck in copper and has a reeded edge. J-1279 is struck in aluminum and has a reeded edge. J-1280 is struck in white metal and has a plain edge.

1873 Trade dollar (J-1281 to 1284): Dies 2-B. *Obverse:* Bailly Head facing left. *Reverse:* Barber's standing eagle holding shield, motto in field above eagle. J-1281 is struck in silver and has a reeded edge. J-1282 is struck in silver and has a plain edge . J-1283 is struck in copper and has a reeded edge. J-1284 is struck in aluminum and has a reeded edge.

1873 Trade dollar (J-1285 and 1286): Dies 2-C. *Obverse:* Bailly Head facing left. *Reverse:* Barber's standing eagle holding shield, motto on ribbon in eagle's beak. J-1285 is struck in copper and has a reeded edge. J-1286 is struck in aluminum and has a reeded edge.

1873 Trade dollar (J-1287): Dies 3-A. *Obverse:* Coronet Head facing right. *Reverse:* Trade Dollar inscription in laurel wreath die. J-1287 is struck in white metal and has a plain edge.

1873 Trade dollar (J-1288): Dies 4-D. *Obverse:* Double Eagle head. *Reverse:* Small stocky eagle perched on shield, facing right. J-1288 is struck in copper and has a reeded edge.

1873 Trade dollar (J-1289): Dies 4-B. *Obverse:* $20 style as preceding. *Reverse:* Barber's standing eagle holding shield, motto in field above eagle. J-1289 is struck in copper and has a reeded edge.

1873 Trade dollar (J-1290 to 1292): Dies 5-B. *Obverse:* Liberty Seated on globe, short plow handles. *Reverse:* Barber's standing eagle holding shield, motto in field above eagle. J-1290 is struck in silver and has a reeded edge. J-1291 is struck in silver and has a plain edge. J-1292 is struck in white metal and has a plain edge.

1873 Trade dollar (J-1293 to 1298): Dies 5-C. *Obverse:* Liberty Seated on globe, short plow handles. *Reverse:* Barber's standing eagle and shield, E PLURIBUS UNUM on ribbon above, held in eagle's beak. J-1293 is struck in silver and has a reeded edge. J-1294 is struck in silver and has a plain edge. J-1295 is struck in copper and has a reeded edge. J-1296 is struck in copper and has a plain edge. J-1297 is struck in aluminum and has a reeded edge. J-1298 is struck in white metal and has a plain edge.

1873 Trade dollar (J-1299): Dies 6-B. *Obverse:* Liberty Seated on globe, long plow handles. *Reverse:* Barber's standing eagle holding shield, motto in field above eagle. J-1299 is struck in white metal and has a plain edge.

1873 Trade dollar (J-1300 to 1303): Dies 6-C. *Obverse:* Liberty Seated on globe, long plow handles. *Reverse:* Barber's standing eagle holding shield, motto on ribbon in eagle's beak. J-1300 is struck in silver and has a reeded edge. J-1301 is struck in copper and has a reeded edge. J-1302 is struck in copper and has a plain edge. J-1303 is struck in aluminum and has a reeded edge.

1873 Trade dollar (J-1304): Dies 6-E. *Obverse:* Liberty Seated on globe, long plow handles. *Reverse:* Small eagle with raised wings, very wide ribbon above head and both wings. J-1304 is struck in white metal and has a plain edge.

1873 Trade dollar (J-1304a to 1306): Dies 6-A. *Obverse:* Liberty Seated on globe, long plow handles. *Reverse:* Trade Dollar inscription in laurel wreath die. J-1304a is struck in silver and has a reeded edge. J-1305 is struck in copper and has a reeded edge. J-1306 is struck in white metal and has a plain edge.

1873 Trade dollar (J-1307): Dies 7-B. *Obverse:* Barber's Indian Princess. *Reverse:* Barber's standing eagle holding shield, motto in field above eagle. J-1307 is struck in white metal and has a plain edge.

1873 Trade dollar (J-1308 and 1309): Dies 7-C. *Obverse:* Barber's Indian Princess. *Reverse:* Barber's standing eagle holding shield, motto on ribbon in eagle's beak. {Earlier listings of J-1326a and b were misdescriptions of J-1308 and 1309.} J-1308 is struck in silver and has a reeded edge. J-1309 is struck in white metal and has a plain edge.

1873 Trade dollar (J-1310 to 1314): Dies 7-E. *Obverse:* Barber's Indian Princess. *Reverse:* Small eagle with raised wings, very wide ribbon above head and both wings. J-1310 is struck in silver and has a reeded edge. J-1311 is struck in silver and has a plain edge. J-1312 is struck in copper and has a reeded edge. J-1313 is struck in aluminum and has a reeded edge. J-1314 is struck in white metal and has a plain edge.

An 1873 pattern trade dollar. (Judd-1311.)

1873 Trade dollar (J-1315 to 1319): Dies 8-D. *Obverse:* Bailly's Liberty Seated die. *Reverse:* Small stocky eagle perched on shield, facing right. J-1315 is struck in silver and has a reeded edge. J-1316 is struck in silver and has a plain edge. J-1317 is struck in copper and has a reeded edge. J-1318 is struck in aluminum and has a reeded edge. J-1319 is struck in white metal and has a plain edge.

1873 Trade dollar (J-1322 to 1326): Dies 9-F. *Obverse:* Similar to regular trade dollar die, but with wider sea. *Reverse:* Small perched eagle with ribbon in beak; ribbon in nearly a closed loop. J-1322 is struck in silver and has a reeded edge. J-1323 is struck in silver and has a plain edge. J-1324 is struck in copper and has a reeded edge. J-1325 is struck in aluminum and has a reeded edge. J-1326[10] is struck in white metal and has a plain edge.

1873 Trade dollar (J-1327 to 1330): Regular dies, Close 3. Dies 10-G. J-1327 is struck in copper and has a reeded edge. J-1328 is struck in aluminum and has a reeded edge. J-1329 is struck in white metal and has a reeded edge. J-1330 is struck in tin and has a reeded edge.

1874 Trade dollar (J-1363 and 1364): Regular dies. J-1363 is struck in copper and has a reeded edge. J-1364 is struck in aluminum and has a reeded edge.

1875 Commercial dollar (J-1423 to 1425): *Obverse:* Liberty Seated at the seashore, similar to J-1396 20-cent piece (complete with illogical depiction of ship), but here with a ribbon below the base inscribed IN GOD WE TRUST. *Reverse:* Commercial Dollar die. Large wreath enclosing COMMERCIAL / DOLLAR / 420 GRS. / 900 FINE. On wreath ribbon is GOD OUR TRUST. At the top border is UNITED STATES OF AMERICA; first seen with 1871 J-1154. By 1875 the COMMERCIAL DOLLAR die was obsolete. The piece is a numismatic delicacy. Judd suggests that six were struck in silver, eight in copper, and three in aluminum, but the statements of Mint officials of this era, probably the source of such information, are completely without credibility. J-1423 is struck in silver and has a reeded edge. J-1424 is struck in copper and has a reeded edge. J-1425 is struck in aluminum and has a reeded edge.

1875 Trade dollar (J-1426 to 1429): *Obverse:* Die as preceding, with illogical ship. *Reverse:* Regular trade dollar of the 1873–1875 design with berry below claw (Type 1, the reverse style of 1873–1876). J-1426 is struck in silver and has a reeded edge. J-1427 is struck in copper and has a reeded edge. J-1428 is struck in aluminum and has a reeded edge. J-1429 is struck in white metal and has a reeded edge.

1875 Trade dollar (J-1430 and 1431): Regular dies. J-1430 is struck in copper and has a reeded edge. J-1431 is struck in aluminum and has a reeded edge.

1876 Commercial dollar (J-1472 and 1473): *Obverse:* Liberty Seated at the seashore, holding a laurel branch in her right hand, her left resting on a globe inscribed LIBERTY in relief. Behind her are two flags and a wheat sheaf. A ship is in the distance. Below the base is IN GOD WE TRUST in a cartouche, below which is the date 1876. *Reverse:* Commercial Dollar die first used in 1871. J-1472 is struck in silver and has a reeded edge. J-1473 is struck in copper and has a reeded edge.

1876 Trade dollar (J-1474 and 1475): *Obverse:* Liberty Seated at the seashore, die as preceding. *Reverse:* The regular die of the Type 2 design, used 1875–1885, without berry below eagle's claw. J-1474 is struck in silver and has a reeded edge. J-1475 is struck in copper and has a reeded edge.

[Attributed to 1876] Undated trade dollar (J-1475a and 1475b): Dies 9-F. *Obverse:* Liberty seated, facing left, somewhat similar to the regular design, but with differences. She is seated on two cotton bales, wears a diadem, holds a laurel branch in her right hand and a ribbon inscribed LIBERTY in her left, wheat sheaf behind. Sea in distance with rounded edges of the sea to the left. IN GOD WE TRUST on base. 13 stars around border, no date. *Reverse:* Large perched eagle with detailed wing feathers, holding three arrows and a laurel branch. Above, E PLURIBUS UNUM on ribbon. Below, 420 GRAINS, 900 FINE. Around the border is UNITED STATES OF AMERICA / TRADE DOLLAR. This undated pattern is believed to have been made in 1876, at which time modifications were being considered. Earlier listed as J-1320 and 1321 of 1873. J-1475a (J-1320 in earlier editions) is struck in silver and has a reeded edge. J-1475b {J-1321 in earlier editions} is struck in copper and has a reeded edge.

1876 Trade dollar (J-1476 and 1477): Regular dies. Specific obverse and reverse varieties (Type 1 or 2) not noted in the literature. J-1476 is struck in copper and has a reeded edge. J-1477 is struck in aluminum and has a reeded edge.

1884 Trade dollar (J-1732): Regular dies. Of special interest as the related silver strikings of the 1884 trade are classic rarities (just ten were struck) and are desired by a wide audience J-1732 is struck in copper and has a reeded edge.

Release and Distribution

Trade dollars shipped to China were received with favor. The new denomination was a resounding success from the start. The demand continued non-stop afterward.

The following review is from the *Carson Daily Appeal* published in Carson City, Nevada, July 22, 1873:

> *The first trade dollar* ever coined west of Philadelphia was shown to us yesterday. Superintendent Hetrich had it all nicely swathed and cuddled in a bit of tissue paper. It is by far the most beautiful silver coin we have ever seen issued from an American mint—handsomest we ever saw of any make, we think. It looks like a beautiful medal—the Mademoiselle Liberty side does. She is just near enough to the scrawny to be classical-like—pre-Raphaelite is the word, to be technical. She seems to have rather got tired of that ostentatious bit of business-like piety of our coinage and scratched 'In God We Trust' on the base of her pedestal of emblematical express packages and let it make a very modest and different showing there. Good taste would cause its entire obliteration, we think. Consider the baseness to which a coin may be put at the hands of godless people, and then somewhat intrusive incongruity of this pious label becomes apparent.
>
> The eagle, on the side which we should say was 'tail' were we tossing trade dollars for keeps, is by all odds the best eagle we have ever seen stamped upon any of our coins. More than any piece of money of Uncle Sam's mintage this looks free from an appearance of being crowded. In most of the others the eagle is too big, too coarse, too evident and lacking in artistic proportions. The man who designed the dies for this trade dollar is an artist. We have always felt an indescribable sense of backwardness in taking any of the more clumsily constructed coins. We would take a million of these and never experience any but the most pleasurable emotions!

In 1875 Superintendent Oscar H. LaGrange of the San Francisco Mint wrote:

> At no time since the commencement of the present calendar year has the mint been able to accumulate a surplus of trade dollars, and the public demand has not been fully met. The limited capacity of the Mint and the unusually large coinage of gold,

which is given precedence over silver, has materially abridged the supply of this international coin at San Francisco, but the favorable introduction of the trade dollar into China has most effectually destroyed the use of the Mexican silver dollar as the medium of exchange between this city and the ports in the Chinese Empire. The city banks report an excessive demand for trade dollar exchange. The coinage capacity of the new Mint, shortly to be occupied, will, it is hoped, fully meet the requirements for all gold and silver coins. Great care has been given in the manufacture of the trade dollar to reach the closest approximate perfection in assay value, weight, and execution.

In 1876 when the price of silver fell and trade dollars were demonetized, they caused problems in domestic commerce. The trade dollar was reported as "fast becoming a drug on the market" in 1876. *The San Francisco Chronicle* noted:

Our banks and money broker offices are becoming glutted with them. Their greater intrinsic value as well as their novelty threatened for a while to crowd the familiar half dollar and the handy quarter out of sight. Chinamen remitting their hard-earned savings to their far distant land would have nothing but trade dollars. Oriental commerce was, and still is to a large extent, conducted on the solid basis of this bright, new, and ringing silver representation of value. But the Orient, like San Francisco, is beginning to find that it is possible to be surfeited with even so much coveted a treasure as the trade dollar. The result is that a reaction has set in against the coin on this market and, it no longer enjoys a preference over other silver.

On the contrary, although a trade dollar is intrinsically worth eight cents more than two half dollars, the two halves will sell in the street from a half to three quarters of a cent more than the dollar. The reason for this is primarily because of the superabundance of the latter. However, there is another reason which is not generally understood. Halves and quarters of the coinage of the United States are legal tender for all debts up to a certain amount; the trade dollar is not legal tender at all for any amount. It is merely a stamped ingot, having a certain value, like an ounce of gold, diamond, or a bushel of wheat. It is a commodity, the value of which fluctuates according to the supply and demand.

Aspects of Striking

Striking varies from issue to issue and is discussed under the various issues below. Many show weakness on the obverse head of Liberty and on some of the stars. On the reverse, weakness is often seen on the eagle's leg and talons to the right.

Cherrypicking can pay good dividends as sharply defined coins cost no more than do those casually struck.

Proof Trade Dollars

The official Mint issue price for Proof trade dollars from 1878 to 1883 was $1.025 each, according to one account, because the coin had been demonetized; most other sources give the figure as $1.25 each, a figure with which R.W. Julian agrees. Earlier, when the coins were worth $1 face value each, 1873 Proofs were sold for $1.75 each in paper money or $1.50 each in silver.

Trade dollars were in no particular favor with numismatists as many considered them to be outside of the regular circulating series, never mind that they were legal tender until that was rescinded on July 22, 1876. Many of the Proofs of the first two years in particular, 1873 and 1874, seem to have been spent. Survivors are at a lower percentage than the mintages would indicate and are usually in lower grades. True choice and gem coins are hard to find. Most often encountered are the Proof-only years of 1878 through 1883. A few 1884 and 1885 Proofs were struck secretly and are great rarities.

Proofs are often mishandled as noted above, and some of the later dates are weakly struck on the head. Others are dark or have questionable toning. With some patience it is possible to assemble a date run from 1873 to 1883, with the keys being the 1873 and 1874.

Grading Trade Dollars

1875-S. Graded MS-61.

MS-60 to 70 (Mint State). *Obverse:* At MS-60, some abrasion and contact marks are evident, most noticeably on the left breast, left arm, and left knee. Luster is present, but may be dull or lifeless. Many of these coins are light in color or even brilliant, having been repatriated from China, and have been cleaned to remove sediment and discoloration. At MS-63, contact marks are very few, and abrasion is minimal. An MS-65 coin has no abrasion in the fields (but may have a hint on the higher parts of the seated figure), and contact marks are trivial. Luster should be full and rich. *Reverse:* Comments apply as for the obverse, except that in lower Mint State grades abrasion and contact marks are most noticeable on the eagle's head, the claws, and the top of the wings. At MS-65 or higher there are no marks visible to the unaided eye. The field is mainly protected by design elements and does not show abrasion as much as does the obverse on a given coin.

Illustrated coin: Some friction in the fields is seen, but much of the original luster remains.

1876. Graded AU-53.

AU-50, 53, 55, 58 (About Uncirculated). *Obverse:* Light wear is seen on the knees, bosom, and head. At AU-58, the luster is extensive but incomplete. At AU-50 and 53, luster is less. *Reverse:* Wear is visible on the eagle's head, the claws, and the top of the wings. An AU-58 coin will have nearly full luster. At AU-50 and 53, there still are traces of luster.

Illustrated coin: This example shows light, even wear. Most of the luster is gone, except in protected areas, but it has excellent eye appeal for the grade.

1876-CC. Graded EF-40.

EF-40, 45 (Extremely Fine). *Obverse:* Further wear is seen on all areas, especially the head, the left breast, the left arm, the left leg, and the bale on which Miss Liberty is seated. Little or no luster is seen on most coins. From this grade downward, strike sharpness on the stars and the head does not matter to connoisseurs. *Reverse:* Further wear is evident on the eagle's head, legs, claws, and wings, although on well-struck coins nearly all feather details on the wings are sharp.

1877-S. Graded VF-30.

VF-20, 30 (Very Fine). *Obverse:* Further wear is seen on the seated figure, although more than half the details of her dress are visible. Details of the wheat sheaf are mostly intact. IN GOD WE TRUST and LIBERTY are clear. *Reverse:* Wear is more extensive; some feathers are blended together, with two-thirds or more still visible.

1873-CC. Graded F-12.

F-12, 15 (Fine). *Obverse:* The seated figure is further worn, with fewer details of the dress visible. Most details in the wheat sheaf are clear. Both mottoes are readable, but some letters may be weak. *Reverse:* Wear is extensive, with about half to nearly two-thirds of the feathers flat or blended with others. The eagle's left leg is mostly flat. Wear is seen on the raised E PLURIBUS UNUM, and one or two letters may be missing.

The trade dollar is seldom collected in grades lower than F-12.

1882. Graded PF-62.

PF-60 to 70 (Proof). *Obverse and Reverse:* Proofs that are extensively cleaned and have many hairlines, or that are dull and grainy, are lower level, such as PF-60 to 62. These are not widely desired. With medium hairlines and good reflectivity, an assigned grade of PF-64 is appropriate, and with relatively few hairlines, Gem PF-65. In various grades hairlines are most easily seen in the obverse field. PF-66 may have hairlines so delicate that magnification is needed to see them. Above that, a Proof should be free of such lines.

Illustrated coin: This coin has medium-gray toning overall.

Collecting Trade Dollars

Considering all of the circulation strike issues in the trade dollar series, a basic set of dates and mintmarks has just one rarity, the 1878-CC, even though it is not all that expensive in the overall scheme of current pricing. Add the obverse and reverse varieties of 1875 and 1876 and the challenge is greater. Going beyond these, there are differences in mintmark sizes and placement.

Trade dollars that circulated in China were often given chopmarks—Chinese characters stamped to indicate their approval by banks, merchants, and others. These are highly collectible in their own right.

Two other trade dollar variations have been popular. Many trade dollars had one side, usually the reverse, routed out. In that space a photograph was placed. A thin sheet of metal, the reverse of another trade dollar with just the top surface remaining, was hinged to the first trade dollar. Upon pressing a spot on the coin the cover would flip open to reveal the photographs. These were sold at the World's Columbian Exposition in 1893 and possibly elsewhere. These are called box dollars or box trade dollars.

Another variation is the "potty dollar" made from carving away portions of the obverse to change the bales on which Liberty is seated to a chamber pot. These were made in fairly large numbers.[14]

Until the 1960s relatively few numismatists collected trade dollars. That changed in 1965 when the Whitman Publishing Co. issued John M. Willem's *The United States Trade Dollar*, one of the most carefully researched texts for any specialized series. Additional attention paid to the series by Walter Breen and others helped increase interest as have articles in the *Gobrecht Journal*.

Today, trade dollars are very popular. Many are very challenging to find in higher grades, and thus there is a sport in the collecting of them.

Being a Smart Buyer

Circulation strikes often have areas of weakness as mentioned above. Luster is sometimes dull or flat. Eye appeal can vary as well. My recommendation is to proceed slowly. If you are building a collection of circulated issues, pick better strikes. If you are opting for a Mint State set the challenges will be strike, luster, and eye appeal. For some varieties this will mean reviewing a half dozen or more offers before finding one that is just right. Proofs, also as noted above, often have problems.

The obverse and reverse types of 1875 and 1876 include rare issues. As these are not widely noticed, rarities can often be found by paying no more. In recent years the

Trade dollar with chopmarks.

A box trade dollar.

A "potty dollar".

circulation strikes (but not the Proofs) have been delineated in *A Guide Book of United States Coins*, but at more or less generic prices not reflecting their rarity—simply because they have not been showcased in the marketplace. In time this may change. The 1876-CC with Doubled-Die reverse and the 1876-S with Doubled-Die obverse are two of the most spectacular blunders in the American series and are worth special attention.

As is the case for other denominations, quality varies widely among trade dollars. Nearly all buyers look at the label on a certified coin. In actuality, there are three, not just one, elements a connoisseur should follow: First, the certified grade is important. In general, the higher the number the more desirable the coin. Second, for most issues, even including some Proofs, the quality of strike differs. It pays to seek a sharp example as these can be found. Third, eye appeal is very important. In my opinion a sharply struck MS-63 or 64 coin with a beautiful appearance is far more desirable than a much more expensive MS-65 or 66 that is dingy or unattractive (and such coins abound). The unswerving quest for high numbers without regard to other factors is driven by the popularity of building Registry Sets, where only numbers count.

1873

Circulation-strike mintage: 396,900

Proof mintage: 600

Availability in Mint State: In 2014 the Eugene H. Gardner Sale featured an example of this coin in MS-65. *MS-60 to 62:* 150 to 250. *MS-63:* 60 to 100. *MS-64:* 50 to 75. *MS-65 or better:* 10 to 15.

actual size: 38.1 mm

Availability in circulated grades: *VF-20 to AU-58:* 1,250 to 2,000. With Chinese chopmarks these are rare. Larry Briggs states: "I have handled dozens of 1873 trade dollars over a span of many years and have seen only two or three with chopmarks."[15]

Characteristics of striking: Many are well struck, though some have light definition on Liberty's head and on the eagle's leg on the right and talons. Some have slight lightness of striking near the bottom of the obverse—an unusual situation among trade dollars. The luster on Mint State coins often is more of a satiny or "greasy" appearance than deeply frosty.

Proofs: *PF-60 to 62:* 200 to 300. *PF-63:* 60 to 100. *PF-64:* 40 to 55. *PF-64 or better:* 20 to 30. Nearly all Proofs of this issue are in lower grades. This is true of 1874 Proofs as well.

Notes: Unlike the situation for other Liberty Seated denominations for which examples of many issues exist in lower-grade ranges, very few trade dollars are less than VF-20. Accordingly, in this chapter the grade ranges for circulated coins are VF-20 to AU-58.

On July 14, 40,000 coins were released. Ensuing months saw strong circulation-strike production, except for October when none was coined. The record output for the year was achieved in September when 103,500 were struck. Trade dollars first reached China in October 1873 where they met a good reception. Nearly all of the 1873 trade dollars went there.

VG-8	F-12	VF-20	EF-40	AU-50	MS-60
$200	$235	$350	$500	$600	$1,250

MS-63	MS-64	MS-65	PF-60	PF-63	PF-65
$3,000	$4,750	$10,000	$2,150	$3,500	$7,000

1873-CC

Circulation-strike mintage: 124,500

Availability in Mint State: In 2014 the Eugene H. Gardner Sale featured an example of this coin in MS-63. *MS-60 to 62:* 40 to 60. *MS-63:* 2 to 4. *MS-64:* 2 or 3. *MS-65 or better:* 0 or 1.

actual size: 38.1 mm

Availability in circulated grades: *VF-20 to AU-58:* 1,000 to 1,500. With Chinese chopmarks these are somewhat rare.

Characteristics of striking: Some coins of this issue have slight weakness of striking on the eagle's leg to the right and on the eagle's claws.

Notes: Four pairs of trade-dollar dies, made in Philadelphia (where all dies for all mints were made), were received in Carson City on July 22, 1873. It is not known if all dies were used; probably most were, as they did not last long, averaging only about 15,000 impressions per die pair. Coinage began immediately, and on the following day, 4,500 pieces were ready for shipment, and 2,580 coins were paid out to local depositors, this being the first circulation of the denomination in the West.

Mintmark varieties include Micro CC with widely spaced (1.2 mm) letters using the same reverse die that was used for 1874-CC and 1876-CC Type 1/1.

Carson Daily Appeal, July 22, 1873: "The new dies for the coinage of the silver trade dollars were received yesterday by the Superintendent of the Carson City Mint and will be put on the press today for the trial. They differ somewhat from the old dollar stamp . . . 8,000 will be coined with the new dies today."

Delivery figures by month: July: 16,500; August: 6,000; September: 8,000; October: 37,000; November: 13,500; December: 43,500.[16]

VG-8	F-12	VF-20	EF-40	AU-50	MS-60	MS-63	MS-64	MS-65
$550	$850	$1,100	$2,250	$2,800	$7,500	$25,000	$45,000	$125,000

1873-S

Circulation-strike mintage: 703,000

actual size: 38.1 mm

Availability in Mint State: In the sale catalog for the John M. Willem Collection, sold on September 5, 1980, Henry Christensen described what was undoubtedly the finest 1873-S Willem had been able to locate: "Unc.-60, with a few light bagmarks. Very scarce without chopmarks." This was in an era when buyers were not as condition conscious. In 2014 the Eugene H. Gardner Sale featured an example of this coin in MS-65. *MS-60 to 62:* 100 to 160. *MS-63:* 30 to 45. *MS-64:* 25 to 32. *MS-65 or better:* 4 to 6.

Availability in circulated grades: *VF-20 to AU-58:* 3,000 to 5,000. With Chinese chopmarks these are available in sufficient numbers to satisfy the numismatic demand, but are notable as the scarcest San Francisco chopmarked variety.[17]

Characteristics of striking: Some coins of this issue have slight weakness on the eagle's leg on the right and on the eagle's claws.

Notes: Production of trade dollars began in San Francisco in July and continued strong throughout the rest of the calendar year, with the peak month of production being December, when 200,000 were struck.

Delivery figures by month: July: 42,000; August: 111,000; September: 137,000; October: 98,000; November: 115,000; December: 200,000. Nearly all were exported to China and the vast majority were melted there or in India.

VG-8	F-12	VF-20	EF-40	AU-50	MS-60	MS-63	MS-64	MS-65
$250	$285	$450	$550	$650	$1,450	$3,800	$4,250	$22,500

1874

Circulation-strike mintage: 987,100

Proof mintage: 700

actual size: 38.1 mm

Availability in Mint State: In 2014 the Eugene H. Gardner Sale featured an example of this coin in MS-65. *MS-60 to 62:* 150 to 250. *MS-63:* 60 to 100. *MS-65 or better:* 6 to 10.

Availability in circulated grades: *VF-20 to AU-58:* 2,500 to 3,500. With Chinese chopmarks these are the most common chopmarked Philadelphia Mint trade dollar, as well as one of the most common of all chopmarked trade dollars. It is scarce, however, in relation to the mintage. One numismatist spent more than 20 years amassing a hoard and obtained about 125 coins.[18]

Characteristics of striking: Some coins of this issue have weakness on the obverse on Liberty's head and at stars six and seven while on others the weakness extends to the stars left and right of these. Some have light striking on eagle's leg on the right.

Proofs: *PF-60 to 62:* 225 to 325. *PF-63:* 70 to 110. *PF-64:* 45 to 65. *PF-64 or better:* 25 to 35. Nearly all are in lower grades. This is true of 1873 Proofs as well.

Notes: In this year a number of Philadelphia Mint 1874 quarters, half dollars, and trade dollars were counterstamped with the advertisement SAGE'S / CANDY / COIN. Today these are known in circulated grades and are rare. The trade dollar is especially elusive. The author has seen only three, the finest of which is shown here.

A counterstamped 1874 dollar.

VG-8	F-12	VF-20	EF-40	AU-50	MS-60
$200	$250	$325	$500	$600	$1,200

MS-63	MS-64	MS-65	PF-60	PF-63	PF-65
$2,400	$4,000	$13,000	$2,150	$3,500	$6,500

1874-CC

Circulation-strike mintage: 1,373,200

Availability in Mint State: In 2014 the Eugene H. Gardner Sale featured an example of this coin in MS-64. *MS-60 to 62:* 150 to 250. *MS-63:* 30 to 45. *MS-64:* 10 to 15. *MS-65 or better:* 0 or 1.

actual size: 38.1 mm

Availability in circulated grades: *VF-20 to AU-58:* 2,500 to 4,000. With Chinese chopmarks this issue ranks as the most available of all chopmarked Carson City trade dollars and fourth most available of *all* chopmarked trade dollars.

Characteristics of striking: Some coins of this issue are lightly or irregularly struck in areas, particularly on the eagle's leg on the right and claws and at the top of the eagle's wing on the left.

Notes: Mintmark varieties include the Micro CC with widely spaced (1.2 mm) letters using the same reverse die that was used for 1873-CC and 1876-CC Type 1/1.
Dangerous modern counterfeits have come on the market in the early 2000s.[19]

VG-8	F-12	VF-20	EF-40	AU-50	MS-60	MS-63	MS-64	MS-65
$350	$425	$550	$925	$1,350	$2,750	$6,000	$15,000	$40,000

1874-S

Circulation-strike mintage: 2,549,000

actual size: 38.1 mm

Availability in Mint State: In 2014 and 2015 the Eugene H. Gardner Sale featured an example of this coin in MS-65. *MS-60 to 62:* 400 to 600. *MS-63:* 30 to 45. *MS-64:* 20 to 25. MS-65: 2 or 3.

Availability in circulated grades: *VF-20 to AU-58:* 2,500 to 4,000. With Chinese chopmarks this is the third most common variety existing with chopmarks.

Characteristics of striking: Many if not most coins of this issue show some weakness at the top of the obverse and/or on the reverse at the eagle's claws on the right.

Notes: Some of these have the reverse rotated about 15° counterclockwise.

VG-8	F-12	VF-20	EF-40	AU-50	MS-60	MS-63	MS-64	MS-65
$200	$235	$325	$425	$475	$1,000	$2,150	$3,250	$15,000

Hub Changes in 1875: Reverse Types 1 and 2

In 1875 Chief Engraver Barber redesigned the reverse master hub, following complaints by Chief Coiner Archibald Loudon Snowden to Superintendent James Pollock about imperfect striking quality of several high points of the design, especially the reverse. The most noticeable differences were at the claws and berries, but the topology of the reverse lettering in relation to the eagle was also altered. Barber sent working dies from the new hub to the coiners at all three mints, but notified only Snowden.

The old and new reverses (Types 1 and 2) are easily identifiable:[11]

Type 1 Reverse: Used from 1873 through 1876, has a berry under the eagle's claw, narrow berries, and broad leaves.

Type 2 Reverse: Used from 1875 through 1885, has no berry under the claw, has larger round berries elsewhere, and narrow leaves.

Type 1 reverse detail.   Type 2 reverse detail.

Both reverses occur on 1875–1876 coins from all three mints.[12]

Reverse 2 Sub-Types

In a study of hundreds of Type 2 reverse coins conducted some years ago certain sub varieties were seen in addition to the regular Type 2. These are hardly new discoveries, for David Proskey knew of certain sub varieties by January 1928. The following were observed. More varieties may exist:

Type 2: Regular type, with comma after GRAINS; rightmost leaf tip in branch is blunt. Seen on the following: 1875 1/2, 1876 2/2, 1877, 1877-CC, 1877-S, 1878-CC, and 1878-S.

Type 2a: Anomalous type, with large period after GRAINS (much larger than the comma on 2a); rightmost leaf tip is pointed. Seen on the following: 1876-S 2/2 and 1877-CC.

Type 2b: Anomalous type, with large period after GRAINS, with a tiny, almost subliminal tail to the bottom of the period (not quite giving it the appearance of a comma); rightmost leaf is blunt. Seen on the following: 1876-S 1/2.

Type 2c: Anomalous type, with comma after GRAINS; leaf tip pointed. Seen on the following: 1875-CC 1/2.

The preceding anomalies, 2a, b, and c, do not represent an alteration of the basic design, as all of the letters, inscriptions, designs, etc., are in the same spatial relationship to each other and to the border dentils. They probably represent alterations to working hubs or dies. Type 2a is very distinctive; Types 2b and 2c are less so. Perhaps additional sub-types are known.

1875, Dies 1/1

Circulation-strike mintage: Small portion of 218,200

Proof mintage: Small portion of 700

Points for identification: *Obverse:* The ribbon ends point left. *Reverse:* The berry is below the claw. The

actual size: 38.1 mm

1875 has the lowest circulation-strike mintage of any trade dollar from this mint. All have a reed count of 190.

Rarity (percent of date and mint, Borckardt study): Circulation strike: 10 percent.[20] Proof: 34 percent.

Availability in Mint State: These are very rare. *MS-60 to 62:* 2 to 4. *MS-63:* 0. *MS-64:* 0. *MS-65 or better:* 0.

Availability in circulated grades: *VF-20 to AU-58:* These are very rare. An estimated 25 to 35 are known. With Chinese chopmarks these are very rare.

Characteristics of striking: This issue is usually well struck.

Proofs: *PF-60 to 62:* 60 to 80. *PF-63:* 60 to 80. *PF-64:* 30 to 45. *PF-64 or better:* 15 to 20.

Notes: In a survey of auction appearances of several thousand 1875 and 1876 circulation-strike and Proof trade dollars conducted in 2014, Mark Borckardt calculated the "Borckardt: percent" figures shown in this chapter.

Some 1/1 Proofs have the reverse with a long arc scratch, the die first used 1873, but now with the scratch partly worn off. The last of these show die failure at the eagle's leg and claws above 900. Other Proofs have a different reverse.

VG-8	F-12	VF-20	EF-40	AU-50	MS-60
$400	$500	$700	$1,150	$1,350	$2,500

MS-63	MS-64	MS-65	PF-60	PF-63	PF-65
$4,500	$7,500	$15,000	$2,150	$3,500	$8,500

1875, Dies 1/2

Circulation-strike mintage: Large portion of 218,200

Proof mintage: Large portion of 700

Points for identification: *Obverse:* The ribbon ends point left. *Reverse:* There is no berry below the claw.

actual size: 38.1 mm

Rarity (percent of date and mint, Borckardt study): Circulation strike: 90 percent. Proof: 66 percent.

Availability in Mint State: *MS-60 to 62:* 150 to 175. *MS-63:* 55 to 75. *MS-64:* 25 to 32. *MS-65 or better:* 10 to 15.

Availability in circulated grades: *VF-20 to AU-58:* 25 to 35. With Chinese chopmarks these are extremely rare.

Characteristics of striking: This issue is usually well struck.

Proofs: *PF-60 to 62:* 90 to 120. *PF-63:* 100 to 130. *PF-64:* 75 to 95. *PF-64 or better:* 30 to 40.

VG-8	F-12	VF-20	EF-40	AU-50	MS-60
$400	$500	$700	$1,150	$1,400	$2,600

MS-63	MS-64	MS-65	PF-60	PF-63	PF-65
$4,650	$9,000	$21,000	$2,150	$3,500	$8,500

1875-CC, Dies 1/1

Circulation-strike mintage: Large portion of 1,573,700

Points for identification: *Obverse:* The ribbon ends point left. *Reverse:* The berry is below the claw.

actual size: 38.1 mm

Rarity (percent of date and mint, Borckardt study): 88 percent.

Availability in Mint State: *MS-60 to 62:* 300 to 450. *MS-60 to 62:* 300 to 450. *MS-63:* 75 to 125. *MS-64:* 5 to 8. *MS-65 or better:* 4 to 6.

Availability in circulated grades: *VF-20 to AU-58:* 4,000 to 6,000. With Chinese chopmarks these are very common.

Characteristics of striking: This issue is usually seen well struck.

Notes: With a total production quantity of 1,573,700 coins, the 1875-CC was produced in larger numbers than any other trade dollar from this mint.

The vast majority of known 1875-CC trade dollars are Type 1/1. Taken as a whole, the 1875-CC is the most available Carson City trade dollar, although in MS-64 or better grade it is a great rarity. A variety formerly known as Doubled-Reverse die is now discredited and is the result of strike doubling.[21]

VG-8	F-12	VF-20	EF-40	AU-50	MS-60	MS-63	MS-64	MS-65
$400	$425	$575	$750	$1,000	$2,500	$4,750	$9,500	$33,500

1875-S, Dies 1/1

Circulation-strike mintage: Large portion of 4,487,000

Points for identification: *Obverse:* The ribbon ends point left. *Reverse:* The berry is below the claw.

actual size: 38.1 mm

Rarity (percent of date and mint, Borckardt study): 86 percent.

Availability in Mint State: *MS-60 to 62:* 1,250 to 2,000. *MS-63:* 400 to 600. *MS-64:* 150 to 250. *MS-65 or better:* 60 to 100.

Availability in circulated grades: *VF-20 to AU-58:* 20,000+. With Chinese chopmarks these ar very common.

Characteristics of striking: This issue is usually seen with some lightness on the head of Liberty.

Notes: The 1875-S Type 1/1 exists with Medium S and Large S mintmarks.

The production quantity of trade dollars at the San Francisco Mint in 1875 was immense and set the record for the series. 80 percent to 90 percent are Type 1/1, and the rest are 1/2. Apparently, the Type 2 reverse dies reached San Francisco late in the year and were not used extensively.

VG-8	F-12	VF-20	EF-40	AU-50	MS-60	MS-63	MS-64	MS-65
$200	$235	$325	$425	$475	$1,000	$1,600	$2,500	$7,500

1875-CC, Dies 1/2

Circulation-strike mintage: Small portion of 1,573,700

Points for identification: *Obverse:* The ribbon ends point left. *Reverse:* There is no berry below the claw.

Rarity (percent of date and mint, Borckardt study): 12 percent.

actual size: 38.1 mm

Availability in Mint State: *MS-60 to 62:* 30 to 45. *MS-60 to 62:* 30 to 45. *MS-63:* 8 to 12. *MS-64:* 1 or 2. *MS-65 or better:* 0 or 1.

Availability in circulated grades: *VF-20 to AU-58:* 400 to 600. With Chinese chopmarks these are elusive.

Characteristics of striking: Most coins of this issue exhibit weakness on the reverse, mainly on the top of the eagle's wing to the left.

VG-8	F-12	VF-20	EF-40	AU-50	MS-60	MS-63	MS-64	MS-65
$400	$425	$575	$750	$1,000	$3,000	$5,500	$11,500	$35,000

1875-S, Dies 1/2

Circulation-strike mintage: Small portion of 4,487,000

Points for identification: *Obverse:* The ribbon ends point left. *Reverse:* There is no berry below the claw.

actual size: 38.1 mm

Rarity (percent of date and mint, Borckardt study): 14 percent.

Availability in Mint State: *MS-60 to 62:* 200 to 300+. *MS-63:* 100 to 200. *MS-64:* 20 to 25. *MS-65 or better:* 15 to 20.

Availability in circulated grades: *VF-20 to AU-58:* 250 to 400. With Chinese chopmarks these are scarce.

Characteristics of striking: Striking of this issue varies.

Notes: The 1875-S Type 1/2 exists with Tall S as well as with Micro S mintmarks, the latter being rare.

VG-8	F-12	VF-20	EF-40	AU-50	MS-60	MS-63	MS-64	MS-65
$200	$235	$325	$425	$475	$1,175	$2,350	$3,400	$11,000

1875-S, S Over CC

Circulation-strike mintage: Small portion of 4,487,000

Availability in Mint State: *MS-60 to 62:* 50 to 75. *MS-63:* 5 to 8. MS-64 4 to 6. MS-65 0 or 1.

Availability in circulated grades: *VF-20 to AU-58:* 200 to 300. Several dozen or more are known with Chinese chopmarks.

actual size: 38.1 mm

Detail of Over Mintmark.

Characteristics of striking: This issue is usually seen well struck.

Notes: The mintage was a small fraction of the above. All are Type 1/1. Rarity is a small percent of that above. This variety is known in different die states up to and including extensively cracked.

For some reason at least two Carson City reverse dies of the Type 1 style, with tall CC letters, had the CC mintmark partially effaced and overpunched with an S mintmark. On the variety most often seen the CC mintmark is more or less centered below the S. This is the variety usually seen. All examined coins are from an extensively cracked die. The variety with CC *far to the right* of the S is much rarer than the coins with the CC centered. These have a differently cracked reverse die.

This issue was generally unknown to numismatists until Bob Medlar found an example in the early 1960s.[22] It is listed by Fivaz-Stanton as FS-T1-1875S-501 and FS-T1-1875S-502.

VG-8	F-12	VF-20	EF-40	AU-50	MS-60	MS-63	MS-64	MS-65
$550	$675	$850	$1,500	$1,900	$6,500	$16,000	$25,000	$40,000

Hub Changes of 1876: Obverse Types 1 and 2

In 1876 Barber redesigned the obverse master hub of the trade dollar and sent new working dies to the coiners of all three mints. The coiners at the Philadelphia and San Francisco mints received at least one Type 2 obverse dated 1876 while the Carson City Mint apparently only received Type 2 dies for 1877 and 1878. If the Type 2 obverse is one of the two new hubs for fiscal year 1877 mentioned in a Mint report of July 7, 1877, cited by R.W. Julian, then it must date to after July 1, 1876, excluding the possibility that 1875-dated coins exist of Type 2/1 or 2/2.

Type 1 obverse details.　　　　　　　Type 2 obverse details.

Type 1: John W. McCloskey, in his article "Obverse Varieties of the U.S. Trade Dollar" in the *Gobrecht Journal*, July 1978, first described in print the two obverse types. The Type 1, he noted:

> has both ribbon tails (the ribbon on which LIBERTY is imprinted) pointing sharply to the left. Three fingers on Liberty's right hand are below the laurel branch (her index finger is missing). Both RT of LIBERTY and ST of TRUST touch.

Type 1 Transitional: In 2005 in the *E-Gobrecht* Dr. Gene Bruder published a new variety—an obverse die resembling Type 1 with the ribbon ends pointing left, but with four fingers and a thumb on Liberty's right hand, as used on Type 2. This enigmatic issue researched by Dan Huntsinger and has been found with the fabric of both Proof and circulation strike formats and with different reed counts (193 and 194). They are very scarce in Proof format. Many of the circulation strike examples are low grade and/or weakly struck and often chopmarked.[13]

Type 2: In the article noted above, McCloskey described the distinguishing features of the Type 2 obverse, which, he stated:

> displays open ribbon ends, the right tail pointing down between the words WE and TRUST. Four fingers on Liberty's right hand are below the laurel branch. Both RT and ST are apart.

1875 and 1876 coins are known with these combinations:

1875 Circulation strikes: 1/1 and 1/2. *Proofs:* 1/1 and 1/2.
1875-CC 1/1 and 1/2.
1875-S 1/1 and 1/2.
1875-S/CC 1/1.
1876 Circulation strikes: 1/1, 1/2, and 2/2. *Proofs:* 1/1, 1/2, and 2/2; and transitional obverse 1.5.
1876-CC 1/1 and 1/2.
1876-S 1/1; 1/2; and 2/2.

1876, Dies 1/1

Circulation-strike mintage: Small portion of 455,000

Proof mintage: Small portion of 1,150

Points for identification: *Obverse:* The ribbon ends point left. *Reverse:* The berry is below the claw.

actual size: 38.1 mm

Rarity (percent of date and mint, Borckardt study)**:** Circulation strike: 14 percent. Proof: 3 percent.

Availability in Mint State: Many Uncirculated coins seen in collections today have deep gray or even black toning. This toning may represent specimens having been saved by the public as a souvenir of the 1876 centennial year, or perhaps there is another explanation. *MS-60 to 62:* 150 to 200. *MS-63:* 40 to 55. *MS-64:* 25 to 35. *MS-65 or better:* 15 to 20.

Availability in circulated grades: *VF-20 to AU-58:* 500 to 700. Coins with Chinese chopmarks are seen more often than coins without chopmarks.

Characteristics of striking: Many coins of this issue are well struck, but many others are lightly struck on the eagle's claws to the left.

Proofs: For the variety specialist this is far and away the rarest Proof of 1876. *PF-60 to 62:* 25 to 35. *PF-63:* 8 to 10. *PF-64:* 3 to 5. *PF-64 or better:* 2 or 3.

1876 Type 1 Transitional 1.5/2: In 2005 in the *E-Gobrecht* Dr. Gene Bruder published a new variety—an obverse die resembling Type 1 with the ribbon ends pointing left, but with four fingers and a thumb on Liberty's right hand, as used on Type 2. Only a few have been discovered since. See discussion on page 500.

Notes: The rare 1876 Type 2/2 (both circulation strikes and Proofs), transitional Type 1.5/2 (both circulation strikes and Proofs), and one circulation-strike Type 1/2 all share the same reverse as noted by a unique die chip in the E PLURIBUS UNUM banner.[23]

Director of the Mint Dr. Henry R. Linderman proposed that a special commemorative reverse be made for 1876 trade dollars, to honor the 100th anniversary of American independence. Had this come to pass—which it didn't—it would have been the first U.S. silver commemorative coin. Elements of the proposed design were used in the 33 mm 1876 Assay Commission medal by William Barber (illustrated), which has the border inscription YEAR ONE HUNDRED / OF AMERICAN INDEPENDENCE enclosing a heavy oak wreath.

VG-8	F-12	VF-20	EF-40	AU-50	MS-60
$215	$250	$350	$450	$500	$1,250

MS-63	MS-64	MS-65	PF-60	PF-63	PF-65
$2,000	$3,200	$10,000	$2,150	$3,500	$6,500

1876, Dies 1/2

Circulation-strike mintage: Large portion of 455,000

Proof mintage: Large portion of 1,150

Points for identification: *Obverse:* The ribbon ends point left.

actual size: 38.1 mm

Reverse: There is no berry below the claw.

Rarity (percent of date and mint, Borckardt study): Circulation strike: 63 percent. Proof: 88 percent.

Availability in Mint State: *MS-60 to 62:* 650 to 800. *MS-63:* 140 to 160. *MS-64:* 90 to 120. *MS-65 or better:* 55 to 70.

Availability in circulated grades: These are common and are readily available with Chinese chopmarks.

Characteristics of striking: Many coins of this issue are well struck, but many others are lightly struck on the eagle's claws to the left.

Proofs: *PF-60 to 62:* 150 to 200. *PF-63:* 80 to 120. *PF-64:* 40 to 55. *PF-64 or better:* 20 to 30. Of the differing die varieties, this is the variety nearly always seen. Although the mintage quantity was large, it is likely that many were sold to visitors to the Centennial Exhibition in Philadelphia and were not preserved.

VG-8	F-12	VF-20	EF-40	AU-50	MS-60
$215	$250	$350	$450	$500	$1,000

MS-63	MS-64	MS-65	PF-60	PF-63	PF-65
$1,850	$2,500	$7,500	$2,150	$3,500	$6,500

1876, Dies 2/2

Circulation-strike mintage: Small portion of 455,000

Proof mintage: Small portion of 1,150

Points for identification: *Obverse:* The ribbon ends point

actual size: 38.1 mm

down. *Reverse:* There is no berry below the claw.

Rarity (percent of date and mint, Borckardt study)**:** Circulation strike: 1 percent (the great rarity among these varieties). Proof: 9 percent.

Availability in Mint State: These are very rare. *MS-60 to 62:* 8 to 12. *MS-63:* 3 to 5. *MS-64:* 2 or 3. *MS-65 or better:* 1 or 2.

Availability in circulated grades: *VF-20 to AU-58:* 40 to 60. With Chinese chopmarks these are exceedingly rare.

Characteristics of striking: Striking of this issue varies.

Proofs: *PF-60 to 62:* 18 to 25. *PF-63:* 10 to 13. *PF-64:* 5 to 8. *PF-64 or better:* 3 to 5.

VG-8	F-12	VF-20	EF-40	AU-50	MS-60
–	–	–	–	–	–

MS-63	MS-64	MS-65	PF-60	PF-63	PF-65
–	–	–	–	–	–

1876-CC, Dies 1/1

Circulation-strike mintage: Portion of 509,000

Points for identification: *Obverse:* The ribbon ends point left. *Reverse:* The berry is below the claw.

actual size: 38.1 mm

Rarity (percent of date and mint, Borckardt study)**:** 46 percent. About three out of four are of the Doubled-Die Reverse.

Availability in Mint State: *MS-60 to 62:* 30 to 40. *MS-63:* 5 to 8. *MS-64:* 2 to 4. *MS-65 or better:* 0.

Availability in circulated grades: *VF-20 to AU-58:* 1,350 to 2,000. Only a small percentage of this issue has Chinese chopmarks.

Characteristics of striking: Striking of this issue varies.

Notes: Delivery figures by month: January: 216,000; February: 80,000; March: 85,000; April: 128,000; May–December: none.

Mintmark varieties for this issue include the Micro CC with widely spaced (1.2 mm) letters using the same reverse die that as used for 1873-CC and 1874-CC Type 1/1, Medium CC, and Large CC.

1876-CC Doubled-Die Reverse, dies 1/1: Of all of the various die repunching, doublings, etc., in the entire American coin series, the 1876-CC 1/1 with doubled-reverse die stands high as a mint gaffe, however, the 1876-S 2/2 with doubled-obverse die gives it a close run for the money.[24] Of this 1876-CC error, Bill Fivaz writes:
"This is probably the strongest and most widely spaced doubled die known in *any* series. The reverse die shows dramatic doubling on the eagle's left wing (on the right side of the coin), the branches, berries, leaves, and much of the lettering. While not exceedingly

rare, once you've found one, this scarce variety is very marketable due to the strength of the doubling."[25] Illustrated is a detail showing doubling of the branch. *Cherrypickers' Guide to Rare Die Varieties* lists this as FS-T1-1876CC-801. Dangerous modern counterfeits exist, having come on the market beginning in the early 2000s. The easiest way to identify such fakes is by a dent or depression on top of Liberty's ankle.[26] In 2015 the Eugene H. Gardner Sale featured an example of this coin in MS-62.

VG-8	F-12	VF-20	EF-40	AU-50	MS-60	MS-63	MS-64	MS-65
$650	$750	$850	$1,450	$2,000	$6,500	$20,000	$40,000	$80,000

1876-CC, Dies 1/2

Circulation-strike mintage: Portion of 509,000

Points for identification: *Obverse:* The ribbon ends point left. *Reverse:* There is no berry below the claw.

actual size: 38.1 mm

Rarity (percent of date and mint, Borckardt study): 54 percent.

Availability in Mint State: *MS-60 to 62:* 35 to 45. *MS-63:* 7 to 10. *MS-64:* 3 to 5. *MS-65 or better:* 0 or 1.

Availability in circulated grades: *VF-20 to AU-58:* 1,500 to 2,250. Most coins of this issue have Chinese chopmarks, however they are slightly scarce.

Characteristics of striking: This issue is usually well struck. A few have prooflike surfaces.

VG-8	F-12	VF-20	EF-40	AU-50	MS-60	MS-63	MS-64	MS-65
$650	$750	$850	$1,450	$2,250	$7,500	$25,000	$45,000	$95,000

1876-S, Dies 1/1

Circulation-strike mintage: Large portion of 5,227,000

Points for identification: *Obverse:* The ribbon ends point left. *Reverse:* The berry is below the claw.

actual size: 38.1 mm

Rarity (percent of date and mint, Borckardt study): 62 percent.

Availability in Mint State: *MS-60 to 62:* 900 to 1,200. *MS-63:* 125 to 200. *MS-64:* 60 to 100. *MS-65 or better:* 15 to 25.

Availability in circulated grades: *VF-20 to AU-58:* These are very common. They are also common with Chinese chopmarks.

Characteristics of striking: Striking of this issue varies, but some are sharp.

Notes: A sample of forty-three 1876-S trade dollars studied by Mark Borckardt in 1992 contained twenty-seven (62 percent) 1/1, eight (19 percent) 1/2, and eight (19 percent) 2/2. Although the data base is small, this seems to provide an indication of relative availability.

This issue has both Medium S (rare) and Large S (common) mintmark varieties.

VG-8	F-12	VF-20	EF-40	AU-50	MS-60	MS-63	MS-64	MS-65
$200	$235	$325	$425	$475	$1,000	$1,750	$2,500	$10,000

1876-S, Dies 1/2

Circulation-strike mintage: Small portion of 5,227,000

Points for identification: *Obverse:* The ribbon ends point left. *Reverse:* There is no berry below the claw.

actual size: 38.1 mm

Rarity (percent of date and mint, Borckardt study): 19 percent.

Availability in Mint State: *MS-60 to 62:* 300 to 450. *MS-63:* 50 to 70. *MS-64:* 30 to 40. *MS-65 or better:* 8 to 10.

Availability in circulated grades: *VF-20 to AU-58:* These are very common. They are also common with Chinese chopmarks, but are seen less often than the issues without.

Characteristics of striking: Striking of this issue varies, but some are sharp.

Notes: These are known with both the Micro S and Large S (scarce) mintmarks, the last thought to have been used for 1875-S as well.[27]

VG-8	F-12	VF-20	EF-40	AU-50	MS-60	MS-63	MS-64	MS-65
$200	$235	$325	$425	$475	$1,000	$2,000	$3,000	$10,000

1876-S, Dies 2/2

Circulation-strike mintage: Small portion of 5,227,000

Points for identification: *Obverse:* The ribbon ends point down. *Reverse:* There is no berry below the claw.

actual size: 38.1 mm

Rarity (percent of date and mint, Borckardt study): 19 percent.

Availability in Mint State: *MS-60 to 62:* 300 to 450. *MS-63:* 50 to 70. *MS-64:* 30 to 40. *MS-65 or better:* 8 to 10.

Availability in circulated grades: *VF-20 to AU-58:* These are very common. They are also common with Chinese chopmarks, but they are the least often seen of the three different die combinations.

Characteristics of striking: Striking of this issue varies, but some are sharp.

Notes: They are known with both the Micro S and Large S (very rare) mintmarks.

Doubled-Die Obverse, dies 2/2 (FS-T1-1876S-101): "Doubling is evident on Liberty's hand, laurel branch, and left foot. Possibly first reported around 1973." Five to eight are estimated to be known.

VG-8	F-12	VF-20	EF-40	AU-50	MS-60	MS-63	MS-64	MS-65
$215	$250	$325	$425	$850	$1,500	$2,650	$3,700	$13,500

1877

actual size: 38.1 mm

Circulation-strike mintage: 3,039,000

Proof mintage: 510

Availability in Mint State: In 2014 the Eugene H. Gardner Sale featured an example of this coin in MS-66. *MS-60 to 62:* 450 to 700. *MS-63:* 150 to 250. *MS-64:* 60 to 100. *MS-65 or better:* 10 to 15.

Availability in circulated grades: *VF-20 to AU-58:* 20,000+. With Chinese chopmarks these are scarcer than the large mintage for this year would suggest, but enough are around that finding one will be no problem.

Characteristics of striking: Many coins of this issue are weakly struck on Liberty's head and certain obverse stars.

Proofs: *PF-60 to 62:* 90 to 120. *PF-63:* 90 to 120. *PF-64:* 65 to 90. *PF-64 or better:* 25 to 45. The mintage may have been 710 (or 510, according to Mint figures).

Delivery figures by month: January: none; February: 400 (probably actually 600; the total of 200 circulation strikes listed in the Mint report for this month were probably Proofs); March–September: none; October: 50; November: none; December: 60. There was an oversupply, and 125 unsold Proofs were distributed for face value on January 11, 1878.

VG-8	F-12	VF-20	EF-40	AU-50	MS-60
$200	$250	$325	$425	$475	$1,000

MS-63	MS-64	MS-65	PF-60	PF-63	PF-65
$1,600	$3,000	$10,000	$2,150	$3,750	$7,000

1877-CC

Circulation-strike mintage: 534,000

actual size: 38.1 mm

Availability in Mint State: Mint State coins are sometimes seen with a "greasy" rather than deeply frosty luster. In 2014 the Eugene H. Gardner Sale featured an example of this coin in MS-64. *MS-60 to 62:* 100 to 160. *MS-63:* 15 to 20. *MS-64:* 5 to 8. *MS-65 or better:* 0 or 1.

Availability in circulated grades: *VF-20 to AU-58:* 400 to 700. With Chinese chopmarks these are scarce, but they are more often seen than those without chopmarks.

Characteristics of striking: Striking of this issue varies, but sharp examples can be found.

Notes: Production resumed at the Carson City Mint, which had not struck trade dollars since April 1876. For a time in June 1877 trade dollars were again minted. The *Territorial Enterprise*, published in Virginia City, Nevada, reported on June 29:

> The work of coining trade dollars will be briskly resumed at the Carson Mint July 1. The 'trades' are not for circulation here. They will be shipped to San Francisco, thence to China. Our people would not object to the big dollars just now, yet if they could get plenty of half dollars they will try to worry along.

By the end of August some 531,000 pieces had been struck at Carson City, and many pieces had found their way into circulation. On September 27, 1877 the *Territorial Enterprise* noted:

> The shoe dealers in this city have all struck against the trade dollar. They all put up cards last evening containing the announcement: 'Trade Dollars Not Taken.' At some of the shoe stores they do not bother with them at all, while at others they are taken at 90 cents. Of late the 'trades' have been circulating to a considerable extent. It is supposed that the brokers were scattering them abroad for the purpose of coming down on them presently and buying them at a discount.[28]

On July 19, 1878, some 44,148 undistributed trade dollars were melted. While it is believed that most of these were of the 1878-CC issue, most likely others, perhaps fewer than 10,000, were of the 1877-CC production.

VG-8	F-12	VF-20	EF-40	AU-50	MS-60	MS-63	MS-64	MS-65
$500	$650	$850	$1,250	$1,750	$5,000	$8,500	$22,500	$75,000

1877-S

Circulation-strike mintage: 9,519,000

actual size: 38.1 mm

Availability in Mint State: In 2014 the Eugene H. Gardner Sale featured an example of this coin in MS-65. *MS-60 to 62:* 2,000 to 3,000. *MS-63:* 350 to 500. *MS-64:* 200 to 300. *MS-65 or better:* 6 to 80.

Availability in circulated grades: *VF-20 to AU-58:* 50,000+. These are the most common in the series with Chinese chopmarks.

Characteristics of striking: Striking of this issue varies, but sharp coins can be found.

Notes: This issue is known to have the Micro S (slightly scarce), Medium S, and Large S mintmark varieties.

The mintage of the 1877-S trade dollar broke all previous records, and no later mintage was ever to equal it, with the result that the production of 9,519,000 pieces stands as the high point of the denomination. In fact, the mintage of 1877-S alone was greater than all combined trade dollar mintages of the Philadelphia and Carson City mints from the first year of circulation-strike production, 1873, until the last, 1878!

Although some coins were distributed within the United States to brokers who bought them at a discount from face value and sold them to industrialists and others, by far the greatest amount of 1877-S trade dollars went to China, where they were plentiful for decades afterward. Many trade dollars struck at the San Francisco Mint and elsewhere were made to the order of Louis McLane, president of the Nevada Bank of San Francisco, who made this statement on August 31, 1877 (reproduced in the *Annual Report of the Director of the Mint*, 1877):

> The benefit of coining trade dollars is that it gives a better market for silver than fine bars would produce. This bank has had coined and sold in the last twenty-two months over six millions of trade dollars, and their sale has netted more than the average of our sales of silver to the government. Returns of trade dollars from the mint have uniformly been made with honesty and fairness. I only remember one case in which the loss by melting was unusually large; but that was afterward explained. Our sales of silver to the government were made direct, through the director of the Mint, mostly by telegraph, except when he was present in person, and were, as specially agreed, free of all commissions or brokerages. In our dealings with the government no commission or brokerage or reward, or any other consideration, has ever been given, in any way, shape, or form, to any officer of the government, or to anyone else. It will happen in seasons of low sterling exchange that silver will rule lower in New York than the equivalent of the London market; but this is quite exceptional. The silver sold the government has been delivered at the mints in San Francisco, Carson, and Philadelphia, in sums as required by the director of the Mint.

VG-8	F-12	VF-20	EF-40	AU-50	MS-60	MS-63	MS-64	MS-65
$200	$235	$325	$425	$475	$1,000	$1,600	$2,250	$7,000

1878

Proof mintage: 900

Characteristics of striking: This issue is usually sharp, but there is sometimes slight weakness above Liberty's ear.

Proofs: Beginning with this year, figures start with PF-58, as

actual size: 38.1 mm

many lightly circulated Proofs are known and are avidly collected. *PF-60 to 62:* 190 to 225. *PF-63:* 125 to 175. *PF-64:* 125 to 175. *PF-64 or better:* 70 to 100.

Notes: On February 22, 1878, Secretary of the Treasury John Sherman, a foe of the trade dollar denomination, mandated that coinage cease. By this time Philadelphia had produced no circulation strikes and made none later, only Proofs. Carson City had made some, production was halted there, and many extant coins were melted. San Francisco ended its coinage, but not immediately, as it wanted to take care of pending business and deposits.

PF-60	PF-63	PF-65
$2,150	$3,500	$7,000

1878-CC

Circulation-strike mintage: 97,000

Net after melting: 52,852

Availability in Mint State: In 2015 the Eugene H. Gardner Sale featured an example of this coin in MS-62. *MS-60 to*

actual size: 38.1 mm

62: 10 to 15. *MS-63:* 15 to 20. *MS-64:* 10 to 15. *MS-65 or better:* 5 to 8.[29]

Availability in circulated grades: *VF-20 to AU-58:* 125 to 225. With Chinese chopmarks these are extremely rare.

Characteristics of striking: This issue is usually well struck.

Notes: Secretary of the Treasury John Sherman, who disliked trade dollars intensely (even though the director of the Mint, Dr. Henry Linderman, believed they were an excellent, useful coin), mandated on February 22, 1878, that no trade dollars would be paid out for deposits of bullion made prior to the order for discontinuance when received at Carson City. When this order reached Carson City, this branch mint had already struck 97,000 pieces; 56,000 in January and 41,000 in February—the smallest circulation strike quantity of the denomination. Thus, a rarity was created.

Apparently, relatively few were sent to China, and most probably remained in the United States. On July 19, 1878, 44,148 undistributed trade dollars went to the melting pot. All must have been dated 1878-CC, many from the 41,000 delivered in February. This leaves a net mintage for distribution of only 52,852 coins.

VG-8	F-12	VF-20	EF-40	AU-50	MS-60	MS-63	MS-64	MS-65
$1,300	$1,650	$2,500	$5,000	$6,500	$16,000	$40,000	$100,000	$200,000

1878-S

actual size: 38.1 mm

Circulation-strike mintage: 4,162,000

Availability in Mint State: In 2015 the Eugene H. Gardner Sale featured an example of this coin in MS-66. *MS-60 to 62:* 1,500 to 2,000. *MS-63:* 300 to 40. *MS-64:* 175 to 250. *MS-65 or better:* 70 to 100.

Availability in circulated grades: *VF-20 to AU-58:* 30,000+. Chopmarked coins are plentiful and are the second most common issue (after 1877-S).

Characteristics of striking: Striking of this issue varies.

Notes: By February 22, 1878, when Secretary of the Treasury John Sherman halted trade dollar mintage, the San Francisco Mint has already made 1,695,819 pieces. This branch did not end production until early April and by then the total was 4,162,000—nearly a record production (the fourth highest in the series).

By the time that the last 1878-S trade dollar fell from the dies, coins of this denomination valued at more than $36 million had been produced, a staggering sum, and an amount more than four times greater than all of the silver dollars that had been coined from 1794 until the denomination was suspended in 1873.

VG-8	F-12	VF-20	EF-40	AU-50	MS-60	MS-63	MS-64	MS-65
$200	$235	$325	$425	$475	$1,000	$1,600	$2,250	$7,000

1879

actual size: 38.1 mm

Proof mintage: 1,541

Proofs: *PF-60 to 62:* 300 to 450. *PF-63:* 250 to 400. *PF-64:* 225 to 300. *PF-64 or better:* 125 to 175.

Notes: There arose in 1879, and continued into 1880, a popular numismatic speculation (later extended to the general public). Word spread that certain coins were of low mintage and would become rare. The "best" condition was considered to be Proofs (circulation strikes were generally ignored and, in any event, were not available in the trade dollar series after 1878). There was also widespread investment interest in the low-mintage dimes, quarters, and half dollars of this year (see information under 1879 dimes in chapter 5).

The fever to squirrel away Proof trade dollars did not develop until later in 1879, as the monthly Proof production figures reveal: January: 122; February: 96; March: 75; April: 119; May: 90; June: 140; July: 40; August: 45; September: 89; October: 64; November: 80; and, finally, December with a whopping 581.

An examination of the monthly figures for the following year, 1880 (see next listing), reveals that production of 1880 Proofs was strongest early in that year, but soon faded. Apparently, the Proof trade dollar boom was very short-lived (reminiscent of some fads today) and extended only from December 1879 through the early part of 1880.

On December 16, 1878, the Engraving Department of the Philadelphia Mint, acting on the orders of Director Horatio Burchard (who seemingly anticipated there would be a coinage of 1879-S trade dollars even though they had been discontinued), shipped five obverse dies dated 1879 to San Francisco, however, no coinage materialized.

PF-60	PF-63	PF-65
$2,150	$3,500	$6,500

1880

Proof mintage: 1,987

Proofs: *PF-60 to 62:* 400 to 600. *PF-63:* 350 to 500. *PF-64:* 250 to 325. *PF-64 or better:* 150 to 200.

Notes: As in all years from 1879 to 1885, the only trade dollars struck in 1880 were

actual size: 38.1 mm

Proofs. This year set a record for Proof trade dollar mintage. The popular speculation in Proof-only trade dollars continued and peaked in March 1880, as the following delivery figures indicate: January: none;[30] February: 488; March: 777; April: 201; May: 58; June: 50; July: 20; August: 25; September: 30; October: 27; November: 40; and December: 271. By year's end some 1,987 Proofs had left the coining press, a record for the denomination and, for that matter, any Proof silver coin before 1936!

From *Mason's Coin Collectors' Herald,* June 1880:

> Trade dollars of this year are still in demand, in Proof condition, at $2. While Proof sets remain at Mint prices the half dollars, quarters and dimes of this year, for general circulation, have not yet been coined, and we shall probably have a repetition of the speculative excitement which attended the distribution of the halves, quarters, and dimes of 1879, in the latter part of the present year.

PF-60	PF-63	PF-65
$2,150	$3,500	$6,500

1881

Proof mintage: 960

Proofs: *PF-60 to 62:* 150 to 250. *PF-63:* 200 to 300. *PF-64:* 150 to 225. *PF-64 or better:* 100 to 150.

Notes: Reflecting the dwindling fad, mintage of 1881 Proof trade dollars was once

actual size: 38.1 mm

again nearly equal to the number of silver Proof sets minted (960 trade dollars versus 975 of other silver denominations).

Monthly figures are as follows: January: none; February: 300; March: 175; April: 85; May: 40; June: 70; July: none; August: 10; September: 25; October: 51; November: 38; and December: 166. The total for the year came to 960.

Most of the Proofs of this year were poorly struck and exhibit flatness in areas, particularly on the head of Liberty and on the upper stars. This was due to incorrect die setting in the press. Poor striking continued to be a problem into 1883.

PF-60	PF-63	PF-65
$2,150	$3,500	$6,500

1882

Proof mintage: 1,097

Proofs: *PF-60 to 62:* 150 to 225. *PF-63:* 200 to 275. *PF-64:* 150 to 200. *PF-64 or better:* 90 to 125.

Notes: For the fifth year in a row, the only trade dollars minted at Philadelphia were

actual size: 38.1 mm

Proofs. The mintage figure of 1,097 Proofs was nearly equal to the number of silver Proof sets (1,100) made of other denominations from the dime to the Morgan dollar.

By year's end 1,097 Proofs had been struck, the third highest Proof mintage in the series, and one of just three Proof production quantities to break the 1,000 mark. Demand for them seems to have been heaviest earlier in the year, as the monthly production figures indicate: January: none; February: 393; March: 277; April: 49; May: 70; June: 23; July: 30; August: 10; September: 20; October: 20; November: 40; and December: 165. There is the possibility that some may have been melted, possibly part of the December mintage. Many Proofs are lightly struck.

PF-60	PF-63	PF-65
$2,150	$3,500	$6,500

1883

Proof mintage: 979

Proofs: *PF-60 to 62:* 100 to 150. *PF-63:* 200 to 300. *PF-64:* 140 to 175. *PF-64 or better:* 75 to 110.

Notes: In this final year of public sales of trade dollars, only Proofs were made.

actual size: 38.1 mm

The figure of 979 Proof trade dollars fell short of the 1,039 Proofs made of other silver denominations. It is likely that many were melted as 1883 is rarer than the mintage would indicate.

PF-60	PF-63	PF-65
$2,150	$3,500	$6,500

1884

Proof mintage: 10

Notes: The trade dollars of 1884 and 1885 furnish a separate situation apart from Mint-authorized trade dollar issues. For many years reference books, catalogs, and

actual size: 38.1 mm

articles have claimed that just 10 specimens were struck dated 1884 and just five dated 1885. These are believed to have been produced secretly at the Mint and were not included in any of the official reports. In fact, the very existence of these coins was not publicized to numismatists until 1908 when Captain John W. Haseltine (in partnership with Stephen K. Nagy), a Philadelphia coin dealer with close connections to the Mint, startled the hobby by announcing they had been found among coins in 1884 and 1885 Proof sets owned by his father-in-law, William K. Idler.[31] However, in 1907, the year before, Haseltine's partner, Nagy, had sold one to Virgil M. Brand in an unannounced transaction.

Farran Zerbe, editor of *The Numismatist*, wrote an article on the subject of 1884 trade dollars and noted that seven of the ten known pieces had been sold within a few months by a single dealer at prices ranging from $150 to $400. It was not revealed by Zerbe, if indeed he knew it, that Virgil Brand was the main buyer.[32]

No one can be sure exactly how many 1884 and 1885 trade dollars were struck, absent official records. What we can be sure of is that only ten 1884s and only five 1885s *are now known.*[33]

Today the 1884 and 1885 trade dollars are recognized as prime rarities. The appearance of a single specimen on the market is a cause for excited publicity.[34] Several "pattern" strikings in copper are known, at least two of which have been silver plated, a deception not discovered until the coins were weighed. One of these was in a "name" collection auctioned in the 1960s. Another was discovered by Larry Briggs when evaluating a Michigan collection. It would seem wise to weigh *all* "silver" 1884 trade dollars.[35] A detailed registry of the known specimens is in the 1997 Eliasberg Collection catalog.

PF-60	PF-63	PF-65
	$650,000	$1,100,000

1885

Proof mintage: 5

Notes: Trade dollars dated 1885 first became known to the numismatic fraternity when five pieces came on the market in 1908, echoing the scenario of the 1884 coins. These had been

actual size: 38.1 mm

"discovered" in 1906 in the estate of William K. Idler as it was being examined by his son-in-law John W. Haseltine. Both were "rascals" in that they were the primary outlet for Mint officials to funnel secret strikes of patterns, restrikes, etc., into the marketplace.

Most likely 1885 Proof trade dollars were struck early in that year, after the January 2, 1885, destruction of the 1884 obverse and reverse die (for the 1885 is from a different reverse than used in 1884), but before Colonel A. Loudon Snowden, superintendent of the Philadelphia Mint since 1879, turned in his resignation in June 1885. His successor as superintendent, Daniel M. Fox, was very circumspect and proper, and no hint of making "fancy pieces" ever surfaced during his administration.[36]

On all five of the known coins the reverse die is doubled.[37] At one time the author had three of the five coins in his office at the same time—the Eliasberg and Norweb coins and one other!

No Proof 1885 trade dollars are listed in Mint reports or records, and it is supposed that the coinage was unofficial. Today, specimens are highly prized as great rarities and are among the most famous and desirable of all U.S. silver coins. A detailed registry of the known specimens is in the 1997 Eliasberg Collection catalog.[38]

PF-60	PF-63	PF-65
	$2,000,000	$3,750,000

EPILOGUE
MARTIN VAN BUREN

It may come as a surprise (unless you are up to date on modern U.S. Mint issues) that the last Liberty Seated coins were minted not in 1891, but in 2008! The scenario began in 2007 with the launch of the First Spouse program of .9999 fine gold coins. Each contains a half ounce of pure gold, an ounce of which in 2008 was selling for around $900. The coins' denomination of $10 was simply to make them legal-tender *coins*, not medals, to enhance their appeal to buyers. On the obverse of each coin was a portrait of a First Lady of the United States, and on the reverse a scene relating to her president husband. Some presidents did not have a wife while in office, so the Mint borrowed from past coin designs to create an obverse. A Draped Bust

design was used for the Thomas Jefferson administration, a Capped Bust motif for Andrew Jackson, and a Liberty Head for James Buchanan. For Martin Van Buren the Mint brought out of its archives the familiar Liberty Seated design.

Van Buren (December 5, 1782 to July 24, 1862), the eighth U.S. president, served from 1837 to 1841, immediately following Andrew Jackson's two terms. He had been Jackson's vice president since 1833. Fiercely loyal to Jackson, he was one of the few high in the administration who stood by him during the shakeup of the Cabinet when certain men recommended by John Calhoun were replaced by the "Kitchen Cabinet" and also during the scandalous Petticoat Affair involving Peggy Eaton.

Van Buren married Hannah Hoes (the family name was Goes earlier), his childhood sweetheart and first cousin once removed, on February 21, 1807, in Catskill, New York. The union produced five sons and one daughter, four of whom lived to adulthood. Hannah contracted tuberculosis, for which there was no cure, and died on February 5, 1819. Contemporary biographies of Van Buren mention her only in passing. A daughter-in-law, Sarah Angelica Singleton Van Buren, would perform many of the hostess functions for the White House during his presidency.

THE VAN BUREN
FIRST SPOUSE COIN

The U.S. Mint started accepting orders for the Martin Van Buren First Spouse gold coin at 12 noon on November 25, 2008. The issue price was set about $75 lower than that of its predecessor coin, following a decrease in the value of bullion on international markets. As with the Andrew Jackson coin that had debuted three months earlier, the Mint set an order limit of 10 coins per format (Mint State and Proof) per household for the first week, reserving the right to evaluate sales and either extend, adjust, or eliminate the limit after that. The total mintage was capped at 40,000 pieces, to be distributed between the Burnished (called Uncirculated by the Mint) and Proof coins according to buyers' demand.

Collector interest waned a bit for this issue, despite its attractive engraving of Christian Gobrecht's famous Liberty Seated design on the obverse. The reverse tableau shows Martin Van Buren as a youth reading a book outside the Kinderhook, New York, tavern run by his father, with a traveler on horseback in the background. When Martin was growing up, the tavern, situated along a post road, was a meeting place for conversation, debate, and voting. Politicians traveling between New York City and the state capital of Albany stopped there. From this exposure young Van Buren developed a taste for politics and the philosophy of law. The coin's detailed scene was designed by Artistic Infusion Program Master Designer Thomas Cleveland and sculpted by Mint sculptor-engraver Jim Licaretz.

The mintage totaled 3,826 Burnished coins and 6,807 Proofs. Even with these fairly low numbers, the Van Buren's Liberty coin was one of the program's last hurrahs, mintage-wise (until Jacqueline Kennedy's turn came in 2015). With the combination of low mintage and ongoing collector demand for the four coins of the Liberty subset, Van Buren's Liberty has emerged as the secondary-market winner among the First Spouse issues of 2007 and 2008. In both Burnished and Proof format it typically carries a premium of 25 to 50 percent over the other coins of those years. Fans of Liberty Seated coinage happily attribute some of that popular demand to Christian Gobrecht's classic American design.

Dennis Tucker
Atlanta, Georgia

APPENDIX

CHRISTIAN GOBRECHT: A CHRONOLOGY

Introduction

Today, numismatists honor Gobrecht as one of the most important engravers ever to work at the Philadelphia Mint. For an entire generation of Americans, his designs were ubiquitous on circulating Liberty Seated silver and Coronet (Liberty Head) half cents, copper "large" cents, and gold coins. The *Gobrecht Journal*, edited by John McCloskey until 2014 and published by the Liberty Seated Collectors Club, is named for him, as are the rare "Gobrecht dollars" of the late 1830s.

1785, DECEMBER 23: Christian Gobrecht was born in Hanover, Pennsylvania, the son of Reverend and Mrs. Johann [anglicized to John] C. Gobrecht, the seventh of ten children born to the couple. His father, Johann Christian Gobrecht (1733–1815), was from Augerstein, Germany. He came to Pennsylvania in 1753 and subsequently served as a minister in the German Reformed Church. Christian Gobrecht's mother, Elisabeth Sands, born in 1746, was a descendant of James Sands, who came from England and settled in Plymouth, Massachusetts, in 1642. James Sands was an early settler of Block Island, where he passed away in 1695.

1794: Not yet a teenager, Christian Gobrecht showed an interest in and an aptitude for art. His sketchbook of this date, preserved by the Historical Society of Pennsylvania, contains many images rendered in pencil and display a remarkable talent. Another sketchbook, advanced in the quality of its contents, is dated 1802.

1800s, EARLY: The teenaged Gobrecht served as an apprentice to a clockmaker in Manheim, Pennsylvania, where he learned to engrave clock faces and metal plates. At the completion of his apprenticeship, he moved to Baltimore. In the early 1800s there were many outlets for the talents of an engraver. In cities such as Baltimore, Philadelphia, New York, and Boston, there was a strong demand for such artisans to work on copper plates and wood blocks to create illustrations for periodicals, vignettes for certificates and bank notes, and to make decorations for calling cards, book plates, watch papers (inserted in the back of watch cases), and other printed items. The making of embossed seals for legal and personal documents, the cutting of stencils for lettering shipping containers and manufactured products, and the making of steel letter stamps were also part of the engraving trade. Still other branches of the art were devoted to making brass plates for doors, for creating designs on clock faces, and for making special items of jewelry or tableware. The demand for engravers to create dies for tokens and medals was very small in comparison to these other areas. For this reason, virtually all of the names we recognize today as important coin or token die engravers also did extensive work in these related disciplines.

1810, CIRCA: Christian Gobrecht worked in Baltimore independently and also with William H. Freeman as an engraver of watch plates, faces, and dials. Around this time, work was begun on his medal-ruling machine by which a three-dimensional medal or bas-relief object could be converted to a two-dimensional illustration for use in a publication using a linear (not slow spiral or circular as in later transfer lathes) process.

1810: In this year he engraved a portrait of George Washington for G. Kingston's *New American Biographical Dictionary*, published in Baltimore. During the decade he also did much other portrait work including images of Dr. B.S. Barton (published in *The Port Folio*), Reverend Andrew Fuller, Reverend Thomas Baldwin, David Rittenhouse, Dr. Benjamin Rush, Benjamin Franklin (for *Delaplaine's Repository*); and Abraham Rees (frontispiece for *Rees's Encyclopedia*), among others.

1811: Christian Gobrecht moved to Philadelphia, where he engaged in the engraving trade, working with bookbinders' dies, calico printing rolls, and other items.

1816: By this time he had joined the staff of Murray, Draper, Fairman & Co., banknote engravers in the same city. An early version of Gobrecht's medal-ruling machine had been improved to the extent that it was practical and was used by artists of the firm.

1817: He perfected his improved engraving machine and used it to copy a medal of Russia's Alexander I to create an image suitable for printing. Soon, the device was used widely in the East including by Alva Mason, Colonel C.G. Childs, the Albany engraving firm of Rawdon, Clark & Co., and others.[1]

1818, MAY 31: Christian Gobrecht married Mary (Hamilton) Hewes, the daughter of Thomas Hamilton and Rebecca Leaming, and the widow of Daniel Hewes. The union produced two sons and two daughters: Christiana Elizabeth (married Dr. William Darrach), Rebecca Mary (never married), Charles Joseph (never married), and William Henry (became a well-known medical surgeon, author, and artist; served in the Civil War as brigade surgeon under General Hancock; and later was professor of anatomy and surgery at the Cincinnati College of Medicine).

1820s: Intrigued by publicity given to Maelzel's automata (of which the chess player is best remembered today), Gobrecht is said to have invented a speaking or automaton doll. He also devised an improvement upon the ancient camera lucida device for projecting images against a screen or wall.

1820–1821, CIRCA: He invented and manufactured a parlor reed organ operated by keys and bellows, the first example of which was sold to a resident of Lancaster, Pennsylvania.

1823, DECEMBER 1: Gobrecht petitioned President James Monroe to appoint him as mint engraver following the death of Robert Scot (letter reproduced in chapter 1).

1823–1824, CIRCA: Gobrecht's talents were admired by Mint Director Robert Patterson.

1824: He was hired as an outside contractor to furnish letter punches for die making.

1824, FEBRUARY 5: Gobrecht was on a committee formed by E. & C. Starr to create an anti-counterfeiting bank-note printing process equal to the one recently created by the Starrs.[2] In reality, the Starr process never proved to be successful. A note of this type is illustrated.

1824, JUNE 11: From the *Statesman*, New York, New York: "From the *Philadelphia Gazette:* Mr. Christian Gobrecht, an ingenious artist of this city and a native of our state, has invented a musical instrument to which he gives the name of *Crescendo-Eolian*. It is a keyed instrument similar to the cottage piano in appearance and has a couple of organ stops connected with it, which the performer can use to his discretion. . . ."[3] Under "General Summary," the *Scioto Gazette*, Chillicothe, Ohio, July 1, 1824, mentioned the instrument and noted, "A new musical instrument has been invented by C. Gobrecht, formerly of Baltimore. . ."

1825: He cut the dies bearing the founding date 1824 for the Franklin Institute medal and signed GOBRECHT F. below the bust of Franklin from a design by Thomas Sully. Upon viewing the medal, John Neagle wrote, "I am delighted with it, and as a specimen of art, am proud to acknowledge it from the hands of a friend. I had an opportunity of comparing it in one hand with the same head by the celebrated Dupré in the other, and it gives me great pleasure to say that, in my opinion, it surpasses the other very far in merit. Yours has more of the genuine character of our great philosopher and statesman." At the third annual exhibition of American Manufacturing held at the Masonic Hall, Philadelphia, October 3–6, 1826, he was awarded a premium (prize) for this medal.

1825, FEBRUARY 14: Mint Director Samuel Moore wrote to President John Quincy Adams "and solicited his permission to introduce Gobrecht (see letter, chapter 1). On the same date, Mint Director Samuel Moore, obviously rising to the subject, wrote to Thomas Jefferson, who was then living in retirement at Monticello near Charlottesville, Virginia, to seek his views:

> What figure or device may be considered as intended by Congress, or the administration, at the establishment of the mint, by words in the law: 'An impression emblematic of liberty?' Was the cap of liberty adopted or alluded to as a fit emblem by any act of the Confederation or any of the states, or by popular usage, during the Revolution, or previous to 1792 [the date of the establishment of the Mint] so that this device may be supposed to have been intended. When emblems or representations of liberty were in those times resorted to, on public occasions, of what description were they? If the liberty cap be the emblem intended in the law; or if it be deemed an Americanized and suitable emblem, is it proper to place it on the head of the figure personifying liberty? Such information or suggestions as you may find it convenient to favor me with will be thankfully received. While I am satisfied as to the impression emblematic of liberty, which can be sustained on the best ground, a few pattern pieces will be struck to be submitted to the consideration of the government, which if approved, or with such modifications as shall be directed, may fix the character of our coins. Supposing the female to be an appropriate figure, three

views in relation to it present themselves. To adhere to the present dress cap, or copy it so nearly as not to exhibit the appearance of any specific change; to exclude the cap and adopt an easy disposition of the hair, with no ornament but the band of liberty; to adopt the classic style of cap, which though resembling the cap of liberty nearly in form, would nevertheless be distinguished from it by being worn on the head of the figure, if it be true that the cap of Liberty is out of place there. The first would be the easiest, being a style familiar to the engraver of the mint. The second if happily executed would perhaps be the most pleasing, as being more true to life and nature. The third has the advantage of a permanent standard in the exquisite models of art derived from classic times.

1826, October 19: Publishers H.C. Carey & I. Lea advertised, "Have in press and will publish in the course of the present month ... *Atlantic Souvenir, a Christmas and New Year's Present*, for 1827. This work will contain about forty articles in prose and poetry by some of the best American writers and will be ornamented with ten engravings executed in the best style by Longacre, Lang, Maverick, Ellis, Childs, Kearney, and Gobrecht."[4]

1826: Gobrecht received $100 as payment for "executing designs and models of dies for the Mint which were not adopted." These are believed to have been dies for "several" Liberty Head medallions at the Mint, descriptions of which are not known today.[5] Gobrecht furnished dies for the U.S. Mint and was accepted as an occasional assistant to Chief Engraver William Kneass. He brought to the Mint an improved version of his 1817 medal-ruling machine. He prepared dies for a medal for the New England Society for the Promotion of Manufactures and Mechanic Arts. Obverse with head of Archimedes; reverse with GENIUS, INTELLIGENCE AND INDUSTRY TRIUMPH. Size 40 (40 sixteenths of an inch). Silver, bronze. Interestingly, Gobrecht himself was the first recipient. His medal was engraved, "For the genius, taste and skill which he evinced in executing the dies therefor." He prepared dies for the Charles Carroll of Carrollton medal, one of the most famous American medallic productions of the era.[6] (Julian PE-6).

1826, circa: Gobrecht prepared dies for two varieties (Julian UN-22 and 23) of the Peale's Museum admission pass.[7]

1828, January, to December 1830: He was a member of the Board of Management of the Franklin Institute, 15 South 7th Street (later numbering system), Philadelphia.[8] A medal he did for the institute is illustrated.

1828, October 8 to 11: Gobrecht was a judge for the awarding of premiums (prizes) to exhibitors at the fifth annual exhibition of the Franklin Institute for the promotion of the mechanical arts.

1829, April 2: Among the subscribers to the $2,200,000 State of Pennsylvania Canal Loan of April 22, 1829, was Christian Gobrecht in the amount of $1,500.

1830, January 25: Gobrecht and Mordecai D. Lewis were elected curators of the Franklin Institute. On February 11 Gobrecht was appointed as a member of the Standing Committee on Inventions. Proceedings of the Franklin Institute mentioned him in a number of connections.

1830s: Gobrecht's embossed business card noted that he was a "die sinker and seal engraver" at 220 Walnut Street, Philadelphia.

1831–1836: A design he created for his own business card was adapted and used to imprint the covers of certain books published by the trade in Philadelphia. Around the same time he is said to have made an "eagle with expanded wings" for use on a token, of which little is known today.

1831, OCTOBER: Gobrecht was one of four judges of silver and plated goods for the Exhibition of American Manufactures held by the Franklin Institute, Philadelphia.

1832: He constructed an improved reed organ for his own use. He was named to the Committee on Inventions of the Franklin Institute.

1834 TO 1844: He was a member of the Committee on Science and the Arts of the Franklin Institute.

1835, JUNE 16: Mint Director Samuel Moore wrote Treasury Secretary Levi Woodbury for permission to hire Christian Gobrecht for the Engraving Department.

1835, AUGUST 28: Engraver William Kneass suffered a major stroke.

1835, AUGUST 29: Mint Director Robert Maskell Patterson, who had been in the post since early July, wrote to Treasury Secretary Woodbury to request emergency permission to hire Gobrecht as second (avoiding the *assistant* name) engraver.

1835, SEPTEMBER: Gobrecht went to work as second engraver at the Mint at a salary of $1,500 per year plus $250 which Mint Director Robert Maskell Patterson had persuaded the incapacitated Kneass to transfer from his salary. This emolument of $1,750 was apparently what Gobrecht required to entice him to leave his private practice of bank-note and illustration engraving.

1835: Gobrecht is believed to have worked with Franklin Peale in the use of an experimental roller-die apparatus.[9]

1836: During the year, Christian Gobrecht prepared various coinage and pattern dies, the most memorable of which was for the Liberty Seated silver dollar. Years later on December 14, 1871, Chief Coiner Archibald Loudon Snowden wrote to rare coin dealer E.L. Mason, Jr., stating, in part: "There are no regular coinage or pattern dies in the Mint, of any denomination whatsoever, except those dated 1871." Snowden reported that shortly after becoming chief coiner, he had found a group of coins that had been labeled years earlier by Franklin Peale. "It was not a complete series of dies, but it embraced either as hubs or dies all the rare pattern pieces executed by Mr. Gobrecht and others. Among the number were several from which no pieces are known to have been struck. Many of the devices were beautiful in design and exquisite in execution. This was particularly the case with a dollar and a half dollar hub by Gobrecht." He designed and engraved dies for the Massachusetts Charitable Mechanic Association (obverse and reverse; Julian AM-33).

1836, OCTOBER 1: *The Athenæum*, published in London, featured an extensive article, "Medallic Engraving," which told of Gobrecht's 1817 invention and related devices. This was reprinted in several American magazines in 1837.

1838: His Liberty Head design was introduced for the $10 gold eagle and was later continued on other denominations until 1908.

1839: Various portrait punches were created and used ephemerally on copper cents; *e.g.*, the *Silly Head* and *Booby Head* varieties. The Braided Hair cent made its debut.

1840: Braided Hair half cents, Liberty Seated silver dollars (with perched eagle reverse), and Coronet, or Liberty Head, $2.50 gold coins designed by Gobrecht were introduced.

1840, August 27: Chief Engraver William Kneass died. After Kneass's death, his widow accused Patterson and Gobrecht of wrongdoing, stating that from 1836 to 1840 $500 per year of her husband's salary had been directed wrongly to Gobrecht. The charges were not acted upon, but the Mint did grant her over $1,000 in "widow's relief."

1840, December 21: Christian Gobrecht was named to the post of "engraver of the Mint of the United States," recognizing what he had been doing *de facto* since Kneass's stroke.

1841, circa: Christian Gobrecht may have designed the reverse die for the 1841-dated medal of John Tyler (Julian PR-8).

1842: The Assay office of the Mint published *A Manual of Gold and Silver Coins of All Nations, Struck Within the Past Century* by Jacob Reese Eckfeldt and William E. Dubois. From page 187: "The whole history of the art of medal ruling, as now practiced, shows that it had its origin in the invention of Mr. Gobrecht."

1843: Gobrecht and Joseph Saxton, a fellow Mint employee, furnished a seal to the American Philosophical Society. The *Official Register of the United States,* issued by the Department of State, gave Gobrecht's annual salary as $2,000. Others at the Mint were: Robert M. Patterson, director, $3,500; Isaac Roach, treasurer, $2,000; Franklin Peale, chief coiner, $2,000; Jacob R. Eckfeldt, assayer, $2,000; Jonas R. McClintock, melter and refiner, $2,000; William E. Dubois, assistant assayer, $1,300; Randal Hutchinson, clerk, $1,100; Edward Sprague, weigh room clerk, $1,200; George W. Edelman, bookkeeper $1,000; and George F. Dunning, director clerk, $1,000.

1844, July 23: Christian Gobrecht died in Philadelphia. "His friends and those of the family are respectfully invited to attend his funeral from his late dwelling, No. 220 Walnut Street, on Friday afternoon, the 25th inst., at four o'clock without further notice."[10] He was succeeded as main engraver on September 6, 1844, by James Barton Longacre, an accomplished engraver of illustration plates. Gobrecht's remains were subsequently interred in the Monument Cemetery in the same city.[11]

APPENDIX B

MINTS FOR THE LIBERTY SEATED COINAGE

Overview of the United States Mints

Coins have been struck at eight different mints over the years. Four of these struck Liberty Seated coins—Carson City, New Orleans, Philadelphia, and San Francisco—and are discussed separately below. The other four are summarized here:

Charlotte Mint (1838–1861): The Coinage Act of 1835 provided for three branch mints to be constructed in Charlotte, North Carolina; Dahlonega, Georgia; and New Orleans, Louisiana. The extent of the United States had expanded greatly since the establishment of the Philadelphia Mint in 1792, and it was felt that additional mints would be beneficial. Charlotte and Dahlonega were in gold-mining districts and would be convenient for that industry. New Orleans on the lower Mississippi River was the center of trade for the Midwest and was the busiest port on the Gulf of Mexico. These three facilities each opened in 1838.

The branch mint was opened in Charlotte, North Carolina, for the purpose of producing gold coins from metals extracted from mines and streams of the area. Gold $1, $2.50, and $5 pieces were produced in Charlotte from 1838 until the Civil War in 1861, at which time the mint closed.

Charlotte coins are identified by the mintmark C, as, for example, 1843-C. All coins struck at Charlotte are either scarce or rare today. Today the Charlotte Mint building, disassembled and re-erected in a park, serves as the Charlotte Art Museum.

Dahlonega Mint (1838–1861): The history of the Dahlonega Mint is similar to that of Charlotte. Gold produced in the Dahlonega area of Georgia was converted into $1, $2.50, $3, and $5 pieces from the 1838 through 1861. The mint closed at the advent of the Civil War. After the war, the building was used as a school, and it later burned.

Dahlonega coins have the mintmark D, not to be confused with the same mintmark later used for Denver coins, for the Dahlonega Mint operated in a different time frame. All Dahlonega gold coins are either scarce or rare, and as a class are more elusive than their Charlotte Mint counterparts.

● 523 ●

Denver Mint (1906 to date): The Denver Mint had its origin in April 21, 1862, when the Treasury Department bought the minting and assaying business of Clark, Gruber & Co. They renamed the facility the Denver Mint, a notation that afterward appeared in all *Annual Reports of the Director of the Mint*. However, that Denver Mint acted only as an assay office and depository. No coins were ever struck there. At the turn of the 20th century construction began for a new Denver Mint at a different location in the city. It officially opened for business on New Year's Day 1906. During the next several weeks, coinage was limited to quarters and half dollars. Coins produced there bear a D mintmark on the reverse, not to be confused with the D for the Dahlonega Mint used from 1838 to 1861. An addition to the Denver Mint was built in 1936 and occupied in 1937.

West Point Mint (1984 to date): Beginning in 1984, a special minting facility in West Point, New York (home of the United States Military Academy), has been used to produce certain gold commemorative coins, silver and gold bullion coins, and a few other issues. The distinguishing mintmark W characterizes these pieces. In the 1960s Lincoln cents without mintmarks were made there to help ease a nationwide coin shortage.

Philadelphia Mint

In 1792 the government acquired a plot of land and several buildings in Philadelphia and set up the first federal facility for the production of coins. In the meantime, in July of that year, about 1,500 silver half dismes were struck in a private shop using equipment intended for the Mint. The foundation stones for a new Mint building were laid on July 31. Equipment was moved into the facility starting in September—two of the buildings remaining from earlier uses. In autumn and early winter of that year, limited numbers of pattern coins were struck there. Copper cents, the first coins made in quantity for general circulation, were issued in March 1793, followed by the first silver coins in 1794, and the first gold coins in 1795.

The Philidelphia Mint.

On July 4, 1829, the cornerstone for the second Philadelphia Mint was laid. A number of silver half dimes were struck for use at the ceremony. In 1832 the new facility opened for operations. In ensuing decades the facility struck coins of many denominations and also supplied dies for the various branches beginning with Charlotte, Dahlonega, and New Orleans in 1838, and continuing with San Francisco in 1854 and Carson City in 1870. Typically, dies for the branch mints were shipped to their destinations late in the preceding year so as to be on hand for use in January.

The Philadelphia Mint also performed assays, storage, and other functions. The engraving department created new designs and motifs. Proof coins for presentation and for collectors were struck there from about 1820 onward, with mintages expanding greatly after 1857 when numismatics became a widely popular hobby. The Mint Cabinet, a display initiated in 1838, was a focal point for numismatists for many years.[1] The office of the director of the Mint was in Philadelphia from 1792 until it was relocated to the Treasury Building in Washington in 1873, after which the Philadelphia Mint was in charge of a superintendent. The last full year of operation of the Second Philadelphia Mint was 1900.

Liberty Seated coins of all denominations in use at a given time were made each year in Philadelphia, as were pattern and Proof coins.

In 1901 the third Philadelphia Mint was opened. The fourth and current Philadelphia Mint was opened in 1969 in Independence Square, not far from the Liberty Bell and other historic attractions.

New Orleans Mint

The New Orleans Mint was opened in 1838. Production continued from that time on until it closed early during the Civil War after being taken over by secessionists who continued coinage for a short time until the supply of bullion ran out. Production consisted of silver and gold coins of all denominations in use at the time. After the war the building was used for various purposes ranging from storage to assaying.

The New Orleans Mint in 1906.

After passage of the Bland-Allison Act on February 28, 1878, which provided from two to four million ounces of silver to be purchased by the Treasury Department and coined into dollars, the New Orleans Mint was refurbished to help meet this challenge. With newly installed coining presses it opened in 1879, in which year dollars and double eagles were minted. Silver dollars continued to be made there through 1904 when the denomination was suspended. The only later gold coins were half eagles in the 1890s and eagles through the early 1900s. Barber dimes, quarters, and half dollars were made at the New Orleans Mint from 1892 until coinage ceased forever in 1909.

Liberty Seated half dimes, dimes, and quarters were first struck in New Orleans in 1838, and half dollars in 1839. Production was continuous through early 1861, but not all denominations were made in all years. Liberty Seated silver dollars were coined in 1846, 1850, 1859, and 1860. Years later in 1891, the New Orleans Mint made dimes and quarters, this being the year that the Liberty Seated design was discontinued. Today most New Orleans Liberty Seated coins are very collectible in circulated grades. Some that are common if worn are extreme rarities in choice or gem Mint State. As a general rule of thumb, the coins minted there have areas of light striking.

San Francisco Mint

The first San Francisco Mint opened in March 1854, in a building that had been slightly expanded after the Treasury purchased it from Curtis, Perry, & Ward, private assayers and minters of gold coins. The gold coining operations of Moffat & Co. and the U.S. Assay Office of Gold had been conducted there earlier. During the first year the San Francisco Mint produced gold $1, $2.50, $5, $10, and $20. The first silver coins were minted in 1855—Liberty Seated quarters and half dollars. Dimes with S mintmarks were first struck in 1856, half dimes in 1863, silver dollars in 1859, trade dollars in 1873, and twenty-cent pieces in 1875.

Cramped and poorly ventilated, the San Francisco facility served its purpose, but from the beginning was unsatisfactory in many ways. During the afternoon of May 25, 1870, the cornerstone for the Second San Francisco Mint was laid. In a special ceremony, gold and silver coins were placed into a one-ton cornerstone at the northeast corner of the building. The contents included "one each of the coins struck off at the San Francisco Branch Mint in the year 1870." The event was conducted by the Masons with a large crowd in attendance.[2] Opened in November 1874, the new mint had the latest equipment. It produced silver and gold coins exclusively until the first

The first (1854–1874) San Francisco Mint.

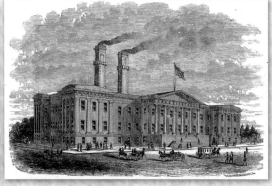

The second (1874–1937) San Francisco Mint.

bronze cents were struck there in 1908 and the first nickel five-cent pieces in 1912. After the earthquake and fire of April 1906, it was the only building left standing in its district. It became the headquarters for security and other government and banking activities while the rubble was cleared and other arrangements were made. In 1937 the Third and current San Francisco Mint was opened on Duboce Street and struck various bronze and silver denominations.

Today Liberty Seated coins from the San Francisco Mint are widely sought. Most of them are affordable, but many range from scarce to rare in higher grades, this being especially true for issues minted prior to 1874, except for the 1873-S trade dollar.

Carson City Mint

In 1870 a branch mint was opened in Carson City, Nevada, to take advantage of silver and gold mined in the Comstock Lode about 15 miles away, discovered in 1858. In the early years, the precious metals were shipped by rail to the San Francisco Mint. It was expected that if a mint was established in Carson City it would offer convenience and take over much of the business. This was done and was opened in 1870 with high expectations. Documents referred to it as the Carson Mint or the Branch Mint at Carson. In modern times, numismatists as well as citizens of the area call it the Carson City Mint.

A description of the structure from Thompson and West's *History of Nevada*, 1881:

> Granite from the prison stone quarry. Pict style of architecture. Portico, Ionic. Hall, 12 feet in width; main hall, 12x40; on the right of the entrance. Paying teller's office, 13x16 feet. Coining room, 19x19. Spiral staircase conducts above. Whitening room 10x14.5, with a vault in solid masonry, 5x6. Annealing furnace and rolling room, 17x24. Gold and silver melting room, 10x24. Melters' and refiners' office, 12x19 feet. Deposit melting room, 14.5x19. Deposit weighing room, 19x19, with a strong vault, 6.5x10.5 feet. Treasurer's office, 13x16, with a vault five feet square. Engine room, 16.5x53 feet. Beside which there is a cabinet, adjusting room, ladies' dressing room, humid assay room, assayer's office, assayer's room, watchman's room, two store-rooms, attic, and basement.
>
> As a preventive against fire the floors are double, with an inch of mortar between. The foundations are seven feet below the basement floor and laid in concrete. Building two and a half stories high. The machinery for the Mint arrived November 22, 1868. The Mint has a front of 90 feet on Carson Street. . . .

The Carson City Mint.

The new facility did not work out as expected as Abram Curry, partner in the largest mine in the area, was the first superintendent—to the displeasure of his competitors in the silver business. Moreover, the greatest call for coins was on the West Coast, not in the mining camps of Nevada. Most coins minted in Carson City had to be shipped to California anyway. As if that was not enough, production at the San Francisco Mint was said to be more efficient. This became particularly so after a new facility was opened there in 1874.

The result was that production of silver and gold coins in Carson City was low in comparison to that of San Francisco. Liberty Seated dimes were struck there from 1871 to 1878, twenty-cent pieces in 1875 and 1876, quarters and half dollars 1870 to 1878, silver dollars from 1870 to 1873, and trade dollars from 1873 to 1878. Gold coins of $5, $10, and $20 were struck intermittently during the mint's existence.

Carson City Liberty Seated silver coins from 1870 to 1874 are for the most part scarce in any grade, and rare to very rare in Mint State. Three notable rarities are the unique 1873-CC, No Arrows, dime; the 1876-CC twenty-cent piece of which about 20 are known; and the 1873-CC, No Arrows, quarter with a population of just five pieces. Most but not all Carson City coins from dimes to half dollars minted from 1875 through 1878 are generally plentiful in the marketplace, and Mint State examples of most varieties are easily enough obtained.

Later coinage consisted only of Morgan-design silver dollars and Liberty Head $5, $10, and $20 gold coins. The mint ceased coining part way through 1885, then opened again in 1889 and closed forever in 1893. On June 30, 1899, the mint designation was officially discontinued, and it became the Carson City Assay Office. In 1900, minting equipment was removed and usable coinage dies for reverses of Morgan dollars were shipped to Philadelphia. Since 1942 the mint building has served as the Nevada State Museum. The Carson City Coin Collectors of America group (www.carsoncitycoinclub.com) specializes in this coinage and issues a magazine, *Curry's Chronicle*.

APPENDIX C

MINT DIRECTORS AND SUPERINTENDENTS – LIBERTY SEATED COINAGE ERA

Mint Directors

The office of the director of the Mint was located in the Treasury Building in Washington, D.C. The appointment was made by the president of the United States, usually nodding to political considerations. The director was responsible for the Denver, Philadelphia, and San Francisco mints. The superintendents of those facilities reported to him or her. The director reported to the secretary of the Treasury. He or she was often called on by various congressional committees regarding coinage and monetary matters.

There was often a small gap between the term of one director and that of his or her successor. These gaps were filled by an appointed acting director. The Mint's fiscal year ran from July 1 of the first year into June 30 of the second. Most accounts and reports were on a fiscal year basis supplemented by some numbers calculated into calendar years (the last necessary for numismatists interested in mintage figures), such as the number of dies used in a calendar year, and related aspects. *The Annual Report of the Director of the Mint* was compiled by staff after the close of the fiscal year and published months later.

Mint Directors and Terms

Robert Maskell Patterson: July 1835 to July 1851.
George N. Eckert: July 1851 to April 1853.
Thomas Pettit: April 1853 to May 1853.
James Ross Snowden: June 1853 to April 1861.
James Pollock: May 1861 to September 1866.

William Millward: October 1866 to April 1867.
Henry Richard Linderman: April 1867 to April 1869.
James Pollock: May 1869 to March 1873.
Henry Richard Linderman: April 1873 to December 1878.
Horatio C. Burchard: February 1879 to June 1885.
James P. Kimball: July 1885 to October 1889.
Edward O. Leech: October 1889 to May 1893.

Mint Superintendents and Terms

Each of the four mints active during the Liberty Seated coinage era was under the direction of an appointed superintendent, again usually a reward for good deeds to the party in control of Congress or to the president. Superintendents reported to the director of the Mint in Washington, D.C. The superintendent had charge of operations of the mint, including the processing of metal and planchets, coining to meet the requirements requested by the Treasury Department, and all other activities and departments.

The most important superintendency was at the Philadelphia Mint, where the engraving department was located and where dies for all mints were made. From 1792 to 1873, the director of the Mint was located there. After that office was moved to Washington, D.C., in 1873, superintendents were appointed for the Philadelphia Mint. The superintendent managed these important departments and corresponded much more frequently with the director than did those of the other mints. Each year he helped organize the Assay Commission to review the previous year's coinage of precious metals.

Philadelphia Mint, 1836–1891
James Pollock: 1873 to 1879.
Colonel A. Loudon Snowden: 1879 to 1885.
Daniel M. Fox: 1885 to 1889.
Colonel O.C. Bosbyshell: 1889 to 1894.

New Orleans Mint, 1838–1861, 1891
David Bradford: 1837 to 1839.
Joseph M. Kennedy: October 1839 to September 1850.
Robert M. McAlpine: September 1850 to May 1853.
Charles Bienvenu: May 1853 to December 1857.
Logan McKnight: January 1858 to May 1858.
John H. Alpuente (acting): May 8, 1858, to May 25, 1858.
Howard Millspaugh (acting): May 25, 1858, to July 9, 1858.
William A. Elmore[1]: July 9, 1859, to January 30, 1861.
Gabriel Montegut: June 24, 1885, to 1893.

San Francisco Mint, 1854–1891
Lewis Aiken Birdsall: June 30, 1853, to July 29, 1855.[2]
Peter Lott: June 30, 1855, to July 29, 1857.
Charles H. Hempstead: June 30, 1857, to June 29, 1861.
Robert Julius Stevens: June 30, 1861, to June 29, 1863.
Robert Bunker Swain: June 30, 1863, to July 31, 1869.

Oscar Hugh LaGrange: August 1, 1869, to December 31, 1877.
Henry Lee Dodge: January 1, 1878, to June 30, 1882.
Edward Freeman Burton: July 1, 1882, to July 31, 1885.
Israel Lawton: July 1, 1885, to July 31, 1889.
William Henry Dimond: August 1, 1888, to July 31, 1893.

CARSON CITY MINT, 1870–1878

There was no Liberty Seated coinage at this mint after 1878.
Abram Van Santwood Curry[3]**:** April 1869 to September 1870.
Henry F. Rice: September 1870 to June 1873.
Frank D. Hetrich: July 1873 to August 1874.
James Crawford: September 1874 to March 1884.

A VISIT TO THE MINT IN 1861

The following is from *Harper's New Monthly Magazine*, December 1861, and gives the reader a tour of the Philadelphia Mint in June 1861. The author, name not given, was a highly observant person who also had an eye for the interesting, was not without humor, and enjoyed giving an occasional piece of philosophy.

This narrative is the most interesting, most valuable I have encountered concerning the operations of the Philadelphia Mint during this era:

MAKING MONEY

Philadelphia Wary of New York City

A stranger in the Quaker City is naturally desirous of visiting the objects of particular interest, one of the greatest of which is the United States Mint. Philadelphians are rather proud of possessing the general Mint, and are a little anxious lest their rival, New York, should succeed in obtaining a branch, which would perform the great bulk of the work, as the United States Sub-Treasury in that city in reality is the nation's banking house. That there is some cause for this feeling, is manifest by the fact that, in 1859, there was received at the New York Assay Office bullion to the value of $8,859,103.93 more than was deposited at the Mint at Philadelphia. In 1860 the deposits were small, but New York had the advantage in nearly two and a quarter million; and it is safe to predict, from the receipts so far, that 1861 will lavish on New York fifty million more than it gives Philadelphia. Whether this is a sufficient cause for duplicating the expensive coining machinery, etc., it is not for us to discuss.[1]

Into the Mint

Leaving our hotel we walk up Chestnut Street, and between Thirteenth and Fourteenth streets come to a fine, substantial, two-story marble building, entirely fireproof, and enclosing within its quadrangular walls a spacious courtyard.

Ascending the massive marble steps, we enter an airy hall, freshened by a gentle breeze which sweeps through into the courtyard beyond. Between the hours of nine and twelve visitors are admitted, who are escorted about the building by gentlemanly conductors, of whom there are seven. Passing through the hall, on one side are the Weigh-Rooms for bullion and the office of the Chief Clerk of the

Treasurer, and on the other the offices of the Cashier and Treasurer. Glance into the latter, to see Mr. James H. Walton, Treasurer, as he is deep in the mysteries of columns of figures so long and broad that Jessie observes, "One must be a *great adder*[2] to run up those columns."

We cross the paved courtyard, spacious and orderly, with boxes piled neatly around, and stacks of copper and nickel ingots ready for rolling. The well-proportioned chimney, 130 feet high—somewhat bullet-marked by pistol practice of the night watchmen—towers above the surrounding roofs, which look low by contrast.

Ingots and Strips

Thus we are conducted into the melting, refining, and assaying rooms. We will linger for a moment only to see the melter run the gold and silver, now reduced to standard quality, into ingots. The standard of nine-tenths fine gold is now adopted by all the principal nations of the world, except England and Russia.

These ingots are bars sharpened at one end like a chisel blade, and are about a foot long, three-fourths to two and half inches broad, and half an inch thick, according to the coin to be cut from them. Continuing our walk through a short entry, we come to the Rolling Room.

Be careful of your dress, Jessie: that light silk had better been left at home, for this is a greasy place; and dirty grease has a magnetic attraction for finery.

Those massive machines are the rolling mills—four of them in a row, with their black heavy stanchions and polished steel rollers. The old man who runs this mill has been in the Mint nearly 40 years, and young girls who came to work are now grandmothers, perhaps, with the tally of their good works marked on their foreheads, a virtue in every wrinkle; and he has gone on rolling out the ingots year after

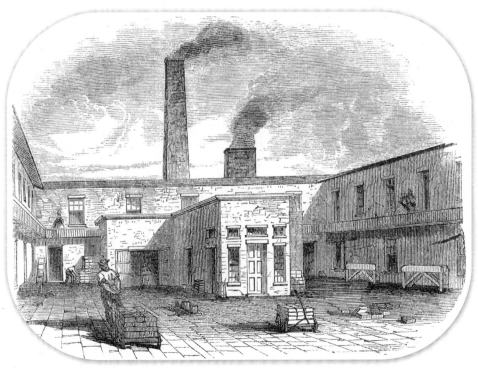

COURTYARD

year, handling more gold in a year than you or I shall see in our lives. He has not tired of showing his machine to visitors, and caresses the surly old iron with a motherly pride and affection.

He measures two ingots, and shows us they are of the same length; puts one of them between the rolls, just above the clock-dial, chisel end first, and it is drawn slowly through. He measures it with the other ingot, and we see it has grown about an inch longer and correspondingly thinner. This is the "breaking down," but it is not yet thin enough; it must be rolled ten times if gold, or eight if silver, to reduce it sufficiently, occasionally annealing it to prevent its breaking. No wonder the rollers look bright, they breakfast on silver and dine on gold.

That dial is not exactly a clock, though it looks like one. Do you see the little crank handle on it, above the hands? That is to regulate the space between the rollers. By turning it the distance is increased or reduced, and the hands of the dial are moved by the same means, to show the interval between them. For instance, when the hands indicate 12 o'clock the rollers are as far apart as they can be. By turning the crank until the hands are at, say, half past one o'clock, the distance is reduced about the sixteenth of an inch. It has been ascertained that when the hands point to, for instance, half past six, the rollers will be at the right distance from each other for rolling the strips thin enough for half eagles. So instead of saying, "Roll that strip the eighth of an inch thick," it is "Roll it to half past six." The rollers can be brought very close together. Give him that visiting card in your hand—there, it is pressed so hard that its texture is destroyed, and it crumbles like crisp pie crust.

ROLLING MILL

This dial arrangement, and some other improvements in the mill, are due to Mr. Franklin Peale, former chief coiner of the Mint, who devised it for the purpose of securing greater accuracy in measuring the distance between the rollers.

The pressure applied is so intense that half a day's rolling heats not only the strips and rollers, but even the huge iron stanchions, weighing several tons, so hot that you can hardly hold your hand on them. Every mill can be altered to roll to any degree of thinness, but usually the ingot passes through several mills, each reducing it slightly. This was quicker than altering the gauge so frequently. When the rolling is completed the strip is about six feet long, or six times as long as the ingot.

It is impossible to roll perfectly true. Now and then there will be a lump of hard gold, which will not be quite so much compressed as the rest. If the coin were cut from this place, it would be heavier and more valuable than one cut from a thinner portion of the strip. It is, therefore, necessary to "draw" the strips, they first being softened by annealing.

Just turn to your right and see those long round copper boxes, into which that clever, plump-looking man is putting the gold strips. He'll tell us all about it.

"Yes, mum; ye see we have to anneal this here gold, to make it soft so we can draw it. Therefore, we put it in these boxes, and puts in the cover and seals it up airtight with clay. It don't do to anneal gold in the open fire like as we can silver; for if we only get a hole in the box no larger than the head of a pin, it will let in the air and turn the color of the whole gold. They call it oxidizing. In that furnace we anneal the silver, but we don't put silver into boxes, 'cause we can heat that in the open fire without its turning. We put these boxes into this furnace—you can look in at the door while I lift it up. Those in there are red-hot, and we keep 'em in about an hour, mum, till all the gold gets red-hot too. It would twist about like a snake if we took out a strip while it was so hot. When it is well *het* we take the boxes out with the tongs, and put 'em into that tank of water to cool 'em, mum. There's from a thousand to twelve hundred dollars in every one of those strips, mum."

It's too hot to stay here long, so pick your way carefully among these boxes of gold, silver, and copper strips, and ingots, to the other end of the room. Be careful of that stand; it is terribly dirty. It is where they are greasing the silver strips and waxing the gold, to enable them to pass through the drawing bench easier. Wax is a better lubricator than grease for gold.

That long table, with the odd-looking, endless chain, running from right to left, making a deafening noise, is the drawing bench. In fact, there are two benches, one on each side of the table. At the right end you see an iron box secured to the table. In this are fastened two perpendicular steel cylinders, firmly supported in a bed, to prevent their bending or turning around, and presenting but a small portion of their circumference to the strip. These are exactly at the same distance apart that the thickness of the strip must be. One end of the strip is pinched somewhat thinner than the rest, to allow it to slip easily between the cylinders.

When through, this end is put between the jaws of a powerful pair of tongs, or pincers, fastened to a little carriage running on the table. One carriage you see has a flag fastened to it, and has drawn a strip nearly through. The carriage to the further bench is up close to the cylinders, ready to receive a strip, which is inserted edgewise. When the end is between the pincers, the operator touches a foot pedal which closes the pincers firmly on the strip, and pressing another pedal, forces down a strong hook at the left end of the carriage, which catches in a link of the moving chain. This draws the carriage away from the cylinders, and the strip being

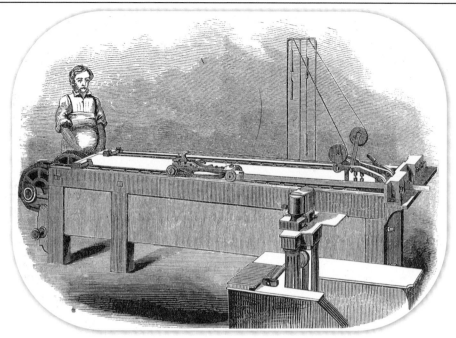

DRAWING BENCH

connected with it has to follow. It is drawn through the cylinders, which, operating on the thick part of the strip with greater power than upon the thin, reduces the whole to an equal thickness.

When the whole is through, the strain on the tongs instantly ceases, which allows a spring to open them and drop the strip. At the same time another spring raises the hook and disengages the carriage from the chain. A cord fastened to the carriage runs back over the wheel near the head of the table, and then up to a couple of combination weights on the wall beyond, which draw the carriage back to the starting-place, ready for another strip.

The original machine was invented by Mr. Barton, controller of the British Mint; but this table has been so far improved by Mr. Peale as to be almost his own creation. Barton's table required two men to operate it, while Peale's requires only one. The arrangement of the combination weights to draw back the carriage, fast at first and slower as it reaches the starting point; the application of the pedals to close the tongs and attach the carriage to the chain, are Mr. Peale's invention. His machine is arranged to run with much less noise than Barton's, and has other minor improvements.

Making Planchets

Just turn around and we shall see the next process the strip undergoes, after being washed free from grease or wax in warm water. Round pieces, called *planchets*, a little larger than the coins they are to make, are being cut from them. Four cutting presses of one kind are in a row; but more being required, Mr. Peale constructed two on about the same principle, but much more compact and handsome. They are not, however, quite so conveniently adjusted as the old ones; and as these show the mode of operating more plainly, we will examine them.

The press consists of a vertical steel punch, which works in a round hole or matrix, cut in a solid steel plate. The action of the punch is obtained by an eccentric wheel. For instance, in an ordinary carriage wheel the axis is in the centre, and the wheel revolves evenly around it. However, if the axis is placed, say four inches from the centre, then it would revolve with a kind of hobble. From this peculiar motion is its name derived. Suppose the tire of the wheel is arranged, not to revolve with, but to slip easily around the wheel, and a rod is fastened to one side of the tire which prevents its turning. Now as the wheel revolves and brings the *long side nearest the rod*, it will push forward the rod, and when the long side of the wheel is *away from the rod*, it draws the rod with it.

The upper shaft, on which are seen the three large wheels, has also fastened to it, over each press, an eccentric wheel. In the first press will be seen three upright rods running from near the table to the top. The middle one is connected with a tire around the eccentric wheel, and rises and falls with each revolution. The eccentric power is very popular among machinists, as it gives great rapidity of motion with but little jerking.

The operator places one end of the strip under the punch and cuts out a couple of planchets, which are a fraction larger than the coin to be struck. As the strips are of uniform thickness, if these two are of the right weight, all cut from the strip will be. They are therefore weighed accurately. If right, or a little too heavy, they are allowed to pass, as the extra weight can be filed off. If too light, the whole strip has to be remelted.

The strips that are correct are quickly cut up, the press striking 220 double eagle planchets, or 250 smaller pieces, in a minute. A man has cut over a million dollars in double eagles [planchets] in a single day.

As fast as cut the planchets fall into a box below, and the perforated strips are folded into convenient lengths to be remelted. From a strip valued at about eleven hundred dollars, eight hundred dollars of planchets will be cut. They are still in a very rough, ragged state, and look but little like coin. The second press, rather smaller than the rest, is the first introduced, and has been in constant use for about 40 years; has never been broken, or had 50 cents' worth of repairs done to it.

We will leave this room, and go into a much more cheerful one for a moment, to see the sorting of the planchets. They are thrown upon a table with

CUTTING PRESSES

two holes in it, and a woman picks out all the imperfect pieces or chips, which are slipped into one hole, and the perfect ones into the other, where they fall into different boxes.

It is not much to see; so come into the entry, up the marble stairs to the second story, past the director's room, out upon a gallery looking down upon the courtyard below. At the further end of the gallery we pass through a small entry, and enter a room. What a peculiar noise, like a young ladies' school at recess, only a strange filing sound withal! Nearly 60 females, some young and pretty, some middle-aged and fine-looking. Jessie will have to do the examination: we cannot stand the 120 eyes brought to a focus on us.

She tells us it is the Adjusting Room. Each operator has on the table before her a pair of assay scales. Seated close to the table, a leather apron, one end tacked to the table, is fastened under her arms to catch any gold that may fall. In short sleeves, to avoid sweeping away the dust, and armed with a fine flat file, she is at work, chatting and laughing merrily. She catches a double eagle planchet from a pile by her side and puts it into the scale. It is too heavy. She files around the edge, and weighs it. Still too heavy. Files it again, and weighs it. Almost right. Just touches it with the file. Right; the index is in the centre. She tosses it into the box, and picks up another to undergo the same operation.

The proper weight of the double eagle is 516 grains, and the smaller gold coins are in the same proportion. Absolute perfection is impossible in the weight of a coin, as in other matters, and the law therefore allows a variation of one half of a grain in the double eagles; therefore, between a heavy and a light piece, there may

ADJUSTING ROOM

be a difference of one grain. This is so slight, however, not two cents in value, as to be deemed sufficiently correct. The weight of the silver half dollar is 192 grains, and smaller pieces in proportion, with the exception of the cent, which, being composed of 88 per cent; copper and 12 per cent; nickel, the weight is 72 grains. The weight of the silver coin was reduced in April 1853. Prior to that date the half dollar was 206-1/4 grains.

To adjust a coin so accurately requires great delicacy and skill, as a too free use of the file would quickly make it too light. Yet by long practice, so accustomed do the operators become, that they work with apparently recklessness, scarcely glancing at planchet or scales, but seemingly guided by their touch. Our artist attempted to obtain a photograph of the room while they were at work, but it was found impossible for 55 out of the 60 to remain quiet long enough for the camera to operate. It was necessary to take the room after they had left, supplying the figures in the drawing.

The exceedingly delicate scales were made under the direction of Mr. Peale, who greatly improved on the old ones in use. So delicate are they that the slightest breath of air affects their accuracy, rendering it necessary to exclude every draft from the room, which, being poorly ventilated, in a hot day is an uncomfortable and probably an unhealthy place. Colonel Childs, the late chief coiner, exercised great care to counteract this difficulty by occasionally stopping work, and opening the windows. The whole process, however, is behind the times. Hand-work cannot compete with machinery. Sixty adjusters cannot keep the coining presses supplied, and genius must find a quicker way of performing the work. It is here that the delay occurs, keeping depositors waiting from 20 to 30 days for the coin they should receive in a week. It is astonishing that our Mint has not made the advancement here that it has in every other department.

Only the gold pieces are adjusted in this manner. The silver has merely the adjustment of the two planchets weighed at the cutting press. A greater allowance is made in the weight of the silver coin, as it is less valuable, and it would be almost impossible to have such a vast number of small pieces separately examined. Mr. Peale ordered from Paris a beautiful and delicate coin-separator, which he intended to apply to silver (although the one received is adapted to the half eagle only), but owing to its not arriving until he had been removed it has never been put into operation. It is so arranged that the planchets, being placed in at one end, are carried through the hopper and dropped singly on a balance. If too light it is tipped into a box at one side; if too heavy, into another box; if exactly right, into a third box. The instrument does not adjust the weight, but merely separates the heavy and light planchets. For silver, however, this would be desirable, as a more uniform weight could be preserved. Why it has never been put into use we are unable to learn.

The females in the adjusting room are paid $1.10 a day for 10 hours' work. They look happy and contented. Behind the screens, at each end of the room, are dining halls, where they eat the dinners they bring with them. On the whole, it is the pleasantest workshop for women we have yet seen, and the pay, in comparison with that ordinarily given to women, is good.

The Milling Machine

If you examine a double eagle, or lacking one, a quarter of a dollar, a slight rim will be noticed around the edge, raised a little higher than the device. It is done to prevent the device being worn by rubbing on counters, etc., and also that the coins may be piled one on another steadily. This edge is raised by a very beautiful piece of mechanism called a milling machine, the invention of Mr. Peale, and vastly superior to any other in use.

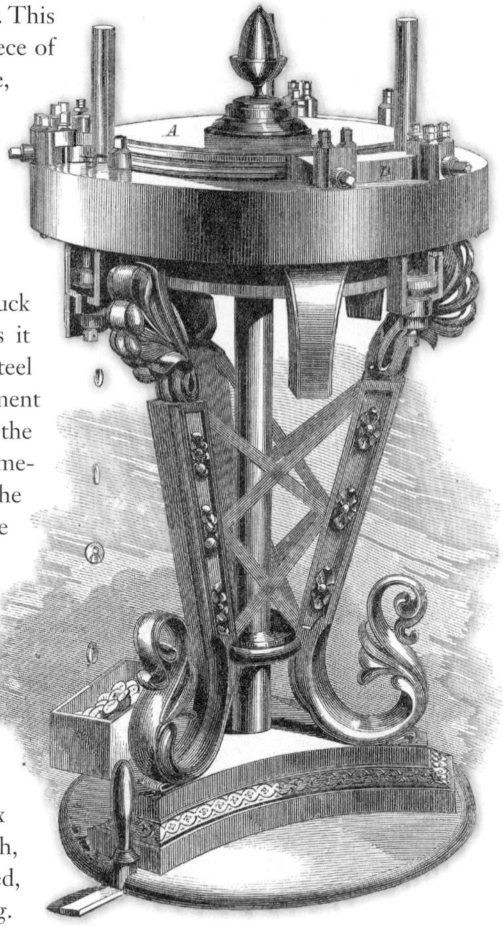

MILLING MACHINE

Some 20 or 30 planchets are placed in one of the brass vertical tubes, of which there are three, for different sized coins. At the bottom of the tube the lowest planchet is struck by a revolving feeder, which drives it horizontally between the revolving steel wheel on one side, and the fixed segment on the other. The segment is on the same curve as the wheel, though somewhat nearer to it at the further end. The planchet is caught in a narrow groove cut in the wheel and segment, and the space being somewhat less than the diameter of the planchet the edge is crowded up about the thirty-second part of an inch.

The planchet makes four revolutions when it reaches the end of the segment, and being released from the grooves falls into a box below. The edge is perfectly smooth, the fluting or "reeding," as it is termed, being put on in the process of coining. The work is so nimbly performed that about 120 double eagles, or 560 half dimes, can be milled in one minute. This is a vast improvement on the English milling machine, worked by hand, and operating on but two planchets at a time.

The planchets being milled are called blanks. They are very dirty and discolored by the processes they have undergone, requiring to be polished before coining. This is done in the Whitening Room, and an exceedingly hot place it is. Sometimes in summer the thermometer will indicate 120°, though the tall man by the furnace declares that it is often at 175°. The room is too small and poorly ventilated for the use to which it is put.

There are two furnaces for annealing the blanks, they being placed in a copper box, with a cover sealed on airtight with clay. Boxes and blanks are heated red-hot, and the blanks tipped into a vat containing a weak solution of sulphuric acid and water, to cleanse them. The stream of water in the other vat is hot, in which the blanks are washed free from the acid, leaving them a beautiful white color, almost like silver.

The curious copper machine, looking like a large revolving squirrel-cage, is the drying drum. Almost half of it is a tight copper drum, into which the blanks from the hot water are placed with a quantity of basswood sawdust. Steam is introduced through the axis to heat the interior, and the drum made to revolve, causing the blanks to roll among the heated sawdust and dry themselves. Basswood dust is used because of its freedom from sap, pitch, or gum of any kind. It is extremely pure. In the language of one of the men, "It ain't got nothing about it but just wood."

When the blankets are dry a door in the end of the drum is opened, allowing them to fall into the sieve, where they tumble about, the dust gradually sifting out, leaving the coin clean. To brighten them they are kept revolving for an hour, and the friction of one upon another gives them a beautiful lustre. It is in this way that pins, brass buttons, and the like are polished.

They are taken from the drying-drum, and heated in a large warming-pan, with steam pipes running under it, until Jessie would hardly hold a handful for the gift of them, though they are all double eagles. They are now ready for coinage, and that prettily painted truck is taking a couple hundred thousand dollars to the other room for the purpose.

How Dies Are Made

Before examining the coining we must visit the Die Room, to learn how the dies are made. A coin has an impression on both sides, requiring, of course, a die for each. These are to be made with extreme care, to be of the finest workmanship and all exactly alike. Their manufacture is one of the most important operations in the Mint.

Look at the bas-relief of Liberty on one side of a coin. It would be exceedingly difficult to design this in hard steel and of so small a size; so they first make the design in wax, probably six times as large as the coin, by which means the beautiful proportions can be obtained. From this a brass cast is taken, and reduced on steel to the size of the coin by a transfer or reducing lathe. This ingenious instrument was introduced from France by Mr. Peale, who also operated it for some time.

The brass cast is fastened to the large wheel at the right-hand side of the lathe. On the small wheel to the left of the cast is fastened a piece of soft steel, on which the design is to be engraved. Both of these wheels revolve in the same way and at the same speed. There is a long iron bar or lever fastened by a joint to an iron support at the extreme left, which runs in front of the two wheels. A spring at the upper end draws it in toward the wheels. Fastened to the lever is a pointed steel stub, which touches the cast.

A very sharp "graver" is fastened to the lever below, which touches the steel. The wheels revolve, and the stub, when it is pushed back by the heavy relief of the cast, forces back the lever, which draws back the graver, and prevents it cutting the steel. So where there is a raised place in the cast the graver is prevented from cutting into the steel, but where there is a depression in the cast the graver cuts the same in steel. As the lever is jointed at the left, the nearer the graver is placed to that end the less motion it will have so that the distance of the steel from the joint regulates the proportion of the reduction from the cast.

After the graver has cut one small shaving around the steel, a screw is turned, which lowers the right end of the lever slightly, just enough to allow the graver to cut another shaving, and the stub to touch the cast a very little further from the centre. Thus the graver cuts a very little at a time; but the work is cut over several times, until the design is sufficiently blocked out. This machine will not finish off the die perfect enough to use; but it reduces the design in perfect proportion; and performs most of the rough work. The original dies for coins being now all made, the lathe is used mostly for medals, of which a great many are struck, by order of Congress, for various purposes. A very fine one was presented to the Japanese while they were in this country. There is now in the machine a cast of Washington's bust, merely to show how the cast is placed.

TRANSFER LATHE

After the die comes from the lathe it is carefully finished off by hand, and when all polished is a beautiful piece of work. It is still very soft, requiring to be hardened before it can be used, which is done by heating it very hot, and holding it under a stream of water until cold. The relief is exactly like the coin—that is, the device is raised as in the coin. It will not do to use this in stamping, as it would reverse the appearance on the coin. Therefore this "hub," or "male die," as it is named, is used only to make other dies.

Round pieces of very soft steel, a little larger than the die, are smoothed off on the top, the centre being brought to a point a little higher than the sides. It is placed on a solid bed, under a very powerful screw-press, and the hub placed on top of it—the centre of the hub on the point of the steel, like a seal on the sealing-wax. The screw is turned with great force by several men, and presses the hub a little into the steel. It is necessary to have the steel higher in the centre, as if the centre impression is not taken first, it cannot be brought out sharp and distinct. The steel is softened again by being heated and allowed

DIES

to cool slowly, and the operation is repeated. This is done several times, until the whole impression is full and distinct.

If there is any little defect it is rectified with the engraver's tool. The surplus steel around the edge is cut off, and the date put in by hand, when it is hardened and ready for use. The date is not cut on the hub or on the first die—which is called "female"— as perhaps the hub will last for two years, and the date cannot be altered. This die is never used to stamp with, but preserved, so that if the hub breaks it can be used to make another. The dies for use are prepared in the same way. About 1,300 a year are made for the various branch mints, and those for the New Orleans Mint were sent on just before the state seceded, which the authorities have not yet had time to return. Sometimes a die will wear for a couple of days, and again they will break in stamping the first coin. Steel is treacherous, and no dependence can be placed in its strength. As nearly as can be ascertained their cost is $16 a pair.

The Coining Room

We will now enter the Coining Room, a light, airy hall, filled with brightly polished machinery, kept as clean as the milk-pans in a New England dairy. Jessie can handle it as freely as her fan without soiling her light gloves, or trail her dress over the floor without a misgiving. A passageway in the middle of the room is separated from the machines on both sides by a neat iron fence. The quantity of gold and silver lying about would make it unwise, especially in these times, to allow strangers to mingle among it. Visitors can see everything from this passageway, but the pleasure of handling is denied.

There are two styles of coining presses, both working on the same principle, but some more compact and handsome than the others. They are the invention of Mr. Peale, the plan being taken from the French press of Thonnelier's [as made by Uhlhorn]. Peale's press works much more perfectly and rapidly, and is a vast improvement over the old-fashioned screw-press still used in England. It seems to be as nearly perfect as anything can be. In the engraving [accompanying the *Harper's* article here reprinted] we have given one of the old presses, as it is more open and exhibits better the working power. There is so little difference, save in form, that, essentially, they are the same. There are eight presses, all turned by a beautiful steam engine at the further end of the room.

The power of the press is known as the "toggle," or, vulgarly, "knee" joint, moved by a lever worked by a crank. The arch is a solid piece of cast iron, weighing several tons, and

COINING PRESS

unites with its beauty great strength. The table is also of iron, brightly polished and very heavy. In the interior of the arch is a nearly round plate of brass, called a triangle. It is fastened to a lever above by two steel bands, termed stirrups, one of which can be seen to the right of the arch.

The stout arm above it, looking so dark in the picture, is also connected with the triangle by a ball-and-socket joint, and it is this arm which forces the end of the lever above by a joint somewhat like that of the knee. One end of the lever can be seen reaching behind the arch to a crank near the large fly-wheel. Now, when the triangle is *raised*, the arm and near end of the lever extend outward, as when one is resting his whole weight on one leg the other bends out at the knee. If the knee is drawn in and the leg straightened, the whole body will be slightly raised.

The press is on exactly the same principle. When the crank lifts the further end of the lever it draws in the knee and forces down the arm until it is perfectly straight. By that time the crank has revolved and is lowering the lever, which forces out the knee again and raises the arm. As the triangle is fastened to the arm it has to follow all its movements. Thus we have got the motion, which is all-important.

Under the triangle, buried in the lower part of the arch, is a steel cap, or technically, a "die stake." Into this is fastened the reverse die, or, according to boys' dialect, the "tail" die. The die stake is arranged to rise about the eighth of an inch, but when down it rests firmly on the solid foundation of the arch. Over the die stake is a steel collar or plate, in which is a hole just large enough to allow a blank to drop upon the die. In the triangle above the obverse die is fastened, which moves with the triangle; and when the knee is straightened the die fits into the collar and presses down upon the reverse die.

Just in front of the triangle will be seen an upright tube made of brass, and of the size to hold the blanks to be coined. The blanks are examined by the girl in attendance, and the perfect ones are placed in this tube. As they reach the bottom they are seized singly by a pair of steel feeders, in motion as similar to that of the finger and thumb as is possible in machinery, and carried over the collar and dropped upon the die. The knee is straightened, forcing the obverse die to enter the collar and press both sides of the blank at once. The sides of the collar are fluted, and the intense pressure expands the blank about the sixteenth of an inch, filling the collar and producing on the coin the fluted or reeded edge. It is put on to prevent any of the gold being filed away.

After the blank has been dropped upon the die, the feeders slide back on the little platform extending in front of the machine, in readiness to receive another. The knee is bent, which raises the die about half an inch above the collar. The die stake is raised at the same time, so as to lift the newly-born coin from the collar, and the feeders coming along with another blank, push the coin over into a sloping channel, whence it slides into a box underneath.

The pressure on the double eagle is about 75 tons; yet so rapid are all these complex motions that 80 double eagles are coined in a minute; and while the reader has been studying out this explanation probably ten or twelve thousand dollars [of value of $20 pieces] could be struck on a single press. The smaller pieces, such as dimes and half dimes, are coined at the rate of 150 a minute. While usually only 75 tons pressure are applied, the large presses will stand a strain of 150 tons. Sometimes government and other large medals are struck, which require this heavy power.

It is a beautiful sight, as the bright glistening coins drop in a golden stream, with the peculiar metallic clink so pleasant to hear. It is as pretty a cascade as one often sees. Jessie remarked to one of the men that it must be exceedingly tantalizing to be handling so much wealth, yet to have so little of it.

"Why, we don't think nothing of this—we just kick it about like so much old iron; but when we get our month's pay in our pockets we feel rich, I—tell—you!"

Production of the Mints

The number of pieces here coined is almost incredible. During the year 1860 there were coined 25,164,467 pieces, amounting in value to $22,781,325.50. Among these were 21,466,000 cents. During the first five months of 1861 there have been coined 12,248,037 pieces, in value $31,123,206. The gold demand has been entirely for double eagles, 1,461,506 having been coined. The present interruption of foreign importations has caused a great influx of gold, to be coined for home use.

Since the commencement of the Mint in 1793 there has not been as much value coined in any *year* (save in 1851), as during the first *five months* in 1861. The smallest coinage was that of 1815, when only 69,869 pieces were struck, in value $16,385.50. The greatest coinage in value, before 1861, was in 1851, when 24,985,716 pieces, including 147,672 half cents, and in value $49,258,058.43 were

COINING ROOM

struck. The largest number of *pieces* were coined in 1853, amounting to 69,770,961. The whole amount of coinage at the Philadelphia Mint, up to June 1860, is 671,904,388 pieces, of a value of $423,426,504.24. The coinage of the branch Mints will add $227,803,096 to this value. Very possibly much of this has been coined over two or three times, our specie having been sent to Europe and there melted and coined; then perhaps returned here in shape of sovereigns, to be reconverted into eagles.

There is a melancholy pleasure in seeing these large figures of unrealized, if not untold wealth; and it seems strange that, with such a vast amount in the world, it is so difficult to collect a few paltry thousands.

Counting and Bagging

After being stamped the coins are taken to the chief coiner's room, and placed on a long table—the double eagles in piles of ten each. It will be remembered that in the Adjusting Room a difference of one half a grain was made in the weight of some of the double eagles. The light and heavy ones are kept separate in coining, and, when delivered over to the treasurer, they are mixed together in such proportions as to give him full weight in every delivery. By law the deviation from the standard weight, in delivering to him, must not exceed three pennyweights in one thousand double eagles.

The gold coins—as small as quarter eagles being counted, and weighed to verify the count—are put up in bags of $5,000 each. The $3 pieces are put up in bags of $3,000, and $1 pieces in $1,000 bags. The silver pieces, and sometimes small gold, are counted on a very ingenious contrivance called a "counting-board," somewhat

DELIVERING COIN TO THE TREASURER

resembling a common wash-board. They are all subsequently weighed, however, to verify the correctness of the counting.

For the various duties of the Mint there are about 200 persons employed as clerks, workmen, etc.—say 140 and 60 women—the number depending, of course, upon the amount of work to be done.

A Tribute to Franklin Peale

We cannot conclude without a tribute to the skill and genius of Mr. Franklin Peale, brother to the late Rembrandt Peale. In 1833 he was appointed assistant assayer, and ordered to spend two years in examining the European mints, which he did, returning in 1835 laden with plans of improvements much needed in our then very imperfect Mint.

In 1836 he was appointed melter and refiner; and while performing those duties introduced the beautiful process, described in the last number of the [*Harper's*] magazine, of precipitating chloride of silver by means of common salt—a much quicker and cheaper process than the old one, requiring the use of copper. He is not the discoverer of this method, but the first to apply it to a practical use on a large scale.

In 1838 [*sic;* actually 1839] Mr. Peale was appointed chief coiner, and we have seen traces of his skill in the various machines employed. It is safe for the visitor to ascribe to his ingenuity—either in design, improvement, or construction—almost any machinery in the Mint which is finished, complete, or compact. In 1854 Mr. Peale was removed by the president.[3]

This removal was certainly unfortunate, as mainly to the efforts of Mr. Peale America is indebted for the finest mint in the world. An attaché of the Royal Mint, London, recently visited ours at Philadelphia. As he was leaving, he remarked to the coiner, "When you come to London, I beg you not to visit our mint. You are a hundred years in advance of us."

APPENDIX E

DIE MAKING IN 1855
Franklin Peale on Die Making

The following report is from the *Proceedings of the American Philosophical Society*, Philadelphia, January–April 1855, pp. 95–100, and contains a description by Franklin Peale on the subject of die making. Peale worked as chief coiner at the Mint from 1839 until he was discharged in 1854 for using Mint facilities for his private profit. More than any other individual at the Mint during his time, he devised many innovations in the fields of die making and coinage. Peale's 1855 report follows:

Mr. Peale made a communication on the subject of coinage, embracing a variety of facts and observations, particularly in relation to the processes of preparing and reproducing dies for monetary and medallic purposes; and, in connection therewith, exhibited electrotype and other copies of coins and medals.

He said, that the observations he was about to offer to the attention of the Society were selected from his notes, upon numismatic operations, and were the result of many years of experience, whilst an officer of the government, in the department to which they refer.

He further observed, that the enthusiasm which had always been an impelling principle whilst endeavoring to fulfill his duties, might have made him overvalue the matter, and that in now asking the attention of the Society, he was committing a similar error; in which case he could ask the indulgence due, and so often granted, under like circumstances.

It cannot be doubted, that the coinage of the country, of high rank in the scale of nations, should bear evidence on its face, in the first place, of the condition and progress both of the fine, and mechanic arts, within its borders; and to insure, in the second place, the greatest degree of security against fraudulent imitations, or counterfeiting, which desirable object can best be secured by the employment of the highest grade of artistic talent in the design of the device, and its execution throughout, to the finished coin as issued from the mint.

A brief notice of die-sinking, and the reproduction of dies for coinage, will be appropriate before proceeding further with the subject.

In the advance of the mechanic arts, in modern times, great facilities have been devised therein. The arts of medal engraving and die-sinking have largely participated; rapid and exact mechanical means now take the place of the laborious and imperfect ones which formerly embarrassed this important art. I will endeavor to exemplify them as briefly as possible.

The artist or designer models in a plastic material, such as wax or clay, a medallion portrait, or other device in relief, of sufficient size to permit freedom of handling, and facile study of effect; from this model a cast can be taken in plaster of Paris, or it may be electrotyped in copper. From the mold thus obtained, copies can be cast in hard metal, bronze, or iron, which may be further retouched or finished, at the will of the artist.

The model, prepared as above, is placed in the portrait lathe, of which we are indebted to the French. By means of mandrels, revolving in equal periods of time, upon one of which the model is placed, and on the other the material for the copy or reduction, in front of which mandrels a *bar* is made to traverse, carrying a *tracer*, which passes over the face of the model, touching, in succession, every part of the model in a spiral line from centre to circumference, or vice versa, a *tool* on the same bar, opposite the mandrel bearing the material, necessarily obeys the same motions, and is thus made to cut a facsimile of the model, the construction of the whole being such as to admit of any proportionate relation in size. By means of this lathe, rapid and exact reductions are made in steel, with an infinitely decreased amount of labor, and having the great advantage as far as coining purposes are concerned, of retaining faithful proportionate relations in the different denominations of pieces bearing the same device. The lettering of legends is usually put in at this stage of proceeding by hand, as well as minor and detached parts.

This, in general but concise terms, is the mode of operating, when a new device is to be executed for a medal or coin; but at this point an important distinction exists, and we must separate, by a very marked division, the two branches of the art, that of medal-striking and the coining of money. In the former, repeated blows upon a disc of metal, with intervening annealings, enable a device, of any degree of elevation, to be brought up, as it is technically termed, whilst in the latter we are restricted to a single blow, or action of the coining press, upon the prepared disc or 'blank,' and hence the necessity of much judicious care and skill in the device and engraving as shall give the strongest effect to the coin, with the least degree of elevation; a most desirable object, when it is known that each pair of dies is required to strike off pieces, numbering from 50 to 200 thousand, with as little injury to the face as possible, as any difference in appearance of coin from the wear of the dies is to be deprecated.

Remarks of importance, in relation to the character of the device, will be introduced in a subsequent part of this communication.

The foregoing relates principally to the execution of new devices, and it is hoped are sufficiently explicit to show the vast saving of labor derived from the process in comparison to the old plans of operating, in prosecuting which, the engraver was obliged to dig out the solid metal by slow and laborious means, taking impressions of parts as he progressed in plastic material, and consuming long periods of time, according to the elaboration, or magnitude of the device.

Equal, if not superior facilities, have been applied to the preparation of the dies for coinage of money; the process in its most improved condition, was learned in the mint of Paris, and introduced by myself into the Mint of the United States, about the year 1836. It is the transfer from an original die, by pressure on a softened steel punch or 'hub,' as it is technically called, a facsimile in relief, which *hub*, after hardening, is used to strike in soft steel properly prepared, the impressions which, after turning off the superfluous metal, hardening, and tempering, and other preparations, form the ordinary coining dies.

By the above described process, dies in indefinite and almost unlimited numbers, can be made complete, with the devices, legends and ornaments in perfect similitude, whilst, by the ancient process, they were separate operations, by hand, and, of course, no two could be made exactly alike, requiring skillful die-sinkers to approximate to such a condition, if at all possible, whereas the present process needs only the manipulation of skillful mechanics.

Where it not for the facilities, of which the above is a condensed notice, the four or five hundred pair of dies, now required for the service of the Mint of the United States and its branches could not be furnished without a very large and expensive engraving establishment.

When new devices are required, the best talent and highest grade of skill, within the command of the government, should be employed at any cost for its execution in the most perfect style. And, further, I do not hesitate to say, that if artistic talents and skill of sufficient eminence cannot be found in this country, to place our coin in the highest rank of the coin issues of the civilized world, we should look for and employ its aid wherever it can be found.

The above views are sustained by the usages of the mints of France and England. In the former the original dies or matrices are procured by competition (concurrence), judged and selected by commissioners appointed for the purpose; and, in the latter, since the late reform, by competent artist selected for the purpose.

Coining dies, it is evident to all acquainted with the subject, as above described, can be procured by the services of mechanics of good ordinary skill; and it is not necessary that they should be diesinkers by profession.

I will not, I hope, be deemed irrelevant to introduce a few remarks on the mechanical relations and exigencies by which the devices of coins are controlled, and which have a most important bearing on the style and execution of them.

It has already been said, and now repeated, that the coiner is limited by the nature of the service, to a single blow of the press in striking pieces of money; it is important, therefore, that the design of the device should be so disposed as to give the strongest effect with the least degree of elevation, not only for the purpose of giving the utmost degree of legibility to the impressions on the coins, and thus prepare them to retain their distinctness, during circulation, to the longest period of time, but also to save the dies as much as possible, under the severe usage to which they are subjected.

Force and strength of expression in a coin are best attained by a judicious outline in strong relief, whilst the general relief is kept as much subdued as possible. In fact, the center of the device should not rise above a plane of which the outline forms the boundary. On the contrary, if a device on coin rises in the middle it compels a reduction of the outline to faintness, producing a weak and unsatisfactory effect, is hard to strike, is soon obscured by abrasion, and entirely deprives the coiner of the opportunity of polishing the *table* or plain part of the dies, and back ground of the coin, the first being the usual technical term, a grave fault very often observed in what, if otherwise executed, would be works of high artistic excellence. The type of the species of relief alluded to, is found in the frieze of the Parthenon, where strong shadows from a bold outline, give the effect of depth by means well understood by the ancients, and of comparatively easy execution.

The obverse of a coin should bear the strongest device, being the most important side, the reverse must be subsidiary, its bearings should therefore be simple, such as broad letters, a shield, wreath or other ornament in low relief, so that the force of the impression may be concentrated on the obverse. By this disposition the best effect is given to the most important side of the coin.

The United States Mint labors under a disadvantage in this respect, the most of our pieces having devices on both sides, of equal depths, in consequence of which the force of the blow, and the necessary metal to supply the impression, is distributed between the two sides, thus making both weak, and losing the effect of a more judicious disposition.

After long experience, observation, and reflection on this subject, I am decidedly of opinion that the *obverse* of all coins should present the device of a *head or profile*, whether it be a 'composition emblematic of Liberty,' or a portrait. The likeness of our glorious Pater Patriæ, Washington, might justly be considered the embodiment of Republican liberty—or the classic head of high art, with the admitted exquisite beauty of the Greek school, are alike applicable. I do no desire to give a decided opinion relative to either, but I say the obverse should be thus engraved because, in the first place, the highest grade of artistic talent and excellence is required for its conception and execution, much more elevated than that required for the usual armorial or inanimate delineations; and, secondly, because its effect, when well and suitably executed for coining purposes, is better adapted to the mechanical exigencies which control the operation. The reverse should, as I believe, be plain and legibly lettered, with the denomination of the piece, in the middle of the field, surrounded by a wreath of rich composition, in low relief, with the usual legend around the border. The design of the wreath might contain the products of the North, West, and South, the wheat, corn, and cotton of our widespread domain.

The disadvantages of the full-length figure of our silver coins, or any other full-length figure, are these. The minute size of the head, hands, limbs and other portions, debars the artist from the ability to give the expression and finish that a high grade of art, under other circumstances, permits, and when executed, however well, interposes difficulty in transferring the impression to the coin.[1]

The various views, above presented, are sustained, and appear to have had their influence, by the best and most recent coinages of Europe.

I have only to fear that I have not brought them in relief (to use an appropriate figure), with the force to which, as I respectfully conceive, they are entitled.

APPENDIX F

MASTER DIES AND HUBS

The early U.S. Mint experimented with hubbed dies, but it was not until Benjamin Franklin Peale returned from his visit to European mints in the 1830s that the Philadelphia Mint used master dies for all coinage. Peale brought back drawings of machinery used in these mints and numerous advancements in technology ensued.

The Contamin portrait lathe in use by early 1837 allowed a metal *galvano* that was three to five times larger than the desired coin to be copied by a stylus rotating in concentric circles from the galvano's center to a steel face either in relief or *intaglio* (usually relief was desired). A series of reducing gears made the cutting tool follow exactly the same path as the stylus on the galvano, thus creating the design at the correct size on

Benjamin Franklin Peale.

the steel rod. The metal galvano was made by electrotyping a plaster (or wax) model.

Once the puncheon (or master hub) was cut, it was touched up by an engraver, hardened, and used to sink a master die. The large-screw press was used until the 1890s, when a hydraulic press was installed in the Mint for hubbing dies and producing medals. Around this time, Proofs were also produced by hydraulic presses—it is believed to be in 1894, as the quality of this format was inconsistent until 1893. From 1894 onward, it is likely all hubbing, medals, and Proofs were produced on hydraulic presses. By 1902, the Mint had two, 450-ton hydraulic presses, a quick-acting, 350-ton press for small medals and Proofs, and a 1,000-ton press for large medals—all powered by electricity.

Once the master die had the major design (head, seated figure, or eagle), the stars and lettering were added by hand-punching them into the die. The denticles were probably added last, but some have opined that they were added first. The smaller dies also had their "plain or false border" added to the master die. The "plain or false border" was the Mint terminology for the rim that was added to the larger dies using a lathe. Once complete, this master die was hardened and tempered.

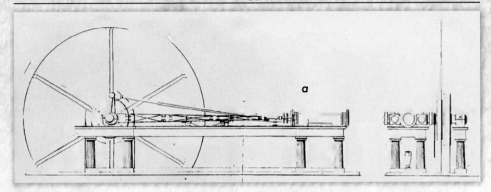

Peale's sketch of the steam engine he designed for the Philadelphia Mint.

From this master die (sans date and mintmark), a working hub was raised using the same large screw press. As noted, the smaller dies had their rims on the master dies, thus they too were transferred to the working hubs. The working hub (positive) was used to make dozens of working dies. It was only replaced after it was damaged or became too worn to produce satisfactory working dies.

Once a working die was produced from the working hub, again using the large-screw press, only the date (and mintmark when necessary) was needed to complete it. These dies were sent to the various branch mints in an unhardened state and without rims on the larger ones. This was to prevent their use if stolen during transit. Each branch mint would basin their dies, lathe rims when required, and then harden them for use. The dies generally were lapped again, as it was realized that the polished dies produced better looking coins. The same procedure was used in Philadelphia, but as each mint basined their own dies, the resulting coins had different looks for each mint.

John Dannreuther
Founder of PCGS

APPENDIX

G

ALTERNATIVE
U.S. CURRENCY

Postage Currency

The presence of Postage Currency arose from the chaos caused by the Civil War and is essentially an emergency currency. By 1862, the financial implications of the Civil War were being felt. The federal government was issuing huge amounts of paper to finance the war and was refusing to redeem any of it in coins. Major banks, therefore, had no choice but to go along with it or be wiped out of their holdings. In December 1861, the banks also suspended payments in coin. The immediate result was a massive hoarding of gold and silver coins in circulation; combine that with the fact that copper was needed for the war, and the result was a total lack of the small change necessary for day-to-day commerce. Merchants and banks, of course, still had business to do, and there soon arose an abundance of creative alternatives, including bartering, promissory notes, private bank notes, postage stamps, and more.

That was when General Francis Elias Spinner, appointed by Lincoln as U.S. treasurer, pasted a few stamps onto a piece of paper in his office, signed his name to it (thinking it would then be more counterfeit-proof), and liked what he saw. He proposed that Congress authorize the printing of small notes that looked like stamps. The president signed the Postage Currency Act on July 17, 1862. The first issue was properly called "Postage Currency" and made its appearance a few months later on August 21. It was issued in 5-, 10-, 25- and 50-cent denominations until May 27, 1863.

Later in 1863, Postage Currency dimes were struck in small numbers to study the feasibility of a special coin taking the place of Postage Currency bills. These coins were lighter than previous coins in order to avoid people hoarding these for their bullion value as well. Listed as patterns J-325 through 330a in the Judd book, the obverse has a small shield in the center with crossed arrows behind and a wreath around the perimeter. EXCHANGED FOR U.S. NOTES is at the border. The reverse is composed entirely of lettering with POSTAGE CURRENCY above, ACT JULY 1862 below, and 10 CENTS 1863 in the center. Research by David Cassel has revealed that an erroneously dated 1868 die was used to strike a handful of 1863 Postage Currency dimes, listed as J-643 through 646. The obverse of this variety is the same as the 1863-dated dimes, but the reverse has a cereal wreath enclosing a six-pointed star with ONE DIME / 1868 in the center (also used on J-641 and 642). Many different alloys and variations

⚫ 554 ⚫

were used, but ultimately the coins were too flimsy and the idea was thrown out in favor of four more issues of Postage Currency bills, now called "Fractional Currency."

The Civil War ended in 1865, another decade passed, and there again was sufficient coin in circulation that the emergency currency was no longer needed. On January 14, 1874, the Specie Resumption Act (repeated in the Act of April 17, 1876) allowed for coins in storage to be exchanged for Fractional Currency and provided for the currency's retirement by redemption into silver coin. By this time, the currency was popular and redemption was slow, so it took a supplemental act—that of July 22, 1876, authorizing the issue of $10 million in silver coin—and other provisions to encourage redemption.

| Shield and "Exchanged For U.S. Notes". 10¢: 1863 and dated 1868. | Regular-issue Barber Liberty Seated design, No Date. 10¢: 1863 and dated 1868. | "Postage Currency . . ." text. 10¢: 1863. | Regular-issue Wreath. 10¢: 1863. | Cereal Wreath enclosing Star, ONE DIME, Date. 10¢: dated 1868. |

Standard Silver

Patterns in the so-called Standard Silver series, inscribed on each coin STANDARD SILVER, do not relate to the standard or regular series half dime, dime, quarter dollar, half dollar, and silver dollar denominations then being made per earlier legislation, but to a new series specifically called Standard Silver. Beginning in 1869, the denominations produced were the dime, quarter dollar, and half dollar, and in 1870 other denominations were added.

The suite of Standard Silver patterns was generally a simple one, appealing then and now to a numismatist's sense of order. For each of the three denominations there were four different obverse dies in combination with a common reverse. In 1869 just one reverse die was made for each denomination, featuring a wreath encircling the value, with STANDARD SILVER 1869 around the border. Sets of nine pieces—three dimes, three quarter dollars, and three half dollars—were made in silver with plain and reeded edges, copper with plain and reeded edges, and aluminum with plain and reeded edges—six varieties per obverse die, 18 coins per denomination, 54 coins in all.

In 1870 certain new Standard Silver dies by Barber were introduced, these featuring his version of Liberty, seated, facing to the left. In this year, illogical combinations and rarities outdid those of 1869, and now Standard Silver issues extended downward to include the trime and half-dime denominations. Never mind that these had been rendered obsolete in circulation by the nickel three-cent piece and five-cent piece, and there was no thought of issuing new designs of these pieces for use in commerce. Some denominations were made with two reverse styles: date within the wreath and date below the wreath. At the Mint the proliferation of unnecessary Standard Silver dime, quarter, and half dollar lightweight patterns continued, to which were added numerous varieties of Standard Silver dollars, although no one at the Mint seriously contemplated a new coinage of lightweight silver dollars. Further, regular-issue dies were combined with Standard Silver dies—with the result that the Philadelphia Mint, the largest "coin dealer" in the United States, albeit unofficially, now had more than 250 different pattern varieties for its officers and insiders to sell.

Among dollar coins of 1870, the Indian Princess design, work of the late Longacre, was used to create several patterns with Standard Silver as well as regular die reverses (J-1008 and 1019), these bearing the full signature, LONGACRE, in the field. Pattern issues were again numerous in 1871, surpassing 100 pieces. Certain Standard Silver pieces were produced, seemingly as numismatic delicacies rather than in sets as earlier, but production of the series ceased by the end of the year.

Liberty Head with
3 Stars on Cap.
10¢ and 25¢:
1869 and 1870.

Liberty Head with
2 Stars on Cap,
Liberty Raised,
With B on Ribbon.
50¢: 1869 and 1870.

Liberty Head with
2 Stars on Cap,
Liberty Raised,
No B on Ribbon.
50¢: 1869 and 1870.

Liberty Head with
2 Stars on Cap,
Liberty Incuse,
No B on Ribbon,
Portrait Rotated
Right. 50¢: 1870.

Liberty Head with
2 Stars on Cap,
Liberty Incuse,
No B on Ribbon.
50¢: 1870.

Liberty Head with
Tiara Without Stars.
10¢, 25¢, and 50¢:
1869 and 1870.

Liberty Head with
Band and One Star.
10¢, 25¢, and 50¢:
1869 and 1870.

Regular-issue
Barber Liberty
Seated design.
Half Dime
and 10¢: 1870.

Barber's Liberty Seated
design With 13 Stars
Around and Date below.
25¢, 50¢, $1: 1870.

Longacre's Indian Princess
design without Stars
Around. Half Dime,
10¢, 25¢, 50¢, $1: 1871.

Longacre's Indian Princess
design with Stars Around,
13 Stars on Flag. Half Dime,
10¢, 25¢, 50¢, $1: 1871.

Longacre's Indian Princess
design with Stars
Around, 22 Stars on
Flag. $1: 1870 and 1871.

Oak and Laurel
Wreath, Date Below.
10¢: 1869 and 1870.

Oak and Laurel
Wreath, Date Below.
25¢: 1869 and 1870.

Oak and Laurel
Wreath, Stars
and Date Below.
50¢: 1869 and 1870.

Agricultural Wreath.
Half Dime:
1870 and 1871.

Agricultural Wreath
with Date. 10¢:
1870 and 1871.

Agricultural Wreath
with Date. 25¢:
1870 and 1871.

Agricultural Wreath
with Date. 50¢:
1870 and 1871.

Agricultural Wreath.
$1: 1870 and 1871.

Agricultural Wreath,
No Date. 10¢:
1870 and 1871.

Agricultural Wreath,
No Date. 25¢:
1870 and 1871.

Agricultural Wreath,
No Date. 50¢:
1870 and 1871.

Goloid Dollars

In addition to the Morgan and Barber suggestions for regular silver dollars, there was an illustrious pattern coinage of experimental dollars made of goloid, an alloy that had been patented by Dr. Wheeler W. Hubbell of Pennsylvania on May 22, 1877. This was a mixture containing 90 percent gold and silver, each of these metals being of equal proportions from the value standpoint, to which 10 percent copper was added to strengthen the alloy. These pieces became known as goloid dollars or goloid metric dollars. Two such coins would contain a total $1 worth of gold and $1 worth of silver.

These pieces were in response to legislation that was introduced into Congress in 1877 to provide for goloid metal as a basic alloy for legal tender coins, and stating that the pieces be struck on the metric system of weights and measures. The dollar was to contain 258 grains (or 16.718 grams), the half dollar 129 grains (8.359 grams), the quarter dollar 64.5 grains (4.179 grams), and the dime 25.8 grains (1.671 grams). The legislation stated that the weight and fineness of the metal and proportion of the gold and silver be stated as part of the inscription.

The Congressional Committee of Coinage, Weights, and Measures wrote to Mint Director Henry R. Linderman on December 29, 1877, to ask for examples of what the goloid dollars, half dollars, and quarter dollars would look like. The request included this:

> We want each dollar to contain 258 grains of the goloid metal, and the same proportions for the half and quarter dollars. That is, the half dollar to have in it 129 grains of goloid and the quarter 64-1/2 grains, etc.
>
> Let the coins, if you please, have stamped these words: on the dollar, GOLOID ONE DOLLAR. 1 G. 24S. .9 FINE. 258 GRAINS. On the half dollar, GOLOID HALF DOLLAR 1 G. 24S. .9 FINE. 129 GRS. On the quarter dollar, GOLOID QUARTER DOLLAR 1 G. 24S. .9 FINE. 64-1/2 GRS.

Accordingly, in early 1878, goloid metric dollars were made, and examples of the coins exist today (J-1557, 1560, 1563). Whether half dollars and quarter dollars were produced is not known, as none have been traced.

The basic fault of the goloid alloy proposal was one that had been discussed at the Mint many times earlier: There would be no way upon sight to determine the metallic content of such coins, the gold would not be visible, and the counterfeits could be made of silver and few would be the wiser.

The goloid proposal did not achieve much interest anywhere—not in Congress, the Mint, or in the general press. However, it did leave a legacy of several interesting pattern varieties of the 1878 year, J-1557 through 1564, and also set the stage for certain goloid issues of 1879 and 1880, the last mostly made as numismatic delicacies.

Barber's Liberty Head
with Broad Band,
1878–1880

Barber's Liberty Head
with Beaded Coronet,
1879 and 1880

Morgan's Liberty Head
with Hair in Bun,
1879 and 1880

Morgan's Liberty Head
with Coiled Hair,
1879 and 1880

Goloid Reverse with
Stars enclosing text,
denomination reads
ONE DOLLAR, 1878

Goloid Reverse with
Wreath enclosing text,
1878

Goloid Reverse with
Stars enclosing text,
denomination reads
100 CENTS, 1878

Goloid Reverse with
DEO EST GLORIA in
cartouche above,
1879 and 1880

Goloid Reverse with
DEO EST GLORIA
below circle of stars,
1879 and 1880

APPENDIX
H

DIE AND HUB TRIALS
AND SPLASHERS

This appendix, based on the work of Saul Teichman, includes pieces, mostly one-sided, struck from uncancelled Mint dies or hubs. Judd numbers have been assigned to these pieces.

A die trial is an impression from a working die with incuse features, resulting in a trial piece with the features raised or in relief, as on a regular coin.

A hub trial is an impression from a hub, with lettering and design raised in the hub, resulting in the features being incuse or recessed on the trial. Some hubs have but a single element, such as the head of Miss Liberty. Others include lettering and numerals. Prior to 1907 and 1908, hubs and master dies did not include dates. These were punched in separately using four-digit logotypes, a practice which began at the Mint in the very late 1830s and was used on all denominations by 1840. Thus, an obverse hub or master die trial with a date reflects two separate impressions on the trial piece: the hub or master die and, separately, the date logotype.

A master die trial is similar to a hub trial and is listed as a hub trial. A master die has features raised and, if made before about 1907 to 1908, includes all features of the working die except the date, which was punched in separately on the working die. Master die impressions are incuse or recessed on the trial.

A whimsy or practice piece is a metal blank on which various date punches or hubs were impressed, perhaps for practice, but are not related to any known pattern issue. Sometimes multiple different date punches were used.

Paper-backed splashers, not specifically identified as such in the descriptions, are impressions on very thin metal (often white metal or lead), backed with paper (plain or from a newspaper) to give a greater body to the metal and to permit a better die impression. Usually, only the layer adhering to the back of the metal remains.

While most trials were struck in metals such as copper, white metal, or lead, some are in other substances, including cardboard and red wax.

Teichman's studies in the field are ongoing as this specialty has not received the scrutiny accorded to regular (two-sided) patterns.

Struck in white metal, these two die trials show early developments in the Liberty Seated design. The example on the left (J-A1836-2) has Liberty's index finger extended on the pole; the right example (J-A1836-3) has the finger wrapped around the pole.

This practice piece struck in white metal (J-A1857-1) shows the reverse outer inscriptions (UNITED STATES OF AMERICA and the date 1857) for the half dime, quarter dollar, and half dollar, set in concentric circles.

Another white metal die trial (J-A1875-1) featuring reverse outer inscriptions, this time for a twenty-cent piece. Dated 1875, it bears the fanciful, if non-existent, country name of UNITED STATES OF NORTH AMERICA.

This fascinating die trial, struck in lead, preceded the Liberty Seated motif's use in two-sided pattern coins. Interesting features include the lack of LIBERTY on the ribbon, the lack of stars, and the date as part of the die (as dates at this time were not present on the final working die, but were struck as separate logotypes). (J-A1837-2)

In these two 1840 hub trials for a silver dollar (J-A1840-5) and a quarter dollar (J-1840-7), one can see the image in reverse and, as to be expected for a hub, no date. Both are struck in white metal.

This paper-backed splasher (J-A1858-5) made of white metal shows reverse lettering as seen on the pattern half dollar J-222, where it is paired with Paquet's Perched Eagle.

NOTES
Chapter 1

1. Sources for the 1835–1836 scenario are many and include Don Taxay, *United States Mint and Coinage* (1966), pp. 170–176; contributions to the *ANA Centennial Anthology* by Elvira Clain-Stefanelli; Dr. J. Hewitt Judd, *United States Patterns*; various publications by Walter H. Breen; the National Archives; R.W. Julian; and John Dannreuther.

2. The Christian Gobrecht papers are courtesy of the Historical Society of Pennsylvania, as examined by Leonard Augsburger (who supplied most of the Historical Society information given here).

3. *Ibid.*

4. Frank Stewart, *History of the First United States Mint*, p. 188.

5. Reminiscence in the letter from Director Patterson to Treasury Secretary Levi Woodbury, June 16, 1835; letter quoted by Walter Breen, *The Secret History of the Gobrecht Coinages 1836–1840* (1954).

6. The definitive reference is by Leonard Augsburger, "Sitting Liberty: The Christian Gobrecht Catalogue Raisonné," *Gobrecht Journal*, March 2008.

7. Christian Gobrecht papers, Historical Society of Pennsylvania.

8. Letter from H.L. Heyl, Actuary of the Franklin Institute to John W. Jordan, Library, Historical Society of Pennsylvania, February 10, 1902. Christian Gobrecht papers, Historical Society of Pennsylvania.

9. For historical details see Kenneth Bressett, "So why a seated Liberty," *Coins* magazine undated (copy sheet furnished by the author).

10. "From the Sketchbook of a Coin Engraver," *American Numismatic Association Centennial Anthology* (1991).

11. From an exchange item in the *Newark Daily Advertiser* on November 11, 1835; this notice was widely published.

12. For details see Craig Sholley, "Some Comments on Early Steam Press Coinage," *Gobrecht Journal*, November 1998.

13. However, an open-mouthed eagle with ruffled neck feathers was used later on certain pattern half dollars of 1838.

14. Peter lived at the Mint for six years. Elizabeth Bryant Johnson, *A Visit to the Cabinet of the United States Mint at Philadelphia* (1876), p. 19.

15. On behalf of the Mint, Franklin Peale had toured the European mints and had seen such a device in use. It was based on Hulot's *tour á portrait* machine of 1766.

16. Documentation from the National Archives furnished by John Dannreuther, communication, March 30, 2015.

17. The effacing was first noticed by John Dannreuther, the addition of feathers by Saul Teichman.

18. Concerning the orientation of stars (from Tom DeLorey): On the twenty-cent piece, half dollar, and dollar (except for 1838 and 1839 Gobrechts) the stars have one point toward the denticles. On the half dime, dime, quarter, and Gobrecht dollars of 1838 and 1839 there are two stars pointing toward the denticles.

19. For a detailed discussion of drapery on various coins see A.G. Heaton, "The

Drapery or 'Sleeve' of the Seated Liberty on United States Silver Coins," *The Numismatist*, October 1901. Robert Ball Hughes, an outside artist, invoiced the Mint for the modest sum of $75 on June 24, 1840, for a model of the figure of Liberty. As Gobrecht was very proud of his work, it is unlikely that Hughes made the major changes seen on the half dimes, dimes, and quarters of this year.

20. Comment in *The Nation*, quoted by the *American Journal of Numismatics*, 1879, p. 55.

21. Letters from the National Archives were provided by Kevin Flynn.

22. Roger W. Burdette, communication, May 11, 2015.

23. *Fractional Money*, p. 218.

24. Weir, p. 138.

25. *Ibid*, p. 151.

Chapter 2

1. The Gardner coins were sold by Heritage Auctions in a series of four sales in 2014 and 2015. Courtesy of Heritage, many Gardner coins are illustrated in the present text.

2. The first of the dollars was auctioned by Bowers and Merena Galleries in January 1992, lot 1283. Michael Hodder's article, "Andrew Jackson's Gobrecht Dollar," *The Numismatist*, January 2003, gives further details.

3. *American Journal of Numismatics*, April 1872. At this time the guest gift pieces were at the Hermitage in Nashville.

4. William Sumner Appleton of Salem, Massachusetts, formed one of the finest collections of United States coins.

5. No 1861-O dollars were coined, an error in the article.

26. Quoted commentary from the *American Journal of Numismatics*, March 1870, p. 87. The "old lady with the broomstick" was a whimsical description of the Liberty Seated half dollar, the "broomstick" being the liberty cap and pole.

27. Weir, p. 159. At the time London was the world's premiere market and price arbiter for gold and silver.

28. Roger W. Burdette, communication, May 11, 2015.

29. Lawrence N. Rogak, "The Circulation Life of Liberty Seated Coinage: Part II," *Gobrecht Journal*, November 1989.

30. *Report of the Director of the Mint*, 1905, p. 22.

31. *Fractional Money*, pp. 259–260, here slightly edited.

6. Provided by Dan Hamelberg from a priced catalog in his library. Modern comments are in brackets.

7. Purchased by John M. Clapp and years later in 1996 it was sold as lot 1195 in the Louis E. Eliasberg Collection sale, VF-30.

8. Clapp: in 1997 it was sold as lot 2048 in the Eliasberg Collection sale, MS-65 or finer. Eliasberg purchased the Clapp Collection *en bloc* in 1942.

9. Clapp: in 1997 it was sold as lot 2330 in the Eliasberg sale, AU-50.

10. Clapp: in 1996 it was sold as lot 1139 in the Eliasberg sale, AU-50.

11. Clapp: in 1997 it was sold as lot 1946 in the Eliasberg sale, MS-65.

12. Clapp: in 1997 it was sold as lot 1233 in the Eliasberg sale, MS-64/65.

13. Clapp: in 1996 it was sold as lot 1236 in the Eliasberg sale, MS-66.

14. Clapp: in 1996 it was sold as lot 1483 in the Eliasberg sale, there as MS-66 "probably the finest known."

15. Clapp: in 1997 it was sold as lot 2016 in the Eliasberg sale, AU-58.

16. David W. Lange, *Coin Collecting Albums A Complete History & Catalog: Volume One. The National Coin Album & Related Products of Beistle, Raymond, & Meghrig*, 2013, is the standard reference on these.

17. Originals, of which only circulation strikes were made, have the date high in the field.

18. Part of an extensive correspondence file furnished by Edwin B. Nash Jr., and was printed in the *Rare Coin Review*, no. 106.

19. This letter suggesting that about 200 to 210 Proof sets were struck in the year 1858 is the only *contemporary* record the author has ever encountered. (Years later the Chapman brothers stated that 80 were struck, a figure that was widely reproduced subsequently.) The 1858 silver Proof sets contained the silver three-cent piece, half dime, dime, quarter dollar, half dollar, and silver dollar.

20. Proof half cents of the 1840s, having been recently restruck at the Mint, were aplenty in Philadelphia numismatic circles. Local dealer William K. Idler

was likely one of the outlets, in addition to Mint officers and their young relatives.

21. Roger W. Burdette, communication, May 11, 2015.

22. John Dannreuther, National Archives research.

23. Again, much of this Proof coin information is from John Dannreuther, conversation of March 27, 2015, and subsequent correspondence.

24. On several occasions a $50 face-value bag of such coins sold for $10,000 to $12,000, creating a sensation in the news media.

25. These hobby groups are all still active and have presences on the Internet: the Token and Medal Society at www.tokenandmedal.org; the Society of Paper Money Collectors at www.spmc.org; the Early American Coppers at www.eacs.org; the John Reich Collectors Society at www.jrcs.org; and the Numismatic Bibliomania Society at www.coinbooks.org.

26. When the dies were first made their faces were lapped by a grinding process with a polishing compound and tool with a very slight convex face that imparted a slightly concave or *basined* surface and removed various marks and imperfections. Relapping was a repetition of the process to increase the quality of the surface of dies that had already been used.

Chapter 3

1. *Commercial Advertiser*, New York, NY.

2. The story of the Stickney exchange with the Mint was related by Henry Chapman in connection with the sale of the Stickney 1804 dollar in Chapman's June 1907 auction. Newman and

Bressett devote a chapter to the transaction.

3. *The Massachusetts First National Bank of Boston, 1784–1934*, by N.S.B. Gras, p. 118.

4. *Banker's Magazine*, January 1852.

5. Senate document dated May 23, 1856.

6. A copy of which was furnished to the author by Charles E. Davis for study.

7. Years earlier in 1837 Lewis Feuchtwanger had proposed a variant German silver alloy with nickel content. These are discussed in *A Guide Book of Hard Times Tokens*, Whitman Publishing, 2015.

8. Today the building houses the Nevada State Museum.

9. *American Journal of Numismatics*, July 1871, p. 24.

10. *Numisma*, Vol. 2, No. 3, May 1878

Chapter 4

1. For detailed information see *The Secret History of the First U.S. Mint*, by Joel J. Orosz and Leonard D. Augsburger.

2. From James Ross Snowden, *A Description of Ancient and Modern Coins in the Cabinet of the Mint of the United States*, 1860, p. 112: "In the present year (1860) a change has been effected in the types of the dime and half dime, the old laurel wreath being displaced by a wreath of *cereals.* . ."

3. John W. McCloskey, "A Study of Half Dime Reeding," *Gobrecht Journal*, March 1978.

4. See page zzz.

5. It has been popular in certain numismatic publications to say that unsold Proof coins were melted. In actuality, it is likely that most were placed into circulation to avoid wasting the time and expense to create them. (Per Roger W. Burdette, communication, May 11, 2015). In other instances unsold Proof coins of various denominations were kept on hand and sold to collectors in later years. (Per National Archives research by John Dannreuther.)

11. Sources were many and include information from John J. Ford Jr., John Dannreuther, and William T. Gibbs, "Dissolving the (half) union Documents in Ford Library auction open windows into government's pursuit of 1877 $50 patterns," *Coin World*, May 17, 2004.

12. Roger W. Burdette, communication, May 11, 2015. Quantities of American gold dollars had been bought by British jewelers since the mid-1870s.

13. Commentary concerning subsidiary silver is adapted from Neil Carothers's *Fractional Money*, p. 269.

6. The *Proof* term was not in use then. "Master coin" was occasionally used, but most often the finish was not revealed in Mint documents.

7. Citation furnished by Kevin Flynn.

8. Stephen A. Crain's study of these appears in *Gobrecht Journal*, July 2002.

9. Population reports may exaggerate the number known.

10. See Jack Marston's study of 1839-O half dimes in *Gobrecht Journal*, November 2011.

11. For a discussion of both letter sizes for this issue see William A. Harmon, "The 1840-O With Drapery Half Dimes," *Gobrecht Journal*, July 1989.

12. For related information see "The 1840-O With Drapery Half Dimes," by William A. Harmon, *Gobrecht Journal*, July 1989.

13. Population reports may exaggerate the number known.

14. Communication, May 7, 2015.

15. John McCloskey, "An 1843 Half Dime with Tripled Date," *Gobrecht Journal*, July 1996.

16. Stephen A. Crain, "The 1843 Shattered Reverse Half Dimes," *Gobrecht Journal*, Spring 2015.

17. Rich Uhrich, communication, May 7, 2015.

18. For additional reading see "Date Styles on 1846 Liberty Seated Coinage," by John W. McCloskey, *Gobrecht Journal*, March 1994. The author relates that across all denominations the dates for this year have peculiarities not found among other issues of the era.

19. Communication, May 13, 2015.

20. Stephen A. Crain, communication, May 7, 2015.

21. Kevin Flynn, communication, March 21, 2015, assisted with this study.

22. One was aligned coin-wise and the other medal-wise.

23. Stephen A. Crain, communication, May 7, 2015.

24. For an in-depth discussion of the varieties see William A. Harmon, "The 1848-O Half Dimes," *Gobrecht Journal*, March 1993.

25. Essay adapted from the author's text as editor of *United States Pattern Coins* (10th edition), by J. Hewitt Judd. Information about the two obverse dies being overdated is from Kenneth Bressett, communication, May 28, 2015.

26. V-8 attribution per Kevin Flynn, communication, May 28, 2015.

27. James Ross Snowden, *A Description of Ancient and Modern Coins in the Cabinet of the Mint of the United States*, 1860, p. 119.

28. Population reports may exaggerate the number known.

29. Stephen A. Crain, communication, May 7, 2015.

30. Population reports may exaggerate the number known.

31. Rich Uhrich and Stephen A. Crain, communications, May 7, 2015. First seen in the John J. Pittman Collection.

32. Stephen A. Crain, communication, May 7, 2015.

33. *The Authoritative Reference on Liberty Seated Half Dimes*, p. 158.

34. Stephen A. Crain, communication, May 7, 2015.

35. *Ibid.*

36. *Ibid.* This corrects certain information in the Blythe text.

37. Stephen A. Crain, communication, May 12, 2015.

38. Discovered by Jess Patrick in the summer of 1963, published by Q. David Bowers in *Coin World*, February 2, 1966.

39. Stephen A. Crain, communication, May 7, 2015.

40. Comment by Stephen Crain in an article by Dennis Fortier, "Overrated and Underrated Liberty Seated Coins, Part 2," *Gobrecht Journal*, Spring 2015.

41. Population reports may exaggerate the number known.

42. Rich Uhrich, communication, May 7, 2015.

43. Stephen A. Crain, communication, May 12, 2015.

44. The information regarding 1867 half dimes differs dramatically from what was stated by Walter Breen in 1988 and in certain later sources. Larry Briggs (communication, May 25, 2015) conferred at length with Stephen A. Crain and Brian Greer to confirm his own opinion that one die was used for Proofs only and another only for circulation strikes.

45. Population reports may exaggerate the number known.

46. *Gobrecht Journal*, November 1995. Discovered by Stephen A. Crain.

47. Population reports may exaggerate the number known.

48. Kevin Flynn, *The Authoritative Reference on Liberty Seated Half Dimes*, pp. 162, 163, 172, 173; the cornerstone information is from Nancy Oliver and Richard Kelly.

49. Q. David Bowers, "The Fabulous 1870-S Half Dime," *Gobrecht Journal*, November 1985.

50. Discussion, March 27, 2015, on many facets of Proof coins. In another context, in the 1870s the Mint had on hand gold Proof sets dating back to the early 1860s and sold them to numismatists.

51. Discovered by Dr. Glenn Peterson and published in *Gobrecht Journal*, Issue 63.

52. Stephen A. Crain, communication, May 12, 2015.

53. *Ibid.*

54. *Ibid.*

55. *Ibid.*

56. Larry Briggs, commentary, May 19, 2015.

Chapter 5

1. John W. McCloskey, "Reeding in Authentication," *Gobrecht Journal*, August 1975.

2. The last was reported on February 20, 2014, to Gerry Fortin's website.

3. May 18, 2015.

4. Gerry Fortin supplied much information about the characteristics of striking on various Liberty Seated dimes.

5. Gerry Fortin, communication, April 14, 2015.

6. Anecdote from Kenneth Bressett, May 19, 2015: "I may have paid the highest price ever for a circulated 1838-O dime. In 1939 I traded a couple of my well-used copies of *Action Comics* for the coin, from a fellow schoolmate. I don't really know if one was the No. 1 (Superman) issue, but I still wonder about it. At the time I was just happy to get my 10 cents cost back for one of the used magazines, and to add something unusual to my budding coin collection. I have no idea where the kid got the coin."

7. The ceremony was held in the early evening and was brief, after which orations were given. The theater closed on January 14, 1843, for lack of patronage. It had been operating at a loss for some time.

8. John McCloskey, "An 1838 Large Stars Proof Dime" *Gobrecht Journal*, Summer 2000.

9. Larry Briggs, communication, May 19, 2015. "I have had 3 or 4 over the years, and Brian Greer has had more than that."

10. Population reports may exaggerate the number known.

11. Larry Briggs, communication, May 19, 2015.

12. Given verbatim below; communication, May 27, 2015.

13. Larry Briggs reported the second in 2011; discussed in the February 2011 *E-Gobrecht*.

14. Population reports may exaggerate the number known.

15. Gerry Fortin, communication, May 11, 2015.

16. Population reports may exaggerate the number known.

17. Larry Briggs, communication, May 19, 2015.

18. Correspondence, April 14, 2015.

19. Population reports may exaggerate the number known.

20. Population reports may exaggerate the number known.

21. Population reports may exaggerate the number known.

22. Larry Briggs, communication, May 19, 2015.

23. Population reports may exaggerate the number known.

24. Joey Lamonte, "A Comprehensive Study of Proof 1856 Small Date Dimes," *Gobrecht Journal*, November 1996. John W. McCloskey, "An 1856 Half Dime with Missing Denticles," *Gobrecht Journal*, March 2005.

25. Larry Briggs, communication, May 19, 2015.

26. Population reports may exaggerate the number known.

27. For an in-depth study see John W. McCloskey, "The 1859-S Seated Dime," *Gobrecht Journal*, March 2007. Fortin-201.

28. Larry Briggs, communication, May 19, 2015.

29. *Ibid.*

30. Rich Uhrich, communication, May 7, 2015.

31. Correspondence, April 14, 2015.

32. For information on this issue in general see "The 1865-S Dime," by John W. McCloskey, *Gobrecht Journal*, July 1989.

33. Larry Briggs, communication, May 19, 2015.

34. Correspondence, April 14, 2015.

35. Population reports may exaggerate the number known.

36. For more information see Jason Carter, "A Study of 1866-S Dimes," *Gobrecht Journal*, March 1995.

37. For additional reading see "The Rare 1867 Dimes," by John W. McCloskey, *Gobrecht Journal*, November 1976.

38. Population reports may exaggerate the number known.

39. Population reports may exaggerate the number known.

40. These are left over from an incompletely machined die face (cf. Craig Sholley, communication, May 26, 2015). This information was used on several other listings here.

41. Population reports may exaggerate the number known.

42. Correspondence, April 14, 2015.

43. Larry Briggs, communication, May 19, 2015.

44. Population reports may exaggerate the number known.

45. Larry Briggs, communication, May 19, 2015.

46. Communication, May 13, 2015.

47. Larry Briggs, communication, May 19, 2015.

48. *Ibid.*

49. Larry Briggs, communication, May 31, 2015.

50. For related information see "The 1873-S Dime," by John W. McCloskey, *Gobrecht Journal*, November 1985.

51. Gerry Fortin, communication, April 14, 2015.

52. Alex Fey and Gerry Fortin, "Missing Arrows on Some 1874 Dimes, a Fascinating Mystery," *Gobrecht Journal*, March 2011.

53. For a detailed study see "The Exceptionally Rare 1874-CC Dime," by John W. McCloskey, *Gobrecht Journal*, November 1980. In the same year Walter Breen called it "extremely rare; possibly six to eight known," a typical lightly researched comment.

54. For related information see "The 1874-S Dime," by John W. McCloskey, *Gobrecht Journal*, July 1986.

55. Population reports may exaggerate the number known.

56. Gerry Fortin, communication, May 11, 2015.

57. Weimar W. White, "Carson City Presentation Pieces," *Gobrecht Journal*, March 1996; and by the same author, "An 1876-CC Dime in Proof-65 Condition Sold at Auction," *Gobrecht Journal*, November 2001. Also, Andy Lustig, communication, May 27, 2015: "With respect to the 'Proof' 1876-CC dimes, most are from striated dies and have at least partial wire rims. I might discount these as ordinary first strikes except for the existence of copper and nickel off-metal strikes, which indicate that something unusual was going on at the CC Mint. There is, however, at least one silver Proof that is not striated, and is as convincing as any Philadelphia Proof."

58. For details see Weimar W. White, "The Chemical Causes of Pitted Dies at the Carson City Mint," *Gobrecht Journal*, March 1995.

59. Larry Briggs, communication, May 31, 2015.

60. Also see "New Dime Overdate Discovered 1877/6-CC," by Gerry Fortin, *E-Gobrecht*, April 2012.

61. For an in-depth study see Gerry Fortin's, "1877-S Seated Dime Varieties," *Gobrecht Journal*, March 1993.

62. Larry Briggs, communication, May 19, 2015.

63. G.W.M. was George Massamore, a Baltimore dentist and rare coin dealer who issued auction catalogs.

64. Correspondence, April 13, 2015.

65. Population reports may exaggerate the number known.

66. Population reports may exaggerate the number known.

67. Larry Briggs, communication, May 19, 2015.

68. Larry Briggs, communication, May 31, 2015.

69. For additional reading see "The 1888-S Dime," by Bill Cregan, *Gobrecht Journal*, July 1992.

70. Population reports may exaggerate the number known.

71. For related information see "The 1890-S Seated Dime," by Bill Cregan, *Gobrecht Journal*, July 1981. The author states that this is "much scarcer than commonly assumed," and that it is "vastly underrated in AU to Uncirculated condition."

Chapter 6

1. The Coinage Act of February 21, 1857, ended the legal-tender status of certain Spanish-American and other foreign silver and gold coins, effective two years later, then extended for a further six months.

2. An example has been certified by the Numismatic Guaranty Corporation of America (NGC) but is no longer listed in reports (cf. Saul Teichman and for NGC, David W. Lange).

3. This was the collection of H.S. Jewett, M.D., of Dayton, Ohio, although his name did not appear on the catalog.

4. Consolidated Virginia was a leading mining and milling company in Virginia City, Nevada, organized in 1871 when William McKay, James Graham Fair, James Clair Flood, and William S. O'Brien consolidated various claims and operations in the area. In 1873 the firm discovered the "big bonanza" lode, which created excitement worldwide.

5. John Frost, communication, May 11, 2015.

6. R.W. Julian, "Mint Supported Creation of 20-Cent Piece," *Numismatic News*, March 2, 2004.

7. Larry Briggs, communication, May 19, 2015.

8. *Ibid.*

9. Larry Briggs, communication, May 31, 2015.

10. *Weekly Nevada State Journal*, Reno, April 6, 1876.

11. Cf. Monfort A. Johnsen, *The Gobrecht Journal*, November 1980. Kevin Flynn, *The Authoritative Reference on Liberty Seated Twenty Cents* has particularly extensive coverage of the 1876-CC.

Chapter 7

1. Citation furnished by Kevin Flynn.

2. John W. McCloskey, "A Study of Seated Quarter Reeding," *Gobrecht Journal*, November 1977.

3. Greg Johnson, communication, May 10, 2015; Larry Briggs, communication, May 19, 2015.

4. Details in Bowers, *American Coin Hoards and Treasures*, 1987, and in *Lost and Found Coin Treasures*, 2015.

5. Larry Briggs, communication, May 19, 2015.

6. Greg Johnson, communication, May 10, 2015.

7. Larry Briggs, communication, May 19, 2015.

8. Population reports may exaggerate the number known.

9. Population reports may exaggerate the number known.

10. Larry Briggs, communication, May 19, 2015.

11. Modern comment by Mark Borckardt, June 2, 2015. Also see P. Scott Rubin, "Three Rare Quarters," *Gobrecht Journal*, April 1975; Eliasberg sale catalog, 1997, lot 1428 for registry.

12. Population reports may exaggerate the number known.

13. Larry Briggs, communication, May 19, 2015. He reports having handled 40 to 50 pieces or more over the years.

14. *Ibid.*

15. Population reports may exaggerate the number known.

16. Communication, June 2, 2015.

17. Rich Uhrich, communication, May 7. 2015.

18. Population reports may exaggerate the number known.

19. John W. McCloskey, "An Analysis of the Seated Quarter Data," *Gobrecht Journal*, July 2008.

20. Larry Briggs, communication, May 19, 2015.

21. John W. McCloskey, "The 1847-O Quarter," *Gobrecht Journal*, November 1981.

22. Greg Johnson, communication, May 10, 2015.

23. Population reports may exaggerate the number known.

24. Communication, May 19, 2015.

25. Also see John W. McCloskey, "The 1849-O Quarter," in *Gobrecht Journal*, March 1980. The writer notes that the issue is a key date and is very seldom offered for sale either at auction or in coin shows.

26. Population reports may exaggerate the number known.

27. Population reports may exaggerate the number known.

28. Population reports may exaggerate the number known.

29. Communication, May 10, 2015.

30. Larry Briggs, communication, May 19, 2015.

31. Greg Johnson, communication, May 10, 2015.

32. Larry Briggs, communication, May 19, 2015.

33. *Ibid.*

34. *Ibid.*

35. From Tom DeLorey, communication, May 14, 2015: "I have a theory that the mint may have backdated an 1854 die in order to pair it with a now-obsolete Without Rays reverse die that would otherwise have to be discarded. This may have happened in early 1853, if indeed it happened."

36. In "Finding the Elusive O Mint Quarters 1840–1891," *Gobrecht Journal*, March 1984, Brian Keefe stated that only two to five specimens were known in the AU to Mint State range of these four quarter varieties: 1840-O, With Drapery; 1852-O; 1853-O, With Arrows and Rays; and 1856-O. Bill Cregan, writing in *Gobrecht Journal*, November 1987, discussed "The 1853-O Quarter," revealing that he only knew of three Uncirculated specimens. He further noted that the 1853-O in worn grades is generally found in condition notably less than those of surrounding issues. The writer concluded with this interesting comment, "I can't explain the reason for its scarcity, but this uncooperative sleeping date is prized by all Seated quarter specialists." In the intervening years since the 1980s more have been studied and classified.

37. John W. McCloskey, "An 1853-O Arrows Quarter with Circular Die Defects," *Gobrecht Journal*, November 1982; the nature of lathe marks was not known at the time. Since then they have been seen on other coins in various denominations.

38. Larry Briggs, communication, May 19, 2015.

39. Communication, May 31, 2015.

40. Population reports may exaggerate the number known.

41. Larry Briggs, communication, May 19, 2015.

42. *Ibid.*

43. *Ibid.*

44. John W. McCloskey, "A Rarity Study for Early San Francisco Quarters 1855-S to 1862-S," *Gobrecht Journal*, July 2014.

45. John McCloskey in "A Rarity Study for Early San Francisco Quarters 1855-S to 1862-S," *Gobrecht Journal*, July 2014, did a survey of these quarters that appeared in the Heritage Auction Archives up to December 2013, not including any damaged pieces.

46. This is an interesting comment from a grading perspective—seemingly flawless from the standpoint of marks but downgraded because of a spot.

47. Larry Briggs, communication, May 19, 2015.

48. Population reports may exaggerate the number known.

49. Larry Briggs, communication, May 19, 2015.

50. Of interest may be the article by James C. Gray, "The 1860-S Quarter, the Most Underrated Seated Coin," in *Gobrecht Journal*, November 1990, and John W. McCloskey, "A Rarity Study for Early San Francisco Quarters 1855-S to 1862-S," *Gobrecht Journal*, July 2014.

51. Larry Briggs, communication, May 19, 2015.

52. *Ibid.*

53. Population reports may exaggerate the number known.

54. For an overview of the situation see Paul Gilkes, "Smithsonian Donation: Receives DuPont Seated Liberty No Motto Coins," *Coin World*, March 9, 2015.

55. Communication, May 19, 2015.

56. Larry Briggs, communication, May 19, 2015.

57. Population reports may exaggerate the number known.

58. Population reports may exaggerate the number known.

59. Larry Briggs, communication, May 19, 2015.

60. Sold by Heritage Auctions in August 2001 for $276,000, resold by HA in August 2013 for $176,250.

61. Larry Briggs, communication, May 19, 2015.

62. For further reading: Larry Briggs in *Gobrecht Journal*, November 1983, "Die Characteristics of the 1870-CC Quarter," which illustrated die finish lines and gave other technical information. Also see "The Underpriced 1870-CC Quarter," by Bob Foster, in the March 1983 number of the same periodical. He notes that this is "one of the most underrated and underpriced coins in the Liberty Seated quarter series."

63. Nancy Oliver and Richard Kelly, "The Missing San Francisco Mint Cornerstone," *Gobrecht Journal*, July 2000; also, communication, May 26, 2015, enclosed copy of the certificate illustrated.

64. Larry Briggs, communication, May 19, 2015.

65. *Ibid.*

66. If you are interested in technical aspects of this series you would do well to examine the motto IN GOD WE TRUST on various issues of this era, to determine common use of reverse dies. More than any other area there are numerous die finish lines, strengthenings and repunchings, etc. Also, the depth at which the motto and ribbon are impressed into the die varies with some dies showing parts of the ribbon missing, particularly in the distant fold near the left side. Die studies in *Gobrecht Journal* are very helpful.

67. Population reports may exaggerate the number known.

68. Larry Briggs, communication, May 31, 2015.

69. Larry Briggs, communication, May 19, 2015.

70. Population reports may exaggerate the number known.

71. Larry Briggs, communication, May 19, 2015.

72. *Ibid.*

73. Larry Briggs, communication, May 12, 2015.

74. Larry Briggs, communication, May 31, 2015.

75. Population reports may exaggerate the number known.

76. Larry Briggs, communication, May 19, 2015.

77. *Ibid.*

78. Larry Briggs, communication, May 12, 2015.

79. Larry Briggs, communication, May 19, 2015.

80. Population reports may exaggerate the number known.

81. Communication, May 31, 2015.

82. Larry Briggs, communication, May 19, 2015.

83. Larry Briggs, communication, May 31, 2015.

84. *Ibid.*

85. Population reports may exaggerate the number known.

86. For an in-depth study see Bill Cregan, "The 1888-S Quarter," *Gobrecht Journal*, July 1982; and in the same journal, July 1984, "Dispute on the 1888-S Quarter," by Larry Briggs.

87. Larry Briggs, communication, May 31, 2015.

88. Larry Briggs, communication, May 19, 2015.

89. Greg Johnson, communication, May 10, 2015.

90. Andy Lustig, communication, May 27, 2015.

Chapter 8

1. Citation furnished by Kevin Flynn.

2. Bill Bugert, communication, May 7, 2015.

3. Ellen Gerth, curator and historian at Odyssey Marine Exploration, Inc., furnished the inventory, illustrations and helped in other ways. For an expanded narrative of the ship and recovered treasure see Q. David Bowers, *Lost and Found Coin Hoards and Treasures*, 2015.

4. These are included in the current NGC population reports.

5. Randall E. Wiley, "1866 Philadelphia Half Dollars *With Motto* from Two Master Tail Dies," *Gobrecht Journal*, March 2008.

6. Manuscript in the editor's library. This is a significant entry, for it seems to suggest that in 1849 this die was being used to make restrikes, possibly for a numismatist on request (the Mint was very accommodating in that era), and it broke.

7. Andrew W. Pollock III, *United States Patterns and Related Issues*, 1994, p. 36.

8. A second example attributed to the Mickley Collection has been discredited (cf. Saul Teichman).

9. Cf. Saul Teichman.

10. A variety earlier listed as J-100a is a regular issue (cf. Saul Teichman).

11. Population reports may exaggerate the number known.

12. Larry Briggs, communication, May 31, 2015.

13. Communication, May 16, 2015.

14. Population reports may exaggerate the number known.

15. Citation furnished by Kevin Flynn.

16. For details see "The 1840 (O) Half Dollar," a study created by Bill Bugert and included in the Louis E. Eliasberg Collection catalog, 1997.

17. Rich Uhrich, communication, May 9, 2015.

18. The writer stated that in 16 years of study he had seen only three true Mint State coins.

19. Population reports may exaggerate the number known.

20. Population reports may exaggerate the number known.

21. Rich Uhrich, communication, May 16, 2015.

22. "Brian Greer, LSCC Hall of Fame Inductee, Class of 2012," Gobrecht Journal, July 2013.

23. Changed from 1 with the Gardner upgrade; hard to keep track of these things.

24. Bill Bugert, communication, May 7, 2015.

25. Population reports may exaggerate the number known.

26. Population reports may exaggerate the number known.

27. Population reports may exaggerate the number known.

28. Population reports may exaggerate the number known.

29. John W. McCloskey, "The 1846 Half Dollar," in Gobrecht Journal, November 1977, describes in detail and illustrates the "Tall Date" and "Small Date" varieties seen.

30. Bill Bugert, communication, May 7, 2015.

31. Rich Uhrich, communication, May 9, 2015.

32. "A Market Analysis for Mint State Pre-1853 Philadelphia Seated Half Dollars," Gobrecht Journal, November 2008.

33. Population reports may exaggerate the number known.

34. Population reports may exaggerate the number known.

35. Population reports may exaggerate the number known.

36. Population reports may exaggerate the number known.

37. Population reports may exaggerate the number known.

38. E-Gobrecht, July 2012 and September 2012, the "Howell coin."

39. Rich Uhrich, communication, May 9, 2015.

40. This rarity has furnished the subject for several articles in Gobrecht Journal. These include: P. Scott Rubin, "Three Rare Half Dollars," November 1976; Roy D. Ash, "Reflections on the 1853-O No Arrows Half Dollar," November 1982; David J. Davis, "Further Reflections on the 1853-O Half Dollar," March 1983; Roy D. Ash, "Further, Further Reflections on the 1853-O No Arrows Half Dollar," March 1983.

41. For discussion see Bill Bugert, "Seated Half Dollar Drapery Die States," *Gobrecht Journal*, March 1982.

42. Bill Bugert, communication, May 7, 2015.

43. Communication, May 11, 2015.

44. Population reports may exaggerate the number known.

45. Population reports may exaggerate the number known.

46. Discussed and illustrated in the *eSylum* issue of January 4, 2015.

47. For additional reading on mintmark sizes, David A. Brase, Ph.D., "Some Varieties of San Francisco Mint Marks on Liberty Seated Halves," in *Gobrecht Journal*, March 1977, is recommended. In the same vein, Randall E. Wiley's exposition, "Mint Mark Varieties of San Francisco Half Dollars (1855–1878)," in the July 1979 number, is worth reviewing as is the same writer's article on mintmark sizes presented in the 1987 Coinage of the Americas Conference publication. Both of these authors provide excellent information.

48. Population reports may exaggerate the number known.

49. Larry Briggs, communication, May 19, 2015.

50. David W. Lange, "The Rare 1858 Type 2 Half Dollar," *Gobrecht Journal*, November 1984.

51. Population reports may exaggerate the number known.

52. Population reports may exaggerate the number known.

53. See *Coin World*, March 30, 2015, p. 38.

54. Rich Ulrich, communication, May 11, 2015.

55. For in-depth studies see Randall E. Wiley "Die Marriages of 1861-O Half Dollars," *Gobrecht Journal*, November 2005, and "Coining Authority and Rarity for Die Marriages of 1861-O Half Dollars," *Gobrecht Journal*, November 2006. Mintage figures for 1861-O are from original records and were furnished by Nancy Oliver and Richard Kelly; they differ from some figures published earlier.

56. For more details see Q. David Bowers, *Lost and Found Coin Hoards and Treasures*, 2015.

57. Population reports may exaggerate the number known.

58. Population reports may exaggerate the number known.

59. Population reports may exaggerate the number known.

60. Population reports may exaggerate the number known.

61. Larry Briggs, communication, May 25, 2015.

62. Population reports may exaggerate the number known.

63. Population reports may exaggerate the number known.

64. Larry Briggs, communication, May 19, 2015.

65. Population reports may exaggerate the number known.

66. Larry Briggs, communication, May 19, 2015.

67. For an in-depth study see Dick Osburn, "Die Marriages for 1873-CC Half Dollars," *Gobrecht Journal*, March 2002, which covers No Arrows and With Arrows types.

68. Population reports may exaggerate the number known.

69. Dennis Fortier, "Diagnostic Notes on the 1874 Large Arrows over Small Arrows Half Dollar," *Gobrecht Journal*, July 2010.

70. Larry Briggs and Brian Greer have handled at least 150 over the years (Larry Briggs, communication, May 25, 2015).

71. As measured and studied by Bill Bugert.

72. Bill Bugert, communication, May 7, 2015; Larry Briggs, communication, May 31, 2015.

73. Larry Briggs, communication, May 31, 2015.

74. Rich Uhrich, communication, May 9, 2015.

75. Bill Bugert has documented the lower range of each MS estimate.

76. Larry Briggs, communication, May 19, 2015; he provided estimates for other half dollars late in the Liberty Seated series.

Chapter 9

1. John Dannreuther was especially helpful and supplied much information on Gobrecht dollars. uspatterns.com and essays there by Mike Carboneau were also used. See chapter 1 for general information on the creation of the design.

2. Pet bank: Nickname for a state-chartered bank that was selected by the Andrew Jackson administration as a depository for federal funds, replacing the earlier policy of placing such funds with the Second Bank of the United States.

3. William L. Stone, editor of the *Commercial Advertiser*.

4. Usually capitalized, Five Points. A seedy district in the Sixth Ward of New York City. The "nymphs" were prostitutes.

5. See David W. Lange, "Upon What Exactly Is Liberty Seated?" *Gobrecht Journal*, July 2012.

6. A new unrelated institution chartered by the Pennsylvania State Legislature on February 18, 1836, and formed by Nicholas Biddle and his associates. It had no connection with the federal Bank of the United States whose charter expired in 1836. The new bank collapsed in fraud a few years later, ruining the reputation of Biddle, a leading figure in high society in the city.

7. Documentation from the National Archives furnished by John Dannreuther, communication, March 30, 2015.

8. Cf. Saul Teichman.

9. Such as: Is there factual information about Peter the Mint eagle, and was he the model for Thomas Sully's eagle? Were 300 Gobrecht dollars made for circulation in 1839, and if so, what die alignment were they? Etc., etc.

10. Bought by A.M. ("Art") Kagin from Louis S. Werner and "shown around" to various dealers and collectors who were suitably impressed. The discovery of this overstrike was noted by Walter H. Breen in *The Numismatist*, May 1957, under title of "Some Unpublished Gobrecht Rarities."

11. Perfect reverse die (cf. Smithsonian Institution). An example, certainly an original, was in the Roper Sale in 1851.

12. Cracked reverse die.

13. Cracked reverse die.

14. Varieties once described as J-86 and 90 are believed to be misdescriptions of J-87 and 89 respectively (cf. Saul Teichman).

15. Perfect reverse die.

16. Cracked reverse die.

17. These pieces came through the estate of William K. Idler (as it was said), John W. Haseltine, and Stephen K. Nagy, and were first announced by Edgar H. Adams in *The Numismatist*, April 1911. Many restrikes and new metal varieties were marketed by Haseltine in particular.

18. Don Taxay, *Counterfeit, Mis-Struck, and Unofficial U.S. Coins*, 1963, pp. 89, 90.

19. Such as Goloid Metric dollars and related coins. For a full listing of patterns see *United States Patterns* (10th edition), by J. Hewitt Judd.

20. During the 1861–1865 Lincoln administration the abuses continued. See Woodward comment.

21. Slightly edited. Reprinted in the *American Journal of Numismatics*, January 1879.

22. Possibly Theodore Eckfeldt (1837–1893), son of George J. Eckfeldt (1805–1864; nephew of Adam Eckfeldt).

23. Letter sold by George F. Kolbe in his auction of the John J. Ford Jr. Library; information courtesy of Saul Teichman.

24. These found eager buyers including Virgil M. Brand, H.O. Granberg, and W.W.C. Wilson.

25. John Dannreuther, communication, May 18, 2015. The Gobrecht dollars are from the Julius Korein Collection at the ANS.

26. John Dannreuther, communication, May 24, 2015.

27. Communication, May 24, 2015.

28. On May 15, 2015, John Dannreuther and Saul Teichman revisited the collection and made further notes.

29. Up to 12 die markers can be found on J-60 dollars delivered on December

31, 1836, these per Saul Teichman: 1, 2: 2 die chips in dentils near second A (AMERICA), the first is nearer the A and appears earlier; 3: Clash mark from eagle pointing toward AT (STATES); 4: Rim mark above the A (STATES); 5, 6: 2 Rim marks above the T (STATES); 7: Die chip in dentils near pellet just above the R (DOLLAR); 8: Rim mark under the same R; 9: Die line through the O (ONE); 10: Die line below the D (DOLLAR); 11: Rim mark at the second A (AMERICA); 12: Rim mark between the pellet and the U (UNITED).

30. This and related documents found by Kevin Flynn in the National Archives. Certain commentary from John Dannreuther, communication, May 28, 2015.

31. Rich Uhrich, communication, May 16, 2015.

32. Communication, May 19, 2015.

33. James Ross Snowden, *The Cabinet Collection of the Mint of the United States*, 1860, p. 111.

34. Usually stored in a special compartment or facility near the captain's cabin. The use of Spanish-American dollars is widely chronicled in literature.

35. See mintage information for 1858 silver sets under half dimes.

36. *Congressional Globe*, April 9, 1872, p. 231. Across the board, numismatic researchers take congressional testimony on any coinage subject with a large grain of salt, as few senators or representatives had much knowledge on the subject.

37. Sources include "Robert Gilmor, Jr. and the Cradle Age of American Numismatics," by Joel J. Orosz, *Rare Coin Review*, No. 58, 1985; his similarly titled article in *The Numismatist*, May 1990; and the same writer's "New Research Illuminates Robert Gilmor,

Jr.," co-authored with Lance Humphries, *The Numismatist*, November and December 1996.

38. This specimen was later owned by a succession of well-known numismatists including Lyman H. Low, Harold P. Newlin, Robert Coulton Davis, John G. Mills, James Ten Eyck, Virgil M. Brand, Robert Friedberg, and Walter Perschke.

39. By 1834 the price of gold bullion had risen to the point at which current gold coins were worth more in melt-down value than face value. Accordingly, vast numbers of coins were melted or exported. On June 28, 1834, Congress lowered the authorized weight of gold coins, such becoming effective on August 1, 1834. As new "Classic Head" $2.50 and $5 coins were minted under the new standard, the older pieces became increasingly scarce. Called "old tenor," the old-style gold coins were quoted at a premium in financial and bullion lists.

40. In 1854, Alfred Hunter prepared a catalog of "extraordinary curiosities" on display by the National Institute at the Patent Office building, which included numismatic items (cf. Emmanuel J. Attinelli, *Numisgraphics*, 1876, p. 82).

41. As the manuscript for the present book was nearing completion a new website, www.seateddollarvarieties.com, was in development by Dick Osburn and Brian Cushing

42. Much information in the *Notes* for Liberty Seated dollars is based on the research of R.W. Julian as published in *Silver Dollars and Trade Dollars of the United States: A Complete Encyclopedia*, 1993.

43. In reviewing this particular section of the book, in which this sentence originally ended as "AU-58 or MS-60," Bill Fivaz made this comment (letter to the author, February 13, 1992): "I have always felt that if a coin is being considered as either an AU-58 or Mint State, it would jump right over the MS-60 to 62 categories and be an MS-63 or better if determined to be Mint State. I feel (and teach thusly at the ANA Summer Conference) that an AU-58 coin is really an MS-63 (or better) coin with just a tad of wear. If an MS-60 coin had the same trace of wear, it should then be graded AU-50, because an MS-60 coin is not an attractive coin, due to contact marks, poor lustre, etc. It is a minor point, but one I feel has a good deal of merit." Fivaz's comment illustrates that numerical grading is not a science but a subjective value judgment. "How many points to take off for problems" translates to "How much to discount the price?"

44. *Times-Picayune*, May 3, 1850.

45. The knowledge of two die pairs for 1851 restrikes represented a new discovery, first confirmed by James C. Gray, Thomas K. DeLorey, and the author, during the examination of a group of 1851 restrike dollars assembled for study at the 1992 ANA convention. Also present were Mark Borckardt, Kenneth E. Bressett, Bill Fivaz, R.W. Julian, Chris Napolitano, and J.T. Stanton.

46. John Dannreuther, communication, May 24, 2015.

47. The sale comprised 140 lots and realized $456.40. Later an edition of 25 copies was printed from a manuscript held by J.N.T. Levick. *Numisgraphics*, p. 14 (cf. Emmanuel J. Attinelli).

48. Nor is the destruction of old logotypes mandated today. On a visit to the Engraving Department of the Philadelphia Mint in 1988, the author examined a logotype date punch used to make 1898 gold quarter eagle dies; it was on a shelf unidentified.

49. Discovered by Frank Van Valen. See the *Gobrecht Journal*, No. 90.

50. Upon reading this comment, J.T. Stanton commented: "The mintmark position may not necessarily match any known position as the struck coin may have been misaligned slightly with the dies, creating the differing position. Other design details may well have been hidden by the strike." Letter to the author, August 23, 1992.

51. Examination of the piece by James C. Gray, Thomas K. DeLorey, the author, and several others, at the August 1992 ANA Convention, reveals that the New Orleans dollar was filed down on the edge (perhaps so it would fit in the collar of the restrike dies) and rim, accounting for its light weight of only 400.3 grains (as compared to the 412.5 grain standard). The O mintmark was flattened by striking. The coin is said to have come from a B. Max Mehl sale years ago, where the overstrike feature was not recognized. The definitive commentary on this is by John Dannreuther in *Gobrecht Journal*, March 2004, where he details how a previously struck New Orleans Mint dollar was used as an undertype.

52. A "Proof" held by the American Numismatic Society is actually a deeply prooflike circulation strike, per John Dannreuther, communication, May 25, 2015.

53. Saul Teichman, communication, May 24, 2015.

54. John Dannreuther, communication, May 24, 2015.

55. The first *copper* restrike was sold in J.W. Haseltine's sale of March 1876. Cf. Saul Teichman, communication, May 24, 2015.

56. *John Sherman's Recollections of Forty Years in the House, Senate, and Cabinet*, Vol. 1, p. 461.

57. *Fractional Money*, footnote p. 120.

58. Frank Van Valen, communication, May 26, 2015, from a study of Perry's reminiscences.

59. David Cohen reported obtaining a group of five Mint State pieces in an article, "The Five Sisters Born 1854," in *Gobrecht Journal*, March 1984. He noted that there seemed to be some overall weakness or flatness in the head and hair, but this varied from coin to coin.

60. As explained in detail in *Silver Dollars and Trade Dollars of the United States: A Complete Encyclopedia*, the owner of a single coin submitted it to PCGS six times, giving six listings in the report.

61. Population reports may exaggerate the number known.

62. Larry Briggs, communication, May 19, 2015: "In all of my life I have only seen one coin below Very Fine."

63. October 1856, p. 303.

64. "Later News from China," *Daily Ohio Statesman*, Columbus, Ohio, December 30, 1856. Normally, patently incorrect accounts are not cited in the present book, but this one is as to date very little other research has been done on the export of Liberty Seated silver dollars, and this account is tagged as misleading.

65. New Orleans *Times-Picayune*, April 9, 1859.

66. Nancy Oliver and Richard Kelly, communication, May 26, 2015.

67. From John M. Willem, in *The United States Trade Dollar*, 1965.

68. "Philadelphia Coinage Statistics: 1853–1873." *Numismatic Scrapbook Magazine*, August 1964.

69. Population reports may exaggerate the number known.

70. The facts are somewhat garbled, common when senators and representatives testified on historical matters involving coinage and finance. Davis stated that all of these silver dollars were minted in San Francisco. In fact, only 20,000 were and only in the year 1859.

71. Population reports may exaggerate the number known.

72. Likely these were 1859-O and 1860-O dollars.

73. Population reports may exaggerate the number known.

74. Population reports may exaggerate the number known.

75. Population reports may exaggerate the number known.

76. Population reports may exaggerate the number known.

77. Population reports may exaggerate the number known.

78. Larry Briggs, communication, May 19, 2015.

79. For a detailed study see Dick Osburn with Brian Cushing, "The 1870-CC Liberty Seated Dollar," *Gobrecht Journal*, Spring 2015.

80. Based on Heritage Auction's listing in the Eugene H. Gardner sale plus information from Saul Teichman and the author's 1993 information in *Silver Dollars and Trade Dollars of the United States: A Complete Encyclopedia*.

81. Displayed at the 2005 ANA Convention in San Francisco.

82. Illustrated in the catalog of the 1914 ANS Exhibition.

83. Menjou was a movie actor who consigned a few coins and lent his name to the sale; nearly all of the coins had belonged to Williams earlier.

84. Walter Breen stated this coin once belonged to 19th century collector Matthew Stickney, but as Stickney stopped collecting before 1870 this is not true. It is possible that Virgil Brand owned this coin at some point.

85. Reported by Frank Van Valen who examined it in the late 1980s at a Long Beach, California, convention.

86. Communication, May 26, 2015. For additional information see Nancy Oliver and Richard Kelly, "The Saga of the 1870-S Silver Dollar," *The Numismatist*, May 2005.

87. Communication, May 19, 2015.

88. *San Francisco Bulletin*, September 13, 1873, stating that coinage was soon to begin.

89. Population reports may exaggerate the number known.

90. Larry Briggs, communication, May 31, 2015.

91. Larry Briggs, communication, May 31, 2015.

92. In addition, there were three "cornerstone" Mint State coins found in 1973; their specific numerical grades are not known but may be in the MS-60 to 63 range.

93. From Nancy Oliver and Richard Kelly, "Telegram reveals fate of 1873-S Seated $1. Researchers find Mint director's order to melt dollars," *Coin World*, July 14, 2008.

Chapter 10

1. Knox was a highly intelligent and well-respected man, an author, numismatist, and man of learning. He was at the epicenter of the issuing of paper money, but it is not known that he collected such, as only his numismatic involvement with *coins* has been recorded. Based in Washington, Knox traveled widely on government business.

2. In actuality, few were shipped to Japan. Most went to Chinese ports.

3. *John Sherman's Recollections of Forty Years in the House, Senate, and Cabinet,* Vol. 1, p. 467. Years later, in 1888, Senator Beck said in an open forum that Sherman was responsible for the Act of 1873 and that it was "secretly passed and surreptitiously done." The charge was easily refuted by Sherman, who produced original documents from the Treasury Department. *Ibid.* Vol. 2, p. 1010.

4. From Willem, *The United States Trade Dollar,* p. 134, and other sources.

5. Most exports of cotton were to Europe, not to eastern Asia.

6. On some coins there is a period after GRAINS in place of the standard comma; this was pointed out by David Proskey in an advertisement in *The Numismatist,* January 1928.

7. The use of the motto GOD OUR TRUST is particularly interesting, as no information has been learned to the effect that the usual motto, IN GOD WE TRUST, needed modification, and GOD OUR TRUST had been rejected years earlier.

8. May not exist; possibly a misdescription of J-1219 (cf. Saul Teichman).

9. A curious style similar to that of the half dollar J-91 of 1839.

10. Pieces earlier listed as J-1326a and 1326b were misdescriptions of J-1308 and 1309 and have been delisted.

11. The existence of two major reverse varieties was discovered by Elliot Landau, December 9, 1952, and published in *The Numismatist,* June 1953.

12. The *Type* 1 and *Type* 2 designations might be better given as *Varieties* 1 and 2, but the "type" nomenclature has been in use for many years, becoming traditional with other denominations, *e.g.,* Types 1 and 2 (instead of Varieties 1 and 2) for 1886 cents, 1913 Buffalo nickels, 1892 and 1917 quarters, etc. In every instance, these "types" represent redesigned hubs.

13. Dan Huntsinger and John Coyle, communication, May 18, 2015.

14. Some years ago Steve Tanenbaum had about two dozen of these.

15. Communication, May 19, 2015.

16. For an in-depth study see Joe Kirchgessner, "Die Combinations for 1873-CC Trade Dollars," *Gobrecht Journal,* July 2001.

17. Dan Huntsinger and John Coyle, communication, May 18, 2015.

18. Larry Briggs, communication, May 19, 2015.

19. *Ibid.*

20. Dan Huntsinger and John Coyle, communication, May 18, 2015.

21. *Ibid.*

22. Described by Don Taxay in *Counterfeit, Mis-struck and Unofficial U.S. Coins,* Arco Publishing Co., 1963; there called unique.

23. Dan Huntsinger and John Coyle, communication, May 18, 2015.

24. Discovered by Jack Beymer. VF-30. Described by Dr. John W. McCloskey and illustrated in the *Gobrecht Journal,* November 1984.

25. Letter to the author, November 30, 1991; another, January 29, 1992, contained additional data.

26. Larry Briggs, communication, May 19, 2015.

27. Dan Huntsinger and John Coyle, communication, May 18, 2015.

28. The reason for this is that the silver in a trade dollar was worth only 95.5¢ at the time, trade dollars had not been legal tender since July 22, 1876, and sharpies deposited silver, obtained trade dollars and then tried to spend them at face value.

29. Population reports are skewed by resubmissions and do not relate to the actual number in existence.

30. In some years the Mint did not begin delivering Proofs until after January.

31. Idler was a professional early in the game. In the 1860s he advertised as a dealer in coins, medals, minerals, paper money, and antiques at No. 109 South 11th Street, Philadelphia.

32. Brand, a wealthy Chicago brewer, began collecting coins in 1879, started keeping extensive records of them (now preserved by the American Numismatic Society, New York) in 1889, and by the time of his death in 1926 had acquired over 350,000 coins of the world. At one time he had five, possibly six, 1884 trade dollars.

33. Stephen K. Nagy, the Philadelphia dealer who was once closely associated with certain officials at the Mint, told me years ago that in some future day the "true story" of the Mint-made rarities such as the 1801–1804 restrike dollars, 1884 and 1885 trade dollars, and 1877 $50 gold pieces would come to light. However, he died without making such information available.

34. For a registry of 1884 and 1885 trade dollars compiled by Mark Borckardt, Q. David Bowers, Walter H. Breen, Carl W.A. Carlson, and P. Scott Rubin see *Silver Dollars and Trade Dollars of the United States: A Complete Encyclopedia,* 1993

35. Larry Briggs, communication, May 19, 2015.

36. Carl W.A. Carlson in his description of the Olsen specimen sold in the French Family Collection, Stack's, 1989, suggests that coinage was accomplished in the first half of the 1885 year.

37. Larry Briggs, communication, May 19, 2015.

38. At one time in 1997 three of the five known 1885 trade dollars were in the office of Bowers and Merena Galleries in Wolfeboro, NH. The author's collection of 1873–1885 trade dollars, including all of the 1/2 combinations, complete in Mint State and Proof was sold in 2011. Details are in an article by James Macor, "The Magnificent New England Collection of United States Trade Dollars," *Gobrecht Journal,* November 2011.

Appendix A

1. In 1923 it was transferred from the Third Philadelphia Mint to the Smithsonian Institution. Today it forms the main part of the National Numismatic Collection there.

2. "The New Mint," *San Francisco Bulletin,* May 26, 1870. A large copper casket measuring 16 inches long, 8 inches wide, and 6 inches deep was placed into a cavity "drilled" in the

five-foot thick stone. The contents are listed including "a piece of Continental paper money dated 1776 valued at $800" (no bills of that year had any such value in 1870). Also see Nancy Oliver and

Richard Kelly, "The Missing San Francisco Mint Cornerstone," *Gobrecht Journal*, July 2000. "A search for the cornerstone was made during renovation work in 1974, but it could not be found.

Appendix B

1. Mint closed 1861–1874; assaying and custodian facilities 1875–1878; Mint commenced coinage again in 1879. Various superintendents were in office until the next, when Liberty Seated coinage took place for a short time.

2. Certain information was provided by Nancy Oliver and Richard Kelly, May 26, 2015.

3. For biographies see the home page of the Carson City Coin Collectors of America at www.carsoncitycoinclub.com.

Appendix C

1. The reference is to the current Liberty Seated design.

Appendix D

1. The campaign to move the Mint facilities to New York City was not a new one. Previously on January 7, 1852, the U.S. Senate considered a letter from the mayor of New York City, A.C. Kingsland, who transmitted a copy of a resolution passed unanimously by both branches of the New York City government requesting the same. A defense, from the Legislature of Pennsylvania, was addressed by the Senate on March 4, 1852. Most proposals (e.g., testimony for H.R. No. 477, May 15, 1862) stated that tremendous amounts of gold arrived in New York from California, and it would be more economical to mint this gold in New York City than in Philadelphia, indeed, as indicated in the *Harper's* article. Desperate, New York later

(1870) proposed that the New Orleans Mint facilities be moved to New York City (41st Congress, 2nd session, Ex. Doc. No. 55).

2. A punning reference to a large snake, an adder.

3. Franklin Peale was discharged from the Mint because of a number of complaints concerning his activities, including the use of Mint facilities to run his extensive and lucrative private business of making medals. He petitioned Congress for $30,000 compensation for the improvements he had made at the Mint over a long period of years, but payment was never received. Taxay, in *The U.S. Mint and Coinage*, addresses the Peale situation in detail.

Appendix F

1. Extensive information about this, including the claims of others, was published in *Mechanics' Magazine*, journals of the American Institute and the Franklin Institute, and elsewhere in the mid-1830s.

2. *Spectator*, New York, New York, February 10, 1824.

3. This account appeared elsewhere as well, one stating he was a *Baltimore artist* and a native of Maryland! The *Boston*

Intelligencer, June 19, 1824, in its article stated that "Mr. Taws of Philadelphia has acquired great skill in performing on it."

4. *Daily National Intelligencer*, Washington, D.C.

5. In *Secret History*, Breen stated that Gobrecht cut dies "1825–6, [for] two medallions for the Mint, which were still preserved there around 1880."

6. When he died Carroll (September 19, 1737 to November 14, 1832) was the last living signer of the Declaration of Independence. His residence, Homewood House, is on the campus of the Johns Hopkins University.

7. Founded by Charles Willson Peale in 1784, the museum experienced many changes. Some of these details are found in the Bowers book, *American Numismatics Before the Civil War (1760–1860)*.

8. Shown here in an early 1900s view, by which time the Institute had long since moved to a larger facility, and the original building housed the Atwater Kent Museum.

9. Details are described by Kenneth E. Bressett in *The ANA Anthology*, 1991.

10. *North American*, Philadelphia, July 25, 1844.

11. Adapted from Q. David Bowers, "Christian Gobrecht: American die engraver *extraordinaire*," *Rare Coin Review*, No. 126, *Autumn 1998*.

SELECTED BIBLIOGRAPHY

Adams, John W. *United States Numismatic Literature.* Vol. 1. Nineteenth Century Auction Catalogs. Mission Viejo, CA: George Frederick Kolbe Publications, 1982.

Adams, John W. *United States Numismatic Literature.* Vol. 2. Twentieth Century Auction Catalogs. Crestline, CA: George Frederick Kolbe Publications, 1990.

Ahwash, Kamal. *Encyclopedia of U.S. Liberty Seated Dimes, 1837–91.* Media, PA: Kamah Press, 1977.

American Journal of Numismatics. New York, NY, and Boston, MA: Various issues of the late 19th century (as cited).

American Numismatic Society. *Exhibition of U.S. and Colonial Coins.* New York, NY: American Numismatic Society, 1914.

Amspacher, Bruce, "United States Trade Dollars: 1873–1885." In *The Comprehensive U.S. Silver Dollar Encyclopedia.* Ch. 62. 1992.

Homren, Wayne. *Asylum, The.* Numismatic Bibliomania Society: Various issues from the 1980s onward.

Attinelli, Emmanuel J. *Numisgraphics, or A List of Catalogues, Which Have Been Sold by Auction in the United States. . . .* New York, NY: Published by the author, 1876.

Augsburger, Len, "Sitting Liberty: The Christian Gobrecht Catalogue Raisonné." *The Gobrecht Journal,* March 2008.

Bankers' Magazine and Statistical Register, The. Boston, MA: Various issues 1846–1880.

Beistle, M.L. *A Register of Half Dollar Die Varieties and Sub-Varieties. Being a description of each die variety used in the coinage of United States Half Dollars.* Shippensburg, PA: The Beistle Company, 1929.

Benton, Thomas Hart. *Thirty Years' View; or, a History of the Working of the American Government for Thirty Years, from 1820 to 1850.* New York, NY: D. Appleton & Co., 1854.

Blythe, Al. *The Complete Guide to Liberty Seated Half Dimes.* Virginia Beach, VA: 1992.

Bolles, Albert S. *The Financial History of the United States from 1774 to 1885.* Vol. 1–3. New York, NY: 1879–1894.

Boosel, Harry X. *1873–1873.* Chicago, IL: Hewitt Brothers, 1960. Summary of articles Boosel created for the *Numismatic Scrapbook Magazine.*

Bosbyshell, Oliver C. *An Index to the Coins and Medals of the Cabinet of the Mint of the United States at Philadelphia.* Philadelphia, PA: Avil Printing and Lithograph Company, 1891.

Bowers and Merena Galleries. Wolfeboro, NH: 1996 and 1997 sales of the Louis E. Eliasberg Collection; other sales as cited.

Bowers, Q. David. *The History of United States Coinage.* Los Angeles, CA: Bowers and Ruddy Galleries, Inc., 1979. Later printings by Bowers and Merena Galleries, Inc. are from Wolfeboro, NH.

———, *American Numismatic Association Centennial History, 1891–1991.* Wolfeboro, NH: Bowers and Merena Galleries, Inc.: 1991.

———, *Silver Dollars and Trade Dollars of the United States*. Vol. 1–2. Wolfeboro, NH: Bowers and Merena Galleries, Inc., 1993.

———, *The History of American Numismatics Before the Civil War, 1760-1860*. Wolfeboro, NH: Bowers and Merena Galleries, 1998.

———, *Lost and Found Coin Hoards and Treasures*. Atlanta, GA: Whitman Publishing, 2015.

Breen, Walter H. "Secret History of the Gobrecht Coinages." *Coin Collectors Journal*, 1954, 157–158.

———, *United States Half Dimes, A Supplement*. New York, NY: Wayte Raymond, Inc., 1958.

———, *Walter Breen's Complete Encyclopedia of U.S. and Colonial Coins*. Garden City, NY: Doubleday, 1988.

———, *A Coiner's Caviar: Walter Breen's Encyclopedia of U.S. and Colonial Proof Coins*. Albertson, NY: FCI Press, 1977. Reprint and update by Bowers and Merena Galleries, Wolfeboro, NH: 1989.

———, *Walter Breen's Encyclopedia of Early United States Cents 1793–1814*, edited by Mark Borckardt. Wolfeboro, NH: Bowers and Merena Galleries, 2000. Posthumous publication, edited and with additions.

Bressett, Kenneth E. (senior editor). *A Guide Book of United States Coins*. Atlanta, GA: Whitman Publishing, various modern editions; earlier editions edited by Richard S. Yeoman.

Bressett, Kenneth E. and A. Kosoff. *The Official American Numismatic Association Grading Standards for United States Coins*. Fourth edition.

Colorado Springs, CO: American Numismatic Association, 1991.

Briggs, Larry. *The Comprehensive Encyclopedia of Liberty Seated Quarters*. Lima, OH: Larry Briggs Rare Coins, 1991.

Brunner, Lane J. and John M. Frost. *Double Dimes———,The United States Twenty-Cent Piece*, 2014. Book and internet forms. <http://www.doubledimes.com>.

Bugert, Bill. *A Register of Liberty Seated Half Dollar Varieties, Volume I, San Francisco Branch Mint*. Gettysburg, PA: Self-published, 2009.

A Register of Liberty Seated Half Dollar Varieties, Volume II, Carson City Branch Mint. Gettysburg, PA: Self-published, 2010.

A Register of Liberty Seated Half Dollar Varieties, Volume III, New Orleans Branch Mint 1840-O to 1853-O NA. Gettysburg, PA: Self-published, 2011.

A Register of Liberty Seated Half Dollar Varieties, Volume IV, New Orleans Branch Mint 1853-O WA to 1861-O. Gettysburg, PA: Self-published, 2013.

A Register of Liberty Seated Half Dollar Varieties, Volume V, Philadelphia Mint 1839–1852. Information from manuscript in progress in early 2015.

Carlson, Carl W.A. and Michael J. Hodder (editors). *The American Numismatic Association Centennial Anthology*. Wolfeboro, NH: Bowers and Merena Galleries, Inc. on behalf of the American Numismatic Association, 1991.

Carothers, Neil. *Fractional Money*. New York, NY: John Wiley & Sons, 1930.

Catalogue of Coins, Tokens, and Medals in the Numismatic Collection of United States at Philadelphia, Pa. Washington, D.C.: Government Printing Office, 1914.

Clain-Stefanelli, Elvira Eliza. "From the Drawingboard of a Coin Engraver." In *The American Numismatic Association Centennial Anthology.* Wolfeboro, NH: Bowers and Merena Galleries, Inc. on behalf of the ANA, 1991.

"Old Friends———,Common Goals: The Evolution of Numismatics in the United States." In *The American Numismatic Association Centennial Anthology.* Wolfeboro, NH: Bowers and Merena Galleries, Inc. on behalf of the ANA, 1991.

Clain-Stefanelli, Vladimir. "History of the National Numismatic Collections." In *Bulletin 229.* Washington, DC: Smithsonian Institution, 1970.

Clapp, John M. and John H. Clapp. Notebook ledger recording their collection through the year 1905 with intermittent entries through 1910 (original notebook furnished by Richard A. Eliasberg).

Coin Collector's Journal, The. New York, NY: Scott & Company. Various issues of the 1870s and 1880s.

Coin World Almanac. Sidney, OH: Coin World, 2010.

Coin World. Sidney, OH: Amos Press, 1960 to date.

COINage. Ventura, CA: Miller Magazines, Inc. Various issues 1970s to date.

Coinage Laws of the United States 1792–1894. Modern foreword to reprint by David L. Ganz. Wolfeboro, NH: Bowers and Merena Galleries, Inc., 1991.

Coinage of Gold and Silver. Washington, D.C.: Government Printing Office, 1891.

Coinage of the Trade Dollar. Washington, D.C., 1878.

Coins Magazine. Iola, WI: Krause Publications, various issues 1962 to date.

CoinWeek. Various issues 2012 to date. Internet site: <http://www.coinweek.com>.

Comparette, T.L. *Catalogue of Coins, Tokens, and Medals in the Numismatic Collection of the Mint of the United States at Philadelphia, Pennsylvania.* Washington, D.C.: Government Printing Office, 1912 (first edition); 1914 (third edition).

Curry's Chronicle. Various issues.

Dannreuther, John W. "Liberty Seated Dollars." In *The Comprehensive U.S. Silver Dollar Encyclopedia.* Chapter 61. 1992.

Davis, Charles E. *American Numismatic Literature: An Annotated Survey of Auction Sales 1980–1991.* Lincoln, MA: Quarterman Publications, Inc., 1992.

Dickeson, Montroville Wilson. *The American Numismatical Manual.* Philadelphia, PA: J.B. Lippincott & Co., 1859. (1860 and 1865 editions were slightly retitled as *The American Numismatic Manual.*)

Dubois, William E. *Pledges of History: A Brief Account of the Collection of Coins Belonging to the Mint of the United States, More Particularly of the Antique Specimens.* First edition: Philadelphia, PA: C. Sherman, Printer, 1846. Second edition: New York, NY: George P. Putnam, 1851.

Dye, John S. *Dye's Coin Encyclopaedia*. Philadelphia, PA: Bradley & Company, 1883.

E-Gobrecht. Online publication of the Liberty Seated Collectors Club.

Eckfeldt, George J. Personal manuscript notebook of die records, formulas, etc., compiled from the 1840s to the 1860s.

Eckfeldt, Jacob Reese and William Ewing Dubois. *A Manual of Gold and Silver Coins of All Nations, Struck Within the Past Century*. Philadelphia, PA: Assay Office of the Mint, 1842.

New Varieties of Gold and Silver Coins, Counterfeit Coins, Bullion with Mint Values. New York, NY: George P. Putnam, 1850 and 1851.

Evans, George G. (publisher). *Illustrated History of the United States Mint*. Philadelphia, PA: 1890.

Fivaz, Bill, and J.T. Stanton. *The Cherrypickers' Guide to Rare Die Varieties*. Fifth edition. Vol. 2. Atlanta, GA: Whitman Publishing, 2012.

The Cherrypickers' Guide to Rare Die Varieties. Sixth edition. Vol. 1. Atlanta, GA: Whitman Publishing, 2015.

Flynn, Kevin. *The Authoritative Reference on Liberty Seated Twenty Cents*. Roswell, GA: Kyle Vick, 2013.

———, *The Authoritative Reference on Liberty Seated Dollars*. Lumberton, NJ: Published by the author, 2014.

———, *The Authoritative Reference on Liberty Seated Half Dimes*. Lumberton, NJ: Published by the author, 2014.

Forrer, Leonard. *Biographical Dictionary of Medallists*. London, England: Spink & Son, Ltd., 1923.

Fortin, Gerry. "Liberty Seated Dimes— ———,Die Varieties, 1837–1891." Internet site: <http://www.seateddimevarieties.com>.

Friedman, Milton and Anna Jacobson Schwartz. *A Monetary History of the United States 1867–1960*. Princeton, NJ: Princeton University Press, 1963.

Gillilland, Cory. "Public Opinion and the Nation's Coinage." In *The American Numismatic Association Centennial Anthology*. Wolfeboro, NH: Bowers and Merena Galleries, Inc. on behalf of the ANA, 1991.

Gobrecht Journal. Various issues 1974 to date.

Greer, Brian. *The Complete Guide to Liberty Seated Dimes*. Virginia Beach, VA: DLRC Press, 1992.

Heritage Auctions. Dallas, TX: 2014 and 2015 sales of the Eugene Gardner and Eric P. Newman collections.

Heaton, Augustus G. *A Treatise on the Coinage of the United States Branch Mints*. Advertised and familiarly known as *Mint Marks*. Washington, D.C.: published by the author, 1893.

Hickson, Howard. *Mint Mark CC: The Story of the United States Mint at Carson City, Nevada*. Carson City, NV: The Nevada State Museum, 1972 and 1990.

Highfill, John W. "The Carson City Mint: A Branch Mint Profile." In *The Comprehensive U.S. Silver Dollar Encyclopedia*. Chapter 11. 1992.

———, "Gobrecht Dollars." In *The Comprehensive U.S. Silver Dollar Encyclopedia*. Chapter 60. 1992.

Historical Statistics of the United States: Colonial Times to 1970. Washington, D.C.: U.S. Department of Commerce, Bureau of the Census, September 1975.

Hodder, Michael J., and Carl W.A. Carlson. *American Numismatic Association Centennial Anthology*. Wolfeboro, NH: Bowers and Merena Galleries, Inc., 1991.

Judd, J. Hewitt, *United States Pattern Coins*. Tenth Edition. Atlanta, GA: Whitman Publishing, 2009.

Julian, R.W., and Ernest E. Keusch. *Medals of the United States Assay Commission, 1860–1977*. Lake Mary, FL: The Token and Medal Society, 1969.

Lange, David W. *Coin Collecting Albums A Complete History & Catalog*. Volume One. The National Coin Album & Related Products of Beistle, Raymond, & Meghrig. Lakewood Ranch, FL: Pennyboard Press, 2013.

Linderman, Henry Richard. *Money and Legal Tender in the United States*. New York, NY: G.P. Putnam's Sons, 1877.

Mason's Monthly Illustrated Coin Collector's Magazine. Philadelphia, PA, and Boston, MA: Ebenezer Locke Mason. Various issues from the 1860s onward.

Niles' Weekly Register. Baltimore, MD: Hezekiah Niles, 1836–1847.

Numismatic Gallery Monthly. New York, NY, and Beverly Hills, CA: Numismatic Gallery, 1948–1953.

Numismatic Guaranty Corporation of America Census Report. Sarasota, FL: Numismatic Guaranty Corporation of America. Various issues.

Numismatic Scrapbook Magazine. Chicago, IL, and Sidney, OH: 1935–1976.

Numismatic News. Iola, WI: Krause Publications, 1952 to date.

Numismatist, The. The American Numismatic Association. Colorado Springs, CO (and other earlier addresses). Various issues 1888 to date.

Orosz, Joel J. "Robert Gilmor, Jr. and the Cradle Age of American Numismatics." Article in *Rare Coin Review*, No. 58. Bowers and Merena Galleries, Inc., 1985.

"Robert Gilmor, Jr. and the Cradle Age of American Numismatics." *The Numismatist*, May 1990 (expansion of 1985 article in the *Rare Coin Review*).

Orosz, Joel J., and Leonard D. Augsburger. *The Secret History of the First U.S. Mint*. Atlanta, GA: Whitman Publishing, 2011.

PCGS Population Report. Newport Beach, CA: Professional Coin Grading Service. Various issues.

Peale, Franklin. "Description of the New Coining Presses Lately Introduced into the U.S. Mint, Philadelphia." In the *Journal of the Franklin Institute*. Vol. 18. November 1837. 307–310.

Pollock, Andrew W. *United States Patterns and Related Issues*. Wolfeboro, NH: Bowers and Merena Galleries, 1994.

Prime, W.C. *Coins, Medals, and Seals*. New York, NY: Harper & Brothers, 1861.

Raymond, Wayte. *Standard Catalogue of United States Coins and Paper Money.* New York, NY: Scott Stamp & Coin Co. (and others), 1934 to 1957 editions.

Records of the Bureau of the Mint and its antecedents, National Archives.

Reiver, Jules. "Variety Identification Manual for United States Half Dimes." 1984.

Rose, F.M. *Chopmarks.* Dallas, TX: Numismatics International, 1987.

Schwarz, Ted, *A History of United States Coinage.* San Diego, CA, and New York, NY: A.S. Barnes and Co., 1980.

Sherman, John. *John Sherman's Recollections of Forty Years in the House, Senate and Cabinet.* Chicago, IL: The Werner Company, 1895.

Smith, A.M. *Coins and Coinage: The United States Mint, Philadelphia, History, Biography, Statistics, Work, Machinery, Products, Officials.* Philadelphia, PA: A.M. Smith, 1885.

Snowden, James Ross. *A Description of Ancient and Modern Coins in the Cabinet of the Mint of the United States.* Philadelphia, PA: J.B. Lippincott & Co., 1860.

Statistical Abstract of the United States. Washington, D.C.: U.S. Department of Commerce, 1987.

Stefanelli, Elvira Eliza, "From the Drawingboard of a Coin Engraver." In the *American Numismatic Association Centennial Anthology.* Wolfeboro, NH: Bowers and Merena Galleries on behalf of the ANA, 1991.

Taxay, Don. *Counterfeit, Mis-Struck, and Unofficial U.S. Coins.* New York, NY: Arco Publishing Co., 1963.

U.S. Mint and Coinage. New York, NY: Arco Publishing Co., 1966.

Scott's Comprehensive Catalogue and Encyclopedia of U.S. Coins, 1971. New York, NY, and Omaha, NE: Scott Publishing Co., 1970.

uspatterns.com. Website conducted by Saul Teichman with updates of the latest news and discoveries.

Treasury Department, United States Mint, *et al. Annual Report of the Director of the Mint.* Philadelphia, PA (later, Washington): 1835 to 1892. Early reports were published in a variety of ways including in presidential messages, in newspaper accounts, and in separate pamphlets. Reports were on a calendar year basis through 1856, and then in 1857 they went to a fiscal year (July 1 through June 30 of the following year) basis. The 1857 report is transitional and covers only January 1 through June 30, 1857, a period of six months.

Tucker, Dennis. *American Gold and Silver: U.S. Mint Collector and Investor Coins and Medals, Bicentennial to Date.* Atlanta, GA: Whitman Publishing, 2015.

Valentine, Daniel W. *The United States Half Dimes.* NY, New York: American Numismatic Society, 1931.

Van Winkle, Mark (editor). *Gobrecht Dollars: Illustrated by the Collection of Julius Korein, M.D.* Dallas, TX: Ivy Press, 2009.

Vermeule, Cornelius. *Numismatic Art in America: Aesthetics of United States Coinage.* First edition: Cambridge, MA: The Belknap Press of Harvard University Press, 1971. Second edition: Atlanta, GA: Whitman Publishing, 2007.

Weir, William. *Sixty Years in Canada.* Montreal, Canada: John Lovell & Son, 1903.

White, Horace. *Money and Banking.* Boston, MA: Ginn & Company, 1896.

White, Weimar W. *The Liberty Seated Dollar 1840–1873.* New York, NY: Sanford J. Durst Numismatic Publications, 1985.

Wikipedia. General information on American history.

Wiley, Randy, and Bill Bugert, *The Complete Guide to Liberty Seated Half Dollars.* Virginia Beach, VA: 1993.

Willem, John M. *The United States Trade Dollar.* Racine, WI: Whitman Publishing, Co., 1965

ACKNOWLEDGEMENTS

The **American Numismatic Association** assisted in several ways. **The American Numismatic Society** was consulted for information. **The American Philosophical Society** provided certain Gobrecht-related images. **Leonard Augsburger** contributed the foreword. The **Bancroft Library** of Berkeley, California, provided images. **Tom Bender** supplied images. **Anne Bentley**, curator of the Massachusetts Historical Society, provided items for photography. **Jack Beymer** made suggestions. **Mark Borckardt** provided research findings on various coins including a survey of thousands of trade dollars (to establish the rarity of chopmarked pieces and also 1875 and 1876 reverse hub combinations), reviewed the manuscript, assisted with mintage and survival figures for pre-1858 Proof coins, provided pricing information, and helped in other ways. **Kenneth Bressett** helped with questions and research including the work of Christian Gobrecht. **Karen Bridges** (Stack's Bowers Galleries) provided many photographs. **Larry Briggs**, well-known for his research on Liberty Seated quarters, reviewed the manuscript for all Liberty Seated denominations and made many suggestions concerning varieties and the numbers known today. **Bill Bugert** provided information on half dollars from the Louis E. Eliasberg Collection, certain of which is used here, and also helped with half dollars in the present text including new counts for obverse and reverse dies, as well as provided pricing information. **Roger W. Burdette** assisted with technical questions, Mint history, and archival information, and supplied extensive files of newspaper clippings and original records—a treasure trove. **Elizabeth Coggan** provided pricing information. **John Coyle**, specialist in trade dollars, reviewed the manuscript. **Stephen A. Crain**, leading specialist in half dimes, reviewed the manuscript and made many corrections and additions to items from earlier literature. **John Dannreuther** answered many questions and helped in other ways; he was a prime source for research and previously unpublished information, wrote appendix F, and provided drafts of a set of three books he is writing on Proof coinage. **Tom DeLorey** contributed much information and also reviewed the manuscript in detail. **Richard A. Eliasberg** provided archival information. **Bill Fivaz** shared research and information on die varieties. **Kevin Flynn** made suggestions and shared documents found in the National Archives. **Gerry Fortin** reviewed the chapter on Liberty Seated dimes, provided pricing information, and made many valuable suggestions. **John Frost** provided pricing information, reviewed the manuscript in detail, and made many valuable suggestions. **Jeff Garrett** helped in several ways. **Ellen Gerth** of Odyssey Marine Exploration provided information about Liberty Seated half dollars recovered from the 1865 wreck of the SS *Republic* and also made suggestions concerning the overall manuscript. **Rusty Goe** provided information concerning Carson City coinage, some of it through the Battle Born Collection auctioned in August 2013. **James C. Gray** corresponded about Liberty Seated coins over a period of years. **Dan Hamelberg** provided information from Ed Frossard's 1894 sale of the William M. Friesner Collection. **Heritage Auctions** provided access to their Permanent Auction Archives, including the comprehensive Eugene H. Gardner Collection, and was the major source of images. **The Historical Society of Pennsylvania** provided images of Gobrecht's bank-note vignettes. **Wayne Homren**, publisher of *E-Sylum*, helped with requests for research information. **Dan Huntsinger** helped with technical information on trade dollars. **Jesse Iskowitz** provided pricing information. **Greg Johnson** reviewed the information on Liberty Seated quarters and made valuable suggestions including about certain varieties and their availability. **Jennifer**

Locke Jones of the Smithsonian Institution facilitated research. **R.W. Julian** furnished much information to Q. David Bowers' *Silver Dollars and Trade Dollars of the United States: A Complete Encyclopedia*, 1993, certain of which is used here. **Thomas Jurkowsky** of the U.S. Mint helped in several ways. **Christine Karstedt** helped in many ways including coordinating communications and suggesting sources. **Richard Kelly** helped in multiple ways including providing information about the San Francisco Mint and its coins and editing. **George F. Kolbe** furnished a photograph of the Chapman brothers. **David W. Lange** assisted with population information, varieties, and illustrations of National and related albums. **The Library Company of Philadelphia** provided certain Gobrecht items to the Smithsonian which were used in the present work. **Denis W. Loring** provided pricing information. **Darrell Low** provided images. **Andy Lustig** sent comments about Gobrecht dollars in particular and other series in general. **Sydney Martin** furnished an image of a 1785 Connecticut copper. **The Massachusetts Historical Society** furnished an image of an original 1836 steam coinage medalet. **John McCloskey** provided much information and answered questions over a period of time. **Jennifer Meers** helped find sources and citations and worked with certain images. **Harry Miller** contributed pricing information. **Bruce Morelan** contributed images from his magnificent collection of silver dollars and trade dollars; these constitute the majority of the coins illustrated. **Karl Moulton** furnished a citation. **Mountvernon.org** provided an image of Mount Vernon. **Tom Mulvaney**'s photographs for Whitman Publishing were used for certain images. **The National Archives** provided most of the quoted correspondence regarding coinage and Mint activities. The **National Numismatic Collection of the Smithsonian Institution** provided certain Gobrecht-related images. **Numismatic Guaranty Corporation of America** (NGC) helped in several ways. **Nancy Oliver** helped in multiple ways including providing information about the San Francisco Mint and its coins and by editing. **Dick Osburn** reviewed the manuscript and made suggestions. **D. Brent Pogue** provided information. **Professional Coin Grading Service** (PCGS) helped in several ways. **Susan Pryor** shared information about the James Bennett Pryor Collection sold in 1996. **Harry Salyards** shared philosophy, ideas, information, and research over a long period of years. **Craig Sholley** corresponded about Mint history and Gobrecht silver dollars. Certain pattern coin illustrations are from the **Robert Simpson Collection**. **Skinner Galleries** provided an image of trade buildings in Canton, China. **Laura Sperber** recommended contacts with her clients for further information. **Stack's Bowers Galleries** furnished many images from its Auction Archives. **David Sundman** provided historical citations. **Eric Tate** of Odyssey Marine Exploration furnished the inventory of Liberty Seated half dollars recovered from the wreck of the SS *Republic* lost at sea in 1865. **Saul Teichman** helped in many ways including with extensive information on Gobrecht dollars and various patterns and Mint practices of the period from spring 1859 to summer 1885. **Frank Trask** contributed a commentary to chapter 5. **Rich Uhrich** provided pricing information, reviewed the manuscript, and made many suggestions, including adding previously unpublished information. **Frank Van Valen** provided pricing information, reviewed the manuscript, and made suggestions and edits. **Alan V. Weinberg** provided photographs of the 1826 Archimedes medal by Gobrecht. **Weimar White** provided information and suggestions. **Randy Wiley** provided information on half dollars for the Louis E. Eliasberg Collection, certain of which is used here. **Ray Williams** reviewed the manuscript and made suggestions.

ABOUT THE AUTHOR

Q. David Bowers has been in the rare-coin business since, he was a teenager starting in 1953. He is chairman emeritus of Stack's Bowers Galleries and is numismatic director of Whitman Publishing. He is a recipient of the Pennsylvania State University College of Business Administration's Alumni Achievement Award (1976); he has served as president of the American Numismatic Association (1983–1985) and president of the Professional Numismatists Guild (1977–1979); he is a recipient of the highest honor bestowed by the ANA (the Farran Zerbe Award); he was the first ANA member to be named Numismatist of the Year (1995); and he has been inducted into the Numismatic Hall of Fame maintained at ANA headquarters. He has also won the highest honors given by the Professional Numismatists Guild. In July 1999, in a poll published in *COINage*, "Numismatists of the Century," Dave was recognized as one of six living people on this list of just 18 names. He is the author of more than 60 books, hundreds of auction and other catalogs, and several thousand articles including columns in *Coin World* (now the longest-running by any author in numismatic history), *The Numismatist*, and other publications. His books have earned more "Book of the Year Award" honors bestowed by the Numismatic Literary Guild than have those of any other author. He and his firms have presented the majority of the most valuable coin collections ever sold at auction. Dave is a trustee of the New Hampshire Historical Society and a fellow of the American Antiquarian Society, the American Numismatic Society, and the Massachusetts Historical Society. He has been a consultant for the Smithsonian Institution, the Treasury Department, and the U.S. Mint, and is research editor of *A Guide Book of United States Coins*. This is a short list of his honors and accomplishments. In Wolfeboro, New Hampshire, he is a former selectman and town historian.

INDEX